THE GAINS FROM TRADE AND THE GAINS FROM AID

When does a country benefit from free trade?

This is one of the oldest questions in economics. Posed by Adam Smith in response to the English Mercantilists, the question has obsessed economists for more than 200 years. *The Gains from Trade and the Gains from Aid* produces some satisfying general answers.

The book is divided into five parts:

- trade under perfect competition;
- restricted trade under perfect competition;
- trade under imperfect competition and other distortions;
- compensation: lumpsum, non-lumpsum or neither?
- international aid

The volume can be viewed as a record of the progress made by Murray Kemp and his co-workers in addressing aspects of normative trade theory over the past 35 years. As such, it will be an invaluable guide for all those interested in the social consequences of international trade and aid.

Murray C. Kemp has for many years been Research Professor of Economics at the University of New South Wales. His principal fields of interest have been the theory of international trade, the economics of welfare and the theory of exhaustible resources.

THE GAINS FROM TRADE AND THE GAINS FROM AID

Essays in International Trade Theory

Murray C. Kemp

London and New York

First published 1995
by Routledge
11 New Fetter Lane, London EC4P 4EE

Simultaneously published in the USA and Canada
by Routledge
29 West 35th Street, New York, NY 10001

Typeset in Garamond by
Pure Tech India Ltd., Pondicherry, India

Printed and bound in Great Britain by
Mackays of Chatham PLC, Chatham, Kent

British Library Cataloguing in Publication Data

A catalogue record for this book is available from the British Library

Library of Congress Cataloguing in Publication Data

Kemp, Murray C.
The gains from trade and the gains from aid: essays in international trade theory / Murray C. Kemp.
p. cm.
Includes bibliographical references and index.
ISBN 0–415–13038–7
1. International trade. 2. International economic relations.
3. Equilibrium (Economics) I. Title.
HF1379.K46 1995
382—dc20

ISBN 0–415–13038–7

CONTENTS

Introduction ix

Part I The gains from free trade under perfect competition

1 THE GAIN FROM INTERNATIONAL TRADE
Economic Journal 72 (December 1962), 803–19. 3

2 THE GAINS FROM FREE TRADE
International Economic Review 13 (October 1972), 509–22. With Henry Y. Wan, Jr. 21

3 AN ELEMENTARY PROPOSITION CONCERNING THE FORMATION OF CUSTOMS UNIONS
Journal of International Economics 6 (February 1976), 95–7. With Henry Y. Wan, Jr. 37

4 THE COMPARISON OF SECOND-BEST EQUILIBRIA: THE CASE OF CUSTOMS UNIONS
In D. Bös and C. Seidl (eds) (1986) *The Welfare Economics of the Second Best*, Supplementum 5 to the *Zeitschrift für Nationalökonomie*, 161–7, Vienna: Springer-Verlag. With Henry Y. Wan, Jr. 41

5 THE GAINS FROM TRADE WHEN MARKETS ARE POSSIBLY INCOMPLETE
With Kar-yiu Wong. 47
A further note on the gains from trade when markets are possibly incomplete 71

6 THE GAINS FROM FREE TRADE FOR A MONETARY ECONOMY
Kobe Economic and Business Review 35 (1990), 27–30. 73

7 THE GAINS FROM TRADE FOR A MONETARY ECONOMY WHEN MARKETS ARE POSSIBLY INCOMPLETE
With Kar-yiu Wong. 78

8 TRADE GAINS IN A PURE CONSUMPTION–LOAN MODEL
Australian Economic Papers 12 (June 1973), 124–6. 101

9 GAINS FROM TRADE WITH OVERLAPPING GENERATIONS
Economic Theory 5 (1995). With Kar-yiu Wong. 105

10 THE GAINS FROM INTERNATIONAL TRADE IN A CONTEXT OF OVERLAPPING GENERATIONS
With Nikolaus Wolik. 129

11 THE WELFARE GAINS FROM INTERNATIONAL MIGRATION
Keio Economic Studies 30 (May 1993), 1–5. 147

12 THE PROBLEM OF SURVIVAL: AN OPEN ECONOMY
In M.C. Kemp and N.V. Long (eds) (1984) *Essays in the Economics of Exhaustible Resources*, pp. 27–35, Amsterdam: North-Holland. With Ngo Van Long. 152

13 THE INTERNATIONAL DIFFUSION OF THE FRUITS OF TECHNICAL PROGRESS
International Economic Review 34 (May 1993), 381–5. With Yew-Kwang Ng and Koji Shimomura. 160

Part II The gains from restricted trade under perfect competition

14 ON THE SHARING OF TRADE GAINS BY RESOURCE-POOR AND RESOURCE-RICH COUNTRIES
Journal of International Economics 8 (February 1978), 93–115. With Michihiro Ohyama. 167

15 THE INTERACTION OF RESOURCE-RICH AND RESOURCE-POOR ECONOMIES
Australian Economic Papers 18 (December 1979), 258–67. With Ngo Van Long. 189

Part III The gains from trade under imperfect competition and other distortions

16 SOME ISSUES IN THE ANALYSIS OF TRADE GAINS
Oxford Economic Papers, New Series, 20 (July 1968), 149–61. 203

17 VARIABLE RETURNS TO SCALE, COMMODITY TAXES, FACTOR-MARKET DISTORTIONS AND THEIR IMPLICATIONS FOR TRADE GAINS
Swedish Journal of Economics 72 (January 1970), 1–11. With Takashi Negishi. 218

18 VARIABLE RETURNS TO SCALE, NON-UNIQUENESS OF EQUILIBRIUM AND THE GAINS FROM INTERNATIONAL TRADE
Review of Economic Studies 58 (July 1991), 807–16. With Albert G. Schweinberger. 230

19 THE GAINS FROM INTERNATIONAL TRADE UNDER IMPERFECT COMPETITION: A CONJECTURAL VARIATIONS APPROACH.
With Masayuki Okawa. 242

20 THE INTERNATIONAL DIFFUSION OF THE FRUITS OF TECHNICAL PROGRESS UNDER IMPERFECT COMPETITION.
With Masayuki Okawa. 253

21 DOES THE SET OF IMPERFECTLY COMPETITIVE GENERAL EQUILIBRIA DEPEND ON THE CHOICE OF PRICE NORMALIZATION? 271

22 LEARNING BY DOING: FORMAL TESTS FOR INTERVENTION IN AN OPEN ECONOMY
Keio Economic Studies 11 (October 1974), 1–7. 274

Part IV Compensation: lumpsum, non-lumpsum or neither?

23 GAINS FROM TRADE WITH AND WITHOUT LUMPSUM COMPENSATION
Journal of International Economics 21 (August 1986), 99–110. With Henry Y. Wan, Jr. 285

24 ON LUMPSUM COMPENSATION
With Henry Y. Wan, Jr. 296

25 LUMPSUM COMPENSATION IN A CONTEXT OF INCOMPLETE MARKETS
With Henry Y. Wan, Jr. 317

26 LUMPSUM COMPENSATION IN A CONTEXT OF OVERLAPPING GENERATIONS
With Nikolaus Wolik. 323

Part V International aid

27 THE STATIC WELFARE ECONOMICS OF FOREIGN AID: A CONSOLIDATION
In D. Savoie and I. Brecher (eds) (1992) *Equity and Efficiency in*

Economic Development: Essays in Honor of Benjamin Higgins, pp. 289–314, Montreal: McGill–Queen's University Press. 333

28 CONDITIONS FOR THE LOCAL IMPOTENCE OF LUMPSUM TRANSFERS TO EFFECT A REDISTRIBUTION OF WELFARE BETWEEN NATIONS 356

29 THE TRANSFER PROBLEM IN A CONTEXT OF PUBLIC GOODS
With Kenzo Abe and Makoto Tawada. Revised version of a paper carrying the same title and published by Abe and Kemp in *Economics Letters* 45 (1994), 223–6. 360

30 ON THE OPTIMAL TIMING OF FOREIGN AID
Kobe Economic and Business Review 35 (1990), 31–49. With Ngo Van Long and Koji Shimomura. 365

31 'TRADE' OR 'AID'?
In A. Takayama, M. Ohyama and H. Ohta (eds) (1991) *Trade, Policy, and International Adjustments*, pp. 19–35, San Diego: Academic Press. With Koji Shimomura. 379

Author index 394

Subject index 397

INTRODUCTION

It has been said that the Torrens–Ricardo doctrine of comparative advantage ranks with the wheel, the violin and the silicon chip among the supreme inventions of mankind. If this be so, I need not strenuously defend the publication of a collection of essays which seek to generalize and delimit the applicability of that doctrine. However, a brief account of the origins of the core essays (Essays 1–10) may be of interest, as may some reflections on the scope of Paretian compensation, upon which many of the essays rely.

A LITTLE HISTORY OF THOUGHT

In the autumn of 1960 Charles Kindelberger went south for a sabbatical year at Howard University leaving in my inexperienced hands both his graduate trade seminar and those who had attended the seminar in earlier years and were then preparing their dissertations. Fortunately the class was more than usually gifted and instruction soon settled into a strictly multilateral pattern. A record of our deliberations later appeared as my *Pure Theory of International Trade* (1964). For me, the year was decisive in at least two respects. By its end, I knew that trade theory, especially the normative aspects of it, would be an abiding interest; and in Henry Wan and Leon Wegge I had found close friends who would later be my colleagues at the University of New South Wales and have been my teachers and co-workers on many occasions. Several of my joint papers with Henry are included in the present collection; some of my work with Leon is represented in my earlier *Three Topics in the Theory of International Trade* (1976).

Professionally speaking, the most significant event of the year 1960–1 was the perception that Paul Samuelson's classical small-country study of the gains from competitive free trade (Samuelson, 1939) could be extended to accommodate trading countries with any degree of market power.[1] The outcome was a paper in the *Economic Journal* for 1962, here reprinted as Essay 1. The essential achievement of that paper was the demonstration that for a single country it is impossible by means of compensating lumpsum transfers in autarky to make everyone better off than in any given free-trade equilibrium. I later realized that from the 1962 finding it could **not** be inferred that it is possible by means of lumpsum transfers under free trade to make everyone better off than in any given autarkic equilibrium and that without the second proposition it is impossible to say that the situation of free trade is unambiguously socially preferable to the situation of autarky.

Some years later, during the autumn of 1969, Henry Wan and I found ourselves together again. He had taken up an appointment at the University of California at Davis; I was visiting the parent institution in Berkeley. It was inevitable that we should set about filling the gap in the 1962 paper. By the time I left California, in late 1970, the job had been done. The paper in which our findings were reported was published in the *International Economic Review* for 1972 and is here reprinted as Essay 2. It provided the first general demonstration that a single country necessarily and unambiguously gains from suitably compensated free trade, whether or not its trading partners are free trading and with generality judged against the Arrow–Debreu standard.

Having achieved a general proof of the traditional gains-from-trade proposition, it was natural for us to turn our attention to the other, newer pillar of our subject, the proposition that **any** group of two or more trading countries, however large the group or however small, can always devise a mutually beneficial compensated customs union which harms no excluded country. This proposition had been discussed in the 1960–1 seminar and later appeared, with a sketch proof, in the *Pure Theory*. It had also been stated, and proved for a special case, by Jaroslav Vanek in his *General Equilibrium of International Discrimination* (1965) and discussed by Michihiro Ohyama in his masterly paper in *Keio Economic Studies* for 1972. However, it lacked a general (Arrow–Debreu) proof. This was essentially achieved in a short note which appeared in the *Journal of International Economics* for 1976; however, some dotting of the i's took place later in the *Zeitschrift für Nationalökonomie* for 1986. The two papers are here reprinted as Essays 3 and 4, respectively.

By the mid 1970s, then, the welfare economics of international trade had completed a transformation, in terms of generality and rigour, made possible by the methods of general equilibrium analysis developed twenty years earlier by Arrow, Debreu, McKenzie and others. Indeed the subject had achieved a generality greater than is commonly appreciated. It is well understood that the two propositions can be given a dynamic interpretation in terms of dated commodities and that they can be made to accommodate costs of transportation by indexing commodities by their place of delivery. It is not well understood that, by indexing factors of production by the industry in which they are employed, the propositions can be made to accommodate the possibility that factors are at each moment industry specific, gradually reallocating themselves in response to interindustrial disparties of factor rewards, with the reallocation resource-using and regulated at each moment by the optimal budget-constrained choices of factor owners.[2] Nor is it well understood that the two central propositions apply not only to international trade in produced goods but also to trade in the services of primary factors of production and to international migration. (The latter point is elaborated in Essay 11.)

Already, however, there had been expressions of dissatisfaction with the complete-markets assumption commonly made in that earlier literature. In particular, Hart (1975) had shown that, in a context of incomplete markets, competitive equilibria may be constrained suboptimal. To a trade theorist, this finding suggested that it might not be always possible to find a scheme of compensation such that free trade (or a customs union) is gainful. Following the appearance of Hart's paper, there came to light several examples of Pareto-inferior free trade; see Kemp and Long (1979), Binh (1985) and Newbery and Stiglitz (1984). All examples involved incompleteness of markets. Their appearance therefore reinforced the earlier Hart-induced doubts about the robustness of standard propositions.

For some years these misgivings lay dormant as I worked on other things. Then, in the winter of 1987–8, I gave a series of lectures on trade gains at the University of Kiel, at the invitation of Horst Herberg. By the end of the series I had convinced myself, if not Horst's graduate students, that the standard propositions were indeed robust in the face of market incompleteness. For every known example in which uncompensated free trade was Pareto-harmful, it was possible to construct a scheme of lumpsum compensation and an associated trading equilibrium which all individuals preferred to autarky. However, a few examples do not constitute a general proof.

Soon after the lectures at Kiel, I entered into a long and fruitful correspondence on the same topic with Kar-yiu Wong, whom I had met some years earlier at Columbia. As we gradually realized, the central issue is not whether an omniscient government could find a scheme of lumpsum compensation such that free trade or a customs union would be gainful; given enough information, there can always be devised a scheme of compensation which will do the work of missing markets and, in addition, compensate potential losers. Rather the issue is whether there can be found schemes of compensation which do not require global knowledge of individuals' preferences and of firms' production sets and yet do enough of the work of missing markets to allow the complete compensation of potential losers. In the end, we were able to show that such schemes always exist. The reasoning is contained in Essay 5. Now if the set of securities markets is incomplete it is unclear just what should be the objective of a firm which will function in more than one period of time. In Essay 5 the ambiguity is eliminated by assuming that production is organized in households; that is, as cottage industry. (Formally, the model then reduces to one of pure exchange.) In Essay 5, the argument accommodates a finite but otherwise arbitrary number of periods.

In the meantime, during a visit to the Research Institute for Economics and Business Administration, Kobe University, in the winter of 1988–9, I had begun to explore the robustness of the two standard theorems to the introduction of fiat money. Taking a money-in-the-utility-function approach, I was able to show that free trade might be harmful. (Money in the production function would have thrown up the same possibility.) The explanation lies in the possibility that an economy is unevenly monetized, with monetary balances more useful in some sectors than in others. The detailed argument was published in the *Kobe Economic and Business Review* for 1990, and is here reproduced as Essay 6.

However, that essay left as an open question the status of the two standard theorems in other types of monetary economies. It was to that question that Kar-yiu Wong and I next turned. Focusing on symmetrical cash-in-advance economies, but retaining the assumption that markets are possibly incomplete, we were able to show that (i) uncompensated free trade might be Pareto-inferior to autarky but that (ii) suitably compensated free trade is always Pareto-preferred to free trade. In other words, the findings of Essay 5 were repeated for monetary economies of the cash-in-advance kind. The details may be found in Essay 7.

Each of Essays 1–7 deals with a world economy in which individual agents and commodities are finite in number. However the Kemp–Long (1979) and Binh (1985) examples of Pareto-harmful free trade involve overlapping generations, an infinite horizon and, therefore, a double infinity of mortal individuals and dated commodities. It still remained unclear whether, in that extended context too, lumpsum-compensated free trade is gainful. The demonstration by Malinvaud (1953) and Samuelson (1958) that economies with overlapping generations and an infinite horizon may have Pareto-inefficient equilibrium paths was an unpromising omen. On the other hand, in a brief note (Kemp, 1973), here reproduced as Essay 8, I had already shown that the gains-from-trade proposition could be extended to pure-exchange economies of the Samuelsonian consumption–loan type. Now, in the last of our joint explorations, here reported in Essay 9, Kar-yiu Wong and I have been able to show that, if commodities and securities are freely traded, then production and capital accumulation can be accommodated, both in the traditional gains-from-trade proposition and in the newer proposition about customs unions, but that if international borrowing and lending are ruled out then the gains from free trade and from customs unions cannot generally be realized without resort to non-lumpsum redistributive devices.

The model of Essay 9 is, in some respects, quite special. In particular, it rests on the assumptions (i) that there are only two commodities, a specialized consumption good and a specialized intermediate good, (ii) that individuals of all generations have the same preferences and (iii) that all contemporaries receive the same endowments and therefore are equally wealthy. These restrictive assumptions have been removed in the last of the ten core essays, written with Nikolaus Wolik. On the other hand, throughout Essay 10 it is assumed that capital is internationally mobile.

That completes my account of the origins of the core essays.[3] Since the initial flawed achievements of 1962, it has been possible to extend considerably the welfare economics of international trade. In particular, it has been possible to enlarge the scope of its two central propositions to embrace the incompleteness of markets, monetization of the economy and the possibility that populations consist of overlapping generations. It remains only to offer two brief remarks concerning the scope of the core essays.

It is customary in approaching the gains from trade to make assumptions which imply that, for each trading country, there is at least one autarkic equilibrium. That tradition has been maintained in the core essays. However, one can imagine economies which, for all distributions of the aggregate endowment, are viable under free trade or under some forms of restricted trade but which cannot survive under autarky, whatever the distribution of the endowment; and we might wish to say that, for such economies, trade is gainful. Essays 12, 14 and 15 contain examples of such economies.

All of the new work reported above has continued to rely on the traditional assumptions of constant returns to scale and imperfect competition. It is true that there is now under way a vigorous search for conditions which suffice for gainful trade even when returns to scale are increasing and competition is imperfect. The point of departure for much of the recent work on these topics has been Kemp and Negishi (1970), here reprinted as Essay 17. To date, however, the outcome of the search has been meagre, consisting for the most part of conditions that (in the absence of complete and global information about preferences and production sets) can be verified only *ex post*, **after** the possibly costly experiment of embarking on free trade or joining a customs union. The pressing need is for restrictions on the specification of the world economy (endowments, preferences and technologies, market structures) which imply or are implied by the gainfulness of free trade or customs unions. Some progress has been made, but it is confined to trading worlds composed of economies which differ in scale only; see, for example, Essays 19 and 20, written jointly with Masayuki Okawa. Even these meagre achievements are under threat. For it has been argued by Volker Böhm (1994) that the set of imperfectly competitive general equilibria, and by implication the extent and possibly the existence of trade gains, depend on the apparently irrelevant choice of price normalization. In Essay 21 Böhm's argument is examined and ultimately rejected.

THE SCOPE OF PARETIAN COMPENSATION

In conclusion I propose to share some of my anxieties about the foundations of our subject.

Much of normative trade theory rests on the Paretian principle that there is an improvement in social welfare if and only if there is an improvement in the well-being of at least one individual and a deterioration in the well-being of no individual. Given this principle, a change in trading arrangements can be appraised only if potential losers are compensated.[4] My work, here displayed, has rested heavily on a particular form of lumpsum compensation, which guarantees to each individual a free-trade income which enables him or her to purchase his or her chosen autarkic consumption bundle at free-trade prices.

This form of compensation might have been called Hicksian. However, Henry Wan and I have instead called it Grandmont–McFadden–Grinols (GMG) compensation, in deference to three respected scholars in our field; see Grandmont and McFadden (1972) and Grinols (1981, 1984).

In recent years – roughly, since the appearance of Diamond and Mirrlees (1971) – there has been some debate over the relative merits of lumpsum and non-lumpsum compensation. That debate continues. My own point of view is expressed in Kemp and Wan (1986a, 1993), the first of which is here reprinted as Essay 23, and in Essays 24–6.[5] I do not wish to add to what is there said on that subject, except to note in passing that the debate has been conducted on the unrealistic supposition that the act of compensation uses no valuable resources. Instead I shall focus on the meaningfulness and relevance of compensation itself.

In careful expositions of the Paretian principle it is explicitly assumed that the population or constituency is independent of the disturbance; and in all valid applications of the principle that assumption must be satisfied. Evidently it is a very restrictive assumption. For some disturbances bear directly on the technology of child bearing and child nurturing; and almost any disturbance, whether or not it is accompanied by compensation, changes equilibrium relative prices and therefore provides an incentive to vary family size. That for so long the assumption has been accepted without regret may stem from the essential timelessness of many formulations of Paretian compensation. In the absence of a time axis, it may have seemed natural to ignore time-consuming adjustments of population.

My purpose here is to draw out some of the implications for Paretian compensation of the recognition that the population or constituency responds, directly or indirectly (through prices), to a disturbance. For concreteness, the disturbance will be taken to be the substitution of free trade for autarky.

Consider then an economy which will run for T periods (T finite), beginning at $t = 0$. Let us suppose that, given a suitable initial condition, the autarkic equilibrium path (including the path of population) is unique. Let us further suppose that the economy is unexpectedly disturbed, say at $t = t_0$ ($0 \leqslant t_0 < T$), by the adoption of free trade. In general, the autarkic and free-trade equilibrium paths differ from each other during the interval $[t_0, T]$. In particular, the autarkic and free-trade paths of population differ from each other. Now suppose that an attempt is made to introduce a scheme of lumpsum compensation during the interval $[t_0, T]$. If this can be achieved, some individual must be better off than in autarky. (I rule out the extreme case in which all indifference curves have a sharp point at the autarkic equilibrium.) Moreover, almost certainly, the new equilibrium relative prices will differ from the old. Some individuals might therefore decide to vary the number of their children. If an individual should decide to **reduce** the size of his or her family in some periods then not all of the individuals who would have been born under autarky will be born under compensated free trade. In that case, the supposition that compensation can be carried out is self-contradictory. If, on the other hand, an individual were to **increase** the number of his or children in some periods then we have to decide what compensation should be paid to individuals who would not have existed under autarky and therefore cannot have left a record of their consumption choices.

This dilemma presents itself whether or not the population is composed of partially overlapping generations and, in the case of overlapping generations, whether or not there is a persistently binding bequest motive. However, if there is a binding bequest motive then the dilemma is, if anything, made more uncomfortable, for the children and grandchildren are not traded goods and therefore cannot be market valued for purposes of compensation.

One might seek to rescue the Pareto principle by restricting the population or constituency of individuals eligible for compensation. For example, one might restrict the constituency to those individuals who are alive at the time of the disturbance. If the purpose of an enquiry is to explain why a social choice has been made or to predict how it will be made, such a restriction may be entirely appropriate. However, from the point of view of a traditional welfare economist or ethical bystander, who does not wish to favour earlier over later generations, the restriction will appear to be much too severe.

It emerges then that the class of comparative statical welfare problems that can be handled on the basis of the weak ethical assumptions implicit in the Paretian principle is quite small, nigh to vanishing. Even questions concerning the gains from trade, for which it has long been thought that the principle suffices, must be attacked with more powerful ethical weaponry. Among the indispensable tools of analysis will be social welfare functions the arguments of which include the populations of each period.

But that is an agenda for the future.

The essays have been written over a period of thirty-five years. Inevitably, there is repetition. This might irritate readers who propose to swallow the essays all at once, but it will, I hope, be accepted as a virtue by those who want to explore in a more selective and intermittent way.

NOTES

1 Chipman (1987: 526) appears to deny that Samuelson had in mind the small-country case. However, Samuelson (1939: 198–9) explicitly assumed that 'there exists an outside market in which there prevail certain arbitrarily established (relative) prices at which this country can buy or sell various commodities in unlimited amounts without changing those quoted prices'.

2 For a statement of this point in the context of a **closed** economy, see Kemp and Wan (1973). Early descriptive treatments of factor reallocation in **open** economies were provided by Kemp *et al.* (1977), Kemp and Kimura (1978) and Neary (1978). However, in those contributions the central equations of adjustment are introduced in an *ad hoc* manner, not as implications of constrained optimization by factor owners. They therefore obscured the fact that the sluggish readjustment of factor allocations is compatible with Arrow–Debreu theory and with our two basic propositions.

3 By virtue of some duplication, the more recent of the essays (Essays 5 and 7–10) can be read independently of each other.
4 This implication of the Paretian principle was noted by Pareto (1894) but became commonplace among English-speaking economists only after the appearance of Samuelson (1950). It is sometimes referred to as the ***non-hypothetical compensation principle.***
5 Essays 23–26 should be read with Dixit and Norman (1980, 1986), where an opposing point of view is developed.

REFERENCES

Binh, T. N. (1985) 'A neo-Ricardian model with overlapping generations', *Economic Record* 61: 707–18.

Binh, T. N. (1986) 'Welfare implications of international trade without compensation', University of New South Wales.

Böhm, V. (1994) 'The foundations of the theory of monopolistic competition revisited', *Journal of Economic Theory* 63: 208–18.

Chipman, J. S. (1987) 'Compensation principle', in J. Eatwell *et al.* (eds) *The New Palgrave: A Dictionary of Economics*, Vol. 1, pp. 524–31, New York: W. W. Norton.

Diamond, P. A. and Mirrlees, J. A. (1971) 'Optimal taxation and public production, I and II', *American Economic Review* 61: 8–27 and 261–78.

Dixit, A. K. and Norman, V. (1980) *The Theory of International Trade*, Cambridge: Cambridge University Press.

Dixit, A. K. and Norman, V. (1986), 'Gains from trade without lumpsum compensation', *Journal of International Economics* 21: 111–22.

Grandmont, J. M. and McFadden, D. (1972) 'A technical note on classical gains from trade', *Journal of International Economics* 2: 109–25.

Grinols, E. L. (1981) 'An extension of the Kemp–Wan theorem on the formation of customs unions', *Journal of International Economics* 11: 259–66.

Grinols, E. L. (1984) 'A thorn in the lion's paw: Has Britain paid too much for common market membership?', *Journal of International Economics* 16: 271–93.

Hart, O. D. (1975) 'On the optimality of equilibrium when the market structure is incomplete', *Journal of Economic Theory* 11: 418–43.

Kemp, M. C. (1962) 'The gains from international trade', *Economic Journal* 72: 803–19.

Kemp, M. C. (1964) *The Pure Theory of International Trade*, Englewood Cliffs, NJ: Prentice Hall.

Kemp, M. C. (1973) 'Trade gains in a pure consumption-loan model', *Australian Economic Papers* 12: 124–6.

Kemp, M. C. (1976) *Three Topics in the Theory of International Trade: Distribution, Welfare and Uncertainty*, Amsterdam: North-Holland.

Kemp, M. C. (1990) 'The gains from free trade for a monetary economy', *Kobe Economic and Business Review* 35: 27–30.

Kemp, M. C. and Kimura, Y. (1978) *Introduction to Mathematical Economics*, New York: Springer-Verlag.

Kemp, M. C. and Long, N. V. (1979) 'The under-exploitation of natural resources: A model with overlapping generations', *Economic Record* 55: 214–21.

Kemp, M. C. and Negishi, T. (1970) 'Variable returns to scale, commodity taxes, factor market distortions, and their implications for trade gains,' *Swedish Journal of Economics* 72: 1–11.

Kemp, M. C. and Wan, H. Y. (1972) 'The gains from free trade', *International Economic Review* 13: 509–22.

Kemp, M. C. and Wan, H. Y. (1973) 'Hysteresis of long-run equilibrium from realistic adjustment costs', in G. Horwich and P.A. Samuelson (eds) *Trade, Stability and*

Macroeconomics. Essays in Honor of Lloyd A. Metzler, pp. 221–42, New York: Academic Press.

Kemp, M. C. and Wan, H. Y. (1976) 'An elementary proposition concerning the formation of customs unions', *Journal of International Economics* 6: 95–7.

Kemp, M. C. and Wan, H. Y. (1986a) 'Gains from trade with and without lumpsum compensation', *Journal of International Economics* 21: 99–110.

Kemp, M. C. and Wan, H. Y. (1986b) 'The comparison of second-best equilibria: The case of customs unions', in D. Bös and C. Seidl (eds) *Welfare Economics of the Second Best*, Suppl. 5 of *Zeitschrift für Nationalökonomie* 161–7, Vienna: Springer-Verlag.

Kemp, M. C. and Wan, H. Y. (1993) *The Welfare Economics of International Trade*, London: Harwood Academic.

Kemp, M. C., Kimura, Y. and Okuguchi, K. (1977) 'Monotonicity properties of a dynamical version of the Heckscher–Ohlin model of production', *Economic Studies Quarterly* 28: 249–53.

Malinvaud, E. (1953) 'Capital accumulation and efficient allocation of resources', *Econometrica* 21: 233–68.

Neary, J. P. (1978) 'Dynamic stability and the theory of factor-market distortions', *American Economic Review* 68: 671–82.

Newbery, D. M. G. and Stiglitz, J. E. (1984) 'Pareto inferior trade', *Review of Economic Studies* 51: 1–12.

Ohyama, M. (1972) 'Trade and welfare in general equilibrium', *Keio Economic Studies* 9: 37–73.

Pareto, V. (1894) 'The maximum of utility given by free competition', *Giornale degli Economisti* 7: 48–66. In Italian.

Samuelson, P. A. (1939) 'The gains from international trade', *Canadian Journal of Economics and Political Science* 5: 195–205.

Samuelson, P. A. (1950) 'Evaluation of real national income', *Oxford Economic Papers*, NS, 1: 1–29.

Samuelson, P. A. (1958) 'An exact consumption–loan model of interest with or without the social contrivance of money', *Journal of Political Economy* 66: 467–82.

Vanek, J. (1965) *General Equilibrium of International Discrimination*, Cambridge, MA: Harvard University Press.

Part I

THE GAINS FROM FREE TRADE UNDER PERFECT COMPETITION

1

THE GAIN FROM INTERNATIONAL TRADE*

1 INTRODUCTION

In a brilliant paper of 1939 Paul Samuelson proved, under certain assumptions concerning technology, that for a small country unable to influence world prices, free trade is, in a clearly defined sense, better than no trade.

In this essay I shall offer a generalization of Samuelson's theorem. In particular, it will be shown that free trade **or trade distorted by (non-negative) import or export duties or quantitative import or export restrictions** is, in Samuelson's sense, better than no trade, **regardless of the size of the trading country**. The theorem will be shown to be valid whether or not the country imports raw materials, or is a net lender or borrower – possibilities from which Samuelson abstracted in his initial exposition.

For the most part my method of proof parallels that introduced by Samuelson. My indebtedness to his 1939 paper will, I hope, be abundantly clear.

2 SAMUELSON'S 1939 THEOREM

It will be convenient to begin with a bare statement of Samuelson's theorem.

> We shall consider a single economy consisting of one or more individuals enjoying a certain unchanging amount of technological knowledge, so that we may take as data the production functions relating the output of each commodity to the amounts of inputs devoted to its production. Any number of commodities is assumed; there may also be any number of inputs or productive services. These are not necessarily fixed in amount, but may have supply functions in terms of various economic prices. Moreover, for our purposes the differentiation of the factors of production can proceed to any degree; thus, labour services of the same man in different occupations are not regarded as the same factor of production unless the provider of these services is indifferent as between these two uses. [As a limiting case, factors may be occupationally completely immobile.] Similarly, in order that the productive services rendered by different individuals may be considered

the same service, it is necessary that in every use they be infinitely substitutable.

In order to ensure that perfect competition is possible, we rule out increasing returns, and assume that all production functions show constant returns with respect to proportional changes of *all* factors. Each individual acts as if he were a small part of the markets which he faces and takes prices as given parameters which he cannot influence by changes in his own supplies or demands. It is assumed that for each individual there exists an *ordinal* preference scale in which enter all commodities and productive services, and that subject to the restraints of fixed prices he always selects optimal amounts of each and every commodity and every productive service (some zero in amount). Each individual is better off if he receives more of every commodity while rendering less of every productive service. No attempt is made to render the 'utilities' and 'disutilities' of different persons comparable.[1]

It is assumed, in addition, that

there exists an outside market in which there prevail certain arbitrarily established (relative) prices at which this country can buy or sell various commodities in unlimited amounts without changing those quoted prices.[2]

The theorem follows:

Although it cannot be shown that every individual *is* made better off by the introduction of trade, it can be shown that through trade every individual *could* [by resort to lump-sum taxes and subsidies] be made better off (or in the limiting case, no worse off). In other words, if a unanimous decision were required in order for trade to be permitted, it would always be possible for those who desired trade to buy off those opposed to trade, with the result that all could be made better off.[3]

3 EXTENSION OF THE THEOREM TO VARIABLE TERMS OF TRADE

I shall demonstrate in this section that Samuelson's theorem can be proved for countries of any size whatever. All other assumptions of section 2 are retained.

The following notation will be useful.[4] The amount consumed of the *i*th commodity is denoted by z_i, the amount produced by $\bar{z}_i$. The consumption vector is then

$$z = (z_1, z_2, \ldots, z_n)$$

and the production vector is

$$\bar{z} = (\bar{z}_1, \bar{z}_2, \ldots, \bar{z}_n).$$

The vector of domestic commodity prices is

$$p = (p_1, p_2, \ldots, p_n).$$

The vector of factor inputs is

$$a = (a_1, a_2, \ldots, a_s)$$

and the vector of factor prices is

$$w = (w_1, w_2, \ldots, w_s).$$

Values of the variables under autarky are indicated by the superscript 0, free-trade values by primes.

In the absence of trade

$$\bar{z}^0 - z^0 = 0. \tag{1}$$

But under balanced free trade the amount consumed of any particular commodity need not equal the amount produced. It is necessary only that the value of imports be equal to the value of exports or, what is the same thing, that the value of consumption be equal to the value of production:[5]

$$p'(\bar{z}' - z') = 0. \tag{2}$$

Turning to the keystone of the proof, we observe that, given constant returns to scale and the possibility of independently carrying on production in separate processes, the set S of production possibilities is convex (Samuelson, 1953). Under perfect competition and free trade, S will be supported by the price plane

$$p'(\bar{z} - \bar{z}') - w'(a - a') = 0 \tag{3}$$

at the free-trade production point $(\bar{z}'; a')$. It follows that $p'\bar{z} - w'a$, considered as a linear function defined on S, reaches a maximum at $(\bar{z}'; a')$. This means that at the free-trade prices the competitive quantities of commodities and factor services maximize for the economy as a whole the algebraic difference between the total value of output and total factor cost, as compared with any other commodity and factor combinations in S, in particular the autarkic combination (Samuelson, 1939: 197). This result may be written

$$0 = p'\bar{z}' - w'a' \geqslant p'\bar{z}^0 - w'a^0 \tag{4}$$

and is illustrated, for the special two-commodities, fixed-factors case, by Figure 1. Substituting from (1) and (2) in (4), we obtain the basic equation

$$p'z' - w'a' \geqslant p'z^0 - w'a^0; \tag{5}$$

at free-trade prices, the community's autarkic consumption pattern would have cost not more than the actual free-trade consumption pattern.

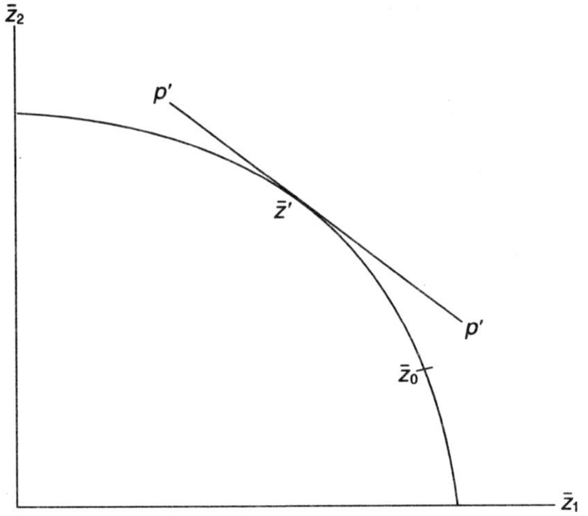

Figure 1

What can be inferred from (5)? Not very much, but enough for our purposes: that it is impossible, by simply redistributing the collection of goods actually chosen under autarky, to make everyone better off than in the chosen free-trade position.[6] This is readily illustrated, for the two-persons case, by means of

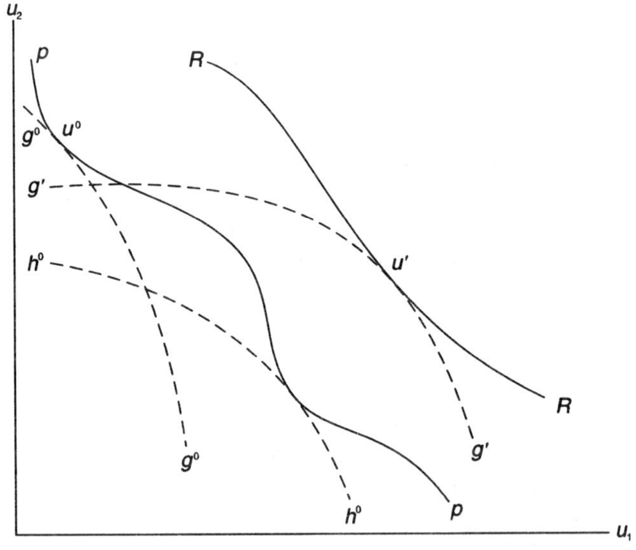

Figure 2

Samuelson's utility possibility curves. In Figure 2 the point u^0 indicates the distribution of utilities which actually emerges under autarky and the dashed curve g^0g^0 is the utility possibility curve corresponding to the collection of goods actually chosen under autarky. g^0g^0 passes south-west of u', the utility mixture of free trade.

Imagine that under autarky some other distribution of income had prevailed. Corresponding to it would be a new set of demands, a new production mixture and hence a new utility possibility curve, say h^0h^0 in Figure 2. If trade is opened up and if, simultaneously, appropriate lumpsum taxes and subsidies are introduced, z' will reappear and, with it, u'. Evidently h^0h^0, like g^0g^0, passes south-west of u'.

Consider now the envelope pp of all **point** utility possibility curves like g^0g^0 and h^0h^0. This envelope is the utility possibility curve of the autarkic **situation** (Samuelson, 1950: 12 ff). It, too, must pass south-west of u'. Thus it is impossible under autarky to make everyone better off than at the particular free-trade point z' (or u'). Put otherwise, it would not be advantageous (it might be impossible) for those who expect to be hurt by the introduction of trade to bribe the rest of the community into foregoing the free-trade point z' (or u').

But evidently a similar statement can be made with respect to **any** free-trade point attainable by means of appropriate lumpsum taxes and transfers. In other words, the utility possibility locus of the free-trade **situation**, say *RR*, cannot lie inside pp, the utility possibility locus of the autarkic situation.[7]

Thus we have proved that, for some systems of taxes and subsidies, (5) would hold for every individual. (z^0, z', a^0 and a' must now be interpreted as vectors of quantities of commodities bought and supplied by individuals.) Every individual would be revealed as better off or (in the limiting case in which $z' = z^0$ and $a' = a^0$) no worse off under compensated free trade than under autarky.

Note that nowhere in the above proof was it assumed that the trading country has no influence on world prices; at no point was it necessary to assume that trade can in fact take place along the $p'p'$ curve of Figure 1. Note also that while inputs and outputs are permitted to vary in response to changes in world prices, the proof does not **require** that such adjustment takes place. Specifically, the theorem holds even for fixed, totally unresponsive inputs and outputs.

4 A FOOTNOTE TO SECTIONS 2 AND 3

It has been stated in section 2 (and proved in section 3) that exposure to world prices which differ from those which happened to prevail under autarky carries with it a clearly defined benefit. Suppose that it is beyond the power of the individual country to influence world prices. Then the following interesting questions arise: (i) Is it possible to show that the benefit increases with an improvement of the terms of trade? (ii) Is it possible to show that the benefit is greater the more prices 'deviate' from those of the autarkic state?[8]

(i) Evidently a prerequisite of any analysis of the first question is agreement on the sense in which in a world of many commodities the terms of trade can be said to improve or deteriorate. Let p' and p'' be two vectors of world commodity prices, w' and w'' the corresponding vectors of domestic factor rewards. Then we shall say that a change from p' to p'' involves an improvement in the terms of trade if and only if

$$p''(\bar{z}' - z') > 0. \tag{6}$$

Now it is clearly impossible to show that everyone is necessarily better off at a chosen consumption point z'' than at any chosen point z'. The analysis of section 2 suggests, however, that the utility possibility locus of the p'' situation might be shown to lie 'outside' that of the p' situation. This is indeed the case.

We wish to show that, if p' consumption is restricted so that inequality (6) is satisfied, then

$$p''z'' - w''a'' \geqslant p''z' - w''a'. \tag{7}$$

From the discussion of section 2,

$$p''\bar{z}'' - w''a'' \geqslant p''\bar{z}' - w''a' \tag{8}$$

and

$$p''(z'' - \bar{z}'') = 0. \tag{9}$$

From these materials the proof may be pieced together:

$$\begin{aligned} p''z'' - w''a'' &= p''\bar{z}'' - w''a'' \text{ [from (9)]} \\ &\geqslant p''\bar{z}' - w''a' \text{ [from (8)]} \\ &= p''z' + p''(\bar{z}' - z') - w''a'' \geqslant p''z' - w''a' \text{ [from (6)].} \end{aligned}$$

Hence equation (7).

Figure 3 illustrates the theorem for the simple two-commodities, fixed-factors case. Assumption (6) means that the chosen point z' cannot lie on the heavy part of the p' line of Figure 3(a). Restricted in this way, the utility possibility curve of the p' situation must lie inside the utility possibility curve of the p'' situation, as in Figure 3(b).

Note that nowhere in the above proof was it assumed that each commodity is either imported or exported: purely domestic goods, for which $z_i = \bar{z}_i$, are admitted.

(ii) If exposure to prices which differ from those which would have prevailed under autarky is beneficial, one might have supposed that the benefit is greater the more prices deviate from those of the autarkic state. Unfortunately, this attractive speculation is false unless heavily qualified.

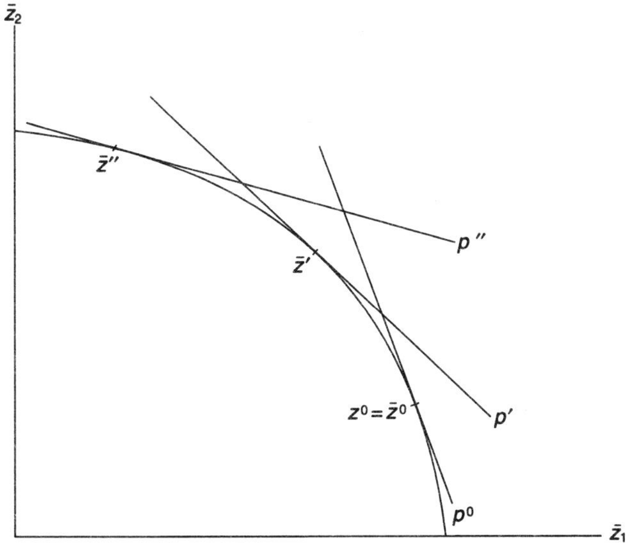

Figure 3(a)

Evidently a prerequisite of any analysis of the question is agreement on the sense in which one set of prices can be said to diverge more than another from the autarkic set. Of several conventions which suggest themselves, the following

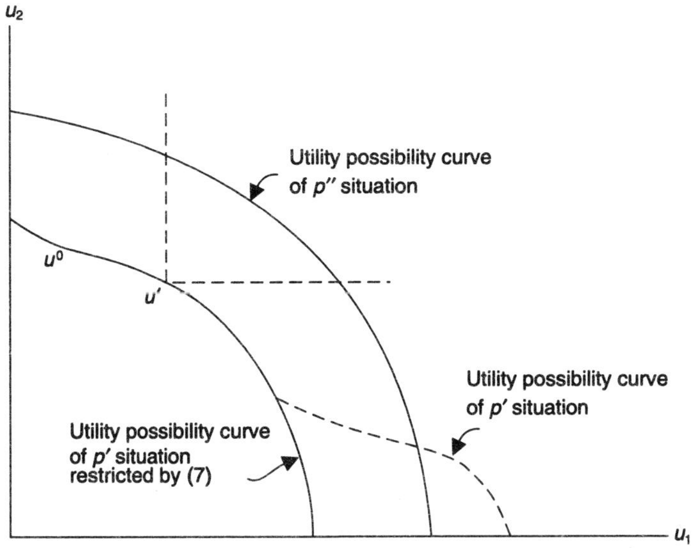

Figure 3(b)

is both plausible and analytically convenient.[9] Again let p' and p'' be two vectors of world prices, w' and w'' the corresponding vectors of domestic factor prices. p'' will be said to deviate from p^0, the autarkic set, by more than does p' if p' can be expressed as a positive linear combination of p^0 and p'':

$$p' = \mu^0 p^0 + \mu'' p'', \quad \mu^0, \mu'' > 0. \tag{10}$$

Given this definition, it can be shown that, provided autarkic and p' consumption points are constrained to satisfy the weak axiom of revealed preference, so that

$$p^0 z^0 - w^0 a^0 < p^0 z' - w^0 a', \tag{11}$$

no possible utility point of the p' situation can lie north-east of a possible utility point of the p'' situation. From the convexity of S we obtain further inequalities analogous to (4):

$$p^0 \bar{z}' - w^0 a' \leqslant 0 \tag{12a}$$

and

$$p'' \bar{z}' - w'' a' \leqslant 0. \tag{12b}$$

From (11) and (12a), and the fact that $p^0 z^0 - w^0 a^0 = 0$,

$$p^0(\bar{z}' - z') < 0. \tag{13}$$

Multiplying (12b) by $\mu > 0$ and (10) by $\mu'' > 0$, and adding, and then applying (10) and (2), we obtain

$$p'' z' - w'' a' < 0 \tag{14}$$

whence

$$0 = p'' z'' - w'' a'' > p'' z' - w'' a', \tag{15}$$

as required.

5 RESTRICTED TRADE IS SUPERIOR TO NO TRADE

So far it has been proved only that for any country compensated free trade is better than no trade. In this section I shall argue the more general proposition that compensated free trade or compensated restricted trade is better than no trade. (It is understood, of course, that the restrictions are not prohibitive.) The manner in which trade is restricted is unimportant; the same conclusions hold for (non-negative) tariffs, quantitative commodity controls or exchange restrictions. The assumption of perfect competition is retained.

If imports are restricted it is necessary to distinguish the domestic and world prices of imports. Imagine that, for any assigned set of trade restrictions and for any assigned system of lumpsum taxes and subsidies, the first m commodities,

$$x = (z_1, z_2, \ldots, z_m)$$

are exported, and that the remainder

$$y = (z_{m+1}, z_{m+2}, \ldots, z_n)$$

are imported.[10] Then

$$z = (x; y).$$

If, as before, p denotes the vector of **domestic** prices, we may write

$$p = (p_1, p_2, \ldots, p_m; p_{m+1}, p_{m+2}, \ldots, p_n) = (p_x; p_y).$$

The vector of world prices is then

$$q = (q_1, q_2, \ldots, q_m; q_{m+1}, q_{m+2}, \ldots, q_n) = (q_x; q_y) = (p_x; q_y),$$

where

$$q_y \leqslant p_y. \tag{16}$$

Primes now indicate the magnitudes of the restricted trade situation.

With the aid of this extended notation, (1) may be expanded as

$$\bar{x}^0 - x^0 = 0, \quad \bar{y}^0 - y^0 = 0 \tag{1a}$$

and (2) may be expanded as

$$p_x'(\bar{x}' - x') + q_y'(\bar{y}' - y') = 0 \quad \text{or} \quad p_x'x' + q_y'y' = p_x'\bar{x}' + q_y'\bar{y}'. \tag{2a}$$

Finally, (4) becomes

$$p_x'\bar{x}' + p_y'\bar{y}' - w'a' \geqslant p_x'\bar{x}^0 + p_y'\bar{y}^0 - w'a^0. \tag{4a}$$

Now it follows from (2a), (11) and the fact that $y' \geqslant \bar{y}'$ that

$$p_x'x' + p_y'y' \geqslant p_x'\bar{x}' + p_y'\bar{y}'. \tag{2b}$$

Substituting from (1a) and (2b) in (4a),

$$p_x'x' + p_y'y' - w'a' \geqslant p_x'x^0 + p_y'y^0 - w'a^0;$$

that is,

$$p'z' - w'a' \geqslant p'z^0 - w'a^0. \tag{5}$$

From this point the proof progresses along familiar lines.

If exports rather than imports are restricted, the proof must be modified, but follows essentially the same lines. The vector of world prices is now

$$q = (q_1, q_2, \ldots, q_m; q_{m+1}, q_{m+2}, \ldots, q_n) = (q_x; q_y) = (q_x; p_y),$$

where

$$q_x \geqslant p_x. \tag{16a}$$

Equation (2) may be expanded as

$$q_x'(\bar{x}' - x') + p_y'(\bar{y}' - y') = 0 \quad \text{or} \quad q_x'x' + p_y'y' = q_x'\bar{x}' + p_y'\bar{y}'. \tag{2c}$$

From (2c), (16a) and the fact that $\bar{x}' \geqslant x'$ we may infer (2b) again. From this point the proof proceeds as for the case of restricted imports.

Note that in constructing the above proofs it has not been found necessary to refer to the tariff proceeds (if any), the profits derived from the sale of import or export licences (if any) or the profits derived from exchange dealings (if any).

6 EXTENSION OF THE PROOF TO COVER IMPORTED RAW MATERIALS

In the proofs of sections 3 and 5 it has been assumed implicitly that the trading country makes no use of imported raw materials. This is, of course, a blatantly unrealistic assumption. Fortunately, as must be intuitively obvious, the proofs can easily be modified to accommodate the possibility of imported materials. It will suffice to prove the proposition that compensated free trade is superior to no trade. The extension to the case of restricted trade is straightforward.

Let $\hat{a} = (\hat{a}_1, \hat{a}_2, \ldots, \hat{a}_t)$ represent the vector of imported raw materials, and $\hat{w} = (\hat{w}_1, \hat{w}_2, \ldots, \hat{w}_t)$ the corresponding vector of raw material prices. Then (2) must be rewritten as

$$p'(\bar{z}' - z') - \hat{w}'\hat{a}' = 0 \tag{2d}$$

and (4) as

$$p'\bar{z}' - w'a' - \hat{w}'\hat{a}' \geqslant p'\bar{z}^0 - w'a^0. \tag{4d}$$

Substituting in (4d) from (1) and (2d), we obtain

$$p'z' - w'a' \geqslant p'z^0 - w'a^0$$

and the proof proceeds as in section 3.

7 THE ACCOMMODATION OF CAPITAL MOVEMENTS

In all proofs furnished so far, balanced trade has been assumed. In this section the implications of capital movements are considered. Attention is confined to the case of free trade and capital **imports**. Extension of the proofs to cover restricted trade and capital exports is straightforward.

In the special and very simple case in which the 'capital' to be moved can be thought of as a constant vector of commodities,[11] $K = (K_1, K_2, \ldots, K_n) \geqslant 0$, equations (1) and (2) become, respectively,

$$\bar{z}^0 - z^0 + K = 0 \tag{1e}$$

and

$$p'(\bar{z}' - z' + K) = 0. \tag{2e}$$

Substitution into (4) from (1e) and (2e) yields (5), as before.

When the object to be transferred is a sum of money, however, the proof becomes slightly more complicated. 'Autarky' must be redefined to permit imports equal in value to the sum to be transferred, say T. Imagine that, under autarky thus defined, the last $(n - m)$ commodities are imported. Exports are, of course, prohibited, so that imports $y^0 - \bar{y}^0$ are limited in value to T:

$$p_y^0(y^0 - \bar{y}^0) = T. \tag{1f}$$

As before,

$$\bar{x}^0 - x^0 = 0. \tag{1g}$$

Equation (2) takes the revised form[12]

$$p_x' x' + p_y' y' = p_x' \bar{x}' + p_y' \bar{y}' + T. \tag{2f}$$

With the introduction of free trade import prices will fall; that is, $p_y' < p_y^0$. Hence, from (1f),

$$p_y'(y^0 - \bar{y}^0) > T. \tag{1h}$$

Substituting in (4a) for $\bar{x}^0$ from (1g), for $p_y'\bar{y}^0$ from (1h), and for $(p_x'\bar{x}' + p_y'\bar{y}')$ from (2f), we obtain

$$p'z' - w'a' \geqslant p'z^0 - w'a^0 \tag{5}$$

as before.

8 THE GAIN FROM RESTRICTING TRADE

It has been shown that situations of free or restricted trade are superior to the autarkic situation. This leaves open the question whether the various trading situations can be ranked. What can be said of the relative desirabilities of the free-trading situation, the trading situation characterized by a uniform 5 per cent import duty, and that characterized by a 10 per cent duty, etc.?

In the special case in which a country's terms of trade are independent of that country's offer, a particularly simple answer can be given: the free-trade situation is superior to the 5 per cent situation, which in turn is superior to the 10 per cent situation, and so on. The reason is very simple: under free trade all the necessary marginal conditions of a Paretian national optimum are satisfied. In particular, the marginal rate of transformation between commodities in production is equal to the marginal rate of transformation between commodities in international trade (the marginal terms of trade) and to their marginal rate of substitution in consumption. A tariff destroys the equality between the marginal terms of trade and the other two marginal rates of transformation. And the greater the rate of duty, the greater the resulting inequality. This is illustrated, for the special two-commodities, fixed-factors case, by Figure 4(a), and for the two-persons case by Figure 4(b). Note that Figure 4(b) allows for the possibility that there exist one or more distributions of income under which no trade takes place. Clearly, if such a distribution exists any tariff will be a dead letter and the utility possibility curves must all touch at one or more points. (In terms of Figure 4(a), W must be recognized as an isolated, tariff-ridden consumption possibility.) Of course, such a distribution need not exist **for the particular terms of trade considered**, in which case the utility possibility curves must lie uniformly one outside the other.

When, however, world prices depend upon the amounts offered and demanded by the tariff-imposing country, complications appear. For in this case the average and marginal rates of transformation through trade diverge; and it is to the average rates that under free trade the marginal rates of substitution and transformation through domestic production are equated. Hence a single-country Paretian optimum is not necessarily reached under free trade. The possibility emerges that an appropriate system of taxes and subsidies on imports and exports, combined with lumpsum redistributive transfers between individuals, would leave everyone in the tariff-ridden country better off than in a particular free-trade situation.

Suppose,[13] then, that world prices in terms of some *numéraire*, which we assume to be the first commodity, are functions of the quantities imported and exported by a particular country,

$$q_i^1 = q_i^1(E_1, E_2, \ldots, E_n), \quad i = 2, 3, \ldots, n$$

(E_i is positive if the country is a net importer of the ith commodity, negative if the country is a net exporter). The necessity of international payments equilibrium is expressed by

$$E_1 + \sum_{i=2}^{n} E_i q_i^1(E_1, E_2, \ldots, E_n) = 0.$$

If follows that the marginal rates of commodity transformation through trade are

$$-\frac{\mathrm{d}E_i}{\mathrm{d}E_j} = \left(q_j^1 + \sum_{s=2}^{n} E_s \frac{\partial q_s^1}{\partial E_j}\right) \Big/ \left(q_i^1 + \sum_{s=2}^{n} E_s \frac{\partial q_s^1}{\partial E_i}\right)$$

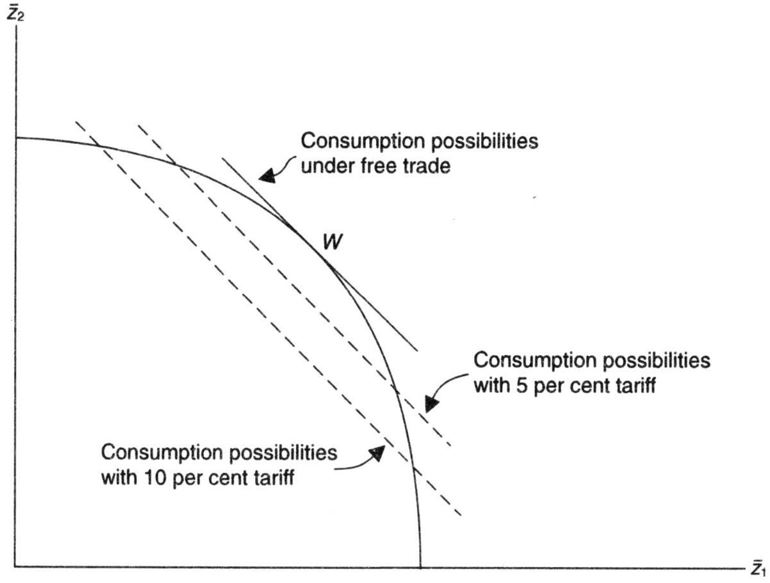

Figure 4(a)

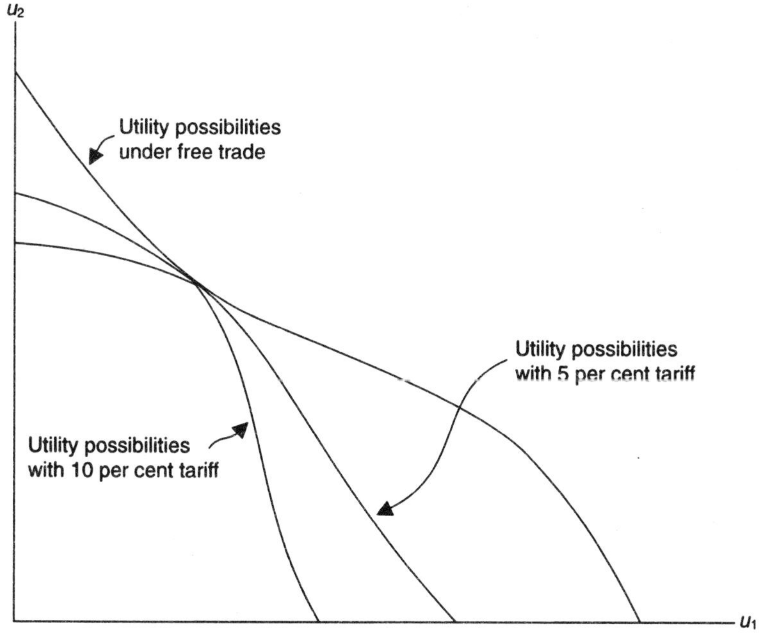

Figure 4(b)

$$= \frac{q_j^1}{q_i^1}\left[\left(1+\sum_s \frac{\alpha_s}{\alpha_j}\cdot\frac{1}{\xi_{js}}\right)\Big/\left(1+\sum_s \frac{\alpha_s}{\alpha_i}\cdot\frac{1}{\xi_{is}}\right)\right], \quad i, j = 1, 2, \ldots, n,$$

where α_s is the value of exports of the sth commodity and ξ_{js} is the cross-elasticity of foreign demand (supply) for the jth export (import) with respect to the sth price. In a Paretian optimum, on the other hand,

$$p_j/p_i = -\,dE_i/dE_j, \quad i, j, = 1, 2, \ldots, n.$$

The conditions of an optimum will be satisfied, therefore, if an *ad valorem* tax of $100[\Sigma_s(\alpha_s/\alpha_i)/(1/\xi_{is})]$ per cent is imposed on the ith commodity as it crosses the frontier, the tax to be reckoned on the **foreign** price.

Note that since no tax need be levied on the *numéraire* commodity, there need be only $(n-1)$ taxes in all. On the other hand, the choice of *numéraire* is arbitrary so that the $(n-1)$-dimensional vector of optimal taxes is not unique. Further, while the taxing authority **need** consider only $(n-1)$ commodities, it may impose taxes on all n commodities. In general, one tax (say, the ith) may be imposed at any arbitrary level; the remaining optimal taxes will then be functions of the ith tax.

Note also that, thanks to the presence of cross-elasticity terms, a Paretian optimum may require that some imports and exports be subsidized.

The special two-commodities case is of some interest. A single tax would suffice, and it could be levied indifferently on the exported or imported commodity. Reckoned on the foreign price, the optimal tax in this case is simply the reciprocal of the elasticity of the foreign supply of imports: $\tau = 1/\xi$. Much attention has been lavished upon this formula.[14] But it provides scant guidance to the discovery of the optimal τ, since it involves two, not one, unknowns. The value of ξ varies with the position on the foreign supply curve; the position on the foreign supply curve depends on the demand by the tariff-imposing country for imports; that, in turn, depends on the internal distribution of income; but, finally, the post-tariff distribution of income depends on the arbitrary pattern of lumpsum taxes and subsidies. There is, then, not a single optimum τ but an infinity. A given τ, say 5 per cent, may be optimal for one distribution of income, but in general will be either greater or smaller than the optimal τ for any other distribution. For the distribution represented by point u'' in Figure 5, for example, a 5 per cent tariff is optimal, whereas the distribution represented by u''' calls for a 10 per cent tariff. (Note that, in contrast to the case previously discussed, the utility possibility curves corresponding to the two tariff levels may intersect; if, as is assumed here, each rate is optimal for **some** distribution of income, they **must** intersect. About all that one can be sure of is that neither curve will loop inside the autarky curve – though they may touch it.) The utility possibility curve for tariff-restricted trade is then the envelope of the set of all utility possibility curves for specific τs. These ideas are illustrated by Figure 5.

The tariff-imposing country is, of course, simply taking advantage of its monopoly position in world markets. What, then, happens to the optimum tariff

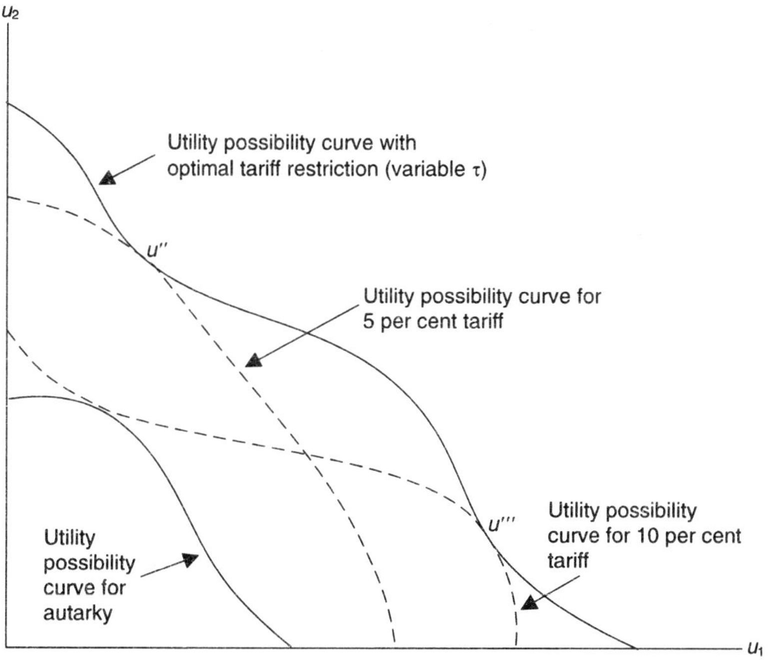

Figure 5

if the production and sale of export commodities are in the hands of a monopolist? The monopolist will seek to equate the marginal cost of exports in terms of importables (i.e. the marginal rate of transformation between exportables and importables) to the marginal revenue of exports in terms of imports (i.e. the marginal terms of trade). Thus the monopolist in pursuit of maximum profit will impose a tax (rate of profit) on the foreigner equal to the optimum tariff rate of competitive conditions. Under conditions of monopoly, then, the optimum tariff is zero (Polak, 1950–1). Note, however, that the full Paretian optimum is not attained under monopoly, for consumers will equate their marginal rates of substitution not to the marginal rate of transformation but to the price ratio. There exists a case for paying a subsidy on sales to the domestic market, at a rate sufficient to equate price and marginal revenue (on home sales only); that is, at a percentage rate equal to (minus) the reciprocal of the elasticity of home demand for the export commodity.

Finally, the reader is reminded that the discussion of this section has been based on the assumption of given trading conditions. In particular, it has been assumed that the import duties levied by its trading partners do not change in response to changes in the home country's tariffs. None of the theorems of this section survive the recognition that the home country's trading partners may retaliate against the erection of a tariff barrier.

9 FINAL COMMENTS

It has been shown, under certain assumptions, that compensated trade, either free or restricted, is better than no trade. It is well, in conclusion, to emphasize that the proofs have been constructed under some fairly severe assumptions. The assumption of stable ordinal preference scales for individuals has ruled out of consideration what Mill considered to be the greatest of the benefits imparted by trade, the destruction of old preferences.[15] Similarly, no attention has been paid to the possible impact of trade on the state of technical knowledge and the rate of its accumulation. It has been assumed, as is customary, that returns to scale are constant, that the full employment of all resources is effected by flexible factor prices, and that there are no external economies or diseconomies, either of production or consumption.[16] Finally, it has been assumed throughout that lumpsum taxes and subsidies are feasible. If the only kinds of taxes and subsidies available are those which carry with them a deadweight loss of allocative efficiency, then the theorems are true but irrelevant. The utility **feasibility** locus of the trade situation may well cut inside the no-trade feasibility locus (Samuelson, 1950).

NOTES

* I have greatly profited from several conversations with Paul Samuelson. I have also had privileged access to the article of Professor Samuelson's published in this issue of the *Economic Journal.*

Sections 1 and 4 are here printed in revised form.

1 Samuelson (1939: 195–6). The sentence in square brackets has been inserted.

2 Samuelson (1939: 198–9).

3 Samuelson (1939: 204). The sentence in square brackets has been inserted.

4 The notation of the present essay conforms as closely as is practicable to that of Samuelson's 1939 paper. There are, however, some discrepancies. In particular, my z corresponds to his x.

5 $p'\bar{z}'$ is to be understood as the inner product $\Sigma_{i=1}^{n} p_i' \bar{z}_i'$, $p'z'$ as $\Sigma_{i=1}^{n} p_i' z_i'$.

6 Samuelson (1950: especially pp. 1–9). Note that it **cannot** be inferred from equation (5) that it is possible, by simply redistributing the collection of goods actually chosen under free trade, to make everyone better off than in the chosen autarkic position.

7 *RR* and *pp* may possibly touch at one or more points. Note that $g'g'$, the **point** utility possibility curve corresponding to the collection of goods actually chosen under free trade, may not only cut *pp* but may pass south-west of u^0 (cf. note 5). This point has been emphasized by Olsen (1958); Olsen went astray, however, in arguing that it is inconsistent with Samuelson's 1939 results. Mr Olsen has indicated in correspondence that he now accepts the analysis of the present essay.

That *RR* cannot lie inside *pp* is denied by Enke (1961) who holds that, given individual indifference curves of 'extreme curvature', 'a change to *free* trade from no trade will . . . lessen welfare for all after compensation'. Mr Enke's mistake is in supposing that the compensated and uncompensated free-trade consumption mixtures (represented by Z' in his fig. 1) are identical and, by implication, denying the necessity of the compensated mixture lying 'above' the autarkic community indifference curve.

8 Samuelson (1939: 203) has stated that this is so for the very special case in which individuals are alike with respect to tastes, abilities and ownership of the factors of production.

9 It should suffice to dispel the doubts expressed by Caves (1960: 266): 'The danger of circularity in reasoning becomes great, unless some way of expressing "greater deviation of world from autarkic prices" can be found which does not *define* an increase in welfare.' Note that preliminary normalization of the price vector is unnecessary. The only weakness of the definition that I can detect is its failure to rank all p' and p''; for some p' and p'' it may not be possible to say that p' deviates from p^0 by more than does p'', or that p'' deviates by more than p', or that p' and p'' deviate equally.

10 The proof could be modified to accommodate non-traded goods.

11 As it can, for example, when reparations are assessed and paid in kind.

12 That when free trade is introduced the list of imports will expand is of no importance here.

13 This paragraph is based on Graaff (1949–50).

14 Mill (1909, 1948) and Sidgwick (1887) drew early attention to the possibility, open to a single country, of gaining by imposing a tariff. It was left for Edgeworth (1925: 15) and Bickerdike (1906) to clinch the matter.

15 Mill (1909: Book III, Ch. XVII, section 5).

16 If external economies of scale are of sufficient strength to reverse the convexity of the production frontier and, withal, are not disturbing of the Paretian optimality conditions – a case which has been studied by Matthews (1949–50) – the following obverse of the proposition of section 2, and 3, may be proved: through trade and lumpsum taxes and subsidies, every individual in an imperfectly specialized country could be made **worse off** (or, in the limiting case, no better off) than in the absence of trade. The welfare implications of factor-price rigidities and external economies have been studied by Haberler (1950).

REFERENCES

Bickerdike, C. F. (1906) 'The theory of incipient taxes', *Economic Journal* 16: 529–35.

Caves, R. E. (1960) *Trade and Economic Structure, Models and Methods*, Cambridge, MA: Harvard University Press.

Edgeworth, F. Y. (1925) *Papers Relating to Political Economy*, II, London: Macmillan.

Enke, S. (1961) 'Trade gains in the short run: A reply to Mr. Kemp', *Canadian Journal of Economics and Political Science* 27: 522–6.

Graaff, J. de V. (1949–50) 'On optimum tariff structures', *Review of Economic Studies* 17(1): 47–59.

Haberler, G. (1950) 'Some problems in the pure theory of foreign trade', *Economic Journal* 60: 223–40.

Matthews, R. C. O. (1949–50) 'Reciprocal demand and increasing returns', *Review of Economic Studies* 17(2): 149–58.

Mill, J. S. (1909) *Principles of Political Economy*, London: Longmans, Green.

Mill, J. S. (1948) *Essays in Some Unsettled Questions of Political Economy*, London School of Economics and Political Science, London.

Olsen, E. (1958) 'Undenrigshandelens gevinst', *Nationaløkonomisk Tidsskrift* 96(1, 2): 76–9.

Polak, J. J. (1950–1) 'The "optimum tariff" and the cost of exports', *Review of Economic Studies* 19(1): 36–41.

Samuelson, P. A. (1939) 'The gains from international trade', *Canadian Journal of Economics and Political Science* 5: 195–205. Reprinted in: Ellis, H. S. and Metzler, L. A. (eds) (1949) *Readings in the Theory of International Trade*, pp. 239–52, Philadelphia: The Blakiston Company.

Samuelson, P. A. (1950) 'Evaluation of real national income', *Oxford Economic Papers, NS*, 2: 1–29.

Samuelson, P. A. (1953) 'Prices of factors and goods in general equilibrium', *Review of Economic Studies*, 21: 1–20.
Sidgwick, H. (1887) *The Principles of Political Economy*, 2nd edn, London: Macmillan.

2

THE GAINS FROM FREE TRADE*

1 INTRODUCTION

The literature concerning the gains from free trade divides naturally into two major parts, that pertaining to the opening of trade and that relating to autonomous variations in the prices facing a small country. In the first part, states of autarky are compared with states of free trade; in the second part, comparisons are made of alternative states of free trade. Almost nothing has been written concerning the welfare implications of variations in foreign demand when the country under consideration is of any size.

In this essay we develop a unified theory which encompasses all of the main known results concerning the gains from free trade, as well as several which appear to be new. In particular, we take a small step towards the welfare analysis of foreign demand variations for countries of any size. In dealing with small countries we find it convenient to introduce a family of price sets each of which is dual to a Scitovsky community indifference surface. The construct will, we think, find applications beyond those demonstrated in this essay.

The scope of the essay is conventional in that externalities and dynamic phenomena are excluded. Section 2 contains a list of the more frequently used notations, as well as a statement of assumptions and a list of key definitions. Section 3 contains a proof of the well-known proposition that for countries of any size free trade is potentially better than no trade. To our knowledge, this is the first complete proof of the proposition under assumptions of any generality. Indeed the proposition is extended to cover trade hindered by non-negative but otherwise arbitrary vectors of import and export duties. In section 4 we state and prove several propositions relating to the trading gains of small countries. Finally, in section 5 we return to the study of countries of any size and prove a theorem concerning the welfare implications of foreign demand variations of a particular type.

2 NOTATION AND ASSUMPTIONS

The notation and assumptions have been kept as close as possible to those now more or less standard in the literature dealing with the existence and optimality of competitive equilibria.[1] However, it is now necessary to distinguish between tradable and non-tradable goods. Moreover, much of the theory relating to trade gains involves comparisons of institutionally constrained or 'second-best' equilibria, or sets of equilibria. To facilitate such comparisons the standard assumptions and notation must be modified and extended.

We distinguish the home country and the rest of the world. Commodities are assumed to be either tradable without cost or non-tradable. We suppose that there are l commodities. The first l^0 of these are internationally tradable, the next l^1 are non-tradables associated with the home country, the last l^2 $(= l - l^0 - l^1)$ are non-tradables associated with the foreign country. (We do not wish to rule out the possibility that the same non-tradable goods are available in both countries.) To avoid triviality, we assume that $l = l^0 + l^1 + l^2 \geq 2$, $l^0 \geq 2$.

It is assumed that in the home country there is a finite number m of consumers. The ith consumer is characterized by a closed, convex and lower-bounded set X_i of viable consumption vectors x_i, an l-dimensional endowment vector $\omega_i = \Delta_i + \underline{x}_i$, where $\underline{x}_i$ is a member of X_i and Δ_i is a vector with the first $(l^0 + l^1)$ elements positive and the remaining l^2 elements zero, and a complete, convex and continuous preference ordering $\succsim_i$ defined over X_i. *Ceteris paribus*, and under all circumstances, each individual prefers more of each of the l^0 tradable commodities to less. Together with our assumption concerning ω_i, this rules out Arrow's counter example (Arrow, 1951: 528). The possibility of consumption saturation is ruled out.

In addition it is assumed that there is a finite number n of producers. The jth producer is characterized by a set Y_j of feasible production vectors y_j; Y_j contains the null vector. The set of feasible aggregate production vectors $Y = \Sigma_j Y_j$ is assumed to be closed and convex and to satisfy the postulates of irreversibility of production and free disposal. We find it convenient to introduce also the set $Y_\omega = Y + \omega$, where $\omega = \Sigma_i \omega_i$, and the aggregate supply correspondence $\eta(p)$, where p is an l-dimensional vector of prices. Evidently Y_ω is closed and convex.

All endowment, consumption and production vectors for the home country have zeros in the last l^2 positions. This is not true of the price vector p. The subvector containing the first l^0 elements of p is denoted by $\tilde{p}$. (The tilde notation will be used consistently to indicate the subvector containing the first l^0 elements of an l-dimensional vector of commodity prices or quantities.)

The aggregate foreign excess demand correspondence is denoted by $\zeta_0(p)$, a set of l-dimensional vectors with zeros in positions $l^0 + 1, \ldots, l^0 + l^1$. It is assumed that ζ_0 (i) is closed, convex and lower-bounded for each p, (ii) is homogeneous of degree 0 in p, (iii) satisfies the budgetary constraint that, for all $z \in \zeta_0(p)$, $p \cdot z \leq 0$ and (iv) is upper semi-continuous in p.[2]

The state is recognized. However, its role is limited to the collection and disbursement of lumpsums (side payments). For our purposes it suffices to consider one special system of side payments. The sums received and given by consumers $2, \ldots, m$ are such that, whatever the disturbance, each of those consumers can enjoy a specified constant level of well-being, usually associated with some initial autarkic or free-trade equilibrium.[3] Let x_i^0 be the initial consumption vector of the ith consumer. Then we may define the not-worse-than-x_i^0 set $X_i(x_i^0) = \{x_i \in X_i\colon x_i \succsim_i x_i^0\}$ and the post-transfer wealth of the ith consumer as $w_i = \min_{x_i \in X_i(x_i^0)} p \cdot x_i$, where $i = 2, \ldots, m$.[4] The first consumer, or *princeps*, then claims the residual income, that is $w_1 = \max_{x_1} p \cdot x_1$, where $x_1 \in [Y_\omega - \Sigma_2^m X_i(x_i^0)]$. We define the aggregate supply correspondence for the rest of the country *vis-à-vis princeps* as that set over which w_1 reaches its maximum, and denote it by $\zeta_-(p)$. The demand correspondence for the ith consumer is denoted by $\xi_i(p, w_i(p))$. In particular, the demand correspondence of *princeps* is denoted by $\xi_1(p, w_1(p))$.

A trading equilibrium exists if there is a pair of price vectors (p', p'') such that

$$\Omega \equiv \xi_1(p', w_1(p')) \cap [\xi_-(p') - \zeta_0(p'')] \neq \emptyset, \tag{1}$$

where p' and p'' are domestic and foreign prices, respectively. A free-trade equilibrium is a trading equilibrium with

$$\tilde{p}' = \tilde{p}''. \tag{2}$$

Free trade is potentially unharmful in relation to some initial equilibrium if Ω contains a vector x_1 such that $x_1 \succsim_i x_1^0$, where x_1^0 is the initial consumption vector of *princeps*.

We now seek to clarify the sense in which an economy will be called 'small'. Let $\tilde{p}$ and $\hat{\hat{p}}$ be two given price subvectors, of dimensions l^0 and l^2 respectively. Let P^1 and P^m be the natural simplexes of dimensions l and m, respectively, and let $\theta \equiv (\theta_1, \ldots, \theta_m) \in P^m$. We define $P(\tilde{p}, \hat{\hat{p}}) = \{p\colon p = (\rho\tilde{p}, \mu\hat{p}, \rho\hat{\hat{p}})$ for some $\hat{p}$, $\mu > 0$, $\rho > 0\}$, also

$$V = \{(p, \theta) \in P(\tilde{p}, \hat{\hat{p}}) \times P^m\colon \xi_i(p, \theta_i \max_{y \in Y} p(y + \omega)) \neq \emptyset \text{ for all } i\}$$

and

$$Z_1 = \left\{ z\colon z = (\tilde{z}, 0) \in \bigcup_{(p, \theta) \in V} \left[\sum_i \xi_i(p, \theta_i \cdot \max_{y \in Y} p(y + \omega)) - \{\omega\} - \eta(p) \right] \right\}. \tag{3}$$

Definition 1. *The domestic economy is small relative to the price* **subvector pair** $(\tilde{p}, \hat{\hat{p}})$ *if* $Z_1 \subseteq -\zeta_0(\tilde{p}, \cdot, \hat{\hat{p}})$.

The foreign excess demand correspondence is written as $\zeta_0(\tilde{p}, \cdot, \hat{\hat{p}})$ to indicate that it does not depend on the prices of home non-tradables. In common-sense terms, a country is small if, whatever the home income distribution (consistent with the survival of each consumer), the resulting equilibria all share the same price subvectors for tradables and foreign non-tradables.

The symbol $a \equiv ((x_i), (y_i))$ denotes a particular **state** of the country. We shall write $a^1 \succsim a^2$ if and only if, for all i, $x_i^1 \succsim_i x_i^2$ and x_i^1 is in a^1, x_i^2 is in

a^2. Similarly, we shall write $a^1 \sim a^2$ if and only if, for all i, $x_i^1 \sim_i x_i^2$ and x_i^1 is in a^1, x_i^2 is in a^2. Finally, we shall write $a^1 \succ a^2$ if and only if $a^1 \succsim_i a^2$ and, for some i, $x_i^1 \succ_i x_i^2$, where x_i^1 is in a^1 and x_i^2 is in a^2. If $a^1 \succsim a^2$ we shall say that the substitution of a^1 for a^2 is Pareto-unharmful; if $a^1 \succ a^2$ we shall say that the substitution is Pareto-beneficial.

An autarkic equilibrium is a pair (a, p) such that

$$\sum_j y_i \in \eta(p), \quad x_i \in \xi_i(p, w_i) \quad \text{for some } w_i, \quad \sum_i x_i = \sum_j y_j + \omega. \tag{4}$$

An autonomous disturbance to the economy (e.g. the freeing of trade, a change in the world prices facing a small country) will be described as potentially unharmful if there exists a system of lumpsum payments which would ensure that no person is harmed by the disturbance. A disturbance will be described as potentially beneficial if it is potentially unharmful and if, in addition, the system of payments would leave at least one person better off than before the disturbance.

Consider three price vectors p^1, p^2 and p^3, each normalized to lie in the natural simplex P^l. We shall say that p^2 is intermediate to p^1 and p^3 if it is possible to write p^2 as a strictly convex linear combination of p^1 and p^3:

$$p^2 = \lambda p^1 + (1 - \lambda)p^3, \quad 0 < \lambda < 1. \tag{5}$$

If (5) is satisfied we shall also say that p^3 deviates more from p^1 than does p^2, and that the replacement of p^1 with p^2 and of p^2 with p^3 involve price changes in the same direction.

Henceforth the superscript 0 will distinguish autarkic quantities and the superscript 1 the quantities of an initial free-trade equilibrium.

3 GAINS FROM THE OPENING OF TRADE – COUNTRIES OF ANY SIZE

We shall prove

Theorem 1. *Given the assumptions of section 2, for any autarkic equilibrium there can be found a free-trade equilibrium in which no one is worse off, that is free trade is potentially unharmful in relation to no trade.*

The proposition is well known (see Kemp, 1962; Samuelson, 1962: conclusion 8), but it seems still to lack proof. Samuelson (1939) showed that for a small country with fixed amounts of the productive factors free trade is potentially unharmful in relation to no trade. Later, Kemp (1962, 1969) provided an 'almost proof' of the more general proposition by showing that no free-trade equilibrium could be improved by returning to autarky, that is by showing that in utility space the autarkic utility possibility frontier could not pass above any free-trade equilibrium point. However, a jump was then made to the conclusion of the theorem, that the free-trade utility possibility frontier must pass above or through every possible autarkic equilibrium point. That the step needs justifica-

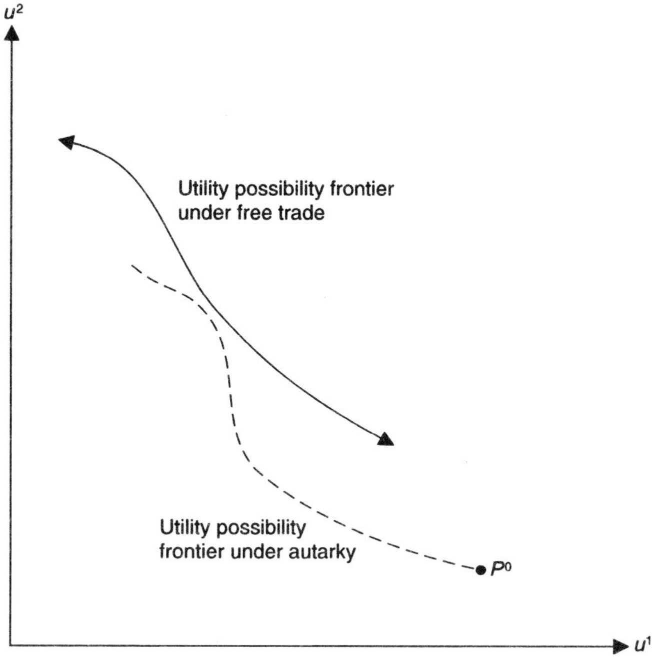

Figure 1

tion is illustrated by Figure 1; evidently the autarkic equilibrium P^0 cannot be equalled or bettered under free trade. It is implicit in the proof we shall give that in drawing Figure 1 we have violated the assumptions of section 2.[5]

Proof of Theorem 1. *It suffices to show that there exists a free-trade equilibrium with prices* p^* *satisfying (1)–(2) and with* $x_1 \in \Omega$, $x_1 \succsim_1 x_1^0$. *The foreign excess demand correspondence is* $\zeta_0(p)$ *and the home excess demand correspondence may be defined as* $\zeta_1(p) \equiv \xi_1(p, w_1(p)) - \zeta_-(p)$. *Both are homogeneous of degree* 0 *in* p. *Following Debreu (1959: Ch. 5), there then exists an equilibrium price vector* p^* *such that* $0 \in [\zeta_0(p^*) + \zeta_1(p^*)]$. *That is,* $x_1^* = z_-^* - z_0^*$, *where* $x_i^* \in \xi_1(p^*, w_1(p^*))$, $z_-^* \in \zeta_-(p^*)$ *and* $z_0^* \in \zeta_0(p^*)$. *We then have*

$$
\begin{aligned}
p^* \cdot x_1^* &= p^* \cdot z_-^* \quad (\textit{since } p^* \cdot z_0^* = 0) \\
&\geqslant p^* \cdot \left(y^0 + \omega - \sum_{i=2}^{m} x_i^0 \right) \\
&= p^* \cdot x_1^0 \quad \left(\textit{since under autarky } y + \omega - \sum_{i=1}^{m} x_i = 0 \right) \qquad (6) \\
&\geqslant \min_{x_1 \in X_1(x_1^0)} p^* \cdot x_1 .
\end{aligned}
$$

Thus x_1^**, the equilibrium consumption vector chosen by princeps under free trade, is not inferior to* x_1^0*, the consumption vector chosen under autarky.* □[6]

We note that theorem 1 accommodates trade in both primary and produced factors of production.

In this paper we focus on the gains from free trade. However, we briefly note the following very substantial but easy generalization of theorem 1.[7]

Theorem 1′. *Given the assumptions of section 2 and any two vectors of non-negative taxes, one vector for imports, the other for exports, and given any autarkic equilibrium, there exists a tax-distorted compensated trade equilibrium in which no one is worse off; that is, trade distorted by fixed non-negative taxes is potentially unharmful in relation to no trade.*

Proof *We begin by noting that there exists a tax-distorted trade equilibrium if and only if there exists a partition of the* l *commodities into imports, exports and non-traded goods such that, given that partition, there exists an equilibrium.*

Consider now **any** *partition of the* l *commodities into imports, exports and non-tradable goods; and suppose for the time being that only imports are taxed. Let* τ_i $(i = 1, \ldots, l^0)$ *be the ad valorem rate of duty on imports of the ith tradable commodity, calculated on the foreign price. Let primes indicate domestic prices and double primes world prices. It has been shown by Sontheimer (1971: theorem 2) that, on the assumptions of the theorem, a trade equilibrium exists. In that equilibrium* $p_i^{*\prime} = \lambda p_i^{*\prime\prime}(1 + \tau_i)$ *if the ith commodity is imported and* $p_i^{*\prime} = \lambda p_i^{*\prime\prime}$ *if it is exported. Let* I *be the l-dimensional unit matrix and* τ *an l-dimensional diagonal matrix with* τ_i *or 0 in the ith diagonal place according as the commodity is or is not imported. Recalling that in equilibrium* $x_1^* = z_-^* + z_0^*$,

$$p^{*\prime} \cdot x_1^* = p^{*\prime} \cdot z_-^* - p^{*\prime} \cdot z_0^*$$

$$= p^{*\prime} \cdot z_-^* - \lambda p^{*\prime\prime} \cdot (I + \tau) \cdot z_0^* \quad \textit{(applying Walras' law to the foreign economy, } p^{*\prime\prime} \cdot z_0 = 0\textit{)}$$

$$\geqslant p^{*\prime} \cdot z_-^* \quad \textit{(from the definition of } \tau\textit{)}$$

$$\geqslant \min_{x_1 \in X_1(x_1^0)} p^{*\prime} \cdot x_1 \quad \textit{(using (6)).}$$

If exports as well as imports are taxed, the same final inequality can be obtained by essentially the same steps. □

If world trade is distorted by subsidies to imports and/or exports it is not generally potentially beneficial. However, it remains potentially beneficial in special cases. Indeed, given any vectors of non-negative import and export duties, it is always possible to find equivalent vectors, each vector containing at least one negative element, such that trade is potentially beneficial. This follows from theorem 1′ and the one-dimensional indeterminacy of any tax vector which supports a given trade equilibrium.

4 VARIATIONS IN FOREIGN DEMAND – SMALL COUNTRIES

We shall prove a series of propositions concerning the implications of an autonomous change in the world price vector, it being assumed that the home country is small in relation to both the initial and the new prices.

In an initial free-trade equilibrium the aggregate home output vector is y^1 and the individual consumption vectors x_i^1, $i = 1, 2, \ldots, m$. The quantities of the new equilibrium are indicated by an asterisk. When prices change a side payment is made to each of individuals $2, \ldots, m$ just sufficient to leave the individual's well-being undisturbed. The price change is then beneficial if and only if *princeps* is better off in the new equilibrium. We know that $p^* \cdot x_1^* = p^* \cdot z_-^*$. Hence *princeps* is better off in the new equilibrium if and only if $p^* \cdot z_-^* > \min_{x_1 \in X_1(x_1^1)} p^* \cdot x_1$, that is if and only if

$$\max_{y \in Y,\, x_i \in X_i(x_i^1)} p^* \cdot \left(y + \omega - \sum_{i=1}^{m} x_i \right) > 0.$$

For this inequality to hold it suffices that

$$\max_{z = (\tilde{z}, 0):\, z \in \left[Y_\omega - \sum_1^m X_i(x_i^1) \right]} p^* \cdot z > 0 \tag{7}$$

and this condition is also necessary. Let $a^1 = ((x_i^1), (y_i^1))$, and let $\tilde{\pi}^*$ be the normalized form of $\tilde{p}^*$, so that $\Sigma_i^{l^0} \tilde{\pi}_i^* = 1$ and $\tilde{\pi}^*$ lies in the l^0-dimensional natural simplex P^{l^0}. Then (7) may be abbreviated to

$$\beta(\tilde{\pi}^*, a^1) > 0. \tag{8}$$

The index β dates back to Marshall (1923) and has been discussed by Viner (n.d.) and by Bhagwati and Johnson (1960). It is known to be a convex function of $\tilde{\pi}$. See Wan (1965), where β is called the maximum bonus.

We next define the set of not-better-than-a^1 world prices $N(a^1) = \{\tilde{\pi}: \beta(\tilde{\pi}, a^1) \leq 0\}$, the set of worse-than-$a^1$ world prices $\mathring{N}(a^1) = \{\tilde{\pi}: \beta(\tilde{\pi}, a^1) < 0\}$, and the set of equivalent-to-a^1 world prices $N(a^1)\backslash\mathring{N}(a^1) = \{\tilde{\pi}: \beta(\tilde{\pi}, a^1) = 0\}$. It will be shown that if $a^1 > a^0$ for some a^0 then $N(a^1)\backslash\mathring{N}(a^1)$ has no interior. The locus $\{\tilde{\pi}: \beta(\tilde{\pi}, a^1) = 0\}$ is dual to the Scitovsky contour, that is the boundary of the set of not-worse-than-a^1 consumption vectors $\Sigma_{i=1}^{m} X_i(x_i^1)$.

We begin by proving three lemmata which collectively characterize the price sets $N(a^1)$ and $\mathring{N}(a^1)$ and which facilitate later proofs.

Lemma 1. *Both* $N(a^1)$ *and* $\mathring{N}(a^1)$ *are convex.*

Proof. *Let* $\tilde{\pi}'$, $\tilde{\pi}''$ *and* $\tilde{\pi}^\lambda$ *be three world price vectors such that* $\tilde{\pi}^\lambda = \lambda\tilde{\pi}' + (1 - \lambda)\tilde{\pi}''$, $0 < \lambda < 1$. *Then*

$$\begin{aligned}\beta(\tilde{\pi}^{\lambda}, a^1) &= \max_{z=(\tilde{z},0):\, z \in \left[Y_\omega - \sum X_i(x_i^1)\right]} (\tilde{\pi}^{\lambda}, 0)\cdot z \\ &= \tilde{\pi}^{\lambda}\cdot\tilde{z}^{\lambda} \quad \text{(say)} \\ &= \lambda\tilde{\pi}'\cdot\tilde{z}^{\lambda} + (1-\lambda)\tilde{\pi}''\cdot\tilde{z}^{\lambda} \\ &\leqslant \lambda\beta(\tilde{\pi}', a^1) + (1-\lambda)\beta(\tilde{\pi}'', a^1).\end{aligned} \tag{9}$$

If both $\beta(\tilde{\pi}', a^1)$ *and* $\beta(\tilde{\pi}'', a^1)$ *are non-positive (negative) so must be* $\beta(\tilde{\pi}^{\lambda}, a^1)$. □

Lemma 2. *Suppose that in a free-trade equilibrium* $\tilde{\pi} = \tilde{\pi}^1$, $a = a^1$ *and* $\underset{\circ}{z} = z^1 = (\tilde{z}^1, 0)$, *where* z *is the excess supply vector of the home country. Then* $\mathring{N}(a^1) \subseteq \{\tilde{\pi} \in P^{l^0} : \tilde{z}^1\cdot\tilde{\pi} < 0\}$.

Proof. *We have* $(\tilde{z}^1, 0) \in [Y_\omega - \Sigma_{i=1}^m X_i(x_i^1)]$. *Moreover, by definition,* $\beta(\tilde{\pi}, a^1) \geqslant \tilde{z}^1\cdot\tilde{\pi}$. *Thus if* $\tilde{z}^1\cdot\tilde{\pi} \geqslant 0$ *then* $\beta(\tilde{\pi}, a^1) \geqslant 0$ *and* $\tilde{\pi} \notin \mathring{N}(a^1)$. □

Lemma 3. *Either (a)* $a^1 \sim a^0$, *an autarkic state, and* $\mathring{N}(a^1) = \mathring{N}(a^0) = \emptyset$ *or (b) the equivalent-to-*a^1 *price set* $[N(a^1)\backslash\mathring{N}(a^1)]$ *has no interior.*

Proof. *(a) If* $a^1 \sim a^0$, *with* $z^0 = 0$, *then, from lemma 2,* $\mathring{N}(a^1) = \mathring{N}(a^0) \subseteq \{\tilde{\pi} \in P^{l^0} : \tilde{\pi}\cdot 0 < 0\} = \emptyset$. *Moreover, if* $a^1 \sim a^0$, *the equivalent-to-*a^1 *price set may have an interior. (b) From (a),* $a^0 > a^1$ *is not possible. Suppose, therefore, that* $a^1 > a^0$ *and that the assertion is false. Then there exists a price vector* $\tilde{\pi}^2 \in 0(\tilde{\pi}^2) \subset [N(a^1)\backslash\mathring{N}(a^1)]$, *where* $0(\tilde{\pi}^2)$ *is an open set. Associated with* $\tilde{\pi}^2$ *there is a state* $a^2 \sim a^1$ *and a trade vector* $\tilde{z}^2 \neq 0$. *Hence*

$$\emptyset \neq \{\tilde{\pi} \in 0(\tilde{\pi}^2) : \tilde{z}^2\cdot\tilde{\pi} > 0\} \not\subset N(a^2) = N(a^1),$$

a contradiction. □

Theorem 2. *Suppose that an initial free-trade equilibrium is disturbed by an autonomous change in world prices.*

(a) If the change in prices is potentially unharmful (potentially beneficial) then any greater change is also potentially unharmful (potentially beneficial) in relation to the initial equilibrium.

(b) If the new price vector is intermediate to some two reference price vectors, where the substitution of the reference prices for the initial prices would not be potentially beneficial, then the change in prices is itself not potentially beneficial. If in addition one of the reference price vectors is such that its substitution for the initial price vector would not be potentially unharmful then the change in prices is itself not potentially unharmful.

(c) If the change in prices implies a non-deterioration of the terms of trade in the Laspeyres sense then the change is potentially unharmful (Krueger and Sonnenschein, 1967: theorem 2). If the change in prices implies an improvement of the terms of trade then the change is potentially beneficial.

Since the initial equilibrium may be one in which no trade takes place, we have:

Corollary. *Whatever the world prices, free trade is potentially unharmful in relation to autarky (Samuelson, 1939).*

Proof of Theorem 2. *(a) Let us denote by* $\tilde{\pi}^2$ *the new world price vector and write* $\tilde{\pi}^\lambda \equiv \tilde{\pi}^2 + \lambda(\tilde{\pi}^2 - \tilde{\pi}^1)$, $\lambda > 0$. *Suppose that* $\beta(\tilde{\pi}^2, a^1) > 0$. *Then* $\beta(\tilde{\pi}^\lambda, a^1) > 0$ *also. For if* $\beta(\tilde{\pi}^\lambda, a^1) \leqslant 0$ *then, from the convexity of* $N(a^1)$ *and the fact that* $\beta(\tilde{\pi}^1, a^1) = 0$, $\beta(\tilde{\pi}^2, a^1) \leqslant 0$, *a contradiction. Thus if the change from* $\tilde{\pi}^1$ *to* $\tilde{\pi}^2$ *is potentially beneficial, so is the change from* $\tilde{\pi}^1$ *to* $\tilde{\pi}^\lambda$. *Suppose alternatively that* $\beta(\tilde{\pi}^2, a^1) \geqslant 0$. *If* $\beta(\tilde{\pi}^\lambda, a^1) < 0$, *then, from (9) and the fact that* $\beta(\tilde{\pi}^1, a^1) \equiv 0$,

$$\beta(\tilde{\pi}^2, a^1) \leqslant [\lambda\beta(\tilde{\pi}^\lambda, a^1) + \beta(\tilde{\pi}^1, a^1)]/(1 + \lambda) < 0,$$

which is a contradiction.

(b) The first statement follows from the convexity of $\overset{\circ}{N}(a^1)$, *the second from lemma 3(b) and the convexity of* $\overset{\circ}{N}(a^1)$.

(c) By definition, the substitution of $\tilde{\pi}^2$ *for* $\tilde{\pi}^1$ *involves the non-deterioration (improvement) of the home country's terms of trade if* $\tilde{\pi}^2 \cdot \tilde{z}^1 \geqslant 0$ *(respectively,* $\tilde{\pi}^2 \cdot \tilde{z}^1 > 0$*) where* $\tilde{z}^1$ *is the initial equilibrium excess supply vector of the home country. From lemma 2* $\tilde{\pi}^2 \cdot \tilde{z}^1 \geqslant 0$ *implies that* $\tilde{\pi}^2 \notin \overset{\circ}{N}(a^1)$. *That proves the first proposition. Suppose that* $\tilde{\pi}^2 \cdot \tilde{z}^1 > 0$ *and that the sum* $\tilde{\pi}^2 \cdot \tilde{z}^1$ *is distributed to princeps. The preferences of princeps are convex and insatiable. Hence it is possible to make princeps better off with no one worse off.* □

Theorem 2 contains a series of statements about comparisons which might be made between two alternative trading situations. In theorem 3, on the other hand, all statements relate to comparisons between three alternative situations. Before proceeding to the theorem, we find it convenient to state and sketch-prove

Lemma 4. *If two states* a^1 *and* a^2 *are Pareto-comparable then:*

(a) $a^2 \succsim a^1$ *implies* $\beta(\tilde{\pi}, a^1) \geqslant \beta(\tilde{\pi}, a^2)$ *for all* $\tilde{\pi}$,

(b) $a^2 \succ a^1$ *implies* $\beta(\tilde{\pi}, a^1) > \beta(\tilde{\pi}, a^2)$ *for all* $\tilde{\pi}$,

(c) $a^2 \sim a^1$ *implies* $\beta(\tilde{\pi}, a^1) = \beta(\tilde{\pi}, a^2)$ *for all* $\tilde{\pi}$,

(d) $\tilde{\pi}^1 \in \overset{\circ}{N}(a^2)$ *if and only if* $\tilde{\pi}^2 \notin N(a^1)$.

Proof. *If* $a^2 \succsim a^1$ *then* $\Sigma_{i=1}^m X_i(x_i^1) \supseteq \Sigma_{i=1}^m X_i(x_i^2)$. *Similarly, if* $a^2 \succ a^1$ *then* $\Sigma_{i=1}^m X_i(x_i^1) \supset \Sigma_{i=1}^m X_i(x_i^2)$*; and if* $a^2 \sim a^1$ *then* $\Sigma_{i=1}^m X_i(x_i^1) = \Sigma_{i=1}^m X_i(x_i^2)$. *Statements (a), (b) and (c) follow straightforwardly from these three set relationships, respectively. Statement (d) follows from (a)–(c) and* $\beta(\tilde{\pi}^1, a^1) = 0 = \beta(\tilde{\pi}^2, a^2)$. □

We can now state

Theorem 3. *(a) Suppose that an initial free-trade equilibrium is disturbed by an autonomous change in world prices. If the change in prices is Pareto-unharmful (Pareto-beneficial) with* *respect to the initial equilibrium then a further change in prices in the same direction is potentially unharmful (respectively, potentially beneficial) with respect to the second equilibrium.*

(b) Consider a sequence of Pareto-unharmful price changes, the economy passing from $(a^1, \tilde{\pi}^1)$ *through* $(a^2, \tilde{\pi}^2)$, $(a^3, \tilde{\pi}^3)$, ... *to* $(a^T, \tilde{\pi}^T)$. *Suppose that* $a^t \succ a^1$ *for some t,* $1 < t \leqslant T$, *so that* $a^T \succ a^1$. *Now consider any convex linear combination of the price vectors* $\tilde{\pi}^1, \ldots, \tilde{\pi}^T$, *say* $\tilde{\pi}^\lambda$. *Then the substitution of* $\tilde{\pi}^\lambda$ *for* $\tilde{\pi}^T$ *is not potentially beneficial with respect to the Tth equilibrium; and, if a positive weight is assigned to* $\tilde{\pi}^t$ *for any t such that* $a^T \succ a^t$, *the substitution is not potentially unharmful with respect to the Tth equilibrium.*

Corollary 1. *Suppose that autarky gives way to free trade, that the free-trade prices differ from those prevailing under autarky and that the change is Pareto-beneficial with respect to autarky. If world prices move farther away from those of autarky then the second change is potentially beneficial with respect to the first free-trade equilibrium.*

Corollary 2. *If an improvement of the terms of trade in the Laspeyres sense is Pareto-beneficial with respect to the initial equilibrium and if* $l^0 = 2$ *then a further improvement in the terms of trade (calculated with the same weights) is potentially beneficial with respect to the second equilibrium.*

Part (a) of the theorem and corollary 2 have been proved by Krueger and Sonnenschein (1967: theorems 1 and 3) under the assumption that primary factors are in fixed supply.

Proof of Theorem 3. (a) *From lemma 4(d),* $\beta(\tilde{\pi}^1, a^2) \leqslant 0$ *(respectively,* $\beta(\tilde{\pi}^1, a^2) < 0$*). The proposition then follows from theorem 2(a).*

(b) *Since* $a^T \succ a^1$, a^T *is not autarkic. Theorem 2(b) may then be applied iteratively to obtain the proof.* □

For the special case in which there are just three traded commodities, the conclusions of this section may be illustrated in terms of the price simplex $P^l = P^3$ depicted in Figure 2. Consider a sequence of five states $a^0, \ldots, a^4$ associated with the normalized world price subvectors $\tilde{\pi}^0, \ldots, \tilde{\pi}^4$ respectively. Suppose that $a^0, \ldots, a^4$ are Pareto-comparable and, in particular, that $a^0 \prec a^1 \prec \ldots \prec a^4$. Then $N(a^0) \subset N(a^1) \subset \ldots \subset N(a^4)$. Moreover, $\mathring{N}(a^0)$ is the only worse-than-*a* set which is empty and $[N(a^0) \backslash \mathring{N}(a^0)]$ is the only equivalent-to-*a* set which has interior points. The remaining constructions in Figure 2 correspond to the assumptions listed in the first column of Table 1.

That theorem 3, corollary 2, cannot be extended to cover the case $l^0 > 2$ follows from the possibility that $\tilde{\pi}^v \cdot \tilde{\zeta}^3 > \tilde{\pi}^4 \cdot \tilde{\zeta}^3$ but $\tilde{\pi} \in \mathring{N}(a^4)$. This is in fact the counter example provided by Krueger and Sonnenschein (1967).

5 DEMAND VARIATIONS – COUNTRIES OF ANY SIZE

Let us suppose that the distributional policy of the home country is such that all equilibria are Pareto-comparable from the point of view of that country. And,

Table 1 Illustration of results

Facts	*Thorem applied*	*Conclusion*
$\tilde{\pi}' = \lambda\tilde{\pi}'' + (1-\lambda)\tilde{\pi}^1,\ \lambda \in (0, 1)$ $\tilde{\pi}' \notin N(a^1)$	Theorem 2(a)	$\tilde{\pi}'' \notin \mathring{N}(a^1)$
$\tilde{\pi}^2 = \lambda\tilde{\pi}''' - (1-\lambda)\tilde{\pi}^1,\ \lambda \in (0, 1)$ $\tilde{\pi}^2 \notin N(a^1)$	Theorem 2(a)	$\tilde{\pi}''' \notin N(a^1)$
$\tilde{\pi}' = \lambda\tilde{\pi}'' + (1-\lambda)\tilde{\pi}^1,\ \lambda \in (0, 1)$ $\tilde{\pi}^1, \tilde{\pi}'' \in N(a^1)$	Theorem 2(b)	$\tilde{\pi}' \in N(a^1)$
$\tilde{\pi}^1 = \lambda\tilde{\pi}' + (1-\lambda)\tilde{\pi}^2,\ \lambda \in (0, 1)$ $\tilde{\pi}^2 \in N(a^2),\ \tilde{\pi}' \in N(a^2)$	Theorem 2(b)	$\tilde{\pi}' \in \mathring{N}(a^2)$
$\tilde{\pi}^{iv} \cdot \tilde{z}^3 \geqslant 0$	Theorem 2(c)	$\tilde{\pi}^{iv} \notin \mathring{N}(a^3)$
$\tilde{\pi}^4 \cdot \tilde{z}^3 > 0$	Theorem 2(c)	$\tilde{\pi}^4_o \notin N(a^3)$
$\tilde{\pi}^0$ is autarkic	Corollary to theorem 2	$N(a^0) = \emptyset$
$\tilde{\pi}' = \lambda\tilde{\pi}'' + (1-\lambda)\tilde{\pi}^1,\ \lambda \in (0, 1)$ $\tilde{\pi}' \notin N(a^1)$	Theorem 3(a)	$\tilde{\pi}'' \notin N(a^1)$ ($N(a')$ not shown)
$\tilde{\pi}^2 = \lambda\tilde{\pi}''' + (1-\lambda)\tilde{\pi}^1,\ \lambda \in (0, 1)$ $\tilde{\pi}^2 \notin N(a^1)$	Theorem 3(a)	$\tilde{\pi}''' \notin N(a^2)$
$\tilde{\pi}^\lambda = \sum_1^3 \lambda_\psi \tilde{\pi}^\psi,\ \lambda_\psi > 0,\ \sum_1^3 \lambda_\psi = 1$ $\tilde{\pi}^2 \notin N(a^1),\ \tilde{\pi}^3 \notin N(a^2)$	Theorem 3(b)	$\tilde{\pi}^\lambda \in \mathring{N}(a^3)$
$\tilde{\pi}^{iv} = \lambda\tilde{\pi}^v + (1-\lambda)\tilde{\pi}^0,\ \lambda \in (0, 1)$ $\tilde{\pi}^{iv} \in N(a^0)$	Corollary to theorem 3	$\tilde{\pi}^v \notin N(a^{iv})$ ($N(a^{iv})$ not shown)

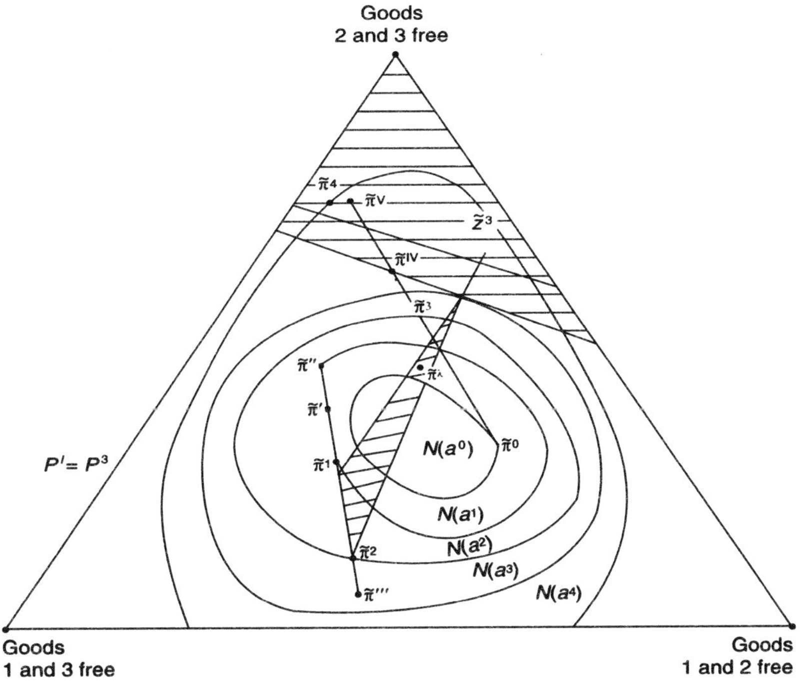

Figure 2

varying our notation slightly, let us now denote the **post-compensation** excess demand correspondence of the home country by $\zeta_1(p)$, a set of l-dimensional vectors the last l^2 components of which are zero. Then $\zeta(p) = \zeta_0(p) + \zeta_1(p)$ is the world excess demand correspondence. Superscripts a and b indicate magnitudes *a*fter and *b*efore a variation of foreign demand. Thus p^a and p^b are equilibrium world price vectors after and before such a change.

It will be assumed that (i) foreign excess demand undergoes an unambiguous expansion, with home demand unchanged:

$$\zeta_0^a(p) \equiv \lambda(p)\zeta_0^b(p), \quad \lambda(p) > 1 \quad \text{for all } p, \quad \zeta_1^a(p) \equiv \zeta_1^b(p).$$

Such an expansion might be associated with the balanced growth of the foreign economy or, less plausibly, with an improvement in the means of international transportation. It will be supposed also that (ii) post-variation world excess demand obeys a 'generalized law of demand', that is

$$z^i \in \zeta^a(p^i), \quad i = 1, 2, \quad \text{implies } (\tilde{p}^2 - \tilde{p}^1)(\tilde{z}^2 - \tilde{z}^1) < 0.$$

We may now state[8]

Theorem 4. *On the above assumptions and if p^b is not autarkic the home country potentially benefits from an expansion of foreign demand. Trivially, if p^b is autarkic the home country is potentially unharmed by an expansion of foreign demand.*

Proof. *Suppose that p^b is not autarkic and let $(\tilde{z}_0^b, \tilde{z}_1^b)$ and $(\tilde{z}_0^a, \tilde{z}_1^a)$ be the foreign and home equilibrium excess demand vectors associated with p^b and p^a respectively. Then*

$$\tilde{z}^b \equiv \tilde{z}_0^b + \tilde{z}_1^b = 0, \quad \tilde{z}_0^b \neq 0 \neq \tilde{z}_1^b, \quad \tilde{z}^a \equiv \tilde{z}_0^a + \tilde{z}_1^a = 0.$$

Let

$$z_0^{ab} \equiv \lambda(p^b) z_0^b \in \zeta_0^a(p^b), \quad z_1^{ab} = z_1^b \in \zeta_1^a(p^b) \equiv \zeta_1^b(p^b),$$

so that

$$z^{ab} = (z_0^{ab} + z_1^{ab}) \in \zeta^a(p^b).$$

Then

$$\begin{aligned} 0 &\geqslant (p^a - p^b)(z^a - z^{ab}) \\ &= -(p^a - p^b)(z_0^{ab} + z_1^{ab}) \\ &= -(p^a - p^b)[(z_0^b + z_1^b) + (\lambda(p^b) - 1)z_0^b] \quad \textit{(assumption (i))} \\ &= [\lambda(p^b) - 1]p^a \cdot z_1^b \quad (p^b \cdot z_0^b = 0 \text{ and } z_1^b = -z_0^b). \end{aligned}$$

That is, the terms of trade of the home country necessarily improve. Then

$$\begin{aligned} p^a x^a &= p^a\omega + p^a y^a + p^a z_1^a \\ &\geqslant p^a\omega + p^a y^b + p^a z_1^a \quad \textit{(convexity of } Y\textit{)} \\ &> p^a\omega + p^a y^b + p^a z_1^b \quad \textit{(improved terms of trade)} \\ &= p^a x^b. \end{aligned}$$

Hence, given the distributional policy of the home country, the new equilibrium is Pareto-preferred to the old. □[9]

It will be noticed that in the statement of theorem 4 the coefficient λ is allowed to depend on world prices. In a special case, for all p, $\lambda(p) = \lambda > 1$.

ADDENDUM: THE GAIN FROM TRADE IN TECHNIQUES OF PRODUCTION

In formal analysis of the gains from trade it has been customary to suppose that in each trading country the set of production possibilities is independent of trading opportunities. It follows that conventional analysis does not cover the trade in productive techniques implicit in licensing agreements based on patents and copyrights.

In seeking to extend existing theory to accommodate this kind of trade one encounters two difficulties. First, patents and copyrights typically confer monopoly–monopsony power on particular individuals or firms; hence techniques of analysis based on the assumption of perfect competition are inapplicable. Second, the privileges conferred by patents and copyrights are typically of finite duration; hence conventional timeless analysis, with its implicit assumption that conditions remain unchanged through time, is inappropriate if post-patent conditions are influenced by earlier licensing decisions. (One thinks here of learning by doing under licence.) These difficulties can be evaded by confining attention to small countries, which take as given both (conventional) commodity prices and the terms of licensing, and by assuming away the possibility that licensing decisions influence post-patent conditions of production or factor supply; and that is what I propose to do.

Let u be a quasi-concave Scitovsky social welfare function of the aggregate consumption vector c, let ω be an aggregate endowment vector, let Y be the net production set with elements y, and let p be a constant vector of world prices. In the absence of trade in techniques, but with free trade in conventional commodities, a small country may be viewed as solving

Problem 1

$$\max_{c,y} u(c) \quad \text{such that } y \in Y, \quad p(c - y - \omega) \leqslant 0, \quad c \geqslant 0.$$

Now suppose that an additional set of production possibilities Y^* is available to the country upon payment of a fee ω^*, a commodity vector which depends on $y^*, y^* \in Y^*$, and let us consider the revised problem,

Problem 2

$$\max_{c,y,y^*} u(c) \quad \text{such that } y \in Y, y^* \in Y^*, \quad p(c - y - y^* - \omega + \omega^*(y^*)) \leqslant 0.$$

The set $Y + Y^*$ can be replaced by a compact subset of itself (Debreu, 1959: sections 5.4 and 5.7); hence the maximum exists. It is easy to see that the solution to problem 2 yields a level of social welfare not less than does the solution to problem 1. In this weak sense, free trade in techniques is gainful.[10]

NOTES

* The essay was written at the University of California, Berkeley, in the summer of 1970. During that period the authors were supported by National Science Foundation Grant GS-3018. Grateful acknowledgement is made to the University and the Foundation. We acknowledge also helpful discussions with Daniel McFadden whose work on a related topic (which has since appeared in a joint article with Grandmont (1972)) inspired our proof of theorem 1.

1 See, for example, Debreu (1959).

2 $\zeta_0(p)$ has these properties if foreign consumers and producers are subject to restrictions similar to those imposed on their home counterparts.

3 In general, such a system of payments may not exist. However, for the disturbances we shall consider, existence is always assured.

4 w_i may not exist for all p. Consider, however, the set of commodity bundles which are not worse than x_i^0 and which, given production techniques, foreign demand and the survival of other consumers, are feasible. This set is a compact subset of $X_i(x_i^0)$. In an equilibrium, as defined below, the chosen x_i must lie in that subset. One therefore may replace $X_i(x_i^0)$ with the compact subset just defined. Then w_i is defined for all p.

5 It may be worth clarifying the relation of the above theorem to the principal propositions of the 1962 companion papers of Kemp (1962) and Samuelson (1962). As we have just noted, Kemp sought to prove what we have here called theorem 1. On the other hand, with the exception of his conclusion 8, Samuelson was concerned with the geometric properties and market attainability of the outward boundary of the country's set of consumption possibilities. In particular, he showed that the autarkic consumption possibility set is a proper subset of the production-cum-trade consumption possibility set and that all Pareto-optimal points on the boundary of the latter set are attainable by means of lumpsum transfers and optimal tariffs. Kemp was chiefly concerned with the welfare properties of second-best free-trade equilibria, Samuelson with those of optimal tariff-restricted equilibria.

6 In a pioneering but neglected paper Vanek (1965: appendix to Ch. iv) has stated a general theorem concerning utility possibility loci and remarked that our theorem 1 is an implication of it. Moreover, in important respects (including the use of the device of *princeps*) he has anticipated our line of argument. Now if one assumes that there always exists a competitive trading equilibrium Pareto-comparable with the autarkic state, his result does imply our theorem 1. However, the assumption of existence is not to be made lightly; indeed it is precisely at this point that Kemp's (1962) proof is defective. Moreover, the proof now offered can be generalized to accommodate **intra**-national externalities (see Wan, 1972); this is not true of Vanek's proof.

7 Theorem 1′ generalizes a proposition put forward by Kemp (1962: section 6).

8 In the famous Ch. 18 of Book III of the *Principles*, J. S. Mill claimed (1909: 604)

> that the countries which carry on their trade on the most advantageous terms, are those whose commodities are most in demand by foreign countries, and which have themselves the least demand for foreign commodities. From which, among other consequences, it follows, that the richest countries, *caeteris paribus*, gain the least by a given amount of foreign commerce: since, having a greater demand for commodities generally, they are likely to have a greater demand for foreign commodities, and thus

modify the terms of interchange to their own disadvantage. Their aggregate gains by foreign trade, doubtless, are generally greater than those of poorer countries, since they carry on a greater amount of such trade, and gain the benefit of cheapness on a larger consumption: but their gain is less on each individual article consumed.

Theorem 4 may be viewed as a restatement of the proposition contained in the first quoted sentence.

9 Theorem 4 has been stated in terms of a finite variation of foreign demand. Confining oneself to infinitesimal changes and differentiable excess demand functions, one may proceed as follows. In an initial equilibrium

$$z_1(p^*) + \lambda z_0(p^*) = 0, \quad \lambda = 1, \quad J \cdot p^* = 1,$$

where p^* is the equilibrium price vector and $J = (1, \ldots, 1)$. Total differentiation with respect to λ yields

$$[\partial z/\partial p]\, \partial p/\partial \lambda = z_1, \quad J \cdot (\partial p/\partial \lambda) = 0.$$

The Laspeyres terms-of-trade test becomes

$$(\partial p/\partial \lambda)' [\partial z/\partial p]\, (\partial p/\partial \lambda) = z_1 \cdot (\partial p/\partial \lambda) < 0$$

for all $(\partial p/\partial \lambda)$ satisfying $J \cdot (\partial p/\partial \lambda) = 0$. This is equivalent to the requirement that the Jacobian $[\partial z/\partial p]$ be quasi-negative semi-definite under constraint. As is well known, the requirement is met if all commodities are gross substitutes for each other.

10 It can be shown also that free trade in techniques is gainful in relation to an initial situation of autarky.

REFERENCES

Arrow, K. J. (1951) 'An extension of the basic theorems of classical welfare economics', in Neyman, J. (ed.) *Proceedings of the Second Berkeley Symposium on Mathematical Statistics and Probability*, pp. 507–32, Berkeley, CA: University of California Press.

Bhagwati, J. and Johnson, H. G. (1960) 'Notes on some controversies in the theory of international trade', *Economic Journal* 70, 74–93.

Debreu, G. (1959) *Theory of Value*, New York: Wiley.

Grandmont, J. M. and McFadden, D. (1972) 'A technical note on classical gains from trade', *Journal of International Economics* 2: 109–26.

Kemp, M. C. (1962) 'The gain from international trade', *Economic Journal* 72: 303–19.

Kemp, M. C. (1969) *The Pure Theory of International Trade and Investment*, Englewood Cliffs, NJ: Prentice Hall.

Krueger, A. O. and Sonnenschein, H. (1967) 'The terms of trade, the gains from trade and price divergence', *International Economic Review* 8: 121–7.

Marshall, A. (1923) *Money, Credit and Commerce*, London: Macmillan.

Mill, J. S. (1909) *Principles of Political Economy*, London: Longmans, Green.

Samuelson, P. A. (1939) 'The gains from international trade', *Canadian Journal of Economics and Political Science* 5: 195–205.

Samuelson, P. A. (1962) 'The gains from international trade once again', *Economic Journal* 72: 820–9.

Sontheimer, K. C. (1971) 'On the existence of international trade equilibrium with trade tax-subsidy distortions', *Econometrica* 39: 1015–36.

Vanek, J. (1965) *General Equilibrium of International Discrimination*, Cambridge, MA: Harvard University Press.

Viner, J. (n.d.) *Studies in the Theory of International Trade*, London: Allen and Unwin.

Wan, H. Y., Jr (1965) 'Maximum bonus – an alternative measure of trading gains', *Review of Economic Studies* 32: 49–58.
Wan, H. Y., Jr (1972) 'A note on trading gains and externalities', *Journal of International Economics* 2: 173–80.

3

AN ELEMENTARY PROPOSITION CONCERNING THE FORMATION OF CUSTOMS UNIONS*

1 INTRODUCTION

In the welter of inconclusive debate concerning the implications of customs unions the following elementary yet basic proposition seems to have been almost lost to sight.[1]

Proposition 1. *Consider any competitive world trading equilibrium, with any number of countries and commodities and with no restrictions whatever on the tariffs and other commodity taxes of individual countries and with costs of transport fully recognized. Now let any subset of the countries form a customs union. Then there exists a common tariff vector and a system of lumpsum compensatory payments, involving only members of the union, such that each individual, whether a member of the union or not, is not worse off than before the formation of the union.*

A detailed list of assumptions, and a relatively formal proof, may be found in section 2. Here we merely note that there exists a common tariff vector which leaves world prices, and therefore the trade and welfare of non-members, at their pre-union levels. If the net trade vector of the union is viewed as a (constant) endowment, it is then plausible that both the union as a whole and (after appropriate internal transfers) each member must be left not worse off by the removal of internal barriers to trade.

The proposition is interesting in that it contains no qualifications whatever concerning the size or number of the countries which are contemplating union, their pre- or post-union trading relationships, their relative states of development or levels of average income, and their propinquities in terms of geography or costs of transportation.

The proposition is also interesting because it implies that an incentive to form and enlarge customs unions persists until the world becomes one big customs union; that is, until world free trade prevails. More precisely, given any initial trading equilibrium, there exist finite sequences of steps, at each step new customs unions being created or old unions enlarged, such that at each step no individual is made worse off and such that after the last step the world is free trading. (In general, at each step some individual actually benefits.) Indeed, on the basis of these observations one might attempt to rehabilitate the vague pre-Vinerian view that to form a customs union is to move in the direction of free trade.[2]

Evidently the incentive is insufficiently strong; tariffs and other artificial obstacles to trade persist. That the real world is not free trading must be explained in terms of:

(1) the game theoretic problems of choosing partners, dividing the spoils and enforcing agreements, and

(2) the non-economic objectives of nations.

A role may be found also for:

(3) inertia and ignorance concerning the implications of possible unions (in particular, concerning the long list of lumpsum compensatory payments required); and, in the short run, for

(4) the restraint exercised by international agreements to limit tariffs.

However (4) can form no part of an explanation of the persistence of trading blocks in the long run.

Topics (1)–(3) form a possible agenda for the further study of customs unions. For a preliminary analysis of (1) the reader may consult Caves (1971); and for suggestive work on (2) the reader is referred to Cooper and Massell (1965), Johnson (1965) and Bhagwati (1968).

2 PROOF OF THE PROPOSITION

Suppose that:

(1a) the consumption set of each individual is closed, convex and bounded below;

(1b) the preferences of each individual are convex and representable by a continuous ordinal utility function;

(1c) each individual can survive with a consumption bundle each component of which is somewhat less than the individual's pre-union consumption bundle;

(2) the production set of each economy is closed, convex, contains the origin and is such that positive output requires at least one positive input (impossibility of free production).

Consider a fictitious economy composed of the member economies but with a net endowment equal to the sum of the member endowments plus the equilibrium pre-union net excess supply of the rest of the world. In view of (1) and (2), the economy possesses an optimum, and any optimum can be supported by at least one internal price vector (Debreu, 1959; 92–3 and 95–6). Either the pre-union equilibrium of the member countries is a Pareto-optimal equilibrium of the fictitious economy (i.e. corresponds to a maximal point of the utility possibility set), or it is not; in the latter case, a preferred Pareto-optimal equilibrium can be attained by means of lumpsum transfers among individuals in the fictitious economy. That essentially completes the proof. It only remains to note that the required vector of common tariffs may be computed as the difference between the vector of pre-union world prices and the vector of internal union prices.

Commodities can be indexed by location. Hence the resource-using activity of moving commodities from one country to another is accommodated in the several production sets; no special treatment of cost of transportation is needed.

3 AN ADDENDUM (1993)

In 1992 the dismantling of tariff and quota restrictions on trade and factor movements between members of the European Economic Community was completed. Uniform quality standards also have been established, at least in principle. In this final section we briefly indicate how quality standards fit into our earlier analysis.

Let G be the universal set of goods which might be produced and/or consumed in some two or more countries, with different qualities of a commodity appearing as different members of G. Initially, before the formation of a customs union, each country may have in place quality controls on production and/or consumption. Let $G_i^p \subset G$ denote the subset of goods which fail to satisfy the production standards of country i and therefore cannot be produced in that country; and let $G_i^c \subset G$ denote the subset of goods which fail to satisfy the consumption standards of country i and therefore cannot be consumed in that country. Possibly, but not necessarily, $G_i^p = G_i^c$; possibly, but not necessarily, G_i^p and/or G_i^c is the null set.

Suppose now that a subset of countries I forms a 'customs union', with a common tariff vector but not necessarily uniform quality standards.

If G_i^p and G_i^c, $i \in I$, are unchanged by the formation of the 'customs union', the Kemp–Wan conclusions remain unchanged. The quality standards merely define for each member country the unchanging sets of goods which can be produced and consumed. It is as though, in member country i, households place no value on the excluded goods in G_i^c and firms are unable to employ or produce the excluded goods in G_i^p. Thus we arrive at a substantial generalization of the Kemp–Wan theorem, the latter emerging from the special case in which $G_i^p = G_i^c = \emptyset$, $i \in I$.

If, on the other hand, the formation of the 'customs union' is accompanied by the replacement of each G_i^p by, say, $\hat{G}_i^p$ and of each G_i^c by, say, $\hat{G}_i^c$, then the Kemp–Wan conclusions survive only in special cases. In the most obvious of such cases, all member countries adopt common and unambiguously less restrictive quality standards, so that $\hat{G}_i^p = \hat{G}^p \subset G_i^p$ and $\hat{G}_i^c = \hat{G}^c \subset G_i^c$, $i \in I$.[3] For, in that case, there is in effect an unambiguous expansion in the production sets of some member countries and an increase in the number of tradable commodities for some member countries. Since there exists a beneficial Kemp–Wan customs union with unchanged quality standards then *a fortiori* there is a Kemp–Wan customs union with relaxed quality standards which is even more beneficial (in the sense that some members are better off, none worse off). Whether Europe 1992 satisfies the requirement that $\hat{G}^p \subset G_i^p$, $\hat{G}^c \subset G_i^c$ remains an interesting empirical question.

NOTES

* We acknowledge with gratitude the useful comments of Jagdish Bhagwati, John Chipman and two referees.

1 The proposition, together with an indication of the lines along which a proof may be constructed, may be found in Kemp (1964: 176). A geometric proof for the canonical three-countries, two-commodities case has been furnished by Vanek (1965: 160–5).

2 We now (1993) add the clarifying remark that, in particular situations, the scheme of international compensatory payments need not embrace all member countries. By way of example, consider an initial world trading equilibrium in which some countries are members of a customs union and the remaining countries are autarkic. If then some of the initially autarkic countries join the existing customs union, no new member need receive from or give to other (new or old) members.

3 Even in that case, the Kemp–Wan conclusions do not hold if existing quality standards serve to protect the health or safety of the public and therefore presuppose the presence of public goods and/or externalities. However, the admission of market imperfections takes us far beyond the conventional context of the theory of customs unions.

REFERENCES

Bhagwati, J. (1968) 'Trade liberalization among LDCs, trade theory, and Gatt rules', in J. N. Wolfe (ed.) *Value, Capital, and Growth. Papers in honour of Sir John Hicks*, pp. 21–43, Edinburgh: Edinburgh University Press.

Caves, R. E. (1971) 'The economics of reciprocity: Theory and evidence on bilateral trading arrangements', Harvard Institute of Economic Research, Discussion Paper No. 166.

Cooper, C. A. and Massell, B. F. (1965) 'Towards a general theory of customs unions for developing countries', *Journal of Political Economy* 73: 461–76.

Debreu, G. (1959) *Theory of Value*, New York: Wiley.

Johnson, H. G. (1965) 'An economic theory of protectionism, tariff bargaining, and the formation of customs unions', *Journal of Political Economy* 73: 256–83.

Kemp, M. C. (1964), *The Pure Theory of International Trade*, Englewood Cliffs, NJ: Prentice Hall.

Vanek, J. (1965) *General Equilibrium of International Discrimination. The Case of Customs Unions*, Cambridge, MA: Harvard University Press.

4

THE COMPARISON OF SECOND-BEST EQUILIBRIA

The case of customs unions*

1 INTRODUCTION

In Kemp and Wan (1976) we stated a proposition concerning the formation of customs unions:[1]

Proposition. *Consider any competitive world trading equilibrium, with any number of countries and commodities, with no restrictions whatever on the tariffs and other commodity taxes of individual countries, and with costs of transport fully recognized. Now let any subset of the countries form a customs union, defined to exclude commodity taxes other than tariffs. Then there exists a common tariff vector and a system of lumpsum compensatory payments, involving only members of the union, such that there is an associated tariff-ridden competitive equilibrium in which each individual, whether a member of the union or not, is not worse off than before the formation of the union.*

The proposition is remarkable for its generality. Thus it contains no qualifications concerning the number or size of countries which are contemplating union, their pre- or post-union trading relationships, their relative states of development or levels of average income, their preferences or relative factor endowments, or their propinquities in terms of geography or costs of transportation.

The proposition is remarkable also for its decisiveness. For, generally speaking, welfare comparisons of second-best equilibria are inconclusive.

Finally, as noted in our earlier paper, the proposition is interesting because it implies that an incentive to form and enlarge customs unions persists until the world becomes one big union, that is until world free trade prevails. More precisely, given any initial world trading equilibrium, there exist finite sequences of steps, at each step new customs unions being created or old unions enlarged, such that at each step no individual is made worse off and such that after the last step the world is free trading. (In general, at each step some individual actually benefits.) Indeed, on the basis of these observations one might attempt to rehabilitate the vague pre-Vinerian view that to form a customs union is to move in the direction of free trade.

However, the proposition lacks proof. The assumptions listed by Kemp and Wan (1976) are now seen to be not quite strong enough to support the conclusions of the theorem. In particular, they do not rule out 'Arrow's corner'[2] and thus do not guarantee that optimal allocations can be decentralized by prices; and they do not ensure the existence of a utility frontier. To overcome the first of these difficulties we now propose a revised form of our assumption (1c) and to overcome the second difficulty we offer a modified form of assumption (2):

(1c′) each individual can survive with somewhat less of every component of any consumption bundle which is not worse than the individual's pre-union consumption bundle;

(2′) the union-wide aggregate production set is closed and convex and is such that positive output requires at least one positive input (impossibility of free production).

2 PROOF OF PROPOSITION

The union-wide economy is the vector[3] $((X_i, \precsim_i), (Y_j), (\omega_i), (\theta_{ij}))$, where Y_j is the production set of country j and X_i, $\precsim_i$, ω_i and (θ_{ij}) are the consumption set, preferences, endowment and vector of profit shares of household i. The pre-union state of the economy is $a^0 = ((x_i^0), (y_j^0))$, where x_i^0 is the consumption vector of household i and y_j^0 is the output vector of country j; it belongs to the set of attainable states

$$A = (\prod_i X_i)\,(\prod_j Y_j) \cap \left\{((x_i), (y_j)): \sum_i x_i - \sum_j y_j = \sum_i \omega_i + z^0\right\}$$

where z^0 is the vector of pre-union net imports from the rest of the world at world prices p^0.

In terms of the above notation, the complete set of revised assumptions is as follows:

(1a) X_i is closed, convex and lower-bounded for $\leq$;
(1b) $\precsim_i$ is convex and can be represented by a continuous utility function u_i;
(1c′) if $x_i \succsim_i x_i^0$ then there is $\underline{x}_i \in X_i$ with $\underline{x}_i \ll x_i$;[4]
(2′) $Y \equiv \Sigma_j Y_j$ is closed and convex, and $Y \cap \Omega = \{0\}$.
(In (2′), Ω is the non-negative orthant.)

Given these assumptions, it can be verified that conditions (a)–(d) of 6.2(i) of Debreu (1959) are satisfied. Thus condition (a) follows from our (1a) and Debreu's 1.9(13), (b) is implied by our (1b) and Debreu's 1.7(3′), (c) is reproduced in our (2′) and (d) follows from the fact that $a^0 \in A$. From a statement in the proof of Debreu's 6.2(i), the set of all attainable vectors of utility levels, $u(A)$, is compact, with its subset of maximal elements being the 'utility frontier'. Therefore there is some $a^* \in A$ which is **both** Pareto-optimal **and** such that a^* is Pareto-not-worse than a^0 (i.e. $a^* \succsim a^0$ in Debreu's notation). Either all households are satiated at a^* and none is worse off than at a^0, so that one can set the intra-union price $p^* = 0$; or one household is not satiated and it can be verified that the conditions of Debreu's 6.4(1) are satisfied.[5] In the latter event, a^* is an equilibrium relative to an intra-union price $p^* \geqslant 0$; hence, from (1c′), $p^* x_i^* > \min_{X_i} p^* x_i$ and (a^*, p^*) is a competitive equilibrium. The lumpsum transfer for i, $p^* x_i^* - p^*(\omega_i + \Sigma_j \theta_{ij} y_j^*)$, and the external tariff, $p^0 - p^*$, are then straightforwardly derived.[6] □

We offer two brief remarks designed to amplify the proof.

Remark 1. *We have constructed a fictitious union-wide economy with an aggregate endowment equal to the true collective endowment $\Sigma_i \omega_i$ modified by the collective net import z^0 from the rest of the world. The sum $\Sigma_i \omega_i + z^0$ need not be non-negative; indeed Theorem 6.2(i) of Debreu (1959) imposes no such requirement. The compact image of the attainable set under u has an outer 'frontier' which either contains the initial utility vector $u(a^0)$ or lies to its north-east, as illustrated by Figures 1 and 2, respectively. That part of the frontier which is Pareto-not-worse than $u(a^0)$ is either $u(a^0)$ itself or a continuum of points north-east of $u(a^0)$. The corresponding efficient attainable states can then be associated with intra-union price vectors to constitute compensated equilibria.*

Remark 2. *Suppose one household is unsatiated at p^*. Without loss of generality we may assume that the world price vector p^0 is a member of the natural simplex*

$$P \equiv \{p \in \mathbb{R}^n_+ : \sum_k p_k = 1\}.$$

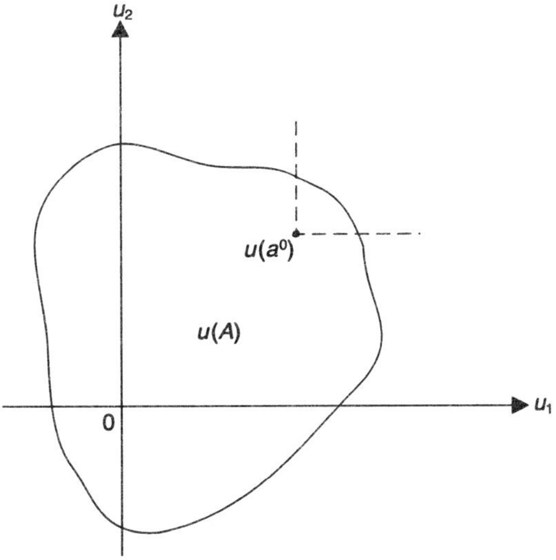

Figure 1

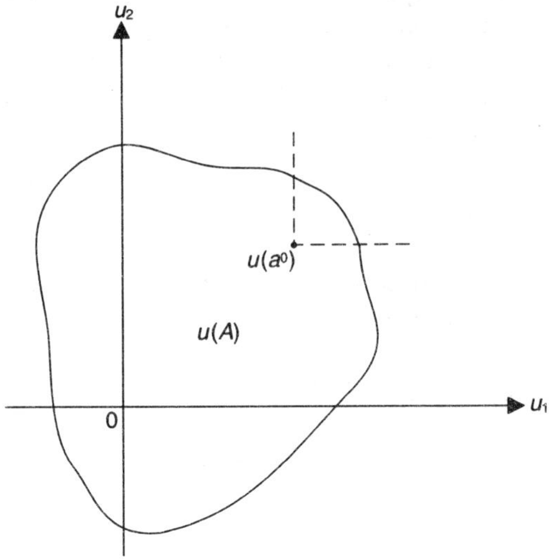

Figure 2

Any equilibrium intra-union price vector p^* is then semi-positive but need not satisfy the restriction

$$\sum_k p_k^* = 1.$$

If p^* is an equilibrium intra-union price vector then, for any $\lambda > 0$, so is λp^*. The change from p^* to λp^* causes nominal profits and incomes in the customs union to change proportionately and causes the vector of tariff rates $p^* - p^0$ to change in an affine way to $\lambda p^* - p^0$, thus causing the net tariff revenue

$$(p^* - p^0)z^0 = p^* z^0 - p^0 z^0$$
$$= p^* z^0$$

to change in the proportion λ, together with all transfer payments.

3 THE NECESSITY AND INFORMATIONAL REQUIREMENTS OF LUMPSUM COMPENSATION

In the proposition of section 1 it is stipulated that intra-union compensation be by lumpsum transfers. We offer two defensive comments.

On the one hand, it seems to be part of the folklore of trade theorists that any scheme of lumpsum compensation requires detailed knowledge of individual preferences and production sets and thus imposes on the policy-maker a practically impossible informational burden. In fact it has been shown by Grinols (1981) that, in the context of customs unions, there always exists a scheme of lumpsum compensation the application of which requires only observable data from the initial equilibrium (roughly, the data required by the income-tax authority) and which, in particular, requires no knowledge of preferences or production sets. Thus let the ith individual receive, as compensation, the commodity vector

$$\sigma_i \equiv x_i^0 - \omega_i^0 - \sum_j \theta_{ij} y_j^0.$$

Under any vector p^* of post-union equilibrium prices, this translates into a price-dependent transfer of $p^*\sigma_i$ and, therefore, an income of

$$w_i^* = p^*(\sigma_i + \omega_i^0) = p^* x_i^0 - \sum_j \theta_{ij} p^* y_j^0$$

$$= p^* x_i^0 + \sum_j \theta_{ij} p^* (y_j^* - y_j^0).$$

Now $y_j^0 \in Y_j^0 \subseteq Y_j^*$ and $p^* y_j^* = \max p^* Y_j^*$; hence $p^*(y_j^* - y_j^0) \geqslant 0$ and $w_i^* \geqslant p^* x_i^0$. It follows that the compensation is adequate.

On the other hand, it is widely believed that the stipulation that compensation be lumpsum is inessential, that if there is a Pareto-improving customs union with lumpsum compensation then there is a Pareto-improving customs union without lumpsum transfers but with compensation effected by means of country-specific commodity taxes and subsidies. The basis of this belief is a passage in Dixit and Norman (1980: 192–4). However, a careful examination of their argument reveals that not even the existence of a compensated post-union equilibrium is established. And we now have several counter examples to the proposition that, in general, compensation need not be lumpsum; see Kemp and Wan (1986).[7]

NOTES

* Thanks are due to J. Bhagwati, M. Yano and E. Grinols for encouragement and advice.

1 The proposition was first stated by Kemp (1964: 176). It may be found also in Vanek (1965) and Ohyama (1972).

2 For 'Arrow's corner', see Arrow (1951) and Chipman (1965).

3 Our notation closely follows Debreu (1959).

4 It follows from (1c′) that the entire set $X^{x_i} \equiv \{x_i \in X_i : x_i \succsim_i x_i^0\}$ is in the interior of X_i.

5 Specifically, Debreu's (a), (b. 1–2) and (c) follow respectively from our (1a), (1b) and (2′); and his assumption that some individual i' is non-satiated is fulfilled in the present case.

6 Professor Earl Grinols has kindly pointed out that there is an alternative way of correcting our earlier (1976) proof. This consists in retaining (1a), (1b) and (1c), and adding the assumption (1d) that all individual preferences are non-satiable. Then one can specify a particular scheme of lumpsum transfers, similar to that of Grinols (1981), to prove the existence of a compensated equilibrium in which no one is worse off than before.

7 The examples of Kemp and Wan were devised to counter the single-country proposition that if free trade is Pareto-beneficial when compensation is by means of lumpsum transfers then it is Pareto-beneficial when compensation is effected by means of commodity taxes and subsidies. However, the examples can be reinterpreted as applying to customs unions with each member initially applying prohibitive tariffs.

REFERENCES

Arrow, K. J. (1951) 'An extension of the basic theorems of classical welfare economics', in J. Neyman (ed.) *Proceedings of the Second Berkeley Symposium on Mathematical Statistics and Probability,* Berkeley, pp. 507–32.

Chipman, J. S. (1965) 'A survey of the theory of international trade: Part 2, the neoclassical theory', *Econometrica* 33: 685–760.

Debreu, G. (1959) *Theory of Value*, New York.

Dixit, A. K. and Norman, V. (1980) *Theory of International Trade*, Cambridge and Welwyn.

Grinols, E. L. (1981) 'An extension of the Kemp–Wan theorem on the formation of customs unions', *Journal of International Economics* 11: 259–66.

Kemp, M. C. (1964) *The Pure Theory of International Trade*, Englewood Cliffs, NJ.

Kemp, M. C. and Wan, H. Y. Jr (1976) 'An elementary proposition concerning the formation of customs unions', *Journal of International Economics* 6: 95–7.

Kemp, M. C. and Wan, H. Y. Jr (1986) 'Gains from trade with and without lumpsum compensation', *Journal of International Economics* 21: 99–110.

Ohyama, M. (1972) 'Trade and welfare in general equilibrium', *Keio Economic Studies* 9: 37–73.

Vanek, J. (1965) *General Equilibrium of International Discrimination*, Cambridge, MA.

5

THE GAINS FROM TRADE WHEN MARKETS ARE POSSIBLY INCOMPLETE*

1 INTRODUCTION

The welfare economics of free trade contains four core propositions:

1 For any single country, large or small, free trade is better than no trade (Samuelson, 1962; Kemp, 1962; Kemp and Wan, 1972; Kemp and Ohyama, 1978).[1]
2 Any subset of trading countries can form a mutually advantageous customs union (Kemp, 1964; Vanek, 1965; Ohyama, 1972; Kemp and Wan, 1976, 1986).
3 For a small open economy, an improvement in the terms of trade is beneficial (Kemp, 1962; Krueger and Sonnenschein, 1967; Wong, 1991).
4 For a small open economy, trade in additional commodities (including primary factors of production) is beneficial (Wong, 1983, 1991; Grossman, 1984).

These propositions are known to be valid whether or not there is uncertainty, provided that there is a complete set of markets, either a complete set of current spot and futures markets for commodities or a complete set of spot markets for commodities in each period and of current securities markets. Whether the propositions remain valid when markets are incomplete remains an open question.

It is well known that when commodity markets are distorted by taxes it may be impossible to find a scheme of lumpsum compensation which supports a free-trade equilibrium in which everyone is better off than in autarky. Since the absence of markets can be viewed as an extreme form of market distortion, it might be expected that the gains-from-trade propositions must be abandoned if markets are incomplete.

Moreover, it is known that, when markets are incomplete, competitive equilibria are generally constrained suboptimal; see Hart (1975) and Geanakoplos and Polemarchakis (1986). This also suggests that free trade may not be gainful if markets are incomplete. Earlier work by trade theorists, in a context of incomplete markets, seems to point in the same direction. Thus it has been argued that, if decisions are taken by a single price-taking consumer or in the light of a social welfare function, the expected well-being of a population may be lower under free trade than under autarky; see Turnovsky (1974), Batra and Russell (1974) and Pomery (1984). Even more strikingly, Newbery and Stiglitz (1984) and Shy (1988) have shown that free trade can be Pareto-inferior to autarky. Furthermore, Helpman and Razin (1978: 137), basing themselves on Hart's (1975) finding that the opening of additional securities markets in a closed economy can harm every household, have argued that free trade in commodities only might be preferred by all countries to free trade in both goods and securities.

The prevailing pessimism about the possibility of extending the gains-from-trade propositions to accommodate incomplete market structures has been succinctly expressed by Grinols (1987: 58): '[N]either the free trade equilibrium nor the autarkic equilibrium need be a Pareto optimum. Either could Pareto dominate the other.'

Our purpose in preparing the present essay has been to demonstrate that, to some extent, this pessimism is misplaced. Thus, for an interesting class of economies with incomplete markets, it is shown that each of propositions 1–4 remains valid when markets are incomplete. In particular, for that class of economies and for the extreme form of market distortion represented by the absence of markets, the 'second-best' expectation, that trade gains may be positive or negative, is falsified.

These propositions are of interest only if the existence of an equilibrium is guaranteed. That existence can be a problem when markets are incomplete was shown by Hart (1975). After describing the class of economies to be studied, therefore, we demonstrate that those economies always have an equilibrium. In this part of the essay (section 3), we build on the work of Geanakoplos and Polemarchakis (1986), extending the scope of their analysis to accommodate production, lumpsum transfers and international trade.

In section 2, we provide a simple example to motivate our analysis and to illustrate the computation of lumpsum transfers. In section 3 we describe our model of a world economy and demonstrate the existence of an equilibrium. In section 4, we state and prove our main propositions. In section 5, we explore the role of lumpsum transfers in improving welfare; and, in a brief final section, we discuss some of the limitations of our analysis.

In the absence of a complete set of securities markets the proper objectives of the firm are, in general, unclear. If the firm's production set satisfies a spanning condition, there can be found a set of weights, one for each state of nature, such that shareholders of the firm unanimously agree to maximize expected profit defined in terms of those weights; see Magill and Shafer (1991: Section 4) and Geanakoplos *et al.* (1990). However, the spanning condition is restrictive. In the present analysis, therefore, it is assumed that, in each national economy, production is carried on by households; that is, attention is confined to cottage industry. In such economies, production decisions are determined in the light of expected utility maximization.[2] One might then wish to say that each household owns its own firm or firms. However, it must be understood that, generally, such firms do not maximize the present values of their cash flows. Moreover, there is no reason why two or more identical households should not combine their productive activities, thus leaving the number of firms indeterminate.

The absence of profit-maximizing firms is reflected in subtle disparities between our conclusions and those of conventional complete-markets analysis. In particular, the familiar 'production gains' associated with the opening of trade (and with other disturbances) are no longer necessarily non-negative. In fact the valuation of production changes has no bearing on questions of trading gain and loss. It matters only that production does change in response to the opening of trade (and to other disturbances). Given that production changes, one may safely rewrite the relevant weak Pareto-inequalities as strong inequalities.

2 AN EXAMPLE[3]

Consider a pure exchange economy with just two commodities and two price-taking households (or two homogeneous and equipopulated classes of price-taking households) and which is expected to last for just two periods of time, labelled 0 and 1. At the beginning of period t, the ith household receives an endowment pair w_t^i, $t = 0, 1$. In each period there is a spot market. However, there are no futures markets and no credit markets; nor can goods be stored from one period to the next. Finally, the ith household has a time-separable utility function

$$U^i(\mathbf{x}_0^i) + \beta^i V^i(\mathbf{x}_1^i) \quad \beta^i > 0, \; i = 1, 2,$$

where $\mathbf{x}_0^i$ and $\mathbf{x}_1^i$ are its first- and second-period consumption pairs.

At first, there is no possibility of trading with other countries. In each period separately, the equilibrium price equates aggregate demand to aggregate endowment:

$$\sum_i \mathbf{x}_0^i = \sum_i \mathbf{w}_0^i, \quad \sum_i \mathbf{x}_1^i = \sum_i \mathbf{w}_1^i.$$

Time preference, indicated by β^1 and β^2, plays no part in the determination of price.

Figure 1 depicts four possible one-period equilibria, two alternative equilibria for each period. The figure also makes clear that there are four possible two-period equilibria: (A, C), (A, D), (B, C) and (B, D). In (B, C) the first household is better off during the first period and worse off during the second period than in (A, D). The opposite is true of the second household. Since the equilibria are independent of β^1 and β^2, these parameters can be chosen arbitrarily. Let us choose β^1 small enough and β^2 large enough that both

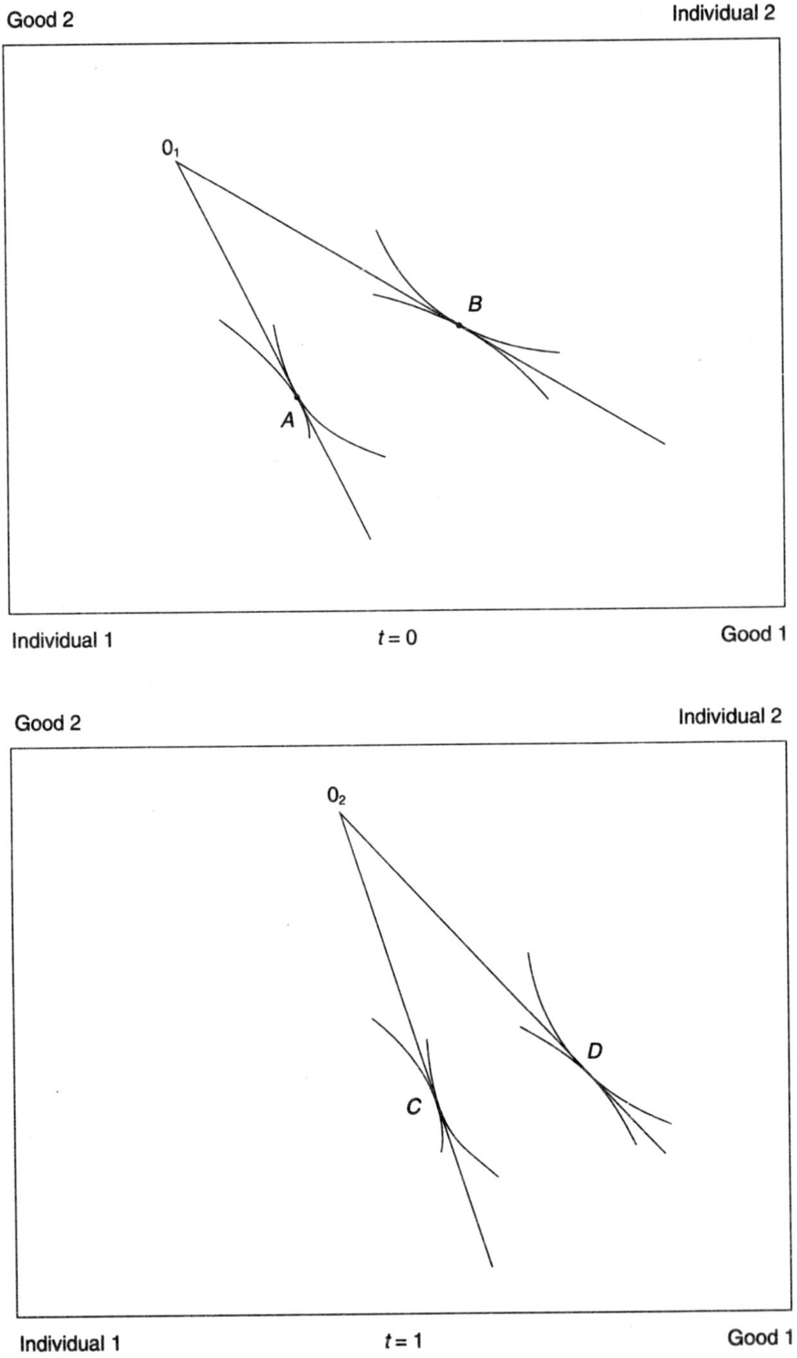
Good 2
Individual 2
0_1
B
A
Individual 1
$t = 0$
Good 1
Good 2
Individual 2
0_2
D
C
Individual 1
$t = 1$
Good 1

Figure 1

households prefer (B, C) to (A, D). And let us suppose that, for whatever reason, (B, C) is the autarkic equilibrium.

Later, our country is given the opportunity to trade at a given world price sufficiently close to (but not identical to) that of the equilibrium (A, D). Then, clearly, some trade takes place. Moreover, both households are worse off under free trade than under autarky; that is, the autarkic equilibrium is Pareto-preferred to the free-trade equilibrium.

Now consider Figure 2. If in period 0 the second household transfers an amount $O_1 O_1'$ of the first good to the first household and if in period 1 the first household reciprocates by transferring $O_2 O_2'$ of the same good to the second household then both households benefit; indeed they find themselves in a new **compensated** free-trade equilibrium which each prefers to autarky. The two-way transfer is a sufficiently good substitute for the missing credit market that compensated free trade is gainful.

Taking one step more, it can be easily verified that, whatever the two-period autarkic equilibrium, there is a scheme of compensation which ensures that free trade is gainful.

Thus, in this example, the traditional proposition is preserved. It remains to be seen whether it is preserved in less special circumstances.

It should be noted that while in the above example we consider an economy with multiple equilibria, other examples with unique equilibria can be constructed to show that free trade is Pareto-inferior to autarky (Newbery and Stiglitz, 1984; Shy, 1988). However, in those examples also, lumpsum transfers can be found to make every household better off under free trade than under autarky.

3 THE MODEL

There are two countries labelled 'home' and 'foreign'; however, the foreign country can be interpreted as the rest of the world. The two countries extend through $T+1$ periods of time, $T \geqslant 1$, beginning with period 0. It is assumed that the values of variables in period 0 are known with certainty, and that which of S mutually exclusive states of nature occurs in period t, $0 < t \leqslant T$, is not known until period t. For simplicity, we assume that there are the same number of states, S, in each period. Define $\mathbf{S} = (1, \ldots, S)$, $\mathbf{T}^a = (0, 1, \ldots, T)$, $\mathbf{T}^b = (0, 1, \ldots, T-1)$, $\mathbf{T}^c = (1, \ldots, T)$ and $\mathbf{T}^d = (1, \ldots, T-1)$.

In each period and each state, there are $N \geqslant 2$ goods in the world. The first $N^0 \geqslant 0$ of these are internationally tradable, while the next $N^1 \geqslant 0$ are non-tradables associated with the home country and the last $N^2 = N - N^0 - N^1 \geqslant 0$ are non-tradables associated with the foreign country. Goods are bought and sold in each period in both countries. The price of the nth good in the home country in period 0 (in period t when state s occurs) is denoted by $p_{0,n}$ ($p_{ts,n}$); and the vector of goods prices in the home country in period 0 (in period t when state s occurs) is denoted by $p_0 \in R_+^N$ ($p_{ts} \in R_+^N$), with the last

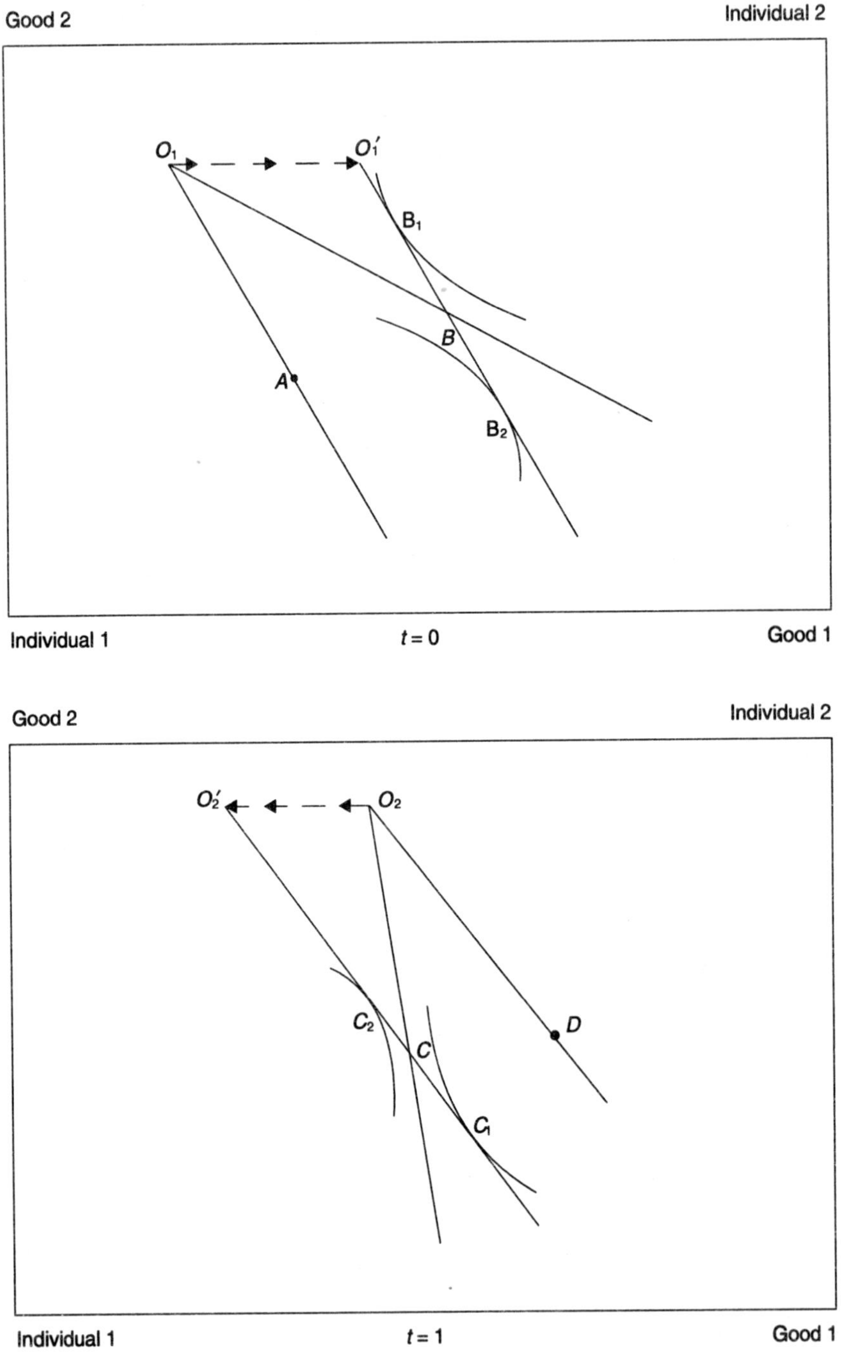
Good 2
Individual 2
O_1
O_1'
B_1
B
A
B_2
Individual 1
$t = 0$
Good 1
Good 2
Individual 2
O_2'
O_2
C_2
C
D
C_1
Individual 1
$t = 1$
Good 1

Figure 2

N^2 elements infinitely large. Similarly, the price of the nth good in the foreign country in period 0 (in period t when state s occurs) is denoted by $q_{0,n}$ ($q_{ts,n}$); and the vector of goods prices in the foreign country in period 0 (in period t and state s) is denoted by $q_0 \in R_+^N$ ($q_{ts} \in R_+^N$), with the $(N^0 + 1)$th to N^1th elements infinitely large. Define $\mathbf{p}_t = \{\mathbf{p}_{ts}\}$, $\mathbf{q}_t = \{\mathbf{q}_{ts}\}$, $\mathbf{p} = (\mathbf{p}_0, \mathbf{p}_1, \ldots, \mathbf{p}_T)$ and $\mathbf{q} = (\mathbf{q}_0, \mathbf{q}_1, \ldots, \mathbf{q}_T)$.

There are M one-period securities in the world. The first $M^0 \geqslant 0$ of these are internationally tradable, while the next M^1 are non-tradables associated with the home country and the last $M^2 = M - M^0 - M^1$ are non-tradables associated with the foreign country. Securities are bought and sold in each period t, $t \in \mathbf{T}^b$, and in both countries. In period t and state s, security m delivers an amount $a_s^m \geqslant 0$ of good 1, the *numéraire* (e.g. gold).[4] The security pays a positive amount of the *numéraire* in at least one of the states. If the price of the *numéraire* in period t and state s is $p_{ts,1} \geqslant 0$, the monetary payment by security m in either country in that period and state is $p_{ts,1} a_s^m \geqslant 0$.[5] Let us define $a_s = \{a_s^m\}$ and the $S \times M$ matrix $\mathbf{A} = \{a_s\}$. $\mathbf{A}$ has full column rank.

The price of the mth security in the home country in period 0 (in period t and state s) is denoted by $r_{0,m}(r_{ts,m})$; and the vector of security prices in the home country is denoted by $r_0 \in R_+^M$ ($r_{ts} \in R_+^M$) with the last M^2 elements infinitely large. Because each security pays non-negative amounts of the *numéraire* in all states with a positive amount in at least one state, and because households are non-satiated, the prices of securities are positive; when securities are free, there is arbitrage. Similarly, the price of the mth security in the foreign country in period 0 (in period t and state s) is denoted by $h_{0,m}$ ($h_{ts,m}$); and the vector of security prices in the foreign country in period 0 (in period t and state s) is denoted by $\mathbf{h}_0 \in R_+^M$ ($\mathbf{h}_{ts} \in R_+^M$), with the $(M^0 + 1)$th to M^1th elements infinitely large. Let us define $\mathbf{r}_t = \{\mathbf{r}_{ts}\}$, $\mathbf{r} = (\mathbf{r}_0, \mathbf{r}_1, \ldots, \mathbf{r}_{T-1})$, $\mathbf{h}_t = \{\mathbf{h}_{ts}\}$ and $\mathbf{h} = (\mathbf{h}_0, \mathbf{h}_1, \ldots, \mathbf{h}_{T-1})$.

Given the positive payment assumption and the assumption that $\mathbf{A}$ has full column rank, Geanakoplos and Polemarchakis (1986) showed that there exists a closed, convex cone $\Theta = \{\mathbf{r}_t \in R_{++}^M\colon \mathbf{r}_t = \mathbf{A}'\mathbf{v}, \mathbf{v} \in R_+^S\}$. The interior of Θ, denoted by Θ^o, is the set of non-arbitrage security prices. It is clear that, in equilibrium, $\mathbf{r}_t, \mathbf{h}_t \in \Theta^o$.

Without loss of generality, it is assumed that those securities available in the home country (the first $M^0 + M^1$ securities) are independent, and that the same is true of those securities available in the foreign country (the first M^0 and the last M^2 securities). Only when M^1 or M^2 is zero is it implied that the M securities available in the world are independent. It is assumed that $S \geqslant M^0 + M^1$ and $S \geqslant M^0 + M^2$. When $S = M^0 + M^1$, markets are complete in the home country; when $S = M^0 + M^2$, markets are complete in the foreign country.

In the home country there are I households. Let us define the set of households as $\mathbf{I} = (1, \ldots, I)$. The ith household is endowed with commodity vectors $\mathbf{w}_0^i$, $\mathbf{w}_{ts}^i \in R_{++}^N$ in periods 0 and t if state s occurs, respectively. The last N^2 elements of $\mathbf{w}_0^i$ and $\mathbf{w}_{ts}^i$ are zero. Moreover, the ith household receives from the government lumpsum transfers $b_0^i \in R$ in period 0, $b_{1s}^i \in R$ in period 1 if state s occurs, and $b_{tss'}^i \in R$ in period t, $t \in \mathbf{T}^c$, if states s and s' occur in periods t and $t-1$, respectively. Define $\mathbf{b}^i = (b_0^i, b_{11}^i, \ldots, b_{1S}^i, b_{211}^i, \ldots, b_{TSS}^i)$. Finally, each household engages in production, making use both of its own and of purchased resources. Let $\mathbf{y}_0^i$, $\mathbf{y}_{ts}^i \in R^N$ be the net output vectors of the ith household in periods 0 and t if state s occurs, respectively; and let $\mathbf{y}_t^i = \{\mathbf{y}_{ts}^i\}$. The choice of net outputs must satisfy the production constraint

$$(\mathbf{y}_0^i, \mathbf{y}_1^i, \ldots, \mathbf{y}_T^i) \in \mathbf{Y}^i \tag{1}$$

where $\mathbf{Y}^i$ is a closed and convex subset of $R^{N(1+ST)}$. Irreversibility and free disposal are assumed. Turning to household expenditure, let $\mathbf{x}_0^i$, $\mathbf{x}_{ts}^i \in R_+^N$ be the consumption vectors of the ith household in periods 0 and t if state s occurs, respectively; and let $\mathbf{z}_0^i$, $\mathbf{z}_{ts}^i \in R^M$ be the vectors of securities purchased in periods 0 and t if state s occurs, respectively. Let $\mathbf{x}_t^i = \{\mathbf{x}_{ts}^i\}$ and $\mathbf{z}_t^i = \{\mathbf{z}_{ts}^i\}$. Then the ith household is subject to the budget constraints

$$\mathbf{p}_0 \cdot (\mathbf{x}_0^i - \mathbf{y}_0^i) + \mathbf{r}_0 \cdot \mathbf{z}_0^i \leqslant \mathbf{p}_0 \cdot \mathbf{w}_0^i + b_0^i \tag{2a}$$

$$\mathbf{p}_{1s} \cdot (\mathbf{x}_{1s}^i - \mathbf{y}_{1s}^i) + \mathbf{r}_{1s} \cdot \mathbf{z}_{1s}^i \leqslant \mathbf{p}_{1s} \cdot \mathbf{w}_{1s}^i + p_{1s,1}\mathbf{a}_s \cdot \mathbf{z}_0^i + b_{1s}^i \tag{2b}$$

$$\mathbf{p}_{ts} \cdot (\mathbf{x}_{ts}^i - \mathbf{y}_{ts}^i) + \mathbf{r}_{ts} \cdot \mathbf{z}_{ts}^i \leqslant \mathbf{p}_{ts} \cdot \mathbf{w}_{ts}^i + p_{1s,1}\mathbf{a}_s \cdot \mathbf{z}_{t-1,s'}^i + b_{tss'}^i \tag{2c}$$

$$\mathbf{p}_{Ts} \cdot (\mathbf{x}_{Ts}^i - \mathbf{y}_{Ts}^i) \leqslant \mathbf{p}_{Ts} \cdot \mathbf{w}_{Ts}^i + p_{Ts,1}\mathbf{a}_s \cdot \mathbf{z}_{T-1,s}^i + b_{Tss'}^i \tag{2d}$$

$$t \in \mathbf{T}^d, \quad s, s' \in \mathbf{S}.$$

Define $\mathbf{x}^i = (\mathbf{x}_0^i, \mathbf{x}_1^i, \ldots, \mathbf{x}_T^i)$, $\mathbf{y}^i = (\mathbf{y}_0^i, \mathbf{y}_1^i, \ldots, \mathbf{y}_T^i)$ and $\mathbf{z}^i = (\mathbf{z}_0^i, \mathbf{z}_1^i, \ldots, \mathbf{z}_{T-1}^i)$. Let us suppose that the preferences of the ith household can be represented by a utility function $U^i(\mathbf{x}^i)$, which is increasing, continuous and concave in all goods and strictly increasing in the *numéraire*. Endowed with perfect conditional foresight, the household chooses $(\mathbf{x}^i, \mathbf{y}^i, \mathbf{z}^i)$ to maximize its utility subject to (1) and (2).

Let us further define $\mathbf{x}_0 = \Sigma_i \mathbf{x}_0^i$, $\mathbf{x}_{ts} = \Sigma_i \mathbf{x}_{ts}^i$, $\mathbf{w}_0 = \Sigma_i \mathbf{w}_0^i$, $\mathbf{w}_{ts} = \Sigma_i \mathbf{w}_{ts}^i$, $\mathbf{y}_0 = \Sigma_i \mathbf{y}_0^i$, $\mathbf{y}_{ts} = \Sigma_i \mathbf{y}_{ts}^i$, $\mathbf{x} = \Sigma_i \mathbf{x}^i$, $\mathbf{y} = \Sigma_i \mathbf{y}^i$, $\mathbf{w} = \Sigma_i \mathbf{w}^i$, and $\mathbf{z} = \Sigma_i \mathbf{z}^i$. Let $\mathbf{0}^p \in R_+^N$ be a vector with the first to the $(N^0 + N^1)$th elements zero and the other elements infinitely large and let $\mathbf{0}^r \in R_+^M$ be a vector with the first to the $(M^0 + M^1)$th elements zero and the other elements infinitely large.

We now introduce the foreign country and international trade. Let us denote the foreign excess demand for goods in period 0 and period t if state s occurs by $\mathbf{f}_0$ and $\mathbf{f}_{ts}$, respectively, and the foreign excess demand for securities by $\mathbf{g}_0$ and $\mathbf{g}_{ts}$. Let $\mathbf{f}_t = \{\mathbf{f}_{ts}\}$, $\mathbf{f} = (\mathbf{f}_0, \mathbf{f}_1, \ldots, \mathbf{f}_T)$, $\mathbf{g}_t = \{\mathbf{g}_{ts}\}$ and $\mathbf{g} = (\mathbf{g}_0, \mathbf{g}_1, \ldots, \mathbf{g}_{T-1})$. The quantity and price vectors are partitioned into three parts: the first part corresponds to internationally tradable goods or securities, the second part to non-tradable goods or securities associated with the home country, and the third part to non-tradable goods or securities associated with the foreign country. For example, $\mathbf{q}_0^0 \in R_+^{N^0}$ contains the first N^0 elements of $\mathbf{q}_0$, $\mathbf{g}_0^2 \in R_+^{M^2}$ contains the last M^2 elements of $\mathbf{g}_0$, and so on. Let $\mathbf{f}_t = \{\mathbf{f}_{ts}\}$. The foreign excess demand correspondence $\mathbf{F}(\mathbf{q}, \mathbf{h}) = \{(\mathbf{f}, \mathbf{g}) \in R^{N(1+TS)} \times R^{M(1+TS-S)}\}$ is assumed to be non-empty, compact, convex valued, upper hemi-continuous for $(\mathbf{q}, \mathbf{h})$ and homogeneous of degree 0 in $(\mathbf{q}, \mathbf{h})$; it is assumed also that, for all $(\mathbf{f}, \mathbf{g}) \in \mathbf{F}(\mathbf{q}, \mathbf{h})$,

$$\mathbf{q}_0^0 \cdot \mathbf{f}_0^0 + \mathbf{h}_0^0 \cdot \mathbf{g}_0^0 = 0 \tag{3a}$$

$$\mathbf{q}_0^2 \cdot \mathbf{f}_0^2 + \mathbf{h}_0^2 \cdot \mathbf{g}_0^2 = 0 \tag{3b}$$

$$\mathbf{q}_{1s}^0 \cdot \mathbf{f}_{1s}^0 + \mathbf{h}_{1s}^0 \cdot \mathbf{g}_{1s}^0 - q_{1s,1} \mathbf{a}_s \cdot \mathbf{g}_0^0 = 0 \tag{3c}$$

$$\mathbf{q}_{1s}^2 \cdot \mathbf{f}_{1s}^2 + \mathbf{h}_{1s}^2 \cdot \mathbf{g}_{1s}^2 - q_{1s,1} \mathbf{a}_s \cdot \mathbf{g}_0^2 = 0 \tag{3d}$$

$$\mathbf{q}_{ts}^0 \cdot \mathbf{f}_{ts}^0 + \mathbf{h}_{ts}^0 \cdot \mathbf{g}_{ts}^0 - q_{ts,1} \mathbf{a}_s \cdot \mathbf{g}_{(t-1)s'}^0 = 0 \tag{3e}$$

$$\mathbf{q}_{ts}^2 \cdot \mathbf{f}_{ts}^2 + \mathbf{h}_{ts}^2 \cdot \mathbf{g}_{ts}^2 - q_{ts,1} \mathbf{a}_s \cdot \mathbf{g}_{(t-1)s'}^2 = 0 \tag{3f}$$

$$\mathbf{q}_T^0 \cdot \mathbf{f}_T^0 - q_{Ts,1} \mathbf{a}_s \cdot \mathbf{g}_{(T-1)s'}^0 = 0 \tag{3g}$$

$$\mathbf{q}_T^2 \cdot \mathbf{f}_T^2 - q_{Ts,1} \mathbf{a}_s \cdot \mathbf{g}_{(T-1)s'}^2 = 0 \tag{3h}$$

$$t \in \mathbf{T}^d, \quad s, s' \in \mathbf{S}.$$

It is necessary to explain eqs (3). Noting that the $(N^0 + 1)$th to $(N^0 + N^1)$th elements of $\mathbf{f}_0$ and the $(M^0 + 1)$th to $(M^0 + M^1)$th elements of $\mathbf{g}_0$ are zero, the sum of eqs (3a) and (3b) gives $\mathbf{q}_0 \cdot \mathbf{f}_0 + \mathbf{h}_0 \cdot \mathbf{g}_0 = 0$, which is the budget constraint in period 0 concerning all goods and securities, or Walras' law. Note that (3a) is the balance-of-payments equation, in which $\mathbf{h}_0^0 \cdot \mathbf{g}_0^0$ is the outflow of foreign portfolio capital. Eqs (3c) to (3h) can be interpreted in a similar way. Because the $(N^0 + 1)$th to $(N^0 + N^1)$th elements of $\mathbf{q}_0$ and $\mathbf{q}_{ts}$, and the $(M^0 + 1)$th to $(M^0 + M^1)$th elements of $\mathbf{h}_0$ and $\mathbf{h}_{ts}$ are infinitely large, the budget constraints in (3) imply that the $(N^0 + 1)$th to $(N^0 + N^1)$th elements of $\mathbf{f}_0$ and $\mathbf{f}_{ts}$, and the $(M^0 + 1)$th to $(M^0 + M^1)$th elements of $\mathbf{g}_0$ and $\mathbf{g}_{ts}$, are zero.

That completes our description of the world economy. Evidently the example of section 2 fits as a special case, as do the examples constructed by Newbery and Stiglitz (1984) and Shy (1988).

Subject to the foreign excess demand correspondence described above, a free-trade equilibrium between the home and foreign countries is said to exist if the following conditions are satisfied:

(a) all households are maximizing their expected utility subject to their production and budget constaints as described above;
(b) $\mathbf{q}_0^0 = \alpha_0 \mathbf{p}_0^0$ and $\mathbf{q}_{ts}^0 = \alpha_{ts} \mathbf{p}_{ts}^0$ for some $\alpha_0, \alpha_{ts} > 0$ and all $t \in \mathbf{T}^c$ and $s \in \mathbf{S}$;
(c) $\mathbf{h}_0^0 = \alpha_0 \mathbf{r}_0^0$ and $\mathbf{h}_{ts}^0 = \alpha_{ts} \mathbf{r}_{ts}^0$ for some $\alpha_0, \alpha_{ts} > 0$ and all $t \in \mathbf{T}^d$ and $s \in \mathbf{S}$;
(d) $\mathbf{x}_t + \mathbf{f}_t \leqslant \mathbf{y}_t + \mathbf{w}_t$ for $t \in \mathbf{T}^a$; and
(e) $\Sigma_i \mathbf{z}_t^i + \mathbf{g}_t \leqslant 0$ for $t \in \mathbf{T}^b$.

Condition (a) is obvious; and (b) and (c) require that, for any internationally tradable good or security, the same price prevails everywhere. Conditions (d) and (e) state that the world excess demands for goods and securities cannot be positive, whether the goods and securities are internationally tradable or not.

Proposition 1. *In the present model and if* $\Sigma_i b_0^i = \Sigma_i b_{ts}^i = 0$ *for all* $t \in \mathbf{T}^c$ *and* $s \in \mathbf{S}$, *a competitive equilibrium exists.*

Proposition 1, which is proved in the appendix, does not rule out the possibility that some of the equilibrium security prices are zero. However, given the assumption of non-satiation and the assumption that all securities pay positive amounts of the *numéraire* in some states, the equilibrium prices of all securities must be positive.

Several special cases of the above framework can be distinguished.

1 Autarky, with or without a transfer scheme. Autarky is the case in which $N^0 = M^0 = 0$. If there is no transfer scheme, $b_0^i = b_{ts}^i = 0$ for all $i \in \mathbf{I}$ and $s \in \mathbf{S}$.
2 Free trade in goods but no trade in securities. In this case, $N^0 \geqslant 2$ and $M^0 = 0$.
3 Free trade in securities but no trade in goods. In this case, $M^0 > 0$ and $N^0 = 0$.
4 Free trade in goods and securities. In this case, $N^0 > 0$ and $M^0 > 0$.

Note that, in case 2, the number of internationally tradable goods is not less than two, while no such restriction is imposed in case 3. The reason is that in case 3 a transfer of the common *numéraire* between the countries is permitted for the purchase of securities and for the payments delivered by the securities, even if no trade in goods is allowed.

4 GAINS FROM TRADE

In this section we explore the effect on the home country of each of four disturbances:

1 The move from autarky to free trade.
2 The formation of a customs union.
3 When it is a small country, an improvement in its terms of trade.
4 When it is a small country, an addition to the list of goods and/or securities which are freely tradable between countries.

We contrast two situations. In the initial situation, the first $N^0 \geqslant 0$ goods and the first $M^0 \geqslant 0$ securities are internationally and domestically tradable while the rest are tradable domestically only, in one or both of the two countries; if $N^0 = M^0 = 0$, both countries are autarkic. In the final situation, either the home country has experienced an improvement in its terms of trade or additional goods and/or securities have become internationally tradable. To allow a meaningful comparison, it is assumed that home-country endowments, preferences, technologies and shareholdings remain unchanged.

Values of variables in the **initial situation** are distinguished by circumflexes. For simplicity only, it is assumed that in the initial situation there are no transfers so that $\hat{b}_0^i = \hat{b}_{ts}^i = 0$ for all $i \in \mathbf{I}$, $t \in \mathbf{T}^c$ and $s \in \mathbf{S}$. The demand of the ith household for goods and securities is $(\hat{\mathbf{x}}^i, \hat{\mathbf{z}}^i)$. Equilibrium in the initial situation is then described by the equations

$$\hat{\mathbf{x}}_0 + \hat{\mathbf{f}}_0 \leqslant \hat{\mathbf{y}}_0 + \mathbf{w}_0 \tag{4a}$$

$$\hat{\mathbf{x}}_{ts} + \hat{\mathbf{f}}_{ts} \leqslant \hat{\mathbf{y}}_{ts} + \mathbf{w}_{ts} \quad t \in \mathbf{T}^c,\ s \in \mathbf{S} \tag{4b}$$

$$\hat{\mathbf{z}}_0 + \hat{\mathbf{g}}_0 \leqslant 0 \tag{4c}$$

$$\hat{\mathbf{z}}_{ts} + \hat{\mathbf{g}}_{ts} \leqslant 0 \quad t \in \mathbf{T}^d,\ s \in \mathbf{S}. \tag{4d}$$

If the economy is closed in the initial situation, $\hat{\mathbf{f}}_0 = \hat{\mathbf{f}}_{ts} = \mathbf{0}^N$ and $\hat{\mathbf{g}}_0 = \hat{\mathbf{g}}_{ts} = \mathbf{0}^M$, where $\mathbf{0}^i \in R^i$, $i = M, N$, is an i-dimensional vector of zeros.

Variables in the **final situation** are distinguished by the absence of circumflexes. For example, $\mathbf{p}_{ts}$ is the price of goods and $\mathbf{y}_{ts}^i$ is the output of the ith household in period t and state s. The period-by-period gains from changes in the terms of trade associated with a move from the initial to the final situation are

$$Q_0 = \mathbf{r}_0 \cdot \hat{\mathbf{g}}_0 + \mathbf{p}_0 \cdot \hat{\mathbf{f}}_0 \tag{5a}$$

$$Q_{1s} = \mathbf{r}_{1s} \cdot \hat{\mathbf{g}}_{1s} + \mathbf{p}_{1s} \cdot \hat{\mathbf{f}}_{1s} - p_{1s,1}\mathbf{a}_s \cdot \hat{\mathbf{g}}_0 \tag{5b}$$

$$Q_{tss'} = \mathbf{r}_{ts} \cdot \hat{\mathbf{g}}_{ts} + \mathbf{p}_{ts} \cdot \hat{\mathbf{f}}_{ts} - p_{ts,1}\mathbf{a}_s \cdot \hat{\mathbf{g}}_{(t-1)s'} \tag{5c}$$

$$Q_{Tss'} = \mathbf{p}_{Ts} \cdot \hat{\mathbf{f}}_{Ts} - p_{Ts,1}\mathbf{a}_s \cdot \hat{\mathbf{g}}_{(T-1)s'} \tag{5d}$$

$$t \in \mathbf{T}^d, \quad s, s' \in \mathbf{S}.$$

In general, the terms-of-trade gains may be of either sign. The ith household receives from the government the lumpsum payments

$$b_0^i = \mathbf{p}_0 \cdot (\hat{\mathbf{x}}_0^i - \hat{\mathbf{y}}_0^i - \mathbf{w}_0^i) + \mathbf{r}_0 \cdot \hat{\mathbf{z}}_0^i + Q_0/I \tag{6a}$$

$$b_{1s}^i = \mathbf{p}_{1s} \cdot (\hat{\mathbf{x}}_{1s}^i - \hat{\mathbf{y}}_{1s}^i - \mathbf{w}_{1s}^i) + \mathbf{r}_{1s} \cdot \hat{\mathbf{z}}_{1s}^i - p_{1s,1}\mathbf{a}_s \cdot \hat{\mathbf{z}}_0^i + Q_{1s}/I \tag{6b}$$

$$b_{tss'}^i = \mathbf{p}_{ts} \cdot (\hat{\mathbf{x}}_{1s}^i - \hat{\mathbf{y}}_{ts}^i - \mathbf{w}_{ts}^i) + \mathbf{r}_{ts} \cdot \hat{\mathbf{z}}_{ts}^i - p_{ts,1}\mathbf{a}_s \cdot \hat{\mathbf{z}}_{(t-1)s'}^i + Q_{tss'}/I \tag{6c}$$

$$b_{Tss'}^i = \mathbf{p}_{Ts} \cdot (\hat{\mathbf{x}}_{Ts}^i - \hat{\mathbf{y}}_{Ts}^i - \hat{\mathbf{w}}_{Ts}^i) - p_{Ts,1}\mathbf{a}_s \cdot \hat{\mathbf{z}}_{(T-1)s'}^i + Q_{Tss'}/I \tag{6d}$$

$$t \in \mathbf{T}^d, \quad s, s' \in \mathbf{S}.$$

In (6), households share uniformly in the gains from changes in the terms of trade. However, any form of sharing would suffice for the purpose of proving propositions 2–5 below.

Lemma 1. *The scheme of lumpsum transfers (6) implies a government deficit of zero and is feasible.*

By lemma 1 and proposition 1, there exists an equilibrium in each situation. Let us say that the final situation weakly Pareto-dominates the initial situation if, under the scheme (6) of lumpsum transfers, no household is worse off in the final situation; and that the final situation Pareto-dominates the initial situation if, under the same scheme of transfers, some households are better off, and none worse off, in the final situation.

Lemma 2. *If the terms-of-trade gains defined in (5) are non-negative, then the final situation weakly Pareto-dominates the initial situation. If, in addition, at least one of the terms-of-trade gains is positive or if consumption and/or production substitution takes place in at least one household then the final situation Pareto-dominates the initial situation.*

From lemmas 1 and 2 it is a short step to our remaining propositions.

Proposition 2. *Given the scheme of lumpsum transfers described by (6), free trade weakly Pareto-dominates autarky; if consumption and/or production substitution takes place in at least one household then free trade Pareto-dominates autarky.*

Proposition 3. *For a small open economy, if free trade exists in both situations and if there is no (time, state) pair in which the terms of trade deteriorate, so that*

$$\mathbf{r}_0 \cdot \hat{\mathbf{g}}_0 + \mathbf{p}_0 \cdot \hat{\mathbf{f}}_0 \geqslant 0 \tag{7a}$$

$$\mathbf{r}_{1s} \cdot \hat{\mathbf{g}}_{1s} + \mathbf{p}_{1s} \cdot \hat{\mathbf{f}}_{1s} - \mathbf{p}_{1s,1} \mathbf{a}_s \cdot \hat{\mathbf{g}}_0 \geqslant 0 \tag{7b}$$

$$\mathbf{r}_{ts} \cdot \hat{\mathbf{g}}_{ts} + \mathbf{p}_{ts} \cdot \hat{\mathbf{f}}_{ts} - \mathbf{p}_{ts,1} \mathbf{a}_s \cdot \hat{\mathbf{g}}_{(t-1)s'} \geqslant 0 \tag{7c}$$

$$\mathbf{p}_{Ts} \cdot \hat{\mathbf{f}}_{Ts} - \mathbf{p}_{Ts,1} \mathbf{a}_s \cdot \hat{\mathbf{g}}_{(T-1)s'} \geqslant 0 \tag{7d}$$

$$t \in \mathbf{T}^d, \quad s, s' \in \mathbf{S}$$

then the final situation weakly Pareto-dominates the initial situation; if in (7) there is at least one strict inequality, or if consumption and/or production substitution takes place, then the final situation Pareto-dominates the initial situation.

Proposition 4. *Consider a small open economy facing fixed world prices and able in the final situation to trade in additional goods and/or securities. The final situation weakly Pareto-dominates the initial situation; and if consumption and/or production substitution takes place in at least one household then the final situation Pareto-dominates the initial situation.*

It should be noted that nothing like proposition 4 holds for a large open economy. Indeed it is possible, when all trading economies are large, that the opportunity to trade in additional goods and/or securities leaves all individuals in all trading countries worse off (even when, in each country, all individuals are identical, so that there is no scope for compensatory transfers). For a simple example, see Kemp and Sinn (1990). Of course, for such an extreme outcome it is necessary that markets remain incomplete even after the opening of trade in additional goods and/or securities.

We now turn to a welfare analysis of the formation of customs unions. There is a fixed number of countries in the world with any constellation of trade restrictions and transport costs. The countries can be divided into two groups. The first group consists of K countries which are about to form a customs union, and the second group consists of all other countries. Countries in the first group are called member countries and are labelled $1, \ldots, K$. Define the set $\mathbf{K} = (1, \ldots, K)$. All other countries are called non-member countries. Member country k has I^k households. We retain our earlier notation, but add a superscript k to denote the variables of country k. For example, $\mathbf{x}_0^{ki}$ is the consumption demand of the ith household in country k.

Consider first the situation before the formation of the customs union. There are, as described above, $T+1$ periods, and in period t, $t \in \mathbf{T}^c$, there are S states. Denote the total volume of goods and services imported by the non-member countries from the member countries in period 0 and period t when state s occurs by $\hat{\mathbf{f}}_0 \in R^N$ and $\hat{\mathbf{f}}_{ts} \in R^N$, respectively. Variables in this situation are distinguished by circumflexes. Similarly, denote the non-member countries' import of securities in period 0 and period t when state s occurs by $\hat{\mathbf{g}}_0 \in R^M$ and $\hat{\mathbf{g}}_{ts} \in R^M$, respectively. Note that the elements of $\hat{\mathbf{f}}_0$ and $\hat{\mathbf{f}}_{ts}$ ($\hat{\mathbf{g}}_0$ and $\hat{\mathbf{g}}_{ts}$) corresponding to the goods and services (securities) that do not flow between member and non-member countries are zero. Denote the corresponding world prices of goods and services by $\hat{\mathbf{q}}_0 \in R_+^N$, and $\hat{\mathbf{q}}_{ts} \in R_+^N$, and the corresponding world prices of securities by $\hat{\mathbf{h}}_0 \in R_+^M$ and $\hat{\mathbf{h}}_{ts} \in R_+^M$. The aggregate balances of payments of these countries are

$$\hat{\mathbf{q}}_0 \cdot \hat{\mathbf{f}}_0 + \hat{\mathbf{h}}_0 \cdot \hat{\mathbf{g}}_0 = 0 \tag{8a}$$

$$\hat{\mathbf{q}}_{1s} \cdot \hat{\mathbf{f}}_{1s} + \hat{\mathbf{h}}_{1s} \cdot \hat{\mathbf{g}}_{1s} - \hat{q}_{1s,1}\mathbf{a}_s \cdot \hat{\mathbf{g}}_0 = 0 \tag{8b}$$

$$\hat{\mathbf{q}}_{ts} \cdot \hat{\mathbf{f}}_{ts} + \hat{\mathbf{h}}_{ts} \cdot \hat{\mathbf{g}}_{ts} - \hat{q}_{ts,1}\mathbf{a}_s \cdot \hat{\mathbf{g}}^0_{(t-1)s'} = 0 \tag{8c}$$

$$\hat{\mathbf{q}}_T \cdot \hat{\mathbf{f}}_T - \hat{q}_{Ts,1}\mathbf{a}_s \cdot \hat{\mathbf{g}}^0_{(T-1)s'} = 0 \tag{8d}$$

$$t \in \mathbf{T}^d, \quad s, s' \in \mathbf{S}.$$

Denote the aggregate consumption of goods and services by households in the member countries in period 0 by $\hat{\mathbf{x}}_0 = \Sigma_k\Sigma_i\hat{\mathbf{x}}_0^{ki}$, their aggregate production by $\hat{\mathbf{y}}_0 = \Sigma_k\Sigma_i\hat{\mathbf{y}}_0^{ki}$, their endowments by $\mathbf{w}_0 = \Sigma_k\Sigma_i\mathbf{w}_0^{ki}$, and their demand for securities by $\hat{\mathbf{z}}_0 = \Sigma_k \Sigma_i \hat{\mathbf{z}}_0^{ki}$. Their aggregate consumption of goods, aggregate production of goods, endowments, and demand for securities in period t and state s are similarly defined and denoted by $\hat{\mathbf{x}}_{ts}$, $\hat{\mathbf{y}}_{ts}$, $\mathbf{w}_{ts}$ and $\hat{\mathbf{z}}_{ts}$. The equilibrium conditions are

$$\hat{\mathbf{x}}_0 + \hat{\mathbf{f}}_0 - \hat{\mathbf{y}}_0 - \mathbf{w}_0 \leqslant 0 \tag{9a}$$

$$\hat{\mathbf{x}}_{ts} + \hat{\mathbf{f}}_{ts} - \hat{\mathbf{y}}_{ts} - \mathbf{w}_{ts} \leqslant 0 \tag{9b}$$

$$\hat{\mathbf{z}}_0 + \hat{\mathbf{h}}_0 \leqslant 0 \tag{9c}$$

$$\hat{\mathbf{z}}_{ts} + \hat{\mathbf{h}}_{ts} \leqslant 0 \tag{9d}$$

$$t \in \mathbf{T}^c,\ s \in \mathbf{S}.$$

Now member countries form a customs union and remove all trade barriers among them. To prove welfare improvement, we follow Kemp and Wan (1976, 1986) and artificially freeze the trade between member countries and non-member countries. The assumption that trade is frozen is for exposition only; it will be shown later that if a suitable common tariff structure is chosen, world prices, and therefore non-member countries' import demands, do not change.

Using the above notation, the budget constraints of the ith household in the kth member country in all periods and states are

$$\mathbf{p}_0 \cdot (\mathbf{x}_0^{ki} - \mathbf{y}_0^{ki}) + \mathbf{r}_0 \cdot \mathbf{z}_0^{ki} \leqslant \mathbf{p}_0 \cdot \mathbf{w}^{ki} + b_0^{ki} \tag{10a}$$

$$\mathbf{p}_{1s} \cdot (\mathbf{x}_{1s}^{ki} - \mathbf{y}_{1s}^{ki}) + \mathbf{r}_{1s} \cdot \mathbf{z}_{1s}^{ki} \leqslant \mathbf{p}_{1s} \cdot \mathbf{w}_{1s}^{ki} + p_{1s,1}\mathbf{a}_s \cdot \mathbf{z}_0^{i} + b_{1s}^{ki} \tag{10b}$$

$$\mathbf{p}_{ts} \cdot (\mathbf{x}_{ts}^{ki} - \mathbf{y}_{ts}^{ki}) + \mathbf{r}_{ts} \cdot \mathbf{z}_{ts}^{ki} \leqslant \mathbf{p}_{ts} \cdot \mathbf{w}_{ts}^{ki} + p_{1s,1}\mathbf{a}_s \cdot \mathbf{z}_{t-1,s'}^{ki} + b_{ts}^{ki} \tag{10c}$$

$$\mathbf{p}_{Ts} \cdot (\mathbf{x}_{Ts}^{ki} - \mathbf{y}_{Ts}^{ki}) \leqslant \mathbf{p}_{Ts} \cdot \mathbf{w}_{Ts}^{ki} + p_{Ts,1}\mathbf{a}_s \cdot \mathbf{z}_{T-1,s}^{ki} + b_{Tss'} \tag{10d}$$

$$t \in \mathbf{T}^d, \quad s, s' \in \mathbf{S}.$$

We now generalize the Kemp–Wan proposition to accommodate markets which are possibly incomplete.

Proposition 5. *Consider any competitive world trading equilibrium, with any number of countries and commodities, with possibly incomplete markets, with no restrictions whatever on the tariffs and other commodity taxes of individual countries, and with costs of transport fully recognized. Now let any subset of the countries form a customs union. Then there exists a common tariff vector and a system of lumpsum compensatory payments involving only members of the union such that each household, whether a member of the union or not, is not worse off than before the formation of the union. Those member households which enjoy consumption and/or production substitution are better off.*

In concluding this section, we note that when $S = M^0 + M^1$, so that markets are complete in the home country, each home household maximizes expected utility only if it maximizes expected profit and our analysis becomes entirely conventional.

That completes the formal presentation of our results. It is therefore a suitable place for a warning sign: all of our welfare propositions are in terms of **prospective** improvements, not in terms of **realized** improvements. The household utility functions $U^i(\mathbf{x}^i)$ have meaning only in period 0, before the states of the world in periods $1,\ldots,T$ are known. After the states are known, utility depends only on consumption planned for the realized states, and that may be less under compensated free trade than it would have been under autarky. The scheme of compensation (6) allows each household to choose free-trade consumption at least as great as autarkic consumption; but it does not require it to do so. Of course, this remark applies whether or not securities markets are incomplete.

5. THE ROLE OF LUMPSUM TRANSFERS

When markets are incomplete, the spreading of risks is suboptimal. What we have shown, in effect, is that the scheme of lumpsum transfers described in section 4 is such that there remains enough risk spreading to ensure the gainfulness of free trade (or of a customs union or of an improvement in the terms of trade or of an addition to the list of tradable goods and/or securities). Can one claim more? Does that scheme of transfers in fact eliminate **all** distortions associated with the incompleteness of markets and generate the same allocation of risks as a complete complement of markets? If that conjecture were valid, propositions 2–5 would be completely uninteresting, for they would simply restate their complete-markets counterparts. In fact, the conjecture is incorrect. Transfers are tied to the equilibrium quantities of the initial situation and therefore cannot be freely chosen to achieve Pareto optimality.

This does not mean that there cannot be found a scheme of lumpsum compensation which eliminates all distortions associated with the incompleteness of markets. However, any such scheme must be based on the trades of households in a **complete-markets** initial equilibrium. Such trades are not observable, even ideally.[6] It is a virtue of the scheme of compensation described in section 4 that it is both efficacious and ideally implementable.[7]

Some readers of our essay have argued that attention should have been restricted to those schemes of compensation which can be effected by prior redistribution of the available securities (and which lie in the cone spanned by the columns of $\mathbf{A}$). Given that restriction, it would have been impossible to prove anything like propositions 2–5. However, we see no good reason to impose such a restriction.

6. FINAL REMARKS

In the introduction, attention was drawn to the fact that in the missing-markets, multiperiod, multistate framework of this essay there is no role for the traditional non-negative 'production gains' associated with the opening of trade and other disturbances. Nevertheless, it is possible to redefine production and consumption gains in an intertemporal sense so that both are non-negative.

Let us denote the ith household's consumption and production under autarky by $\hat{\mathbf{x}}^i$ and $\hat{\mathbf{y}}^i \in R^{N(TS+1)}$, respectively, and its consumption and production under free trade by x^i and $y^i \in R^{N(TS+1)}$. Consider now the trade situation. Note that with the transfers, the autarky consumption and production are still feasible. Suppose that the production of the household is frozen at $\hat{\mathbf{y}}^i$. Denote its consumption by $x^{i\prime}$. Then the compensating variation associated with the shift in consumption from $\hat{\mathbf{x}}^i$ to $x^{i\prime}$ can be interpreted as the consumption gain. When the household is allowed to shift its production from $\hat{\mathbf{y}}^i$ to $y^{i\prime}$, with its consumption shifting from $x^{i\prime}$ to x^i, the corresponding compensating variation defines the production gain.

Finally, two limitations of our analysis should be noted.

First, the set of missing markets has been taken as given. In a more complete analysis, the set would be endogenously determined in the light of the costs of establishing and running each market, the sharpness with which property rights are defined and the distribution of information among market participants. It is possible that in such an analysis the set of missing markets might depend on the possibility of trade.

Second, we have followed tradition in assuming that compensation is effected by lumpsum transfers between households. Depending on the supplementary story told about the process of introducing trade, this form of compensation may or may not raise problems of incentives. For a detailed discussion of these problems, see Kemp and Wan (1992a, b).

APPENDIX

In this appendix, we prove the lemmas and propositions stated in the paper. Before proving proposition 1, we first state and prove the following additional lemma.

Lemma 3. *Consider the truncated excess demand correspondence*

$$\mathbf{D}^i(\mathbf{p}, \mathbf{r}; H, \mathbf{b}^i) = \{(\mathbf{x}^i - \mathbf{y}^i, \mathbf{z}^i)\colon (\mathbf{x}^i, \mathbf{y}^i, \mathbf{z}^i) \text{ satisfies (1) and (2), and } U^i(\mathbf{x}^i) \geqslant U^i(\mathbf{x}^{i\prime}) \text{ for all } (\mathbf{x}^{i\prime}, \mathbf{y}^{i\prime}, \mathbf{z}^{i\prime}) \text{ which satisfy (1) and (2)}\},$$

where $H \subseteq R^{N(1+TS)} \times R^{M(1+TS-S)}$ is a closed rectangle with centre at the origin. The demand correspondence $\mathbf{D}^i(\mathbf{p}, \mathbf{r}; H, \mathbf{b}^i)$ is non-empty, compact, convex valued and upper hemi-continuous at each $(\mathbf{p}, \mathbf{r}) \in R_+^{N(1+TS)} \times R_+^{M(1+TS-S)}$ with $\mathbf{p}_0 \neq \mathbf{0}^p$, $\mathbf{p}_{ts} \neq \mathbf{0}^p$, $\mathbf{r}_0 \neq \mathbf{0}^r$, and $\mathbf{r}_{ts} \neq \mathbf{0}^r$ for all $s \in \mathbf{S}$.

Proof. *Non-emptiness, compactness and convexity of the demand correspondence are obvious. To establish upper hemi-continuity, define the sequences*

$$(\mathbf{p}^j, \mathbf{r}^j) \rightarrow (\mathbf{p}, \mathbf{r})$$

and

$$((\mathbf{x}^i - \mathbf{y}^i)^j, (\mathbf{z}^i)^j) \to (\mathbf{x}^i - \mathbf{y}^i, \mathbf{z}^i),$$

where $((\mathbf{x}^i - \mathbf{y}^i)^j, (\mathbf{z}^i)^j) \in \mathbf{D}^i(\mathbf{p}^j, \mathbf{r}^j; K, \mathbf{b}^i)$. *Suppose that there exists*

$$(\bar{\mathbf{x}}^i, \bar{\mathbf{y}}^i, \bar{\mathbf{z}}^i) \in \{(\mathbf{x}^{i\prime}, \mathbf{y}^{i\prime}, \mathbf{z}^{i\prime}): \text{(1) and (2) are satisfied}\}$$

such that $U^i(\bar{\mathbf{x}}^{i\prime}) > U^i(\mathbf{x}^i)$. *Take* $\lambda < 1$ *but sufficiently large that* $U^i(\lambda\bar{\mathbf{x}}^i) > U^i(\mathbf{x}^i)$. *By continuity, for j large,* $U^i(\lambda\bar{\mathbf{x}}^i) > U^i((\mathbf{x}^i)^j)$. *Define*

$$(\bar{\mathbf{z}}_0^i)^j = \arg\min_{\mathbf{z}_0^{i\prime}} \{\|\bar{\mathbf{z}}_0^i - \mathbf{z}_0^{i\prime}\|: \mathbf{r}_0 \cdot \mathbf{z}_0^{i\prime} = \mathbf{p}_0 \cdot (\mathbf{w}_0^i - \mathbf{x}_0^i + \mathbf{y}_0^i) + b_0^i\}$$

$$(\bar{\mathbf{z}}_{ts}^i)^j = \arg\min_{\mathbf{z}_{ts}^{i\prime}} \{\|\bar{\mathbf{z}}_{ts}^i - \mathbf{z}_{ts}^{i\prime}\|: \mathbf{r}_{ts} \cdot \mathbf{z}_{ts}^{i\prime} = \mathbf{p}_{ts} \cdot (\mathbf{w}_{ts}^i - \mathbf{x}_{ts}^i + \mathbf{y}_{ts}^i) + p_{ts,1}\mathbf{a}_s \cdot \mathbf{z}_{t-1,s}^i + b_{ts}^i\}.$$

Note that, for $\mathbf{r}_0 \neq \mathbf{0}^r$, $(\bar{\mathbf{z}}_0^i)^j \to \bar{\mathbf{z}}_0^i$; *and that, for* $\mathbf{r}_{ts} \neq \mathbf{0}^r$, $(\bar{\mathbf{z}}_{ts}^i)^j \to \bar{\mathbf{z}}_{ts}^i$. *Now the budget constraint (2) implies that, for j large,*

$$\lambda\mathbf{p}_0 \cdot \bar{\mathbf{x}}_0^i \leqslant \mathbf{p}_0 \cdot (\mathbf{w}^i + \mathbf{y}_0^i) + b_0^i - \mathbf{r}_0 \cdot (\mathbf{z}_0^i)^j$$

$$\lambda\mathbf{p}_{1s} \cdot \mathbf{x}_{1s}^i \leqslant \mathbf{p}_{1s} \cdot (\mathbf{w}_{1s}^i + \mathbf{y}_{1s}^i) + p_{1s,1}\mathbf{a}_s \cdot (\mathbf{z}_0^i)^j + b_{1s}^i - \mathbf{r}_{1s} \cdot (\mathbf{z}_{1s}^i)^j$$

$$\lambda\mathbf{p}_{ts} \cdot \mathbf{x}_{ts}^i \leqslant \mathbf{p}_{ts} \cdot (\mathbf{w}_{ts}^i + \mathbf{y}_{ts}^i) + p_{1s,1}\mathbf{a}_s \cdot (\mathbf{z}_{t-1,s'}^i)^j + b_{tss'}^i - \mathbf{r}_{ts} \cdot (\mathbf{z}_{ts}^i)^j$$

$$\lambda\mathbf{p}_{Ts} \cdot \mathbf{x}_{Ts}^i \leqslant \mathbf{p}_{Ts} \cdot (\mathbf{w}_{Ts}^i + \mathbf{y}_{Ts}^i) + p_{Ts,1}\mathbf{a}_s \cdot (\mathbf{z}_{T-1,s}^i)^j + b_{Tss'}^i$$

$$t \in \mathbf{T}^d, \quad s, s' \in \mathbf{S}.$$

These inequalities imply that, for j large, $(\lambda\bar{\mathbf{x}}^i, \bar{\mathbf{y}}^i, \bar{\mathbf{z}}^i)$ *is feasible when prices are* $(\mathbf{p}^j, \mathbf{r}^j)$, *but it contradicts the condition that* $U^i(\lambda\bar{\mathbf{x}}^i) > U^i((\mathbf{x}^i)^j)$. □

By lemma 3, the aggregate excess demand correspondence $\mathbf{D} = \Sigma_i \mathbf{D}^i$ is non-empty, compact, convex valued, and upper hemi-continuous.

Proof of Proposition 1. *Let us define* $\mathbf{0}^q \in R_+^N$ *as a vector with the first* N^0 *elements and the last* N^2 *elements zero and the remaining elements infinitely large, and* $\mathbf{0}^h \in R_+^M$ *as a vector with the first* M^0 *elements and the last* M^2 *elements zero and the remaining elements infinitely large. Let us define the simplices*

$$\Delta_0 = \left\{\mathbf{p}_0 \in R_+^N, \mathbf{r}_0 \in \Theta^0: \mathbf{p}_0 \neq \mathbf{0}^p, \mathbf{r}_0 \neq \mathbf{0}^r, \sum_{\ell=1}^{N^0+N^1} p_{0,\ell} + \sum_{\ell=1}^{M^0+M^1} r_{0,\ell} = 1\right\}$$

$$\Delta_{ts} = \left\{ \mathbf{p}_{ts} \in R_+^N, \mathbf{r}_{ts} \in \Theta^{\circ}: \mathbf{p}_{ts} \neq \mathbf{0}^p, \mathbf{r}_{ts} \neq \mathbf{0}^r, \sum_{\ell=1}^{N^0+N^1} p_{ts,\ell} + \sum_{\ell=1}^{M^0+M^1} r_{ts,\ell} = 1 \right\}$$

$$t \in \mathbf{T}^d, s \in \mathbf{S};$$

$$\Delta_{Ts} = \left\{ (\mathbf{p}_{Ts}) \in R_+^N : \mathbf{p}_{Ts} \neq \mathbf{0}^p, \sum_{\ell=1}^{N^0+N^1} p_{Ts,\ell} = 1 \right\}$$

$$\Gamma_0 = \left\{ \mathbf{q}_0 \in R_+^N, \mathbf{h}_0 \in \Theta^{\circ}: \mathbf{q}_0 \neq \mathbf{0}^q, \mathbf{h}_0 \neq \mathbf{0}^h, \right.$$

$$\left. \sum_{\ell=1}^{N^0} q_{0,\ell} + \sum_{\ell=N^0+N^1+1}^{N} q_{0,\ell} + \sum_{\ell=1}^{M^0} h_{0,\ell} + \sum_{\ell=M^0+M^1+1}^{M} h_{0,\ell} = 1 \right\}$$

$$\Gamma_{ts} = \left\{ \mathbf{q}_{ts} \in R_+^N, \mathbf{h}_{ts} \in \Theta^{\circ}: \mathbf{q}_{ts} \neq \mathbf{0}^q, \mathbf{h}_{ts} \neq \mathbf{0}^h, \right.$$

$$\left. \sum_{\ell=1}^{N^0} q_{ts,\ell} + \sum_{\ell=N^0+N^1+1}^{N} q_{ts,\ell} + \sum_{\ell=1}^{M^0} h_{ts,\ell} + \sum_{\ell=M^0+M^1+1}^{M} h_{ts,\ell} = 1 \right\}$$

$$t \in \mathbf{T}^d, s \in \mathbf{S}$$

$$\Gamma_{Ts} = \left\{ (\mathbf{q}_{Ts}) \in R_+^N : \mathbf{q}_{Ts} \neq \mathbf{0}^q, \sum_{\ell=1}^{N^0} q_{Ts,\ell} + \sum_{\ell=N^0+N^1+1}^{N} q_{Ts,\ell} = 1 \right\}.$$

The strategy of the proof is to show that when households are maximizing their expected utilities, and when prices are equalized across countries according to conditions (b) and (c), equilibrium conditions (d) and (e) are also satisfied.

Let us define the aggregate excess demand correspondence as $\mathbf{E}(\mathbf{p}, \mathbf{r}, \mathbf{q}, \mathbf{h}; K) = \mathbf{D} + \mathbf{F} - (\mathbf{w}, \mathbf{0}^{M(1+TS-S)})$, *where* $\mathbf{0}^{M(1+TS-S)} \in R^{M(1+TS-S)}$ *has elements zero and* K *is sufficiently large that it contains any feasible aggregate supply in any period and any state of nature, and let us write*

$$\mathbf{e} = (\mathbf{x} - \mathbf{y} - \mathbf{w} + \mathbf{f}, \mathbf{z} + \mathbf{g}) \in \mathbf{E}.$$

Let us also define $\tilde{\mathbf{f}}_0, \tilde{\mathbf{f}}_{ts} \in R^N$, *with the first* N^0 *elements identical to the corresponding elements of* $\mathbf{f}_0$ *and* $\mathbf{f}_{ts}$, *respectively, and with the last* $N^1 + N^2$ *elements zero. Let us similarly define* $\tilde{\mathbf{g}}_0, \tilde{\mathbf{g}}_{ts} \in R^M$, *with the first* M^0 *elements identical to the corresponding elements of* $\mathbf{g}_0$ *and* $\mathbf{g}_{ts}$, *respectively, and with the last* $M^1 + M^2$ *elements zero. In view of lemma 1 and the restrictions placed on* $\mathbf{F}$, $\mathbf{E}(\mathbf{p}, \mathbf{r}, \mathbf{q}, \mathbf{h}; K)$ *is non-empty, compact, convex valued and upper hemi-continuous.*

Now consider the correspondence $\mathbf{\Phi}$:

$$\Delta_0 \times \Delta_{11} \times \ldots \times \Delta_{TS} \times \Gamma_0 \times \Gamma_{11} \times \ldots \times \Gamma_{TS} \times \mathbf{E}.$$

Choosing arbitrary finite $\alpha_0, \alpha_{11}, \ldots, \alpha_{TS} > 0$*, the first* $2(1 + TS)$ *components of* Φ *are given as*

$$\Phi_1 = \{(\mathbf{p}_0, \mathbf{r}_0) \in \Delta_0 : (\mathbf{p}_0, \mathbf{r}_0) \text{ maximizes } \mathbf{p}_0 \cdot (\mathbf{x}_0 + \tilde{\mathbf{f}}_0 - \mathbf{y}_0 - \mathbf{w}_0)$$

$$+ \mathbf{r}_0 \cdot (\mathbf{z}_0 + \tilde{\mathbf{g}}_0)\}$$

$$\Phi_{ts+1} = \{(\mathbf{p}_{ts}, \mathbf{r}_{ts}) \in \Delta_{ts} : (\mathbf{p}_{ts}, \mathbf{r}_{ts}) \text{ maximizes } \mathbf{p}_{ts} \cdot (\mathbf{x}_{ts} + \tilde{\mathbf{f}}_{ts} - \mathbf{y}_{ts} - \mathbf{w}_{ts})$$

$$+ \mathbf{r}_{ts} \cdot (\mathbf{z}_{ts} + \tilde{\mathbf{g}}_{ts}) \text{ for all } t \in \mathbf{T}^d \text{ and } s \in \mathbf{S}\}$$

$$\Phi_{Ts+1} = \{(\mathbf{p}_{Ts}) \in \Delta_{Ts} : (\mathbf{p}_{Ts}) \text{ maximizes } \mathbf{p}_{Ts} \cdot (\mathbf{x}_{Ts} + \tilde{\mathbf{f}}_{Ts} - \mathbf{y}_{Ts} - \mathbf{w}_{Ts})$$

$$\text{for all } s \in \mathbf{S}\}$$

$$\Phi_{Ts+2} = \{(\mathbf{q}_0, \mathbf{h}_0) \in \Gamma_0 : (\mathbf{q}_0^2, \mathbf{h}_0^2) \text{ maximizes } \mathbf{q}_0^2 \cdot \mathbf{f}_0^2 + \mathbf{h}_0^2 \cdot \mathbf{g}_0^2,\ \mathbf{q}_0^0 = \alpha_0 \mathbf{p}_0^0,$$

$$\text{and } \mathbf{h}_0^0 = \alpha_0 \mathbf{r}_0^0\}$$

$$\Phi_{TS+2+ts} = \{(\mathbf{q}_{ts}, \mathbf{h}_{ts}) \in \Gamma_{ts} : (\mathbf{q}_{ts}^2, \mathbf{h}_{ts}^2) \text{ maximizes}$$

$$\mathbf{q}_{ts}^2 \cdot \mathbf{f}_{ts}^2 + \mathbf{h}_{ts}^2 \cdot \mathbf{g}_{ts}^2,\ \mathbf{q}_{ts}^0 = \alpha_{ts} \mathbf{p}_{ts}^0, \text{ and } \mathbf{h}_{ts}^0 = \alpha_{ts} \mathbf{r}_{ts}^0, \text{ for all } s \in \mathbf{S}\}$$

$$\Phi_{TS+2+Ts} = \{\mathbf{q}_{Ts} \in \Gamma_{Ts} : \mathbf{q}_{Ts}^2 \text{ maximizes } \mathbf{q}_{Ts}^2 \cdot \mathbf{f}_{Ts}^2,\ \mathbf{q}_{Ts}^0 = \alpha_{Ts} \mathbf{p}_{Ts}^0, \text{ for all } s \in \mathbf{S}\}.$$

Φ *is non-empty, compact, convex valued and upper hemi-continuous. By Kakutani's fixed-point theorem, there is some point* $(\mathbf{p}^*, \mathbf{r}^*, \mathbf{q}^*, \mathbf{h}^*, \mathbf{E}^*)$ *such that*

$$(\mathbf{p}^*, \mathbf{r}^*, \mathbf{q}^*, \mathbf{h}^*, \mathbf{E}^*) \in \Phi(\mathbf{p}^*, \mathbf{r}^*, \mathbf{q}^*, \mathbf{h}^*, \mathbf{E}^*). \tag{11}$$

We now show that the point in (11) represents an equilibrium in the sense that $\mathbf{E}^* \leqslant 0$*. First, look at* Φ_1*. By definition,*

$$\mathbf{p}_0^* \cdot (\mathbf{x}_0^* + \tilde{\mathbf{f}}_0^* - \mathbf{y}_0^* - \mathbf{w}_0) + \mathbf{r}_0^* \cdot (\mathbf{z}_0^* + \tilde{\mathbf{g}}_0^*) \geqslant \mathbf{p}_0 \cdot (\mathbf{x}_0^* + \tilde{\mathbf{f}}_0^* - \mathbf{y}_0^* - \mathbf{w}_0)$$

$$+ \mathbf{r}_0 \cdot (\mathbf{z}_0^* + \tilde{\mathbf{g}}_0^*) \text{ for all } (\mathbf{p}_0, \mathbf{r}_0) \in \Delta_0. \tag{12}$$

Let us choose $(\mathbf{p}_0, \mathbf{r}_0)$ *so that it equals* $(\mathbf{p}_0^*, \mathbf{r}_0^*)$ *except for any two elements* ℓ *and* k *of* $\mathbf{r}_0$*, where* $1 \leqslant \ell, k \leqslant (M^0 + M^1)$ *and where at least* $r_{0,\ell}^*$ *or* $r_{0^*,k}$ *is positive. Without loss of generality, assume that* $r_{0,\ell}^* > 0$*. Then (12) reduces to*

$$(r_{0,\ell}^* - r_{0,\ell})(z_{0,\ell}^* + \tilde{g}_{0,\ell}^*) + (r_{0,k}^* - r_{0,k})(z_{0,k}^* + \tilde{g}_{0,k}^*) \geqslant 0. \tag{13}$$

Since $(\mathbf{p}_0^*, \mathbf{r}^*), (\mathbf{p}_0, \mathbf{r}) \in \Delta_0$, $(r_{0,\ell}^* + r_{0,k}^*) = (r_{0,\ell} + r_{0,k})$*. Hence (13) further reduces to*

$$(r_{0,k}^* - r_{0,k})[(z_{0,k}^* + \tilde{g}_{0,k}^*) - (z_{0,\ell}^* + \tilde{g}_{0,\ell}^*)] \geqslant 0. \tag{14}$$

If $r_{0,k}^* = 0$ *then, since* $r_{0,k}$ *can be any non-negative number, (14) implies that* $(z_{0,k}^* + g_{0,k}^*) \leqslant (z_{0,\ell}^* + \tilde{g}_{0,\ell}^*)$*. If* $r_{0,k}^* > 0$ *then, since* $r_{0,k}$ *can be chosen to be greater or smaller* *than* $r^*_{0,k}$, *the only condition under which (14) holds is that* $(z^*_{0,\ell} + \tilde{g}^*_{0,\ell}) = (z^*_{0,k} + \tilde{g}^*_{0,k})$. *The same argument can be extended to other values of* ℓ *and* k. *For the sake of exposition, assume that* $r^*_{0,1} > 0$, *renumbering the securities if necessary. We then have*

$$(z^*_{0,1} + \tilde{g}^*_{0,1}) = \ldots = (z^*_{0,m} + \tilde{g}_{0,m}) = \ldots$$

for all securities m *whose optimal prices are positive, while*

$$(z^*_{0,i} + \tilde{g}^*_{0,i}) \leqslant (z^*_{0,1} + \tilde{g}^*_{0,1})$$

for all i *where* $r^*_{0,i} = 0$. *The same argument can be applied to commodity prices and to commodity and security prices together. Thus let us choose* $(\mathbf{p}_0, \mathbf{r}_0)$ *so that it equals* $(\mathbf{p}^*_0, \mathbf{r}^*_0)$ *except for any two elements* ℓ *and* k *of* $\mathbf{p}_0$, *where* $1 \leqslant \ell, k \leqslant (N^0 + N^1)$ *and where at least one price is positive; and let us choose* $(\mathbf{p}_0, \mathbf{r}_0)$ *so that it equals* $(\mathbf{p}^*_0, \mathbf{r}^*)$ *except for any element* ℓ *of* $\mathbf{p}_0$ *and* k *of* $\mathbf{r}_0$, *where* $1 \leqslant \ell \leqslant (N^0 + N^1)$ *and* $1 \leqslant k \leqslant (M^0 + M^1)$ *and where at least one of* $p^*_{0,\ell}$ *and* $r^*_{0,k}$ *is positive. Then*

$$(z^*_{0,1} + \tilde{g}^*_{0,1}) = \ldots = (z^*_{0,m} + \tilde{g}^*_{0,m}) = \ldots = (x^*_{0,n} + \tilde{f}^*_{0,n} - y^*_{0,n} + w_{0,n}) = \ldots \quad (15a)$$

for all securities m *and goods* n *whose optimal prices are positive, while*

$$(z^*_{0,i} + \tilde{g}^*_{0,i}), (x^*_{0,j} + \tilde{f}^*_{0,j} - y^*_{0,j} + w_{0,j}) \leqslant (z^*_{0,1} + \tilde{g}^*_{0,1}) \quad (15b)$$

for all securities i *and goods* j *with optimal prices zero. Summing the household budget constraints, and recalling the foreign budget constraint (3a), we have*

$$\mathbf{p}^*_0 \cdot (\mathbf{x}^*_0 + \tilde{\mathbf{f}}^*_0 - \mathbf{y}^*_0 - \mathbf{w}_0) + \mathbf{r}^*_0 \cdot (\mathbf{z}^*_0 + \tilde{\mathbf{g}}^*_0) = 0. \quad (16)$$

Expressions (15) and (16) can be combined to give

$$(z^*_{0,1} + \tilde{g}^*_{0,1}) = \ldots = (z^*_{0,m} + \tilde{g}^*_{0,m}) = \ldots = (x^*_{0,n} + \tilde{f}^*_{0,n} - y^*_{0,n} + w_{0,n}) = 0$$

$$(z^*_{0,i} + \tilde{g}^*_{0,i}), (x^*_{0,j} + \tilde{f}^*_{0,j} - y^*_{0,j} + w_{0,j}) \leqslant 0.$$

A similar argument can be developed to show that other markets are in equilibrium. □

Proof of Lemma 1. *We need to show that the sum of transfers is zero in each period and state:*

$$\begin{aligned}\sum_i b^i_0 &= \sum_i [\mathbf{p}_0 \cdot (\hat{\mathbf{x}}^i_0 - \hat{\mathbf{y}}^i_0 - \mathbf{w}^i_0) + \mathbf{r} \cdot \hat{\mathbf{z}}^i_0] + Q_0 \\ &= \mathbf{p}_0 \cdot (\hat{\mathbf{x}}_0 - \hat{\mathbf{y}}_0 - \mathbf{w}_0) + \mathbf{r}_0 \cdot \hat{\mathbf{z}}_0 + \mathbf{r}_0 \cdot \hat{\mathbf{g}}_0 + \mathbf{p}_0 \cdot \hat{\mathbf{f}}_0 \\ &= \mathbf{p}_0 \cdot (\hat{\mathbf{x}}_0 + \hat{\mathbf{f}}_0 - \hat{\mathbf{y}}_0 - \mathbf{w}_0) + \mathbf{r}_0 \cdot (\hat{\mathbf{z}}_0 + \hat{\mathbf{g}}_0) \\ &= 0 \quad \textit{[from (4a, c)]}.\end{aligned}$$

$$\begin{aligned}\sum_i b^i_{1s} &= \sum_i [\mathbf{p}_{1s}\cdot(\hat{\mathbf{x}}^i_{1s} - \hat{\mathbf{y}}^i_{1s} - \mathbf{w}^i_{1s}) + \mathbf{r}_{1s}\cdot\hat{\mathbf{z}}^i_{1s} - p_{1s,1}\mathbf{a}_s\cdot\hat{\mathbf{z}}^i_0] + Q_{1s}\\
&= \mathbf{p}_{1s}\cdot(\hat{\mathbf{x}}_{1s} - \hat{\mathbf{y}}_{1s} - \mathbf{w}_{1s}) + \mathbf{r}_{1s}\cdot(\hat{\mathbf{z}}_{1s} + \hat{\mathbf{g}}_{1s}) - p_{1s,1}\mathbf{a}_s\cdot(\hat{\mathbf{z}}_0 + \hat{\mathbf{g}}_0) + \mathbf{p}_{1s}\cdot\hat{\mathbf{f}}_{1s}\\
&= \mathbf{p}_{1s}\cdot(\hat{\mathbf{x}}_{1s} + \hat{\mathbf{f}}_{1s} - \hat{\mathbf{y}}_{1s} - \mathbf{w}_{1s}) + \mathbf{r}_{1s}\cdot(\hat{\mathbf{z}}_{1s} + \hat{\mathbf{g}}_{1s}) - p_{1s,1}\mathbf{a}_s\cdot(\hat{\mathbf{z}}_0 + \hat{\mathbf{g}}_0)\\
&= 0 \quad \textit{[from (4b, c, d)].}\end{aligned}$$

$$\begin{aligned}\sum_i b^i_{tss'} &= \sum_i [\mathbf{p}_{ts}\cdot(\hat{\mathbf{x}}^i_{ts} - \hat{\mathbf{y}}^i_{ts} - \mathbf{w}^i_{ts}) + \mathbf{r}_{ts}\cdot\hat{\mathbf{z}}^i_{ts} - p_{ts,1}\mathbf{a}_s\cdot\hat{\mathbf{z}}^i_{(t-1)s'}] + Q_{tss'}\\
&= \mathbf{p}_{ts}\cdot(\hat{\mathbf{x}}_{ts} - \hat{\mathbf{y}}_{ts} - \mathbf{w}_{ts}) + \mathbf{r}_{ts}\cdot(\hat{\mathbf{z}}_{ts} + \hat{\mathbf{g}}_{ts}) - p_{ts,1}\mathbf{a}_s\cdot(\hat{\mathbf{z}}_{(t-1)s'} + \hat{\mathbf{g}}_{(t-1)s'})\\
&\quad + \mathbf{p}_{ts}\cdot\hat{\mathbf{f}}_{ts}\\
&= \mathbf{p}_{ts}\cdot(\hat{\mathbf{x}}_{ts} + \hat{\mathbf{f}}_{ts} - \hat{\mathbf{y}}_{ts} - \mathbf{w}_{ts}) + \mathbf{r}_{ts}\cdot(\hat{\mathbf{z}}_{ts} + \hat{\mathbf{g}}_{ts}) - p_{ts,1}\mathbf{a}_s\cdot(\hat{\mathbf{z}}_{(t-1)s'}\\
&\quad + \hat{\mathbf{g}}_{(t-1)s'})\\
&= 0 \quad \textit{[from (4b, d)].}\end{aligned}$$

$$\begin{aligned}\sum_i b^i_{Tss'} &= \sum_i [\mathbf{p}_{Ts}\cdot(\hat{\mathbf{x}}^i_{Ts} - \hat{\mathbf{y}}^i_{Ts} - \mathbf{w}^i_{Ts}) - p_{Ts,1}\mathbf{a}_s\cdot\hat{\mathbf{z}}^i_{(T-1)s'}] + Q_{Tss'}\\
&= \mathbf{p}_{Ts}\cdot(\hat{\mathbf{x}}_{Ts} - \hat{\mathbf{y}}_{Ts} - \mathbf{w}_{Ts}) - p_{Ts,1}\mathbf{a}_s\cdot(\hat{\mathbf{z}}_{(T-1)s'}\\
&\quad + \hat{\mathbf{g}}_{(T-1)s'}) + \mathbf{p}_{Ts}\cdot\hat{\mathbf{f}}_{Ts}\\
&= \mathbf{p}_{Ts}\cdot(\hat{\mathbf{x}}_{Ts} + \hat{\mathbf{f}}_{Ts} - \hat{\mathbf{y}}_{Ts} - \mathbf{w}_{Ts}) - p_{Ts,1}\mathbf{a}_s\cdot(\hat{\mathbf{z}}_{(T-1)s'}\\
&\quad + \hat{\mathbf{g}}_{(T-1)s'})\\
&= 0 \quad \textit{[from (4b, d)].}\end{aligned}$$

□

Proof of Lemma 2. *Substituting from (6) into the household budget constraint (2), we obtain*

$$\mathbf{p}_0\cdot(\mathbf{x}^i_0 - \mathbf{y}^i_0) + \mathbf{r}_0\cdot\mathbf{z}^i_0 \leqslant \mathbf{p}_0\cdot(\hat{\mathbf{x}}^i_0 - \hat{\mathbf{y}}^i_0) + \mathbf{r}_0\cdot\hat{\mathbf{z}}^i_0 + Q_0/I \tag{17a}$$

$$\begin{aligned}\mathbf{p}_{1s}\cdot(\mathbf{x}^i_{1s} - \mathbf{y}^i_{1s}) + \mathbf{r}_{1s}\cdot\mathbf{z}^i_{1s} - p_{1s,1}\mathbf{a}_s\cdot\mathbf{z}^i_0 &\leqslant \mathbf{p}_{1s}\cdot(\hat{\mathbf{x}}^i_{1s} - \hat{\mathbf{y}}^i_{1s}) + \mathbf{r}_{1s}\cdot\hat{\mathbf{z}}^i_{1s}\\
&\quad - p_{1s,1}\mathbf{a}_s\cdot\hat{\mathbf{z}}^i_0 + Q_{1s}/I\end{aligned} \tag{17b}$$

$$\begin{aligned}\mathbf{p}_{ts}\cdot(\mathbf{x}^i_{ts} - \mathbf{y}^i_{ts}) + \mathbf{r}_{ts}\cdot\mathbf{z}^i_{ts} - p_{ts,1}\mathbf{a}_s\cdot\mathbf{z}^i_{(t-1)s'} &\leqslant \mathbf{p}_{ts}\cdot(\hat{\mathbf{x}}^i_{ts} - \hat{\mathbf{y}}^i_{ts}) + \mathbf{r}_{ts}\cdot\hat{\mathbf{z}}^i_{ts}\\
&\quad - p_{ts,1}\mathbf{a}_s\cdot\hat{\mathbf{z}}^i_{(t-1)s'} + Q_{ts}/I\end{aligned} \tag{17c}$$

$$\begin{aligned}\mathbf{p}_{Ts}\cdot(\mathbf{x}^i_{Ts} - \mathbf{y}^i_{Ts}) - p_{Ts,1}\mathbf{a}_s\cdot\mathbf{z}^i_{(T-1)s'} &\leqslant \mathbf{p}_{Ts}\cdot(\hat{\mathbf{x}}^i_{Ts} - \hat{\mathbf{y}}^i_{Ts})\\
&\quad - p_{Ts,1}\mathbf{a}_s\cdot\hat{\mathbf{z}}^i_{(t-1)s'} + Q_{Ts}/I.\end{aligned} \tag{17d}$$

By assumption, $Q_0 \geqslant 0$ and $Q_{ts} \geqslant 0$. Hence each household can maintain its initial consumption, production and portfolio sequences at final prices and therefore is not worse off *in the final situation; if consumption and/or production substitution takes place, the household is better off, and if* $Q_0 > 0$ *and/or* $Q_{ts} > 0$ *for some t and s, all households are better off.*

By virtue of lemma 1, the scheme of lumpsum transfers is feasible. □

Proof of Proposition 2. *Since the initial situation is autarky,* $\hat{\mathbf{f}}_0 = \hat{\mathbf{f}}_{ts} = \mathbf{0}^N$ *and* $\hat{\mathbf{g}}_0 = \hat{\mathbf{g}}_{ts} = \mathbf{0}^M$*, which in turn implies that the terms-of-trade gains are zero. The proposition then follows from lemmas 1 and 2.* □

Proof of Proposition 3. *From the given condition (7), the terms-of-trade gains are non-negative. The proposition follows from lemmas 1 and 2.* □

Proof of Proposition 4. *World prices are fixed; hence by (3), the terms-of-trade gains are zero. The proposition then follows from lemmas 1 and 2.* □

Proof of Proposition 5. *Let the ith household in country k receive from its government the transfers*

$$b_0^{ki} = \mathbf{p}_0 \cdot (\hat{\mathbf{x}}_0^{ki} - \hat{\mathbf{y}}_0^{ki} - \mathbf{w}_0^{ki}) + \mathbf{r}_0 \cdot \hat{\mathbf{z}}_0^{ki} \quad (18a)$$

$$b_{1s}^{ki} = \mathbf{p}_{1s} \cdot (\hat{\mathbf{x}}_{1s}^{ki} - \hat{\mathbf{y}}_{1s}^{ki} - \mathbf{w}_{1s}^{ki}) + \mathbf{r}_{1s} \cdot \hat{\mathbf{z}}_{1s}^{ki} - p_{1s,1}\mathbf{a}_s \cdot \hat{\mathbf{z}}_0^{ki} \tag{18b}$$

$$b_{tss'}^{ki} = \mathbf{p}_{ts} \cdot (\hat{\mathbf{x}}_{ts}^{ki} - \hat{\mathbf{y}}_{ts}^{ki} - \mathbf{w}_{ts}^{ki}) + \mathbf{r}_{ts} \cdot \hat{\mathbf{z}}_{ts}^{ki} - p_{ts,1}\mathbf{a}_s \cdot \hat{\mathbf{z}}_{(t-1)s'}^{ki} \tag{18c}$$

$$b_{Tss'}^{ki} = \mathbf{p}_{Ts} \cdot (\hat{\mathbf{x}}_{Ts}^{ki} - \hat{\mathbf{y}}_{Ts}^{ki} - \mathbf{w}_{Ts}^{ki}) - p_{Ts,1}\mathbf{a}_s \cdot \hat{\mathbf{z}}_{(T-1)s'}^{ki} \tag{18d}$$

$$t \in \mathbf{T}^d, \quad s, s' \in \mathbf{S}.$$

These transfers are substituted into the household's budget constraint (10). It is easy to see that the original consumption and portfolio choice is still feasible in the new situation. Hence the household is not worse off; in fact, it is better off if consumption and/or production substitution occurs. It remains to show that the above transfer scheme is feasible.

The common tariffs imposed by member countries on goods and services from non-member countries in period 0 and period t when state s occurs are $\mathbf{p}_0 - \hat{\mathbf{q}}_0$ *and* $\mathbf{p}_{ts} - \hat{\mathbf{q}}_{ts}$*, respectively, and the common tariffs on imported securities are* $\mathbf{r}_0 - \hat{\mathbf{h}}_0$ *and* $\mathbf{r}_{ts} - \hat{\mathbf{h}}_{ts}$*, respectively. However, no tariff is imposed on the repatriation of security payments. This means that the domestic price of good 1, the numéraire, equals the world price of good 1 in all periods and states, that is* $p_{ts,1} = q_{ts,1}$*. Because world prices remain unchanged, the volumes of trade of non-member countries with member countries, that is* $\hat{\mathbf{f}}_0$*,* $\hat{\mathbf{f}}_{ts}$*,* $\hat{\mathbf{g}}_0$ *and* $\hat{\mathbf{g}}_{ts}$*, are not changed. For example, the tariff revenue in period t and state s collected by member countries from the import of goods and securities is* $-(\mathbf{p}_{ts} - \hat{\mathbf{q}}_{ts}) \cdot \hat{\mathbf{f}}_{ts} - (\mathbf{r}_{ts} - \hat{\mathbf{h}}_{ts}) \cdot \hat{\mathbf{g}}_{ts}$.

Member countries share the tariff revenues according to the transfers they must make to their residents. Thus, the above transfer scheme is feasible if the sum of tariff revenue and total transfers to all households in the member countries is non-negative in all periods and states; in period t and state s, for example, feasibility implies that $-\Sigma_k\Sigma_i b_{ts}^{ki} - (\mathbf{p}_{ts} - \hat{\mathbf{q}}_{ts}) \cdot \hat{\mathbf{f}}_{ts} - (\mathbf{r}_{ts} - \hat{\mathbf{h}}_{ts}) \cdot \hat{\mathbf{g}}_{ts} \geqslant 0$. *We have*

$$-\sum_k \sum_i b_0^{ki} - (\mathbf{p}_0 - \hat{\mathbf{q}}_0)\cdot\hat{\mathbf{f}}_0 - (\mathbf{r}_0 - \hat{\mathbf{h}}_0)\cdot\hat{\mathbf{g}}_0$$

$$= -\sum_k \sum_i [\mathbf{p}_0\cdot(\hat{\mathbf{x}}_0^{ki} - \hat{\mathbf{y}}_0^{ki} - \mathbf{w}_0^{ki}) + \mathbf{r}_0\cdot\hat{\mathbf{z}}_0^{ki}] - (\mathbf{p}_0 - \hat{\mathbf{q}}_0)\cdot\hat{\mathbf{f}}_0 - (\mathbf{r}_0 - \hat{\mathbf{h}}_0)\cdot\hat{\mathbf{g}}_0$$

$$= -[\mathbf{p}_0\cdot(\hat{\mathbf{x}}_0 - \hat{\mathbf{y}}_0 - \mathbf{w}_0) + \mathbf{r}_0\cdot\hat{\mathbf{z}}_0 - (\mathbf{p}_0 - \hat{\mathbf{q}}_0)\cdot\hat{\mathbf{f}}_0 - (\mathbf{r}_0 - \hat{\mathbf{h}}_0)\cdot\hat{\mathbf{g}}_0]$$

$$= -[\mathbf{p}_0\cdot(\hat{\mathbf{x}}_0 - \hat{\mathbf{y}}_0 - \mathbf{w}_0) + \mathbf{r}_0\cdot\hat{\mathbf{z}}_0 - \mathbf{p}_0\cdot\hat{\mathbf{f}}_0 - \mathbf{r}_0\cdot\hat{\mathbf{g}}_0) \quad \textit{[using (8a)]}$$

$$\geqslant 0 \quad \textit{[using (9a)]}$$

$$-\sum_k \sum_i b_{1s}^{ki} - (\mathbf{p}_{1s} - \hat{\mathbf{q}}_{1s})\cdot\hat{\mathbf{f}}_{1s} - (\mathbf{r}_{1s} - \hat{\mathbf{h}}_{1s})\cdot\hat{\mathbf{g}}_{1s}$$

$$= -\sum_k \sum_i [\mathbf{p}_{1s}\cdot(\hat{\mathbf{x}}_{1s}^{ki} - \hat{\mathbf{y}}_{1s}^{ki} - \mathbf{w}_{1s}^{ki}) + \mathbf{r}_{1s}\cdot\hat{\mathbf{z}}_{1s}^{ki} - p_{1s,1}\mathbf{a}_s\cdot\hat{\mathbf{z}}_0^{ki}] - (\mathbf{p}_{1s} - \hat{\mathbf{q}}_{1s})\cdot\hat{\mathbf{f}}_{1s}$$

$$- (\mathbf{r}_{1s} - \hat{\mathbf{h}}_{1s})\cdot\hat{\mathbf{g}}_{1s}$$

$$= -[\mathbf{p}_{1s}\cdot(\hat{\mathbf{x}}_{1s} - \hat{\mathbf{y}}_{1s} - \mathbf{w}_{1s}) + \mathbf{r}_{1s}\cdot\hat{\mathbf{z}}_{1s} - p_{1s,1}\mathbf{a}_s\cdot\hat{\mathbf{z}}_0) - (\mathbf{p}_{1s} - \hat{\mathbf{q}}_{1s})\cdot\hat{\mathbf{f}}_{1s}$$

$$- (\mathbf{r}_{1s} - \hat{\mathbf{h}}_{1s})\cdot\hat{\mathbf{g}}_{1s}$$

$$= -\mathbf{p}_{1s}\cdot(\hat{\mathbf{x}}_{1s} - \hat{\mathbf{y}}_{1s} - \mathbf{w}_{1s}) + \mathbf{r}_{1s}\cdot\hat{\mathbf{z}}_{1s} - \mathbf{p}_{1s}\cdot\hat{\mathbf{f}}_{1s} - \mathbf{r}_{1s}\cdot\hat{\mathbf{g}}_{1s} \quad \textit{[using (8b)]}$$

$$\geqslant 0 \quad \textit{[using (9b)]}$$

$$-\sum_k \sum_i b_{ts'}^{ki} - (\mathbf{p}_{ts} - \hat{\mathbf{q}}_{ts})\cdot\hat{\mathbf{f}}_{ts} - (\mathbf{r}_{ts} - \hat{\mathbf{h}}_{ts})\cdot\hat{\mathbf{g}}_{ts}$$

$$= -\sum_k \sum_i [\mathbf{p}_{ts}\cdot(\hat{\mathbf{x}}_{ts}^{ki} - \hat{\mathbf{y}}_{ts}^{ki} - \mathbf{w}_{ts}^{ki}) + \mathbf{r}_{ts}\cdot\hat{\mathbf{z}}_{ts}^{ki} - p_{ts,1}\mathbf{a}_s\cdot\hat{\mathbf{z}}_{(t-1)s'}^{ki}]$$

$$- (\mathbf{p}_{ts} - \hat{\mathbf{q}}_{ts})\cdot\hat{\mathbf{f}}_{ts} - (\mathbf{r}_{ts} - \hat{\mathbf{h}}_{ts})\cdot\hat{\mathbf{g}}_{ts}$$

$$= -\mathbf{p}_{ts}\cdot(\hat{\mathbf{x}}_{ts} - \hat{\mathbf{y}}_{ts} - \mathbf{w}_{ts}) + \mathbf{r}_{ts}\cdot\hat{\mathbf{z}}_{ts} - \mathbf{p}_{ts}\cdot\hat{\mathbf{f}}_{ts} - \mathbf{r}_{ts}\cdot\hat{\mathbf{g}}_{ts} \quad \textit{[using (8b)]}$$

$$\geqslant 0 \quad \textit{[using (9b)]}$$

$$-\sum_k \sum_i b_{Ts}^{ki} - (\mathbf{p}_{Ts} - \hat{\mathbf{q}}_{Ts})\cdot\hat{\mathbf{f}}_{Ts} - (\mathbf{r}_{Ts} - \hat{\mathbf{h}}_{Ts})\cdot\hat{\mathbf{g}}_{Ts}$$

$$= -\sum_k \sum_i [\mathbf{p}_{Ts}\cdot(\hat{\mathbf{x}}_{Ts}^{ki} - \hat{\mathbf{y}}_{Ts}^{ki} - \mathbf{w}_{Ts}^{ki}) + \mathbf{r}_{Ts}\cdot\hat{\mathbf{z}}_{Ts}^{ki} - p_{Ts,1}\mathbf{a}_s\cdot\hat{\mathbf{z}}_{(T-1)s'}^{ki}]$$

$$- (\mathbf{p}_{Ts} - \hat{\mathbf{q}}_{Ts})\cdot\hat{\mathbf{f}}_{Ts} - (\mathbf{r}_{Ts} - \hat{\mathbf{h}}_{Ts})\cdot\hat{\mathbf{g}}_{Ts}$$

$$= -\mathbf{p}_{Ts}\cdot(\hat{\mathbf{x}}_{Ts} - \hat{\mathbf{y}}_{Ts} - \mathbf{w}_{Ts}) + \mathbf{r}_{Ts}\cdot\hat{\mathbf{z}}_{Ts} - \mathbf{p}_{Ts}\cdot\hat{\mathbf{f}}_{Ts} - \mathbf{r}_{Ts}\cdot\hat{\mathbf{g}}_{Ts} \quad \textit{[using (8b)]}$$

$$\geqslant 0 \quad \textit{[using (9b)]}$$

$t \in \mathbf{T}^d, \quad s, s' \in \mathbf{S}.$ □

NOTES

* We acknowledge with gratitude the helpful comments of Henry Y. Wan, Jr.

1 One might substitute the following proposition, which we owe to Grandmont and McFadden (1972): 1′ For any group of two or more countries, free trade is better than no trade. However, 1 is the more general proposition: 1 implies 1′, but 1′ does not imply 1 because 1 allows any or all of the other countries to be non-free-traders.

2 Indeed production economies of this kind are isomorphic to pure exchange economies.

3 The example is based on an earlier example of Hart's (1975).

4 In assuming that the yield of securities is in terms of a single commodity, we follow Geanakoplos and Polemarchakis (1986). This assumption is important in proving the existence of equilibrium. In the model of Hart (1975), equilibrium may not exist because the yield of securities is in terms of several commodities.

5 The assumption that each security pays a non-negative amount of the *numéraire* in all states and a positive amount of the *numéraire* in at least one state greatly simplifies the analysis. With preferences which are non-satiated in the *numéraire*, and with arbitrage, the prices of the securities are positive. This assumption, however, is stronger than is needed. An alternative assumption is that the expected payment of each security is positive. A more general analysis, without these two assumptions, is provided by Geanakoplos and Polemarchakis (1986).

6 A simple example might be useful. Consider a closed pure-exchange economy. Let $\mathbf{w}^i$ be the endowment vector of the ith household, with subvectors $\mathbf{w}_0^i$ corresponding to period 0 and $\mathbf{w}_{ts}^i$ corresponding to period t and state s. Now consider hypothetically an economy with the same endowments and preferences but a full set of Arrow–Debreu markets. Suppose that there is a unique equilibrium, with the allocation $(\mathbf{x}^i)$ and the full vector of Arrow–Debreu prices $\mathbf{p}$. Let us now return to the economy with incomplete markets and consider the scheme of compensation

$$b_{ts}^i = \mathbf{p}_{ts} \cdot (\mathbf{x}_{ts}^i - \mathbf{w}_{ts}^i). \tag{19}$$

For each t and s, the compensatory transfers add to zero (recall that there is no production). Given (19), there is an equilibrium which relies on spot markets only, with price vector $\mathbf{p}$ and allocation $(\mathbf{x}^i)$. Thus the full Pareto-optimum of the complete-markets equilibrium can be achieved as a compensated incomplete-markets equilibrium with spot markets only. The only problem is that, given the incompleteness of markets, the $\mathbf{x}^i$ are unobservable.

7 For a careful discussion of the implementability of alternative schemes of lumpsum compensation, see Kemp and Wan (1992a, b).

REFERENCES

Batra, R. N. and Russell, W. R. (1974) 'Gains from trade under uncertainty', *American Economic Review* 64: 1040–8.

Geanakoplos, J. and Polemarchakis, H. (1986) 'Existence, regularity, and constrained suboptimality of competitive allocations when markets are incomplete', in W. Heller, R. Starr and D. Starrett (eds), *Essays in Honor of Kenneth Arrow*, Vol. 3, pp. 65–95, Cambridge: Cambridge University Press.

Geanakoplos, J., Magill, M. Quinzii, M. and Drèze, J. (1990) 'Generic inefficiency of stock market equilibrium when markets are incomplete', *Journal of Mathematical Economics* 19: 113–51.

Grandmont, J. M. and McFadden, D. (1972) 'A technical note on classical gains from trade', *Journal of International Economics* 2: 109–25.

Grinols, E. L. (1987) *Uncertainty and the Theory of International Trade*, New York: Harwood Academic.

Grossman, G. M. (1984) 'The gains from international factor movements', *Journal of International Economics* 17: 73–83.

Hart, O. D. (1975) 'On the optimality of equilibrium when the market structure is incomplete', *Journal of Economic Theory* 11: 418–43.

Helpman, E. and Razin, A. (1978) *A Theory of International Trade under Uncertainty*, New York: Academic Press.

Kemp, M. C. (1962) 'The gains from international trade', *Economic Journal* 72: 803–19.

Kemp, M. C. (1964) *The Pure Theory of International Trade*, New York: Prentice Hall.

Kemp, M. C. and Ohyama, M. (1978) 'The gain from trade under conditions of uncertainty', *Journal of International Economics* 8: 139–41.

Kemp, M. C. and Sinn, H.-W. (1990) 'A simple model of privately profitable but socially harmful speculation', University of Munich.

Kemp, M. C. and Wan, H. Y. Jr (1972) 'The gains from free trade', *International Economic Review* 13: 509–22.

Kemp, M. C. and Wan, H. Y. Jr (1976) 'An elementary proposition concerning the formation of customs unions', *Journal of International Economics* 6: 95–7.

Kemp, M. C. and Wan, H. Y. Jr (1986) 'The comparison of second-best equilibria: The case of customs unions', in D. Bös and C. Seidl (eds) *Welfare Economics of the Second Best*, Suppl. 5 of *Zeitschrift für Nationalökonomie* 161–7, Vienna: Springer-Verlag.

Kemp, M. C. and Wan, H. Y. Jr (1992a) *The Welfare Economics of International Trade*, London: Harwood Academic

Kemp, M. C. and Wan, H. Y. Jr (1992b) 'On lumpsum compensation', University of New South Wales.

Krueger, A. O. and Sonnenschein, H. (1967) 'The terms of trade, the gains from trade and price divergence', *International Economic Review* 8: 121–7.

Magill, M. and Shafer, W. (1991) 'Incomplete markets', in W. Hildenbrand and H. Sonnenschein (eds) *Handbook of Mathematical Economics*, Vol. IV. pp. 1523–614, Amsterdam: North-Holland.

Newbery, D. M. G. and Stiglitz, J. E. (1984) 'Pareto inferior trade', *Review of Economic Studies* 51: 1–12.

Ohyama, M. (1972) 'Trade and welfare in general equilibrium', *Keio Economic Studies* 9: 37–73.

Pomery, J. (1984) 'Uncertainty in trade models', in R. W. Jones and P. B. Kenen (eds) *Handbook of International Economics*, Vol. I, pp. 419–65, Amsterdam: North-Holland.

Samuelson, P. A. (1962) 'The gains from trade once again', *Economic Journal* 72: 820–9.

Shy, O. (1988) 'A general equilibrium model of Pareto inferior trade', *Journal of International Economics* 25: 143–54.

Turnovsky, S. J. (1974) 'Technological and price uncertainty in a Ricardian model of international trade', *Review of Economic Studies* 41: 201–17.

Vanek, J. (1965) *General Equilibrium of International Discrimination*, Cambridge, MA: Harvard University Press.

Wong, K.-Y. (1983) 'On choosing among trade in goods and international capital and labor mobility: A theoretical analysis', *Journal of International Economics* 14: 223–50.

Wong, K.-Y. (1991) 'Welfare comparison of trade situations', *Journal of International Economics*, 30: 49–68.

A FURTHER NOTE ON THE GAINS FROM TRADE WHEN MARKETS ARE POSSIBLY INCOMPLETE

It is now known that, even when markets are incomplete, the substitution of free trade for autarky is potentially beneficial for a country, in the sense that there exist schemes of lumpsum compensation which, if implemented, would make all households better off under free trade. Moreover, it is known that among such schemes of compensation there is one which, for its implementation, requires less information than any scheme of non-lumpsum compensation.

However, in existing proofs of those propositions (Kemp and Wong, 1995; Kemp and Wan, 1995) it is assumed that all goods which are **internationally** tradable **after** the abolition of trade barriers are **internally** tradable **before** the abolition of barriers. (The world allocation **after** the abolition of barriers is the same whether or not goods are internally tradable.) This leaves as an open question the validity of the proposition in the absence of the assumption; that is, when allowance is made for the possibility that some goods which are internationally tradable after the abolition of trade barriers are internally non-tradable before the abolition of barriers. It will be shown that, when allowance is made for that possibility, both propositions remain valid.

Let G be the universal set of goods, let G^i ($G^i \subset G$) be the set of goods which are untraded in country i when that country is autarkic, and let G^t ($G^t \subset G$, $G^t \cap G^i \neq \emptyset$) be the set of goods tradable by country i on world markets after the removal of its barriers to trade. Then the opening of trade can be viewed as occurring in two steps. In the first step, new internal markets are created for all goods in the set $G^t \cap G^i$. In the second step, free international trade becomes possible in goods in G^t. Now it is known that, in a closed economy, the replacement of some but not all of the missing markets might harm all households (see Hart, 1975); that is, it is known that the first step might be harmful. This suggests the possibility that, under some circumstances, the change in welfare associated with the first step might dominate that associated with the second step, so that, on a balance of considerations, international trade is harmful.

However, reflection reveals that this possibility can be ruled out. For, while the addition of markets might harm all households, there can always be found a scheme of lumpsum compensation such that, after the addition of markets, all households are better off. Thus the **first** step is potentially beneficial. Moreover, for implementation of the scheme of compensation, the authorities need only the initial net-purchase vector of each agent; they need no information about preferences or technologies. It is already known from the cited references that the **second** step is potentially beneficial and that there is associated with it an efficacious and informationally parsimonious scheme of compensation. Thus we may conclude that, taken together, the two steps have the same properties.

References

Hart, O. D. (1975) 'On the optimality of equilibrium when the market structure is incomplete', *Journal of Economic Theory* 11: 418–43.

Kemp, M. C. and Wan, H. Y. (1995) 'On lumpsum compensation', this volume.

Kemp, M. C. and Wong, K.-Y. (1995) 'The gains from trade when markets are possibly incomplete', this volume.

6

THE GAINS FROM FREE TRADE FOR A MONETARY ECONOMY*

1 INTRODUCTION

The classical gains-from-trade proposition has been proved in a barter context only. It has been taken for granted that the same proposition is valid for monetary economies.

In the present essay it is shown that, for economies of a standard monetary type, free trade may be disadvantageous; the traditional production and consumption gains may be swamped by a loss of satisfaction from holding cash when relative prices change.

2 ANALYSIS

Consider a small country which produces, consumes and trades two commodities and which derives satisfaction from its holding of cash balances. To avoid inessential complications, suppose that all households are alike in preferences, endowments and family composition. Let p_i denote the domestic price of the ith commodity, c_i the domestic demand for the ith commodity, $I(p_1, p_2)$ the maximum value of output at prices p_1 and p_2, $\pi(p_1, p_2)$ a suitable price index (positive, increasing, concave and homogeneous of degree 1), m the stock of money demanded, and $\bar{m}$ the given stock of money. Then the community can be viewed as maximizing a utility function

$$u[c_1, c_2, m/\pi(p_1, p_2)] \tag{1}$$

subject to a budget constraint

$$p_1c_1 + p_2c_2 + m = I(p_1, p_2) + \bar{m}. \tag{2}$$

The solution to the problem may be written

$$c_i = c_i(p_1, p_2, \bar{m}), \quad i = 1, 2 \tag{3a}$$

$$m = m(p_1, p_2, \bar{m}). \tag{3b}$$

In balance-of-payments equilibrium,

$$m(p_1, p_2, \bar{m}) = \bar{m}. \tag{4}$$

Moreover, since the country has no influence on the terms of international trade,

$$p_1 = \lambda p_2 \quad (\lambda > 0, \text{ constant}). \tag{5}$$

Equations (4) and (5) form a complete system in p_1 and p_2. Let us assume that it has a unique solution

$$p_i = p_i(\lambda, \bar{m}) \quad i = 1, 2. \tag{6}$$

By varying the terms of trade parametrically, one can generate alternative feasible output, consumption and export pairs. Presumably there is a critical value of λ, say λ^*, at which trade is extinguished. This value is equal to $p_1(\bar{m})/p_2(\bar{m})$, where $p_i(\bar{m})$, $i = 1, 2$, is the solution to

$$c_i = c_i(p_i, \bar{m}) = I_i(p_1, p_2) \quad i = 1, 2$$

and $I_i \equiv \partial I/\partial p_i$. Suppose that, initially, $\lambda = \lambda^*$.

The initial no-trade equilibrium is disturbed by a small increase in λ. What happens to the well-being of the typical household? From (1),

$$du = u_1 dc_1 + u_2 dc_2 + u_{m/\pi} d(m/\pi) \tag{7}$$

where $u_i \equiv \partial u/\partial c_i$ and $u_{m/\pi} \equiv \partial u/\partial(m/\pi)$. However, from the first-order conditions associated with (1) and (2),

$$u_i/u_{m/\pi} = p_i/\pi(p_1, p_2). \tag{8}$$

Hence

$$\pi \frac{du}{u_{m/\pi}} = (p_1 dc_1 + p_2 dc_2) - \frac{m}{\pi}(\pi_1 dp_1 + \pi_2 dp_2) \tag{9}$$

where $\pi_i \equiv \partial\pi/\partial p_i$. Finally, from constraint (2) and equilibrium condition (4), and bearing in mind that consumption equals production in the initial (autarkic) equilibrium,

$$p_1 dc_1 + p_2 dc_2 = 0, \tag{10}$$

implying that[1]

$$\pi \frac{du}{u_{m/\pi}} = -\frac{m}{\pi}(\pi_1 dp_1 + \pi_2 dp_2). \tag{11}$$

Evidently expression (11) may be of either sign. If (11) does not vanish, there can be found a world terms of trade, say $\hat{\lambda}$, which is near but not equal to λ^*

and such that trade is harmful, and there can be found a world terms of trade, say $\tilde{\lambda}$, such that trade is beneficial. If $|\lambda - \lambda^*|$ is sufficiently large, trade is necessarily gainful.

It might be thought that the possibility of harmful trade flows from a failure to make use of all relevant properties of the price index π. In particular, it might be thought that the possibility will go away if π is required to be a true cost of living index, so that

$$\pi_i = \gamma c_i \quad (\gamma > 0, \text{ constant}). \tag{12}$$

However, it is easy to show that there is no escape along that route. Thus, availing ourselves of (6), $\Sigma \pi_i \mathrm{d}p_i = 0$ if and only if

$$\frac{\mathrm{d}}{\mathrm{d}\lambda} \pi(\lambda p_2(\lambda, \bar{m}), p_2(\lambda, \bar{m})) = 0 \tag{13}$$

or, in view of (12), if and only if

$$(\lambda c_1 + c_2)(\mathrm{d}p_2/\mathrm{d}\lambda) = -\, c_1 p_2 \tag{14}$$

which may or may not be satisfied.

To remove the troublesome finding, it suffices to assume, in addition, that the income velocity of circulation is a constant:

$$I(\lambda p_2, p_2)/\bar{m} = k \quad (k > 0, \text{ constant}). \tag{15}$$

For then

$$\frac{\mathrm{d}p_2}{\mathrm{d}\lambda} = \frac{-\, p_2 I_1}{\lambda I_1 + I_2} = \frac{-\, p_2 x_1}{\lambda x_1 + x_2} \tag{16}$$

where x_i is the output of the ith commodity. Since $x_i = c_i$ in the initial equilibrium, the right-hand side of (16) reduces to $-\,p_2 c_1/(\lambda c_1 + c_2)$ and (14) is satisfied. Evidently (15) is a very strong and implausible assumption, since it rules out the possibility that consumption of one good requires larger cash balances, per unit of value, than consumption of the other good.

Suppose that $\lambda = \hat{\lambda} > \lambda^*$, as in Figure 1. What can the government do to cancel or reverse the loss associated with $\hat{\lambda}$? Tinkering with the nominal stock of money will be ineffective. Given any λ, the homogeneity of $\pi(p_1, p_2)$ ensures that real cash balances (and therefore u) are independent of $\bar{m}$. On the other hand, the government could kill all trade by imposing a sufficiently heavy duty on imports (of the second commodity). That would eliminate the loss but it would not convert the loss into a gain. To achieve the latter objective it will be necessary, I suppose, to destroy the motive for holding cash. How that is to be done cannot be determined without laying the monetary foundations much more carefully.

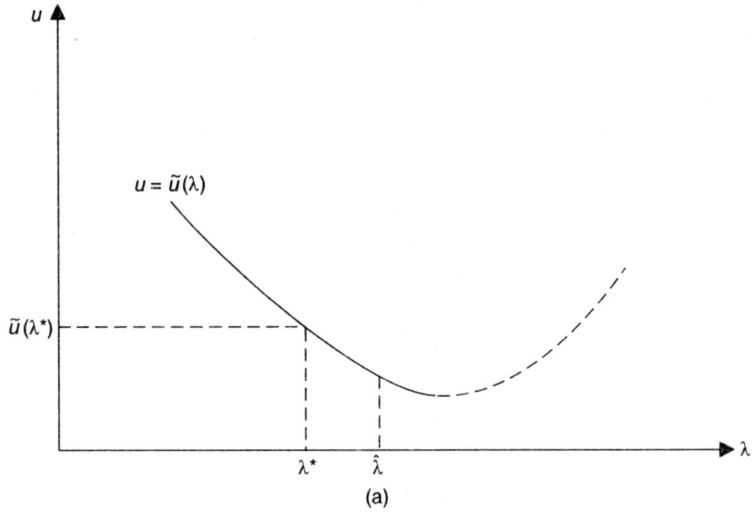

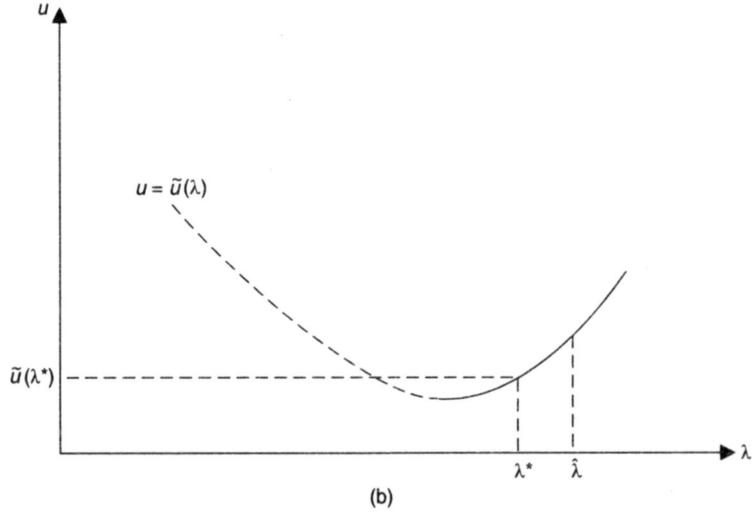

Figure 1

3 FINAL REMARK

How seriously one takes the possibility of harmful trade depends on one's confidence in the utility function (1). Here it suffices to note that (1) can be derived from any of several alternative microfoundations; see Croushore (1993) and his references to the earlier investigations of Brock, Drazen, McCallum and Feenstra.

NOTES

* I acknowledge with gratitude the useful suggestions of Ngo Van Long, Koji Shimomura and Kar-yiu Wong. The present essay was written during my visit to the Research Institute for Economics and Business Administration at Kobe University, December 1989 to February 1990. I am grateful to the members of the Institute, especially the Director, Professor Hiromasa Yamamoto, for their generous and friendly hospitality.

1 It might be wondered why there is no term on the right side of (11), to represent the traditional gains from barter trade. The reason is that in the situation described there are no such gains. In a barter world, $du/d\lambda = 0$ when λ takes its autarkic value.

REFERENCE

Croushore, D. (1993) 'Money in the utility function: Functional equivalence to a shopping-time model', *Journal of Macroeconomics* 15: 175–82.

7

THE GAINS FROM TRADE FOR A MONETARY ECONOMY WHEN MARKETS ARE POSSIBLY INCOMPLETE*

1 INTRODUCTION

The welfare economics of free trade contains four core propositions:

a For any single country, large or small, free trade is better than no trade (Samuelson, 1962; Kemp, 1962; Kemp and Wan, 1972; Kemp and Ohyama, 1978).[1]

b For a small open economy, an improvement in the terms of trade is beneficial (Kemp, 1962; Krueger and Sonnenschein, 1967; Wong, 1991).

c For a small open economy, trade in additional commodities (including primary factors of production) is beneficial (Wong, 1983, 1991; Grossman, 1984).

d Any subset of trading countries can form a mutually advantageous customs union (Kemp, 1964; Vanek, 1965; Ohyama, 1972; Kemp and Wan, 1976, 1986).

These propositions have been shown to be valid for general-equilibrium barter economies of the Arrow–Debreu type, with a well-behaved social utility function or appropriate compensation among individuals, whether or not uncertainty is present as long as a set of complete markets is present. Of course, it is a feature of such economies that markets are complete. The fairly recent work of Newbery and Stiglitz (1984) and Shy (1988), which presents examples in which free trade is Pareto-inferior to autarky for barter economies with suboptimal risk sharing, has raised questions about the validity of these propositions when markets are incomplete. However, Kemp and Wong (1991) have shown that feasible lumpsum compensating transfers are always available for these economies to guarantee welfare improvement in the cases considered by these propositions.

Whether these propositions still hold for monetary economies with possibly incomplete markets is still an open question, and has never been closely examined. It is well known that in the Arrow–Debreu general-equilibrium framework money as a medium of exchange is neutral. However, in general-equilibrium models with incomplete markets and of the cash-in-advance kind, it has been shown that money can have real effects (Magill and Quinzii, 1989a, b). This leads to the suspicion that free trade may not be better than no trade.

The purpose of this essay is to analyze the role of money in international trade when markets may be incomplete, and to examine the validity of these propositions. The first question we will answer is whether free trade can be Pareto-inferior to no trade. In the only treatment of this question known to the authors, Kemp (1990) showed that, for monetary economies of a particular type, proposition **a** is invalid: free trade is not necessarily gainful. However, his result depends crucially on the fact that, in the economies he studied, money balances yield utility directly. That formulation allows for the possibility that money balances are more valuable in some sectors than others. In the present essay, we show with a counter example that, in cash-in-advance economies with incomplete markets, uncompensated free trade can be Pareto-inferior to autarky.

The second question is whether the governments of these economies can find appropriate compensation schemes to ensure welfare improvement in the cases considered in propositions **a** to **d**: do these propositions remain valid for monetary economies with possibly incomplete markets? The answer to this question, as the present essay shows, is in the affirmative.

Propositions concerning the gains from trade are of interest only if the existence of a world trading equilibrium is assured. After describing the class of economies to be studied, therefore, we demonstrate that those economies always have an equilibrium. In this part of the essay (section 3) we build on the closed-economy analysis of Magill and Quinzii (1989a, b), extending the scope of their model to accommodate lumpsum transfers and international trade. In section 4 we state and prove our main propositions; and in a brief final section we discuss some of the limitations of our analysis.

2 PARETO-INFERIOR TRADE

Newbery and Stiglitz (1984) and Shy (1988) have shown that, in a world with barter trade and incomplete markets, for any particular economy, uncompensated free trade can be Pareto-dominated by autarky. We now demonstrate that the same outcome is possible in a cash-in-advance monetary economy.

Consider a pure-exchange economy in which money is the medium of exchange and, possibly, a store of value. Let us call it the home economy. There are two periods, '0' and '1', and two states of nature in period 1, '1' and '2'. There are two households, '1' and '2'. At the beginning of each period, the households receive state-dependent endowments of goods, but no money. Variables in period 0 are known with certainty while those in period 1 are not known until period 1. There are no securities other than money.

Denote the consumption of the ith household in period 0 by $\mathbf{x}_0^i \in R_+^2$ and that in period 1 when state s occurs by $\mathbf{x}_s^i \in R_+^2$, $i, s = 1, 2$. Suppose that the preferences of the ith household are represented by the utility function

$$U^i(\mathbf{x}_0^i, \mathbf{x}_1^i, \mathbf{x}_2^i) = \alpha^i u^i(\mathbf{x}_0^i) + \beta^i u^i(\mathbf{x}_1^i) + \gamma^i u^i(\mathbf{x}_2^i),$$

$$\alpha^i, \beta^i, \gamma^i > 0,$$

where $u^i(.)$ is increasing, concave and continuous. We assume that α^i is sufficiently small in relation to β^i and γ^i so that, as far as the welfare of both households is concerned, we can concentrate on the equilibria in period 1.

In the presence of money, the exchange of goods between the households is indirect. In each period and state, each household first sells its endowment to the government for money and then spends the proceeds on the basket of goods which maximizes utility.

Suppose for the time being that money is used as a medium of exchange but cannot be used as a store of value. This means that in period 0 each household spends the entire proceeds from the sale of its endowment.

Initially, the home economy is closed. There are two possible equilibria in each state in period 1. Let us label the two equilibria in state 1 as *A* and *B*, and the two equilibria in state 2 as *C* and *D*, as shown in Figure 1. In each state, the equilibria are on the contract curve. Combining these equilibria, there are four possible two-state equilibria in period 1: (*A*, *C*), (*A*, *D*), (*B*, *C*), and (*B*, *D*).

We further assume that γ^1 is sufficiently small in relation to β^1, and β^2 sufficiently small in relation to γ^2. This implies that both households prefer equilibrium (*B*, *C*) to (*A*, *D*). Assume further that, for whatever reason, (*B*, *C*) is the autarkic equilibrium.

Free trade is now permitted between the home country and the rest of the world at a given world price sufficiently close to (but not identical to) that of the equilibrium (*A*, *D*). Some trade takes place, but both households are worse off under free trade than under autarky; that is, the free-trade equilibrium is Pareto-inferior to the autarkic equilibrium.

So far, money has been used only as a medium of exchange. We now allow for the possibility that money is held as a store of value and show that Pareto-inferior free trade is still possible.

Since both households prefer period 1 consumption to period 0 consumption, they may save by holding money at the end of period 0.[2] If no saving occurs in period 0, the above analysis remains unchanged. If saving does take place then, because the endowments of the households in period 0 are insignificant and because preferences are continuous, there are four equilibria in period 1 close to those examined above: (*A*, *C*), (*A*, *D*), (*B*, *C*), and (*B*, *D*). We assume again that the one close to (*B*, *C*) is the autarkic equilibrium.

Free trade with the rest of the world under the prevailing prices is now allowed. Both households export their endowments in period 0 and hold the proceeds to be spent in period 1. Again, if they do save then, since their period 0 endowments are sufficiently small, the free-trade equilibrium in period 1 is close to (*A*, *D*). Thus, uncompensated free trade is Pareto-inferior to autarky.

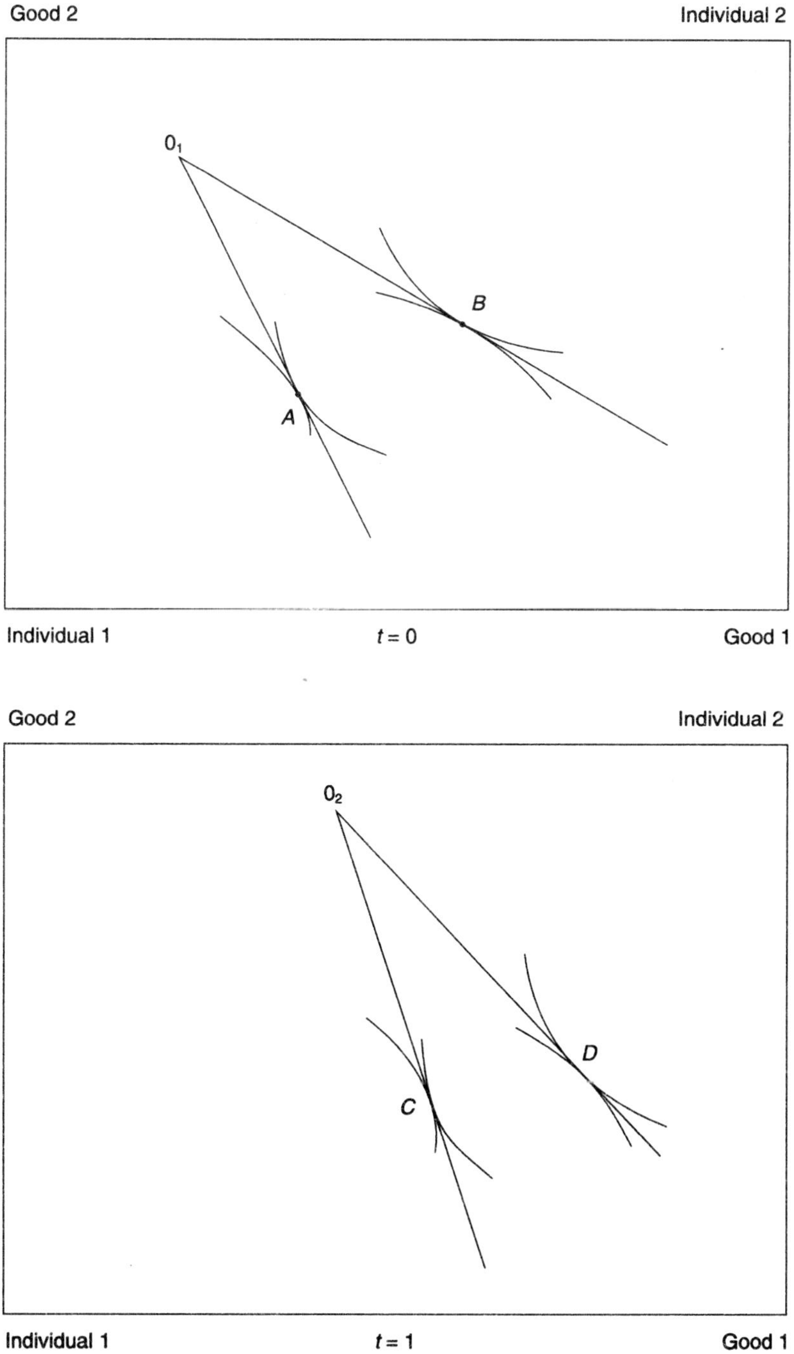
Good 2
Individual 2
0₁
B
A
Individual 1
t = 0
Good 1
Good 2
Individual 2
0₂
D
C
Individual 1
t = 1
Good 1

Figure 1

3 THE MODEL

There are two countries labelled 'home' and 'foreign'; however, the foreign country can be interpreted as the rest of the world. The two countries extend through two periods, 0 and 1. It is assumed that the values of variables in period 0 are known with certainty, and that which of S mutually exclusive states of nature occurs in period 1 is not known until period 1. We associate state 0 with period 0 and label the states in period 1 as $1, \dots, S$. Let $\mathbf{S} = (1, \dots, S)$ and $\mathbf{S}' = (0, 1, \dots, S)$.

In each period and each state, there are $N \geqslant 2$ goods in the world. The first $N^0 \geqslant 0$ of these are internationally tradable, while the next $N^1 \geqslant 0$ are non-tradables associated with the home country and the last $N^2 = N - N^0 - N^1 \geqslant 0$ are non-tradables associated with the foreign country. Goods are sold and purchased in each period in both countries. The vector of goods prices in the home country in state s is denoted by $\mathbf{p}_s \in R_+^N$, $s \in \mathbf{S}'$ with the last N^2 elements infinitely large, and the vector of goods prices in the foreign country in state s is denoted by $\mathbf{q}_s \in R_+^N$, with the $(N^0 + 1)$th to $(N^0 + N^1)$th elements infinitely large. Define $\mathbf{p}_s^0 \in R^N$ and $\mathbf{q}_s^0 \in R^N$ so that their first N^0 elements are identical to those of $\mathbf{p}_s$ and $\mathbf{q}_s$, respectively, while the rest of their elements are zero. Vectors $\mathbf{p}_s^0$ and $\mathbf{q}_s^0$ correspond to the prices of the tradable goods. Suppose that the home country imposes exogenously determined tariffs on goods and services so that the tariff rates in state s are $\mathbf{t}_s^p \in R^N$ of which the last $N^1 + N^2$ elements are zero.[3] Define $\mathbf{t}^p \equiv (\mathbf{t}_0^p, \mathbf{t}_1^p, \dots, \mathbf{t}_S^p) \in R^{N(S+1)}$. Then, in equilibrium, $\mathbf{p}_s^0 = \varepsilon_s \mathbf{q}_s^0 + \mathbf{t}_s^p$, where ε_s is the exchange rate defined as the price of the foreign money. Define $\boldsymbol{\varepsilon} = (\varepsilon_0, \dots, \varepsilon_S)$.

There are H securities, $H \leqslant S$. Define $\mathbf{H} \equiv (1, \dots, H)$. All securities are tradable and can be issued in either country.[4] Securities are purchased and sold in period 0. In period 1 and if state s occurs, security h delivers an amount $a_{sh} \geqslant 0$ units of domestic money in the home country or a'_{sh} units of foreign money in the foreign country.[5] Assuming the presence of an income tax t_{sh}^a imposed by the home government on the hth security payment, in equilibrium we have $a_{sh} = \varepsilon_s a'_{sh} + t_{sh}^a$. Let us define $\mathbf{a}_s \equiv \{a_{sh}\} \in R_+^H$, $\mathbf{a}'_s \equiv \{a'_{sh}\} \in R_+^H$, $\mathbf{t}_s^a \equiv \mathbf{a}_s - \varepsilon_s \mathbf{a}'_s \in R_+^H$ and $\mathbf{t}^a \equiv (\mathbf{t}_1^a, \dots, \mathbf{t}_S^a) \in R^{SH}$. All securities are independent in the sense that the $S \times H$ matrices $\{\mathbf{a}_s\}$ and $\{\mathbf{a}'_s\}$ have full column rank H. The vector of security prices of the home country is denoted by $\mathbf{r} \in R_+^H$, while that of the foreign country is denoted by $\mathbf{d} \in R_+^H$. Because securities deliver non-negative payoffs in period 1, non-satiation of households' preferences implies that equilibrium security prices are non-negative. Denote the non-prohibitive tariffs on securities trade imposed by the home country by $\mathbf{t}^r \in R^H$. Then in equilibrium we have $\mathbf{r} = \varepsilon_s \mathbf{d} + \mathbf{t}^r$.

There are I price-taking households. Define $\mathbf{I} = (1, \dots, I)$. The ith household, $i \in \mathbf{I}$, has an endowment of goods $\mathbf{w}_s^i \in R_+^N$ in state s, $s \in \mathbf{S}'$. The last N^2 elements of $\mathbf{w}_s^i$ are zero; all other elements are positive. For simplicity, it is assumed that the household enters period 0 with zero endowments of domestic and foreign money. During period 0 the household issues securities $\mathbf{z}^i \in R^H$, positive elements corresponding to purchases; and in state s, $s \in \mathbf{S}$, it pays out $\mathbf{a}_s \cdot \mathbf{z}^i$. Moreover, in state s, $s \in \mathbf{S}'$, the household receives from the government a lumpsum transfer $b_s^i \in R$; a negative b_s^i means a transfer from the household to the government.

The ith household engages in a cottage industry. In period 0, it chooses its inputs, $\mathbf{y}_0^i \in R_-^N$ at prices $\mathbf{p}_0$. Those elements of $\mathbf{y}_0^i$ which correspond to inputs chosen are non-positive, while all other elements are zero. Production is then carried out, and the output realized in period 1 depends on the inputs and on the state of nature. Denote the outputs in period 1 and if state s occurs by $\mathbf{y}_s^i \in R_+^N$. Elements corresponding to outputs are positive, while all other elements are zero. The last N^2 elements of $\mathbf{y}_0^i$ and $\mathbf{y}_s^i$ are zero. The production possibility set $\mathbf{Y}^i \equiv \{\mathbf{y}_0^i, \mathbf{y}_s^i\}$ is assumed to be closed, continuous and convex. Irreversibility and free disposal are assumed.

It remains to explain how the cash-in-advance requirement is built into the model and to indicate the means by which monetary control is exercised. To ensure that for all households 'cash' is always available 'in advance' of purchases, it is required that, within each period, the several types of transactions take place in a strict sequence. Following Magill and Quinzii (1989a, b), each of the two periods is subdivided into several subperiods. Each type of transaction is then assigned to one subperiod.

Let us begin with period 0. In the first subperiod, the ith household sells the whole of its endowment $\mathbf{w}_0^i$ to a Central Exchange, abbreviated as CE, at prices $\mathbf{p}_0'$.[6] In the same subperiod, the CE purchases from its foreign counterpart an amount C_0 of foreign money. (It is assumed that each CE has a zero endowment of the other country's money.) In the second subperiod, the ith household receives the transfer b_0^i from the CE. In the third subperiod, the ith household purchases foreign money from the CE, in preparation for its later purchases of foreign goods and securities. Finally, in the fourth subperiod the ith household purchases its consumption basket $\mathbf{x}_0^i$ and its factor inputs $-\mathbf{y}_0^i$, at prices $\mathbf{p}_0$. Let us denote the foreign excess demand for goods and services by $\mathbf{f}_0 \in R^N$, with the (N^0+1)th to (N^0+N^1)th elements zero; and let us define $\mathbf{f}_0^0 \in R^N$ so that its first N^0 elements are identical to those of $\mathbf{f}_0$ and the rest of its elements zero. Then $\mathbf{f}_0^0$ is the vector of net purchases of home goods and services by the foreign country. Let us denote the foreign excess demand for securities by $\mathbf{g} \in R^H$. At the end of period 0, the ith household holds, as a store of value, an amount $m^i \in R_+$ of domestic money and an amount $c^i \in R_+$ of foreign money. At the same time, foreign residents hold m' units of domestic money, and possibly foreign money too. These amounts will be spent during period 1. The household's budget constraint for period 0 is

$$\mathbf{p}_0 \cdot (\mathbf{x}_0^i - \mathbf{y}_0^i) + \mathbf{r} \cdot \mathbf{z}^i + m^i + \varepsilon_0 c^i \leq \mathbf{p}_0' \cdot \mathbf{w}_s^i + b_0^i. \tag{1a}$$

During period 1 transactions take place in a similarly stipulated order. In the first subperiod of state s, $s \in \mathbf{S}$, the CE purchases the ith household's endowment $\mathbf{w}_s^i$ at prices $\mathbf{p}_s'$. It also purchases from its foreign counterpart an amount C_s of foreign money. Production which starts in period 0 is complete in the second subperiod so that the ith household sells its outputs $\mathbf{y}_s^i$ to the CE at prices $\mathbf{p}_s$. In the third subperiod, the CE transfers b_s^i to the ith household. In the same subperiod, households in both countries receive or make payments on the securities purchased or sold during period 0. In the fourth subperiod, the ith household purchases foreign money from the CE, in preparation for its later purchases of foreign goods. In the fifth subperiod, the ith household purchases its consumption basket $\mathbf{x}_s^i$ at prices $\mathbf{p}_s$. In conformity with $\mathbf{f}_0$ and $\mathbf{f}_0^0$, we define $\mathbf{f}_s$ and $\mathbf{f}_s^0$. Thus, $\mathbf{f}_s^0$ represents the net purchase of domestic goods and services by the foreign country in this subperiod. At the end of this subperiod, the ith household will have exhausted its holdings of domestic and foreign money. Its budget constraint for period 1 is

$$\mathbf{p}_s \cdot (\mathbf{x}_s^i - \mathbf{y}_s^i) \leqslant \mathbf{p}_s' \cdot \mathbf{w}_s^i + b_s^i + \mathbf{a}_s \cdot \mathbf{z}^i + m^i + \varepsilon_s c^i \quad \text{for all } s \in \mathbf{S}. \tag{1b}$$

It is apparent that monetary control is exercised through the scheme of lumpsum transfers and through the prices $\mathbf{p}_s$ and $\mathbf{p}_s'$ set by the CE. Thus in state s, $s \in \mathbf{S}'$, the ith household receives an amount of money $M_s^i \equiv \mathbf{p}_s' \cdot \mathbf{w}_s^i + b_s^i$. We may define $M_s \equiv \Sigma_i M_s^i$, $s \in \mathbf{S}$. All money issued, in whatever period, is returned to the CE before the end of period 1.

To economize on the use of symbols, we adopt the following hierarchy of notation. Variables without superscript i denote aggregate variables, summing over all households; for example, $\mathbf{x}_0 = \Sigma_i \mathbf{x}_0^i$, $\mathbf{y}_s = \Sigma_i \mathbf{y}_s^i$, $b_s \equiv \Sigma_i b_s^i$, $m = \Sigma_i m^i$, $c = \Sigma_i c^i$ and so on. Variables without a subscript for the state of nature refer to the vectors of the corresponding variables in different states; for example, $\mathbf{w}^i = (\mathbf{w}_0^i, \ldots, \mathbf{w}_S^i)$, $\mathbf{x}^i = (\mathbf{x}_0^i, \ldots, \mathbf{x}_S^i)$, $\mathbf{f} = (\mathbf{f}_0, \ldots, \mathbf{f}_S)$ and so on.

We further define $\mathbf{F} \equiv \{\mathbf{f}_s, \mathbf{g}\}$ as the foreign excess demand correspondence which is assumed to be non-empty, compact, convex valued, and upper hemi-continuous.

We now turn to the consumption and production choices of the home country. It is assumed that the ith household's preferences can be represented by a utility function $U^i(\mathbf{x}^i)$ which is increasing, continuous and concave in all goods. Non-satiation in income in all periods and states is assumed. The vector $(\mathbf{x}^i - \mathbf{y}^i, m^i, c^i, \mathbf{z}^i)$ is chosen to maximize the household's utility subject to budget constraints (1a) and (1b), and the production possibility sets. As pointed out by Magill and Quinzii (1989a), no household will hold money as a store of value if there exists a riskless security with a positive rate of interest.

Let us denote by $\Theta \in R_+^H$ the convex cone in the non-negative-price orthant spanned by $\mathbf{a}_1, \mathbf{a}_2, \ldots, \mathbf{a}_S$, and by Θ° the interior of Θ. Then Θ° is the set of non-arbitrage prices of securities. For, if $\mathbf{r} \notin \Theta^\circ$, there exists a portfolio of securities $\mathbf{z}'$ such that $\mathbf{r} \cdot \mathbf{z}' \leqslant 0$, $\mathbf{a}_s \cdot \mathbf{z}' \geqslant 0$ for $s = 1, \ldots, S$ and $\mathbf{a}_s \cdot \mathbf{z}' > 0$, for at least one s. It is clear that if $\mathbf{r}$ is an equilibrium security price vector then $\mathbf{r} \in \Theta^\circ$.

Let us therefore define $\mathbf{Z}^i \equiv (m^i, c^i, \mathbf{z}^i) \in R^{H+2}$, $\mathbf{R} \equiv (1, \varepsilon_0, \mathbf{r})$, and $\mathbf{A}_s \equiv (1, \varepsilon_s, \mathbf{a}_s) \in R^{H+2}$ for all $s \in \mathbf{S}$. The budget constraints of the ith household in the two periods, in terms of the amount of money received in the first subperiod, are

$$\mathbf{p}_0 \cdot (\mathbf{x}_0^i - \mathbf{y}_0^i) + \mathbf{R} \cdot \mathbf{Z}^i \leq M_0^i \tag{2a}$$

$$\mathbf{p}_s \cdot (\mathbf{x}_s^i - \mathbf{y}_s^i) \leq M_s^i + \mathbf{A}_s \cdot \mathbf{Z}^i \quad \text{for all } s \in \mathbf{S}. \tag{2b}$$

Following Magill and Quinzii (1989a, b), we assume that, for the households, the selling prices and buying prices of goods are related to each other by the condition

$$\mathbf{p}_s = v_s \mathbf{p}_s' \quad \text{for all } s \in \mathbf{S}'. \tag{3}$$

Equation (3) implies the following expressions for the money supplies in period 0 and state $s \in \mathbf{S}$:

$$(M_0 - b_0)\, v_0 = \mathbf{p}_0 \cdot \mathbf{w}_0 \tag{4a}$$

$$(M_s - b_s)\, v_s = \mathbf{p}_s \cdot \mathbf{w}_s. \tag{4b}$$

Equation (4) is analogous to the traditional quantity theory of money. For this reason, we adopt the terminology of Magill and Quinzii (1989a, b) and call v_s the velocity of circulation.[7] Let us define $\mathbf{v} \equiv (v_0, v_1, \dots, v_S)$.

The tariff revenue from the import of goods and securities in period 0 and that from the import of goods and security payments in state s are, respectively,

$$T_0 = -(\mathbf{p}_0 - \varepsilon_0 \mathbf{q}_0) \cdot \mathbf{f}_0^0 - (\mathbf{r} - \varepsilon_0 \mathbf{d}) \cdot \mathbf{g} \tag{5a}$$

$$T_s = -(\mathbf{p}_s - \varepsilon_s \mathbf{q}_s) \cdot \mathbf{f}_s^0 + (\mathbf{a}_s - \varepsilon_s \mathbf{a}_s') \cdot \mathbf{g}. \tag{5b}$$

The balance of trade in goods and services, excluding the investment income of the home country in state s, $s \in \mathbf{S}'$, is $\varepsilon_s \mathbf{q}_s \cdot \mathbf{f}_s^0$. The balances on current account, which include investment incomes, are $\varepsilon_0 \mathbf{q}_0 \cdot \mathbf{f}_0^0$ in state 0 and $\varepsilon_s \mathbf{p}_s \cdot \mathbf{f}_s' - \varepsilon_s \mathbf{a}_s' \cdot \mathbf{g}$ in state s, $s \in \mathbf{S}$. Because the net foreign purchase of domestic securities is $\varepsilon_0 \mathbf{d} \cdot \mathbf{g}$, the balance on non-reserve capital account in period 0 is $\mathbf{r} \cdot \mathbf{g} + m' - \varepsilon_0 c$ and $-m' + \varepsilon_s c$ in state s, $s \in \mathbf{S}$. The sums of current account and non-reserve capital account balances, which are the balances of payments in different states in units of domestic currency, are given by

$$B_0 = \varepsilon_0 \mathbf{q}_0 \cdot \mathbf{f}_0^0 + \varepsilon_0 \mathbf{d} \cdot \mathbf{g} + m' - \varepsilon_0 c \tag{6a}$$

$$B_s = \varepsilon_s \mathbf{q}_s \cdot \mathbf{f}_s^0 - \varepsilon_s \mathbf{a}_s' \cdot \mathbf{g} - m' + \varepsilon_s c \quad \text{for all } s \in \mathbf{S}. \tag{6b}$$

Let us define $\mathbf{B} \equiv (B_0, B_1, \dots, B_S)$. Using tariff/tax revenues given in (5), the balances of payments can be written as

$$B_0 = T_0 + \mathbf{p}_0 \cdot \mathbf{f}_0^0 + \mathbf{r} \cdot \mathbf{g} + m' - \varepsilon_0 c \tag{7a}$$

$$B_s = T_s + \mathbf{p}_s \cdot \mathbf{f}_s^0 - \mathbf{a}_s \cdot \mathbf{g} - m' + \varepsilon_s c \quad \text{for all } s \in \mathbf{S}. \tag{7b}$$

Recall that the foreign country makes a net purchase of domestic money of $\varepsilon_s C_s$ in state s. This money is spent on goods, securities or security payments, and on tariffs and income taxes; the balance m' is held. Thus, the balances of payments are alternatively given by

$$B_0 = \varepsilon_0 C_0 - \varepsilon_0 c \tag{8a}$$

$$B_s = \varepsilon_s C_s + \varepsilon_s c \quad \text{for all } s \in \mathbf{S}. \tag{8b}$$

Conditions (8) state that the balances of payments equal the increases in the foreign reserve held by the CE.

Recall that during the first subperiod in period 0 the CE spends $\mathbf{p}_0' \cdot \mathbf{w}_0$ on households' endowments, transfers b_0 to households, and purchases C_0 foreign money. Therefore the total domestic money issued is $\mathbf{p}_0' \cdot \mathbf{w}_0 + b_0 + \varepsilon_0 C_0 = M_0 + \varepsilon_0 C_0$. Later, domestic and foreign households spend $\mathbf{p}_0 \cdot \mathbf{w}_0$ to buy back the aggregate endowment and $\varepsilon_0 c$ to purchase the amount of foreign money c that they want to hold. The foreign country pays T_0 in tariffs and taxes. The rest of the money in circulation is held partly by domestic residents, m, and partly by foreign residents, m'. Therefore

$$M_0 + \varepsilon_0 C_0 = \mathbf{p}_0 \cdot \mathbf{w}_0 + T_0 + m + m' + \varepsilon_0 c,$$

which, recalling (8a), gives

$$M_0 + B_0 = \mathbf{p}_0 \cdot \mathbf{w}_0 + T_0 + m + m'. \tag{9a}$$

Similarly, during the first subperiod of period 1 when state s occurs, $s \in \mathbf{S}$, the domestic government issues $\mathbf{p}_s' \cdot \mathbf{w}_s$ of domestic money in purchasing households' endowments and in effecting transfers b_s to households; $M_s = \mathbf{p}_s' \cdot \mathbf{w}_s + b_s$. Domestic households hold m of domestic money and c of foreign money, while foreigners hold m' of domestic money. At the same time, the foreign government sells C_s of foreign money to the home country at the exchange rate ε_s. Later, domestic and foreign households purchase the endowment $\mathbf{w}_s$ from the CE at the price $\mathbf{p}_s$ while the foreign country pays T_s in tariffs and other taxes. Therefore

$$M_s + \varepsilon_s C_s = \mathbf{p}_s \cdot \mathbf{w}_s + T_s - m - m' - \varepsilon_s c$$

which, recalling (8b), gives

$$M_s + B_s = \mathbf{p}_s \cdot \mathbf{w}_s + T_s - m - m'. \tag{9b}$$

Conditions (9a) and (9b) have a nice interpretation which is consistent with the monetary approach to the balance of payments. For example, (9a) can be written as

$$B_0 = \mathbf{p}_0 \cdot \mathbf{w}_0 + T_0 + m + m' - M_0. \tag{10}$$

In (10), $\mathbf{p}_0 \cdot \mathbf{w}_0 + T_0$ can be interpreted as the total domestic and foreign transaction demand for money because it is the amount of domestic money needed to buy back the endowment from the CE. m and m' are respectively the domestic and foreign speculative and precautionary demands for domestic money. Thus, $\mathbf{p}_0 \cdot \mathbf{w}_0 + m + m'$ is the total demand for money, and the balance of payments is seen to equal the excess demand for money. Condition (9b) can be interpreted in a similar way.

Conditions (9a) and (9b) can be substituted into (4) to give an alternative expression for the velocity of circulation. Thus, in period 0,

$$(M_0 - b_0)v_0 = M_0 + B_0 - T_0 - m - m',$$

or

$$v_0 = \frac{M_0 + B_0 - T_0 - m - m'}{M_0 - b_0}. \tag{11a}$$

Similarly, for state s, $s \in \mathbf{S}$, we have, after substitution and rearrangement of terms,

$$v_s = \frac{M_s + B_s - T_s + m + m'}{M_s - b_s}. \tag{11b}$$

In the special case in which $m = m' = B_s = b_s = T_s = 0$, we have $v_0 = v_s = 1$.

Two exchange rate regimes are considered separately. Under a fixed exchange rate regime, the exchange rate ε_s is fixed at $\bar{\varepsilon}_s$, $s \in \mathbf{S}'$. The CE must rely on its foreign reserve to maintain the officially set exchange rates, and there is no guarantee that the balance of payments in each state is zero. Under a flexible exchange rate regime, the exchange rate will adjust so that the balance of payments is zero.

The monetary rule of the government is defined as $\mathbf{M} \equiv (M_0, \ldots, M_S)$, and the transfer scheme as $\mathbf{b} \equiv (b_0, \ldots, b_S)$. Let us partition all vectors related to goods into three parts. The first part has N^0 elements, which corresponds to internationally tradable goods, the second part has N^1 elements and corresponds to non-tradable goods associated with the home country, and the third part has N^2 elements and corresponds to non-tradable goods associated with the foreign country. Let us define $\boldsymbol{\phi} \equiv (1, -1, \ldots, -1) \in R^{(S+1)}$. The conditions which must be satisfied in a world monetary equilibrium can now be stated.

Definition 1. *Given the monetary rule* $\mathbf{M}$, *endowment* $\mathbf{w}$ *and transfer scheme* $\mathbf{b}$, *a monetary equilibrium for the home and foreign countries under a* **fixed** *exchange rate regime is the action* $(\mathbf{x}, \mathbf{y}, \mathbf{Z}, \mathbf{f}, \mathbf{g}, m')$ *and the prices* $(\mathbf{p}, \mathbf{R}, \mathbf{q}, \mathbf{d}, \mathbf{v})$ *such that:*

(a) Households everywhere maximize utility subject to budget constraints and the production possibility sets.
(b) $\mathbf{x} + \mathbf{f} \leqslant \mathbf{w} + \mathbf{y}$.
(c) $\mathbf{z} + \mathbf{g} \leqslant \mathbf{0}$.
(d) $\mathbf{p}^0 = \boldsymbol{\varepsilon} \,\square\, \mathbf{q}^0 + \mathbf{t}^p$.

(*e*) $\mathbf{r} = \varepsilon \,\square\, \mathbf{d} + \mathbf{t}^r$.
(*f*) $\mathbf{M} + \mathbf{B} = \mathbf{p} \,\square\, \mathbf{w} + (m + m')\phi$.
(*g*) $(\mathbf{M} - \mathbf{b}) \,\square\, \mathbf{v} = \mathbf{p} \,\square\, \mathbf{w}$.
(*h*) $\varepsilon = \bar{\varepsilon}$.

Note that $\bar{\varepsilon}$ is a vector of exogenously fixed exchange rates. The box-product operator $\square$ provides a compact way of writing a system of equations. For example, $(\mathbf{M} - \mathbf{b}) \,\square\, \mathbf{v} = \mathbf{p} \,\square\, \mathbf{w}$ represents the $S + 1$ equations: $(M_s - b_s)\, v_s = \mathbf{p}_s \cdot \mathbf{w}_s$ for all $s \in \mathbf{S}'$. Also note that, since the balance of payments may not be zero, the total money supply $\hat{M}_s$ will be determined endogenously, although the government can exogenously choose the amount of money supplied to domestic residents, M_s. A similar definition can be given for an equilibrium under a flexible exchange rate regime.

Definition 2. *Given the monetary rule* **M**, *endowment* **w** *and transfer scheme* **b**, *a monetary equilibrium for the home and foreign countries under a* **flexible** *exchange rate regime is the action* (**x**, **y**, **Z**, **f**, **g**, m') *and the prices* (**p**, **R**, **q**, **d**, **v**) *such that:*

(*a*) *Households everywhere maximize utility subject to budget constraints and the production possibility sets.*
(*b*) $\mathbf{x} + \mathbf{f} \leqslant \mathbf{w} + \mathbf{y}$.
(*c*) $\mathbf{z} + \mathbf{g} \leqslant 0$.
(*d*) $\mathbf{p}^0 = \varepsilon \,\square\, \mathbf{q}^0 + \mathbf{t}^p$.
(*e*) $\mathbf{r} = \varepsilon \,\square\, \mathbf{d} + \mathbf{t}^r$.
(*f*) $\mathbf{M} + \mathbf{B} = \mathbf{p} \,\square\, \mathbf{w} + (m + m')\phi$.
(*g*) $(\mathbf{M} - \mathbf{b}) \,\square\, \mathbf{v} = \mathbf{p} \,\square\, \mathbf{w}$.
(*h'*) $\mathbf{B} = \mathbf{0}$.

Condition (h′) states that the balances of payments in all states are zero. By (9), the total money supply is the same as the amount of money supplied to domestic residents; it therefore can be controlled by the government as a policy tool.

The preferences and technologies of the foreign country are similar to those of the home country so that the (truncated) foreign net demand correspondence for goods and securities, $\mathbf{F}(\mathbf{q}, \mathbf{d}, K) \in R^{N(S+1)+M}$, is non-empty, compact, convex valued and upper hemi-continuous. The elements of **F** corresponding to the $(N^0 + 1)$th to the $(N^0 + N^1)$th goods are zero.

Proposition 1. *Under a fixed exchange rate regime as described above, an equilibrium exists.*

Proposition 2. *Under a flexible exchange rate regime as described above, an equilibrium exists.*

The proofs of propositions 1 and 2 are given in the appendix.

4 THE GAINS FROM TRADE

Consider two situations. In each situation, there are two periods, 0 and 1. Values of variables in period 0 are known with certainty while values of variables in period 1 are not certain until the state is known. However, the two situations differ in terms of foreign trade. In the initial situation, the first $N^0 \geqslant 0$ goods are internationally tradable while the other goods are tradable only within either the home or foreign country. If the initial situation is autarky, $N^0 = 0$ and $\mathbf{g}$ is constrained to be zero. In the final situation, either the home country has experienced an improvement in its terms of trade or additional goods have become internationally tradable. Until we turn our attention to customs unions, it is assumed that, if trade is allowed, no policy restrictions are present. This means that $\mathbf{p}_s = \varepsilon_s \mathbf{q}_s$, $\mathbf{r} = \varepsilon_s \mathbf{d}$ and $\mathbf{a}_s = \varepsilon_s \mathbf{a}_s'$, $s \in \mathbf{S}'$. Thus, the tariff/tax revenue is zero: $T_s = 0$. To allow meaningful comparison, it is assumed that the home country's preferences, endowments and technologies remain unchanged in these two situations.

Values of variables in the initial situation, except households' endowments, which are fixed in both situations, are distinguished by circumflexes. For simplicity, assume that transfers to households and firms are zero in the initial situation, that is $\hat{b}_s^i = 0$, for all $s \in \mathbf{S}'$. The demand for goods and securities of the ith household is $(\mathbf{x}^i - \mathbf{y}^i, \mathbf{z}^i)$. In equilibrium, the following conditions are satisfied:

$$\hat{\mathbf{x}} + \hat{\mathbf{f}} \leqslant \hat{\mathbf{y}} + \mathbf{w} \tag{12a}$$

$$\hat{\mathbf{z}} + \hat{\mathbf{g}} \leqslant 0. \tag{12b}$$

With non-satiation, the above inequalities can be replaced by equalities.

Now consider the final situation. Define the gains from changes in the terms of trade in periods 0 and 1, respectively, as

$$Q_0 = \mathbf{p}_0 \cdot \hat{\mathbf{f}}_0^0 + \mathbf{r} \cdot \hat{\mathbf{g}} + \hat{m}' - \varepsilon_0 \hat{c} \tag{13a}$$

$$Q_s = \mathbf{p}_s \cdot \hat{\mathbf{f}}_s^0 - \mathbf{a}_s \cdot \hat{\mathbf{g}} - \hat{m}' + \varepsilon_s \hat{c} \quad \text{for all } s \in \mathbf{S}, \tag{13b}$$

where $\hat{m}'$ is the amount of domestic money held by the foreign country and $\hat{c}$ is the amount of foreign money held by the home country in period 0 in the initial situation. In general, the terms-of-trade gains may be positive or negative.

Transfers are made by the government in the first subperiod of each period. In periods 0 and 1, respectively, the ith household receives from the government the transfers

$$b_0^i = \mathbf{p}_0 \cdot (\hat{\mathbf{x}}_0^i - \hat{\mathbf{y}}_0^i) + \hat{m}^i + \varepsilon_0 \hat{c}^i + \mathbf{r} \cdot \hat{\mathbf{z}}^i - \mathbf{p}_0' \cdot \mathbf{w}_0^i + Q_0/I \tag{14a}$$

$$b_s^i = \mathbf{p}_s \cdot (\hat{\mathbf{x}}_s^i - \hat{\mathbf{y}}_s^i) - \hat{m}^i - \varepsilon_s \hat{c}^i - \mathbf{a}_s \cdot \hat{\mathbf{z}}^i - \mathbf{p}_s' \cdot \mathbf{w}_s^i + Q_s/I \quad \text{for all } s \in \mathbf{S}. \tag{14b}$$

In (14), households share uniformly in the terms-of-trade gains.

The sums of the transfers given by the government in different states are

$$b_0 = \mathbf{p}_0 \cdot (\hat{\mathbf{x}}_0 - \hat{\mathbf{y}}_0) + \hat{m} + \varepsilon_0 \hat{c} + \mathbf{r} \cdot \hat{\mathbf{z}} - \mathbf{p}_0' \cdot \mathbf{w}_0 + Q_0$$

$$= \mathbf{p}_0 \cdot \mathbf{w}_0 + \hat{m} + \hat{m}' - \mathbf{p}_0' \cdot \mathbf{w}_0 \quad (15a)$$

$$b_s = \mathbf{p}_s \cdot (\hat{\mathbf{x}}_s - \hat{\mathbf{y}}_s) - \hat{m} - \varepsilon_s \hat{c} - \mathbf{a}_s \cdot \hat{\mathbf{z}} - \mathbf{p}_s' \cdot \mathbf{w}_s + Q_s$$

$$= \mathbf{p}_s \cdot \mathbf{w}_s - \hat{m} - \hat{m}' - \mathbf{p}_s' \cdot \mathbf{w}_s, \quad (15b)$$

where the equilibrium conditions (12) and the definitions of the production and terms-of-trade gains have been used. Note that the net transfer from the government to households in each state is not necessarily zero. By rearranging terms, (15a) and (15b) imply that

$$M_0 = \mathbf{p}_0' \cdot \mathbf{w}_0 + b_0 = \mathbf{p}_0 \cdot \mathbf{w}_0 + \hat{m} + \hat{m}' \quad (16a)$$

$$M_s = \mathbf{p}_s' \cdot \mathbf{w}_s + b_s = \mathbf{p}_s \cdot \mathbf{w}_s - \hat{m} - \hat{m}'. \quad (16b)$$

Next, we need to define feasibility of the transfer scheme given by (14) and to determine whether the scheme is feasible. As explained above, money supplied by the government in state s consists of three parts: the net transfer, b_s, the money used to purchase endowments, $\mathbf{p}_s' \cdot \mathbf{w}_s$, and the balance of payments, B_s. On the other hand, the government receives money equal to $\mathbf{p}_s \cdot \mathbf{w}_s$. Thus, the net amount of money issued is $b_s + \mathbf{p}_s' \cdot \mathbf{w}_s + B_s - \mathbf{p}_s \cdot \mathbf{w}_s$, which, by (9a) and (9b), equals $m + m'$ in period 0 and $-(m + m')$ in period 1. Thus we may say that the transfer scheme is feasible if and only if $m + m'$ equals $\hat{m} + \hat{m}'$. Of course, other definitions of feasibility can be imagined.

To show that the above transfer scheme is feasible, we make the following assumptions.

Assumption 1. *In the presence of the transfers (14), the balance of payments in each state is zero:* $B_s = 0$, $s \in \mathbf{S}'$.

Assumption 2. *The home government maintains the same monetary policy in both situations:* $M_0 = \hat{M}_0$ *and* $M_s = \hat{M}_s$.

Assumption 1 generally requires a flexible exchange rate regime.[8]

Lemma 1. *Under assumptions 1 and 2 the transfer scheme (14) is feasible. Furthermore, if* $\hat{m} + \hat{m}' = 0$, $b_s = 0$, $s \in \mathbf{S}'$.

The special case treated in lemma 1, with $\hat{m} + \hat{m}' = B_s = 0$, is the one usually found in real trade models.

We now compare the welfare levels of home-country households in these two situations. We say that the final situation weakly Pareto-dominates the initial situation if, under the above scheme of lumpsum transfers, nobody is worse off in the final situation; and that the final situation Pareto-dominates the initial situation if, under the same scheme of transfers, some households are better off, and none worse off, in the final situation.

Lemma 2. *If the terms-of-trade gains defined by (13) are non-negative then the final situation weakly Pareto-dominates the initial situation under the compensation scheme (14). If, in addition, at least one of the terms-of-trade gains is positive, or consumption and/or production substitution takes place in at least one household, then the final situation Pareto-dominates the initial situation.*

Proposition 3. *Given the scheme of lumpsum transfers described by (14), free trade weakly Pareto-dominates autarky; if consumption and/or production substitution takes place in at least one household then free trade Pareto-dominates autarky.*

Proposition 4. *For a small open economy, if free trade exists in both situations and if there is an improvement in the terms of trade in some states, so that*

$$\mathbf{p}_0 \cdot \hat{\mathbf{f}}_0^0 + \mathbf{r} \cdot \hat{\mathbf{g}} + \hat{m}' - \varepsilon_0 \hat{c} \geqslant 0$$

$$\mathbf{p}_s \cdot \hat{\mathbf{f}}_s^0 - \mathbf{a}_s \cdot \hat{\mathbf{g}} - \hat{m}' + \varepsilon_s \hat{c} \geqslant 0, \quad s \in \mathbf{S},$$

with some strict inequalities, then the final situation Pareto-dominates the initial situation.

Proposition 5. *Consider a small open economy facing fixed world prices and able in the final situation to trade in additional goods and/or securities. Given the compensation scheme (14), the final situation weakly Pareto-dominates the initial situation; if consumption and/or substitution occurs for at least one household then the final situation Pareto-dominates the initial situation.*

We now turn to a welfare analysis of customs unions. Let an initial world trading situation be constrained by any conceivable trade restrictions. For simplicity, however, transport costs are neglected.[9] The countries are divided into two groups. The first group consists of K countries which are about to form a customs union, and the second group consists of all other countries. Countries in the first group are called member countries and labelled 1, ..., K. Define the set $\mathbf{K} = (1, \ldots, K)$. All other countries are called non-member countries. We retain our earlier notation, but add a superscript k to distinguish the variables of country k. For example, member country k has I^k households and $\mathbf{x}_s^{ki}$ is the consumption demand of the ith household in the country in state s. Let $I \equiv \Sigma_k I^k$.

Consider the situation before the formation of the customs union. Denote the total volume of goods and services (securities) imported by non-member countries from member countries in state s by $\hat{\mathbf{f}}_s^0 \in R^N$ ($\hat{\mathbf{g}}_s \in R^H$), $s \in \mathbf{S}'$; variables in this situation are distinguished by circumflexes. The elements of $\hat{\mathbf{f}}_s^0$ corresponding to goods that do not flow between member and non-member countries are zero. Assuming perfect currency arbitrage, we choose as the **world money** the money of a non-member country; the exchange rate of any country is then defined as the price of the world money in terms of that country's money. Thus, if households in the member countries want to hold foreign money, they hold the world money. Denote the corresponding world prices of goods and services by $\hat{\mathbf{q}}_s \in R_+^N$ and the world prices of securities by $\hat{\mathbf{d}}_s \in R_+^H$, all in terms of world money.

Denote the amounts of country k's money and world money, expressed in **units of world money**, held by the ith household in country k, $k \in \mathbf{K}$, by $\hat{m}^{ki}/\varepsilon_s^k$ and $\hat{c}^{ki}$, respectively, where ε_s^k is the country's exchange rate in state s. Define $\hat{m} \equiv \Sigma_k \Sigma_i (\hat{m}^{ki}/\varepsilon_s^k)$ and $\hat{c} \equiv \Sigma_k \Sigma_i \hat{c}^{ki}$. The aggregate balance of payments of the member countries, in **units of the world money**, are

$$\hat{B}_0^w = \hat{\mathbf{q}}_0 \cdot \hat{\mathbf{f}}_0^0 + \hat{\mathbf{d}}_0 \cdot \hat{\mathbf{g}} + \hat{m} - \hat{c} = 0 \tag{17a}$$

$$\hat{B}_s^w = \hat{\mathbf{q}}_s \cdot \hat{\mathbf{f}}_s^0 - \mathbf{a}_s' \cdot \hat{\mathbf{g}} - \hat{m} + \hat{c} = 0. \tag{17b}$$

The superscript w in $\hat{B}_s^w$ is to remind us that it is measured in units of the world money.

Denote the aggregate endowments, demand for goods and securities by households in the member countries in state s, $s \in \mathbf{S}'$, by $\mathbf{w}_s$, $\hat{\mathbf{x}}_s - \hat{\mathbf{y}}_s$, and $\hat{\mathbf{z}}_s$, respectively; for example, $\hat{\mathbf{x}}_s = \Sigma_k \Sigma_i \hat{\mathbf{x}}_s^{ki}$. The equilibrium conditions are

$$\hat{\mathbf{x}}_s + \hat{\mathbf{f}}_s - \hat{\mathbf{y}}_s - \mathbf{w}_s \leqslant 0 \tag{18a}$$

$$\hat{\mathbf{z}}_s + \hat{\mathbf{g}}_s \leqslant 0, \quad s \in \mathbf{S}'. \tag{18b}$$

Now member countries form a customs union and remove all trade barriers among them. To prove welfare improvement, we follow Kemp and Wan (1976, 1986) and artificially freeze the volume of trade between member countries and non-member countries. We further assume that the exchange rates of all countries are not changed. The assumption that the volume of trade is frozen is for exposition only; it will be shown later that if a suitable common tariff structure is chosen, world prices, and therefore non-member countries' import demands, do not change. Variables in this situation do not have circumflexes.

Denote the prices of goods in state s in the kth country by $\mathbf{p}_s^k$, the prices of securities by $\mathbf{r}^k$, and the yields of the securities in state s by $\mathbf{a}_s^k$. Because of the existence of free trade among member countries, we can define the following prices expressed in the world money: $\mathbf{p}_s \equiv \mathbf{p}_s^k/\varepsilon_s^k$, $\mathbf{r} \equiv \mathbf{r}^k/\varepsilon_s^k$ and $\mathbf{a}_s \equiv \mathbf{a}_s^k/\varepsilon_s^k$. These are the common prices and security yields within the customs union.

We now generalize the Kemp–Wan proposition to accommodate money and markets which are possibly incomplete.

Proposition 6. *Consider any competitive world trading equilibrium, with any number of countries and commodities, with possibly incomplete markets, with no restrictions whatever on* *the tariffs and other commodity taxes of individual countries. Now let any subset of the countries form a customs union. Then there exists a common tariff vector and a system of lumpsum compensatory payments involving only members of the union such that each household, whether a member of the union or not, is not worse off than before the formation of the union. Those households which substitute in consumption and/or production are better off.*

5 CONCLUDING REMARKS

In recent general-equilibrium analysis of economies with incomplete securities markets it has been customary to assume that the economies extend over just two periods of time. The explanation is straightforward: in the absence of a complete set of securities markets it is unclear what should guide the investment decisions of firms. In this respect we have been quite conventional, and this might be thought to be a serious limitation of our analysis. It is therefore worth emphasizing that our analysis can be extended to accommodate any finite number of time periods. Propositions **a–d** of section 1 emerge essentially unchanged by the appendage of additional periods of time.

More serious, perhaps, we have implicitly assumed that, per dollar of transactions, money is equally efficacious in all markets. It does not allow for the possibility that sectors are not uniformly monetized. It is a merit of Kemp's (1990) analysis that uneven monetization is accommodated. It remains to provide a more general multiperiod analysis of an explicitly cash-in-advance kind but with non-uniformity of monetization allowed for.

APPENDIX

In our proof of the existence of equilibrium, we shall make use of the following lemmas.

Lemma 3. *Consider the truncated excess demand correspondence of the ith household*

$$\mathbf{X}^i(\mathbf{p}, \mathbf{R}\,;\, K, \mathbf{M}^i, \{\mathbf{A}_s\}) = \{(\mathbf{x}^i - \mathbf{y}^i, \mathbf{Z}^i) \mid U^i(\mathbf{x}^i) \geqslant U^i(\mathbf{x}^{i'})$$
$$\textit{for all } (\mathbf{x}^{i'} - \mathbf{y}^{i'}, \mathbf{Z}^{i'}) \textit{ which satisfy constraints (2) for all } s \in \mathbf{S}\},$$

where $K \subseteq R_+^{N(S+1)} \times R^H$ *is a closed rectangle with centre at the origin. The demand correspondence in non-empty, compact, convex valued and upper hemi-continuous at each* $(\mathbf{p}, \mathbf{R}) \in R_+^{N(S+1)} \times R_+^H$ *with* $\mathbf{p}_s \neq \mathbf{0}^p$ *for all* $s \in \mathbf{S}'$, *where* $\mathbf{0}^p \in R_+^N$ *is a vector with the first to the* $(N^0 + N^1)$*th elements zero and the other elements infinitely large.*

Proof. *Non-emptiness, compactness, and convexity of the demand correspondence are obvious. To establish upper hemi-continuity, define the sequences*

$$(\mathbf{p}^n, \mathbf{r}^n) \rightarrow (\mathbf{p}, \mathbf{r}) \quad \textit{and} \quad ((\mathbf{x}^i - \mathbf{y}^i)^n, (\mathbf{Z}^i)^n) \rightarrow (\mathbf{x}^i - \mathbf{y}^i, \mathbf{Z}^i),$$

where $((\mathbf{x}^i - \mathbf{y}^i)^n, (\mathbf{Z}^i)^n) \in \mathbf{X}^i(\mathbf{p}^n, \mathbf{R}^n; K, \mathbf{M}^i, \{\mathbf{A}_s\})$. *Note that the first element of* $\mathbf{R}^n$ *is unity and that, under a fixed exchange rate regime, the second element of* $\mathbf{R}^n$ equals $\bar{\varepsilon}_0$. *We wish to show that* $(\mathbf{x}^i - \mathbf{y}^i, \mathbf{Z}^i) \in \mathbf{X}^i(\mathbf{p}, \mathbf{R}; K, \mathbf{M}^i, \{\mathbf{A}_s\})$. *Suppose not. Let there exist*

$$(\bar{\mathbf{x}}^i - \bar{\mathbf{y}}^i, \bar{\mathbf{Z}}^i) \in \{(\mathbf{x}^{i\prime} - \mathbf{y}^{i\prime}, \mathbf{Z}^{i\prime}) | \text{ constraints (2) are satisfied at } (\mathbf{p}, \mathbf{R})\}$$

and such that $U^i(\bar{\mathbf{x}}^i) > U^i(\mathbf{x}^i)$. *By continuity, for n large,*

$$\mathbf{p}_0^n \cdot (\bar{\mathbf{x}}_0^i - \bar{\mathbf{y}}_0^i) + \mathbf{R}^n \cdot \bar{\mathbf{Z}}^i \leqslant M_0^i \tag{19a}$$

$$\mathbf{p}_s^n \cdot (\bar{\mathbf{x}}_s^i - \bar{\mathbf{y}}_s^i) \leqslant M_s^i + \mathbf{A}_s \cdot \bar{\mathbf{Z}}^i, \tag{19b}$$

for all $s \in \mathbf{S}$. *Take* $\alpha < 1$ *but sufficiently large so that* $U^i(\alpha\bar{\mathbf{x}}^i) > U^i(\mathbf{x}^i)$. *For n large,* $U^i(\alpha\bar{\mathbf{x}}^i) > U^i((\mathbf{x}^i)^n)$ *and, by* (19),

$$\alpha\mathbf{p}_0^n \cdot \bar{\mathbf{x}}_0^i < M_0^i - \mathbf{R}^n \cdot \bar{\mathbf{Z}}^i + \mathbf{p}_0^n \cdot \bar{\mathbf{y}}_0^i$$

$$\alpha\mathbf{p}_s^n \cdot \bar{\mathbf{x}}_s^i < M_s^i + \mathbf{A}_s \cdot \bar{\mathbf{Z}}^i + \mathbf{p}_s^n \cdot \bar{\mathbf{y}}_s^i$$

for all $s \in \mathbf{S}$. *This means that* $(\alpha\bar{\mathbf{x}}^i - \bar{\mathbf{y}}^i, \bar{\mathbf{Z}}^i)$ *is feasible when prices are* $(\mathbf{p}^n, \mathbf{R}^n)$ *for n large, but it contradicts the condition that* $U^i(\alpha\bar{\mathbf{x}}^i) > U^i((\mathbf{x}^i)^n)$. □

By lemma 3, the aggregate demand correspondence

$$\mathbf{X}(\mathbf{p}, \mathbf{R}; K, \mathbf{M}) = \sum_i \mathbf{X}^i(\mathbf{p}, \mathbf{R}; K, \mathbf{M}^i, \{\mathbf{A}_s\})$$

is non-empty, compact, convex valued and upper hemi-continuous.

Proof of Lemma 1. *Comparison of (9) and (16) shows that* $m + m' = \hat{m} + \hat{m}'$. *By the above definition, therefore, the transfer scheme is feasible. Furthermore, if* $\hat{m} + \hat{m}' = 0$, *and since* $B_s = 0$, *by (11),* $v_s = 1$, $s \in \mathbf{S}'$. *This implies that* $\mathbf{p}_s = \mathbf{p}_s'$, *and, by (15), that* $b_s = 0$. □

Proof of Lemma 2. *The budget constraints of the ith household, given the transfers described by (14), are*

$$\mathbf{p}_0 \cdot (\mathbf{x}_0^i - \mathbf{y}_0^i) + \mathbf{r} \cdot \mathbf{z}^i + m^i + \varepsilon_0 c^i \leqslant \mathbf{p}_0 \cdot (\hat{\mathbf{x}}_0^i - \hat{\mathbf{y}}_0^i) + \mathbf{r} \cdot \hat{\mathbf{z}}^i + \hat{m}^i + \varepsilon_0 \hat{c}^i + Q_0/I \tag{20a}$$

$$\mathbf{p}_s \cdot (\mathbf{x}_s^i - \mathbf{y}_s^i) \leqslant \mathbf{p}_s \cdot (\hat{\mathbf{x}}_s^i - \hat{\mathbf{y}}_s^i) + \mathbf{a}_s \cdot \mathbf{z}^i + m^i + \varepsilon_s c^i - \mathbf{a}_s \cdot \hat{\mathbf{z}}^i - \hat{m}^i - \varepsilon_s \hat{c}^i + Q_s/I, \quad s \in \mathbf{S}. \tag{20b}$$

Because the terms-of-trade gain is shared equally among households, if it is non-negative then, by (20), the initial demand for goods, money and securities $(\hat{\mathbf{x}}^i - \hat{\mathbf{y}}^i, \hat{m}^i, \hat{c}^i, \hat{\mathbf{z}}^i)$ *is still* *affordable. Thus the household cannot be worse off. It is better off if (i) $Q_s > 0$ for some $s \in \mathbf{S}'$, or (ii) consumption and/or production substitution takes place.* □

Proof of Proposition 1. *We will show that when households are maximizing their utilities and firms maximizing their expected profits, and when conditions (e), (f) and (h) in definition 1 are satisfied, then conditions (c) and (d) are also satisfied, with the velocities of circulation being obtained from condition (g) and equilibrium prices. Let us introduce the aggregate (world) excess demand correspondence* $\mathbf{E}(\mathbf{p}, \mathbf{R}, \mathbf{q}, \mathbf{d}, K) \equiv \mathbf{X} + \mathbf{F} - (\mathbf{w}, \mathbf{0}^H)$ *where* $\mathbf{0}^H \in R^H$ *has elements zero and K is sufficiently large that it contains any feasible aggregate supply in any state, and where* $\mathbf{F} \equiv \{\mathbf{f}_s, \mathbf{g}\}$ *is the foreign excess demand correspondence. Note that the officially imposed exchange rates have been substituted into* $\mathbf{R}$. *The aggregate excess demand is denoted by* $\mathbf{e} \equiv (\mathbf{x} - \mathbf{y}, \mathbf{z}) + (\mathbf{f}, \mathbf{g}) - (\mathbf{w}, \mathbf{0}^H) \in \mathbf{E}$. *Recalling lemma 3 and the restrictions imposed on* $\mathbf{F}$, $\mathbf{E}(\mathbf{p}, \mathbf{R}, \mathbf{q}, \mathbf{d}, K)$ *is non-empty, compact, convex valued and upper hemi-continuous. Define* $\mathbf{f}_s^2$, $\mathbf{q}_s^2 \in R^N$ *so that their last* N^2 *elements are identical to* $\mathbf{f}_s$ *and* $\mathbf{q}_s$, *respectively, while all other elements are zero.*

Let us choose a positive real number L sufficiently large that it exceeds the greatest possible nominal price of any good or security,[10] *and define the sets*

$$\Delta \equiv \{(\mathbf{p}, \mathbf{r}) \mid \mathbf{p} \in R_+^{N(S+1)}, \mathbf{r} \in \Theta^\circ, p_{sn}, r_h \leqslant L, \text{ for all } s \in \mathbf{S}', n \in \mathbf{N}, h \in \mathbf{H}\}$$

$$\Gamma \equiv \{(\mathbf{q}, \mathbf{d}) \mid \mathbf{q} \in R_+^{N(S+1)}, \mathbf{d} \in \Theta^\circ, q_{sn}, t_h \leqslant L, \text{ for all } s \in \mathbf{S}', n \in \mathbf{N}, h \in \mathbf{H}\}$$

where $\mathbf{N} = (1, \ldots, N)$.

Consider the correspondence $\boldsymbol{\Phi}$: $\Delta \times \Gamma \times \mathbf{E}$. *The first two components of* $\boldsymbol{\Phi}$ *are*

$$\boldsymbol{\Phi}_1 = \{(\mathbf{p}, \mathbf{r}) \in \Delta \mid (\mathbf{p}_0, \mathbf{r}) \text{ maximizes } \mathbf{p}_0 \cdot (\mathbf{x}_0 + \mathbf{f}_0^0 - \mathbf{y}_0 - \mathbf{w}_0) + \mathbf{r} \cdot (\mathbf{z} + \mathbf{g}), \text{ and } \mathbf{p}_s \text{ maximizes } \mathbf{p}_s \cdot (\mathbf{x}_s + \mathbf{f}_s^0 - \mathbf{y}_s - \mathbf{w}_s) \text{ for all } s \in \mathbf{S}\}$$

$$\boldsymbol{\Phi}_2 = \{(\mathbf{q}, \mathbf{d}) \in \Gamma \mid (\mathbf{q}_0^2) \text{ maximizes } \mathbf{q}_s^2 \cdot \mathbf{f}_s^2 \text{ for all } s \in \mathbf{S}'; \; \mathbf{p}^0 = \varepsilon \,\square\, \mathbf{q}^0 + \mathbf{t}^p \text{ and } \mathbf{r} = \varepsilon \,\square\, \mathbf{d} + \mathbf{t}^r\}.$$

It is easy to see that $\boldsymbol{\Phi}$ *is non-empty, compact, convex valued and upper hemi-continuous. By Kakutani's fixed-point theorem, there is some point* $(\mathbf{p}^*, \mathbf{R}^*, \mathbf{q}^*, \mathbf{d}^*, \mathbf{e}^*)$ *such that*

$$(\mathbf{p}^*, \mathbf{R}^*, \mathbf{q}^*, \mathbf{d}^*, \mathbf{e}^*) \in \boldsymbol{\Phi}(\mathbf{p}^*, \mathbf{R}^*, \mathbf{q}^*, \mathbf{d}^*, \mathbf{e}^*). \tag{21}$$

Note that in view of the money supply equations, we can rule out the following values as an equilibrium point: $\mathbf{p}_s^* = \mathbf{0}^p$, $\mathbf{q}_s^* = \mathbf{0}^q$ *for all* $s \in \mathbf{S}'$, *and* $\mathbf{r} = \mathbf{0}^r$ *and* $\mathbf{d}^* = \mathbf{0}^t$. *We now show that the point in (21) represents an equilibrium in the sense that* $\mathbf{e}^* \leqslant 0$. *Consider* $\boldsymbol{\Phi}$ *and state 0. By definition*

$$\mathbf{p}_0^* \cdot (\mathbf{x}_0^* + \mathbf{f}_0^{0*} - \mathbf{y}_0^* - \mathbf{w}_0) + \mathbf{r}^* \cdot (\mathbf{z}^* + \mathbf{g}^*) \geqslant \mathbf{p}_0 \cdot (\mathbf{x}_0^* + \mathbf{f}_0^{0*} - \mathbf{y}_0^* - \mathbf{w}_0) + \mathbf{r} \cdot (\mathbf{z}^* + \mathbf{g}^*), \text{ for all } (\mathbf{p}, \mathbf{r}) \in \Delta.$$

Let us choose $(\mathbf{p}_0, \mathbf{r})$ *so that it equals* $(\mathbf{p}_0^*, \mathbf{r}^*)$ *except for any two elements* ℓ *and* k *of* $\mathbf{r}$, *where* $1 \leqslant \ell, k \leqslant H$, *and where at least* r_ℓ^* *or* r_k^* *is positive, and let us assume, without loss of generality, that* $r_\ell^* > 0$. *Then (6) reduces to*

$$(r_\ell^* - r_\ell)(z_\ell^* + g_\ell^*) + (r_k^* - r_k)(z_k^* + g_k^*) \geqslant 0. \tag{22}$$

Since $(\mathbf{p}^*, \mathbf{r}^*), (\mathbf{p}, \mathbf{r}) \in \Delta$, $(r_\ell^* + r_k^*) = (r_\ell + r_k)$. *Applying this result, (22) reduces to*

$$(r_k^* - r_k)[(z_k^* + g_k^*) - (z_\ell^* + g_\ell^*)] \geqslant 0. \tag{23}$$

If $r_k^* = 0$ *then, since* r_k *can be any non-negative number, (23) implies that* $(z_k^* + g_k^*) \leqslant (z_\ell^* + g_\ell^*)$. *If* $r_k^* > 0$ *then, since* r_k *can be chosen to be greater or smaller than* r_k^*, *(23) holds only if* $(z_\ell^* + g_\ell^*) = (z_k^* + g_k^*)$. *The same argument can be extended to other values of* ℓ *and* k. *For the sake of exposition, let us assume that* $r_1^* > 0$, *renumbering the securities if necessary. We then have*

$$(z_1^* + g_1^*) = \ldots = (z_h^* + g_h^*) = \ldots$$

for all securities h *whose optimal prices are positive, while*

$$(z_i^* + g_i^*) \leqslant (z_1^* + g_1^*)$$

for all i *such that* $r_i^* = 0$. *The same argument can be applied in the following way. First, choose* $(\mathbf{p}_0, \mathbf{r})$ *so that it equals* $(\mathbf{p}_0^*, \mathbf{r}^*)$ *except for any two elements* ℓ *and* k *of* $\mathbf{p}_0$, *where* $1 \leqslant \ell, k \leqslant (N^0 + N^1)$ *and where at least one price is positive. Second, choose* $(\mathbf{p}_0, \mathbf{r})$ *so that it equals* $(\mathbf{p}_0^*, \mathbf{r}^*)$ *except for any element* ℓ *of* $\mathbf{p}_0$ *and* k *of* $\mathbf{r}$, *where* $1 \leqslant \ell \leqslant (N^0 + N^1)$ *and* $1 \leqslant k \leqslant (M^0 + M^1)$ *and where at least one price is positive. Then*

$$(z_1^* + g_1^*) = \ldots = (z_h^* + g_h^*) = \ldots = (x_{0n}^* + f_{0n}^{0*} - y_{0n}^* + w_{0n}) = \ldots \tag{24a}$$

for all securities h *and goods* n *whose optimal prices are positive, while*

$$(z_i^* + g_i^*), (x_{0j}^* + f_{0j}^{0*} - y_{0j}^* + w_{0j}) \leqslant (z_1^* + g_1^*) \tag{24b}$$

for all securities i *and goods* j *with optimal prices zero. Add together the aggregate budget constraint of the home country and its balance of payments at point* $(\mathbf{p}^*, \mathbf{R}^*, \mathbf{q}^*, \mathbf{d}^*, \mathbf{e}^*)$ *to give*

$$\mathbf{p}_0^* \cdot (\mathbf{x}_0^* + \mathbf{f}_0^{0*} - \mathbf{y}_0^*) + \mathbf{r}^* \cdot (\mathbf{z}^* + \mathbf{g}^*) + m^* + m'^* = M_0 + B_0,$$

which, recalling (9a) and rearranging terms, gives

$$\mathbf{p}_0^* \cdot (\mathbf{x}_0^* + \mathbf{f}_0^{0*} - \mathbf{y}_0^* - \mathbf{w}_0) + \mathbf{r}^* \cdot (\mathbf{z}^* + \mathbf{g}^*) = 0. \tag{25}$$

Expressions (24) and (25) combine to yield

$$(z_1^* + g_1^*) = \ldots = (z_h^* + g_h^*) = \ldots = (x_{0n}^* + f_{0n}^{0*} - y_{0n}^* + w_{0n}) = 0$$

$$(z_i^* + g_i^*), (x_{0j}^* + f_{0j}^{0*} - y_{0j}^* + w_{0j}) \leqslant 0.$$

A similar argument can be developed to show that other markets are in equilibrium. □

Proof of Proposition 2. *The proof of this proposition is similar to that of proposition 1, except that the exchange rates in all states have to be determined endogenously. Moreover, it must be shown that if households are maximizing utilities, and if the free-trade price equalization conditions (e) and (f) are satisfied, then there exists a set of endogenous prices at which conditions (c), (d), and (h′) are satisfied. Again, condition (g) is used to determine the velocities of circulation, once the equilibrium* $\mathbf{p}$ *has been derived.*

We retain the notation used in proving proposition 1, except that the demand and supply correspondences depend not just on prices of goods and securities but also on exchange rates. Let us define the correspondence Φ*:* $\Delta \times \Gamma \times \Pi \times \mathbf{E}$. Δ *and* Γ *are defined above, except that* ε *is an endogenous variable, and*

$$\Pi \equiv \{\varepsilon \in R_+^{S+1} \mid \varepsilon_s < L, \ \varepsilon_s \text{ maximizes } \varepsilon_s B_s \text{ for all } s \in \mathbf{S}'\}.$$

Again by Kakutani's fixed-point theorem, there is some point $(\mathbf{p}^*, \mathbf{R}^*, \mathbf{q}^*, \mathbf{d}^*, \varepsilon^*, \mathbf{e}^*)$ *such that*

$$(\mathbf{p}^*, \mathbf{R}^*, \mathbf{q}^*, \mathbf{d}^*, \varepsilon^*, \mathbf{e}^*) \in \Phi(\mathbf{p}^*, \mathbf{R}^*, \mathbf{q}^*, \mathbf{d}^*, \varepsilon^*, \mathbf{e}^*). \tag{26}$$

Again note that, because of the money supply equations, we can rule out the following values as an equilibrium point: $\mathbf{p}_s^* = \mathbf{0}^p$, $\mathbf{q}_s^* = \mathbf{0}^q$ *for all* $s \in \mathbf{S}'$, *and* $\mathbf{r} = \mathbf{0}^r$ *and* $\mathbf{d}^* = \mathbf{0}^t$. *This result, together with conditions (e) and (f), implies that* $\varepsilon > 0$. *We now show that* $(\mathbf{p}^*, \mathbf{R}^*, \mathbf{q}^*, \mathbf{d}^*, \varepsilon^*, \mathbf{e}^*)$ *represents an equilibrium in the sense that* $\mathbf{e} \leqslant \mathbf{0}$ *and* $\mathbf{B} = \mathbf{0}$. *That* $\mathbf{e} \leqslant \mathbf{0}$ *can be proved using the techniques above. To show that* $\mathbf{B} = \mathbf{0}$, *consider first period 0. By definition,*

$$\varepsilon_0^* B_0^* \geqslant \varepsilon_0 B_0^* \quad \text{for all } \varepsilon \in \Pi,$$

which implies that

$$(\varepsilon_0^* - \varepsilon_0) B_0^* \geqslant 0. \tag{27}$$

Since $\varepsilon_0^* > 0$, *and* ε_0 *can be either greater or smaller than* ε_0^*, *the only condition under which (27) holds is* $B_0^* = 0$. *The same argument can be used to show that* $B_s^* = 0$ *for all* $s \in \mathbf{S}$. □

Proof of Proposition 3. *Since the initial situation is autarky,* $\hat{\mathbf{f}}_0^0 = \hat{\mathbf{f}}_s^0 = \mathbf{0}^N$, $\hat{\mathbf{g}} = \mathbf{0}^H$, *and* $\hat{m}' = \hat{c} = 0$, *which in turn implies that the terms-of-trade gains in different states are zero. The proposition then follows from lemmas 1 and 2.* □

Proof of Proposition 4. *From the given conditions in (13), the terms-of-trade gains are positive. The proposition follows from lemmas 1 and 2.* □

Proof of Proposition 5. *Since world prices are fixed, by (13) and assumption 1, the terms-of-trade gains are zero. The proposition then follows from lemmas 1 and 2.* □

Proof of Proposition 6. *Let the ith household in country k receive from its government the transfers*

$$b_0^{ki} = \mathbf{p}_0^k \cdot (\hat{\mathbf{x}}_0^{ki} - \hat{\mathbf{y}}_0^{ki}) + \mathbf{r}^k \cdot \hat{\mathbf{z}}^{ki} + \hat{m}^{ki} + \varepsilon_0^k \hat{c}^{ki} - \mathbf{p}_0' \cdot \mathbf{w}^{ki} \tag{28a}$$

$$b_s^{ki} = \mathbf{p}_s^k \cdot (\hat{\mathbf{x}}_s^{ki} - \hat{\mathbf{y}}_s^{ki}) + \mathbf{a}_s^k \cdot \hat{\mathbf{z}}^{ki} - \hat{m}^{ki} - \mathbf{p}_s^{k\prime} \cdot \mathbf{w}_s^{ki} \tag{28b}$$

$$s' \in \mathbf{S}.$$

Define the aggregate transfer of the member countries to households, measured in **units of world money**, *in state s, as* $b_s^w = \Sigma_k(\Sigma_i b_s^{ki}/\varepsilon_s^k)$, *where the superscript w in* b_s^w *is to remind us that it is measured in units of the world money.*

These transfers are substituted into the household's budget constraint (1). It is easy to see that the original consumption and portfolio choice is still feasible in the new situation. Hence the household is not worse off; in fact, it is better off if consumption and/or production substitution occurs.

The common tariff imposed by member countries on goods and services from non-member countries in state s and measured in units of world money is $\mathbf{p}_s - \hat{\mathbf{q}}_s$. *Similarly the common tariff on imported securities is* $\mathbf{r} - \hat{\mathbf{d}}$ *and the common tax on repatriation of security payments is* $\mathbf{a}_s - \mathbf{a}_s'$, *recalling that* $\mathbf{p}_s$, $\mathbf{r}$ *and* $\mathbf{a}_s$ *are measured in units of world money. Because world prices remain unchanged, the volumes of trade of non-member countries with member countries, that is* $\hat{\mathbf{f}}_s^0$ *and* $\hat{\mathbf{g}}$, *are not changed. The total tariff revenue in units of world money received by all member countries in period 0 is* $T_0^w = -(\mathbf{p}_0 - \hat{\mathbf{q}}_0) \cdot \hat{\mathbf{f}}_0^0 - (\mathbf{r}_0 - \hat{\mathbf{d}}_0) \cdot \hat{\mathbf{g}}$, *and that in period 1 and state s is* $T_s^w = -(\mathbf{p}_s - \hat{\mathbf{q}}_s) \cdot \hat{\mathbf{f}}_s^0 + (\mathbf{a}_s - \mathbf{a}_s') \cdot \hat{\mathbf{g}}$. *Furthermore, in state s the aggregate balance of payments of the non-member countries, which is the negative of that of the member countries, remains zero.*

The net revenues of the governments of the member countries in different states are, in units of world money,

$$\begin{aligned} -b_0^w + T_0^w &= -\mathbf{p}_0 \cdot (\hat{\mathbf{x}}_0 - \hat{\mathbf{y}}_0) + \mathbf{p}_0' \cdot \mathbf{w}_0 - \hat{m} - \hat{c} - \mathbf{r} \cdot \hat{\mathbf{z}} - (\mathbf{p}_0 - \hat{\mathbf{q}}_0) \cdot \hat{\mathbf{f}}_0^0 \\ &\quad - (\mathbf{r} - \hat{\mathbf{d}}) \cdot \hat{\mathbf{g}} \\ &= -\mathbf{p}_0 \cdot \mathbf{w}_0 + \mathbf{p}_0' \cdot \mathbf{w}_0 - \hat{m} - \hat{c} + \hat{\mathbf{q}} \cdot \hat{\mathbf{f}}_0^0 + \hat{\mathbf{d}} \cdot \hat{\mathbf{g}} \\ &= -\mathbf{p}_0 \cdot \mathbf{w}_0 + \mathbf{p}_0' \cdot \mathbf{w}_0 - \hat{m} - \hat{m}' \end{aligned} \tag{29a}$$

$$\begin{aligned} -b_s^w + T_s^w &= -\mathbf{p}_s \cdot (\hat{\mathbf{x}}_s - \hat{\mathbf{y}}_s) + \mathbf{p}_s' \cdot \mathbf{w}_s + \hat{m} + \hat{c} + \mathbf{a}_s \cdot \hat{\mathbf{z}} - (\mathbf{p}_s - \hat{\mathbf{q}}_s) \cdot \hat{\mathbf{f}}_s^0 \\ &\quad + (\mathbf{a}_s - \mathbf{a}_s') \cdot \hat{\mathbf{g}} \\ &= -\mathbf{p}_s \cdot \mathbf{w}_s + \mathbf{p}_s' \cdot \mathbf{w}_s + \hat{m} + \hat{c} + \hat{\mathbf{q}} \cdot \hat{\mathbf{f}}_s^0 - \mathbf{a}_s' \cdot \hat{\mathbf{g}} \\ &= -\mathbf{p}_s \cdot \mathbf{w}_s + \mathbf{p}_s' \cdot \mathbf{w}_s + \hat{m} + \hat{m}' \end{aligned} \tag{29b}$$

where the equilibrium conditions (18) and the zero balance-of-payments conditions have been used. Rearrangement of the terms in (29a) and (29b) yields

$$M_0 = \mathbf{p}_0' \cdot \mathbf{w}_0 + b_0' = \mathbf{p}_0 \cdot \mathbf{w}_0 + \hat{m} + \hat{m}' + T_0 \tag{30a}$$

$$M_s = \mathbf{p}_s' \cdot \mathbf{w}_s + b_s' = \mathbf{p}_s \cdot \mathbf{w}_s - \hat{m} - \hat{m}' + T_s \tag{30b}$$

where $M_s \equiv \Sigma_k M_s^k/\varepsilon_s^k$ *is the total money supply in the member countries, measured in* **units of world money**. *By comparing (30) with (9), and recalling that money supplies are fixed and balances of payments are zero, we see that* $m + m' = \hat{m} + \hat{m}'$. *Using the above criterion, we see that the compensation scheme is feasible.* □

NOTES

* We acknowledge with gratitude the helpful comments of Jürgen Eichberger.

1 One might substitute the following proposition, which we owe to Grandmont and McFadden (1972): **a**′ For any group of two or more countries, free trade is better than no trade. However, **a**′ is the more general proposition: **a** implies **a**′ but **a**′ does not imply **a** because **a** allows any or all of the other countries to be non-free-traders.

2 If the demand of both households for any good is positive when its price is zero, then under autarky at most one household may hold money as a store of value at the end of period 0.

3 If the foreign country also imposes tariffs on goods and securities, and income taxes on security payments, $\mathbf{q}_s$, $\mathbf{d}_s$ and $\mathbf{a}_s'$ can be interpreted as the world prices of goods, world prices of securities, and world security payments which may or may not be the same as the domestic prices in the foreign country.

4 We can make the model slightly more general by assuming that some of the domestic and foreign securities are non-tradable. However, this does not add much to the model and results.

5 For simplicity, we assume that a security delivers a non-negative payment in all states. A more general model in which negative payments are allowed may be found in Geanakoplos and Polemarchakis (1986).

6 Some goods such as labour services cannot be stored. Thus they do not have to be delivered until the households purchase them in the last subperiod.

7 The meaning of the circulation of money in the present model is quite restricted because it refers to the flow of money from the government to local residents and then back to the government in each period.

8 We do not consider the use of foreign reserves to import foreign goods and services to maintain the welfare levels of households.

9 There are gainful customs unions whatever the pattern of transport costs. However, to prove it would require much more complicated notation.

10 With a finite supply of money, the price of any good and the non-arbitrage price of any security are bounded from above.

REFERENCES

Geanakoplos, J. and Polemarchakis, H. (1986) 'Existence, regularity, and constrained suboptimality of competitive allocations when markets are incomplete', in W. Heller, R. Starr and D. Starrett (eds) *Essays in Honor of Kenneth Arrow*, Vol. 3, Cambridge: Cambridge University Press.

Grandmont, J. M. and McFadden, D. (1972) 'A technical note on classical gains from trade', *Journal of International Economics* 2: 109–25.

Grossman, G. M. (1984) 'The gains from international factor movements', *Journal of International Economics* 17: 73–83.

Kemp, M. C. (1962) 'The gains from international trade', *Economic Journal* 72: 803–19.

Kemp, M. C. (1964) *The Pure Theory of International Trade*, New York: Prentice Hall.

Kemp, M. C. (1990) 'The gains from free trade for a monetary economy', *Kobe Economic & Business Review*, 35th Annual Report: 27–30.

Kemp, M. C. and Ohyama, M. (1978) 'The gain from trade under conditions of uncertainty', *Journal of International Economics* 8: 139–41.

Kemp, M. C. and Wan, H. Y. Jr (1972) 'The gains from free trade', *International Economic Review*, 13: 509–22.

Kemp, M. C. and Wan, H. Y. Jr (1976) 'An elementary proposition concerning the formation of customs unions', *Journal of International Economics* 6: 95–7.

Kemp, M. C. and Wan, H. Y. Jr (1986) 'The comparison of second-best equilibria: The case of customs unions', in D. Bös and C. Seidl (eds) *Welfare Economics of the Second Best*, Suppl. 5 of *Zeitschrift für Nationalökonomie* 161–7, Vienna: Springer-Verlag.

Kemp, M. C. and Wong, K.-Y. (1991) 'Gains from trade with possibly incomplete markets', University of Washington. Essay 5 of this volume.

Krueger, A. O. and Sonnenschein, H. (1967) 'The terms of trade, the gains from trade and price divergence', *International Economic Review* 8: 121–7.

Magill, M. and Quinzii M. (1989a) 'Real effects of money in general equilibrium', mimeo.

Magill, M. and Quinzii, M. (1989b) 'The non-neutrality of money in a production economy with nominal assets', mimeo.

Newbery, D. M. G. and Stiglitz, J. E. (1984) 'Pareto inferior trade', *Review of Economic Studies* 51: 1–12.

Ohyama, M. (1972) 'Trade and welfare in general equilibrium', *Keio Economic Studies* 9: 37–73.

Samuelson, P. A. (1962) 'The gains from trade once again', *Economic Journal* 72: 820–9.

Shy, O. (1988) 'A general equilibrium model of Pareto inferior trade', *Journal of International Economics* 25: 143–54.

Vanek, J. (1965) *General Equilibrium of International Discrimination*, Cambridge, MA: Harvard University Press.

Wong, K.-Y. (1983) 'On choosing among trade in goods and international capital and labor mobility: A theoretical analysis', *Journal of International Economics* 14: 223–50.

Wong, K.-Y. (1991) 'Welfare comparison of trade situations', *Journal of International Economics* 30: 49–68.

8

TRADE GAINS IN A PURE CONSUMPTION–LOAN MODEL*

1 INTRODUCTION

The question of trading gains has been discussed almost always in the context of a static model of international trade. Here I consider the question in relation to a consumption–loan model of the Samuelson type (see Samuelson, 1958; Gale, 1973) and show that, in spite of the propensity of that model to generate paradoxes (see, for example, Gale, 1971), the familiar welfare propositions of static trade theory carry over to it.

The essence of the argument can be put very simply. Any closed-economy competitive equilibrium involves a market redistribution of the community's aggregate endowment for each period among the individuals surviving into that period. In any open economy it is possible to achieve the closed-economy competitive allocation by means of taxes and subsidies. Any open-economy 'trading' away from that allocation must then be to the advantage of each individual.

2 A CLOSED ECONOMY

There is only one commodity, a perishable consumption good which cannot be produced and cannot be stored from one period to another. In each period of his finite life span, each individual receives a fixed amount of that commodity. Each individual is born with perfect foresight and with stable preferences defined over his or her lifetime consumption profile. In particular, the individual knows with certainty his or her own life span, own income profile and all prices or interest rates which will prevail during his or her lifetime. Individuals may differ in preferences, life span, date of birth and income profile. The birth rate may be constant or variable.

There exists a clearing house or market secretariat which buys and sells (against some unit of account) at prices (rates of interest) which clear the market, that is equate to zero the net purchases of the secretariat during each period.

Let n be the maximum life expectancy of any individual; let $y^j_{ht} \geq 0$ and $c^j_{ht} \geq 0$ be respectively the income and consumption during the jth period of the individual's life of the ith individual born in period t; and let r_t be the one-period rate of interest during period t. Then we have, for period t, the market-clearance condition

$$\begin{aligned}\sum_i c_{it}^1(r_t, r_{t+1}, \ldots, r_{t+n-2}) + \sum_i c_{i,t-1}^2(r_{t-1}, \ldots, r_{t+n-3}) \\ + \cdots + \sum_i c_{i,t-n+1}^n(r_{t-n+1}, r_{t-n+2}, \ldots, r_{t-1}) \\ = \sum_i y_{it}^1 + \sum_i y_{i,t-1}^2 + \cdots + \sum_i y_{i,t-n+1}^n.\end{aligned} \qquad (1)$$

This is a difference equation of order $2(n-1)-1$ in the rate of interest. To solve, we need $2(n-1)-1$ boundary restrictions on the c or the r. Only the details of our argument, not our qualitative conclusions, depend on the manner in which these restrictions are generated and on their content.[1] We may suppose that some $2(n-1)-1$ consecutive r are arbitrarily chosen by the secretariat, so that the equations (1) can be used to determine recursively all earlier and later r.

3 AN OPEN ECONOMY

Suppose now that from period $t = t_0$ the country under study is opened to 'trade' (free or restricted) with other countries and (in keeping with the assumption of perfect foresight) that the opening of trade in period t_0 is perfectly foreseen throughout their lives by all individuals who are born under the old regime but will live for at least two periods under the new regime (so that r_{t_0} will influence their decisions); that is, all individuals born not earlier than period $t_0 - n + 2$ and not later than period $t_0 - 1$. Suppose further that the post-trade profile of interest rates is forced through the same grid of boundary values as the autarkic profile. It is then clear that the opening of trade potentially affects all rates of interest prevailing, during and after period $t_0 - n + 2$.

Is it possible on welfare grounds to compare the free-trade and autarkic equilibria? The answer seems to be 'Yes'. For during and after period $t_0 - n + 2$ it is possible so to redistribute the country's aggregate endowment for that period that each individual has exactly what he or she would have consumed under autarky. If after redistribution an individual engages in borrowing and lending, consuming either more or less than under autarky, the individual does so by choice and is therefore not worse off than under autarky. Of course, the trade-with-redistribution profile of interest rates will differ from the trade-without-redistribution profile (from period $t_0 - n + 2$ on) and from the autarky-without-redistribution profile.

Technically, the above argument is incomplete without a demonstration that autarkic and (post-redistribution) trading equilibria exist. However, that demonstration poses no problems which have not been handled in the literature (see, for example, Kemp and Wan, 1972).

4 CONCLUDING REMARKS

The assumption that there is only one consumption good is inessential to our conclusions. In fact, all c^j_{it} and y^j_{it} can be as well interpreted as vectors as scalars. Thus our conclusion that free trade is gainful comprehends both the conventional atemporal exchange of commodities as well as the intertemporal exchange emphasized above.

On the other hand, the market secretariat has been endowed with perfect foresight concerning future excess demands. Even for a Samuelson–Gale world, with identical individuals born in each period and a constant relative age distribution of the population, this assumption might be thought a little extravagant.

NOTES

* The helpful comments of Henry Y. Wan, Jr and a referee are gratefully acknowledged.

1 One might suppose that at some specific point in time the first births miraculously took place, trading with the market secretariat being possible from this biological time origin, $t = 1$. Then the system of market-clearance equations becomes

$$\sum_i c^1_{i1}(r_1, r_2, \ldots, r_{n-1}) = \sum y^1_{i1},$$

$$\sum_i c^2_{i1}(r_1, r_2, \ldots, r_{n-1}) + \sum_i c^1_{i2}(r_2, r_3, \ldots, r_n) = \sum y^2_{i1} + \sum y^1_{i2},$$

$$\vdots$$

$$\sum_i c^n_{i1}(r_1, r_2, \ldots, r_{n-1}) + \ldots + \sum_i c^1_{in}(r_n, r_{n+1}, \ldots, r_{2(n-1)}) = \sum y^n_{i1} + \ldots + \sum y^1_{in}, \quad (2)$$

$$\sum_i c^n_{i2}(r_2, r_3, \ldots, r_n) + \ldots + \sum_i c^1_{i,\,n+1}(r_{n+1}, r_{n+2}, \ldots, r_{2(n-1)+1})$$

$$= \sum y^n_{i2} + \ldots + \sum y^1_{i,\,n+1},$$

etc.

One might then suppose that the secretariat simply supplies arbitrary values for $r_1, r_2, \ldots, r_{n-2}$, leaving $r_{n-1}, r_n, \ldots$ to be determined recursively by the first, second, . . . equation. Or one might suppose that time has a foreseen biological end, as well as a beginning.

Let doomsday be the period $t = T$. Births might continue right up to doomsday or, more consistently with the assumption of perfect foresight, the last births might occur during period $T - n + 1$. In the latter case, the system (2) terminates with the equation

$$\sum c^n_{i,\,T-n}(r_{T-n}, \ldots, r_{T-2}) + \sum c^{n-1}_{i,\,T-n+1}(r_{T-n+1}, \ldots, r_{T-1})$$

$$= \sum y^n_{i,\,T-n} + \sum y^{n-1}_{i,\,T-n+1}.$$

Instead of starting the system at the biological time origin, one might imagine that the possibility of trading is introduced only during some period $t = t_1$ after the biological zero and that until then individuals simply consume their incomes. If the trading origin is at least n periods after the biological origin, the system of market-clearance equations is of the form (1) with $t = t_1, t_1 + 1, \ldots$. Then sufficient boundary conditions could be provided by the secretariat. For example, the secretariat might simply announce arbitrary values for $r_{t_1}, r_{t_1+1}, \ldots, r_{t_1+n-3}$.

REFERENCES

Gale, D. (1971) 'General equilibrium with imbalance of trade', *Journal of International Economics* 1: 141–58.

Gale, D. (1973) 'Pure exchange equilibrium of dynamic economic models', *Journal of Economic Theory* 6: 12–36.

Kemp, M. C. and Wan, H. Y. Jr (1972) 'The gains from free trade', *International Economic Review* 13: 509–22.

Samuelson, P. A. (1958) 'An exact consumption–loan model of interest with or without the social contrivance of money', *Journal of Political Economy* 66: 467–82.

9

GAINS FROM TRADE WITH OVERLAPPING GENERATIONS*

1 INTRODUCTION

The welfare economics of free trade contains four core propositions:

1 For any economy, large or small, free trade is better than no trade (Samuelson, 1962; Kemp, 1962; Grandmont and McFadden, 1972; Kemp and Wan, 1972; Kemp and Ohyama, 1978).
2 For a small open economy, an improvement in the terms of trade is beneficial (Kemp, 1962; Krueger and Sonnenschein, 1967; Wong, 1991).
3 For a small open economy, trade in additional commodities (including primary factors of production) is beneficial (Wong, 1983, 1991; Grossman, 1984).[1]
4 Any subset of trading countries can form a mutually advantageous customs union (Kemp, 1964; Vanek, 1965; Ohyama, 1972; Kemp and Wan, 1976, 1986).

These propositions are known to be valid for economies in a static world with complete markets and with finite numbers of agents and commodities.[2] For the most part, the welfare economics of international trade has neglected the obvious and regrettable fact of life that populations comprise overlapping generations of mortal individuals. It seems to have been taken for granted that, in essentials, the propositions carry over to a world of overlapping generations.

However, popular models of economies with overlapping generations are characterized by Pareto-suboptimal competitive equilibria;[3] and it is well known that, for economies with distortions, free trade may be worse than no trade.

Moreover, we now have several published examples of competitive economies with overlapping generations for which, in the absence of government compensation policies, autarky is Pareto-preferred to free trade; see Kemp and Long (1979), Binh (1985, 1986) and Serra (1991). These examples cast doubt on the robustness not only of the gainfulness of free trade but of all the core welfare propositions associated with free trade.

The purpose of this essay is to show that, for a class of economies with overlapping generations, and for a class of disturbances which includes the substitution of free trade for autarky, an improvement in a small country's terms of trade, an enlargement of a small country's set of tradable goods and factors, and the formation of a customs union, there can always be found one or more policies which are effective in compensating those who otherwise would have been harmed by the disturbance. Depending on the conditions of trade and on the range of available government instruments, four different compensation policies may be considered. Thus, if free international trade in goods and capital movements are allowed, there exists an efficacious scheme of lumpsum compensation. If international capital movements are prohibited, the government can combine lumpsum transfers and a saving subsidy to regulate private saving, or it can supplement private saving with public saving to redistribute welfare over generations; alternatively, the government may resort to commodity taxes similar to those suggested by Dixit and Norman (1980) in a different context.

Our essay thus helps remove the pessimism about the benefits of free trade created by the work of Kemp and Long, Binh and Serra. It shows that, although in the absence of appropriate compensation free trade may be Pareto-inferior to autarky, nevertheless under certain conditions there exists feasible compensation which ensures that free trade is beneficial in the sense of Pareto.

The essay is organized as follows. In section 2, we present a model incorporating overlapping generations. The model is similar to that of Serra (1991), but the dual approach we take allows us easily to extend the model to higher dimensions. Section 3 presents a compensation scheme and some sufficient conditions under which losers can be compensated when the economy experiences a shock such as the movement from autarky to free trade, the improvement of the terms of trade or an addition to the list of tradable goods and factors for a small open economy, or the formation of a customs union. In the next section, four types of government policy are suggested. In sections 4 and 5 our several gains-from-trade propositions are stated and discussed. In section 6 it is argued that all propositions of sections 4 and 5 remain valid for monetary economies. Section 7 contains some concluding remarks. The existence, stability and uniqueness of equilibrium in the present model are discussed in an appendix.

2 AN OVERLAPPING-GENERATIONS MODEL

This section describes a simple overlapping-generations framework with two goods, consumption and investment goods, and two factors, labour and capital. The focus will be on a single trading country. In period t, the amounts of capital k_t and labour ℓ_t are given. Factors are perfectly mobile across sectors. Denote the outputs of the consumption and investment goods by m_t and i_t, respectively, and the prices of the consumption and investment goods by p_t and q_t, respectively. Later, we will find it convenient to choose the investment good as the *numéraire* and set $q_t = 1$ for all t. Assuming perfect price flexibility, full employment of factors exists at all times. Treating the labour endowment as a parameter, the production possibility set of the economy for period t can be defined as

$$\Phi(\ell_t) = \{(m_t, i_t, k_t): (m_t, i_t, k_t, \ell_t) \text{ is feasible}\}.$$

The economy is characterized by perfect competition, convex, linearly homogeneous and continuously differentiable technologies, and the absence of any static distortions. Taking factor endowments as given, the firms choose their production as if they are jointly maximizing the gross domestic product (GDP) function given by[4]

$$D(p_t, q_t, k_t, \ell_t) = \max_{m_t, i_t} \{p_t m_t + q_t i_t: (m_t, i_t, k_t) \in \Phi(\ell_t)\}.$$

Technologies are stationary over time. It is well known that the GDP function is increasing, differentiable, convex and linearly homogeneous in commodity prices and increasing, differentiable, concave and linearly homogeneous in factor endowments, and has the following derivatives:

$$\frac{\partial D}{\partial p_t} = m_t \tag{1a}$$

$$\frac{\partial D}{\partial q_t} = i_t \tag{1b}$$

$$\frac{\partial D}{\partial k_t} = r_t \tag{1c}$$

$$\frac{\partial D}{\partial \ell_t} = w_t \tag{1d}$$

where r_t and w_t are the market rental and wage rates, respectively.

Each individual lives for two periods. In the first period, the young individual works and earns an income given by the wage rate. In addition, the individual receives a transfer of b_t^y from the government (negative for a transfer to the government). The income is devoted partly to consumption, and partly to saving. In the next period, the old individual retires but receives an income from earlier saving and a transfer from the government, b_{t+1}^0. A subsidy τ_{t+1} on saving may be provided by the government. Thus each unit of saving yields a return of $(r_{t+1} + \tau_{t+1})$ in period $t + 1$. With perfect foresight, there is no difference between expected and realized values of variables in period $t + 1$.

To focus our analysis on capital formation, we assume that the population has a zero net growth rate so that, in each period, the same number of individuals are born and die. Because the labour force remains constant, we can normalize it so that $\ell_t = 1$ for all t. The population in any period is then 2, the sum of young and old people.

Denote the demand for the consumption good of the young individual in period t by c_t^y, saving by s_t and the demand for consumption when the individual is old in period $t+1$ by c^o_{t+1}. The individual's budget constraints are (with non-satiation)

$$p_t c^y_t + s_t = w_t + b^y_t \tag{2a}$$

$$p_{t+1} c^o_{t+1} = (r_{t+1} + \tau_{t+1}) s_t + b^o_{t+1} \tag{2b}$$

where we have chosen the investment good as the *numéraire*. The preferences of the individual born in period t can be represented by a utility function $U(c^y_t, c^o_{t+1})$ which is increasing, continuously differentiable and strictly quasi-concave. Thus the bequest motive is neglected. Moreover, preferences are uniform across generations. However, the benefits and feasibility of the compensation scheme to be introduced later do not require the existence of a steady state and thus do not require uniform preferences.[5] The individual born in period t chooses (c^y_t, s_t, c^o_{t+1}) to maximize $U(c^y_t, c^o_{t+1})$ subject to the budget constraints in (2). It is easy to show that, in the absence of satiation and if the individual has positive saving,[6] the first-order conditions give

$$\lambda^y_t = \lambda^o_{t+1}(r_{t+1} + \tau_{t+1}) \tag{3}$$

where $\lambda^y_t > 0$ is the marginal utility of income of the individual when young in period t and $\lambda^o_{t+1} > 0$ is the marginal utility of income of the individual when old in period $t+1$. Evidently $\lambda^y_t/\lambda^o_{t+1}$ can be interpreted as one plus the subjective rate of discount.

Denote the individual's indirect utility function by $v(w_t + b^y_t, p_t, r_{t+1} + \tau_{t+1}, p_{t+1}, b^o_{t+1})$. By the envelope theorem, the indirect utility function has the following derivatives:

$$\frac{\partial v}{\partial w_t} = \frac{\partial v}{\partial b^y_t} = \lambda^y_t \tag{4a}$$

$$\frac{\partial v}{\partial p_t} = -\lambda^y_t c^y_t \tag{4b}$$

$$\frac{\partial v}{\partial p_{t+1}} = -\lambda^o_{t+1} c^o_{t+1} \tag{4c}$$

$$\frac{\partial v}{\partial r_{t+1}} = \frac{\partial v}{\partial \tau_{t+1}} = \lambda^o_{t+1} s_t \tag{4d}$$

$$\frac{\partial v}{\partial b^o_{t+1}} = \lambda^o_{t+1}, \tag{4e}$$

The derivatives in (4d) and (4e) can be used to give the saving function:

$$s_t = s(w_t + b^y_t, p_t, r_{t+1} + \tau_{t+1}, p_{t+1}, b^o_{t+1}) = \frac{\partial v/\partial r_{t+1}}{\partial v/\partial b^o_{t+1}}.$$

The capital stock used in period t depreciates completely in one period.[7] The capital stock in the next period comes from the production of the investment good in period t, i_t, less any possible export of the good, e_t^i, and plus any possible foreign capital inflow in period $t+1, f_{t+1}$ (f_{t+1} being negative for domestic capital outflow); that is,

$$k_{t+1} = i_t - e_t^i + f_{t+1}. \tag{5}$$

Denoting the export of the consumption good in period t by e_t^c, the equilibrium conditions for the commodity markets are

$$c_t^y + c_t^o + e_t^c = m_t \tag{6a}$$

$$s_t + e_t^i = i_t. \tag{6b}$$

In view of equations (5) and (6b), in equilibrium

$$k_{t+1} = s_t + f_{t+1}. \tag{5'}$$

For the time being, we assume that the government refrains from intervening, so that $b_t^y = b_{t+1}^o = \tau_{t+1} = 0$. With positive demand for each good, production is diversified. This implies that, locally, factor prices depend on the relative price of the consumption good but not on factor endowments. A steady state is defined as a state in which the growth of the capital stock is zero, that is $k_{t+1} = k_t$. Because the labour force is constant over time, because preferences are identical across generations, and because the technologies are stationary, in a steady state variables like prices are also stationary; for example, $p_{t+1} = p_t = p^a$ for all t.

The indirect utility function of a representative individual in any steady-state equilibrium, whether or not the economy is closed, reduces to

$$V(w, p, r, p) \equiv v(w + 0, p, r + 0, p, 0).$$

Using (2)–(4), the dependence of utility on relative price is given by

$$\frac{\mathrm{d}V}{\mathrm{d}p} = \lambda^y \left\{\frac{\mathrm{d}w}{\mathrm{d}p} - \frac{w}{p} + \frac{s}{r}\frac{\mathrm{d}r}{\mathrm{d}p}\right\}. \tag{7}$$

Because the GDP function is linearly homogeneous in commodity prices and also in factor endowments, $w = pD_{\ell p} + D_{\ell q}$, $r = pD_{kp} + D_{kq}$ and $i = D_{\ell q} + kD_{kq}$, where subindices of D represent partial derivatives. Substitute these relations into (7) and rearrange terms to give[8]

$$\frac{\mathrm{d}V}{\mathrm{d}p} = \frac{\lambda^y}{p}\left[\left(k - \frac{s}{r}\right)D_{kq} + (s - i)\right]. \tag{7'}$$

Because the consumption good is capital intensive, $D_{kq} < 0$.

Consider first a closed economy so that $e_t^c = e_t^i = f_t = 0$. In a steady state, $s = i = k$; hence (7′) reduces to

$$\frac{\mathrm{d}V^a}{\mathrm{d}p} = \frac{s\lambda^y}{p}\left(1 - \frac{1}{r}\right)D_{kq} \tag{7''}$$

where the superscript a denotes the autarkic value. The Golden Rule path is defined to be that steady-state path along which the utility of each individual is at a maximum. Let the corresponding relative price of the consumption good be p^*. The first-order condition for a Golden Rule path is that, at p^*, $\mathrm{d}V/\mathrm{d}p = 0$ or, by (7″), that $r = 1$. This rule implies that the interest rate, which is defined as $r - 1$, is equal to zero. (Note that in the present framework the rate of growth of population is zero.)

The above model is of interest only if the existence of equilibrium is guaranteed. There are two types of equilibrium, the temporary equilibrium of any period t and the steady-state equilibrium. Unfortunately, little is known about the existence of either type of equilibrium in a context of overlapping generations, production and physical capital.[9] However, it is shown in the appendix that at any date t, given $k_t > 0$, the present model possesses an equilibrium; and it is shown that there are interesting sufficient conditions under which a steady-state equilibrium exists. The appendix also analyzes the stability and uniqueness of equilibrium.

3 THE COMPENSATION SCHEME

In the examples constructed by Kemp and Long (1979), Binh (1985, 1986) and Serra (1991), to demonstrate that free trade may be Pareto-inferior to autarky, none of the individuals in the economy concerned is compensated when free trade prevails. This raises the question: can one find a feasible compensation scheme that leaves all individuals not worse off, with at least one individual better off, under free trade than under autarky?

Serra (1991) has studied the special case of a small country with the opportunity of trading at the given and constant world price ratio p^w, and has suggested a scheme of compensation for that case. However, this scheme has a serious weakness. It works if (i) $p^a > p^*$ and (ii) $p^w > p^*$ but not necessarily for other specifications of the economy. An example in which (i) and (ii) are not satisfied will be provided below.

We know that a competitive steady-state equilibrium need not be on a Golden Rule path. Suppose that there exists an autarkic steady state and that the steady-state price of the consumption good is slightly smaller than the Golden Rule price, that is $p^a < p^*$. Because the consumption good is capital intensive, the assumption that $p^a < p^*$ implies that the autarkic rental rate is less than unity, $r^a < 1$. Substituting the value of r^a into condition (7″), we get $\mathrm{d}V/\mathrm{d}p < 0$ in a sufficiently small region around the autarkic price.

Suppose now that, at the beginning of period $t = t'$, free trade is allowed with the rest of the world. The rest of the world is in a steady state, with the price of the consumption good equal to p^w. Suppose further that the economy is a small one, taking world prices as given, and that p^w is slightly smaller than the economy's autarkic price ratio, that is $p^w < p^a$. Because the economy is a price-taker, it will move to the new steady state with $p = p^w$ in one period.

To evaluate the welfare effects of free trade on this economy, we must examine the change in the steady-state utility of a representative individual, and that of a representative individual during the transitional period, that is period t'. First, let us look at the change in steady-state welfare. Because $\mathrm{d}V/\mathrm{d}p < 0$, a fall in the price of the consumption good under free trade will lower the steady-state utility level of a representative individual. This means that free trade hurts all individuals who are born during or after period t'. Moreover, free trade is detrimental to individuals who were born in period $t' - 1$ and who are old during the transitional period t'; for the income of the latter group comes entirely from the rental rate of capital, which falls under free trade.

In the above example, which shows that free trade may be Pareto-inferior to autarky, we have $p^a < p^*$ and $p^w < p^*$. Thus the two conditions needed for Serra's compensation scheme are violated and it remains an open question whether one can find other schemes which do not depend on these conditions.

In this section we describe a particular scheme of compensation and establish several preliminary propositions about the welfare effects of disturbances of the four types distinguished in section 1.

Suppose that the economy receives an unanticipated shock in period t'. The shock may be a shift from autarky to free trade, or acceptance as a member of a customs union, or, in the case of a small country, a change in its terms of trade or an increase in the number of its tradable goods (including capital services). We need to compare the pre- and post-shock welfares of all generations in period t' and beyond.

We shall say that, at and after t', the economy is in situation 2 if a shock occurs at t', otherwise in situation 1. The values taken by variables in situation 1 are distinguished by circumflexes. For example, $\hat{k}_t$ is the level of the capital stock in period t in situation 1 (when no shock has occurred). For convenience, we sometimes call situations 1 and 2 the initial and final situations, respectively. However, we must bear in mind that the two situations do not exist one after the other; instead, the final situation (situation 2) is the observed situation starting from period t' after the shock, while the initial situation (situation 1) is a hypothetical one that will prevail, also from period t', **if by then the shock has not occurred**. For simplicity, it is assumed that, in situation 1, government transfers and the saving subsidy are zero: $\hat{b}^y_t = \hat{b}^o_t = \hat{\tau}_t = 0$.

Recall that equation (5′) shows how the capital stock in period $t + 1$ depends on the saving of the previous period and on the foreign capital inflow of the same period. Let us define $\bar{f}_t$ so that

$$s_{t-1} + \bar{f}_t \equiv \hat{s}_{t-1} + \hat{f}_t = \hat{k}_t. \tag{8}$$

This is, $\bar{f}_t$ is the amount of foreign capital that, when added to savings, would ensure that the total capital stock is the same in situation 2 as in situation 1.

Let us define the production gain associated with the shock as

$$P_t \equiv p_t m_t + i_t - r_t \bar{f}_t - (p_t \hat{m}_t + \hat{i}_t - r_t \bar{f}_t). \tag{9}$$

If no international capital movement is allowed in either situation, $f_t = \bar{f}_t = 0$.

Let us also define the terms-of-trade gain associated with the shock as

$$Q_t \equiv p_t \hat{e}_t^c + \hat{e}_t^i - r_t \hat{f}_t. \tag{10}$$

In general, P_t and Q_t can be positive or negative. Sufficient conditions under which P_t is non-negative will be stated later.

Consider now a permanent transfer scheme and saving subsidy (b_t^y, τ_t, b_t^o) in the presence of the shock (situation 2), where the scheme may vary over time. The budget constraints of young and old individuals in period t are, respectively,

$$p_t c_t^y + s_t \leqslant w_t + b_t^y \tag{11a}$$

and

$$p_t c_t^o \leqslant (r_t + \tau_t) s_{t-1} + b_t^o. \tag{11b}$$

Individuals take the policy parameters and prices as given.

The transfers are chosen to be

$$b_t^y = p_t \hat{c}_t^y + \hat{s}_t - w_t + (P_t + Q_t)/2 \tag{12a}$$

$$b_t^o = p_t \hat{c}_t^o - r_t \hat{s}_{t-1} - \tau_t s_{t-1} + (P_t + Q_t)/2 \tag{12b}$$

with the two generations sharing the production and terms-of-trade gains equally. However, any form of sharing would suffice for our purposes.

Lemma 1. *The scheme of transfers (12) is feasible.*

Proof. *We need to show that the government budget balance is zero. Indeed, it is the case, for*

$$\begin{aligned} b_t^y + b_t^o + \tau_t s_{t-1} &= p_t(\hat{c}_t^y + \hat{c}_t^o) + \hat{s}_t - w_t - r_t \hat{s}_{t-1} - \tau_t s_{t-1} + P_t \\ &\quad + Q_t + \tau_t s_{t-1} \\ &= 0 \end{aligned}$$

where the equilibrium conditions (6) for situation 1, the definition of $\bar{f}_t$ in (8), the production gain in (9), the terms-of-trade gain in (10), equation (5′), *and the zero-profit condition are used.* □

Let us say that situation 2 weakly Pareto-dominates situation 1 if, under the above scheme of transfers, nobody is worse off in situation 2; and that situation 2 Pareto-dominates situation 1 if, under the same scheme of transfers, some individuals are better off, and none is worse off, in situation 2.

Lemma 2. *If the production gain and the terms-of-trade gain are non-negative then situation 2 weakly Pareto-dominates situation 1 under the compensation scheme described by*

(12). If, in addition, at least one of the gains is positive or consumption substitution takes place in at least one generation, then, under the compensation scheme (12), situation 2 Pareto-dominates situation 1.

Proof. *Substitute the transfers defined by (12) into the individual's budget constraints to give*

$$p_t c_t^y + s_t \leqslant p_t \hat{c}_t^y + \hat{s}_t + (P_t + Q_t)/2 \tag{13a}$$

$$p_t c_t^o \leqslant r_t s_{t-1} + p_t \hat{c}_t^o - r_t \hat{s}_{t-1} + (P_t + Q_t)/2. \tag{13b}$$

Although (13a) gives only one of the budget constraints for the young generation, it should be noted that similar schemes of compensation are available in future periods. Thus we may conclude that if $P_t \geqslant 0$ and $Q_t \geqslant 0$ then both generations can still afford their initial consumption and saving choices, and are not worse off. If P_t or Q_t is positive for some t, or if consumption substitution exists for some individuals, then situation 2 Pareto-dominates situation 1. □

It should be noted that the feasibility and benefits of the above compensation scheme exist for every period, and thus do not require the existence of a steady state. This implies that similar schemes can be applied to economies with heterogeneous preferences and non-stationary technologies, and to economies with technologies that are always productive so that $r > 1$, as long as an equilibrium (not necessarily a steady-state equilibrium) exists in each period.

Sufficient conditions under which $P_t \geqslant 0$ will be given below. In the meantime, we have the following propositions.

Proposition 1. *Given the scheme of lumpsum transfers described by (12), if $P_t \geqslant 0$ for all t then free trade weakly Pareto-dominates autarky; if in addition $P_t > 0$ for some t or if consumption substitution occurs for at least one individual then free trade Pareto-dominates autarky.*

Proof. *Since situation 1 is autarky, $\hat{e}_t^c = \hat{e}_t^i = \hat{f}_t = 0$; that is, the terms-of-trade gain is zero. The proposition then follows from lemmas 1 and 2.* □

Note that a zero terms-of-trade gain under free trade and a non-negative production gain as assumed in the proposition do not rule out the possibility that the competitive equilibrium of the economy is Pareto-suboptimal. This means that uncompensated free trade may still be Pareto-inferior to autarky. What proposition 1 shows is that if the production gain is non-negative, the government can find a feasible compensation scheme to make all individuals – those who will live out their lives under free trade and those who have spent their youth under autarky and their old age under free trade – at least as well off as under autarky.

Proposition 2. *For a small, open, free-trading economy, if $P_t \geqslant 0$ for all t and if there is an improvement in the terms of trade in the sense that $Q_t \geqslant 0$ for all t, with strict inequalities for some t, then, under the compensation scheme (12), situation 2 Pareto-dominates situation 1.*

Proof. *The proposition follows directly from lemmas 1 and 2.* □

Proposition 3. *Consider a small, open, free-trading economy able in situation 2 to trade in additional goods and/or capital. Given the scheme of lumpsum transfers described by (12), if $P_t \geqslant 0$ for all t, situation 2 weakly Pareto-dominates situation 1; if $P_t > 0$ for some t or if consumption substitution occurs for at least one individual then situation 2 Pareto-dominates situation 1.*

Proof. *Since the prevailing world prices are fixed, the terms-of-trade gain equals the trade balance of the economy in the initial situation and is thus zero. The proposition then follows from lemmas 1 and 2.* □

We now turn to the formation of a customs union. Let an initial world trading situation be constrained by any conceivable trade restrictions and transport costs. $J \geqslant 2$ countries, called member countries, agree to form a customs union. Member countries are indexed by j, $j = 1, \ldots, J$. Circumflexes are again used to denote values of variables in the initial situation with no customs union, while values in the final situation have no circumflexes. The following modifications of our earlier notation are needed.

1. A superscript j is added to distinguish the variables of country j. For example, c_t^{jy} is the demand of the young in country j for the consumption good in period t.
2. Variables without superscript j now represent the aggregate variables of the member countries; for example, $c_t^y = \Sigma_j c_t^{jy}$ and p_t is the common relative price of the consumption good in the member countries after the formation of the customs union.
3. Variables of (the rest of) the world are denoted by tildes; for example, $\tilde{p}_t$ is the world relative price of the consumption good.

Following Kemp and Wan (1976, 1986), we artificially freeze the volume of trade between member countries and non-member countries, and therefore world prices in the presence of the customs union. This assumption is for exposition only, for member countries will choose common tariffs to keep world prices and thus their volume of trade unchanged. This assumption implies that the world price $\tilde{p}_t$ and the volumes of trade $\hat{e}_t^c$ and $\hat{e}_t^i$ are fixed.

The production gain for the member countries is defined by (9), recalling that quantity variables such as m_t are now aggregates over member countries. In the presence of a common tariff on goods traded with non-member countries, the member countries receive in period t an aggregate tariff revenue of $T_t = -(p_t - \tilde{p}_t)\hat{e}_t^c$. Note that the import demand of non-member countries and the world price remain at their pre-union levels. Balanced trade means that $\tilde{p}_t\hat{e}_t^c + \hat{e}_t^i = 0$. This implies that the tariff revenue reduces to $T_t = -p_t\hat{e}_t^c - \hat{e}_t^i$.

Proposition 4. *Consider any competitive world trading equilibrium with no restrictions whatever on the tariffs and other commodity taxes of individual countries, or on transport* *costs. Now let any subset of the countries form a customs union. If the production gain defined by (9) is non-negative then there exists a common tariff vector and a system of lumpsum compensatory payments involving only members of the union such that each individual, whether a member of the union or not, is not worse off than before the formation of the union.*

Proof. *Let the young and old in country j in period t receive from their government the transfers*

$$b_t^{jy} = p_t\hat{c}_t^{jy} + \hat{s}_t^j - w_t^j + P_t/(2J) \tag{14a}$$

$$b_t^{jo} = p_t\hat{c}_t^{jo} - r_t\hat{s}_{t-1}^j - \tau_t s_{t-1}^j + P_t/(2J). \tag{14b}$$

Because the total number of individuals in the member countries in each period is 2J, conditions (14) mean that they share the production gains equally in period t.

These transfers are substituted into the individual's budget constraints (2). It is easy to see that, if the production gain is non-negative, the original consumption choice is still feasible for the individual in the new situation. Hence the individual is not worse off; in fact, the individual is better off if consumption and/or production substitution occurs.

We need to show that the above transfers are feasible for the governments of the member countries. This is indeed the case, because the sum of all transfers paid by the governments less the tariff revenue in period t is zero:

$$\begin{aligned} b_t^y + b_t^o - T_t &= \sum_j [p_t(\hat{c}_t^{jy} + \hat{c}_t^{jo}) + \hat{s}_t^j - w_t^j - r_t\hat{s}_{t-1}^j - \tau_t s_{t-1}^j + P_t] - p_t\hat{e}_t^c - \hat{e}_t^i \\ &= 0, \end{aligned}$$

where use has been made of the equilibrium conditions (6), condition (8), and the definition of P_t. □

4 GAINS FROM TRADE

It is clear from the analysis in the previous section that if the production gain is non-negative then, in the cases described in propositions 1 to 4, situation 2 (weakly) Pareto-dominates situation 1. This section describes several cases in which the production gain is non-negative.

4.1 International capital movement

Suppose that capital can flow freely across countries. Then, taking the labour endowment as given, firms will choose their outputs and capital owners will allocate their capital as if they are jointly maximizing the gross national product (GNP) function

$$\begin{aligned} N(p_t, q_t, r_t, s_{t-1}, \ell_t) &= \max_{m_t, i_t, f_t} \{p_t m_t + q_t i_t - r_t f_t\colon (m_t, i_t, s_{t-1} + f_t) \in \Phi\} \\ &= \max_{f_t} \{D(p_t, q_t, k_t, \ell_t) - r_t f_t\colon (m_t, i_t, s_{t-1} + f_t) \in \Phi\}. \end{aligned}$$

Recalling that $s_{t-1} + \bar{f}_t$ equals the initial capital stock, we see that $(\hat{m}_t, \hat{i}_t, s_{t-1} + \bar{f}_t)$ equals the initial production point, and is feasible. By the definition of the GNP function, therefore,

$$p_t m_t + i_t - r_t f_t \geqslant p_t \hat{m}_t + \hat{i}_t - r_t \bar{f}_t. \tag{15}$$

Expression (15) implies that $P_t \geqslant 0$ for all t.

Thus if capital is internationally mobile in the final situation, propositions 1–4 can be considerably sharpened.

Proposition 1′. *Given the scheme of lumpsum transfers described by (12), free trade weakly Pareto-dominates autarky; if $P_t > 0$ for some t or if consumption substitution occurs for at least one individual then free trade Pareto-dominates autarky.*

Proposition 2′. *For a small, open, free-trading economy, if free trade exists in both situations and if there is an improvement in the terms of trade in the sense that $Q_t \geqslant 0$ for all t, with some strict inequalities for some t, then situation 2 Pareto-dominates situation 1.*

Proposition 3′. *Consider a small, open, free-trading economy able in situation 2 to trade in additional goods and/or capital. Given the scheme of lumpsum transfers described by (12), situation 2 weakly Pareto-dominates situation 1; if $P_t > 0$ for some t or if consumption substitution occurs for at least one individual then situation 2 Pareto-dominates situation 1.*

Proposition 4′. *Consider any competitive world trading equilibrium with no restrictions whatever on the tariffs and other commodity taxes of individual countries and on transport costs. Now let any subset of the countries form a customs union. There exists a common tariff vector and a system of lumpsum compensatory payments involving only members of the union such that each individual, whether a member of the union or not, is not worse off than before the formation of the union.*

These propositions can be intuitively appreciated by reflecting that, if capital is internationally mobile, the economy can choose a final inflow such that the amount of capital available is not less than in the initial situation; and that the initial production point is therefore feasible in the final situation. In general, the economy can do better than the original production plan, for firms and owners of capital jointly and indirectly maximize the gross national production function. This ensures that the production gain is not negative.

If, on the other hand, capital is internationally immobile, domestic investors might so change their investment plans in the final situation that the production set would shrink and the production gain turn negative. For the remainder of this section, it will be assumed that capital is internationally immobile.

4.2 Public saving

Under this policy, the government supplements private saving in situation 2, $\{s_t\}$, with public saving, $\{g_t\}$, subject to the government's budget constraint and to the scheme of compensation (12). The purpose of the policy is to ensure that the production possibility set (PPS) in situation 1 is a subset of the production possibility set in situation 2. If that purpose is achieved, the production gain is non-negative for all t and, by a familiar argument, the scheme (12) leaves all individuals not worse off in situation 2 than in situation 1.

Turning to the detail of the policy,

$$g_t = \max\{\hat{s}_t - s_t, 0\} \quad \text{for all } t, \tag{16}$$

where, of course, $\hat{s}_t$ is the private saving by the young of period t in situation 1 and s_t is the private saving by the young of period t in situation 2. According to (16), the government saves if and only if private saving in situation 1 exceeds private saving in situation 2; and, if the government saves, it saves just enough to bring total saving up to the level of situation 1. If the government saves during period t, it will receive an income of $r_{t+1}g_t$ in the next period.

It must be shown that policy (16) is feasible. If no public saving is needed, feasibility is ensured by lemma 1. We therefore focus on the case in which the required public saving is positive during period t and/or period $t-1$.

Suppose that both g_t and g_{t-1} are positive. Making use of the budget constraint (13a),

$$g_t = \hat{s}_t - s_t = p_t c_t^y - p_t \hat{c}_t^y - (P_t + Q_t)/2. \tag{17a}$$

Similarly, from (13b),

$$-r_t g_{t-1} = -r_t(\hat{s}_{t-1} - s_{t-1}) = p_t c_t^o - p_t \hat{c}_t^o - (P_t + Q_t)/2. \tag{17b}$$

Combining (17) and (12), the latter with $\tau_t = 0$, we find that

$$\begin{aligned} b_t^y + b_t^o + g_t - r_t g_{t-1} &= p_t(c_t^y + c_t^o) + \hat{s}_t - w_t - r_t\hat{s}_{t-1} \\ &= p_t m_t - p_t e_t^c + \hat{s}_t - w_t - r_t\hat{s}_{t-1} \quad \text{[condition (6a)]} \\ &= p_t m_t + c_t^i + \hat{s}_t - w_t - r_t\hat{s}_{t-1} \quad \text{[trade balance]} \\ &= p_t m_t + i_t - w_t - r_t\hat{s}_{t-1} \quad \text{[condition (6b)]} \\ &= 0. \quad \text{[zero profit]} \end{aligned}$$

Thus the policy is feasible.

Suppose now that $g_t = 0$ while $g_{t-1} > 0$, so that $s_t \geqslant \hat{s}_t$. In view of (12) and (17b), the net expenditure of the government in period t is

$$\begin{aligned} b_t^y + b_t^o - r_t g_{t-1} = {} & p_t(\hat{c}_t^y + \hat{c}_t^o) + \hat{s}_t - w_t - r_t\hat{s}_{t-1} + (P_t + Q_t) \\ & - r_t(\hat{s}_{t-1} - s_{t-1}) + p_t c_t^o - p_t\hat{c}_t^o - (P_t + Q_t)/2 \end{aligned}$$

$$= p_t(\hat{c}_t^y + \hat{c}_t^o) - w_t - r_t\hat{s}_{t-1} + (P_t + Q_t) - r_t(\hat{s}_{t-1} - s_{t-1}) + p_t c_t^o - p_t\hat{c}_t^o$$
$$- (P_t + Q_t)/2 + s_t + p_t c_t^y - p_t\hat{c}_t^y - (P_t + Q_t)/2 \quad \text{[condition (13a)]}$$
$$= p_t(c_t^y + c_t^o) + s_t - w_t - r_t\hat{s}_{t-1}.$$

From this point the proof coincides with that of the preceding paragraph. The same argument can be applied to the case in which $g_t > 0$ and $g_{t-1} = 0$.

4.3 Saving subsidy

Suppose that the government relies not on public saving but on the stimulation of private saving by means of a subsidy, supported again by the scheme of compensation (12). Since both international capital movement and public saving are now ruled out, $f_t = g_t = 0$ and $k_t = s_{t-1}$.

We seek a rate of subsidy which ensures that the production gain is non-negative. Taking the policy parameters as given, the saving function of the individual born in period t is

$$s_t = s(w_t + b_t^y, p_t, r_{t+1} + \tau_{t+1}, p_{t+1}, b_{t+1}^o) = \frac{\partial v/\partial r_{t+1}}{\partial v/\partial b_{t+1}^o}.$$

where the derivatives of function v are given by (4). The required rate is then given implicitly by the condition

$$\hat{s}_t = s(w_t + b_t^y, p_t, r_{t+1} + \tau_{t+1}, p_{t+1}, b_{t+1}^o). \tag{18}$$

It is assumed that (18) can be solved for τ_{t+1}.

Since the technology and population are stationary, and since in each period the subsidized saving of situation 2 is equal to the saving of situation 1, the PPS of period t is the same in situation 2 as in situation 1. Profit maximization by firms and convexity of the PPS imply that the production gain is non-negative in each period. The gainfulness of the shocks then follows from propositions 1 to 4.

4.4 Commodity taxation

There is yet another policy by means of which the government can make everyone better off (or not worse off) as the economy shifts from situation 1 to situation 2. Suppose that the government imposes taxes on the consumption good, labour services and capital services. In particular, a specific tax of $(\hat{p}_t - p_t)$ is imposed on the purchase of the consumption good, $(w_t - \hat{w}_t)$ on labour services, and $(r_t - \hat{r}_t)$ on capital services. Recall that variables with circumflexes are those in situation 1, without the shock. Firms are facing world prices because there are no production taxes.

Consider any period t. Because consumers are facing the initial prices, they are willing to make the same consumption and saving choice: $(\hat{c}_t^y, \hat{s}_t)$ by the young generation and $(\hat{c}_t^o)$ by the old generation. Their budget constraints in that period are

$$\hat{p}_t\hat{c}_t^y + \hat{s}_t = \hat{w}_t \tag{19a}$$

$$\hat{p}_t\hat{c}_t^o = \hat{r}_t\hat{s}_{t-1}. \tag{19b}$$

Note that lumpsum transfers and a saving subsidy are not considered.

The firms employ the amounts of labour and capital services supplied by the consumers. Because the firms are facing the world price ratio p_t, they choose (m_t, i_t) to maximize the GDP function, even though the original outputs $(\hat{m}_t, \hat{i}_t)$ are still feasible. This implies that

$$p_tm_t + i_t \geqslant p_t\hat{m}_t + \hat{i}_t. \tag{20}$$

Lemma 4. *If $Q_t \geqslant 0$ for all t then the above commodity tax policy is feasible.*

Proof. *Tax revenue* $= (\hat{p}_t - p_t)(\hat{c}_t^y + \hat{c}_t^o) + (w_t - \hat{w}_t) + (r_t - \hat{r}_t)\hat{s}_{t-1}$

$$\begin{aligned}
&= -p_t(\hat{c}_t^y + \hat{c}_t^o) - \hat{s}_t + w_t + r_t\hat{s}_{t-1} \quad \textit{[by (19)]}\\
&= -p_t\hat{m}_t - \hat{i}^t + p_t\hat{e}_t^c + \hat{e}_t^i + w_t + r_t\hat{s}_{t-1} \quad \textit{[by (6)]}\\
&\geqslant -p_tm_t - i_t + p_t\hat{e}_t^c + \hat{e}_t^i + w_t + r_t\hat{s}_{t-1} \quad \textit{[by (20)]}\\
&= p_t\hat{e}_t^c + \hat{e}_t^i \quad \textit{[zero-profit condition]}\\
&= Q_t.
\end{aligned}$$

Thus if $Q_t \geqslant 0$ then the tax revenue is non-negative. □

We have shown that under the conditions described in propositions 1′ to 4′, $Q_t \geqslant 0$. Thus every individual can be made at least as well off as before.

5 ANTICIPATED SHOCKS

In the previous sections, we assumed that the shocks are unexpected. Thus individuals and firms make new decisions about consumption and production after the shocks occur. There are, however, cases in which the occurrence of a shock is anticipated. For example, the government may make a credible announcement concerning the future opening of free trade or the future formation of a customs union with other countries. Let us assume that individuals know in period t'' that one of the shocks analyzed above will occur with certainty in period t', $t' < \infty$, $t'' \leqslant t'$.[10]

Since prices in any period depend on future prices, the anticipation of the shock will change the prices in periods from t'' to t'. As a result, without compensation some generations may be hurt. If compensation is allowed then, under the conditions examined in the previous sections, all generations, including those occupying the transitional periods before the shock occurs, will be made not worse off, or better off when consumption substitution or production substitution is present, or when the terms-of-trade gain is positive.

6 MONETARY ECONOMIES

To this point we have focused on non-monetary or barter economies. Let us now extend our model to accommodate a constant stock of fiat money in each country so that, if the equilibrium price of money is positive, individuals may hold their wealth either as money or as productive capital.

Let us suppose for the time being that residents of country k can hold the money of country k only, and let the disturbance be the replacement of autarky by free trade. Before the opening of trade there may or may not exist a monetary equilibrium, with the price of money in terms of the investment good always positive; see, for example, Bose and Ray (1992). Similarly, after the opening of trade there may or may not exist a monetary equilibrium in any particular country. If after the opening of trade there is a monetary equilibrium in **no** country, our earlier analysis applies in its entirety. The interesting case is that in which, after the opening of trade, there is a monetary equilibrium in some (possibly all) countries. Then the detail of our analysis changes. In particular, each young individual must choose not only the level of his or her savings but the form in which to hold his or her wealth; and the money market in each country, as well as the two world commodity markets, must clear. Nevertheless, all of our earlier conclusions remain intact.[11]

The same is true even when residents of one country can hold the money of other countries. However, in that case, either there is a monetary equilibrium in every country or there is a monetary equilibrium in **no** country.

7 CONCLUDING REMARKS

It is well known that competitive equilibria in models with overlapping generations are generally not Pareto-efficient. For the type of economies considered, however, we have shown that, when free trade and free international capital movement are allowed, there always exists a feasible lumpsum transfer scheme which enables every individual to attain a utility level at least as high as in autarky. If international capital movement does not exist, the government can still use either public saving or a saving subsidy to supplement lumpsum transfers. Finally, given non-negative terms-of-trade gains, suitable commodity taxes will induce the economy to replicate the autarkic consumption choice and thus maintain autarkic welfare.

Throughout the essay we assume that technologies are stationary, that preferences are the same within and across generations, that the population is constant, and that the consumption good is capital intensive. These assumptions can be relaxed without affecting the validity of the propositions for, as mentioned in section 3, the feasibility and benefits of the compensation schemes do not depend on the existence of a steady state.

APPENDIX

This appendix analyzes the existence, stability and uniqueness of equilibrium in the above framework. For simplicity, we consider only a competitive equilibrium for a closed economy with no government intervention. A world with trading countries with or without the policies considered above can be analyzed in the same way.

There are two levels of equilibrium, the equilibrium in any period t and the steady-state equilibrium. Consider the equilibrium in period t, given $k_t > 0$. The equilibrium condition for a closed economy in that period is

$$s(w_t, p_t, r_{t+1}/p_{t+1}) = i(p_t, k_t), \tag{A1}$$

where, for simplicity, all policy parameters are dropped from the saving function. Choose any arbitrary value of $p_{t+1} \in (0, \infty)$. As shown later, an equilibrium in period t implies diversification in production. Therefore there is no harm in assuming that both goods are produced in period $t + 1$, so that p_{t+1} determines r_{t+1}. Define $\bar{p}_t$ and $\underline{p}_t$ so that $\bar{p}_t > \underline{p}_t \geqslant 0$ and that for all p_t, $\underline{p}_t < p_t < \bar{p}_t$, the economy is diversified in production.

For $p_t \leqslant \underline{p}_t$, the economy is completely specialized in the production of the investment good. The wage rate w_t is less than the value of output i_t. By the budget constraint of a representative individual, $s_t \leqslant w_t$, implying that $s_t < i_t$. When $p_t \geqslant \bar{p}_t$, the economy is completely specialized in the production of the consumption good, that is $i_t = 0$. When the wage rate remains positive, the individual gets a positive income. Therefore when p_t is sufficiently high, that is the consumption good is sufficiently expensive, the individual will have positive saving, $s_t > 0 = i_t$. By strict convexity and continuity of technologies and preferences, function s_t is continuous in p_t, as long as the economy is diversified. Thus, there exists some p_t' so that $\underline{p}_t < p_t' < \bar{p}_t$ and (A1) is satisfied. The equilibrium is shown in Figure 1 for the case in which $\underline{p}_t = 0$ and $\bar{p}_t \to \infty$. The equilibrium is at point E.

To check the Walrasian stability of the equilibrium p_t when p_{t+1} is given, we assume that p_t moves in response to excess demand for the consumption good. Alternatively, by Walras' law, we assume that the rate of change of price, denoted by $\dot{p}_t$, is an increasing function of the excess supply of the investment good, that is $\dot{p}_t = f(i_t - s_t)$, where $f' > 0$. For stability, we require that

$$\frac{d\dot{p}_t}{dp_t} = f' \left(\frac{\partial i_t}{\partial p_t} - \frac{\partial s_t}{\partial w_t}\frac{\partial w_t}{\partial p_t} - \frac{\partial s_t}{\partial p_t} \right) < 0. \tag{A2}$$

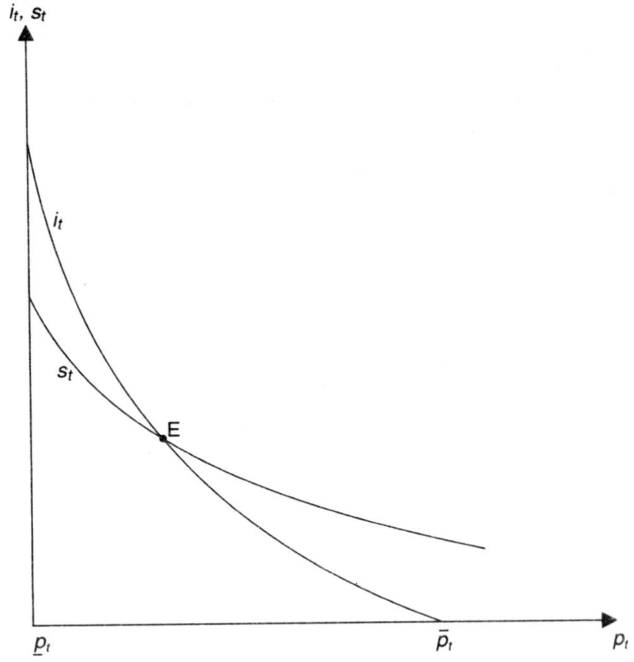

Figure 1

In terms of Figure 1, condition (A2) means that the saving schedule cuts the investment schedule from below. With strictly convex technologies, $\partial i_t/\partial p_t < 0$. Therefore a sufficient condition for stability is that

$$\frac{\partial s_t}{\partial w_t}\frac{\partial w_t}{\partial p_t}+\frac{\partial s_t}{\partial p_t}>0 \tag{A3}$$

at the equilibrium point.

If condition (A3) holds globally then the saving schedule in Figure 1 is downward sloping. By the above analysis, the equilibrium is stable and unique.

Assuming invertibility of the functions, condition (A1) can be stated in either of the following ways:

$$p_t = B_t(p_{t+1}) \tag{A4}$$

$$p_{t+1} = F_{t+1}(p_t). \tag{A5}$$

In (A4), function B_t defines the dependence of p_t on p_{t+1}, while in (A5), function F_{t+1} defines the dependence of p_{t+1} on p_t. Similar analysis can be extended to other periods. Note that the number of prices to be determined is greater than the number of conditions by one. An additional condition is provided if, for example, the price in any one period is given exogenously, or if a steady state exists and the economy is converging to the steady state, or if the last period is known and provides one more condition. In any of these cases, the entire adjustment path of p_t can be derived.

Next we turn to a steady-state equilibrium in which all prices and the capital stock in the economy remain stationary; for example, $p_t = p_{t+1} = p$ and $k_t = k_{t+1} = k$. The conditions of equilibrium are

$$s(w, p, r/p) = i(p, k) \tag{A6}$$

$$k = i(p, k). \tag{A7}$$

We need to find (p, k) at which (A6) and (A7) are simultaneously satisfied. Consider first condition (A7). In Figure 2, schedule ORQ shows the relationship between the output of the investment good i and capital stock k. On line OP condition (A7) is satisfied. Given the diminishing marginal productivity of capital, a necessary condition for (A7) is that the marginal product of capital (i.e. the slope of ORP) when k is sufficiently small is greater than unity.

Schedule ORQ cuts line OP at point P. Given the above necessary condition and the diminishing marginal productivity of capital, the point of intersection

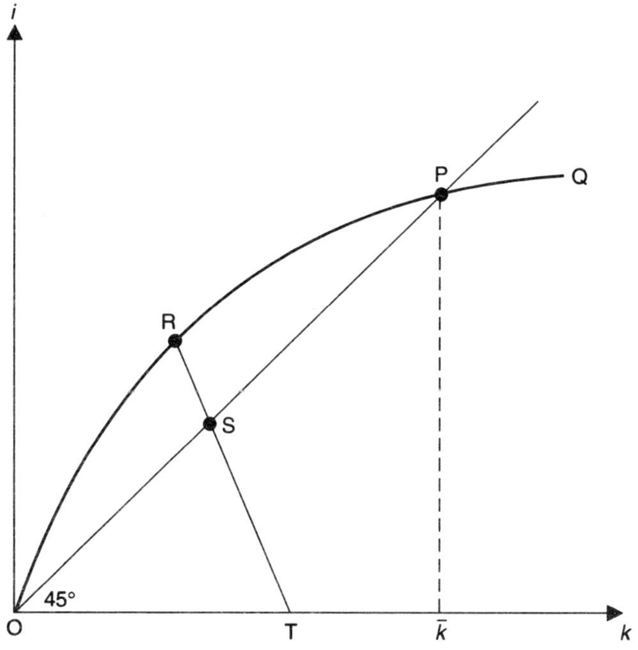

Figure 2

between ORQ and OP is unique. Thus the corresponding capital stock $\bar{k}$ is the critical capital stock beyond which condition (A7) cannot be satisfied.

Line RST is the Rybczynski line which shows the changes in output i under constant prices when k increases and when both goods are produced. Assuming that the investment good is labour intensive, RST is negatively sloped.[12] An increase in p will shift line RST down so that at any given level of k a smaller output of the investment good is produced at a higher level of p.

Point S on the 45° line OP in the figure shows the value of k at which $i = k$ under the given p. The point also shows diversification in production. Therefore points O and P define two critical values of p which satisfy condition (A7) and diversification. For example, $\underline{p}$ is the price corresponding to the Rybczynski line passing through point P (not shown).[13] The Rybczynski line corresponding to prices $p \geqslant \bar{p}$ degenerates to the origin, point O. When $p < \underline{p}$, condition (A7) cannot be satisfied, and when $p \geqslant \bar{p}$, no investment good is produced.

When $\underline{p} \leqslant p \leqslant \bar{p}$, there exists one and only one k, $0 \leqslant k \leqslant \bar{k}$, so that (A7) is satisfied. Inverting $i(p, k)$ with respect to k in (A7) gives

$$k = i(p, k) = I(p). \tag{A8}$$

Function $I(p)$ is shown in Figure 3. Given convex technologies, $I(p)$ is a decreasing function.

We now focus on condition (A6). Note that if the economy is diversified, factor prices are functions of p but not of factor endowments. Thus we can define $S(p) \equiv s[w(p), p, r(p)/p]$ and replace (A6) with

$$S(p) = I(p). \tag{A6$'$}$$

Suppose that p is greater than but sufficiently close to $\underline{p}$. By Figure 2, the economy is nearly completely specialized in the production of the investment good with (A7) satisfied. The wage rate is less than the output of the investment good, $w < I(\underline{p})$. By the budget constraint of an individual, $s \leqslant w$, implying that $S(\underline{p}) < (I(\underline{p})$.

Proposition A1. *Each of the following conditions is sufficient for the existence of a steady state with diversification in the present model.*

(a) *There exists a price p', $\underline{p} < p' < \bar{p}$, such that $S(p') > I(p')$.*
(b) *Labour alone can produce a positive amount of the consumption good and when $\underline{p} < p < \bar{p}$ the consumption good is desirable both to the young and the old, in the sense that, when income is positive, an individual will demand a positive amount of the good, whether he or she is young or old.*
(c) *Both the utility function of a representative individual and the production function for the investment good are of the Cobb–Douglas type.*

Proof. *(a) By continuity and strict convexity (quasi-convexity) of technologies and preferences, both $S(p)$ and $I(p)$ are continuous. Since $S(\underline{p}) < I(\underline{p})$, the given condition implies that there*

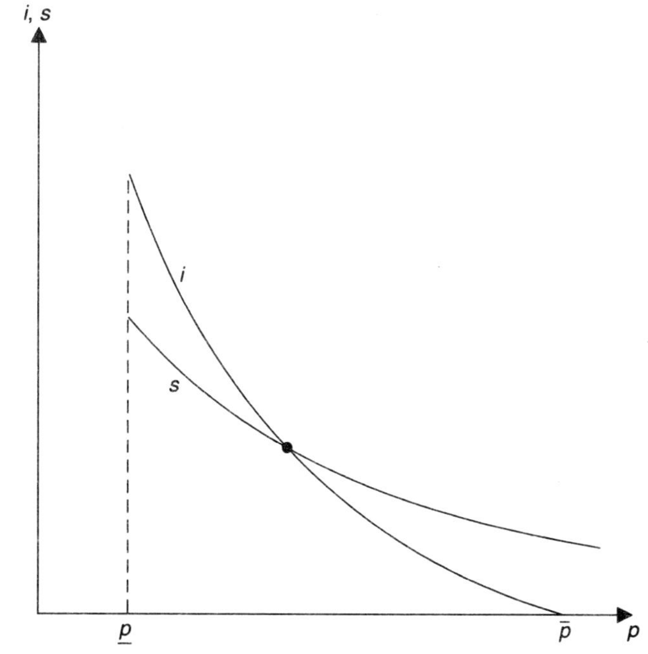

Figure 3

exists at least one p so that $S(p) = I(p)$. *For (b), suppose that p is smaller than but close to* $\bar{p}$, *that is* $k = I(p)$ *is small and is approaching zero. Since labour is productive even without capital, the output of the consumption good is positive, giving a positive income to the individual. By the desirability assumption, saving is positive, that is* $S(p) > I(p) = 0$. *By result (a), a steady state exists.*

For (c), denote by $1 > \alpha > 0$ *the constant share of income spent on consumption when an individual is old, by* $1 > \beta > 0$ *the constant share of labour in the investment sector, and by* $0 \leqslant \theta \leqslant 1$ *the proportion of labour working in the investment sector. The two budget constraints of an individual can be combined to give*

$$pc^y + \frac{p}{r} c^o \leqslant w.$$

Using the properties of a Cobb–Douglas function, we have

$$\alpha = \frac{pc^o/r}{w}. \qquad \text{(A9)}$$

Since $s = pc^o/r$, *(A9) gives*

$$s = \alpha w. \qquad \text{(A10)}$$

Because the investment sector has a Cobb–Douglas production function, $\beta = w\theta/i$, *where* i *is the output of the investment good satisfying condition (A7). Thus*

$$i = \frac{w\theta}{\beta}. \tag{A11}$$

By (A10) and (A11),

$$s \gtreqless i \text{ if } \alpha\beta \gtreqless \theta.$$

Thus when p *is greater than but close to* $\underline{p}$, θ *is close to unity and* $s < i$. *When* p *is smaller than but close to* $\bar{p}$, θ *is close to zero and* $s > i$. *There exists one* θ *so that* $\alpha\beta = \theta$ *and* $s = i$. □

Proposition A2. *If (i) both the utility function of a representative individual and the production function of the investment good are of the Cobb–Douglas type and (ii) the production function of the consumption good is convex, the steady-state equilibrium is unique.*

Proof. *In the proof of proposition A1, we show that, if condition (i) holds, there is only one value of* θ *and thus one value of* i *and* k *for a steady state. A Cobb–Douglas production function of the investment good is strictly convex; if, in addition, the consumption-good production function is convex then there is only one price* p *corresponding to the steady-state output of the investment good. Hence the equilibrium is unique.* □

NOTES

* We acknowledge with gratitude the helpful comments of Henry Y. Wan, Jr.

1 Wong (1983), using a special model, observed that for a small open economy free trade in goods and free movement of either capital or labour are better than just free trade in goods or just free movement of that factor. Grossman (1984), as far as we know, is the first one to generalize this result using a social utility function. Wong (1991) showed that the proposition is also valid for a many-household, small open economy, provided that either lumpsum transfers or commodity taxation can be used.

2 Fairly recently, these propositions have been extended to barter and monetary economies with possibly incomplete markets (Kemp and Wong, 1991a, b).

3 Samuelson (1958). See Geanakoplos (1987) for a more recent survey.

4 The function is called gross domestic product instead of gross national product because later we will allow international capital movement. If no international capital movement exists, gross domestic product is equivalent to gross national product.

5 In fact the validity of the propositions in this essay does not depend on the factor intensities of sectors or require the assumptions of constant population and steady technologies.

6 If the transfer in period $t+1$ is zero ($b^o_{t+1} = 0$) and if satiation is ruled out, saving is positive. Saving may be zero if b^o_{t+1} is sufficiently large. However, in the interesting cases studied below, b^o_{t+1} will not be chosen to be so large that saving is zero.

7 We make the simplifying assumption that a capital stock depreciates completely in one period because we want to avoid the need to analyze what each individual has to do with his or her capital before he or she dies.

8 Because $D_{\ell p} \equiv dw/dp$ and $w = pD_{\ell p} + D_{\ell q}$, we have $dw/dp - w/p = -D_{\ell q}/p$. Because $D_{kp} \equiv dr/dp$ and $r = pD_{kp} + D_{kq}$, we have $dr/dp = (r - D_{kq})/p$. Substitute these results into (7). Since $k = i = D_{\ell q} + kD_{kq}$, equation (7′) then follows.

9 Serra (1991: 31) suggested that, whatever the factor-intensity ranking of the sectors, a sufficient condition for the existence of a steady-state equilibrium is that

$$\lim_{p \to 0} S(p)/I(p) = 1 + \varepsilon \qquad (*)$$

where $S(p) \equiv s[w(p), p, r(p)/p]$, $k = i(p, k) = I(p)$ and ε is a positive number. Unfortunately, condition $(*)$ is not generally satisfied. When p is sufficiently small, the economy is completely specialized in the production of the investment good. The wage rate in terms of the investment good, which equals the wage bill, is not greater than the output, $w \leqslant I(p)$, and by the budget constraint of an individual, $S(p) \leqslant w$. Thus $S(p) \leqslant I(p)$, or $\lim_{p \to 0} S(p)/I(p) \leqslant 1$.

10 The case in which the perceived probability of the occurrence of the shock is less than unity but positive can be analyzed in the same way. If t' approaches zero, the impacts of the shock during the current and near-future periods approach zero.

11 A list of the principal equations which must be satisfied in a monetary equilibrium may be obtained from either author.

It may be noted that, in a closed-economy monetary equilibrium, money and productive capital must yield the same rate of return. This condition has the implication that in a steady state, with the price of money constant, the economy must be on the Golden Rule path, with $r = 1$. Similarly, in any world steady state each economy in monetary equilibrium must satisfy the Golden Rule.

12 If the investment good is capital intensive, line RST is positively sloped.

13 If ORQ cuts the 45° line at infinity, $\underline{p}$ is equal to 0.

REFERENCES

Binh, T. N. (1985) 'A neo-Ricardian model with overlapping generations', *Economic Record* 61: 707–18.

Binh, T. N. (1986) 'Welfare implications of international trade without compensation', University of New South Wales.

Bose, A. and Ray, D. (1992) 'Monetary equilibrium in an overlapping generations model with productive capital', mimeo.

Dixit, A. and Norman, V. (1980) *Theory of International Trade*, Cambridge: Cambridge University Press.

Geanakoplos, J. (1987) 'Overlapping generations models of general equilibrium', in J. Eatwell, M. Milgate and P. Newman (eds) *The New Palgrave: A Dictionary of Economics*, New York: W. W. Norton. Also in J. Eatwell, M. Milgate and P. Newman (eds) (1989) *General Equilibrium*, pp. 205–33, New York: W. W. Norton.

Grandmont, J. M. and McFadden, D. (1972) 'A technical note on classical gains from trade', *Journal of International Economics* 2: 109–25.

Grossman, G. M. (1984) 'The gains from international factor movements', *Journal of International Economics* 17: 73–83.

Kemp, M. C. (1962) 'The gains from international trade', *Economic Journal* 72: 803–19.

Kemp, M. C. (1964) *The Pure Theory of International Trade*, New York: Prentice Hall.

Kemp, M. C. and Long, N. V. (1979) 'The under-exploitation of natural resources: A model with overlapping generations', *Economic Record* 55: 214–21.

Kemp, M. C. and Ohyama, M. (1978) 'The gain from trade under conditions of uncertainty', *Journal of International Economics* 8: 139–41.

Kemp, M. C. and Wan, H. Y. Jr (1972) 'The gains from free trade', *International Economic Review* 13: 509–22.

Kemp, M. C. and Wan, H. Y. Jr (1976) 'An elementary proposition concerning the formation of customs unions', *Journal of International Economics* 6: 95–7.

Kemp, M. C. and Wan, H. Y. Jr (1986) 'The comparison of second-best equilibria: The case of customs unions', in D. Bös and C. Seidl (eds) *Welfare Economics of the Second Best*, Suppl. 5 of *Zeitschrift für Nationalökonomie* 161–7, Vienna: Springer-Verlag.

Kemp, M. C. and Wong, K.-Y. (1991a) 'Gains from trade with possibly incomplete markets', mimeo.

Kemp, M. C. and Wong, K.-Y. (1991b) 'Gains from trade for a monetary economy with possibly incomplete markets', mimeo.

Krueger, A. O. and Sonnenschein, H. (1967) 'The terms of trade, the gains from trade and price divergence', *International Economic Review* 8: 121–7.

Ohyama, M. (1972) 'Trade and welfare in general equilibrium', *Keio Economic Studies* 9: 37–73.

Samuelson, P. A. (1958) 'An exact consumption loan model of interest, with or without the social contrivance of money', *Journal of Political Economy* 66: 467–82.

Samuelson, P. A. (1962) 'The gains from trade once again', *Economic Journal* 72: 820–9.

Serra, P. (1991) 'Short-run and long-run welfare implications of free trade', *Canadian Journal of Economics* 24: 21–33.

Vanek, J. (1965) *General Equilibrium of International Discrimination*, Cambridge, MA.: Harvard University Press.

Wong, K.-Y. (1983) 'On choosing among trade in goods and international capital and labor mobility: A theoretical analysis', *Journal of International Economics* 14: 223–50.

Wong, K.-Y. (1991) 'Welfare comparison of trade situations', *Journal of International Economics* 30: 49–68.

10

THE GAINS FROM INTERNATIONAL TRADE IN A CONTEXT OF OVERLAPPING GENERATIONS*

1 INTRODUCTION

The welfare economics of international trade contains two core propositions of global scope:

1 For any economy, large or small, free trade is better than no trade (Samuelson, 1962; Kemp, 1962; Grandmont and McFadden, 1972; Kemp and Wan, 1972; Kemp and Ohyama, 1978).
2 Any subset of trading countries can form a mutually advantageous customs union without harming any excluded country (Kemp, 1964; Vanek, 1965; Ohyama, 1972; Kemp and Wan, 1976, 1986a).

These propositions are known to be valid for finite world economies, that is for economies with finite numbers of households and (dated) commodities. Whether they survive the recognition that economies go on for ever, with populations composed of overlapping generations of mortal individuals, is a relatively novel question. It seems to have simply been taken for granted that, in essentials, the propositions carry over to a world of overlapping generations.

However, popular models of economies with overlapping generations are characterized by Pareto-suboptimal competitive equilibria;[1] and it is well known that, for economies with distortions, free trade may be worse than no trade. Moreover, we now have several examples of competitive economies with overlapping generations for which, in the absence of government-sponsored compensatory schemes, autarky is Pareto-preferred to free trade; see Kemp and Long (1979: Section IV), Binh (1985, 1986) and Serra (1991). These examples raise questions about the robustness of each of the two core welfare propositions listed above.

The purpose of this essay is to show that, for a class of economies with overlapping generations, and for a class of disturbances which includes the substitution of free trade for autarky and the formation of a customs union, there can always be found a scheme of lumpsum transfers which is effective in compensating those who otherwise would have been harmed by the disturbance. In particular, it is shown that, although in the absence of compensation free trade may be inferior to autarky, nevertheless there always exists feasible lumpsum compensation which ensures that free trade is beneficial in the sense of Pareto. Thus our essay may serve to stifle the pessimism about the benefits of free trade created by the earlier work of Kemp and Long, Binh and Serra.

The essay is organized in the following way. In section 2 there is set out a model of an open economy with overlapping generations. It will sometimes be referred to as the OLG economy. Section 3, supported by a technical appendix, contains careful statements, and proofs, of our principal propositions. Those proofs rest on the assumption that all goods are perishable within one period of time so that, in particular, only circulating capital is recognized. However, in section 4, it is argued that the proofs can be extended to accommodate goods that last for any finite number of periods. The final section relates our paper to that of Kemp and Wong (1993), which deals with the same topic; and it indicates one possible path for future exploration.

2 A MODEL OF AN OLG ECONOMY

There are two countries, the 'home' and the 'foreign'. However, for the time being we focus on the home country.

2.1 The home country

Time is discrete. In every period of time $t \in \mathbf{N}$, where $\mathbf{N}$ is the set of all positive integers, there is a constant finite number $N \geq 2$ of completely perishable goods. These are bought and sold in spot markets in each period. The price of good n in period t is denoted by p_n^t; and the vector of goods prices in period t is denoted by $p^t \in \mathbf{R}_+^N$. The set of all possible price sequences is then $\mathbf{P} = \{p: p = (p^1, p^2, \ldots) \in \times_{t=1}^{\infty} \mathbf{R}_+^N\}$.

At the beginning of any period $t \in \mathbf{N}$, a generation of finitely many households H_t appears; let us define $\mathbf{H}_t = \{1, \ldots, H_t\}$. Each member of each generation lives for two periods. In addition, therefore, there is a single generation $\mathbf{H}_0$ that survives into period 1. Thus the set of all households is $\mathbf{H} = \cup_{t \in \mathbf{N}_0} \mathbf{H}_t$ where $\mathbf{N}_0$ is the set of non-negative integers. Sometimes reference will be made to the subset $\mathbf{H}_{\leq T} = \cup_{t=0}^{t=T} \mathbf{H}_t$, where $T \in \mathbf{N}$.

Household h chooses its lifetime consumption vector x_h from its consumption set $\mathbf{X}_h$, which is simply the non-negative orthant of the relevant finite-dimensional Euclidean space. Specifically,

$$x_h = (x_h^t, x_h^{t+1}) \in \mathbf{X}_h = \mathbf{R}_+^{2N} \quad \text{for } h \in \mathbf{H} \backslash \mathbf{H}_0$$

$$x_h = x_h^t \in \mathbf{X}_h = \mathbf{R}_+^N \quad \text{for } h \in \mathbf{H}_0$$

where the superscripts refer to the time period in which consumption takes place. Whenever it is convenient, we also denote by x_h the sequence

$(0, \ldots, x_h, 0, \ldots)$. Throughout the essay, and without further mention, this convention will be applied to other symbols too. The preferences of household h are represented by a complete, transitive and reflexive binary relation $\succcurlyeq_h$ on $\mathbf{X}_h$.

Each generation $t \in \mathbf{N}$ establishes a finite set of firms $\mathbf{F}_t$. The set $\mathbf{F}_t$ is taken as given, as is the ownership of firms. Each firm survives for two periods. In addition, during period 1 there is a set $\mathbf{F}_0$ of all firms owned by the members of $\mathbf{H}_0$. The set of all firms is $\mathbf{F} = \cup_{t \in \mathbf{N}_0} \mathbf{F}_t$. Sometimes reference will be made to the subset $\mathbf{F}_{\leqslant T} = \cup_{t=0}^{t=T} \mathbf{F}_t$. Firm $f \in \mathbf{F}$ chooses a profit-maximizing point y_f in its production possibility set $\mathbf{Y}_f$. In particular,

$$y_f = (y_f^t, y_f^{t+1}) \in \mathbf{Y}_f \subset \mathbf{R}^{2N} \quad \text{for } f \in \mathbf{F} \backslash \mathbf{F}_0$$

$$y_f = y_f^1 \in \mathbf{Y}_f \subset \mathbf{R}^N \quad \text{for } f \in \mathbf{F}_0.$$

The social production possibility set is $\mathbf{Y} = \Sigma_{f \in \mathbf{F}} \mathbf{Y}_f$.

Household $h \in \mathbf{H}_t$ is endowed with a vector of resources $e_h = (e_h^t, e_h^{t+1}) \in \mathbf{X}_h$. Included in e_h may be labour of several types. Any profits made by firms $f \in \mathbf{F}_t$ are completely distributed among the households $h \in \mathbf{H}_t$ according to the given shares $\theta_{hf} \geqslant 0$ $(\Sigma_{h \in \mathbf{H}_t} \theta_{hf} = 1)$. Given prices p and the profit-maximizing production plans $(y_f)_{f \in \mathbf{F}}$, the wealth of household h is

$$w_h(p) = p \cdot e_h + \textstyle\sum_{f \in \mathbf{F}} \theta_{hf} p \cdot y_f. \tag{1}$$

This provides an upper bound for the household's expenditure on consumption. Thus the household's budget set is

$$B_h(p) = \{x \in \mathbf{X}_h : p \cdot x_h \leqslant w_h(p)\}. \tag{2}$$

The aggregate resource vector of period t is $e^t = \Sigma_{h \in H_{t-1} \cup \mathbf{H}_t} e_h^t$; similarly $x^t = \Sigma_{h \in H_{t-1} \cup \mathbf{H}_t} x_h^t$ and $y^t = \Sigma_{f \in F_{t-1} \cup F_t} y_f^t$ denote the aggregate consumption and production vectors of period t. Resources aggregated to period T are denoted by $e_{\leqslant T} = \Sigma_{h \in H_{\leqslant T}} e_h$. This notation is extended to other quantities in an obvious way.

Assumption H. *The preferences of each household are continuous and convex. There is no satiation.*

Assumption F. *The production possibility sets of firms are closed and convex and include the origin. Free production is impossible* $(\mathbf{Y} \cap \mathbf{R}_+^\infty \subset \{0\})$.

Assumption S. *For each household h, $e_h > 0$.*[2]

Assumption I. *For every $T \in \mathbf{N}$, there is $\bar{y} \in \mathbf{Y}_{\leqslant T}$: $e_{\leqslant T} + \bar{y} \gg 0$.*

Assumption I requires that the resources and technologies of the subeconomies with time horizon T permit the supply of a positive amount of each good.

Definition (feasible allocation). *A feasible allocation is a pair of sequences* $(x, y) = ((x_h)_{h \in \mathbf{H}}, (y_f)_{f \in \mathbf{F}})$ *such that* $x_h \in \mathbf{X}_h$ *for all h,* $y_f \in \mathbf{Y}_f$ *for all f and* $x^t = y^t + e^t$ *for all t.*

Definition (competitive equilibrium). *A competitive equilibrium is a feasible allocation* $(x^*, y^*) = ((x^*_h)_{h \in \mathbf{H}}, (y^*_f)_{f \in \mathbf{F}})$ *and a non-zero price sequence* $p^* \in \mathbf{P}$ *such that, for all h and f,*

(a) $p^* y^*_f \geqslant p^* y_f$ *for all* $y_f \in \mathbf{Y}_f$.
(b) x^*_h *is a greatest element of* $B_h(p^*)$ *for* $\succcurlyeq_h$.

It should be noted that competitive equilibrium as defined is compatible with intra-generational borrowing and lending. Intergenerational borrowing and lending are, of course, ruled out by the assumption of two-period life expectancy.

Definition (irreducibility). *The economy is said to be irreducible if and only if for any feasible allocation* (x, y) *and for any non-trivial partition of households* $\mathbf{H}^1$, $\mathbf{H}^2$ *there is a* $\bar{t} \in \mathbf{N}$ *and an* $\bar{h} \in \mathbf{H}_{\bar{t}} \cap \mathbf{H}^1$ *such that*

$$x'_{\bar{h}} \succ_{\bar{h}} x_{\bar{h}}$$

where

$$x'_{\bar{h}} = x_{\bar{h}} + \sum_{\mathbf{H}^2 \cap \mathbf{H}_{\bar{t}-1}} e^{\bar{t}}_h + \sum_{\mathbf{H}^2 \cap \mathbf{H}_{\bar{t}}} e_h + \sum_{\mathbf{H}^2 \cap \mathbf{H}_{\bar{t}+1}} e^{\bar{t}+1}_h .$$

McKenzie (1959) developed the concept of an irreducible economy to ensure that every household has positive wealth in equilibrium: 'In loose firms, an economy is irreducible if it cannot be divided into two groups of consumers where one group is unable to supply any goods which the other group wants.' The present definition is an adaptation of McKenzie's to accommodate overlapping generations. It is similar to the definition introduced by Geanakoplos and Polemarchakis (1991) in their study of abstract exchange economies.

We can now state our basic existence theorem.

Theorem 1. *If the economy is irreducible and if assumptions* **H, F, S** *and* **I** *are satisfied then there exists a competitive equilibrium.*

Proofs of theorem 1 and other propositions may be found in the appendix.

2.2 The world economy

We now add the foreign country and, with it, the possibility of international trade and investment. Foreign magnitudes will be indicated by a tilde. Not all commodities need be internationally tradable. Thus we continue to assume that there are N commodities in each period but now suppose that only the first

$N^1 \geqslant 0$ are tradable while the next $N^2 \geqslant 0$ are non-tradables associated with the home country and the last $N^3 = N - N^1 - N^2 \geqslant 0$ are non-tradables associated with the foreign country. The quantity and price vectors of each country may be partitioned accordingly, with the convention that in each country the prices of non-tradables associated with the other country are equated to infinity. Thus

$$p = (p^{\mathrm{I}}, p^{\mathrm{II}}, p^{\mathrm{III}})$$

$$\tilde{p} = (\tilde{p}^{\mathrm{I}}, \tilde{p}^{\mathrm{II}}, \tilde{p}^{\mathrm{III}})$$

where p^{I} $(\tilde{p}^{\mathrm{I}})$ is a sequence of home (foreign) prices for internationally traded goods, p^{II} $(\tilde{p}^{\mathrm{II}})$ is a sequence of home (foreign) prices for the purely domestic goods of the home country, and p^{III} $(\tilde{p}^{\mathrm{III}})$ is a sequence of home (foreign) prices for the purely domestic goods of the foreign country.

Definition (competitive free-trade world equilibrium). *A competitive free-trade world equilibrium is a feasible allocation* $(x^*, \tilde{x}^*, y^*, \tilde{y}^*) = ((x^*_h)_{h \in \mathbf{H}}, (\tilde{x}_h)_{h \in \tilde{\mathbf{H}}}, (y^*_f)_{f \in \mathbf{F}}, (\tilde{y}^*_f)_{f \in \tilde{\mathbf{F}}})$ *and non-zero price sequences* $p^*, \tilde{p}^* \in \mathbf{P}$ *such that*

(a1) $p^* y^*_f \geqslant p^* y_f$ *for all* $y_f \in \mathbf{Y}_f$
(a2) $\tilde{p}^* \tilde{y}^*_f \geqslant \tilde{p}^* \tilde{y}_f$ *for all* $\tilde{y}_f \in \tilde{\mathbf{Y}}_f$
(b1) x^*_h *is a greatest element of* $B_h(p^*)$ *for* $\succcurlyeq_h$, $h \in \mathbf{H}$
(b2) $\tilde{x}^*_h$ *is a greatest element of* $\tilde{B}_h(\tilde{p}^*)$ *for* $\tilde{\succcurlyeq}_h$, $h \in \tilde{\mathbf{H}}$
(c) $p^{\mathrm{I}*} = \alpha \tilde{p}^{\mathrm{I}*}$ *for some positive scalar* α
(d) $p^{\mathrm{I}*} \neq 0$.

Condition (c) states that, for internationally tradable goods, the same prices prevail everywhere. It should be especially noted that world equilibrium as defined is compatible with intra-generational borrowing and lending and therefore with international borrowing and lending.

For the world economy we have, as a corollary of theorem 1,

Theorem 2. *If the world economy is irreducible and if assumptions* **H**, **F**, **S** *and* **I** *are satisfied in each country then there exists a competitive world equilibrium.*

Of course not all goods are internationally tradable. Hence the assumption of irreducibility is more stringent when applied to the world economy.

Later we shall want to introduce a particular scheme of lumpsum compensatory transfers in each country. Let b_h be the vector of transfers to household h in the home country, with positive elements for quantities received, negative elements for quantities taken, and zero elements in the positions reserved for the non-tradables of the foreign country. Then

$$b_h = (b^t_h, b^{t+1}_h) \in \mathbf{R}^{2N} \quad \text{for } h \in \mathbf{H}_t,\ t \in \mathbf{N}$$

$$b_h = b^1_h \in \mathbf{R}^N \quad \text{for } h \in \mathbf{H}_0.$$

A pair of schemes of lumpsum compensatory transfers, one for each trading country, is **balanced** if

$$\sum_{h \in \mathbf{H}_{t-1} \cup \mathbf{H}_t} b_h^t + \sum_{h \in \tilde{\mathbf{H}}_{t-1} \cup \tilde{\mathbf{H}}_t} \tilde{b}_h^t = 0.$$

Provided that assumptions **S** and **I** are suitably generalized, theorem 2 remains valid even when a balanced scheme of lumpsum transfers is in place.

Assumption S′. *For each household* $h \in \mathbf{H}$, $e_h + b_h > 0$; *and for each household* $h \in \tilde{\mathbf{H}}$, $\tilde{e}_h + \tilde{b}_h > 0$.

Assumption I′. *For each* $T \in \mathbf{N}$ *there is* $\bar{y} \in \mathbf{Y}_{\leq T}$: $(e + b)_{\leq T} + \bar{y} \gg 0$ *and* $\bar{\tilde{y}} \in \tilde{\mathbf{Y}}_{\leq T}$: $(\tilde{e} + \tilde{b})_{\leq T} + \bar{\tilde{y}} \gg 0$.

Theorem 2′. *If the world economy is irreducible, if any scheme of transfers is balanced and if assumptions* **H, F, S′** *and* **I′** *are satisfied then there exists a competitive world equilibrium.*

Clearly theorem 2′ is valid for a world economy containing any finite number of countries, not just two. We record also, as the basis of our study of customs unions, that, given the assumptions of theorem 2′, existence is ensured even in a context of commodity taxes, including taxes on international trade.

3 THE GAINS FROM TRADE

In this section we explore the effect on the home country of each of two disturbances.

1 The move from autarky to free trade.
2 The formation of a customs union.

Accordingly, we contrast two conterminous situations, the **initial** or without-disturbance situation and the **final** or cum-disturbance situation. To allow meaningful comparisons of situations, it is assumed that all endowments, preferences, technologies and shareholdings remain unchanged; that is, are common to the two situations.

Values of variables in the initial situation are distinguished by circumflexes. For simplicity only, it is assumed that in the initial situation there are no transfers, so that $\hat{b}_h = 0$ for all $h \in \mathbf{H}$. Values of variables in the final situation are distinguished by the absence of circumflexes.

Suppose now that, in the final situation, household h ($h \in \mathbf{H}_t$, $t \in \mathbf{N}$) receives the lumpsum transfers

$$b_h^t = \hat{x}_h^t - \sum_{f \in \mathbf{F}_t} \theta_{hf} \hat{y}_f^t - e_h^t \tag{3a}$$

$$b_h^{t+1} = \hat{x}_h^{t+1} - \sum_{f \in \mathbf{F}_t} \theta_{hf} \hat{y}_f^{t+1} - e_h^{t+1} \tag{3b}$$

while household h ($h \in \mathbf{H}_0$) receives

$$b_h^1 = \hat{x}_h^1 - \sum_{f \in \mathbf{F}_0} \theta_{hf} \hat{y}_f^1 - e_h^1. \tag{3c}$$

In this scheme, households share uniformly in the terms-of-trade gains. However any form of sharing would suffice for the purpose of proving theorems 3 and 4 below.

Lemma 1. *The scheme of transfers (3), combined with a similar scheme for the foreign country, is balanced and feasible.*

In view of lemma 1 and theorem 2′, there exists a transfer-ridden world equilibrium in the final situation.

Definition (Pareto dominance). *The final situation weakly Pareto-dominates the initial situation if, given the scheme of transfers (3), and a similar scheme for the foreign country, no household is worse off in the final situation; and the final situation Pareto-dominates the initial situation if, under the same scheme of transfers, some households are better off, and none worse off, in the final situation.*

Now it is a short step to the remaining propositions.

Theorem 3. *Given the scheme of lumpsum transfers (3) and a similar scheme for the foreign country, free trade weakly Pareto-dominates autarky; moreover, the scheme of transfers is, for each country, balanced and feasible. If consumption and/or production substitution takes place in at least one household and/or firm then free trade Pareto-dominates autarky.*

Finally, we turn to a welfare analysis of customs unions. There are now at least three countries, with any initial constellation of trade restrictions and transport costs. The countries can be divided into two groups. The first group consists of $K \geqslant 2$ countries which are about to form a customs union; and the second group consists of all other countries, at least one in number. Those in the first group are called member countries and are labelled $1, \ldots, K$. Let us define the set $\mathbf{K} = \{1, 2, \ldots, K\}$. All other countries are called non-member countries. Generally speaking, we retain our earlier notation but sometimes add a superscript k to relate the variable to country k, $k \in \mathbf{K}$. For example, H_t^k will denote the number of new households in member country k in period t, and x_h^{kt} will denote the consumption vector of household h in member country k in period t.

Consider the initial situation, without a customs union. Let us define

$$\hat{m}^t = -\sum_{k \in \mathbf{K}} (\hat{x}^{kt} - \hat{y}^{kt} - \hat{e}^{kt}),$$

the vector of total imports by non-member countries from member countries in period t, $t \in \mathbf{N}_0$. (Of course, those elements of $\hat{m}^t$ which correspond to goods that do not flow between member and non-member countries are zero.) And let us denote by $\hat{q}^t$ the world prices of goods in period t. The aggregate balance of payments of non-member countries is then $\hat{q}^t \cdot \hat{m}^t$, $t \in \mathbf{N}$.

Now k countries, $k \in \mathbf{K}$, form a customs union. To demonstrate that a world-wide welfare improvement is possible, we follow Kemp and Wan (1976, 1986a) in artificially freezing trade between member and non-member countries at its initial level. The assumption that trade is frozen is for exposition only; it will be shown in the appendix that, if a suitable common tariff structure is chosen, world prices, and therefore the import demands of non-member countries, do not change. And it will be shown that the scheme of intra-union compensation is exactly financed by revenue from the common tariff.

Theorem 4. *Consider any competitive world trading equilibrium, with any number of countries and commodities, with no restrictions whatever on the tariffs and other commodity taxes of individual countries, and with costs of transport fully recognized. Now let any proper subset of the countries form a customs union. Then there exists a common tariff vector and a system of lumpsum compensatory payments involving only members of the union such that each household, whether a member of the union or not, is not worse off than before the formation of the union. Those member households which engage in consumption substitution and/or own shares of firms which engage in production substitution are better off.*

4 DURABLE CAPITAL GOODS

We have advanced to this point with the help of the fiction that all marketable goods perish within one period of time. However, the fiction was introduced merely as a simplifier; none of the conclusions requires it.

For suppose that, in addition to the N perishable goods already distinguished, there are M produced capital goods, each with a fixed and finite lifetime of θ periods. Then, admitting age as an economically relevant characterestic of such goods, we may distinguish θM additional goods, M of them newly produced and the remainder used or second-hand. In the first period of their existence, firms buy vectors of such goods; then, in their maturity, they either scrap the goods (if the latter have reached age θ) or sell them to a new generation of firms. They may or may not be tradable internationally.

It is straightforward but cumbersome to demonstrate that theorems 2′, 3 and 4 remain valid when the list of marketable goods is extended in this way.

Similarly, stocks of exhaustible resources can be accommodated without disturbing our conclusions. For example, in any period, a deposit of iron ore can be left underground (transformed by storage into the same stock with a later time subscript), or it can be extracted and stored above ground (transformed, with the aid of other inputs, into an intermediate good), or it can be extracted and used as an input to a conventional productive process.

5 FINAL REMARKS

In conclusion we offer three brief remarks. The first of these is designed to clarify the relationship of the present essay to that of Kemp and Wong (1993); the second remark places the gains-from-trade proposition 1 in the context of global Paretian comparative-statical welfare economics; and the third indicates possible directions of future research.

Kemp and Wong worked with a model which, in some respects, is quite special. In particular, it rests on the assumptions (i) that there are only two commodities, a specialized consumption good and a specialized intermediate good, (ii) that individuals of all generations have the same preferences, and (iii) that all contemporaries hold the same assets and therefore are equally wealthy. None of these assumptions has been needed in the present study. On the other hand, Kemp and Wong went beyond the present essay in allowing for the possibility that international borrowing and lending are forbidden or, for some other reason, infeasible. They found that, in those circumstances, individual countries cannot always rely on schemes of lumpsum compensation alone to deliver the gains from free trade and customs unions. Thus suppose that a particular economy gives up initial autarky for final free trade. Then, if capital is internationally mobile, the economy can choose a final inflow such that the amount of capital available is not less than in the initial situation and, therefore, such that the initial production point is feasible in the final situation. In general, the economy can do better than the initial production plan, for firms and owners of capital jointly and indirectly maximize gross national product. This ensures that the production gain is not negative. If, on the other hand, capital is internationally immobile, domestic investors might so change their investment plans after the opening of trade that the production set would shrink and the production gain turn negative.

In two earlier papers (Kemp and Wan, 1992, 1993) it was shown that if the production sets of some firms unexpectedly expand while those of all other firms remain unchanged, or if the endowment vectors of some households unexpectedly expand while those of all other households remain unchanged, then it is possible by means of lumpsum compensation to achieve a strict Pareto improvement; and it was shown that both propositions are valid whether or not there is a complete set of markets. Together, the two propositions form the centrepiece of Paretian comparative-statical welfare economics. Moreover, it was noted that the traditional gains-from-trade proposition 1 is an implication of the first of the two welfare propositions. Now, in the present essay, it has been shown that the gains-from-trade proposition is valid even in a context of overlapping generations and an infinite horizon, and we note without proof that the proposition can be viewed as an implication of two global comparative-statical welfare propositions suitably phrased to accommodate overlapping generations and an infinite horizon.

In the present essay markets have been assumed to be complete. However, in view of Kemp and Wong (1991), it should be straightforward to extend our present results to accommodate market incompleteness. It should be straightforward also to allow for lifetimes which extend beyond two periods.[3] Of greater importance, in the present essay we have ruled out intergenerational gifts, whether from parents to children or from children to parents. An urgent next step is that of introducing intergenerational links of this kind, links which may be intermittent, sometimes binding and sometimes not binding.

APPENDIX[4]

The purpose of this appendix is to provide careful statements and proofs of our main propositions. In particular, it focuses on the existence of a competitive equilibrium in an economy with overlapping generations, production and a scheme of lumpsum compensation, as described in our essay. The question of existence is interesting in its own right. Moreover, once the existence of an equilibrium is ensured, it is a short step to our principal welfare conclusions.

For the most part, the question of existence has been tackled in the severely restricted context of pure exchange. Within that context the problem is well understood. See, for the basic analysis, Balasko and Shell (1980) and Balasko *et al.* (1980) and, for generalizations, Wilson (1981), Burke (1988), Aliprantis *et al.* (1989) and Geanakoplos and Polemarchakis (1991). Those few who have allowed for production in models with overlapping generations have been content to examine very special cases; moreover, they have failed to consider the question of existence. See, for example, Muller and Woodford (1988), Galor and Ryder (1989) and Stephan and Wagenhals (1990).

Our own model is composed of assumptions borrowed from the finite-horizon models of Debreu (1959), McKenzie (1959) and Arrow and Hahn (1971) and adapted to the dynamic structure of populations with overlapping generations. However, these adaptations leave unchanged the economic content of the assumptions.

Our principal task is to prove theorem 1. Our approach to the theorem will be indirect. As a first, intermediate step, we establish the existence of a compensated equilibrium, in which attention is restricted to the behaviour of households $h \in \mathbf{H}_{\leqslant T}$ and firms $f \in \mathbf{F}_{\leqslant T}$. For that step, in turn, several preliminary results are needed.

Definition (compensated T-period equilibrium). *A feasible allocation* $(x^*, y^*) = ((x_h^*)_{h\in \mathbf{H}}, (y_f^*)_{f\in \mathbf{F}})$ *and a price sequence* $p^* \in \mathbf{P}$ *constitute a compensated T-period equilibrium if*

(a) $(p^{*1}, \ldots, p^{*T-1}) > 0$

(b) *for every* $f \in \mathbf{F}_{\leqslant T}$, $p^* y_f^* \geqslant p^* y_f$ *for all* $y_f \in \mathbf{Y}_f$

(c) *for every* $h \in \mathbf{H}_{\leqslant T}$, $x_h \succcurlyeq_h x_h^* \Rightarrow p^* x_h \geqslant p^* x_h^*$

(d) $p^* x_h^* = w_h(p^*)$.

Definition (compensated equilibrium). *A compensated equilibrium is a feasible allocation* $(x^*, y^*) = ((x_h^*)_{h \in \mathbf{H}}, (y_f^*)_{f \in \mathbf{F}})$ *and a non-zero price sequence* $p^* \in \mathbf{P}$ *such that the above conditions (b), (c) and (d) hold for all* $h \in \mathbf{H}$ *and* $f \in \mathbf{F}$.

The difference between compensated and competitive equilibria lies in the assumed behaviour of households. In a compensated equilibrium each household minimizes the cost of achieving a given level of satisfaction, with an income sufficient to cover that cost. In a competitive equilibrium, on the other hand, each household maximizes its satisfaction given its budget constraint. However, it is well known that the latter is implied by the former if the wealth of every household is positive; see Debreu (1959: Chapter 5) and Arrow and Hahn (1971: Theorem 5.2). And it turns out that the assumption of irreducibility ensures the positivity of wealth.

Proposition A1. If (x^*, y^*, p^*) *is a compensated equilibrium in an irreducible economy then it is a competitive equilibrium.*

Proof. Let $\mathbf{H}^1 \equiv \{h \in \mathbf{H} : w_h(p^*) \geqslant 0\}$ and $\mathbf{H}^2 \equiv \{h \in \mathbf{H} : w(p^*) = 0\}$. *Irreducibility implies the existence of* $t \in \mathbf{N}$ *and* $\bar{h} \in \mathbf{H}_t \cap \mathbf{H}^1$ *such that* $x'_{\bar{h}} \succ_h x^*_{\bar{h}}$. *Since* $w_{\bar{h}}(p^*) > 0$, *this implies that*

$$0 < p^* \, (x'_{\bar{h}} - x^*_h) = p^* \left(\sum_{\mathbf{H}^2 \cap \mathbf{H}_{t-1}} e_h^t + \sum_{\mathbf{H}^2 \cap \mathbf{H}_t} e_h + \sum_{\mathbf{H}^2 \cap \mathbf{H}_{t+1}} e_h^{t+1} \right)$$
$$\leqslant \sum_{\mathbf{H}^2 \cap (\mathbf{H}_{t-1} \cup \mathbf{H}_t \cup \mathbf{H}_{t+1})} w_h(p^*).$$

Hence there is a household $h \in \mathbf{H}^2$ *such that* $w_h(p^*) > 0$. *This contradicts the choice of* $\mathbf{H}^2$. *Consequently* $w_h(p^*) > 0$ *for all* $h \in \mathbf{H}$ *and* (x^*, y^*, p^*) *is a competitive equilibrium.* □

Notice that irreducibility in a closed OLG economy does not imply the irreducibility of its finite subeconomies. The reason is that members of, say, generation $\mathbf{H}_S$ may be able to achieve higher levels of satisfaction only by consuming additional goods which are exclusively owned by members of generation $\mathbf{H}_{S+1}$ and which therefore are unavailable to the subeconomy E_S consisting of households and firms up to period S.

We now introduce the finite augmented economy $\mathring{E}_S$ by adding to E_S a fictitious household $\mathring{h}_S$ with the endowment

$$e_{\mathring{h}_S} = \sum_{h \in \mathbf{H}_{S+1}} e_h^{S+1}$$

and with strictly increasing preferences.

Lemma A1. $\mathring{E}_S$ *is irreducible.*[5]

Proof. *It must be checked whether for every non-trivial partition* $\mathbf{H}^1, \mathbf{H}^2$ *of* $\mathbf{H}_{\leq S} \cup \{\mathring{h}_S\}$ *and every (finite) feasible allocation in* $\mathring{E}_S$ *there is at least one household in* $\mathbf{H}^1$ *that can be made better off by the additional consumption of resources owned by members of* $\mathbf{H}^2$.

Only two cases need be investigated: case 1, in which $\mathbf{H}^1 = \{\mathring{h}_S\}$, *and case 2, in which* $\mathbf{H}^2 = \{\mathring{h}_S\}$. *For all remaining, intermediate instances the claim is directly implied by the irreducibility of the whole economy.*

Case 1

Since the whole economy is irreducible,

$$\sum_{h \in \mathbf{H}_0} e_h^1 > 0$$

and

$$\sum_{h \in \mathbf{H}_t} e_h^\tau > 0 \quad \textit{for } \tau = t, t+1 \textit{ and every } t \in \mathbf{N}.$$

Moreover, the preferences of $\mathring{h}_S$ *are strictly increasing. Hence the welfare of* $\mathring{h}_S$ *is enhanced by the additional consumption of* $\Sigma_{h \in \mathbf{H}_S} e_h^{S+1}$.

Case 2

Suppose that there is no household in $\mathbf{H}_S$ *that can be made better off by the additional consumption of* $e_{\mathring{h}_S}$. *Then the whole economy must be reducible for, by definition,*

$$e_{\mathring{h}_S} = \sum_{h \in \mathbf{H}_{S+1}} e_h^{S+1} .$$

Thus all cases have been verified and the proof is complete. □

Since $\mathring{E}_S$ has all the needed properties, there is a finite feasible allocation

$$((x_h)_{h \in \mathbf{H}_{\leq S}}, x_{\mathring{h}_S}, (y_f)_{f \in \mathbf{F}_{\leq S}})$$

and a vector of prices $p_S = (p_S^1, \ldots, p_S^{S+1}) > 0$ that constitutes a competitive equilibrium in $\mathring{E}_S$. As is well known, this is also a compensated equilibrium for the finite subeconomy. It can be extended to a compensated S-period equilibrium (x_S, y_S, p_S). By construction, $w_h(p_S) > 0$ for $h \in \mathbf{H}_{\leq S}$, which implies that $p_S^1 > 0$.

Summarizing, we have a sequence $(x_S, y_S, p_S)_{S \in \mathbf{N}}$ of compensated S-period equilibria such that $p_S^1 > 0$ for all $S \in \mathbf{N}$. From the analysis of Arrow and Hahn (1971), it can be easily deduced that the set of feasible allocations is compact in the product topology. Hence we may assume without loss of generality that this sequence converges to a limit (x^*, y^*) which is itself a feasible allocation. We focus attention on this limit.

Lemma A2. *For every $T \in \mathbf{N}$, there is a sequence of prices*

$$p_T \equiv (p_T^1, p_T^2, \ldots, p_T^{T+1}, 0, \ldots)$$

such that (x^*, y^*, p_T) is a compensated T-period equilibrium.

Proof. *Fix any $T \in \mathbf{N}$ and consider the sequence $(x_S, y_S, p_S)_{S \in \mathbf{N}}$ of compensated S-period equilibria. The limit of the feasible allocations is (x^*, y^*). Since by construction $p_S^1 > 0$ for every $S \in \mathbf{N}$, for every sufficiently large S a compensated S-period equilibrium is also a compensated T-period equilibrium. Hence every p_S can be normalized in its $T+1$ leading vectors:*

$$\|p_S^1, \ldots, p_S^{T+1}\| = 1.$$

Thus without loss of generality, we can assume that

$$(p_S^1, \ldots, p_S^{T+1}) \to (p_T^1, \ldots, p_T^{T+1}) > 0.$$

Let us now define the sequences of price vectors

$$p_T \equiv (p_T^1, \ldots, p_T^{T+1}, 0, \ldots).$$

For *any $f \in \mathbf{F}_{\leqslant T}$ and every S such that $p_S y_{Sf} \geqslant p_S y_f$ for all $y_f \in \mathbf{Y}_f$, we have $p^* y_f^* \geqslant p^* y_f$ for all $y_f \in \mathbf{Y}_f$. Hence, given prices p^*, the production plans y_f^* are profit maximizing for every $f \in \mathbf{F}_{\leqslant T}$.*

Since $(x_S, y_S; p_S)$ is a compensated T-period equilibrium for sufficiently large S and since, as is well known, compensated demand correspondences are upper semi-continuous, the limit $(x^*, y^*; p^T)$ exists and is also a T-period equilibrium. □

The following lemma provides a growth estimate for the price sequences $(p_S)_{S \in \mathbf{N}}$. It is based on a lemma of Wilson's (1981).

Lemma A3. *For every $h_1, h_2 \in \mathbf{H}$,*

$$\liminf_{S \to \infty} \frac{w_{h_1}(p_S)}{w_{h_2}(p_S)} > 0.$$

Proof. *Suppose, to the contrary, that there are $h_1, h_2 \in \mathbf{H}$ such that*

$$\liminf_{S \to \infty} \frac{w_{h_1}(p_S)}{w_{h_2}(p_S)} = 0$$

and consider

$$\mathbf{H}^1 \equiv \left\{ h \in \mathbf{H} : \liminf_{S \to \infty} \frac{w_{h_1}(p_S)}{w_{h_2}(p_S)} > 0 \right\}$$

and

$$\mathbf{H}^2 \equiv \left\{ h \in \mathbf{H} : \liminf_{S \to \infty} \frac{w_{h_1}(p_S)}{w_{h_2}(p_S)} = 0 \right\}.$$

By assumption, $h_1 \in \mathbf{H}^2$ *and* $h_2 \in \mathbf{H}^1$. *Thus* $\mathbf{H}^1, \mathbf{H}^2$ *is a non-trivial partition of* $\mathbf{H}$.

Since the economy is irreducible, there is an $\bar{h} \in \mathbf{H}^1 \cap \mathbf{H}_{\bar{t}}$ *such that*

$$x^*_{\bar{h}} + z \succ_{\bar{h}} x^*_{\bar{h}}$$

where

$$z \equiv \sum_{\mathbf{H}^2 \cap \mathbf{H}_{\bar{t}-1}} e^{\bar{t}}_h + \sum_{\mathbf{H}^2 \cap \mathbf{H}_{\bar{t}}} e_h + \sum_{\mathbf{H}^2 \cap \mathbf{H}_{\bar{t}+1}} e^{\bar{t}+1}_h.$$

By construction,

$$\lim_{S \to \infty} (x_{\bar{h}})_S = x^*_{\bar{h}}.$$

From the continuity of preferences, there is a $\lambda \in \mathbf{R}$, $0 < \lambda < 1$, *such that, for sufficiently large S,*

$$\lambda(z + x_{\bar{h}})_S \succ_{\bar{h}} (x_{\bar{h}})_S.$$

Again by construction, if S is sufficiently large then $(x_{\bar{h}})_S$ *is a greatest element of* $B_h(p_S)$ *with respect to the preferences* $\preccurlyeq_{\bar{h}}$ *of household* $\bar{h}$. *For large S, therefore,*

$$\lambda p_S(z + (x_{\bar{h}})_S) > p_S(x_{\bar{h}})_S$$

$$\Leftrightarrow \lambda p_S z > (1 - \lambda) p_S(x_{\bar{h}})_S = (1 - \lambda) w_{\bar{h}}(p_S).$$

Now

$$\sum_{\mathbf{H}^2 \cap (\mathbf{H}_{\bar{t}-1} \cup \mathbf{H}_{\bar{t}} \cup \mathbf{H}_{\bar{t}+1})} w_h(p_S) > (1 - \lambda) w_{\bar{h}}(p_S).$$

Hence, dividing by $w_{h_2}(p_S) > 0$ *and going to the limit,*

$$0 = \lambda \liminf_{S \to \infty} \sum_{\mathbf{H}^2 \cap (\mathbf{H}_{\bar{t}-1} \cup \mathbf{H}_{\bar{t}} \cup \mathbf{H}_{\bar{t}+1})} \frac{w_h(p_S)}{w_{h_2}(p_S)}$$

$$\geqslant (1 - \lambda) \liminf_{S \to \infty} \frac{w_{\bar{h}}(p_S)}{w_{h_2}(p_S)} > 0,$$

a contradiction. □

Finally, we restate and prove Theorem 1.

Theorem 1. *If the economy is irreducible and if assumptions* **H**, **F**, **S** *and* **I** *are satisfied then there exists a competitive equilibrium.*

Proof. *We already know that, for every $S \in \mathbf{N}$, there is a compensated S-period equilibrium (x_S, y_S, p_S) such that $\lim_{S \to \infty} (x_S, y_S) = (x^*, y^*)$ in the product topology and such that $p_S^1 > 0$. By lemma A2, therefore, for every $T \in \mathbf{N}$ there is*

$$p_T \equiv (p_T^1, \ldots, p_T^{T+1}, 0, \ldots)$$

such that (x^*, y^*, p_T) is a compensated T-period equilibrium.

We now show that $w_h(p) > 0$ for $h \in \mathbf{H}_{\leq T}$. Suppose by way of contradiction that there are households $h_1, h_2 \in \mathbf{H}_{\leq T}$ such that $w_{h_1}(p_T) = 0$ and $w_{h_2}(p_T) > 0$. By construction,[6]

$$w_{h_1}(p_T) = \lim_{S \to \infty} \frac{1}{\|(p_T^1, \ldots, p_T^{T+1})\|} w_{h_1}(p_S)$$

and

$$w_{h_2}(p_T) = \lim_{S \to \infty} \frac{1}{\|(p_T^1, \ldots, p_T^{T+1})\|} w_{h_2}(p_S).$$

Hence

$$\liminf_{S \to \infty} \frac{w_{h_1}(p_S)}{w_{h_2}(p_S)} = 0,$$

contradicting lemma A3. Hence $p_T^1 > 0$.

Lemma 3 of Wolik (1991) permits the supposition that, for every $t, T \in \mathbf{N}$, $\|p_T^1\| = 1$ and $\|p_T^t\| \leq M^t$, where M^t is a finite constant. Hence there exists a subsequence $(p_{T_k})_{k \in \mathbf{N}}$ such that $\lim_{k \to \infty} p_{T_k} \equiv p^* > 0$ with respect to the product topology. This subsequence has the property that (x^*, y^*, p_{T_k}) is a compensated T_k-period equilibrium for every $k \in \mathbf{N}$. As in the proof of lemma A2, it can be shown that (x^*, y^*, p^*) is a compensated H-period equilibrium for every finite time horizon H. Hence, by definition, it is a compensated equilibrium. The irreducibility of the economy, together with proposition A1, then yields the required conclusion. □

In summary, we have found that, for our OLG economy, in which the time horizon is infinite but in which households and firms exist for a finite time only, the existence of a competitive equilibrium is guaranteed under assumptions that are commonly employed to establish existence in models with finite horizons.

Proof of Theorem 2′. *If the scheme of transfers is balanced, the set of feasible allocations remains unchanged. Moreover, assumptions* **S′** *and* **I′** *simply ensure that the purposes of assumptions* **S** *and* **I** *are achieved even in the presence of transfers. Taking into the reckoning the 'net' endowments of households, that is their endowments plus transfers,* **S′** *ensures that every household can survive in the sense that it is left with a positive amount of at least one good. Assumption* **I′**, *on the other hand, requires that, for each country, the transfers, resources and technologies of the subeconomies with time horizon T permit the supply of positive amounts of all goods. Thus, like theorem 2, theorem 2′ is little more than a corollary of theorem 1.* □

Proof of Lemma 1. *From (3), for given $t \in \mathbf{N}$,*

$$
\begin{aligned}
b^t &\equiv \sum_{h \in \mathbf{H}_{t-1} \cup \mathbf{H}_t} b_h^t \\
&= \sum_{h \in \mathbf{H}_{t-1}} \left(\hat{x}_h^t - \sum_{f \in \mathbf{F}_{t-1}} \theta_{hf} \hat{y}_f^t - e_h^t \right) + \sum_{h \in \mathbf{H}_t} \left(\hat{x}_h^t - \sum_{f \in \mathbf{F}_t} \theta_{hf} \hat{y}_f^t - e_h^t \right) \\
&= \hat{x}^t - \hat{y}^t - e^t.
\end{aligned}
$$

Similarly,

$$\tilde{b}^t = \hat{\tilde{x}}^t - \hat{\tilde{y}}^t - \tilde{e}^t.$$

However, in a world free-trade equilibrium,

$$(\hat{x}^t - \hat{y}^t - e^t) + (\hat{\tilde{x}}^t - \hat{\tilde{y}}^t - \tilde{e}^t) = 0.$$

Hence $b^t + \tilde{b}^t = 0$ for all $t \in \mathbf{N}$. Each scheme of lumpsum transfers is balanced and thus feasible and self-financing. □

Remark. *If the initial situation is autarky, $b^t = \tilde{b}^t = 0$ for all $t \in \mathbf{N}$.*

Proof of Theorem 3. *By lemma 1, the pair of transfer schemes, one for each country, is balanced. By theorem 2′, therefore, there is a competitive free-trade equilibrium. Setting $b_h^t = 0$ when $t = 0$, the expenditures of household $h \in \mathbf{H}_t$ ($t \in \mathbf{N}$) are, in equilibrium,*

$$
\begin{aligned}
px_h &= p\left(e_h + \sum_{f \in \mathbf{F}_t} \theta_{hf} y_f + b_h^t + b_h^{t+1} \right) \\
&= p\left(e^h + \sum_{f \in \mathbf{F}_t} \theta_{hf} y_f + \hat{x}_h - \sum_{f \in \mathbf{F}_t} \theta_{hf} \hat{y}_f - e_h \right) \\
&= p\left(\hat{x}_h + \sum_{f \in \mathbf{F}_t} \theta_{hf} (y_f - \hat{y}_f) \right).
\end{aligned}
$$

However, from profit maximization, $p(y_f - \hat{y}_f) \geqslant 0$. Hence each household could still purchase its initial consumption at final prices. Hence, by the maximum theorem, no household is worse off in the final situation. □

Proof of Theorem 4. *As in the proof of theorem 3, it can be verified that for household h ($h \in \mathbf{H}^k$, $k \in \mathbf{K}$) initial consumption is still feasible in the final equilibrium. Hence the household is not worse off in the customs union; indeed it is better off if consumption substitution takes place or if there is production substitution in firms partly owned by it.*

It remains to be shown that the scheme of transfers adopted by member governments collectively is exactly financed, period by period, by revenue from the common tariff. The tariff revenue of period t is

$$-(p^t - \hat{q}^t)\hat{m}^t = -p^t \hat{m}^t$$

and the net transfer of the member governments is $\Sigma_h b_h^t$, *where the summation is over all households in the customs union in period t. Spelling it out, we obtain*

$$\sum_{k\in \mathbf{K}} p^t \left[\sum_{h\in \mathbf{H}_t^k} \left(\hat{x}_h^{kt} - \sum_{f\in \mathbf{F}_t^k} \theta_{hj}^k \hat{y}_f^{kt} - e_h^{kt} \right) \right] + \sum_{h\in \mathbf{H}_{t-1}^k} \left(x_h^{kt} - \sum_{f\in \mathbf{F}_{t-1}^k} \theta_{hj}^k \hat{y}_f^{kt} - e_h^{kt} \right)$$

$$= \sum_{k\in \mathbf{K}} p^t (\hat{x}^{kt} - \hat{y}^{kt} - e^{kt})$$

$$= -p_t \hat{m}_t. \qquad \square$$

NOTES

* We acknowledge with gratitude the helpful comments of Ngo Van Long.

1 For a recent account, see Geanakoplos (1987).

2 The vector inequality $\mathbf{x} > \mathbf{0}$ means that each element of $\mathbf{x}$ is non-negative, with at least one element positive. The inequality $\mathbf{x} \gg \mathbf{0}$ means that all elements of $\mathbf{x}$ are positive.

3 Indeed Balasko *et al.* (1980) have provided an algorithm for converting a pure-exchange overlapping-generations economy with finite but otherwise arbitrary lifetimes into an economy with lifetimes of at most two periods.

4 The appendix is based on Wolik (1992).

5 Irreducibility in a finite economy is closely analogous to irreducibility in an infinite economy. See the definition in section 2.

6 The method of proof employed in lemma A2 requires that the price sequences be normalized in their first $T + 1$ vector components.

REFERENCES

Aliprantis, C. D., Brown, D. Y. and Burkinshaw, O. (1989) *Existence and Optimality of Competitive Equilibria*, Berlin, Heidelberg: Springer-Verlag.

Arrow, K. J. and Hahn, F. H. (1971) *General Competitive Analysis*, San Francisco: Holden-Day.

Balasko, Y. and Shell, K. (1980) 'The overlapping-generations model I: The case of pure exchange without money', *Journal of Economic Theory* 23: 281–306.

Balasko, Y., Cass, D. and Shell, K. (1980) 'Existence of equilibrium in a general overlapping-generations model', *Journal of Economic Theory* 23: 307–22.

Binh, T. N. (1985) 'A neo-Ricardian model with overlapping generations', *Economic Record* 61: 707–18.

Binh, T. N. (1986) 'Welfare implications of international trade without compensation', University of New South Wales.

Burke, J. (1988) 'On the existence of price equilibria in dynamic economies', *Journal of Economic Theory* 44: 281–300.

Debreu, G. (1959) *Theory of Value*, New York: Wiley.

Galor, O. and Ryder, H. E. (1989) 'Existence, uniqueness and stability of equilibrium in an overlapping generations model with productive capital', *Journal of Economic Theory* 49: 360–75.

Geanakoplos, J. (1987) 'Overlapping generations models of general equilibrium', in J. Eatwell, M. Milgate and P. Newman (eds) *The New Palgrave: A Dictonary of Economics*, pp. 767–79, New York: W. W. Norton.

Geanakoplos, J. D. and Polemarchakis, H. M. (1991) 'Overlapping generations', in W. Hildenbrand and H. Sonnenschein (eds) *Handbook of Mathematical Economics*, Vol. IV, 1899–960, Amsterdam: North-Holland.

Grandmont, J. M. and McFadden, D. (1972) 'A technical note on classical gains from trade', *Journal of International Economics* 2: 109–25.

Kemp, M. C. (1962) 'The gains from international trade', *Economic Journal* 72: 803–19.

Kemp, M. C. (1964) *The Pure Theory of International Trade*, New York: Prentice Hall.

Kemp, M. C. and Long, N. V. (1979) 'The under-exploitation of natural resources: A model with overlapping generations', *Economic Record* 55: 214–21.

Kemp, M. C. and Ohyama, M. (1978) 'The gain from trade under conditions of uncertainty', *Journal of International Economics* 8: 139–41.

Kemp, M. C. and Wan, H. Y., Jr (1972) 'The gains from free trade', *International Economic Review* 13: 509–22.

Kemp, M. C. and Wan, H. Y., Jr (1976) 'An elementary proposition concerning the formation of customs unions', *Journal of International Economics* 6: 95–7.

Kemp, M. C. and Wan, H. Y., Jr (1986a) 'The comparison of second-best equilibria: The case of customs unions', in D. Bös and C. Seidl (eds) *Welfare Economics of the Second Best*, Suppl. 5 of *Zeitschrift für Nationalökonomie* 161–7, Vienna: Springer-Verlag.

Kemp, M. C. and Wan, H. Y., Jr (1986b) 'Gains from trade with and without lumpsum compensation', *Journal of International Economics* 21: 99–110.

Kemp, M. C. and Wan, H. Y., Jr (1992) 'On lumpsum compensation', University of New South Wales, this volume.

Kemp, M. C. and Wan, H. Y., Jr (1993) 'Lumpsum compensation in a context of incomplete markets', University of New South Wales, this volume.

Kemp, M. C. and Wong, K.-Y. (1991) 'The gains from trade when markets are possibly incomplete', mimeo.

Kemp, M. C. and Wong, K.-Y. (1993) 'Gains from trade with overlapping generations', University of Washington.

McKenzie, L. W. (1959) 'On the existence of general equilibrium for a competitive market', *Econometrica* 27: 54–71.

Muller, W. J. and Woodford, M. (1988) 'Determinacy of equilibrium in stationary economies with both finite and infinite lived consumers', *Journal of Economic Theory* 46: 225–90.

Ohyama, M. (1972) 'Trade and welfare in general equilibrium', *Keio Economic Studies* 9: 37–73.

Samuelson, P. A. (1962) 'The gains from trade once again', *Economic Journal* 72: 820–9.

Serra, P. (1991) 'Short-run and long-run welfare implications of free trade', *Canadian Journal of Economics* 24: 21–33.

Stephan, G. and Wagenhals, G. (1990) 'Innovation, decentralization and equilibrium', *Swiss Journal of Economics and Statistics* 126: 129–45.

Vanek, J. (1965) *General Equilibrium of International Discrimination*, Cambridge, MA: Harvard University Press.

Wilson, C. A. (1981) 'Equilibrium in dynamic models with an infinity of agents', *Journal of Economic Theory* 24: 95–111.

Wolik, N. (1991) 'Innovation, decentralization and equilibrium: A comment', *Swiss Journal of Economics and Statistics* 127: 767–73.

Wolik, N. (1992) 'On the existence of competitive equilibria in OLG economies', University of Dortmund.

11

THE WELFARE GAINS FROM INTERNATIONAL MIGRATION*

1 INTRODUCTION

The welfare economics of international migration has developed more or less independently of the welfare economics of international trade and investment. Why this has been so is not entirely clear; however, part of the explanation may be found in the many non-economic motives for international migration and in the fact that migration often (but not always) involves the movement of both a factor and its owner.

Moreover, each of the two topics has been tackled with its own distinctive technical apparatus. Whereas the gains from international trade and investment have typically been examined in terms of quite abstract general-equilibrium models, the gains from international migration have usually been analyzed in terms of partial-equilibrium or simple $2 \times 2 \times 2$ general-equilibrium models.

In the present essay it will be shown that a core of quite general propositions about the gains from international migration can be deduced from the two leading gains-from-trade theorems. Moreover, the reader will be reminded that the gains-from-trade theorems are now known to be valid not only under the familiar assumptions of Arrow–Debreu general-equilibrium theory but also in the presence of incomplete markets, in a context of overlapping generations and infinite horizons, and in some types of monetary economies. Thus a strong link will be established between the welfare economics of international trade and the welfare economics of international migration, a link which holds firm over a very considerable domain.[1]

2 THE GAINS FROM INTERNATIONAL TRADE AND INVESTMENT

The welfare economics of international trade contains two core propositions which are valid for countries of any size.

Proposition α (The Gainfulness of Trade for a Single Free-Trading Country). *If some closed country s abandons all artificial obstacles to international trade, either in the* *whole set of potentially tradable goods or in some proper subset, and if the preferences, technologies and endowments of the trading partners are suitably restricted then there is a scheme of lumpsum compensation in s and an associated competitive world equilibrium such that no individual in s is worse off than in autarky.*

Proposition β (The Existence of Gainful Customs Unions). *If an arbitrary world trading equilibrium is disturbed by the formation of a customs union comprising any subset of two or more countries then there exists a common external tariff vector, a scheme of lumpsum compensation, restricted to individuals in the union, and an associated world trading equilibrium in which (a) no individual, whether a member of the union or not, is worse off than before the union, and (b) the net tariff revenue of the union is at least as large as the net compensation accruing to individual members of the union.*

In both propositions, the list of tradable goods may include primary and produced factors of production, including labour, as well as pure consumption goods.

Propositions α and β are remarkable for their robustness to respecification of the economy. Originally demonstrated for a world of Arrow–Debreu economies (Kemp and Wan, 1972, 1976, 1986) they are now known to be valid for economies with incomplete markets, for at least some types of monetary economies, and for economies with overlapping generations and infinite horizons (Kemp and Wong, 1990a, b, 1991a, b).

3 THE GAINS FROM INTERNATIONAL MIGRATION

(α) Suppose that the residents of a closed economy are presented with the opportunity to trade and invest internationally and with the opportunity to emigrate and/or to receive immigrants. Then proposition α applies, provided that emigrants are included in the scheme of compensation and immigrants excluded. (Of course, the compensation of emigrants must be calculated on the basis of the **country-of-origin** consumption and prices.)

The fact that, in the case of labour migration, the owners move with the factor does not affect the applicability of the proposition, provided that the preferences of emigrants do not change with their country of residence. In particular, whether or not emigrants remit part of their earnings, to support their families or for investment, is of no theoretical significance. (Its administrative significance is another matter. After an emigrant's departure, and in the absence of remittances, it may be legally impossible to secure a contribution to a scheme of compensation. In that case, the migrant's departure may be made conditional upon the prior completion of the transfer.)

What happens to the preferences of immigrants, on the other hand, has no bearing on the applicability of proposition α (although it obviously affects the extent of the gains). Immigrants are merely foreign suppliers of labour, on a par with foreign exporters of any other commodity. The fact that they happen to consume their wages in the host country is of no significance.

It does not matter whether migration takes place at the beginning of the (finite) period of time covered by our analysis, or is delayed. Nor does it matter whether migration is permanent or temporary or, indeed, repeated or periodical. For each individual, and for each moment of time, compensation is so calculated that, if the individual were living in his or her country of origin, he or she could consume the bundle that he or she would have chosen under continued autarky. If for some part or parts of the interval covered by our analysis the individual chooses to reside in the country of destination, it is because he or she prefers to do so.

Nor does it matter if emigration and immigration take place simultaneously, even to the point where a country loses its entire initial or autarkic population. Compensation is always **of** the initial population, including emigrants but excluding immigrants, and **on the basis of** country-of-origin consumption and prices.

It might be thought that non-traded consumption goods invalidate the above reasoning, but this is not so. Suppose that non-traded goods form part of the initial consumption bundle of an emigrant and that not all of those goods are produced in the country of destination. Then, after compensation, the migrant can purchase his or her initial bundle only if he or she returns to his or her country of origin. If the migrant chooses to not return, however, he or she is revealed as **preferring** an attainable post-trade post-migration bundle to the initial bundle. Similar reasoning applies if the same non-traded goods are available in each country but at different relative prices.

Finally, nothing can be said about the change in well-being of an immigrant who is not part of a scheme of compensation in his or her country of origin. Of course, given the world equilibrium after the elimination of restrictions on trade and migration, an immigrant is revealed as preferring to live in his or her country of destination. But that reveals nothing about the immigrant's ranking of the **pre**-trade situation in his or her country of origin and the **post**-trade situation in his or her country of destination.

Suppose alternatively that, initially, there is free trade in some goods but the world's frontiers are closed to migration. Subsequently, the frontiers are opened. In effect, it is possible to trade in another commodity. Except in the uninteresting small-country case, one cannot be sure that, after compensation, a particular country will benefit from the enlarged trading opportunities. After the opening of the frontiers, however, the world enjoys a more efficient allocation of its resources. It follows that, for at least one country, there is a potential enhancement of welfare.[2]

(β) Turning to the interpretation of proposition β, let us now suppose that a world equilibrium of international trade, investment and migration is disturbed by the formation, by some proper subset of countries, of a common market embracing produced commodities as well as primary factors of production like labour. Then proposition β applies, it being understood that the common vector of external tariffs may include a tax on migration between member and non-member countries.[3] Thus if the tariff vector and the scheme of compensation are carefully calculated then all individuals initially in the common market, including those who choose to leave it, benefit from its formation.

If in the initial world equilibrium all factor movements are ruled out, one can imagine the formation of a common market as proceeding in two stages. In the first stage, a customs union, embracing produced commodities only, is formed; in the second stage, all restrictions on the intra-union movement of factors, including labour, are removed. If at **each** stage the common external tariff and the scheme of compensation are carefully chosen then at **each** stage all individual members of the union are made better off. This is in contrast to our earlier finding that the enlargement of the list of freely traded goods may harm some individuals and some countries.[4] The present sharper result is made possible by the international character of compensation within the union.

4 FINAL REMARKS

In spite of appearances, none of the conclusions of section 3 is inconsistent with the findings of the best recent treatments of our topic. Thus when Johnson (1967), Wong (1986), Quibria (1988) and Tu (1991) demonstrate that a country of origin cannot gain from migration, they do so on the implicit assumption that emigrants are excluded from the scheme of compensation adopted by that country.[5]

On the other hand, when Wong (1986), Quibria (1988), Tu (1991) and Clarke and Ng (1991) rely on special models to demonstrate that the initial residents of a country of destination necessarily benefit from free trade and migration, they overlook the more general demonstration implicit in the standard proposition α.

NOTES

* The author is grateful to Koji Shimomura, Henry Wan, Kar-yiu Wong and a referee for their comments.

1 The link is already implicit in Ohyama (1972), where it is understood that the list of tradable commodities includes primary and produced factors of production.

2 Even this is not true if labour is the last on the list of goods (primary factors and products) to become mobile and if the same constant-returns technology is available to all countries. In that case, the mobility of labour leaves the world's allocation unchanged, and that is true whether the individual countries are large or small.

3 From Lerner's symmetry theorem, one tariff can be arbitrarily chosen. In particular, the tax on migration might be set equal to zero (as in the European Economic Community).

4 See the final paragraph of section 3(α).

5 Johnson (1967) and Wong (1986) consider the possibility that their conclusion may be reversed if the migrants leave behind a sufficient amount of their capital. However, the capital remains the property of the migrants and continues to earn income for them. Hence the separation of the migrants from their capital cannot be interpreted as a compensatory transfer to those left behind.

REFERENCES

Clarke, H. R. and Ng, Y.-K. (1991) 'Are there valid economic grounds for restricting immigration?', *Economic Papers* 10: 71–6.

Johnson, H. G. (1967) 'Some economic aspects of brain drain', *Pakistan Development Review* 7: 379–409.

Kemp, M. C. and Wan, H. Y. (1972) 'The gains from free trade', *International Economic Review* 13: 509–22.

Kemp, M. C. and Wan, H. Y. (1976) 'An elementary proposition concerning the formation of customs unions', *Journal of International Economics* 6: 95–7.

Kemp, M. C. and Wan, H. Y. (1986) 'The comparison of second-best equilibria', in D. Bös and C. Seidl (eds) *Welfare Economics of the Second Best*, Suppl. 5 of *Zeitschrift für Nationalökonomie* 161–7, Vienna: Springer-Verlag.

Kemp, M. C. and Wong, K.-Y. (1990a) 'The gains from trade when markets are possibly incomplete', University of Washington, this volume.

Kemp, M. C. and Wong, K.-Y. (1990b) 'The gains from trade when markets are possibly incomplete: A more general analysis', University of Washington.

Kemp, M. C. and Wong, K.-Y. (1991a) 'Gains from trade with overlapping generations', University of Washington, this volume.

Kemp, M. C. and Wong, K.-Y. (1991b) 'Gains from trade for a monetary economy when markets are possibly incomplete', University of Washington, this volume.

Ohyama, M. (1972) 'Trade and welfare in general equilibrium', *Keio Economic Papers* 9: 37–73.

Quibria, M. G. (1988) 'On generalising the economic analysis of international migration: A note', *Canadian Journal of Economics* 21: 874–6.

Tu, P. N. V. (1991) 'Migration: Gains or losses?', *Economic Record* 67: 153–7.

Wong, K.-Y. (1986) 'The economic analysis of international migration: A generalisation', *Canadian Journal of Economics* 19: 357–62.

12

THE PROBLEM OF SURVIVAL

An open economy*

1 INTRODUCTION

Suppose that a small country is totally dependent upon its trading partners for an essential raw material derived from an exhaustible and non-renewable resource stock. Suppose, further, that the net price (i.e. price less average cost of extraction) of the raw material is rising exponentially. (Hotelling (1931) has shown that the net price of the raw material must behave in this way if the rest of the world is competitive and enjoys perfect myopic foresight.) Such a country will progressively economize in its use of the material by substituting for it the services of durable produced inputs or capital. Can the strategy of substitution succeed, in the restricted sense of imposing a positive lower bound on per capita consumption? Can it succeed in the sense of making possible ever-growing per capita consumption?

It will be shown that, for a Cobb–Douglas economy, a positive and growing level of per capita consumption is possible if and only if technical progress takes place at a sufficiently rapid rate, the required rate depending on the rate of growth of consumption. For a modest defence of the use of Cobb–Douglas production functions in the analysis of exhaustible resources, see Kemp and Long (1980, appendix).

Questions similar to ours have been posed and answered in a splendid paper of Mitra *et al.* (1982). However, their model of production is rather different from ours. On the one hand, they work with general no-joint-products production functions and allow the terms of trade to be non-exponential functions of time. On the other hand, they do not recognize labour as a factor of production and assume that production functions are homogeneous of degree 1 in capital and the raw material alone. Thus, a precise comparison of our conclusions with theirs is not possible.

2 ANALYSIS

A small country produces a single commodity with the aid of capital, labour and an imported raw material. The production function is of the Cobb–Douglas type. Thus

$$y(t) = k(t)^{\alpha} r(t)^{\beta} l(t)^{\gamma} \exp(\beta\lambda t), \quad 0 < \alpha, \beta, \gamma < 1; 1 - \alpha - \beta > 0, \tag{1}$$

where $y(t)$ is total output at time t, $k(t)$ is the stock of capital at time t, $r(t)$ is the input of the imported raw material at time t, $l(t)$ is the input of labour at time t, and λ is the constant rate of resource-saving technical progress. Thus, there are no restrictions on returns to scale with respect to all three factors jointly, but it is required that returns to scale with respect to capital and the raw material alone are declining. The labour force is assumed to be constant and, by choice of units, equated to one, so that (1) reduces to

$$y(t) = k(t)^{\alpha} r(t)^{\beta} \exp(\beta\lambda t), \quad 0 < \alpha, \beta < 1; 1 - \alpha - \beta > 0. \tag{2}$$

The produced commodity can be consumed, invested or exported in exchange for the raw material. The net world price of the raw material, in terms of output, grows exponentially. Thus, if $p(t)$ is the gross price of the material and ε is the constant average cost of extraction,

$$p(t) - \varepsilon = [p(0) - \varepsilon] \exp(\delta t), \quad \delta \text{ constant.}$$

However, the cost of extraction plays only a nuisance role in our analysis: none of the conclusions of the essay depends on the value assigned to ε; indeed, they remain unchanged if ε declines monotonically under the pressure of technical improvements in extraction. We therefore simplify at the outset by setting $\varepsilon = 0$ and writing

$$p(t) = p(0) \exp(\delta t), \quad \delta \text{ constant.} \tag{3}$$

International trade is always balanced; moreover, imports of the raw material are immediately fed into the productive process. Thus

$$y(t) = c(t) + \dot{k}(t) + p(t) r(t), \tag{4}$$

where $c(t)$ is the rate of consumption at time t.

If there is a feasible programme which allows for survival (or survival cum growth) then there must be an efficient programme with the same property. Hence, we may impose the efficiency condition that at each moment of time the marginal product of the raw material is equated to the price of the raw material:

$$\partial y(t)/\partial r(t) = \beta y(t)/r(t) = p(t). \tag{5}$$

Solving (2), (3) and (5) for $r(t)$:

$$r(t) = [p(0)/\beta]^{1/(\beta - 1)} [k(t)]^{\alpha/(1 - \beta)} \exp[(\beta\lambda - \delta)t/(1 - \beta)]. \tag{6}$$

Substituting from (6) into (4), and recalling (2) and (3),

$$\dot{k}(t) = a[k(t)]^{\alpha/(1 - \beta)} \exp(\theta t) - c(t), \tag{7}$$

where

$$\theta \equiv \beta(\lambda - \delta)/(1 - \beta) \tag{8}$$

and

$$a \equiv (1 - \beta)\,[p(0)/\beta]^{-\beta/(1-\beta)} > 0. \tag{9}$$

Finally, if attention is confined to positive exponential paths of consumption, we have

$$c(t) = c(0)\exp(gt), \quad c(0) > 0, \tag{10}$$

and (7) reduces to

$$\dot{k}(t) = a[k(t)]^{\alpha/(1-\beta)}\exp(\theta t) - c(0)\exp(gt), \quad c(0) > 0, \tag{11}$$

whence

$$\dot{k} = 0, \quad \text{iff } k(t) = [c(0)/a]^{(1-\beta)/\alpha}\exp[(g - \theta)(1 - \beta)t/\alpha] > 0. \tag{12}$$

Equation (11) will be the focus of our attention. In particular we must determine the conditions under which it has a positive solution with $g \geqslant 0$.

We begin by showing that such a solution does not exist if θ is negative.[1]

Lemma 1. *If equation (11) has a positive solution with $g \geqslant 0$, then $\theta \geqslant 0$. If (11) has a positive solution with $g > 0$, then $\theta > 0$.*

Proof. *Suppose that*

$$g \geqslant 0 \geqslant \theta, \quad \textit{with at least one strict inequality.} \tag{13}$$

It will be shown that $k(t)$ must go to zero in finite time. The proof contains three steps.

First, we note, as an implication of (11) and of the assumption that $g > \theta$ (but independently of the sign of θ), that any trajectory which cuts the curve $\dot{k} = 0$ will hit the time axis in finite time (see Figure 1).

Next we note that the path of pure accumulation defined by

$$\dot{z}(t) = a[z(t)]^{\alpha/(1-\beta)}\exp(\theta t), \quad z(0) = k(0), \tag{14}$$

provides an upper bound for $k(t)$.

Solving (14),

$$z(t) = \begin{cases} \left(\dfrac{1-\alpha-\beta}{1-\beta}\,\dfrac{a}{\theta}\,[\exp(\theta t) - 1] + [k(0)]^{(1-\alpha-\beta)/(1-\beta)}\right)^{(1-\beta)/(1-\alpha-\beta)} & \textit{if } \theta \neq 0, \\[2ex] \left(\dfrac{1-\alpha-\beta}{1-\beta}\,at + [k(0)]^{(1-\alpha-\beta)/(1-\beta)}\right)^{(1-\beta)/(1-\alpha-\beta)} & \textit{if } \theta = 0. \end{cases} \tag{15}$$

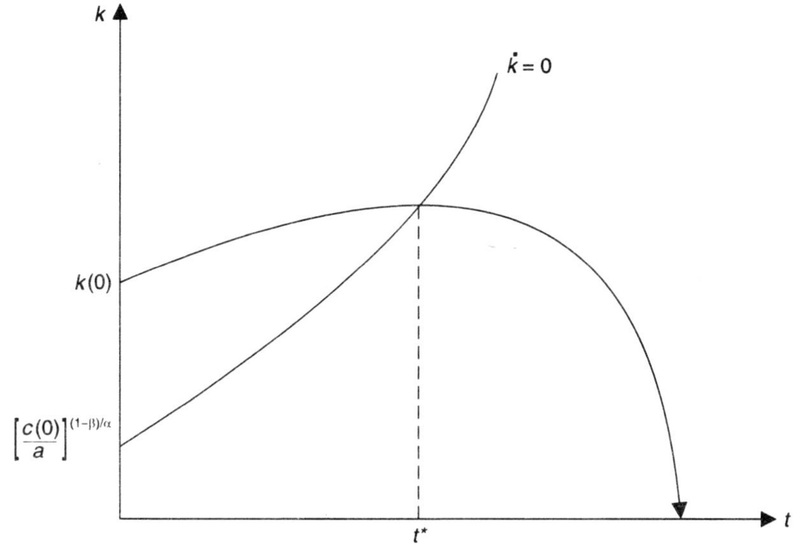

Figure 1 $g \geqslant 0 > \theta$

From (12) and (14), bearing in mind (13), the locus $(z(t), t)$ *intersects the locus* $\dot{k} = 0$ *from above in finite time.*

P*ulling together the above pieces of information we see that any trajectory* $\{k(t)\}$ *beginning above the locus* $\dot{k} = 0$ *must cut that locus and proceed to the time axis in finite time.* □

Lemma 1 eliminates all but the following three cases: (a) $g = \theta \geqslant 0$, (b) $\theta > g \geqslant 0$ and (c) $g > \theta > 0$.

Lemma 2(a). *If* $g = \theta \geqslant 0$, *then equation (11) has a positive solution if and only if* $c(0) \leqslant a[k(0)]^{\alpha/(1-\beta)}$.

Proof. *Consider (11). If* $c(0) > a[k(0)]^{\alpha/(1-\beta)}$, *then* $\dot{k}(t) < 0$ *for all* $t \geqslant 0$; *indeed,* $\dot{k}(t)$ *goes to* $-\infty$ *as* t *goes to* ∞, *implying that* $k(t) = 0$ *in finite time. Hence,* $c(0) > a[k(0)]^{\alpha/(1-\beta)}$ *is infeasible. If, on the other hand,* $c(0) \leqslant a[k(0)]^{\alpha/(1-\beta)}$, *then* $\dot{k}(t) \geqslant 0$. *Hence* $c(0) \leqslant a[k(0)]^{\alpha/(1-\beta)}$ *is feasible.* □

Remark. *From lemma 2(a), if* $g = \theta \geqslant 0$, *then the largest maintainable rate of consumption is* $a[k(0)]^{\alpha/(1-\beta)}$. *If consumption is maintained at that level,* $k(t) = k(0)$ *and, in view of (6), the rate of input of the raw material rises at the rate* $(\beta\lambda - \delta)/(1 - \beta)$, *which is negative if and only if* $\theta > \delta$.

Lemma 2(b). *If* $\theta > g \geq 0$, *then there exists* $\hat{c}^*(0)$, $\hat{c}^*(0) > a[k(0)]^{\alpha/(1-\beta)}$ *such that (11) has a positive solution if and only if* $c(0) \leq \hat{c}^*(0)$.

Proof. *Consider (11). If* $c(0) \leq a[k(0)]^{\alpha/(1-\beta)}$, *then* $\dot{k}(t) > 0$ *for all* $t > 0$. *If* $c(0)$ *exceeds* $a[k(0)]^{\alpha/(1-\beta)}$ *by a sufficiently small quantity, then* $k(t)$ *declines at first and later increases, with* k *always positive. If* $c(0)$ *exceeds* $a[k(0)]^{\alpha/(1-\beta)}$ *by a sufficiently large amount, then* $k(t)$ *will reach zero in finite time. There is a largest value of* $c(0)$, *say* $\hat{c}^*(0)$, *such that* $k(t)$ *remains positive for all t. If that value is chosen,* $k(t)$ *declines asymptotically to zero (the upturn in* $k(t)$ *is at infinity).* □

Lemma 2(c). *If* $g > \theta > 0$, *then (11) has a positive solution provided that* $c(0)$ *is sufficiently small and* $(1-\beta)\theta/(1-\alpha-\beta) > g$.

Proof. *From earlier reasoning (the first step in the proof of lemma 1), a programme is feasible if and only if the path* $\{k(t)\}$ *lies everywhere above the locus* $\dot{k} = 0$ *that is everywhere above the curve*

$$\tilde{k}(t) = [c(0)/a]^{(1-\beta)/\alpha} \exp[(g-\theta)(1-\beta)t/\alpha]. \tag{16}$$

Comparing (15) and (16), and bearing in mind that $g > \theta > 0$, *we see that if* $c(0)$ *is positive but sufficiently small and if*

$$(1-\beta)\theta/(1-\alpha-\beta) > (g-\theta)(1-\beta)/\alpha$$

or, equivalently,

$$g < (1-\beta)\theta/(1-\alpha-\beta), \tag{17}$$

then, for all $t \geq 0$, $z(t) \geq \tilde{k}(t)$. □

Pulling together the salient features of lemmas 1 and 2, we have the following:

Proposition. *Under the general assumptions of this section (stationary population, Cobb–Douglas technology), a constant and positive level of consumption can be maintained if and only if* $\lambda - \delta \geq 0$, *that is if and only if the rate of exogenous resource-saving technical progress at least matches the rate of deterioration of the terms of trade, and an exponentially growing positive level of consumption is attainable if and only if* $(\lambda - \delta)/(1-\alpha-\beta) > g/\beta$.

Remark 1. *Solow (1974) showed that a closed economy with a constant population, a finite deposit of an essential, costlessly storable resource, and a stationary, constant-returns Cobb–Douglas production function can maintain a positive level of consumption if and only if the share of capital exceeds the share of the resource, that is if and only if* $\alpha > \beta$. *And, of course, even if Solow's condition is not met, survival is possible if there is steady technical progress, at however modest a rate. In contrast, it has emerged that for the survival of a small open economy with deteriorating terms of trade, technical progress is always necessary, whether* *or not Solow's condition is met and whether or not returns to scale are constant, and that technical progress is sufficient only if it accrues at a rate which depends on the share of the resource and on the rate of decline of the terms of trade.*

Remark 2. *The condition for a constant and positive level of consumption is quite independent of the nature of returns to scale in capital and the resource. The intuitive explanation may be found in the fact that if* $g = 0$*, then output is constant and returns to scale never come into play. The conditions for a growing level of consumption, on the other hand, depend intimately on the nature of returns to scale: the larger is* $\alpha + \beta$*, the measure of returns to scale, the less severe the requirements placed on technical progress.*

3 THE POSSIBILITY OF STORAGE

Throughout the argument of section 2 it was assumed that imports of the raw material are immediately used in production. The assumption would be inescapable if storage of the extracted resource were impossible. But in general extracted resources can be stored, at some cost. Does the possibility of storage make any difference to our conclusion that survival is impossible without technical progress? We proceed to sketch-argue that in the canonical case of exponential storage costs survival is impossible without technical progress.

Let a stock $R(t)$ of imported raw material be held and let the stock decay at the constant rate ε. Suppose, for the sake of the argument, that there is no technical progress, but that nevertheless there is an efficient trajectory $\{k^*(t), R^*(t), r^*(t)\}$ with $c(t) = c(0) > 0$. Along that trajectory the stock $R^*(t)$ must eventually decline. Let us suppose that it begins to decline at $t = T$. We pick up the evolution of the economy at T.

Consider two fictitious economies. The first is closed, with $k^{(1)}(T) = k^*(T) > 0$, $R^{(1)}(T) = R^*(T) > 0$, and $l^{(1)}(t) = l(t) = 1$ given and with the capacity to store the raw material subject to exponential decay; the second is open, with $k^{(2)}(T) = k^*(T) > 0$ and $l^{(2)}(T) = l(T) = 1$ given, able to trade at $p(0)\exp(\delta t)$ but unable to store the raw material. The economies share the production function (1). The first economy uses up its stock of raw material at the rate $-\dot{R}^*(t)$; the second economy imports the raw material at the rate $r^*(t)$. The first economy makes available goods for consumption at the rate $c^{(1)}(t) = \alpha^{(1)}(t)c(0)$, the second at the rate $c^{(2)}(t) = \alpha^{(2)}(t)c(0)$, where $\alpha^{(1)}(t) \equiv -\dot{R}^*(t)/[r^*(t) - \dot{R}^*(t)]$, $\alpha^2(t) \equiv r^*(t)/[r^*(t) - \dot{R}^*(t)]$, and $\alpha^{(1)}(t) + \alpha^{(2)}(t) = 1$. Thus, collectively, the two fictitious economies yield consumption at the same rate as our small open economy. Moreover, from the concavity of the production function, $\dot{k}^{(i)}(t) > \dot{k}(t)$ and $k^{(i)}(t) > k(t)$ $(i = 1, 2)$ for all $t > T$; and, of course, $R^{(1)}(t) = R^*(t)$ for $t > T$. It follows that if the programme $\{k^*(t), R^*(t), r^*(t)\}$ is feasible, then so are the programmes, just described, of the two fictitious economies and, *a fortiori*, so are those programmes modified by the substitution of the positive constant $\bar{\alpha}^{(i)} \equiv \inf_t \alpha^{(i)}(t)$ for $\alpha^{(i)}(t)$. But it is known that such modified programmes are infeasible: that the first is infeasible has been shown by Kemp and Long (1982); that the second is infeasible has been demonstrated in section 2. Hence, the trajectory $\{k^*(t), R^*(t), r^*(t)\}$ is infeasible and we arrive at a contradiction. Our small open economy cannot survive.

4 AN ALTERNATIVE MODEL

We have considered conditions for the survival of a small country which depends on foreign sources for an essential raw material. It was found in section 2 that survival is impossible if the rate of resource-saving technical progress is less than the rate of deterioration of the terms of trade. Suppose instead that the imported good is an essential consumption good. What then are the conditions of survival?

Sticking as close as possible to the formulation of section 2, we might write utility as

$$u(t) = y(t)^{\omega} r(t)^{\beta} \exp(\beta\lambda t), \quad 0 < \omega, \beta < 1; \omega + \beta < 1,$$

and

$$y(t) = k(t)^{\mu} \quad 0 < \mu < 1, \tag{1*}$$

so that, substituting from the second equation into the first,

$$u(t) = k(t)^{\alpha} r(t)^{\beta} \exp(\beta\lambda t), \quad 0 < \alpha \equiv \mu\omega < 1.$$

The analysis and conclusions of section 2 now apply, with $u(t)$ playing the role of $y(t)$.

Alternatively we might write

$$u(t) = y(t)^{\omega} r(t)^{\beta}$$

and

$$y(t) = k(t)^{\mu} \exp(\beta\lambda t/\omega),$$

so that, substituting from the second equation into the first, we again obtain (1*).

NOTES

* The authors gratefully acknowledge the constructive comments of Carl Chiarella, Koji Okuguchi and Makoto Tawada. An earlier version of the essay appeared in the *Journal of International Economics* 13: 135–42 (1982).

1 Shimomura (1983) has shown that lemma 1 is valid without the restriction that the production function be Cobb–Douglas.

REFERENCES

Hotelling, H. (1931) 'The economics of exhaustible resources', *Journal of Political Economy* 38: 137–75.

Kemp, M. C. and Long, N. V. (eds) (1980) *Exhaustible Resources, Optimality, and Trade*, Amsterdam: North-Holland.

Kemp, M. C. and Long, N. V. (1982) 'On the possibility of surviving when an essential natural resource depreciates through time', University of New South Wales.

Mitra, T., Majumdar, M. and Ray, D. (1982) 'Feasible alternatives under deteriorating terms of trade', *Journal of International Economics* 13: 105–34.

Shimomura, K. (1983) 'A note on the survival of a small economy', Kobe University.

Solow, R. M. (1974) 'Intergenerational equity and exhaustible resources', *Review of Economics Studies, Symposium on the Economics of Exhaustible Resources*, pp. 39–45.

13

THE INTERNATIONAL DIFFUSION OF THE FRUITS OF TECHNICAL PROGRESS

The Hicks–Ikema theorem, that a uniform expansion of a trading country's production set must benefit its trading partner if the preferences of the expanding country are homothetic, has been demonstrated under assumptions of the Lerner–Samuelson kind. It is here shown that the theorem remains valid if one of the trading partners imposes an optimal tariff, if there are produced inputs, and if factors of production are internationally mobile.

1 INTRODUCTION

Hicks (1953) suggested that any uniform expansion of a country's production set would normally benefit its trading partners via an enhancement of the partners' terms of trade. More precise statements, and formal proofs, were provided by Kemp (1955), for economies suffering from Keynesian unemployment, and by Ikema (1969), for economies with homothetic preferences, full employment of resources and incomplete specialization of production. More recently, Kemp and Shimomura (1988) have observed that, as an important implication of the Hicks–Ikema (H–I) theorem, neither country can hold a continuing global absolute advantage over the other. Any temporary advantage would be dissipated by self-serving gifts of technical information by the owners of firms in the more advanced country.

Ikema's (1969) analysis was conducted in the narrow textbook setting of two countries, two produced goods, no produced inputs and internationally immobile primary factors of production; moreover, it is implicit in Ikema's demonstration that all markets are competitive and that trade is completely free of tariffs and other artificial obstacles to trade. Since then it has been shown by Shimomura (1991) that the theorem can accommodate more than two goods, not all of which need be tradable. Moreover Kemp and Shimomura (1988) have noted that allowance can be made for additional trading partners. (The theorem then asserts only that a uniform expansion of one country necessarily benefits at least one other country.) In the present essay we further clarify the scope of the H–I theorem by showing that it remains valid when capital is internationally mobile, when there are produced inputs and when one of the trading partners takes advantage of its market power by imposing an optimal tariff.

2 FREE TRADE

Let us begin with the conventional world in which two countries α and β trade in two commodities produced under constant returns by means of two or more primary factors of production. Let α be technically progressive, β unprogressive, and let preferences in α (but not necessarily in β) be homothetic. The second commodity will serve as *numéraire*.

The following notation will be used:

p_j the world price of the first commodity in terms of the second,
u^j the well-being of the jth country, $j = \alpha, \beta$,
$e^j(p, u^j)$ the expenditure function of the jth country, $j = \alpha, \beta$,
$r^j(p)$ the revenue or GNP function of the jth country, $j = \alpha, \beta$,
z^{j1} the excess demand of the jth country for the first commodity,
λ a technical parameter, initially equal to one.

Recalling Shepherd's lemma,

$$z^{j1}(p, u^j) = e^j_p(p, u^j) - r^j_p(p), \quad j = \alpha, \beta \tag{1}$$

where subscripts indicate partial or total differentiation.

Our model contains the two national budget constraints

$$e^\alpha(p, u^\alpha) - \lambda r^\alpha(p) = 0 \tag{2}$$

and

$$e^\beta(p, u^\beta) - r^\beta(p) = 0 \tag{3}$$

as well as the market-clearing condition which, recalling (1), can be written as

$$e^\alpha_p(p, u^\alpha) - \lambda r^\alpha_p(p) + e^\beta_p(p, u^\beta) - r^\beta_p(p) = 0. \tag{4}$$

This formulation is sufficiently general to accommodate produced inputs; if there are produced inputs, r^j must be interpreted as the value of net outputs and r^j_p as the possibly negative net output of the first commodity. The formulation also allows for the possibility of complete specialization in production, that is for zero gross output of either commodity.

We seek to show that an unbiased technical improvement in α necessarily benefits β. Differentiating (2) through (4) with respect to λ,

$$\begin{bmatrix} e^\alpha_u & 0 & e^\alpha_p - r^\alpha_p \\ 0 & e^\beta_u & e^\beta_p - r^\beta_p \\ e^\alpha_{pu} & e^\beta_{pu} & e^\alpha_{pp} - r^\alpha_{pp} + e^\beta_{pp} - r^\beta_{pp} \end{bmatrix} \begin{bmatrix} \mathrm{d}u^\alpha \\ \mathrm{d}u^\beta \\ \mathrm{d}p \end{bmatrix} = \begin{bmatrix} r^\alpha \\ 0 \\ r^\alpha_p \end{bmatrix} \mathrm{d}\lambda. \tag{5}$$

Solving,

$$\Delta(\mathrm{d}u^{\beta}/\mathrm{d}\lambda) = -\,(e^{\beta}_{p} - r^{\beta}_{p})(e^{\alpha}_{u}r^{\alpha}_{p} - e^{\alpha}_{pu}r^{\alpha}) \tag{6}$$

where Δ is the determinant of the Jacobian matrix in (5) and, as a sufficient and almost necessary condition of Walrasian stability, is negative. Now

$$\begin{aligned} 0 &= e^{\alpha}_{p} - r^{\alpha}_{p} + e^{\beta}_{p} - r^{\beta}_{p} \quad \text{[from (4)]} \\ &= (e^{\alpha}_{p}/e^{\alpha})\,e^{\alpha} - r^{\alpha}_{p} + e^{\beta}_{p} - r^{\beta}_{p} \\ &= (e^{\alpha}_{pu}/e^{\alpha}_{u})\,r^{\alpha} - r^{\alpha}_{p} + e^{\beta}_{p} - r^{\beta}_{p} \quad \text{[homotheticity of } \alpha\text{-preferences]} \\ &= (1/e^{\alpha}_{u})(e^{\alpha}_{pu}r^{\alpha} - r^{\alpha}_{p}e^{\alpha}_{u}) + e^{\beta}_{p} - r^{\beta}_{p}. \end{aligned}$$

Hence

$$(e^{\beta}_{p} - r^{\beta}_{p})(e^{\alpha}_{pu}r^{\alpha} - r^{\alpha}_{p}e^{\alpha}_{u}) < 0$$

and $\mathrm{d}u^{\beta}/\mathrm{d}\lambda > 0$.

It has been implicit in our analysis that primary factors are internationally immobile. Suppose, however, that one of two distinct industries employs just one factor (capital) to produce (capital) services which may be used as inputs to the other industry and imported or exported. Then it becomes clear that the analysis can be interpreted as accommodating international factor mobility.

3 TRADE RESTRICTED BY OPTIMAL TARIFFS

We now vary our analysis by allowing for the possibility that one of the two countries imposes an optimal tariff.

Suppose that the progressive country α imposes a tariff. For concreteness, let us assume that α imports the first commodity. If the tariff-inclusive relative price of that commodity in α is denoted by q then the tariff revenue of α in terms of the second commodity (the *numéraire*) is $-\,(q-p)\,z^{\beta 1} = -\,(q-p)(e^{\beta}_{p} - r^{\beta}_{p})$ and equations (2) and (4) must be replaced by

$$e^{\alpha}(q, u^{\alpha}) - \lambda r^{\alpha}(q) - (q-p)[-\,z^{\beta 1}(p, u^{\beta})] = 0 \tag{7}$$

and

$$e^{\alpha}_{q}(q, u^{\alpha}) - \lambda r^{\alpha}_{q}(q) + e^{\beta}_{p}(p, u^{\beta}) - r^{\beta}_{p}(p) = 0 \tag{8}$$

respectively. To complete the model, we introduce an implication of the assumption that α imposes an optimal tariff, by way of[1]

$$z^{\beta 1} - (q-p)(z^{\beta 1}_{p} - z^{\beta 1}z^{\beta 1}_{u}) \equiv z^{\beta 1} - (q-p)\,\tilde{z}^{\beta 1}_{p} = 0 \tag{9}$$

where $\tilde{z}^{\beta 1}_{p}$ is the price slope of β's Marshallian excess demand function for the first commodity. Thus we have the four equations (3), (7)–(9) in the four variables u^{α}, u^{β}, p, q and the parameter λ.

Differentiating that system with respect to λ, we obtain

where use is made of (1) and the normalizations $e_u^{\alpha} = 1 = e_u^{\beta}$, and where $x^{\alpha 1} \equiv r_p^{\alpha}$ is the output in α of the first commodity. Solving,

$$\Delta'(\mathrm{d}u^{\beta}/\mathrm{d}\lambda) = r^{\alpha} z^{\beta 1} \tilde{z}_p^{\beta 1} [z_u^{\alpha 1} - x^{\alpha 1}/r^{\alpha}]$$

where Δ' is the Jacobian determinant of the system and as a sufficient condition of Walrasian stability is positive. Moreover, $z^{\beta 1} < 0$ by assumption; $\tilde{z}_p^{\beta 1} < 0$ as an implication of α's optimal tariff; and the square-bracketed term is positive as an implication of the homotheticity of α-preferences and of the assumption that α imports the first commodity. Hence $\mathrm{d}u^{\beta}/\mathrm{d}\lambda > 0$.

The above finding can be understood in terms of Meade's trade indifference curves. After the technical improvement there emerges a new family of α-trade indifference curves. However, the new curve through the old tariff-ridden equilibrium trading point represents greater welfare than the old curve through that point. Moreover, the two curves generally differ in slope at that point, implying that the old tariff is no longer optimal and that further gains can be achieved by resetting it at its new optimal level.

If β instead of α maintains an optimal tariff, and if α-preferences are homothetic, it remains true that a technical improvement in α benefits β. A mathematical proof, of the type provided above, could be fashioned. For a proof based on simple offer-curve techniques, see Kemp *et al.* (1990).

4 IMPLICATIONS

It has been shown that the H–I theorem is valid under quite general conditions. It follows from the reasoning of Kemp and Shimomura (1988) that, under the same general conditions, no country can hold a global advantage over all other countries.

NOTES

1 See Bhagwati *et al.* (1983).

REFERENCES

Bhagwati, J. N., Brecher, R. A. and Hatta, T. (1983) 'The generalized theory of transfers and welfare: Bilateral transfers in a multilateral world', *American Economic Review* 83: 606–18.

Hicks, J. R. (1953) 'An inaugural lecture', *Oxford Economic Papers* 5: 117–35.

Ikema, M. (1969) 'The effect of economic growth on the demand for imports: A simple diagram', *Oxford Economic Papers* 21: 66–9.

Kemp, M. C. (1955) 'Technological change, the terms of trade and welfare', *Economic Journal* 65: 457–74.
Kemp, M. C. and Shimomura, K. (1988) 'The impossibility of global absolute advantage in the Heckscher–Ohlin model of trade', *Oxford Economic Papers* 40: 575–6.
Kemp, M. C., Ng, Y.-K. and Shimomura, K. (1990) 'The international diffusion of the fruits of technical progress', mimeo, Univerity of New South Wales.
Shimomura, K. (1991) 'A note on the Hicks–Ikema–Kemp proposition', *Kobe Economic and Business Review* 36: 27–32.

Part II

THE GAINS FROM RESTRICTED TRADE UNDER PERFECT COMPETITION

14

ON THE SHARING OF TRADE GAINS BY RESOURCE-POOR AND RESOURCE-RICH COUNTRIES*

1 INTRODUCTION

Our concern in the present essay is with a view of world production and trade enjoying an extraordinarily mixed ancestry. One may find it in the turn-of-the-century and later writings on economic imperialism; in some of the immediate post-Second World War modelling of the process of economic development (Prebisch, 1950, 1959; Singer, 1950); and, by implication, in the agenda of recent international conferences for economic co-operation between industrialized and developing nations.

According to this view, to a useful approximation one may divide the world into two complementary groups of countries. In one group are the resource-rich providers of raw materials; in the other group are the resource-poor processors of raw materials. Until recent cautionary events in the world markets for oil and other raw materials, it was held by adherents of this view that the 'imperial' processors of raw materials enjoy a special, one-sided collective power to 'exploit', and interest in 'exploiting', their economic 'colonies'. Now there are those who believe that the boot really is on the other foot.

In section 2 we offer a particular formalization of the above view. We then, in section 3, proceed to examine the extent to which, within the framework of the model, imperial countries can, and might wish to, exploit their colonies. In section 4 we face the other way and seek to define the extent to which colonies can, and might wish to, exploit their masters; that is, we seek to determine the scope of 'resource nationalism'. The chief conclusion emerging from sections 2–4 is that, in the context of our model, imperial exploitation will be complete while the scope for resource nationalism is necessarily limited.

In section 5 we seek to relate our analysis to the well-known works of Prebisch and Singer by examining the implications of technical improvements in the context of the model of section 2.

The more substantial of our conclusions are collected as propositions 1 and 2 of sections 3 and 4, respectively.

In pursuit of a concise and simple analysis we introduce some stiff assumptions. For example, we recognize only two economies, the imperial and the colonial, and (departing from the production symmetry of Heckscher and Ohlin) we suppose that neither country is both provider and processor of raw materials. In a final section we examine the robustness of our conclusions under relaxed assumptions.

2 AN ASYMMETRICAL WORLD ECONOMY[1]

We consider a world of only two countries, the 'home' and the 'foreign'. The foreign country produces just one commodity, a raw material, by means of labour and equipment. The home country also produces just one commodity, but a consumption good and by means of labour and equipment and of the imported raw material. The foreign country cannot produce the consumption good; the home country cannot produce the raw material. The consumption good cannot be produced without the raw material; the raw material cannot be produced by labour alone. The consumption good is called the first commodity, the raw material the second commodity. The home country exports the first commodity, imports the second. The home country may be a capital-poor borrower or a capital-rich lender; for concreteness it is now assumed that it is a capital-rich lender (like Victorian Britain), but it will be shown later that nothing hinges on this assumption. Individual producers and consumers behave competitively. Factors of production are fully employed in each country. International payments balance, that is there is no involuntary or 'compensatory' borrowing or lending by governments.

Seeking its own advantage, and unmindful of the welfare of the foreigner, the capital-rich home country may impose taxes on any two or all three of imports, exports and the rentals of equipment invested abroad. We suppose that it taxes its exports and rentals, distributing the proceeds (positive or negative) in lumpsum fashion to its residents. The self-seeking foreign country, on the other hand, is supposed to impose taxes on its exports and on the foreign earnings of home capital.

The following notation will be employed throughout sections 3–5:

D_i the home demand for the *i*th commodity,
X_i the home production of the *i*th commodity,
p the home price of the second commodity in terms of the first,
r the home rental of capital in terms of the first commodity,
$\bar{K}$ the home stock of capital,
K the stock of capital lent abroad by the home country,
τ the *ad valorem* rate of tax imposed by the home country on its exports,
t the rate of tax imposed by the home country on the rentals of that part of its equipment invested abroad.

The corresponding foreign variables are distinguished by an asterisk. For example, D_i^* is the foreign demand for the *i*th commodity and τ^* is the *ad* *valorem* rate of tax imposed by the foreign country on its exports. Notice that, by assumption, $X_2 \equiv 0$, $X_1^* \equiv 0$ and $D_2^* \equiv 0$.

Suppressing the constant labour inputs, the two production functions are

$$X_1 = \tilde{X}_1(\bar{K} - K, D_2) \tag{1}$$

and

$$X_2^* = \tilde{X}_2^*(\bar{K}^* + K), \tag{2}$$

and are supposed to satisfy the restrictions

$$\frac{\partial \tilde{X}_1}{\partial(\bar{K} - K)} > 0, \quad \frac{\partial \tilde{X}_1}{\partial D_2} > 0, \tag{3a}$$

$$\frac{\partial^2 \tilde{X}_1}{\partial(\bar{K} - K)^2} < 0, \quad \frac{\partial^2 \tilde{X}_1}{\partial D_2^2} < 0, \tag{3b}$$

$$\frac{\partial^2 \tilde{X}_1}{\partial(\bar{K} - K)\partial D_2} \geqslant 0, \tag{3c}$$

$$\frac{\mathrm{d}\tilde{X}_2}{\mathrm{d}(\bar{K}^* + K)} > 0, \tag{4a}$$

$$\frac{\mathrm{d}^2\tilde{X}_2^*}{\mathrm{d}(\bar{K}^* + K)^2} < 0. \tag{4b}$$

In the present context, all of these restrictions (even (3c)) seem plausible. Under the assumed competitive conditions,

$$r = \frac{\partial \tilde{X}_1}{\partial(\bar{K} - K)}, \tag{5}$$

$$p = \frac{\partial \tilde{X}_1}{\partial D_2}, \tag{6}$$

and

$$r^* = p^* \frac{\mathrm{d}\tilde{X}_2^*}{\mathrm{d}(\bar{K}^* + K)}. \tag{7}$$

3 THE SCOPE OF ECONOMIC IMPERIALISM

Suppose that the home country imposes taxes τ and t and seeks to set them at levels which yield the greatest home consumption. Suppose further that the foreign country is completely passive, imposing no taxes of any kind.[2] What is the scope for intervention in this form; that is, to what extent can home consumption be raised above its *laissez-faire* level? And what are the implications for foreign consumption?

Our consideration of these questions proceeds from a pair of market-equilibrium conditions. The conditions of equilibrium in world commodity markets are

$$D_1 + D_1^* = X_1 \tag{8}$$

and

$$D_2 = X_2^*. \tag{9}$$

However, in view of the two countries' budget constraints, one of these equations is redundant. Under the assumptions of this section, the home and foreign constraints are, respectively,

$$(D_1 - X_1) + p^* D_2 = r^* K \tag{10}$$

and

$$D_1^* - p^* X_2^* = - r^* K. \tag{11}$$

Equation (8) is implied by (9)–(11) and therefore can be discarded. Proceeding, as a condition of equilibrium in the world capital market,

$$\frac{\partial \tilde{X}_1}{\partial(\bar{K} - K)} = (1 - t)p \frac{\mathrm{d}\tilde{X}_2^*}{\mathrm{d}(\bar{K}^* + K)}. \tag{12}$$

However, as an implication of competitive arbitrage, we have

$$p = (1 + \tau)p^*. \tag{13}$$

Together with (5) and (7), (12) and (13) imply that

$$r = (1 - t)(1 + \tau)r^*. \tag{14}$$

Finally, we notice that the home demand for the second commodity is a function of the home price ratio and the stock of capital in use at home:

$$D_2 = \tilde{D}_2(p, \bar{K} - K). \tag{15}$$

Thus, from (6),

$$\mathrm{d}p = \frac{\partial^2 \tilde{X}_1}{\partial D_2^2} \mathrm{d}D_2 + \frac{\partial^2 \tilde{X}_1}{\partial(\bar{K} - K)\partial D_2} \mathrm{d}(\bar{K} - K), \tag{16}$$

which, together with (3b) and (3c), yields

$$\frac{\partial \tilde{D}_2}{\partial p} < 0, \quad \frac{\partial \tilde{D}_2}{\partial(\bar{K} - K)} \geqslant 0. \tag{17}$$

It follows that (9) and (14) can be treated as our equilibrium conditions. Given τ, t, $\bar{K}$ and $\bar{K}^*$ they determine p^* and K; (13) then yields p.

We next introduce an adjustment mechanism for the key variables p^* and K and show that any equilibrium defined by (9) and (14) is locally stable. The mechanism is described by the pair of differential equations

$$\dot{p}^* = f[\tilde{D}_2(p, \bar{K} - K) - \tilde{X}_2^*(\bar{K}^* + K)], \tag{18}$$

$$\dot{K} = g[(1 - t)(1 + \tau)r^* - r], \tag{19}$$

where an overdot denotes the time derivative and where

$$f'(\cdot) > 0, \quad g'(\cdot) > 0,$$

$$f(0) = 0, \quad g(0) = 0. \tag{20}$$

In words, the foreign relative price of the second commodity rises or falls as the excess demand for that commodity is positive or negative; and the stock of home capital lent abroad rises or falls as the home rental falls short of or exceeds the foreign rental net of taxes. Consider now the Jacobian matrix J of the equilibrium equations (9) and (14). From (1), (5), (7) and (13),

$$J = \begin{pmatrix} -D_2\eta_2 & -(\lambda + r^*) \\ (r + D_2\eta_2\mu)K & -(\delta\varepsilon + \delta^*\varepsilon^*)p^*r \end{pmatrix}, \tag{21}$$

where

$$\eta_2 \equiv -\frac{p}{D_2}\frac{\partial \tilde{D}_2}{\partial p},$$

$$\lambda \equiv p^*\frac{\partial \tilde{D}_2}{\partial(\bar{K} - K)},$$

$$\mu \equiv \frac{\partial r}{\partial D_2},$$

$$\delta \equiv \frac{K}{\bar{K} - K},$$

$$\delta^* \equiv \frac{K}{\bar{K}^* + K},$$

$$\varepsilon \equiv -\frac{\bar{K}-K}{r}\left(\frac{\partial r}{\partial(\bar{K}-K)}+\frac{\partial r}{\partial D_2}\cdot\frac{\partial \tilde{D}_2}{\partial(\bar{K}-K)}\right),$$

$$\varepsilon^* \equiv -\frac{\bar{K}^*+K}{r^*}\cdot\frac{\partial r^*}{\partial(\bar{K}^*+K)}.$$

In view of (3)–(5), (7) and (17),

$$\eta_2 > 0,\quad \lambda \geqslant 0,\quad \mu \geqslant 0,\quad \varepsilon^* > 0. \tag{22a}$$

Moreover, since $K > 0$,

$$\delta > 0,\quad \delta^* > 0. \tag{22b}$$

Finally, we shall assume that the home marginal productivity of capital is diminishing in the total or *mutatis mutandis* sense, with induced changes in the input of raw material allowed for:

$$\frac{\partial r}{\partial(\bar{K}-K)}+\frac{\partial r}{\partial D_2}\cdot\frac{\partial \tilde{D}_2}{\partial(\bar{K}-K)} < 0.$$

It then follows that

$$\varepsilon > 0 \tag{22c}$$

also. From (22), the determinant of J is positive and its trace is negative. Hence any equilibrium defined by (9) and (14) is locally stable if the adjustment mechanism is described by (18) and (19). In fact, J is stable everywhere, not just in stationary equilibrium; hence, by Olech's theorem (Hartman and Olech, 1962) the adjustment mechanism is globally stable.

Now we can turn to the main business of this section, the examination of the effect on home consumption of changes in τ and t. Differentiating (9) and (14) totally, we obtain

$$-D_2\eta_2 \mathrm{d}p^* - (\lambda + r^*)\mathrm{d}K = \frac{p^* D_2\eta_2}{1+\tau}\mathrm{d}\tau \tag{23}$$

and

$$(r + D_2\eta_2\mu)K\,\mathrm{d}p^* - (\delta\varepsilon + \delta^*\varepsilon^*)p^* r\mathrm{d}K = pr^* K\,\mathrm{d}t - \frac{(r + D_2\eta_2\mu)p^* K}{1+\tau}\mathrm{d}\tau, \tag{24}$$

whence

$$\frac{\partial p^*}{\partial t} = \frac{p(\lambda + r^*)r^* K}{\Delta} > 0, \tag{25}$$

$$\frac{\partial K}{\partial t} = -\frac{pD_2 r^* K\eta_2}{\Delta} < 0, \tag{26}$$

$$\frac{\partial p^*}{\partial \tau} = -\frac{p^*}{1+\tau} < 0, \tag{27}$$

$$\frac{\partial K}{\partial \tau} = 0, \tag{28}$$

where $\Delta \equiv \det J > 0$.

The first three of these conclusions are not surprising. Equation (28), however, displays a remarkable feature of the present model, that is the invariance of the world allocation of resources and choice of production technique to changes in the rate of export tax and to the consequential changes in world prices. Confirming this feature of the model, we have, from (27) and (28), together with (5), (7) and (13),

$$\frac{\partial p}{\partial \tau} = 0, \tag{29}$$

$$\frac{\partial r}{\partial \tau} = 0 \tag{30}$$

and

$$\frac{\partial r^*}{\partial \tau} = \frac{r^*}{p^*} \cdot \frac{\partial p^*}{\partial \tau} < 0. \tag{31}$$

(Alternatively, we may note that (9) and (14) can be solved for p and K in terms of t, independently of τ.)

Thus an increase in the home country's export tax merely redistributes income (consumption) from the foreign country to the home. Moreover, the home country can secure for itself any proper fraction of world consumption simply by choosing a sufficiently high but finite export tax. In the limit, as the rate of tax goes to infinity, the fraction goes to one. Thus there is no finite optimal rate of export tax.[3] We can make this point clearer, perhaps, by considering the foreign country's budget constraint (11). This can be rewritten as

$$D_1^* = \frac{1}{1+\tau}\left(pX_2^* - \frac{rK}{1-t}\right). \tag{11'}$$

Given t, $t \neq 1$, the bracketed term is a finite constant; hence foreign consumption D_1^* goes to zero as the rate of export tax τ goes to infinity.

Several conclusions can be drawn from the above discussion. First, it is optimal for the self-seeking home country to exploit the foreign country to the limit. Second, the act of exploitation does not involve manipulation of international borrowing and lending. Indeed, it is an implication of complete exploitation that international indebtedness remains at its pre-intervention level. Finally, the desired degree of exploitation can be achieved by means of an export tax only. The second policy instrument, the tax on foreign rentals, may be used in a supplementary role, but it need not be used. However, one can imagine political or institutional considerations which impose an upper bound on the rate of export tax and which therefore activate the tax on foreign rentals. Suppose then that the rate of export tax rests at its political–institutional upper bound $\bar{\tau}$. We seek the second-best, $\bar{\tau}$-dependent optimal t. Differentiating the foreign budget constraint (11), we find that

$$\frac{\partial D_1^*}{\partial t} = \frac{D_1^*}{p^*}\frac{\partial p^*}{\partial t} + \delta^*\varepsilon^* r^* \frac{\partial K}{\partial t}. \tag{32}$$

Applying the commodity-market equilibrium conditions (8) and (9), substituting for $\partial p^*/\partial t$ and $\partial K/\partial t$ from (25) and (26), and equating the end product to zero, we find that

$$t = \tilde{t}(\bar{\tau}) \equiv \frac{1}{1+\bar{\tau}}\left(\delta^*\varepsilon^* - \frac{(\lambda + r^*)D_1^*}{r^* p^* D_2 \eta_2}\right). \tag{33}$$

There seems to be no reason why t should not be negative,[4] in contrast to the usual argument for the restriction of foreign lending.

That completes our calculations. They have been conducted on the assumption that the resource-poor home country is also capital rich, so that K is positive. It remains to note that none of our conclusions rests on that assumption. Of course, if K is negative then so are δ and δ^*, and we can conformably reinterpret all the results. The capital-rich OPEC and Scandinavian countries are not excluded from our analysis merely by virtue of their capital-richness. Thus, pulling together our main conclusions, we have

Proposition 1. *Within the framework of the model, the resource-poor imperial economy can exploit the resource-rich colonial economy to any desired degree and can do this by means of just one policy instrument, the export tax. Exploitation involves only a redistribution of a constant world consumption; it is not accompanied by a reallocation of productive factors. Hence the self-regarding imperial economy will choose to exploit fully the colonial economy.*

It perhaps bears remarking that, while (under the special assumptions of this essay) the home country can achieve any desired degree of exploitation by means of an export tax only, there is no **need** for it to rely on that instrument. Any degree of exploitation can be achieved by an appropriate choice of import tax and subsidy to foreign earnings. (In general, if there is trade in n commodities, possibly including the services of capital, then any trading equilibrium attainable by the exercise of n import–export tax subsidies is also attainable by the exercise of $n - 1$ such instruments.) On the other hand, it is not the case that any desired degree of exploitation can be achieved by an import tax alone. For an import tax creates no gap between the home and foreign nominal prices of the first commodity, the *numéraire* in terms of which capital rents are measured. It follows that if only an import tax is imposed then the condition of capital-market equilibrium is $r = r^*$, which is inconsistent with (14) when $t = 0$ and $\tau \neq 0$. Does this mean that Lerner's symmetry theorem (Lerner, 1936) cannot be extended to a world with mobile capital? Not at all. In such a world, counting in the services of capital, there are not two but three traded commodities. The extended symmetry theorem then becomes as follows: uniform *ad valorem* export and import taxes, at the same rate on imports and exports, are consistent with the same real producing–trading–consuming equilibrium.

Finally, and obviously, our conclusion that the self-seeking resource-poor country will exploit the resource-rich country to the limit can be modified to accommodate the fact that some positive level of consumption is necessary for the survival of the resource-rich (and therefore the resource-poor) country. Only a change of origin is involved.

4 THE SCOPE OF RESOURCE NATIONALISM

Reversing the assumptions of section 3, we suppose that the foreign country imposes taxes τ^* and t^* and seeks to set them at levels which yield the greatest foreign consumption, with the home country now playing the passive role. To what extent can foreign consumption be raised above its *laissez-faire* level? And what are the implications of resource nationalism for home consumption?

Each country produces a commodity without which the other's consumption is pinned to zero – each country has the power to beggar the other. One might expect therefore that the resolution of the above questions would follow familiar lines; that, in particular, the foreign country would be revealed as not only capable of completely exploiting the home but also with an interest in doing so, symmetry of conclusions emerging from a highly asymmetrical model. This expectation is not realized.

Omitting detailed derivations, we note that the condition of arbitrage equilibrium is now

$$p = (1 + \tau^*)p^*, \tag{34}$$

that the home and foreign budget constraints are

$$(D_1 - X_1) + pD_2 = rK \tag{35}$$

and

$$D_1^* - pX_2^* = -rK, \tag{36}$$

and that, by implication, our equilibrium conditions are (9) and, in place of (14),

$$r = (1 - t^*)r^*. \tag{37}$$

Notice that (37) is simpler than its counterpart (14); the reason is that the *numéraire* (the consumption good) is now untaxed. Local stability is assured.

Differentiating (9) and (37) totally, we obtain

$$-D_2\eta_2 dp - \frac{p}{p^*}(\lambda + r^*)dK = 0 \tag{38}$$

and

$$(r + D_2\eta_2\mu)Kdp - (\delta\varepsilon + \delta^*\varepsilon^*)prdK = pr^*Kdt^* + \frac{prK}{1+\tau^*}d\tau^*, \tag{39}$$

whence

$$\frac{\partial p}{\partial t^*} = \frac{(1+\tau^*)p(\lambda + r^*)r^*K}{\Delta^*} > 0, \tag{40}$$

$$\frac{\partial K}{\partial t^*} = -\frac{pD_2r^*K\eta_2}{\Delta^*} < 0, \tag{41}$$

$$\frac{\partial p}{\partial \tau^*} = \frac{p(\lambda + r^*)rK}{\Delta^*} > 0, \tag{42}$$

$$\frac{\partial K}{\partial \tau^*} = -\frac{pD_2rK\eta_2}{(1+\tau^*)\Delta^*} < 0, \tag{43}$$

where Δ^* is the determinant of the Jacobian matrix of (9) and (37) with respect to p and K and is positive.

We notice immediately that changes in τ^* and t^* disturb the endogenous variables in essentially the same way. Thus, as in section 3, one of the two policy instruments is redundant.

Next, combining the conditions of factor-market equilibrium (8) and (9) with the budget constraints (35) and (36), we obtain an expression for the change in each country's consumption in terms of changes in the two policy instruments:

$$dD_1 = -(p + K\eta_2\mu)\frac{D_2}{p}dp + \delta\varepsilon r dK, \tag{44}$$

$$dD_1^* = (p + K\eta_2\mu)\frac{D_2}{p}dp + \left[\left(\frac{p}{p^*}r^* - r\right) - \delta\varepsilon r\right]dK \tag{45}$$

From (39)–(45) we then obtain

$$\begin{aligned}\frac{\partial D_1^*}{\partial \tau^*} &= \frac{r}{r^*(1+\tau^*)}\frac{\partial D_1^*}{\partial t^*}\\ &= \frac{D_2rK}{(1+\tau^*)\Delta^*}\left\{(\lambda + r^*)(p + K\eta_2\mu)(1+\tau^*)\right.\\ &\quad \left. - \left[\left(\frac{p}{p^*}r^* - r\right) - \delta\varepsilon r\right]p\eta_2\right\}.\end{aligned} \tag{46}$$

Equating this expression to zero, we obtain an equation which can be solved for the optimal τ^*, given t^*, or for the optimal t^*, given τ^*. In the special separable case in which at home the marginal product of each factor is independent of the amount of the other factor employed, so that $\mu = \lambda = 0$,

$$\text{opt. } \tau^* = \frac{1 + \delta\varepsilon\eta_2}{\eta_2 - 1}, \quad \text{when } t^* = 0, \tag{47}$$

and

$$\text{opt. } t^* = \frac{1 + \delta\varepsilon\eta_2}{(1 + \delta\varepsilon)\eta_2}, \quad \text{when } \tau^* = 0. \tag{48}$$

It is clear that, in general, the foreign country is able to increase its consumption at the expense of the home country. However, the incentive to exploit is limited. Moreover, if international capital movements are ruled out, the foreign country is deprived of all power to exploit by means of taxes. For if $K \equiv 0$ then (9) is the only equilibrium condition and determines the international terms of trade, and therefore the international division of world consumption, independently of foreign tax policy. Thus, whereas for complete exploitation by the resource-poor home country it is necessary that there be no change in the level of international indebtedness, for any exploitation by the resource-rich foreign country it is essential that the level of indebtedness be free to assume a non-zero value. The common sense of this asymmetry may be found in the assumption that the foreign country (but not the home country) produces an intermediate good. With labour and equipment inputs unchanged in the home country, any change in the nominal price of the raw material must be transmitted to the nominal price of the consumer good, leaving relative prices unchanged.

As in section 3, none of our conclusions rests on the assumption that K is positive. Thus we have the following proposition.

Proposition 2. *Within the framework of the model, the resource-rich colonial economy has a limited incentive to exploit the resource-poor imperial economy and it can achieve an optimum by means of a single policy instrument. Exploitation involves a reallocation of world resources, with an attendant drop in world consumption. In the special case in which international investment is ruled out, the colonial economy loses all power to exploit by means of taxes.*

We note that, while the self-seeking resource-poor country will exploit to the limit and the self-seeking resource-rich country only partially, it is not implied by our analysis that exploitation by the resource-poor country is greater in absolute terms (i.e. in terms of additional consumption acquired). The resource-rich country may be close to beggary even in the absence of intervention.

5 TO WHOM THE FRUITS OF PROGRESS?

The asymmetry of the effects of home and foreign tax policies is attributable to differences in the productive structures of the two countries. One therefore might expect similar asymmetries in the effects of any paired structural changes. In the present section we take up the comparative statics of technical improvement, a focus of controversy in the post-war literature concerning the appropriate paths of economic development.

To avoid merely obscuring complications, all kinds of taxation are now assumed away, so that the conditions of arbitrage and capital-market equilibrium reduce to

$$p = p^* \tag{49}$$

and

$$r = r^*. \tag{50}$$

To accommodate the possibility of technical improvements, the two production functions are rewritten more elaborately as

$$X_1 = \tilde{X}_1(\bar{K} - K, D_2; \alpha), \tag{51}$$

$$X_2^* = \tilde{X}_2^*(\bar{K}^* + K; \alpha^*), \tag{52}$$

and the home demand for the raw material as

$$D_2 = \tilde{D}_2(p, \bar{K} - K; \alpha), \tag{53}$$

where increases in the parameters α and α^* indicate technical improvement $(\partial\tilde{X}_1/\partial\alpha > 0,\ \partial\tilde{X}_2^*/\partial\alpha^* > 0,\ \partial\tilde{D}_2/\partial\alpha \gtreqless 0)$.

Differentiating (9) and (50) totally, bearing in mind (49) and (51), we obtain

$$-D_2\eta_2\,\mathrm{d}p - (\lambda + r^*)\mathrm{d}K = -p\frac{\partial\tilde{D}_2}{\partial\alpha}\,\mathrm{d}\alpha + p\frac{\partial\tilde{X}_2^*}{\partial\alpha^*}\,\mathrm{d}\alpha^*, \tag{54}$$

$$(r + D_2\eta_2\mu)K\mathrm{d}p - (\delta\varepsilon + \delta^*\varepsilon^*)pr\mathrm{d}K = pK\left(\frac{\partial r}{\partial\alpha}\,\mathrm{d}\alpha - \frac{\partial r^*}{\partial\alpha^*}\,\mathrm{d}\alpha^*\right); \tag{55}$$

whence

$$\frac{\partial p}{\partial\alpha} = \frac{p}{\Gamma}\left((\delta\varepsilon + \delta^*\varepsilon^*)pr\frac{\partial\tilde{D}_2}{\partial\alpha} + (\lambda + r^*)K\frac{\partial r}{\partial\alpha}\right), \tag{56}$$

$$\frac{\partial K}{\partial\alpha} = \frac{p}{\Gamma}\left((r + D_2\eta_2\mu)K\frac{\partial\tilde{D}_2}{\partial\alpha} - KD_2\eta_2\frac{\partial r}{\partial\alpha}\right), \tag{57}$$

$$\frac{\partial p}{\partial \alpha^*} = -\frac{p}{\Gamma}\left((\delta\varepsilon + \delta^*\varepsilon^*)pr^* \frac{\partial \tilde{X}_2^*}{\partial \alpha^*} + (\lambda + r^*)K\frac{\partial r^*}{\partial \alpha^*}\right), \tag{58}$$

$$\frac{\partial K}{\partial \alpha^*} = \frac{p}{\Gamma}\left(KD_2\eta_2 \frac{\partial r^*}{\partial \alpha^*} - (r + D_2\eta_2\mu)K\frac{\partial \tilde{X}_2^*}{\partial \alpha^*}\right), \tag{59}$$

where Γ is the determinant of the Jacobian matrix of the equilibrium equations (9) and (50) and is positive.

The change in each country's consumption may be related to the changes in the terms of trade, in the level of international indebtedness and in the two production technologies. Thus we have

$$\mathrm{d}D_1 = -\frac{D_1^*}{p}\,\mathrm{d}p - \delta^*\varepsilon^* r^*\,\mathrm{d}K + \frac{\partial \tilde{X}_1}{\partial \alpha}\,\mathrm{d}\alpha + K\frac{\partial r^*}{\partial \alpha^*}\,\mathrm{d}\alpha^* \tag{60}$$

and

$$\mathrm{d}D_1^* = \frac{D_1^*}{p}\,\mathrm{d}p + \delta^*\varepsilon^* r^*\,\mathrm{d}K + \left(p\frac{\partial \tilde{X}_2^*}{\partial \alpha^*} - K\frac{\partial r^*}{\partial \alpha^*}\right)\mathrm{d}\alpha^*. \tag{61}$$

Inspection of the general expressions (60) and (61) already reveals the expected asymmetry of the effects of technical improvement at home and abroad. However, to sharpen the picture let us consider the separable case in which $\lambda = \mu = 0$, and let us suppose that technical improvement bears only on the marginal products of domestic inputs, leaving the marginal products of imported or borrowed inputs unchanged. Then

$$\frac{\partial r}{\partial \alpha} \geqslant 0, \tag{62}$$

$$\frac{\partial \tilde{D}_2}{\partial \alpha} = 0, \tag{63}$$

$$\frac{\partial r^*}{\partial \alpha^*} = 0, \tag{64}$$

so that, from (56)–(61),

$$\frac{\partial p}{\partial \alpha} \geqslant 0, \tag{65}$$

$$\frac{\partial K}{\partial \alpha} \leqslant 0, \tag{66}$$

$$\frac{\partial p}{\partial \alpha^*} < 0, \tag{67}$$

$$\frac{\partial K}{\partial \alpha^*} < 0. \tag{68}$$

That is, technical improvement in any country depresses its terms of trade and reduces international indebtedness.

If $\partial r/\partial\alpha = 0$, applying (56)–(59) to (60) and (61),

$$\frac{\partial D_1}{\partial\alpha} = \frac{\partial\tilde{X}_1}{\partial\alpha}, \tag{69}$$

$$\frac{\partial D_1^*}{\partial\alpha} = 0, \tag{70}$$

$$\frac{\partial D_1}{\partial\alpha^*} = \frac{1}{\Gamma}\,[(\delta\varepsilon + \delta^*\varepsilon^*)D_1^* + \delta^*\varepsilon^* r^* K]\,rp\,\frac{\partial\tilde{X}_2^*}{\partial\alpha^*}, \tag{71}$$

$$\frac{\partial D_1^*}{\partial\alpha^*} = \frac{1}{\Gamma}\left[\delta^*\varepsilon^*(\eta_2 - 1) + \delta\varepsilon\left|\eta_2 - \frac{D_1^*}{pD_2}\right| + \left|1 - \frac{D_1^*}{pD_2}\right|\right]p^2 D_2 r\,\frac{\partial\tilde{X}_2^*}{\partial\alpha^*}. \tag{72}$$

Thus technical improvement, wherever it occurs, benefits the home country; and the foreign country is untouched by improvement at home, necessarily benefits from local foreign improvement if the home import demand is elastic but otherwise may suffer immiseration.

If international investment is ruled out, equilibrium condition (50) drops out and the analysis takes a much simpler form. We then have

$$-D_2\eta_2\,\mathrm{d}p = -p\,\frac{\partial\tilde{D}_2}{\partial\alpha}\,\mathrm{d}\alpha + p\,\frac{\partial\tilde{X}_2^*}{\partial\alpha^*}\,\mathrm{d}\alpha^* \tag{73}$$

$$\mathrm{d}D_1 = -\frac{D_1^*}{p}\,\mathrm{d}p + \frac{\partial\tilde{X}_1}{\partial\alpha}\,\mathrm{d}\alpha \tag{74}$$

$$\mathrm{d}D_1^* = \frac{D_1^*}{p}\,\mathrm{d}p + \frac{\partial\tilde{X}_2}{\partial\alpha^*}\,\mathrm{d}\alpha^* \tag{75}$$

so that, under (62)–(64),

$$\frac{\partial p}{\partial\alpha} = 0,$$

$$\frac{\partial p}{\partial\alpha^*} < 0.$$

That is, an improvement at home does not affect the terms of trade but a foreign improvement turns them in favour of the home country. Immiserizing growth is impossible at home. However,

$$\frac{\partial D^*}{\partial\alpha^*} = \frac{\eta_2 - 1}{\eta_2}\cdot p\,\frac{\partial\tilde{X}^*}{\partial\alpha^*},$$

so that foreign growth is immiserizing if and only if the home country's demand for the raw material is inelastic.

The foregoing analysis seems to bear on some of the controversial propositions advanced by Prebisch (1950) and Singer (1950). Thus Singer wrote:

> the fruits of technical progress may be distributed either to producers (in the form of rising incomes) or to consumers (in the form of lower prices). In the case of manufactured commodities produced in more developed countries, the former method, i.e., distribution to producers through higher incomes, was much more important relatively to the second method, while the second method prevailed more in the case of food and raw material production in the underdeveloped countries. Generalizing, we may say that technical progress in manufacturing industries showed in a rise in incomes while technical progress in the production of food and raw materials in underdeveloped countries showed in a fall in prices. Now in the general case, there is no reason why one or the other method should be generally preferable.... In a closed economy the general body of producers and the general body of consumers can be considered as identical, and the two methods of distributing the fruits of technical progress appear merely as two formally different ways of increasing real incomes.
>
> When we consider foreign trade, however, the position is fundamentally changed. The producers and consumers can no longer be considered as the same body of people. The producers are at home; the consumers are abroad. Rising incomes of home producers to the extent that they are in excess of increased productivity are an absolute burden on the foreign consumer. Even if the rise in the income of home producers is offset by increases in productivity, this is still a relative burden on foreign consumers, in the sense that they lose part or all of the potential fruits of technical progress in the form of lower prices. On the other hand, where the fruits of technical progress are passed on by reduced prices, the foreign consumer benefits alongside with the home consumer. Nor can it be said, in view of the notorious inelasticity of demand for primary commodities, that the fall in their relative prices has been compensated by its total revenue effects.
>
> (Singer, 1950: 478–9)

6 A LESS ASYMMETRICAL WORLD ECONOMY

We have consistently assumed that there are just two commodities and that the resource-rich foreign country produces no consumption goods. Not only are these assumptions highly unrealistic but one fears that at least the second may be crucial to some of the strong conclusions of sections 3 and 4. In the present section we seek to allay the reader's misgivings by showing that our assumptions can be substantially relaxed without disturbing propositions 1 and 2. Specifically, it can be shown that our conclusions remain valid even if each country produces many consumption goods and many raw materials provided only that the foreign consumption-good industries divide into two disjoint subsets, with members of one subset producing only for the home or export market and members of the other subset producing (with fixed resources) only for the local foreign market. If the second subset of industries is empty, the foreign country is the purest kind of 'export enclave'. If the first subset of industries is empty, we have an instance of a dual economy. We shall focus on the first of these extreme situations (that of the export enclave), leaving the other extreme (as well as the general situation) to the reader.

Let us begin by reconsidering the scope of economic imperialism in the broader context just sketched. The home country is assumed to impose taxes on its exports at the uniform *ad valorem* rate τ and a tax on its capital earnings abroad at the rate t. For given t, let us consider the effect of an increase of τ on the several endogenous variables. Suppose tentatively that the foreign prices of home goods all increase in the same proportion $\Delta\tau/(1 + \tau)$, leaving home prices undisturbed. With all other prices unchanged, there would be no change in the supply of any commodity nor in the level of international indebtedness. On the other hand, the tax revenue represents an international redistribution of income. If the two countries were to possess identical homothetic preferences then the redistribution would exert no influence on the world demand for any commodity and the real world equilibrium would be unchanged. However, such a severe restriction on preferences is not needed. The essential thing is that the effects of an increase in the export tax are identical to those of an international transfer of income from the foreign to the home country. From that fact we can infer that, even under the present greatly relaxed assumptions, the home country is able to exploit the foreign in any desired degree by imposing a sufficiently heavy tax on its exports.

We return now to the scope of resource nationalism. The foreign country is assumed to impose taxes on its exports at the uniform *ad valorem* rate τ^* and a tax on home capital earnings abroad at the rate of τ^*. It is easy to see that if there is no international indebtedness, and if capital is internationally immobile, then an increase in τ^* has no effect at all on the real equilibrium of either country. For suppose that the foreign prices of all foreign products were to decline uniformly at the rate $\Delta\tau^*/(1 + \tau^*)$, leaving the home prices of foreign goods unchanged. With every other price unchanged, all demands and supplies would remain at their old levels provided only that foreign consumers are reimbursed from the additional foreign tax revenue. With capital mobile internationally the implications of an increase in τ^* would be complex, as they were even in the context of the simple model of section 4. However, the introduction of many commodities would not nullify our earlier observation: the foreign country lacks the incentive to exploit the home country completely by means of an export tax because of its harmful effect on international indebtedness and eventually on foreign imports of consumption goods.

Similarly, it is possible to extend some of the more important of our conclusions concerning the sharing of the fruits of technical improvements. That too is left to the reader.

APPENDIX

In sections 3 and 4 it was supposed that one country is the aggressor, the other completely passive in the sense of persistent *laissez-faire.* Here we briefly consider the alternative possibility that one country responds to the other's aggression again passively but with a passivity of the Cournot type, always choosing a policy which is optimal in the light of the given policy of the aggressor. Again we find that there is a sense in which the resource-poor country has an advantage over its resource-rich trading partner.

Two cases are studied. In one the aggressive country does and in the other does not allow for a reaction by the passive country. In other words, we study both a pure Cournot process and a Stackelberg leader–follower process.

It follows from the analysis of sections 3 and 4 that only export taxes need be considered.

The Cournot process

Suppose that the resource-poor home country is the aggressor. Our first task is to derive the foreign 'reaction function', which tells us the foreign country's choice of export tax for any given value of the home country's tax. Let p_i be the nominal home price of the *i*th commodity and p_i^* the nominal foreign price, in a common unit of account. Then, in arbitrage equilibrium,

$$(1+\tau)p_1 = p_1^*, \quad (1+\tau^*)p_2^* = p_2, \tag{A1}$$

and the international terms of trade π are given by

$$\begin{aligned}\pi &\equiv p_2/p_1^* \\ &= p/(1+\tau) = (1+\tau^*)p^*.\end{aligned} \tag{A2}$$

The budget constraints of the home and foreign countries are, respectively,

$$D_1 = X_1 + r^*K - \pi D_2 \tag{A3}$$

and

$$D_1^* = \pi X_2^* - r^*K, \tag{A4}$$

and the conditions of equilibrium are

$$\tilde{D}_2(p, \bar{K} - K) = \tilde{X}_2(\bar{K}^* + K), \tag{A5}$$

$$r = (1+\tau)r^*. \tag{A6}$$

Totally differentiating (A5) and (A6), we obtain

$$- D_2\eta_2 \,d\pi - (1 + \tau^*)(\lambda + r^*)dK = \frac{\pi D_2\eta_2}{1 + \tau}\, d\tau, \tag{A7}$$

and

$$(r + D_2\eta_2\mu)K d\pi - (\delta\varepsilon + \delta^*\varepsilon^*)\pi r dK = \frac{\pi r K}{1 + \tau^*}\, d\tau^* - \frac{(r + D_2\eta_2\mu)\pi K}{1 + \tau}\, d\tau, \tag{A8}$$

which, in turn, yield

$$\frac{\partial\pi}{\partial\tau} = - \frac{\pi}{1 + \tau} < 0, \tag{A9}$$

$$\frac{\partial K}{\partial\tau} = 0, \tag{A10}$$

$$\frac{\partial\pi}{\partial\tau^*} = \frac{(\lambda + r^*)\pi r K}{\Delta'} < 0, \tag{A11}$$

$$\frac{\partial K}{\partial\tau^*} = - \frac{D_2\eta_2\pi r K}{\Delta'(1 + \tau^*)} < 0, \tag{A12}$$

where Δ' is the positive determinant of the coefficient matrix of (A7) and (A8). Not surprisingly, these conclusions are qualitatively the same as those obtained under the simpler assumption that the passive country is *laissez-faire.* (Compare (A9) and (A10) with (27) and (28), (A11) and (A12) with (42) and (43).)

Next, differentiating (A3), we obtain

$$dD_1 = - D_2\,[1 + \tau\eta_2 + (\mu\eta_2K/\pi)]\,d\pi + [r\delta\varepsilon + (\tau\lambda\pi/p^*)]\,dK$$

$$- D_2\eta_2(\tau\pi + K\mu)\,\frac{d\tau}{1 + \tau}, \tag{A13}$$

$$dD_1^* = dX_1 - dD_1$$

$$= D_2\,[1 + \tau\eta_2 + (\mu\eta_2K/\pi)]\,d\pi + [(\tau^* - \delta\varepsilon)r - (\tau\lambda\pi/p^*)]\,dK$$

$$+ D_2\eta_2(\tau\pi + K\eta_2)\,\frac{d\tau}{1 + \tau}, \tag{A14}$$

whence, substituting from (A9)–(A12),

$$\frac{\partial D_1}{\partial\tau} = \frac{\pi D_2 - r^* K}{1 + \tau} > 0, \tag{A15}$$

$$\frac{\partial D_1^*}{\partial\tau} = - \frac{\pi D_2}{1 + \tau} < 0, \tag{A16}$$

$$\frac{\partial D_1}{\partial \tau^*} = \frac{\pi D_2 rK}{\Delta'(1+\tau^*)}\{[1 + \tau\eta_2 + (\mu K\eta_2/\pi)](1+\tau^*)(\lambda + r^*)$$
$$+ [r\delta\varepsilon + (\tau\lambda\pi/p^*)]\eta_2\} < 0, \quad \text{(A17)}$$

$$\frac{\partial D_1^*}{\partial \tau^*} = \frac{\pi D_2 rk}{\Delta'(1+\tau^*)}\{[1 + \tau\eta_2 + (\mu K\eta_2/\pi)](1+\tau^*)(\lambda + r^*)$$
$$- [(\tau^* - \delta\varepsilon)r - (\tau\lambda\pi/p^*)]\eta_2\}. \quad \text{(A18)}$$

Setting $dD_1^*/d\tau^* = 0$, we obtain at last the foreign reaction function $\tau^* = \tilde{\tau}^*(\tau)$. In the special, separable case, in which $\lambda = \mu = 0$, the function is

$$\tau^* = \frac{1 + \delta\varepsilon\eta_2 + (1+\delta\varepsilon)\eta_2\tau}{\eta_2 - 1} \equiv \tilde{\tau}^*(\tau). \quad \text{(A19)}$$

Consider Figure 1. Point F shows the international division of consumption under free trade. Suppose now that the aggressive home country disturbs an initial free-trade equilibrium by imposing an export tax at that rate τ_1, $0 < \tau_1 < \infty$, which, in the absence of any foreign policy response, drives the foreign country to its subsistence level D_1^* (= OC). The new equilibrium lies at

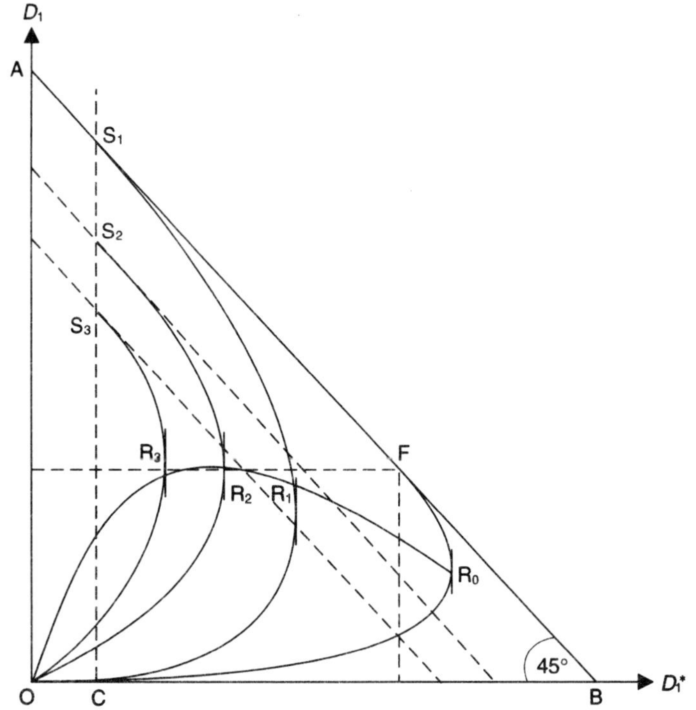

Figure 1

S_1, with the home country consuming more, the foreign country less, than under free trade. Given $\tau = \tau_1$, however, the foreign country can move to any point on the curve S_1R_1O by choosing τ^* appropriately. (An increase in τ^* forces the equilibrium point along S_1R_1O towards O.) Evidently the foreign country will choose τ_1^*, that value of τ^* which establishes R_1 as the equilibrium point. The home country then chooses a rate of export tax τ_2 which, given τ_1^*, drives the world economy to S_2. (Evidently $\tau_2 > \tau_1$.) The foreign country responds by raising τ^* and forcing the economy to R_2. And so on. The Cournot process goes on indefinitely, pushing the economy through the sequence of points S_1, R_1, S_2, R_2, S_3, R_3, ... Foreign consumption will converge to the subsistence level D^* (= OC) and home consumption to an associated positive value. Figure 1 illustrates the possibility that home consumption eventually falls below its free-trade level, so that in the long run neither country gains. But this outcome is not inevitable. The home country might end up with a level of consumption greater than under free trade; it all depends on the underlying structure of preferences and technology.

It remains to note that the final outcome of the Cournot process (but not the path traced) is the same when it is triggered by an aggressive foreign country. (The first temporary equilibrium then lies at R_0.)

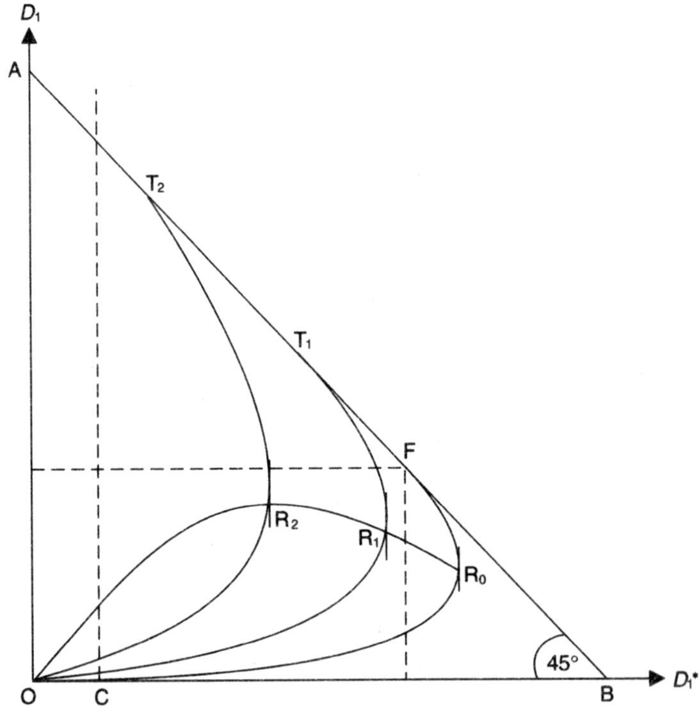

Figure 2

The Stackelberg process

In describing the Cournot process one needs to mention only a subset of all non-negative values of τ. Let us now consider all non-negative values of τ. To each value of τ there can be associated a unique value of τ^* by means of the foreign reaction function $\tilde{\tau}^*(\tau)$. With the set of all such pairs is associated the continuous curve $R_0R_1R_2R_3O$ of Figure 1. In the world of Cournot this curve is unknown to the home country.

In the world of Stackelberg, however, the curve is both known to the home country and taken into the reckoning when that country chooses a value of τ. Analytically, the home country must solve the equation

$$\frac{dD_1}{d\tau} = \left.\frac{dD_1}{d\tau^*}\right|_{\tau \text{ const.}} \cdot \frac{d\tilde{\tau}^*}{d\tau} + \left.\frac{dD_1}{d\tau}\right|_{\tau^* \text{ const.}} = 0. \tag{A20}$$

In terms of Figure 1 it is optimal for the home country to choose the value τ_2 for then, after the passive reaction of the foreign country, the equilibrium will lie at R_2.

The Stackelberg solution is, in general, superior to the Cournot solution for both countries. In the case illustrated by Figure 1, the home country (the leader)

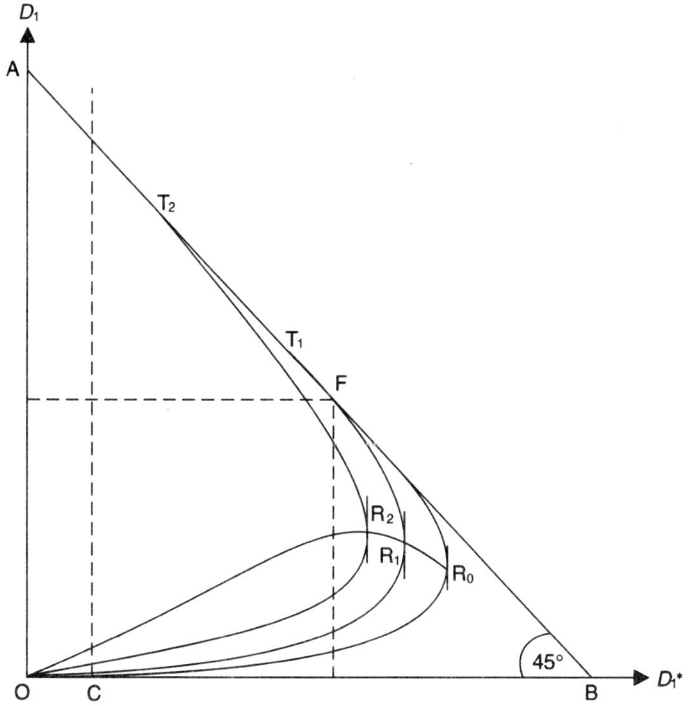

Figure 3

ends up better off than in the initial free-trade equilibrium and the foreign country (the follower) ends up worse off. However, that outcome is not inevitable. Both may be worse off, as in Figure 2, or the home country may be worse off, the foreign country better off, as in Figure 3. Evidently the home country would have no incentive to act as leader in either of these cases. Moreover, even in the case of Figure 3, the foreign country has no incentive to lead; R_2 can be attained only under the leadership of the home country. We may conclude then that only in the circumstances of Figure 1 will a Stackelberg process be observed.

NOTES

* The authors are grateful to Bent Hansen for a long and constructive correspondence and to Koichi Hamada, Daniel Léonard, Yew-Kwang Ng and Richard Snape for many helpful suggestions.

1 See Kemp (1962) for an earlier version of the model developed in this section.

2 In an appendix the questions tackled in sections 3 and 4 are re-examined under alternative assumptions about the behaviour of the passive trading partner.

3 This implication was overlooked in Kemp (1962).

4 On the supposition that each country specializes in the production of a consumption good and that the home country imposes no taxes on imports and exports, Jones has arrived at a similar conclusion (see Jones, 1967: 23).

REFERENCES

Hartman, P. and Olech, C. (1962) 'On global asymptotic stability of solutions of ordinary differential equations', *Transactions of American Mathematical Society* 14: 154–78.

Jones, R. W. (1967) 'International capital movements and the theory of tariffs and trade', *Quarterly Journal of Economics* 81: 1–38.

Kemp, M. C. (1962) 'Foreign investment and the national advantage', *Economic Record* 38: 56–62.

Lerner, A. P. (1936) 'The symmetry between import and export taxes', *Economica* 3: 306–13.

Prebisch, R. (1950) 'The economic development of Latin America and its principal problems', The United Nations Economic Commission for Latin America, New York.

Prebisch, R. (1959) 'Commercial policy in underdeveloped countries', *American Economic Review* 49: 261–4.

Singer, H. W. (1950) 'The distribution of gains between investing and borrowing countries', *American Economic Review* 40: 477–89.

15

THE INTERACTION OF RESOURCE-RICH AND RESOURCE-POOR ECONOMIES

1 INTRODUCTION

Economists have begun to ponder some of the problems posed by the exhaustibility of an essential resource.[1] However, the problems so far studied have been formulated in global terms, with no allowance for the possibility that decision-making may be dispersed among many countries nor for the possibility that the resource may be unevenly distributed over those countries. In fact, of course, the international distribution of many exhaustible resources is extremely uneven. This suggests the possibility that some countries are non-viable under autarky but viable under free trade. It also suggests that those countries especially favoured by nature might seek to take advantage of their position as collective monopolists, and that the resource-deprived countries might seek to exploit their position as collective monopsonists, each group by concerted action endeavouring to twist the international terms of trade in its favour. And even in the absence of such aggressive behaviour there remains an interesting question: in a *laissez-faire* world how may we expect the terms of trade and the international distribution of consumption to evolve?

We shall be concerned for the most part with a model world which is very simple but within which it is possible to study the above issues in their purest form. Two countries trade in a raw material, extracted from an exhaustible stock, and in a consumption good, the latter produced by means of the raw material and of other factors. The first country owns the entire world stock of the resource but has neither the physical facilities nor the aptitudes and skills needed to produce the consumption good. The second country has both facilities and aptitudes but, of course, lacks the resource. International borrowing is ruled out.

To begin, it is assumed that each country ignores its monopoly–monopsony position. The path of the equilibrium competitive terms of trade under world-wide *laissez-faire* is described, as are the time paths of consumption in each country. It is shown that the international distribution of consumption can move in favour of either country and in the Cobb–Douglas case is constant. The assumption of universal *laissez-faire* is then relaxed and provision made for aggressive behaviour on the part of first one and then the other country. The vehicle of aggression is a tax on imports or exports. In each case the path of the equilibrium terms of trade and the path of consumption in each country are described. It is shown that it always is both possible and optimal for the resource-poor country to exploit completely its trading partner whereas it may be impossible for the resource-rich country to exploit its partner and, where exploitation is possible, it is never optimal to carry exploitation to the limit of feasibility.

2 A SINGLE CLOSED ECONOMY

We begin by considering the competitive outcome in a single closed economy. The exercise is of interest in its own right. Moreover, it will be shown later that if the resource-poor country is aggressive then the world economy behaves like a single closed economy.

We consider an economy with a known stock of the resource $\bar{M}$. Ownership of the resource is shared by a large number of identical firms. The firms produce a single perishable consumption good with a production function f defined on the rate of resource use m and possibly on other constant (and therefore suppressed) factors. The production function is supposed to be increasing and strictly concave, and the resource is supposed to be essential to production, so that $f(0) = 0$; it is assumed also that $f'(0) = \infty$. The firms are owned by a constant population of individuals who are identical in their shareholdings and in their preferences. In particular, individuals have in common an increasing and concave utility function u, defined on the rate of consumption c, and a constant and positive rate of time preference ρ; it is assumed also that $u'(0) = \infty$.

The firms seek to maximize their present value in terms of the consumption good. That is, given the path of the momentary rate of interest $r(t)$, firms seek

$$\max_{\{m\}} \int_0^\infty \exp\left(- \int_0^t r(s)\,\mathrm{d}s \right) f(m)\,\mathrm{d}t$$

subject to

$$\dot{M} = m, \qquad M \leqslant \bar{M}, \qquad M(0) = 0, \tag{I}$$

where M is the cumulative planned resource use. Among the necessary conditions for an interior solution we have

$$f'(m) + \mu = 0, \tag{1}$$

$$\dot{\mu} - r\mu = 0, \tag{2}$$

$$\lim_{t \to \infty} M = \bar{M}. \tag{3}$$

Given the time profiles $\{m\}$ and $\{r\}$, consumers in their turn seek to maximize the present value of their utility stream, that is, they seek

$$\max_{\{c\}} \int_0^\infty \exp(-\rho t) u(c)\, dt$$

subject to

$$\dot{A} = -c + rA,$$

$$A(0) = \int_0^\infty \exp\left(-\int_0^t r(s)\, ds\right) f(m)\, dt, \tag{II}$$

$$\lim_{t \to \infty} A(t) \geqslant 0,$$

where $A(t)$ is consumers' wealth (in terms of the consumption good at time t). Among the necessary conditions for an interior solution we have

$$u'(c) - \lambda = 0, \tag{4}$$

$$\dot{\lambda} - (\rho - r)\lambda = 0. \tag{5}$$

Finally, as a condition of market equilibrium,

$$c = f(m). \tag{6}$$

From (1), (2) and (4)–(6),

$$u'(f(m))f'(m) = -\mu(0)\lambda(0)\exp(\rho t). \tag{7}$$

Together with (3), equation (7) determines $\{m\}$ and $\mu(0)\lambda(0)$. Given $\{m\}$, we can calculate $\{\mu\}$ from (1) and then $\{r\}$ from (2); and, since $\mu(0)\lambda(0)$ is known, we can calculate $\lambda(0)$ also.

Equation (7) tells us that along the equilibrium trajectory, the marginal utility product of the resource, $u'f'$, increases exponentially at the rate of time preference, provided something is produced. Given the restrictions placed on u and f, we can be sure that extraction, and therefore production and consumption, is positive for all t but declines to zero. Differentiating (4) logarithmically with respect to time, and applying (5), we find that

$$r = \rho - (u''/u')\dot{c}. \tag{8}$$

Since $\dot{c} < 0$ and $u'' < 0$, the rate of interest is always less than the rate of time preference.

In the special Cobb–Douglas case

$$f(m) = m^{\alpha}, \quad 0 < \alpha < 1, \tag{9a}$$

$$u(c) = c^v/v, \quad 0 < v < 1, \tag{9b}$$

and it is possible to be more explicit. Differentiating (7) totally with respect to time, and substituting from (9), we obtain

$$(\alpha v - 1)(\dot{m}/m) \equiv (\alpha v - 1)(\ddot{M}/\dot{M}) = \rho. \tag{10}$$

The characteristic roots of the equation in M are $\rho/(\alpha v - 1)$ and 0, implying that

$$M(t) = A_1 + A_2 \exp[-\rho t/(1 - \alpha v)].$$

Now $M(0) = 0$, whence $A_1 + A_2 = 0$; and $M(\infty) = \bar{M}$, implying that $A_1 = \bar{M}$ and, therefore, that $A_2 = -\bar{M}$. Thus,

$$M(t) = \bar{M}\{1 - \exp[-\rho t/(1 - \alpha v)]\} \tag{11a}$$

and

$$m(t) \equiv \dot{M}(t) = [\rho/(1 - v)]\bar{M} \exp[-\rho t/(1 - \alpha v)]. \tag{11b}$$

Thus, m changes at the negative exponential rate $-\rho/(1 - \alpha v)$ and therefore output and consumption at the rate $-\alpha\rho/(1 - \alpha v)$. It then follows from (8) that the rate of interest is a positive constant:

$$r = \rho + (1 - v)(\dot{c}/c)$$

$$= \rho(1 - \alpha)/(1 - \alpha v) < \rho. \tag{12}$$

From (11b) and (12) it is easy to calculate $dm(t)/d\alpha$, $dc(t)/d\alpha$, $dr/d\alpha$, etc.

Finally, we notice that the equilibrium path defined by (7) is also the solution to the problem

$$\max_{\{c,\, m\}} \int_0^\infty \exp(-\rho t) u(c)\, dt$$

subject to

$$c = f(m), \quad \dot{M} = m, \quad M \leqslant \bar{M}, \quad M(0) = 0. \tag{III}$$

That is, the competitive outcome is optimal and the optimal trajectory can be mimicked by a competitive economy. This is so for all economies studied in this essay, a fact of which we shall make much use in the sections to follow.

3 BOTH COUNTRIES ARE PRICE-TAKERS

Let there now be two countries, as described in section 1. Let c_i be the rate of consumption, $u_i(c_i)$ the utility and ρ_i the constant rate of time preference of the ith country, where u_i is an increasing and strictly concave function with $u_i'(0) = \infty$; let m now be the rate of resource extraction (and the rate of exportation) by the resource-rich first country; let M again be the cumulative extraction of the resource and $\bar{M}$ the initial stock of the resource; let p be the world price of the raw material in terms of the consumption good; let f again be the rate of output of the consumption good, an increasing and strictly concave function of the raw-material input m with $f(0) = 0$ and $f'(0) = \infty$.

The resource-rich first country seeks

$$\max_{\{m\}} \int_0^\infty \exp(-\rho_1 t) u_1(c_1)\, dt$$

subject to

$$c_1 = pm, \quad \dot{M} = m, \quad M \leqslant \bar{M}, \quad M(0) = 0, \tag{IV}$$

where p is treated as a known and given function of time and where the first constraint gives expression to the assumption that the balance of trade is always zero (so that international borrowing and lending are ruled out). Among the necessary conditions for an interior maximum we have

$$u_1'(pm)p + \mu_1^c = 0, \tag{13}$$

$$\dot{\mu}_1^c - \rho_1 \mu_1^c = 0. \tag{14}$$

The resource-poor second country, on the other hand, seeks a solution to the conventional static problem

$$\max_{\{m\}} \int_0^\infty \exp(-\rho_2 t) u_2(c_2)\, dt \tag{V}$$

subject to

$$c_2 = f(m) - pm,$$

where again p is treated as an uncontrollable but known function of time. As a necessary condition for an interior maximum we have

$$f'(m) - p = 0. \tag{15}$$

Notice that by employing the same symbol m for the first country's exports and the second country's imports of the raw material we have built in the assumption that world commodity markets are in equilibrium.

Equations (13)–(15), together with the transversality condition

$$\lim_{t \to \infty} M(t) = \bar{M}, \tag{3}$$

suffice to determine the equilibrium time paths of all variables. **Survival, impossible under autarky, is feasible under free trade.**

We notice at once that the equilibrium paths depend on the preferences (utility function and rate of time preference) of the first or resource-rich country only. The second country, with no resource to husband, has no decisions of an intertemporal nature to make; hence its time preference has no role to play. And, since the resource-poor country is a price-taker, short-run utility maximization yields the same decisions as short-run profit maximization, implying that the form of its utility function is irrelevant.

The rate of resource use goes asymptotically to zero. One might have expected m to decline (and p to increase) uniformly over time, as in the case of a single country. It appears, however, that there may be intervals of time over which m is constant or even increasing. Thus, differentiating (13) with respect to time and making use of (14) and (15), we obtain

$$[\varepsilon(1+\delta)+\delta](\dot{m}/m)=\rho_1, \tag{16}$$

where

$$\varepsilon(c_1)\equiv c_1u_1''(c_1)/u_1'(c_1)<0 \tag{17}$$

and

$$\delta(m)\equiv mf''(m)/f'(m)<0 \tag{18}$$

are the elasticities of marginal utility (in the first country) and marginal productivity, respectively. Evidently the square-bracketed term in (16) may be positive, and therefore $\dot{m}$ also positive, even though both ε and δ are negative. (For a steady decline in m it suffices that δ be bounded below by -1.)

It remains to consider the time path of consumption in each country. Since f is strictly concave we can solve (15) for m and write

$$m=m(p),\quad m'(p)=1/f''<0. \tag{19}$$

From (13), then,

$$(u_1''/u_1')\dot{c}_1+\dot{p}/p=\rho_1, \tag{20}$$

where

$$\begin{aligned}\dot{c}_1&=(m+pm')\dot{p}\\&\equiv[m+m/\delta(m)]\,\dot{p}.\end{aligned} \tag{21}$$

It follows that $\dot{c}_1$ can be of either sign. In particular, $\dot{c}_1<0$ if $\dot{p}>0$ (as it must be eventually) and if $m[1+(1/\delta)]<0$ (as it must be if δ is greater than -1). From (20), if $\dot{c}_1<0$ then $\dot{p}/p<\rho_1$. Thus, eventually, the relative price of the raw material grows at a rate smaller than the rate of time preference. On the other hand, $c_2=f(m)-pm$. Differentiating with respect to time, and making use of (15), we find that

$$\dot{c}_2=-m\dot{p}. \tag{22}$$

Thus, $\dot{c}_2$ has the sign of $-\dot{p}$. Comparing (21) and (22) we see that c_1 and c_2 can move in opposite directions. In particular, if $\dot{p} > 0$ then c_2 necessarily declines but c_1 rises or falls as δ is less than or greater than -1.

In the special Cobb–Douglas case in which

$$u_i(c_i) = c_i^{v_i}v_i, \quad 0 < v_i < 1, \tag{23a}$$

and

$$f(m) = m^{\alpha}, \quad 0 < \alpha < 1, \tag{23b}$$

we regain many of the features of the single-economy outcome described in section 2. Thus, from (16) we obtain the explicit solutions

$$M(t) = \bar{M}\{1 - \exp[-\rho_1 t/(1 - \alpha v_1)]\} \tag{24a}$$

and

$$m(t) = [\rho/(1 - \alpha v_1)]\bar{M}\exp[-\rho_1 t/(1 - \alpha v_1)]. \tag{24b}$$

We deduce that in this case m changes at the negative exponential rate $-\rho_1/(1 - \alpha v_1)$ and that therefore output, as well as consumption in each country, changes at the rate $-\alpha\rho_1/(1 - \alpha v_1)$. Thus, in one sense of the term, trade becomes neither more nor less 'unequal'. We deduce also that the price ratio, $p = f'(m) = \alpha m^{\alpha - 1}$, changes at the rate $\rho_1(1 - \alpha)/(1 - \alpha v_1)$, which is positive but smaller than ρ_1. Finally, the rate of interest is constant in each country:

$$r_i = \rho_i - (v_i - 1)(\dot{c}_i/c_i) = \rho_i - (1 - v_i)\alpha\rho_1/(1 - \alpha v_1). \tag{25}$$

4 THE RESOURCE-RICH COUNTRY IS AGGRESSIVE

We now disturb this tranquil world by supposing that the resource-rich first country recognizes and exploits its monopoly–monopsony power. That country now seeks

$$\max_{\{p\}} \int_0^{\infty} \exp(-\rho_1 t)u_1(c_1)\,dt$$

subject to

$$c_1 = pm(p), \quad \dot{M} = m, \quad M \leq \bar{M}, \quad M(0) = 0, \tag{VI}$$

where $pm(p)$ is the revenue, in terms of the consumption good, received by the first country and is assumed to be a concave function. Among the conditions which must be satisfied along an optimal internal trajectory, we have

$$u_1'(pm(p)) \cdot [p + m(p)/m'(p)] + \mu_1 = 0, \tag{26}$$

$$\dot{\mu}_1 - \rho_1\mu_1 = 0, \tag{27}$$

where the new term $[p + m(p)/m'(p)]$ is, of course, the marginal revenue from sales of the raw material.

The still-passive resource-poor country, on the other hand, again seeks to solve problem (V), with p treated as a known and given function of time. As a necessary condition we again have (15).

We can now compare the outcome under *laissez-faire* with the outcome under aggression by the resource-rich country. From (13)–(15), the *laissez-faire* outcome satisfies

$$u_1'(mf'(m))f'(m) = -\mu_1^c(0)\exp(\rho_1 t). \tag{28}$$

From (15), (26) and (27), the outcome under aggression satisfies

$$u_1' \cdot (mf'(m)) \cdot f'(m) \cdot [1 + \delta(m)] = -\mu_1(0)\exp(\rho_1 t). \tag{29}$$

(Since $-\mu_1(0)$ is positive, δ must be greater than -1 along the optimal path of aggression. The restrictions imposed on f imply that this condition is satisfied for all sufficiently small m.) Comparing (28) and (29) we see that in general the path of extraction when both countries passively accept price differs from the path generated by aggressive behaviour on the part of the resource-rich country.[2] It follows that in general the paths of world prices and of the internal rates of interest also differ. The manner in which the two extraction paths differ depends in a complicated way on the properties of the elasticity $\delta(m)$. However, in one special case all complications vanish. Thus, if δ is a constant, as when f is Cobb–Douglas, the two paths of extraction coincide, the initial value of μ_1 under aggression being $1 + \delta$ times its value under *laissez-faire*. In that case the resource-rich country has no effective monopoly power. (Notice that for this conclusion it suffices that the production function be Cobb–Douglas; it is not necessary that the utility function u also be Cobb–Douglas. If in addition the utility function is Cobb–Douglas then, as in the preceding section, output and consumption change at the rate $\alpha\rho_1/(1 - \alpha v_1)$ and price at the rate $(1 - \alpha)\rho_1/(1 - \alpha v_1)$.)

An important question remains. It has been assumed that the government of the resource-rich country exercises direct control over the rate of extraction and therefore over the world price ratio. Could the same objective be achieved by means of a tax on the imports or exports of a competitive economy? If so, what is the time profile of the optimal tax?

To enable us to examine these questions we return to the assumptions of section 2. Thus, it is assumed that the resource is owned by many price-taking firms which, in turn, are owned by the consumers; and it is assumed that consumers are identical in their preferences, in their ownership of firms, and in their claims on the proceeds of the tax.

The government of the resource-rich country knows the optimal path of extraction $\{m^*\}$ and the associated path of world prices $\{p^* \equiv f'(m^*)\}$. It wishes to announce paths of the internal price ratio, say $\{p^{(1)}\}$, and of the momentary rate of interest which, allowance being made for the tax proceeds, induce paths of extraction and consumption $\{m^*\}$ and $\{p^*m^*\}$. It will be shown that the required paths are given by

$$p^{(1)}(t) = \beta[1 + \delta(m^*)]\, p^*(t) \quad (\beta \text{ a positive constant}), \tag{30}$$

$$r_1(t) = \dot{p}^{(1)}(t)/p^{(1)}(t). \tag{31}$$

Present-value-maximizing firms seek

$$\max_{\{m\}} \int_0^\infty \exp\left(-\int_0^t r_1(s)\,\mathrm{d}s\right) \cdot p^{(1)}(t) m(t)\,\mathrm{d}t$$

subject to

$$\dot{M} = m, \quad M(0) = 0, \quad M(\infty) \leqslant \bar{M}. \tag{VII}$$

For a positive interior solution, with firms content to hold the outstanding stock of the resource, it is necessary that (31) be satisfied; and, if (31) is satisfied, the rate of extraction is indeterminate.

The tax proceeds, in terms of the consumption good, are

$$T(t) \equiv [p^*(t) - p^{(1)}(t)]m^*(t) \tag{32}$$

and are distributed to consumers in lumpsum fashion. The initial wealth of consumers is therefore

$$A(0) = \int_0^\infty \exp\left(-\int_0^t r_1(s)\,\mathrm{d}s\right)(T + p^{(1)}m^*)\,\mathrm{d}t \tag{33}$$

and the consumers' problem is to find

$$\max_{\{c_1\}} \int_0^\infty \exp(-\rho_1 t) u_1(c_1)\,\mathrm{d}t$$

subject to

$$\dot{A} = -c_1 + r_1 A, \quad \lim_{t\to\infty} A(t) \geqslant 0, \tag{VIII}$$

and to (33), where r_1, T and m^* are taken to be known functions of time. Among the necessary conditions for an interior solution we have

$$u_1'(c_1) = \psi_1, \tag{34}$$

$$\dot{\psi}_1 = \psi_1(\rho_1 - r_1), \tag{35}$$

$$A(t) \geqslant 0. \tag{36}$$

From (34) and (35)

$$u_1'(c_1) = \psi_1(0) \cdot \exp(\rho_1 t) \cdot \exp\left(-\int_0^t r(s)\,ds\right), \tag{37}$$

where $\psi_1(0)$ is the positive and calculable initial value of ψ_1.
Let

$$p^{(1)}(0) = -\beta\mu_1(0)/\psi_1(0). \tag{38}$$

Then

$$\begin{aligned} u_1'(c_1)\exp(-\rho_1 t) &= -\beta\mu_1(0)/p^{(1)}(t) \quad [\text{from (31) and (37)}] \\ &= -\mu_1(0)/p^*(t)[1+\delta(m^*(t))] \quad [\text{from (30)}] \\ &= -\mu_1(0)/f'(m^*)[1+\delta(m^*(t))] \quad [\text{from (15)}], \end{aligned}$$

which is the condition of optimality (29), as required.

Let $\tau_1(t)$ be the *ad valorem* rate of export tax. From (30) and the condition of arbitrage equilibrium

$$p^{(1)}(t) \cdot [1 + \tau_1(t)] = p(t) \tag{39}$$

we can calculate the optimal rate of tax:

$$1/[1 + \tau_1^*(t)] = \beta[1 + \delta(m_1^*(t))]. \tag{40}$$

What can we say about the behaviour of $\tau_1^*(t)$? First, we notice that, since β and therefore $p^{(1)}(0)$ can be freely chosen, the time path $\{\tau_1^*\}$ is not unique. Many 'different' policies generate the same optimal paths $\{p^*\}$ and $\{m^*\}$. It is not the level of $\{p^{(1)}\}$ but its time shape which determines the choice of extraction path by firms; if $\{p^{(1)}\}$ is multiplied by any positive number, the extraction path remains unchanged. Similarly, it is a matter of indifference to consumers whether they receive their income in the form of dividends or tax hand-outs. Second, we notice that if $\delta(m)$ is constant, as in the Cobb–Douglas case, so is the optimal tax. Indeed, for a suitable choice of β and therefore of $p^{(1)}(0)$, the optimal tax is identically zero. In this special case, as we already know, the power to exploit vanishes.

5 THE RESOURCE-POOR COUNTRY IS AGGRESSIVE

We now take the opposite tack by supposing that the resource-poor country seeks to exploit its monopoly–monopsony power, with the resource-rich country resuming its role of passive trading partner.

It is immediately apparent that the optimal policy for the resource-poor country is simply to offer a zero price at all times. For then the resource-rich country is indifferent concerning the rate of extraction and the aggressive resource-poor country is faced with a single-country problem of type (II). In a competitive market setting, the optimal outcome can be approached as closely as desired by imposing an import or export tax at a sufficiently high *ad valorem* level.

We have assumed that the resource-rich country is completely passive. However, our conclusion is independent of that assumption. For suppose, in Nash–Cournot fashion, that the resource-rich country 'reacts' to each choice of tax by the resource-poor country by choosing its own best tax. Then, in the extreme situation studied, whatever the choice of tax by the resource-rich country it is optimal for the resource-poor country to offer a zero price at all times.

6 FINAL REMARKS

For the austerity of our model we offer no apology. Only by concentrating on an extreme case could we hope to isolate the implications of world imbalance in endowments and productive facilities. However, our pathology completed, we can now reveal some of the consequences of relaxing our assumptions. Suppose that not only the resource-poor but also the resource-rich country can produce the consumption good. Then the more extreme of our conclusions in section 4 must be softened. Specifically, the optimal export tax is both uniquely determined and positive, and this is so even when the production function of the resource-poor country is Cobb–Douglas. The explanation is that, under the relaxed assumptions, domestic absorption of the raw material by the resource-rich country, and therefore the extraction path, are no longer independent of the internal price ratio. Similarly, the extreme conclusion of section 5, that the aggressive resource-poor country could exploit its trading partner to the limit of beggary and would choose to do so, must be abandoned. Under no circumstances can the resource-rich country be depressed below its (positive) autarkic level, and in general it will be optimal for the resource-poor country to allow its partner positive gains from trade.

NOTES

1 See, for example, the Symposium in the *Review of Economic Studies* (1974).

2 This is also true in a finite horizon model. In that case it might be optimal for the aggressive resource-rich country to plan to exploit less than fully its resource stock. This is the case if δ is less than -1 for all but very low rates of extraction. We wish to thank John Spraos for this observation.

Part III

THE GAINS FROM TRADE UNDER IMPERFECT COMPETITION AND OTHER DISTORTIONS

16

SOME ISSUES IN THE ANALYSIS OF TRADE GAINS*

1 INTRODUCTION

It is well known that for a small country, with no power to influence world prices, free trade is optimal. From this it has seemed reasonable to infer (i) that any tariff-ridden situation is suboptimal and (ii) that the higher is the tariff the smaller is the gain from trade. That, at any rate was the position I adopted in my *Pure Theory of International Trade*.[1]

> What can be said of the relative desirabilities of the free trading situation, the trading situation characterized by a uniform 5% import duty, that characterized by a 10% duty, etc.?
>
> In the special case in which world prices are virtually independent of the volume of a country's imports and exports, a particularly simple answer can be given: the free trade situation is superior to the 5% situation, which in turn is superior to the 10% situation, and so on.

After reading Bhagwati's (1968) paper – and Vanek's book on customs unions[2] – I see no need to modify my 1962–4 conclusions. I should not, however, seek to defend the logic by which I once tried to establish them. The best I can now say of the argument provided is that it is not so much wrong as lamentably incomplete.

What I now hope to show, in section 2, is that the maximum feasible utility of one individual, given arbitrary minimum feasible utilities of all other individuals, is greater in a low-tariff than in a high-tariff situation. As a by-product, the derivation and possible shapes of the utility feasibility locus will be considered in some detail. I hope also to be able to set out conditions under which tariff-ridden equilibria are dynamically stable.

In the course of my 1962–4 discussion of trade gains I proved that trade restricted by tariffs, quantitative controls or exchange restrictions is better than no trade at all. On the other hand, Jagdish Bhagwati (1968) argues in his companion paper that for a small country the trade gain may be negative if trade is distorted by a tax on domestic production of either commodity or by a tax on domestic consumption of the imported commodity (or, equivalently, if trade is distorted by a subsidy to domestic production of either commodity or by a subsidy to domestic consumption of the exported commodity).

In calculating the gain or loss from trade, however, Bhagwati compares an autarkic equilibrium unencumbered by taxes or subsidies of any kind with a tax- or subsidy-ridden free-trade equilibrium. The gain or loss is then the joint result of the opening of trade and the imposition of taxes or subsidies. Without wishing to mount a methodological high horse or cast any doubt on the value of Bhagwati's calculations, it does seem to me that an equally interesting comparison is that of a tax- or subsidy-ridden free-trade situation with an equally tax- or subsidy-ridden autarkic situation. Only that comparison can reveal the gains **from trade alone**. The comparison is made in section 3.

Moreover, Bhagwati's practice of considering a tax or subsidy on the production or consumption of the **imported** or **exported** commodity may be found slightly confusing. For the superposition of an arbitrarily large tax or subsidy on an initial tax-free free-trade situation may reverse the direction of trade: the pre-tax imported commodity may be the post-tax exported commodity. It seems preferable to consider the implications for trade gains of a tax or subsidy on a specific commodity, leaving the market to determine its export–import status. That at any rate will be our procedure in section 3. It will be shown that, even in the face of a consumption tax or (subject to a mild qualification) a production tax, free trade is potentially gainful.[3]

In section 4 I consider a further question closely related to those considered in sections 2 and 3: does an improvement in a tariff-ridden country's terms of trade imply a potential gain?

2 IS A HIGHER TARIFF WORSE THAN A LOWER TARIFF?

Suppose that a competitive economy produces two goods and trades one for the other at constant world prices. In Figure 1 the terms of trade are indicated by the slope of PC, and the free-trade production and consumption equilibria lie, respectively, at P and C.[4]

If an import duty is imposed, the internal price ratio turns in favour of the imported commodity. Production now takes place at P' and consumption at C', a point on the new trading line $P'C'''$ at which the slope of the intersecting community indifference curve is equal to the slope of the internal or domestic price line.

If the import duty is raised the internal price ratio moves even further in favour of the imported commodity; production moves to P'' and consumption to C''. As the figure makes clear, high-tariff welfare may be either greater or less than low-tariff welfare; moreover, for high-tariff welfare to exceed low-tariff welfare it is necessary that low-tariff consumption of the exported commodity exceed high-tariff consumption. But if consumption is greater at a higher price and lower real income the exported commodity must be inferior in

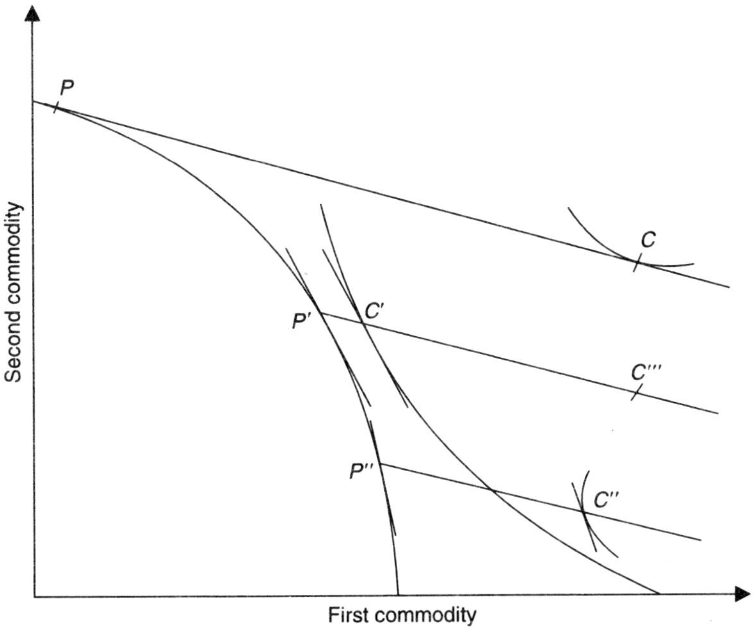

Figure 1

consumption. However, while inferiority of the exported commodity is necessary to the paradoxical outcome it is not by itself sufficient.

In terms of utility feasibilities (Figure 2), we have shown that U', a point attainable in the low-tariff situation, may lie inside or south-west of U'', a point attainable in the high-tariff situation.

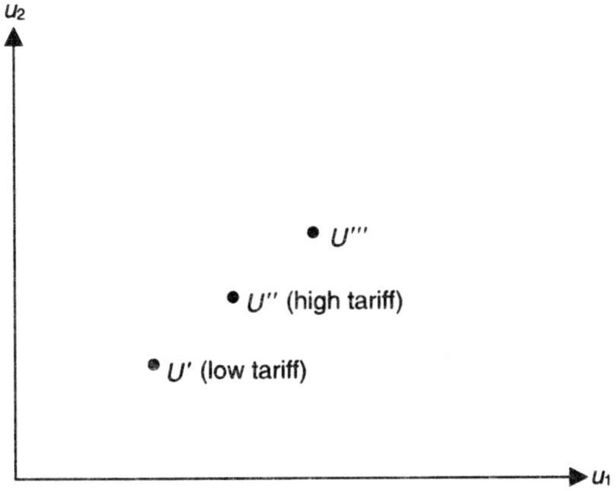

Figure 2

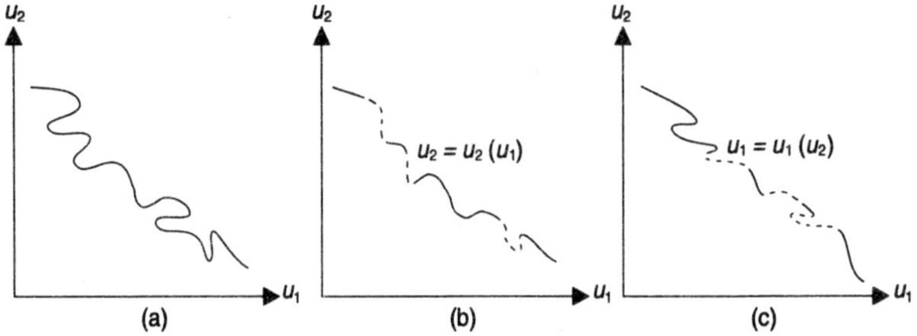

Figure 3

It is not difficult to see, however, that there also exists a feasible low-tariff point U''' north-east of U''. Thus, in terms of Figure 1, the income–consumption curve of the low-tariff situation passes south of C''. Therefore it must intersect $P'C'$ extended, possibly on the horizontal axis. The point of intersection, say C''', corresponds to U'''. A similar argument applies to each feasible high-tariff point. Thus every high-tariff equilibrium is dominated by at least one low-tariff equilibrium.

Let us define the utility feasibility locus as the locus of possible equilibrium utilities, given the rate of import duty. If inferiority is present this locus may incorporate several positively sloped stretches; it may even include one or more disconnected loops. Figures 3(a) and A2 illustrate.[5]

From this locus we may derive two further loci. The first of these tells us the maximum attainable values of u_2 for given minimum values of u_1 and is illustrated by Figure 3(b). The second locus is defined analogously. From it we may read off the maximum attainable values of u_1 for given minimum values of u_2 illustrated by Figure 3(c). We call these derived loci the **optimal loci**. In general the two optimal loci possess discontinuities and are not identical. If and only if the utility feasibility locus is monotonic are the optimal loci continuous and coincident.

In terms of these constructions we may paraphrase our main conclusion by saying that each low-tariff optimal locus lies uniformly outside both high-tariff optimal loci.

Thus we have confirmed that the paradoxical Vanek–Bhagwati outcome is possible, and have shown that it can emerge only if the exported commodity is inferior in consumption **and** if society is content with equilibria inside the optimal loci.

Does that conclusion carry over to a world of many traded commodities? The answer is yes, provided the tariff is not prohibitive for any non-exported commodity. For when tariffs are raised uniformly, the domestic prices of imported goods all rise in the same proportion, with the prices of exported goods unchanged. Within each commodity group relative prices are constant, leaving only one relative price free to change – the price of imports in terms of exports. In effect we are back in a world of just two commodities to which the preceding analysis applies unchanged.[6]

The stability or instability of an equilibrium can be investigated only in relation to a specific dynamic adjustment process. In this section we seek to show only that the Vanek–Bhagwati equilibrium may be stable. The process considered is therefore very simple: we assume that international payments are always in balance, so that the low-tariff consumption point of the country under consideration always lies on the trading line $P'C'''$ of Figure 1; we assume that there are no lags or frictions in the collection and distribution of tariff proceeds; and we assume that, whenever the slope of the community indifference curve exceeds that of the internal price line, the community tries to substitute the imported good for the exported good and vice versa. Suppose then that an initial equilibrium at C' is displaced slightly to the right along $P'C'''$, say to Z. If at C' the low-tariff Engel or income–consumption curve is steeper than $P'C'''$, the relevant indifference curve at Z must be steeper than the internal price line; hence the community will attempt to substitute the imported for the exported good, and consumption will move further away from C'. Evidently C' is in this case a point of locally unstable equilibrium.

If, on the other hand, the slope of the income–consumption curve at C' is less than that of $P'C'''$ we find by analogous reasoning that C' is a point of stable equilibrium. In this case, however, the income–consumption curve must cut $P'C'''$ again, to the right of C', before passing south of C''. This implies the existence of at least one additional low-tariff equilibrium which is Pareto-inferior to C''. Suppose we confine our attention to that low-tariff equilibrium point farthest to the right yet still inferior to C''. Clearly at that point the income–consumption curve must have steeper slope than $P'C'''$, so that the point is one of unstable equilibrium. Thus we may conclude that, if attention is confined to 'adjacent' low- and high-tariff equilibria, the Vanek–Bhagwati paradox requires that the low-tariff equilibrium be unstable.

In general, there may be any number of low-tariff equilibria which are Pareto-inferior to C''. Counting from the right, they must be alternately unstable, stable, unstable, ...

It is not difficult to show that the dividing line between stability and instability is defined by the relation $1 + tm = 0$, where t is the rate of import duty and m is the marginal propensity to consume the exported commodity. If $m < -1/t$ equilibrium is unstable; if the inequality points the other way, equilibrium is stable.

3 THE GAINS FROM TAX- OR SUBSIDY-RIDDEN TRADE

Suppose that taxes (subsidies) are levied on (paid to) consumers of either or both of the two commodities. The country's budget constraint may be written

$$\sum_{i=1}^{2} p_i'(X_i' - D_i') = 0, \tag{1}$$

where p_i' is the world price of the ith commodity, X_i' is the free-trade production of the ith commodity and D_i' is the free-trade consumption of the ith commodity. Free-trade prices as seen by producers are the same as world prices. From the convexity of the production set, therefore,

$$\sum_{i=1}^{2} p_i'(X_i' - X_i^0) \geqslant 0, \tag{2}$$

where X_i^0 is the autarkic production of the ith commodity. Moreover,

$$X_i^0 - D_i^0 = 0, \tag{3}$$

where D_i^0 is the autarkic consumption of the ith commodity. It follows from (1)–(3) that

$$\sum_{i=1}^{2} p_i'(D_i' - D_i^0) \geqslant 0.$$

That is, at world prices the community's autarkic consumption pattern would cost not more than the actual free-trade consumption pattern. Since the p_i' are given, we may infer that the consumption possibility line of the free-trade situation cuts (in an extreme case, touches) the autarkic indifference curve and that the community conceivably could consume more (not less) of both commodities than in the autarkic equilibrium. It only remains to show that there exists a competitive equilibrium on an indifference curve lying above (not below) the autarkic curve. Suppose that there does not exist such an equilibrium but that there exists an equilibrium on a lower indifference curve. Figure 4 illustrates the possibility for the case in which a tax is imposed on the consumption of the first commodity. Since world prices are the same as producers' prices, trade takes place along the producers' price line $P'C'$. The free-trade consumption equilibrium is represented by point C', on an indifference curve below the indifference curve II′ which corresponds to the autarkic equilibrium at P^0. Note, however, that the Engel curve passing through C' must cut II′ to the right of P^0, say in C'', so that over the relevant range the second commodity is inferior. The Engel curve, therefore, must eventually cut the line $P'C'$ a second time, above II′, possibly on the horizontal axis. Thus there must exist at least one additional consumption equilibrium superior to the initial autarkic equilibrium. The geometric argument can be adjusted to cope with a tax on the consumption of the second commodity; the same conclusion (that trade is necessarily gainful) emerges. Moreover, the entire argument of this paragraph can be extended algebraically to cover an arbitrary number of commodities.

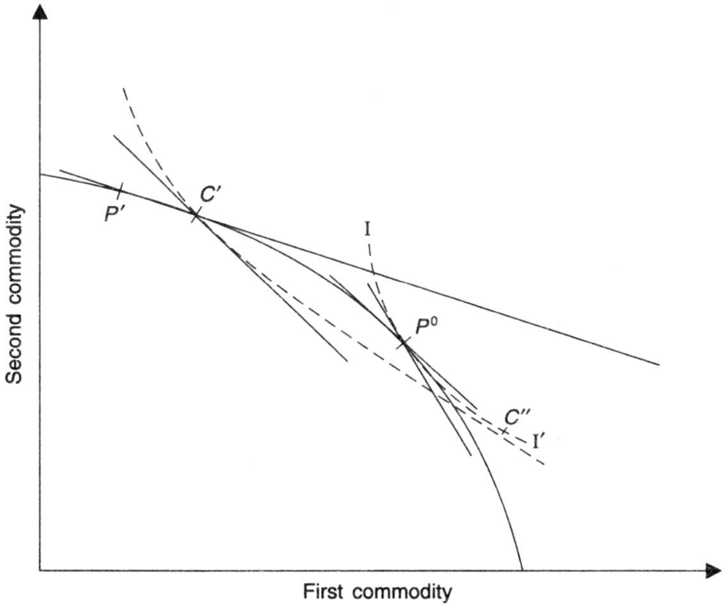

Figure 4

When we turn our attention to production taxes the picture which emerges is a little less tidy. We may suppose without loss that a tax is imposed on the production of the first commodity. (Equivalently, we may suppose that the production of the second commodity is subsidized.) An initial pre-trade equilibrium is indicated by point P^0 in Figure 5. The dashed Scitovsky indifference curve II′ is based on the distribution of earned incomes in the initial equilibrium. The price ratio as seen by consumers is indicated by the slope of II′ at P^0, the producers' price ratio by the slope of the production frontier. Suppose now that trade is opened and that, as a result, both price ratios move in favour of the first or taxed commodity. Then, as Figure 5 makes clear, trade is necessarily gainful.

If, however, the opening of trade moves the two price ratios in favour of the second or untaxed commodity, the welfare outcome does not emerge so clearly. In this case trade shifts resources to the overproducing tax-protected industry. The implicit subsidy to that industry is passed on to foreign as well as to local consumers, suggesting that sometimes the subsidization of the foreigner may outweigh any gain from international **exchange**. The precise condition for this outcome is easy to find. If, as in Figure 6, the rate of tax is small enough to ensure that the world price line $P'C'$ intersects II′, trade is gainful. If, as in Figure 7, the rate of tax is large enough to ensure that $P'C'$ does not intersect or touch II′, trade is harmful. The critical rate of tax, for which trade is neither

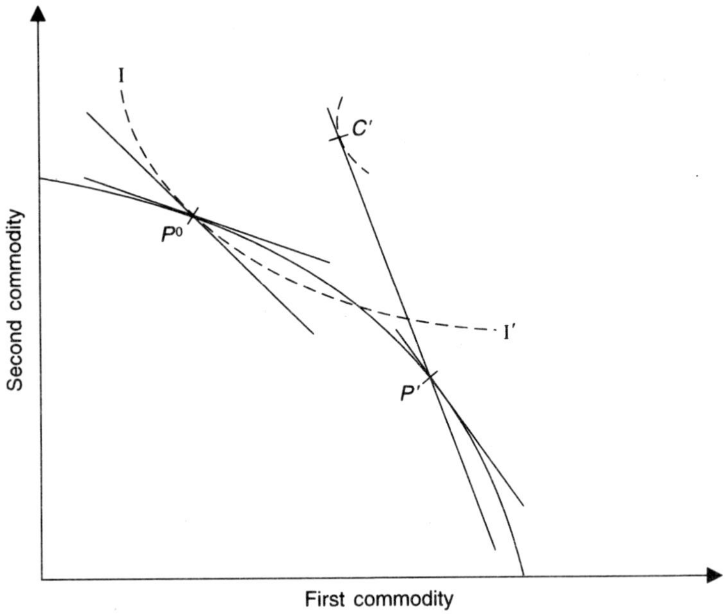

Figure 5

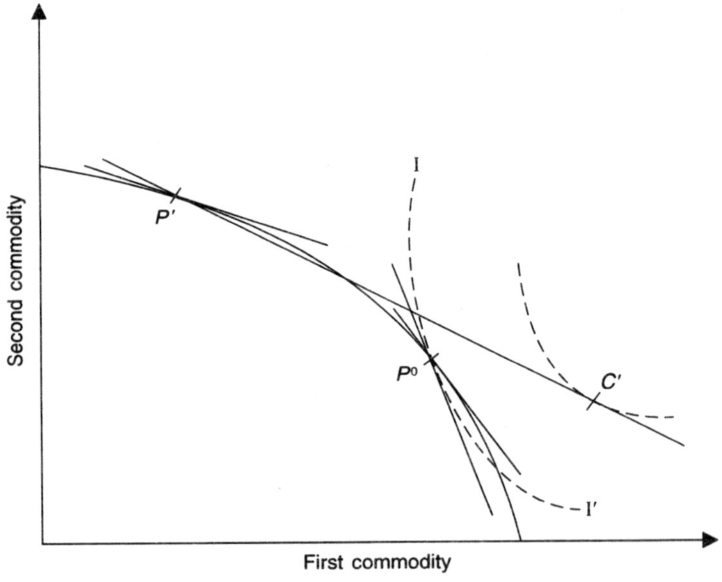

Figure 6

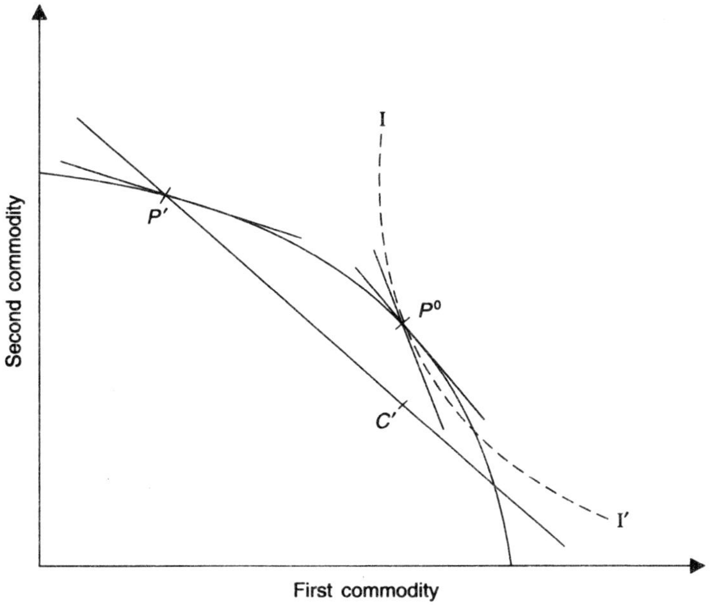

Figure 7

harmful nor gainful, depends on the difference between the world price ratio and the autarkic consumers' price ratio, and on the curvatures of the production frontier and II'.

We conclude that tax-distorted trade is necessarily gainful (i) if the opening of trade moves prices in favour of the relatively heavily taxed commodity or (ii) if the rate of tax is sufficiently small. Since the critical tax rate depends on other things, however, only in case (i) can one infer from observable price changes alone that a gain has accrued.

4 THE EFFECT ON WELFARE OF AN IMPROVEMENT IN THE TERMS OF TRADE

We owe to Anne Krueger and Hugo Sonnenschein the first rigorous demonstration that an improvement in a small country's terms of trade implies a potential gain for that country (Krueger and Sonnenschein, 1967). A potential gain accrues if the set of consumption bundles attainable after the change in the terms of trade includes one which dominates the initial consumption bundle in that it contains at least as much (algebraically) of every commodity and more of at least one commodity. (It is understood that factor supplies are listed in each bundle with a negative sign.) It follows from the Krueger–Sonnenschein theorem that the utility–feasibility surface of the situation with improved terms of trade lies uniformly outside that corresponding to the initial terms of trade.

The proof provided by Krueger and Sonnenschein is based on the assumption of free and balanced trade. Suppose, however, that trade is not free but impeded by tariffs. Is the theorem still valid? It can be shown that an improvement in a tariff-ridden country's terms of trade may leave everyone worse off, that for this outcome it is necessary that at least one good be inferior in consumption, and that in any case it is always possible to find an equilibrium after the improvement in the terms of trade which is Pareto-superior to an initial equilibrium.

After the discussion of section 2, these conclusions will not be found surprising. The nature of the reasoning will be sufficiently indicated if we consider a very simple case: a small country with no appreciable influence on its terms of trade produces just one commodity, in constant amount; it exports part of its production in exchange for a second commodity; and it levies a duty on imports at a constant *ad valorem* rate. In terms of Figure 8, the country's output is *OP* and its trading and consumption opportunities are indicated by the straight line *PQ*. Under conditions of free trade, equilibrium would be reached at *C*, where a community indifference curve is tangent to the terms-of-trade line. But the effect of the tariff is to raise the internal relative price of imports above the world level. Therefore, the internal price ratio is represented by the slope of a line less steep than *PQ*, say *RS*, and the actual equilibrium is found on *PQ* at the point where the slope of the intersecting indifference curve is equal to that of *RS*. Suppose that *C′* is that point.

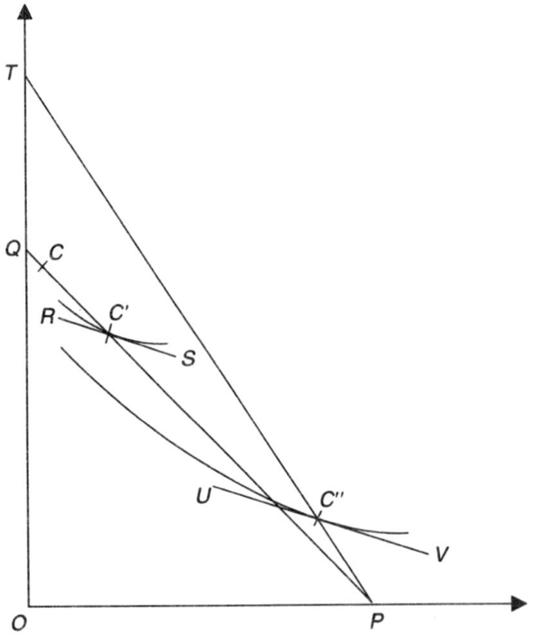

Figure 8

Now the terms of trade improve. The new trading possibilities are indicated by *PT* and the new internal price ratio by the slope of *UV*. The new equilibrium is found on *PT* at that point C'' where the slope of the intersecting indifference curve is equal to that of *UV*. The new indifference curve may represent either an improvement or a deterioration of welfare.

Figure 8 illustrates the possibility of deterioration. This anomalous result emerges, however, only when the export good is inferior (over the relevant range). This is clear enough from Figure 8 if it is borne in mind that the slope of *RS* is **less** than that of *UV*. If neither good is inferior, an improvement in the terms of trade must increase welfare.

Moreover, even if a new equilibrium C'' involves a deterioration of welfare, there exists an alternative final equilibrium C''' such that everyone is better off than at C'. To see this, consider the income–consumption curve corresponding to the new domestic price ratio. Evidently it passes through C'' and to the left of C'. It therefore must eventually cut *PT* a second time, possibly at *T*. It follows that an alternative final equilibrium exists and that welfare is greater there than at C'.

5 CONCLUDING REMARKS

The analysis of section 2 suggests a general proposition. Consider an initial competitive equilibrium which is a Paretian optimum. Now drive any number of wedges into the Paretian marginal equalities (and inequalities): a 5 per cent sales tax on commodity 4, a 20 per cent tax on commodity 7, etc. Evidently the new situation is Pareto-inferior to the initial situation. Finally, double the size of every wedge, so that the tax on the fourth commodity stands at 20 per cent, etc. Then **the final situation is Pareto-inferior both to the initial situation and to the intermediate situation**. I have not proved this proposition – section 2 merely illustrates it for the case of a single wedge.

The paradoxes discussed in sections 2 and 3 are members of a very large set. A single further example, from public finance, must suffice.[7] A simple closed economy, producing just two goods, is disturbed by the imposition of a 5 per cent sales tax on one good. This depresses the price received by producers and reduces the output of the taxed good. It also reduces welfare: the initial situation is Pareto-preferred to the tax-ridden situation. If now the tax is raised to 10 per cent it is possible that the producers' price of the taxed good will rise, that output will rise, and that everybody will be better off than before the tax increase. For this outcome, however, it is necessary that the untaxed good be inferior in consumption. Moreover, among possible final equilibria there is one which is Pareto-preferred to that described.

APPENDIX: DERIVATION OF THE UTILITY–FEASIBILITY LOCUS

Consider an economy with just two individuals and with a fixed output of each of two commodities. Trade with the rest of the world takes place at fixed terms

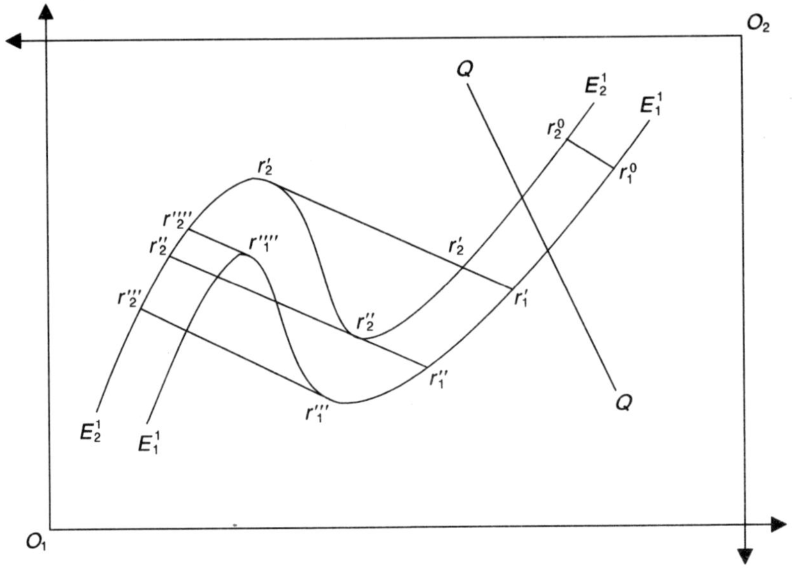

Figure A1

of trade $\pi = \pi_1/\pi_2$. Let τ_i be the rate of import duty on the ith commodity. Then the internal price ratio is

$p = \pi(1 + \tau_1)$ if the first commodity is imported,

$p = \pi/(1 + \tau_2)$ if the second commodity is imported,

$\pi(1 + \tau_1) \leqslant p \leqslant \pi/(1 + \tau_2)$ otherwise.

For such an economy we may construct a box diagram with dimensions given by the fixed outputs. Within this box we may draw four Engel curves, one for each individual for each of the two extreme price ratios, $\pi(1 + \tau_1)$ and $\pi/(1 + \tau_2)$. In Figure A1 are drawn the curves corresponding to $\pi(1 + \tau_1)$. $E_i^1 E_i^1$ is the Engel curve of the ith individual. The internal price ratio is represented by the slope of QQ; the international terms of trade are indicated by the common slope of the other straight lines.

Consider r_1^0 and r_2^0 in Figure A1. These represent a possible trading equilibrium with $r_1^0 r_2^0$, the net foreign trade vector, revealing that the first commodity is imported, the second exported. Corresponding to r_1^0 and r_2^0 in Figure A1 is r^0 on the utility–feasibility curve in Figure A2. Now let r_1 move in a south-westerly direction along $E_1^1 E_1^1$, beginning at r_1^0, and let us trace out the corresponding equilibrium r_2 points on $E_2^1 E_2^1$. Until r_1 reaches r_1' this is a simple matter; the utility of the first individual steadily declines and that of the second individual steadily grows. To r_1', however, there correspond not one but two r_2 points; and to r_1 points between r_1' and r_1'' there correspond three equilibrium

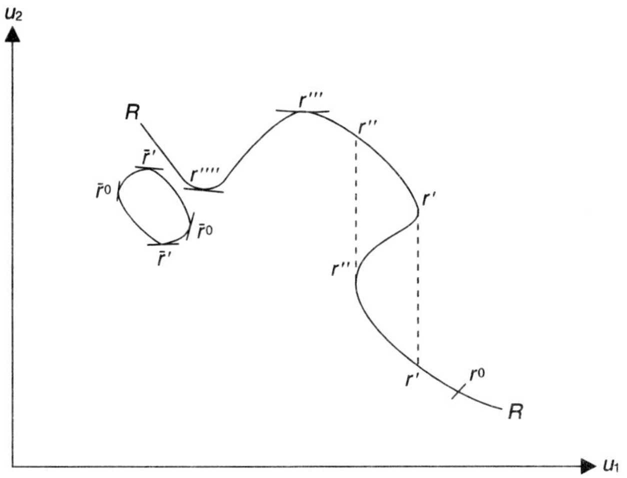

Figure A2

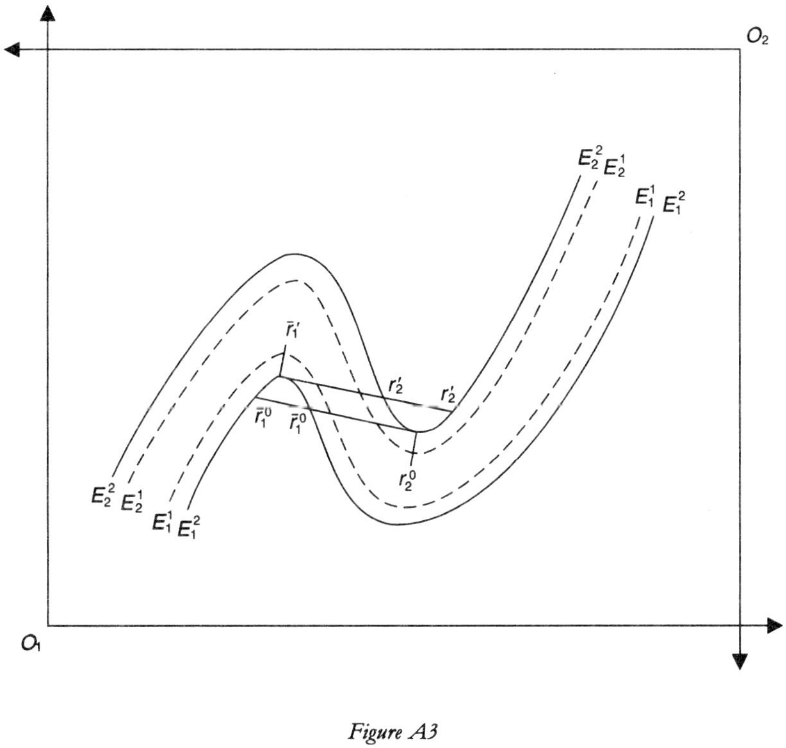

Figure A3

r_2 points, each with its associated trading vector and level of utility for the second individual. Continuing in this way we eventually trace out the *RR* curve of Figure A2.

The above construction was based on the assumption that the first commodity is imported. It is possible, however, that for some income distributions the second commodity will be imported. To explore this possibility we need the remaining pair of Engel curves, corresponding to an internal price ratio of $\pi/(1 + \tau_2)$. These are drawn in Figure A3 and labelled $E_i^2E_i^2$, with the old $E_i^1E_i^1$ curves included for comparison. It is not difficult to see that only those r_1 points which lie between $\overline{r}_1^0$ and $\overline{r}_1^0$ and the corresponding r_2 points represent possible trading equilibria, with net imports of the second commodity. As we allow r_1 to run through this restricted range, r_2 moves between the two $\overline{r}_2'$ points and traces out in Figure A2 a closed loop of utility possibilities. When added to the *RR* curve this loop gives us our complete set of feasible utility combinations. In the case illustrated the set is not connected.

That completes the derivation. It is to be emphasized that inferiority is necessary but not by itself sufficient to produce positively sloped stretches in the utility–feasibility locus. And even when inferiority is sufficiently strong to produce positive slopes it may not be strong enough, or may not prevail over a sufficiently wide range of incomes, to produce a closed loop. Finally, even if the loop exists, it is disconnected only if $E_1^2E_1^2$ and $E_2^2E_2^2$ do not intersect. If $E_1^1E_1^1$ and $E_2^1E_2^1$ intersect, and if $E_1^2E_1^2$ and $E_2^2E_2^2$ intersect, the loop and *RR* can be connected by movements along the contract locus, with net foreign trade zero.

NOTES

* I am grateful to Jagdish Bhagwati, Harry Johnson and Paul Samuelson for helpful correspondence.

1 Kemp (1964: 169). A similar passage appears in Kemp (1962: 814).

2 Vanek (1965). In Ch. 4 and in the appendix Vanek has anticipated many of the points made in Bhagwati's (1968) section 3 and in section 2 of this essay. Of special relevance and interest are passages on pp. 80 and 202.

3 It is I think fair to say also that in section 2 of his paper Bhagwati (1968) shows not that 'Kemp's theorem is . . . invalid' but that the theorem cannot be extended in the particular direction he considers.

4 All indifference curves in Figure 1 are of the Scitovsky variety, but non-intersecting.

5 The construction of the utility feasibility locus is described in the appendix.

6 This paragraph contains a particular application of the well-known Leontief–Hicks theorem on composite commodities.

7 This example is being worked out in detail by Professors Hugo Sonnenschein and Edward Foster of the University of Minnesota. [Since this essay was first published, their findings have been reported in Foster and Sonnenschein (1970) – M. K., 1995].

REFERENCES

Bhagwati, J. N. (1968) 'The gains from trade once again', *Oxford Economic Papers*, New Series, 20: 137–48.

Foster, E. and Sonnenschein, H. (1970) 'Price distortions and economic welfare', *Econometrica* 38: 281–97.

Kemp, M. C. (1962) 'The gain from international trade', *Economic Journal* 72: 803–19.

Kemp, M. C. (1964), *The Pure Theory of International Trade*, Englewood Cliffs, NJ: Prentice Hall.

Krueger, A. O. and Sonnenschein, H. (1967) 'The terms of trade, the gains from trade and price divergence', *International Economic Review* 8: 121–7.

Vanek, J. (1965) *General Equilibrium of International Discrimination. The Case of Customs Unions*, Cambridge, MA: Harvard University Press.

17

VARIABLE RETURNS TO SCALE, COMMODITY TAXES, FACTOR-MARKET DISTORTIONS AND THEIR IMPLICATIONS FOR TRADE GAINS

The gains from international trade have been analyzed under restrictive assumptions concerning scale returns, taxes and other market distortions. It is shown that theorems of considerable sweep and generality can be proved even when those assumptions are relaxed.

1 INTRODUCTION

The contemplation of the static theory of the gains from international trade may induce a response of breathless admiration or a mood of deep despair, or both. It all depends on one's point of view: the subject is difficult and one cannot fail to admire the elegance and glitter of the theorems which have been established; on the other hand, the theorems rest on very special assumptions.

Specifically, it has been shown that, in the absence of external or internal economies and diseconomies of scale, in the absence of factor-market distortions, and in the absence of consumption and production taxes,

(1) free trade is better (strictly, not worse) than no trade, in the sense that there always exists a system of ideal lumpsum taxes and subsidies which would leave everybody not worse off after trade than before, and that
(2) an improvement in a country's barter terms of trade is desirable, in the same sense.

We owe the first proposition to Paul Samuelson, the second to Anne Krueger and Hugo Sonnenschein.[1] The assumptions listed above will be referred to as the **standard assumptions**.

When the standard assumptions are relaxed we are reduced to erroneous generalization[2] or the dissection of highly special cases.[3] The field is in a mess, littered with the debris of earlier debate yet empty of satisfactory generalizations.

Of course we are in this field occupied with comparisons of second-best situations, and for some this observation will serve both as explanation and expiation. In the world of second best many strange things are possible. Nevertheless one need not jump overboard in the belief that literally anything can happen and that generalization is impossible; at least, that is what we hope to show.

2 VARIABLE RETURNS TO SCALE[4]

It is assumed that in industries, $1, \ldots, k$ returns to scale are decreasing, that in industries $k+1, \ldots, q$ returns to scale are constant, and that in industries $q+1, \ldots, n$ returns are increasing. It is assumed, moreover, that entry to each industry is perfectly free so that, in equilibrium, profit is zero. If returns to scale are decreasing, they must be accompanied by diseconomies external to the firm; for internal diseconomies combined with freedom of entry imply constant returns to the industry (and firms of infinitesimal size). If, on the other hand, returns are increasing, the economies may be either internal to the firm or external to it. The form taken by the economies in this case, however, has no bearing on the analysis to follow: if the economies are of the internal variety, the industry will contain a single firm, but a firm constrained by the prospect of new entrants to equate price to average cost; and if the economies are external to the firm price will in any case be forced to the level of average cost. We therefore need not specify the nature of the process generating the economies.

The assumptions just listed will be maintained throughout the section and will not be repeated in the statement of theorems.

The following notation will be employed:

$X = (X_1, \ldots, X_n)$ vector of outputs
$D = (D_1, \ldots, D_n)$ consumption vector
$A = (A_1, \ldots, A_m)$ vector of total inputs
$A_j = (A_{1j}, \ldots, A_{mj})$ vector of inputs in the jth industry
$p = (p_1, \ldots, p_n)$ vector of commodity prices
$w = (w_1, \ldots, w_m)$ vector of factor rentals.

Values of the variables under autarky will be indicated by the superscript 0, free-trade values will be indicated by primes, and alternative free-trade values will be indicated by double primes.

Theorem 1. *If the opening of trade results in the non-expansion of every industry $j = 1, \ldots, k$ and in the non-contraction of every industry $j = q+1, \ldots, n$, so that*

$$\begin{aligned} X_j' &\leqslant X_j^0, \quad j = 1, \ldots, k, \\ X_j' &\geqslant X_j^0, \quad j = q+1, \ldots, n, \end{aligned} \tag{1}$$

then trade is necessarily non-harmful, in the sense that those who benefit from trade could afford to compensate those who suffer.

Proof. *Suppose the contrary, that there exists an autarkic equilibrium which, in terms of individual utilities, cannot be reproduced or bettered under free trade. Then for all relevant free-trade distributions of income, that is distributions such that either everyone is not worse off or everyone is not better off than under autarky, the inequality*

$$p'D' - w'A' < p'D^0 - w'A^0 \tag{2}$$

must be satisfied. Otherwise, free trade would be revealed as preferred to autarky. However, $X^0 = D^0$ *and free trade is balanced so that*

$$p'D' = p'X'. \tag{3}$$

Hence (2) may be rewritten as

$$p'X' - w'A < p'X^0 - w'A^0; \tag{4}$$

that is, as

$$\sum_{j=1}^{k} (p_j'X_j' - w'A_{.j}') + \sum_{j=k+1}^{q} (p_j'X_j' - w'A_{.j}') + \sum_{j=q+1}^{n} (p_j'X_j' - w'A_{.j}')$$

$$< \sum_{j=1}^{k} (p_j'X_j^0 - w'A_{.j}^0) + \sum_{j=k+1}^{q} (p_j'X_j^0 - w'A_{.j}^0) + \sum_{j=q+1}^{n} (p_j'X_j^0 - w'A_{.j}^0). \tag{5}$$

However, freedom of entry ensures that in free-trade equilibrium profit is zero in each industry:

$$p_j'X_j' - w'A_{.j}' = 0, \quad j = 1, \ldots, n.$$

If, faced with free-trade prices and rentals, producers in the jth constant-returns industry hold their outputs and factor inputs at levels appropriate to autarkic prices and rentals, their profit must be non-positive, that is

$$0 = p_j'X_j' - w'A_{.j}' \geqslant p_j'X_j^0 - w'A_{.j}^0, \quad j = k+1, \ldots, q. \tag{6a}$$

A fortiori, given (1),

$$0 = p_j'X_j' - w'A_{.j}' \geqslant p_j'X_j^0 - w'A_{.j}^0, \quad j = 1, \ldots, k; j = q+1, \ldots, n. \tag{6b}$$

Inequalities (6) contradict inequalities (5). □

We shall say that a country's barter terms of trade have improved if

$$p''X' > p''D'. \tag{7}$$

Theorem 2. *If an autonomous improvement in a country's barter terms of trade results in the non-expansion of every industry* $j = 1, \ldots, k$ *and in the non-contraction of every industry* $q + 1, \ldots, n$ *then the change is necessarily non-harmful, in the sense that those who benefit from the change could afford to compensate those who suffer.*

Proof. *Suppose the contrary, that there exists an initial free-trade equilibrium which, in terms of individual utilities, cannot be reproduced or improved upon in the new free-trade situation. Then for all relevant distributions of income the inequality*

$$p''D'' - w''A'' < p''D' - w''A' \tag{8}$$

is satisfied. However, (7) holds and trade is balanced, so that

$$p''D'' = p''X''. \tag{9}$$

Hence (8) may be rewritten as

$$p''X'' - w''A'' < p''X' - w''A'; \tag{10}$$

that is, as

$$\sum_{j=1}^{k} (p_j''X_j'' - w''A_{.j}'') + \sum_{j=k+1}^{q} (p_j''X_j'' - w''A_{.j}'') + \sum_{j=q+1}^{n} (p_j''X_j'' - w''A_{.j}'')$$

$$< \sum_{j=1}^{k} (p_j''X_j' - w''A_{.j}'') + \sum_{j=k+1}^{q} (p_j''X_j' - w''A_{.j}')$$

$$+ \sum_{j=q+1}^{n} (p_j''X_j' - w''A_{.j}'). \tag{11}$$

By an argument similar to that which justified (6), however,

$$0 = p_j''X_j'' - w''A_{.j}'' \geqslant p_j''X_j' - w''A_{.j}', \quad j = 1, \ldots, n. \tag{12}$$

Inequalities (12) contradict inequalities (11). □

Perhaps the most surprising features of theorem 1 are that it requires no assumptions about either the autarkic or free-trade state of specialization, that it sidesteps any reference to the shape of either the locus of production possibilities or the locus of competitive outputs, and that no mention is made of the import–export status of any industry. It is perhaps worth drawing attention to the fact that in the statement of the theorem no restrictions are placed on the outputs of the $q - k$ constant-returns industries.

Theorems 1 and 2 can be extended without difficulty to cover trade which is not free but restricted by tariffs, import quotas or exchange restrictions.

On the other hand, some plausible analogues to theorems 1 and 2 turn out to be false. Those theorems enable us to compare situations (pre- and post-trade, for example) which are characterized not only by variable returns to scale but also by the allocative distortions associated with average cost pricing. The theorems therefore tell us little about the implications for trade gains of variable returns *per se*. To get at that question one must imagine that, before and after the hypothetical disturbance (the opening of trade, for example), the distortions are precisely offset by a suitable system of taxes and subsidies. **But then theorems 1 and 2 are no longer true.** Even when (1) is satisfied the opening of trade (or an improvement in the terms of trade) may be harmful. Figure 1 provides an illustration from the world of two products and inelastic factor supplies.

Suppose that all industries enjoy increasing returns to scale and that they can be unambiguously divided into those with less strongly and those with more strongly increasing returns, each member of the second group enjoying more strongly increasing returns than every member of the first group. Suppose, moreover, that the opening of trade (or an improvement in the terms of trade) results in the non-expansion of the output of each industry in the first group, and in the non-contraction of the output of each industry in the second group.

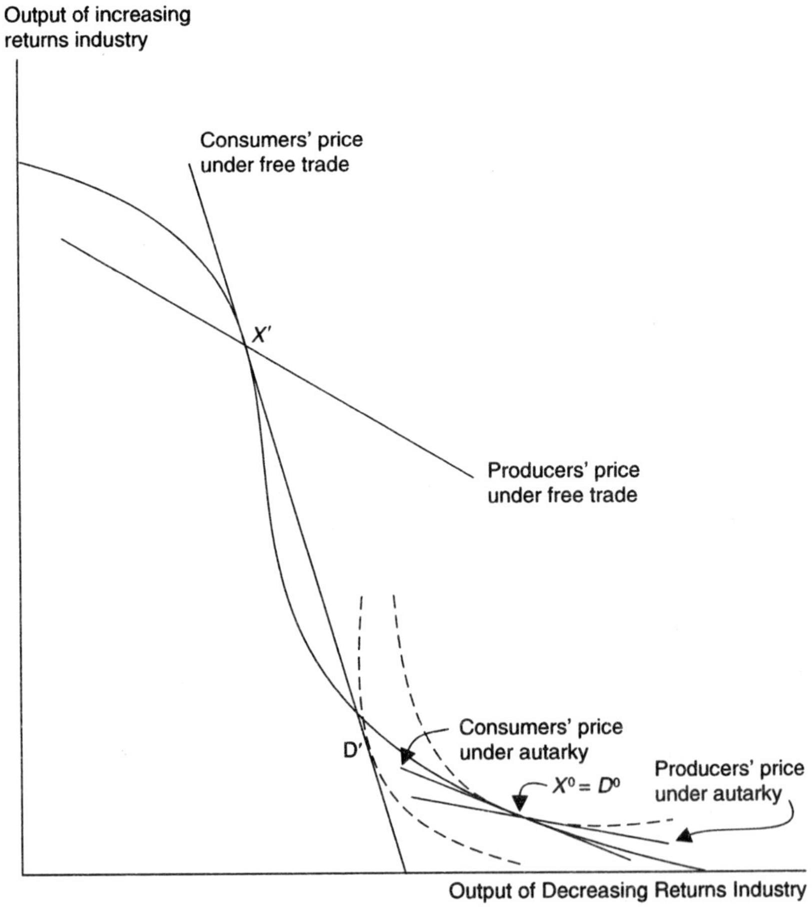

Figure 1

One is tempted to conjecture, in analogy to theorems 1 and 2, that under these conditions trade is necessarily gainful. Unfortunately the conjecture cannot be confirmed by the kind of argument used so far. Indeed there are reasons for believing the conjecture to be false. For when all industries enjoy increasing returns the contracting industries suffer a **loss** of efficiency, and whether this is outweighed in the welfare balance by the improvement in the efficiency of the expanding industries cannot be determined without a closer specification both of preferences and technology.

3 COMMODITY TAXES

We now revert to the assumption of constant returns to scale but vary the standard assumptions by introducing commodity taxes.

Our notation must be extended to include consumption and production taxes and to admit the distinction between prices as seen by consumers and prices as seen by producers:

$T_j \gtreqless 0$ *ad valorem* tax on the consumption of the *j*th commodity

$$T = \begin{bmatrix} T_1 & 0 & \dots & 0 \\ 0 & T_2 & \dots & 0 \\ \vdots & & & \vdots \\ 0 & 0 & \dots & T_n \end{bmatrix}$$ diagonal matrix with T_j as the *j*th diagonal element

$T_j^* \gtreqless 0$ *ad valorem* tax on the production of the *j*th commodity

$$T^* = \begin{bmatrix} T_1^* & 0 & \dots & 0 \\ 0 & T_2^* & \dots & 0 \\ \vdots & & & \vdots \\ 0 & 0 & \dots & T_n^* \end{bmatrix}$$

$p = (p_1, \dots, p_n)$ vector of consumers' prices

$p^* = (p_1^*, \dots, p_n^*)$ vector of producers' prices.

Suppose that the government has imposed a vector of consumption taxes but that all other standard assumptions hold. Then we have:

Theorem 3. *If the opening of trade results in the non-contraction of net tax revenue, calculated on the basis of pre-trade prices, then trade is necessarily non-harmful, in the sense that those who benefit from trade could afford to compensate those who suffer. Net tax revenue cannot decline if consumption of the jth good fails to contract when T_j is positive and fails to expand when T_j is negative.*

Proof. *Suppose the contrary, that there exists an autarkic equilibrium which, in terms of individual utilities, cannot be reproduced or bettered under free trade. Then, for all relevant free-trade distributions of income, the inequality*

$$p'D' - w'A' < p'D^0 - w'A^0 \tag{2}$$

must hold. Now

$$p' = p^{*\prime}(I + T) \tag{13}$$

where I is the unit matrix. Hence

$$p^{*\prime}(I + T)D' - w'A' < p^{*\prime}(I + T)D^0 - w'A^0, \tag{14}$$

that is

$$p^{*\prime}D' + p^{*\prime}T(D' - D^0) - w'A' < p^{*\prime}D^0 - w'A^0. \tag{15}$$

Now $p^{*\prime}T(D' - D^0)$ *is the increase in tax revenue calculated on the basis of pre-trade prices. By assumption it is non-negative; hence*

$$p^{*\prime}D' - w'A' < p^{*\prime}D^0 - w'A^0. \tag{16}$$

But free trade is balanced:

$$p^{*\prime}D' = p^{*\prime}X'; \tag{17}$$

and autarkic production is equal to autarkic consumption:

$$D^0 = X^0. \tag{18}$$

Hence,

$$p^{*\prime}X' - w'A' < p^{*\prime}X^0 - w'A^0. \tag{19}$$

Under constant returns and freedom of entry, however,

$$0 = p_j^{*\prime}X_j' - w'A_j' \geqslant p^{*\prime}X^0 - w'A_j^0, \quad j = 1, \ldots, n. \tag{20}$$

Inequalities (19) and (20) are in conflict; hence the main part of the theorem is proved. The second part of the theorem is obvious. □

Theorem 4. *If an autonomous improvement in a country's barter terms of trade results in the non-contraction of net tax revenue calculated on the basis of unchanged prices then the change is necessarily non-harmful in the sense that those who benefit from the change could afford to compensate those who suffer. Net tax revenue cannot decline if consumption of the jth good fails to contract when* T_j *is positive and fails to expand when* T_j *is negative.*

Proof. *Suppose the contrary, that there exists an initial free-trade equilibrium which, in terms of individual utilities, cannot be reproduced or bettered in the new free-trade situation. Then for all relevant distributions of income the inequality*

$$p''D'' - w''A'' < p''D' - w''A' \tag{8}$$

must hold. Now

$$p'' = p^{*''}(I + T) \tag{21}$$

so that (8) may be rewritten as

$$p^{*''}D'' + p^{*''}T(D'' - D') - w''A'' < p^{*''}D' - w''A'. \tag{22}$$

But by assumption the change in net tax revenue, $p^{*''}T(D'' - D')$, *is non-negative; hence*

$$p^{*''}D'' - w''A'' < p^{*''}D' - w''A'. \tag{23}$$

Free trade is balanced:

$$p^{*''}D'' = p^{*''}X''; \tag{24}$$

and the terms of trade have improved:

$$p^{*''}(X' - D') > 0. \tag{25}$$

Hence

$$p^{*''}X'' - w''A'' < p^{*''}X' - w''A'. \tag{26}$$

Under constant returns and freedom of entry, however,

$$0 = p_j^{*''}X_j'' - w''A_{.j}'' \geqslant p_j^*X_j' - w''A_{.j}'', \quad j = 1, \ldots, n. \tag{27}$$

Inequalities (26) and (27) are in conflict and the non-trivial part of the theorem is proved. □

Suppose alternatively that the government has imposed a vector of production taxes but that all other standard assumptions hold. Then the following theorems, companion to theorems 3 and 4, can be proved. The proofs contain no novelties and are withheld.

Theorem 5. *If the opening of trade results in the non-contraction of net tax revenue, calculated on the basis of pre-trade prices, then trade is necessarily non-harmful, in the sense that those who benefit from trade could afford to compensate those who suffer. Net tax revenue cannot decline if production of the jth good fails to contract when* T_j^* *is positive and fails to expand when* T_j^* *is negative.*

Theorem 6. *If an autonomous improvement in a country's barter terms of trade results in the non-contraction of net tax revenue, calculated on the basis of pre-trade prices, then the change is necessarily non-harmful, in the sense that those who benefit from the change could afford to compensate those who suffer. Net tax revenue cannot decline if production of the jth good fails to contract when* T_j^* *is positive and fails to expand when* T_j^* *is negative.*

4 FACTOR-MARKET DISTORTIONS

Let us now assume that in each industry returns to scale are constant but that the reward of any particular factor, say the mth, may vary from industry to industry. The rental paid by the jth industry to the mth factor is denoted by w_{mj}, $j = 1, \ldots, n$. Without loss of generality we can renumber industries so that under free trade each industry pays to the mth factor not more than its predecessor:

$$w_{m,j+1} \leqslant w_{mj}, \quad j = 1, \ldots, n-1 \tag{28}$$

with a strong inequality for some j.

Before proceeding to the substance of this section we clear out of the way two preliminary matters. First we note that the interindustrial differentials create a merely sham problem if they accurately reflect non-pecuniary advantages and disadvantages of employment in particular industries. To see this, we need only divide the mth factor into n subfactors according to the industry supplied, so that there are $n + m - 1$ factors in all. To avoid inessential complications, therefore, we assume that the owners of the mth factor are completely insensitive to the non-pecuniary aspects of employment.

We notice next that the persistence of the differentials is inconsistent with rational household choice; if in the circumstances described by (28) households behaved rationally, the mth factor would be supplied only to the first industry. Accordingly, we now abandon an assumption we have carried through sections 2 and 3 – that the supply of each factor is a variable, depending on product prices and factor rewards – and assume instead that A_m, the supply of the mth factor, is a constant. The supplies of other factors remain variable.

Theorem 7. *If for any h, $1 < h < n$, the opening of trade results in the non-expansion of the employment of the mth factor in every industry $j = h, \ldots, n$ and in the non-contraction of the employment of the mth factor in every industry $j = 1, \ldots, h-1$, so that*

$$A'_{mj} \leqslant A^0_{mj}, \quad j = h, \ldots, n,$$

$$A'_{mj} \geqslant A^0_{mj}, \quad j = 1, \ldots, h-1,$$

then trade is necessarily non-harmful, in the sense that those who benefit from trade could afford to compensate those who suffer.

Proof. *Suppose the contrary, that there exists an autarkic equilibrium which, in terms of individual utilities (which are, this time, functions of the individual's consumption of n goods and of his or her supply of $m-1$ factors of production), cannot be reproduced or bettered under free trade. Then, since the household choice of D and $\bar{A}$ is assumed to be rational, for all relevant free-trade distributions of income,*

$$p'D' - \bar{w}'\bar{A}' < p'D^0 - \bar{w}'\bar{A}^0 \tag{29}$$

where $\bar{A} = (A_1, \ldots, A_{m-1})$ *and* $\bar{w} = (w_1, \ldots, w_{m-1})$. *Otherwise, free trade would be revealed as preferred to autarky. On the other hand, from the assumptions of the theorem,*

$$\sum_{j=1}^{h-1} w'_{mj}(A'_{mj} - A^0_{mj}) + \sum_{j=h}^{n} w'_{mj}(A'_{mj} - A^0_{mj}) > 0$$

which in turn yields

$$\sum_{j=1}^{n} w'_{mj}A'_{mj} > \sum_{j=1}^{n} w'_{mj}A^0_{mj} \tag{30}$$

From (29) and (30)

$$p'D' - w'A' < p'D^0 - w'A^0 \tag{2}$$

and the argument proceeds as in the second half of the proof of theorem 1. □

Theorem 8. *If for any h,* $1 < h < n$, *an autonomous improvement in a country's barter terms of trade results in the non-expansion of the employment of the mth factor in every industry* $j = h, \ldots, n$ *and in the non-contraction of the employment of the mth factor in every industry* $j = 1, \ldots, h-1$, *so that*

$$A''_{mj} \leqslant A'_{mj}, \quad j = h, \ldots, n,$$

$$A''_{mj} \geqslant A'_{mj}, \quad j = 1, \ldots, h-1,$$

then the change is necessarily non-harmful, in the sense that those who benefit from trade could afford to compensate those who suffer.

Proof. *Suppose the contrary, that there exists an initial free-trade equilibrium which, in terms of individual utilities (which, again, are functions of the individual's consumption of n goods and of his or her supply of* $m-1$ *factors), cannot be reproduced or improved on in the free-trade situation. Then, for all relevant distributions of income, the inequality*

$$p''D'' - \bar{w}''\bar{A}'' < p''D' - \bar{w}'\bar{A} \tag{31}$$

is satisfied. From the assumptions of the theorem, we have

$$\sum_{j=1}^{n} w''_{mj}A''_{mj} > \sum_{j=1}^{n} w''_{mj}A'_{mj} \tag{32}$$

which, in conjunction with (31), yields again the inequality (8). The rest of the proof parallels that of theorem 2. □

Like theorems 1 and 2, these theorems bypass many questions which to earlier writers seemed central. For example, no mention is made of the import–export status of any industry, and no assumptions are made about the shape of the locus of competitive outputs. It may be noted also that nothing has been said about the hierarchy of rewards to the *m*th factor in the initial situation (autarky in theorem 7, the first of two free-trade positions in theorem 8), and that nothing has been said about changes in the employment of factors other than the *m*th.

Theorems 7 and 8 have been stated in terms of interindustrial differences in the reward of a single factor. However, both theorems can be extended to cover interindustrial differences in the rewards of several (but not all) factors provided industries are ranked in the same way by each of the several factors.

5 FINAL REMARKS

In some of our proofs we have relied on the assumption that in each industry entry is completely free. This assumption is extreme, and may be thought crucial. We note therefore that all theorems carry over, with inessential changes, to the other polar world in which, in each industry, the number of firms is constant.

NOTES

1 See Samuelson (1939, 1962) and Krueger and Sonnenschein (1967).

2 Only in the case of variable returns to scale has there been a serious attempt to generalize the standard propositions. The essential references are to Graham (1923) and Tinbergen (1945, 1954). Most recent treatments contain simple variations on Tinbergen's theme, or parrot him quite uncritically.

In fact Tinbergen's treatment is wrong in essentials. His much-reproduced diagram (Fig. 4, 1954: 181) is constructed on the assumption that the price ratio is equal to the ratio of marginal social costs, which it clearly cannot be. Moreover, the locus of competitive outputs in that diagram has a shape which is inconsistent with the assumptions made about scale returns in the two industries. For more detail, see Herberg and Kemp (1969).

3 See Kemp (1969: Ch. 12).

4 Some of the problems discussed in this section are treated also in Negishi (1969).

REFERENCES

Graham, F. D. (1923) 'Some aspects of protection further considered', *Quarterly Journal of Economics* 37: 199–227.

Herberg, Horst and Kemp, Murray C. (1969) 'Some implications of variable returns to scale', *Canadian Journal of Economics* 2: 403–15.

Kemp, Murray C. (1969) *The Pure Theory of International Trade and Investment*, Englewood Cliffs, NJ: Prentice Hall.

Krueger, Anne O. and Sonnenschein, Hugo (1967) 'The terms of trade, the gains from trade and price divergence', *International Economic Review* 8: 121–7.

Negishi, Takashi (1969) 'Marshallian external economies and gains from trade between similar countries', *Review of Economic Studies* 36: 131–5.

Samuelson, Paul A. (1939) 'The gains from international trade', *Canadian Journal of Economics and Political Science* 5: 195–205.

Samuelson, Paul A. (1962) 'The gains from international trade once again', *Economic Journal* 72: 820–9.
Tinbergen, J. (1945) *International Economic Cooperation*, Amsterdam: Elsevier.
Tinbergen, J. (1954) *International Economic Integration*, Amsterdam: Elsevier.

18

VARIABLE RETURNS TO SCALE, NON-UNIQUENESS OF EQUILIBRIUM AND THE GAINS FROM INTERNATIONAL TRADE

1 INTRODUCTION

If production takes place under variable returns to scale, the exposure of a country to foreign trade may or may not be gainful. However, trade theorists have managed to scrape together a miscellany of sufficient conditions for gain. Most of these conditions relate to a model of production in which individual firms perceive that they produce under constant returns and in which variable returns to the industry arise from interfirm externalities. In such a model variable returns are consistent with perfect competition; it is therefore possible to study the effects of variable returns in isolation, uncontaminated by the distortions associated with imperfect competition. The best known of the conditions was formulated by Kemp and Negishi (1970, 1971); but see also Ohyama (1972), Negishi (1972) and Helpman (1983, 1984). Roughly, trade is gainful if it induces an expansion of industries which enjoy increasing returns and a contraction of industries which produce under decreasing returns. Other sufficient conditions were obtained by Negishi (1969, 1972: Ch. 5) and Krugman (1979), who showed that even two identical countries can gain from trade, and by Ethier (1982), who showed that a country gains from trade if there are two industries, one subject to constant returns, the other to increasing returns which accrue at a constant rate, and if the dynamic adjustment mechanism is of Marshallian type.

Nevertheless the present state of affairs is unsatisfactory. The available conditions for gainful trade are merely sufficient, and very special. On the other hand, while confining themselves to the 'externalities' model of production, trade theorists have failed to avail themselves of one of its more pertinent properties, that given product prices may be associated with several distinct production equilibria, so that neither supply functions nor convex-valued supply correspondences generally exist. Indeed it is customary to work with special assumptions which guarantee the existence of supply functions; see, for example, Ethier (1982) and Markusen and Wigle (1989). Similarly, trade theorists have neglected the possibility that, in a context of distorting production externalities, there may be multiple **and Pareto-rankable** autarkic and free-trade equilibria.

In the present essay we re-examine the awkward old question of trade gains under variable returns to scale. We retain the externalities model of production, but avail ourselves of the hitherto neglected properties of that model. However, it may be noted that our conclusions remain valid if scale economies are internal to the firm and if entry to each industry is open. In that case, as in the case of external economies, price is equal to average cost in equilibrium; see Kemp (1969: 155, n. 2) and Kemp and Negishi (1970: Section 2), also Ethier (1982).

Taking advantage of recent developments in factor-content and duality theory, we derive a necessary and sufficient condition for trade gains which is both novel and global in scope: trade is gainful if and only if any loss of productivity as a consequence of trade is more than offset by the improvement in the factoral terms of trade. Moreover, it is shown that trade gains do not imply changes in product prices, that changes in factor prices can alone suffice for gain, and that this is so even when trade exacerbates the distortion associated with externalities. Indeed trade may be less gainful when it brings about a change in product prices than when prices are unchanged.

2 CONCEPTS AND ASSUMPTIONS

We begin with a brief description of the production-externalities model. Each of $n \geqslant 2$ industries consists of a large number of identical firms. Associated with each firm there is a production function which is differentiable, linearly homogeneous and strictly quasi-concave in factor inputs. The output of the firm depends also on the outputs of all industries (which may be defined on a world-wide basis), but the firm treats all outputs but its own as parameters. Factor markets are perfectly competitive and all firms face the same factor prices. Hence there exist implicit industry production functions

$$\mathbf{y}_j = f_j(\mathbf{v}_j; \mathbf{y}), \quad j = 1, \ldots, n, \tag{1}$$

where $\mathbf{y}_j$ and $\mathbf{v}_j$ denote the output and the input vector of the jth industry, and $\mathbf{y}$ is the vector of industry outputs; see, for example, Helpman (1984). These functions have the same properties as the production functions of firms; that is, they are strictly quasi-concave and linearly homogeneous in factor inputs.

Each firm, and therefore each industry and the production sector as a whole, chooses a technique of production which, for given factor prices $\mathbf{w}$ and outputs $\mathbf{y}$, minimizes the cost of production. For the economy as a whole, there is an aggregate cost function, defined as the envelope function

$$C(\mathbf{w}, \mathbf{y}) \equiv \min_{\mathbf{v}_1 \ldots \mathbf{v}_n} \left\{ \sum_j \mathbf{w}\mathbf{v}_j : f_j(\mathbf{v}_j; \mathbf{y}) \geqslant y_j \text{ and } \mathbf{v}_j \geqslant 0, \ j = 1, \ldots, n \right\}. \tag{2}$$

The aggregate cost function has the following properties:

(1) the partial derivatives $C_{\mathbf{w}}(\mathbf{w}, \mathbf{y})$ are the demand functions for factors,

(2) the partial derivatives $C_{\mathbf{y}}(\mathbf{w}, \mathbf{y})$ represent the marginal costs to the economy,
(3) C is increasing in each element of $\mathbf{w}$ and $\mathbf{y}$, and
(4) C is linearly homogeneous and concave in $\mathbf{w}$.

In the context of production externalities, the aggregate cost function has substantial advantages over the national product or revenue functions. In particular, it is differentiable in $\mathbf{w}$ whatever the numbers of factors and products; and factor demand functions exist even though product supply functions generally do not exist.

From problem (2) we obtain the solution functions

$$\mathbf{v}_j = \mathbf{v}_j(\mathbf{w}, \mathbf{y}), \quad j = 1, \ldots, n, \tag{3}$$

and the unit cost functions

$$c_j = c_j(\mathbf{w}, \mathbf{y}) \equiv \mathbf{w}\mathbf{v}_j(\mathbf{w}, \mathbf{y})/y_j, \quad j = 1, \ldots, n. \tag{4}$$

In (2) the factor prices $\mathbf{w}$ are exogenous. However, in a competitive economy, the equilibrium $\mathbf{w}$ solves the problem

$$\min_{\mathbf{w}} \mathbf{w}\mathbf{v} \text{ s.t. } c_j(\mathbf{w}, \mathbf{y}) \geqslant p_j \quad (j = 1, \ldots, n) \quad \text{and} \quad \mathbf{w} \geqslant 0 \tag{5}$$

where $\mathbf{v}$ denotes the vector of factor endowments and p_j denotes the price of the jth commodity. The unique solution to (5) is

$$\mathbf{w} = \mathbf{w}(\mathbf{p}, \mathbf{y}, \mathbf{v}) \tag{6}$$

where $\mathbf{p} \equiv (p_1, \ldots, p_n)$.

Assuming that all factors are fully employed, we can write

$$C_{\mathbf{w}}(\mathbf{w}(\mathbf{p}, \mathbf{y}, \mathbf{v}), \mathbf{y}) = \mathbf{v}. \tag{7}$$

Normally, (7) cannot be uniquely solved for outputs, given output prices. Nor can we be sure that the set of solutions is convex. This is in sharp contrast to the outcome under constant returns. Suppose, for example, that products and factors are equal in number and that the matrix $C_{\mathbf{wy}}$ is non-singular. Under universal constant returns to scale, factor prices are fully determined by the zero-profit conditions (5) and the given factor supplies; moreover, if the cone of diversification is non-degenerate, there exist variations in factor endowments which leave factor prices unchanged. Thus, differentiating (7),

$$C_{\mathbf{wy}}(\mathbf{w})d\mathbf{y} = d\mathbf{v}. \tag{8}$$

With production externalities, on the other hand, we have

$$[C_{\mathbf{ww}}(\mathbf{w}, \mathbf{y})\mathbf{w}_{\mathbf{y}} + C_{\mathbf{wy}}(\mathbf{w}, \mathbf{y})]d\mathbf{y} = d\mathbf{v}. \tag{9}$$

Expressions (8) and (9) clarify the nature of the complications introduced by variable returns. Thus under constant returns $C_{\mathbf{wy}}$ depends only on factor prices (the property of separability), and outputs can change without associated changes in factor prices (non-degeneracy of the cone of diversification); under variable returns neither of these things is true.[1]

The description of the autarkic economy is completed by the addition of the product-market equilibrium conditions

$$y_j = X_j(\mathbf{p}, \mathbf{py}), \quad j = 1, \ldots, n, \tag{10}$$

where X_j is the uncompensated or Marshallian demand for the jth produced commodity.

One of equations (7) and (10) may be deleted, by appeal to Walras' law; and one of the factors of production or one of the produced commodities (or a basket of them) may be chosen as *numéraire*. Even after the choice of *numéraire*, however, the solution (if it exists) may lack uniqueness; and, if there are several solutions, it may be possible to rank them in the sense of Pareto.

Finally, we introduce the **factor trade expenditure function**, defined as

$$B(\mathbf{w}, \mathbf{y}, \mathbf{v}, \mathbf{u}) \equiv E(\mathbf{c}(\mathbf{w}, \mathbf{y}), u) - \mathbf{wv} \tag{11}$$

where u is the level of national well-being, $E(\mathbf{p}, u)$ is the ordinary expenditure function and, for simplicity, it is assumed that all goods are produced.[2] (For closely related concepts see Neary and Schweinberger (1986) and Lloyd and Schweinberger (1988).) The function B has properties which make it useful in normative analysis against a background of production externalities.

Lemma 1. (i) *The first-order partial derivatives of B with respect to* $\mathbf{w}$ *are the (Hicksian) factor-content functions; they indicate the factor content of imports.*

(ii) *The function B is concave in* $\mathbf{w}$ *and, given the autarkic levels of output and utility, reaches a maximum at autarkic factor prices.*

Proof. (i) *From (11),*

$$B_{\mathbf{w}} = E_{\mathbf{p}}\mathbf{c}_{\mathbf{w}} - \mathbf{v} \equiv \mathbf{M}(\mathbf{w}, \mathbf{y}, \mathbf{v}, \mathbf{u}) \tag{12}$$

and, from standard duality theory, $E_{\mathbf{p}}\mathbf{c}_{\mathbf{w}}$ is the factor content of the consumption vector.

(ii) *To establish the concavity of B in* $\mathbf{w}$ *it suffices to prove that the reduced-form expenditure function $E(\mathbf{c}(\mathbf{w}, \mathbf{y}), u)$ is concave in* $\mathbf{w}$.[3] *From the concavity of the (unreduced) expenditure function in* $\mathbf{p}$ *and of the unit cost functions in* $\mathbf{w}$, *recalling that expenditure is an increasing function of* $\mathbf{p}$,

$$\theta E(\mathbf{c}(\mathbf{w}^1, \mathbf{y}), u) + (1 - \theta)E(\mathbf{c}(\mathbf{w}^2, \mathbf{y}), u) \leqslant E[\theta\mathbf{c}(\mathbf{w}^1, \mathbf{y}) + (1 - \theta)\mathbf{c}(\mathbf{w}^2, \mathbf{y}), u]$$

$$\leqslant E\{\mathbf{c}[\theta\mathbf{w}^1 + (1 - \theta)\mathbf{w}^2, \mathbf{y}], u\}.$$

Let us distinguish autarkic and free-trade quantities by the superscripts 0 *and* 1, *respectively.*

It remains to show that B reaches a maximum at $\mathbf{w}^0$, given $\mathbf{y}^0$ and u^0. At autarkic factor prices the factor content of consumption cannot exceed the factor endowment:

$$B_{\mathbf{w}}(\mathbf{w}^0, \mathbf{y}^0, \mathbf{v}, u^0) = \mathbf{M}(\mathbf{w}^0, \mathbf{y}^0, \mathbf{v}, u^0) \leqslant 0. \tag{13}$$

Given the concavity of B in $\mathbf{w}$, however, (13) is necessary and sufficient for a maximum. □

3 ANALYSIS

We can now state our main proposition.

Proposition 1. *The movement to free trade is welfare enhancing if and only if*

$$B(\mathbf{w}^1, \mathbf{y}^1, \mathbf{v}, u^0) < 0. \tag{14}$$

Proof. Suppose that (14) is satisfied. Then, since $B(\mathbf{w}^1, \mathbf{y}^1, \mathbf{v}, u^1) = 0$,

$$B(\mathbf{w}^1, \mathbf{y}^1, \mathbf{v}, u^1) - B(\mathbf{w}^1, \mathbf{y}^1, \mathbf{v}, u^0) > 0. \tag{15}$$

However, B is an increasing function of u; hence $u^1 > u^0$ and trade is gainful.

Suppose that trade is gainful, so that $u^1 > u^0$. Then (15) is satisfied and, since $B(\mathbf{w}^1, \mathbf{y}^1, \mathbf{v}, u^1) = 0$, (14) also is satisfied. □

The standard gains-from-trade result can be derived from proposition 1 and lemma 1(ii) by considering the special case in which B is independent of $\mathbf{y}$.

Proposition 1 is mathematically trivial. However, it is globally valid, and it provides a condition for gainful trade which is both necessary and sufficient. Moreover, it has the virtue of making clear that for gainful trade it is necessary that the equilibrium (wage, output) pair change when the move to free trade is made. It is **not** always necessary that commodity prices change, as is the case under constant returns to scale. For it is possible that with any given vector of commodity prices the conditions of factor-market equilibrium (7) associate many distinct (wage, output) pairs all but one of which are ruled out by the conditions of autarkic product-market equilibrium (10). Indeed mutually profitable trade with unchanged commodity prices is sometimes possible even when the trading partners are identical in all respects; the appendix contains a worked example. This possibility was overlooked by earlier writers, including such notable contributors as Negishi (1969, 1972: Ch. 5), Krugman (1979), Ethier (1982), Helpman (1983, 1984) and Markusen and Melvin (1984). Hence a few words of elaboration may be useful. In a context of production externalities, agents react to both price and quantity signals, as with rationing. More precisely, shadow prices play a role in the determination of output similar to that of market prices in constant-returns economies. Shadow prices in turn depend on market prices and quantities. When a country is opened to trade, the set of feasible quantities changes so that, even if market prices are constant, the set of possible shadow prices changes.

Nor is a change in commodity prices sufficient for gainful trade. It is possible for a country to benefit from trade with unchanged commodity prices but suffer a loss when free-trade and autarkic prices differ.

To assist further understanding of these possibilities we introduce two new concepts and offer a reformulation of proposition 1. Thus, first, we define the movement from autarky to free trade to be **productivity increasing (decreasing)** if

$$B(\mathbf{w}^1, \mathbf{y}^0, \mathbf{v}, u^0) > (<)\ B(\mathbf{w}^1, \mathbf{y}^1, \mathbf{v}, u^0). \tag{16}$$

In words, free trade is productivity increasing (decreasing) if and only if, at free-trade factor prices, the change in outputs associated with the movement to free trade reduces (raises) the cost of financing autarkic utility.[4] Next, we define the movement from autarky to free trade as inducing **an improvement (a deterioration) in the implicit factoral terms of trade** if

$$B(\mathbf{w}^0, \mathbf{y}^0, \mathbf{v}, u^0) - B(\mathbf{w}^1, \mathbf{y}^0, \mathbf{v}, u^0) > (<)\ 0; \tag{17}$$

that is, if the transfer needed to maintain the autarkic level of utility at free-trade factor prices and autarkic outputs is negative (positive).[5] We recall from lemma 1(ii) that when trade is introduced the implicit factoral terms of trade can only improve.

In terms of the new concepts, proposition 1 becomes

Proposition 1′. *The movement to free trade is welfare enhancing if and only if the change in the implicit factoral terms of trade and the trade-induced change in productivity add to a positive number.*

Proof. *The changes in the implicit factoral terms of trade and in productivity sum to*

$$[B(\mathbf{w}^0, \mathbf{y}^0, \mathbf{v}, u^0) - B(\mathbf{w}^1, \mathbf{y}^0, \mathbf{v}, u^0)] + [B(\mathbf{w}^1, \mathbf{y}^0, \mathbf{v}, u^0) - B(\mathbf{w}^1, \mathbf{y}^1, \mathbf{v}, u^0)]$$

$$= B(\mathbf{w}^0, \mathbf{y}^0, \mathbf{v}, u^0) - B(\mathbf{w}^1, \mathbf{y}^1, \mathbf{v}, u^0)$$

$$= -\ B(\mathbf{w}^1, \mathbf{y}^1, \mathbf{v}, u^0)$$

which, from proposition 1, is positive if and only if free trade is welfare enhancing. □

Suppose that the movement from autarky to free trade is productivity reducing. In these circumstances theorists have been agnostic about the gainfulness of trade. Proposition 1′, on the other hand, provides a precise necessary and sufficient condition for gainfulness: the reduction in productivity must be dominated by the improvement in the implicit factoral terms of trade. Moreover, the slopes of the Hicksian factor-content functions can be derived from the slopes of the Marshallian factor-content functions; see Neary and

Schweinberger (1986). Hence changes in the implicit factoral terms of trade can be estimated.

We have noticed that, when trade is introduced, the implicit factoral terms of trade necessarily improve. Let us try to clarify the mechanism by which trade, on this account, is unambiguously beneficial. Suppose, then, that outputs, and therefore productivity, are unaffected by the opening of trade. Figure 1 displays two level curves of $E(\mathbf{c}(\mathbf{w}, \mathbf{y}^0), u^0)$. In autarkic equilibrium, represented by point A, the vector $E_{\mathbf{w}}(.)$ of factors embodied in autarkic consumption must equal the vector $\mathbf{v} = (v_1, v_2)$ of factor endowments. It follows that the minimum expenditure needed to maintain the autarkic level of utility, given output, reaches a maximum at the autarkic factor prices.

Relaxing for a moment our insistence on necessary and sufficient conditions for gain, we may derive a sufficient condition which relates our analysis to earlier work mentioned in the introduction. Thus, defining $\bar{\mathbf{y}} \equiv \theta\mathbf{y}^0 + (1 - \theta)\mathbf{y}^1$ and applying the mean-value theorem to (16), we find that

$$B(\mathbf{w}^1, \mathbf{y}^1, \mathbf{v}, u^0) - B(\mathbf{w}^1, \mathbf{y}^0, \mathbf{v}, u^0) = B_{\mathbf{y}}(\mathbf{w}^1, \bar{\mathbf{y}}, \mathbf{v}, u^0)(\mathbf{y}^1 - \mathbf{y}^0)$$

$$= \left(\sum_j X_j(\partial c_j/\partial y_1), \ldots, \sum_j X_j(\partial c_j/\partial y_n)\right) \cdot (\mathbf{y}^1 - \mathbf{y}^0) < 0$$

is a sufficient condition for an expenditure-reducing change and hence a sufficient condition for trade gains. In other words, for gainful trade it suffices that there be a negative correlation between $\Sigma_j X_j(\partial c_j/\partial y_i)$ and changes in output y_i. This provides a general statement of the intuitive idea that trade is beneficial if 'on average' it increases the output of industries subject to increasing returns.[6]

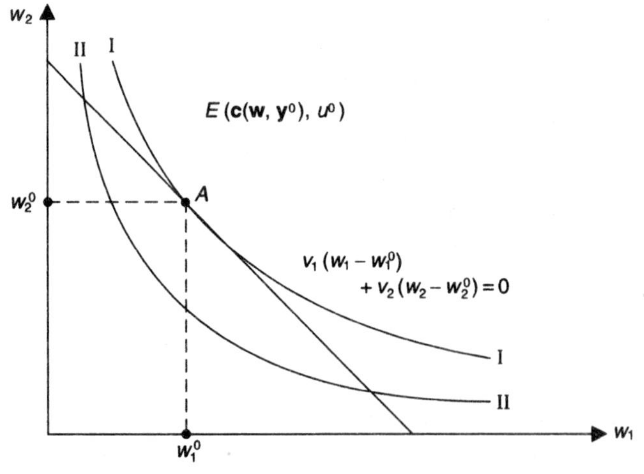

Figure 1

To this point it has been assumed that, in the free-trade equilibrium, all goods are produced. The assumption has allowed us to highlight the hitherto neglected role of factor-price changes in the achievement of trade gains. However, in a context of increasing returns to scale, it is to be expected that free-trade production will be partially or completely specialized. Accordingly, we now extend the analysis to accommodate the possibility of specialization.

To allow for that possibility, the factor trade expenditure function must be redefined as

$$\hat{B}(\hat{\mathbf{p}}, \mathbf{w}, \mathbf{y}, \mathbf{v}, u) \equiv \hat{E}(\hat{\mathbf{p}}, \hat{\mathbf{c}}(\mathbf{w}, \mathbf{y}), u) - \mathbf{wv}$$

where $\hat{\mathbf{p}}$ is the vector of prices of goods not produced in the free-trade equilibrium and $\hat{\mathbf{c}}$ is the vector of unit costs of goods produced in the free-trade equilibrium (cf. Neary and Schweinberger 1986: Section V). By familiar reasoning, $\hat{B}$ is concave in $\hat{\mathbf{p}}$ and $\mathbf{w}$. Moreover, $\hat{B}_{\hat{\mathbf{p}}}(\hat{\mathbf{p}}^0, \mathbf{w}^0, \mathbf{y}^0, \mathbf{v}, u^0) \leqslant 0$ and $\hat{B}_{\mathbf{w}}(\hat{\mathbf{p}}^0, \mathbf{w}^0, \mathbf{y}^0, \mathbf{v}, u^0) \leqslant 0$, where $\hat{B}_{\mathbf{w}}$ is the factor content of goods consumed in the free-trade equilibrium less the factor endowment; hence $\hat{B}(\hat{\mathbf{p}}, \mathbf{w}, \mathbf{y}^0, \mathbf{v}, u^0)$ reaches a maximum at the autarkic prices $\hat{\mathbf{p}}^0$ and $\mathbf{w}^0$.

Conformably, the implicit factoral terms of trade must be redefined as

$$\hat{B}(\hat{\mathbf{p}}^0, \mathbf{w}^0, \mathbf{y}^0, \mathbf{v}, u^0) - \hat{B}(\hat{\mathbf{p}}^1, \mathbf{w}^1, \mathbf{y}^0, \mathbf{v}, u^0) \tag{18}$$

which decomposes into (i) the implicit factoral terms of trade with respect to factors employed in the free-trade production of goods and (ii) the novel terms of trade with respect to goods not produced in the free-trade equilibrium. By an earlier argument, expression (18) cannot be negative. The principal new finding, then, is that trade may be gainful even if the improvement of the implicit factoral terms of trade (i) is insufficient to offset a loss of productivity: the new gains from specialization (ii) may reverse the balance.

In concluding this section we note that, under variable returns to scale, not only alternative free-trade equilibria but also alternative autarkic equilibria may be Pareto-ranked. Many output and factor-price vectors which satisfy the cum-trade factor-market equilibrium conditions (7) are ruled out by the autarkic product-market equilibrium conditions (10); but the possibility of Pareto-rankable multiple equilibria remains. Thus propositions 1 and 1′ can be usefully given a closed-economy interpretation. On the other hand, our analysis applies with only slight reinterpretation to movements from one free-trade equilibrium to another, whether or not the movements are associated with changes in commodity prices.

4 FINAL REMARK

We have worked with the 'externalities' model of production, thereby keeping at bay the complicating distortions associated with imperfect competition. However, our method can be applied also in a context of imperfect competition and monopoly. Under conditions of monopoly, for example, we can define

$$\tilde{B} \equiv B(\mathbf{w}, \mathbf{y}, \mathbf{v}, u) + E(\mathbf{p}, u) - E(\mathbf{c}(\mathbf{w}, \mathbf{y}), u) - \Pi$$

where the new term $E(\mathbf{p}, u) - E(\mathbf{c}(\mathbf{w}, \mathbf{y}), u) - \Pi$ is a **general-equilibrium** measure of the **net** welfare cost of monopoly and comprises the net welfare cost to consumers $E(\mathbf{p}, u) - E(\mathbf{c}(\mathbf{w}, \mathbf{y}), u)$ less monopoly profit $\Pi = \mathbf{py} - \mathbf{wv}$. Proceeding as in section 3, on the basis of $\tilde{B}$ rather than B, it can be shown that trade may be gainful even if it causes the net social cost of monopoly to increase and productivity to fall. Moreover, this statement remains valid even if consumers' prices $\mathbf{p}$ and average production costs $\mathbf{c}(\mathbf{w}, \mathbf{y})$ fail to respond to the opening of trade. Of course, for gainful trade it is necessary that the change in the implicit factoral terms of trade outweigh the other changes.

In section 3 we have touched on issues which deserve further examination. In particular, the possibility of multiple Pareto-rankable world equilibria suggests a role for government in moving the economy to a preferred equilibrium. This may require the co-operation of national governments.

APPENDIX

Given conventional constant returns to scale, for a country to benefit from the opportunity to trade freely with the rest of the world in a given list of goods it is necessary that

(1) the vector of pre-trade domestic prices of those goods differs intrinsically from the corresponding vector of post-trade domestic (and world) prices, so that one vector cannot be obtained from the other by positive scalar multiplication.

Moreover, (1) can be satisfied only if

(2) the vector of pre-trade domestic prices of those goods differs intrinsically from the vector of pre-trade rest-of-the-world prices of those goods.

In this appendix it is shown by example that, in a context of increasing returns to scale, trade can be advantageous when neither (1) nor (2) is satisfied, even if all trading countries are identical. That (2) is not implied by trade gains has been known for some time; see Negishi (1969). That (1) is not implied seems to be new.

The example is of additional interest in exposing the possible role of international trade in bridging the non-convex portions of production sets.

Example. In each of two trading countries there is just one homogeneous factor of production (labour), available in given amount $L = 1$. Each of two industries has the same production function. Individual firms perceive themselves to be producing under constant returns. However, external economies ensure that, at the industry level, returns to scale are increasing. Specifically,

$$y_j = g(y_j)L_j, \quad j = 1, 2,$$

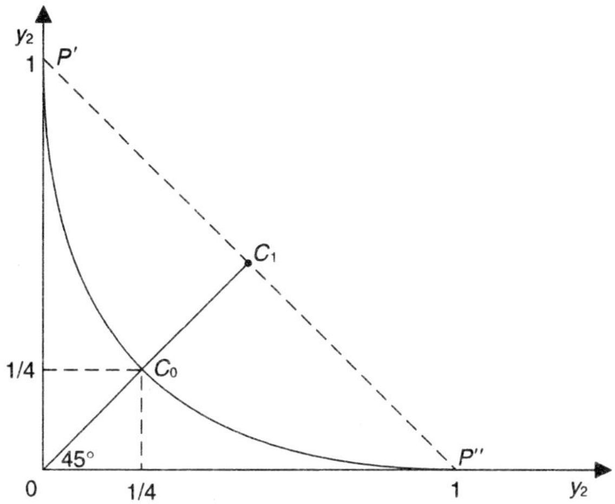

Figure A1

where L_j is the amount of labour employed by the jth industry. Hence the production transformation surface is described by

$$y_1/g(y_1) + y_2/g(y_2) = 1.$$

Now consider the special form of g:

$$g(x) = x^{1/2}.$$

This yields the transformation curve $P'C_0P''$ of Figure A1. At C_0 the ratio of marginal private costs is equal to the ratio of average private costs and to the ratio of marginal social costs, and all are equal to one. Evidently we can find an indifference curve (not shown) which is tangential to the transformation curve at C_0 and such that the two curves do not intersect or touch elsewhere. Given such an indifference curve, C_0 represents the unique autarkic equilibrium of each country, with a price ratio of one.

Now suppose that at C_1 a higher indifference curve is tangential to the chord $P'C_1P''$. Then C_1 represents a possible free-trade consumption equilibrium for each country, with the production of one country represented by P' and the production of the other country by P''. Evidently this free-trade equilibrium is preferred to the autarkic equilibrium by all individuals, even though the common autarkic prices prevail under free trade.

Of course there is also a tradeless (and therefore gainless) free-trade equilibrium at C_0. However, given the world price ratio, C_0 is unstable in the sense of Marshall. To ensure that production moves to P' and P'', therefore, all that is needed is a small displacement of the two economies (in opposite directions) from C_0. It remains to establish the instability of C_0. At C_0 demand prices are equal to supply prices (average costs). A small increase in y_2 lowers the supply price of the second good and therefore raises the excess demand price for that good. Hence y_2 continues to increase. Indeed it goes to P' monotonely and in finite time. Similarly, a small decrease in y_2 sets off a monotone transition to P''.

The example disposes of (1) and (2) as necessary conditions for trade gains when returns to scale are increasing. Moreover, as noted in our introductory remarks, the example clarifies the role of international trade in bridging the non-convex portions of production sets. We have focused on non-convexities associated with increasing returns. However, trade can play a bridging role whatever the source of non-convexities, whether on the supply side or the demand side. Finally, the example shows that, in non-convex world economies, it may be suboptimal to treat identical countries identically.

ACKNOWLEDGEMENTS

Grateful acknowledgement is made of the support of the Alexander von Humboldt Stiftung and the Research Institute for Economics and Business Administration, Kobe University, also of the very helpful comments of a referee.

NOTES

1 For a general analysis of the descriptive properties of models with output-generated externalities, see Markusen and Schweinberger (1990).
2 The assumption will be relaxed in section 4.
3 For the following concise proof we are indebted to a referee.
4 A productivity-increasing change from autarky to free trade, as here defined, should not be confused with a productivity-improving change in tariffs, as recently defined by Diewert *et al.* (1989: 204). The latter concept relates to a small country in which production is subject to constant returns to scale.
5 That the terminology associated with (19) is appropriate may be confirmed by recalling that $B_{\mathbf{w}}\,\mathbf{dw} = \mathbf{M}\,\mathbf{dw}$; see (12).
6 For this observation we are indebted to a helpful referee.

REFERENCES

Diewert, W. E., Turunen-Red, A. H. and Woodland, A. D. (1989) 'Productivity- and Pareto-improving changes in taxes and tariffs', *Review of Economic Studies* 56: 199–216.

Ethier, W. J. (1982) 'Decreasing costs in international trade and Frank Graham's argument for protection', *Econometrica* 53: 1243–68.

Helpman, E. (1983) 'Variable returns to scale and international trade: Two generalizations', *Economics Letters* 11: 167–74.

Helpman, E. (1984) 'Increasing returns, imperfect markets and trade theory', in R. W. Jones and P. B. Kenen (eds) *Handbook of International Economics, Volume 1: International Trade Theory*, Amsterdam: North-Holland.

Kemp, M. C. (1969) *The Pure Theory of International Trade and Investment*, Englewood Cliffs, NJ: Prentice Hall.

Kemp, M. C. and Negishi, T. (1970) 'Variable returns to scale, commodity taxes, factor market distortions, and their implications for trade gains', *Swedish Journal of Economics*, 72: 1–11.

Kemp, M. C. and Negishi, T. (1971) 'Variable returns to scale, commodity taxes, factor market distortions, and their implications for trade gains: A clarification', *Swedish Journal of Economics* 73: 257–8.

Krugman, P. R. (1979) 'Increasing returns, monopolistic competition and international trade', *Journal of International Economics* 9: 469–79.

Lloyd, P. J. and Schweinberger, A. G. (1988) 'Trade expenditure functions and the gains from trade', *Journal of International Economics* 24: 275–97.

Markusen, J. R. and Melvin, J. R. (1984) 'The gains from trade theorem with increasing returns to scale', in H. Kierzkowski (ed.) *Monopolistic Competition and International Trade*, Oxford: Oxford University Press.

Markusen, J. R. and Schweinberger, A. G. (1990) 'The positive theory of production externalities under perfect competition', *Journal of International Economics* 29: 69–91.

Markusen, J. R. and Wigle, R. M. (1989) 'Nash equilibrium tariffs for the United States and Canada: The roles of country size , scale economics, and capital mobility', *Journal of Political Economy* 97: 368–86.

Neary, J. P. and Schweinberger, A. G. (1986) 'Factor content functions and the theory of international trade', *Review of Economic Studies* 53: 421–32.

Negishi, T. (1969) 'Marshallian external economies and gains from trade between similar economies', *Review of Economic Studies* 36: 131–5.

Negishi, T. (1972) *General Equilibrium Theory and International Trade*, Amsterdam: North-Holland.

Ohyama, M. (1972) 'Trade and welfare in general equilibrium', *Keio Economic Papers* 9: 37–73.

19

THE GAINS FROM INTERNATIONAL TRADE UNDER IMPERFECT COMPETITION

A conjectural variations approach

1 INTRODUCTION

Very little is known about the gains from trade under conditions of imperfect competition. The little that is known is unsatisfactory as a guide to the formation of policy. For a typical proposition relates trade gains to trade-induced changes in commodity outputs, which can be known only after a possibly costly social experiment; see, for example, Kemp and Negishi (1970, 1971) and Helpman and Krugman (1985: 96–100). What we need are propositions which relate trade gains to the underlying characteristics of the world economy (national endowments, preferences, technologies and market structures).

Recently we made a modest attack on the problem of relating trade gains to those underlying characteristics, especially market structure; see Kemp and Okawa (1992). In that paper, attention was focused on a world economy composed of national economies which differ in scale only.

Under the conventional assumption that perfect competition prevails in all industries and that the equilibrium is unique, this case is of little interest. For, under the conventional assumption, (i) all countries have the same autarkic equilibrium, with equilibrium defined in terms of relative prices and of quantities produced and consumed per capita. If the countries should agree to trade freely, the agreement would be without force: (ii) there would be no international trade and, therefore, (iii) there would be no gains from trade.

All of this changes if the conventional assumption is modified to allow a single oligopolistic industry. In general, (i′) the sets of autarkic equilibria are not independent of scale; indeed they have no elements in common. Nevertheless, if the countries should agree to trade freely, the agreement would be without force, in the sense that (ii″) there would be no trade. However, the agreement would be operative in the sense that (iii′) the opportunity to trade would be gainful. As a by-product of our analysis we learned that equilibrium factor prices are everywhere the same.

In our earlier paper oligopolists were assumed to be of the uncooperative Cournot–Nash type. In the present essay we take a more general approach, in terms of conjectural variations. The advantage of this approach is that particular static oligopoly solutions, such as the Cournot–Nash and collusive solutions, emerge as special cases.[1] In all other respects, the model of the present essay is identical to that of Kemp and Okawa.

It will be shown that whether the opportunity to trade is gainful or not crucially depends on the conjectures oligopolists make. In particular it will be shown that if the conjectural variations parameter, to be defined, lies between plus one and a calculable negative number then, in any world trading equilibrium,

(1) all countries are incompletely specialized,
(2) all oligopolists, wherever they are, produce the same output,
(3) factor prices, as well as product prices, are everywhere the same, and
(4) international trade is zero.

It is shown also that if the trading equilibrium is unique then

(1′) each oligopolist produces more under free trade than in autarky,
(2′) at least in the case of identical homothetic preferences, the equilibrium world price of the good produced under imperfect competition is lower than either equilibrium autarkic price, and
(3′) in each country, the allocational distortion is smaller than in autarky, so that free trade is potentially gainful.

If, on the other hand, the conjectural variation parameter is equal to one (the case of perfect collusion) then there are no gains from trade.

Thus the conclusions of Kemp and Okawa (1992) remain valid under expectational assumptions much more general than those of Cournot.

2 THE MODEL

Each of two consumable commodities, 1 and 2, is produced under conditions of constant returns to scale by means of two primary factors, labour and capital, in each of two countries, α and β. The same production functions prevail in each country. The first commodity is produced under conditions of free entry and perfect competition, and is chosen as the *numéraire*. The second commodity is produced by a fixed number m^i ($i = \alpha, \beta$) of oligopolists. The production functions are

$$X_1^i = G(L_1^i, K_1^i), \quad i = \alpha, \beta \tag{1}$$

$$X_{2k}^i = F(L_{2k}^i, K_{2k}^i), \quad i = \alpha, \beta; \ k = 1, \ldots, m^i, \tag{2}$$

where X_j^i ($j = 1, 2$) is the total output of the jth good in the ith country, X_{2k}^i is the output of the second good from the kth oligopolist in the ith country, L_j^i (K_j^i) is the total amount of labour (capital) employed by the jth industry in the ith country and L_{2k}^i (K_{2k}^i) is the amount of labour (capital) employed by the

kth oligopolist in the ith country. In each country the factors of production are inelastically supplied, move freely between industries and are fully employed.

In each country there are two classes of agents, the class of factor owners and the class of oligopolists. All agents, wherever they live, have the same preferences. The oligopolists own their own firms but possess no capital and supply no labour. Each oligopolist seeks to maximize his or her utility. If in equilibrium good 2 is produced, and consumed by all individuals (including the oligopolists), then utility maximization and profit maximization are incompatible. Each oligopolist is a perfect competitor in the factor markets. The cost function of the typical oligopolist in the ith country may be derived from the production function (2) and is written as

$$C_2(w^i, r^i, X^i_{2k}) = c_2(w^i, r^i)X^i_{2k}, \quad i = \alpha, \beta, \tag{3}$$

where w^i (r^i) is the wage rate (rental rate) in the ith country and $c_2(w^i, r^i)$ is the oligopolist's average cost of production which, under the assumption of perfect competition in the factor markets, is also his or her **perceived** marginal cost of production.

All factor owners, whatever their country of residence, own the same amount of each factor. Thus the national capital : labour ratio is everywhere the same. Each factor is supplied inelastically.

The two countries are identical except possibly in scale. Let n^i be the number of factor owners in country i. Then $\mu = m^\beta/m^\alpha = n^\beta/n^\alpha$, where μ is some positive number.

3 AUTARKIC EQUILIBRIUM

As noted in the introduction, we present our analysis in the framework of conjectural variations, thus capturing in one formulation a variety of behavioural assumptions. However, it is not necessary to assume that the conjectural variations are consistent.

The kth oligopolist in the ith country seeks

$$\max_{X^i_{2k}} V(p^i, \pi^i_k) \tag{4}$$

subject to

$$\pi^i_k = p^i X^i_{2k} - C_2(w^i, r^i, X^i_{2k}) \tag{5}$$

where $V(,)$ is the indirect utility function of each agent, p^i is the relative price of good 2 in the ith country, and π^i_k is the profit of the kth oligopolist. From (4) and (5) we obtain the first-order condition

$$p^i + (X^i_{2k} - D^i_{2mk})(\mathrm{d}p^i/\mathrm{d}X^i_{2k}) = c_2(w^i, r^i) \tag{6}$$

where D^i_{2mk} is the demand by the kth oligopolist for good 2.

To elucidate the feedback term ($\mathrm{d}p^i/\mathrm{d}X^i_{2k}$) of (6), we resort to the market-clearing condition for good 2:

$$n^i D_2(p^i, y^i_f) + \sum_{\ell=1}^{m^i} D_2(p^i, \pi^i_\ell) = \sum_{\ell=1}^{m^i} X^i_{2\ell} \tag{7}$$

where $y^i_f \equiv w^i L + r^i K$ is the income of a typical factor owner in the ith country, $L(K)$ is the labour (capital) endowment of the typical factor owner in the ith country and $D_2(\,,)$ is the Marshallian demand function for good 2. Differentiating (7), keeping factor prices constant,

$$\mathrm{d}p^i/\mathrm{d}X^i_{2k} = -(p^i/A^i)\left\{[1-(\phi^i_k/p^i)(p^i-c^i_2)] + \sum_{\substack{\ell=1\\ \ell\neq k}}^{m^i}[1-(\phi^i_\ell/p^i)(p^i-c^i_2)]\lambda^i_\ell\right\} \tag{8}$$

where

$$A^i \equiv n^i D^i_{2f}\eta^i_f + \sum_{\ell=1}^{m^i} D^i_{2m\ell}\eta^i_{m\ell} - \sum_{\ell=1}^{m^i}\phi^i_\ell X^i_{2\ell} \tag{9}$$

$$\eta^i_f \equiv -(p^i/D^i_{2f})(\partial D^i_{2f}/\partial p^i) > 0 \tag{10}$$

$$\eta^i_m \equiv -(p^i/D^i_{2m\ell})(\partial D^i_{2m\ell}/\partial p^i) > 0 \tag{11}$$

$$\phi^i_\ell \equiv p^i(\partial D^i_{2m\ell}/\partial \pi^i_\ell) \tag{12}$$

$$\lambda^i_\ell \equiv \mathrm{d}X^i_{2\ell}/\mathrm{d}X^i_{2k} \quad \text{for } \ell \neq k,\ \ell = 1,\ldots, m^i \tag{13}$$

and where it is assumed that $A^i \neq 0$.

Let us consider the conjectural variations term $\lambda^i_\ell \equiv \mathrm{d}X^i_{2\ell}/\mathrm{d}X^i_{2k}$, which describes the change in the ℓth ($\ell \neq k$) oligopolist's output anticipated by the kth oligopolist in response to a unit change in the latter's output. Let us assume that λ^i_ℓ is constant. Since in each country all oligopolists are identical in all respects,

$$\lambda^i_1 = \lambda^i_2 = \ldots = \lambda^i_{m^i} = \lambda, \quad i = \alpha, \beta. \tag{14}$$

In principle, λ can take any value, with special interest attaching to the values one (the fully collusive case) and zero (the Cournot case). However, we now proceed to restrict its range somewhat.

It is shown in the appendix that the perceived marginal cost of each oligopolist is equal to the marginal rate of transformation evaluated at X^i_2:

$$c_2(w^i, r^i) = -\,\mathrm{d}X^i_1/\mathrm{d}X^i_2. \tag{15}$$

Moreover, in each country all oligopolists are identical in all respects; hence any autarkic equilibria are bound to be symmetrical. Thus, substituting from (8) into (7) we obtain the first-order condition for the kth oligopolist in the ith country:

$$p^i \{1 - [(X_2^i - D_{2m}^i)/A^i][1 + (m^i - 1)\lambda][1 - (\phi^i/p^i)(p^i - c_2^i)]\}$$
$$= c_2(w^i, r^i) \qquad (16)$$

where

$$A^i \equiv n^i D_{2f}^i \eta_f^i + m^i D_{2m}^i \eta_m^i - m^i \phi^i X_2^i.$$

From (16) we see that if $m^i > 1$ and $\lambda = -(m^i - 1)^{-1}$ then each oligopolist, when contemplating a change in his or her output, conjectures that the change will be exactly absorbed by an equal but contrary change in the aggregate output of other oligopolists, leaving him or her powerless to influence market price but able to vary his or her share of total output; this is the perfectly competitive case. On the other hand, if $\lambda = 1$ then each oligopolist conjectures that any change in his or her output will be matched by identical changes in the outputs of other oligopolists, leaving him or her powerless to influence his or her share of total output but able to control market price; this is the case of perfect collusion. It is normally assumed that λ lies between those values which correspond to perfect competition and perfect collusion; see, for example, Bresnahan (1981), Perry (1982) and Seade (1980). However, when countries differ in scale, the value of λ associated with perfect competition varies from country to country. To overcome this ambiguity it will be assumed that λ is not less than $-(m^\alpha + m^\beta - 1)^{-1}$ and not greater than one:[2]

$$-[(1 + \mu)m^\alpha - 1] \leqslant \lambda \leqslant 1. \qquad (17)$$

We can now compare the equilibrium autarkic allocations of the two countries. Consider the cost side of (16). We have already observed that the perceived marginal cost of a typical oligopolist is equal to the marginal social opportunity cost of producing the second commodity which, in turn, is equal to the marginal rate of transformation along the production possibility locus. We now note that, since returns to scale are constant, the marginal rate of transformation is an increasing function of the total output of the second commodity. It follows that the typical oligopolist's actual marginal cost is an increasing function of total output of the second commodity. Moreover, the two countries share a common technology, the factor markets are perfectly competitive and, since the countries differ at most in scale, $n^\beta K = \mu n^\alpha K$, $n^\beta L = \mu n^\alpha L$ and $m^\beta = \mu m^\alpha$. It follows that if all oligopolists, whatever their location, produce the same amount then factor prices must be equalized internationally and all oligopolists must perceive the same marginal and average cost of production. Thus if attention is confined to symmetrical allocations, we may drop the country subscript i and write the **actual** marginal cost function of each oligopolist as

$$C(X_2) \equiv c_2(w(X_2), r(X_2)), \quad \mathrm{d}C/\mathrm{d}X_2 > 0. \tag{18}$$

Let us turn now to the marginal benefit associated with an increase in the output of an oligopolist; it is described by the left-hand side of (16). Suppose that all oligopolists, whatever their nationalities, produce the same amount, so that autarkic factor and product prices are the same in each country. Then marginal benefit can be written as a function, the same for all oligopolists, of output X_2, of a scale parameter

$$\delta(i) = \begin{cases} 1 & \text{if } i = \alpha \\ \mu & \text{if } i = \beta \end{cases} \tag{19}$$

and of the conjectural variations parameter λ:

$$B(X_2, \delta, \lambda) = p(X_2)\,\{1 - [X_2 - D_2(p(X_2), \pi(X_2))] \times [1 + (\delta m^{\alpha} - 1)\lambda]\,H(X_2)(\delta\tilde{A}(X_2))^{-1}\} \tag{20}$$

where

$$\tilde{A} \equiv n^{\alpha} D_2(p(X_2), y_f(X_2))\eta_f(X_2) + m^{\alpha} D_2(p(X_2), \pi(X_2))\eta_m(X_2) - m^{\alpha} X_2 \phi(X_2) \tag{21}$$

$$H(X_2) \equiv 1 - (\phi(X_2)/p(X_2))[p(X_2) - c_2(w(X_2), r(X_2))] \tag{22}$$

$$\pi(X_2) \equiv p(X_2)X_2 - c_2(w(X_2), r(X_2))X_2 \tag{23}$$

$$y_f(X_2) \equiv w(X_2)L + r(X_2)K \tag{24}$$

$$\eta_f(X_2) \equiv -[p(X_2)/D_2(p(X_2), y_f(X_2))][\partial D_2(p(X_2), y_f(X_2))/\partial p(X_2)] \tag{25}$$

$$\eta_m(X_2) \equiv -[p(X_2)/D_2(p(X_2), \pi(X_2))][\partial D_2(p(X_2), \pi(X_2))/\partial p(X_2)] \tag{26}$$

$$\phi(X_2) \equiv p(X_2)[\partial D_2(p(X_2), \pi(X_2))/\partial \pi(X_2)]. \tag{27}$$

Let us define the marginal **net** benefit function

$$F(X_2, \delta, \lambda) \equiv B(X_2, \delta, \lambda) - C(X_2). \tag{28}$$

Then the optimal output of the typical oligopolist in country α (β) is obtained as the solution of $F(X_2, 1, \lambda) = 0$ ($F(X_2, \mu, \lambda) = 0$). Moreover, differentiating $F(X_2, \delta, \lambda) = 0$, holding λ constant,

$$\mathrm{d}X_2/\mathrm{d}\delta = -(\partial B/\partial\delta)/[(\partial B/\partial X_2) - (\mathrm{d}C/\mathrm{d}X_2)] \tag{29}$$

where

$$\partial B/\partial\delta = p(X_2 - D_{2m})(1 - \lambda)[1 - (\phi/p)(p - c_2)]\delta^{-2}\tilde{A}^{-1}. \tag{30}$$

In view of (20), for positive profits it is necessary and sufficient that

$$(X_2 - D_{2m})[1 + (\delta m^{\alpha} - 1)\lambda](\delta\tilde{A})^{-1}H > 0. \tag{31}$$

Moreover, since $X_2 - D_{2m} > 0$, $\delta > 0$ and $\delta m^{\alpha} \geqslant 1$,

$$\text{sign}\,\{H\} = \text{sign}\,\{\tilde{A}\}. \tag{32}$$

From (30), therefore,

$$\partial B/\partial\delta \gtreqless 0 \Leftrightarrow \lambda \lesseqgtr 1. \tag{33}$$

This implies that, for given X_2, an increase in the scale of a country increases the marginal benefit of each oligopolist in the country. This further implies that the marginal benefit curve of each oligopolist shifts up, shifts down, or remains unchanged as λ is less than, greater than, or equal to one; see Figure 1.[3] It follows that

$$\mathrm{d}X_2/\mathrm{d}\delta \gtreqless 0 \Leftrightarrow \lambda \lesseqgtr 1. \tag{34}$$

We can now state our first proposition.

Proposition 1. *(i) If* $-[(1+\mu)m^{\alpha}-1]^{-1} \leqslant \lambda < 1$ *(including the Cournot model as a special case), the sets of autarkic equilibria are not independent of scale. Moreover, if the autarkic equilibria are unique, every individual in the larger country, whether a resource owner or an oligopolist, is better off than his or her counterparts in the smaller country. (ii) If* $\lambda = 1$, *the oligopolists are fully collusive and the sets of autarkic equilibria are independent of scale.*

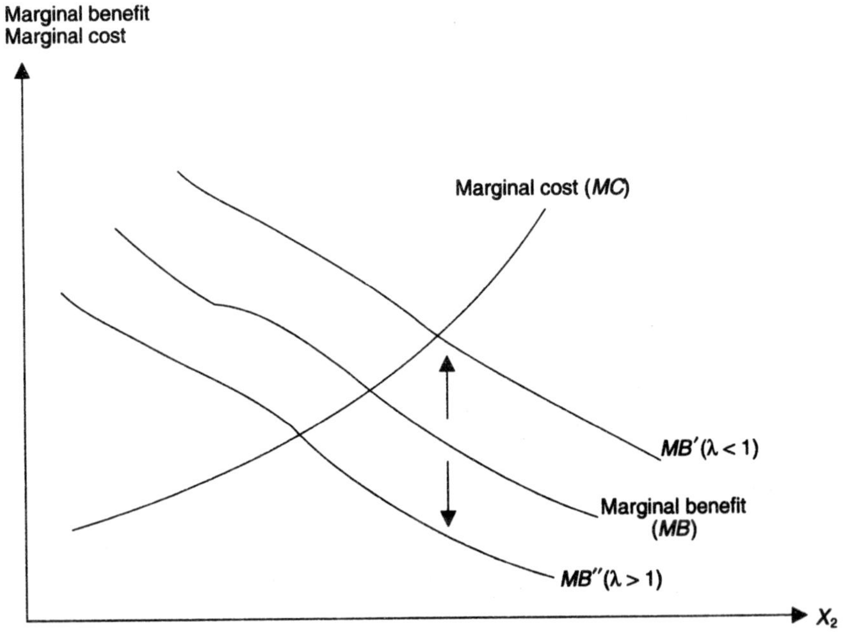

Figure 1

4 THE TRADING EQUILIBRIUM

Suppose that there is free trade between α and β. Let us consider the optimal behaviour of the kth oligopolist in the ith country ($i = \alpha, \beta$).

The world market-clearing condition for the second commodity is

$$n^{\alpha}D_2(p, y_f^{\alpha}) + n^{\beta}D_2(p, y_f^{\beta}) + \sum_{\ell=1}^{m^{\alpha}} D_2(p, \pi_{\ell}^{\alpha}) + \sum_{\ell=1}^{m^{\beta}} D_2(p, \pi_{\ell}^{\beta}) = X_2^{\alpha} + X_2^{\beta} \quad (35)$$

where p is now the world price of the second commodity.

Differentiating (35), keeping factor prices constant, we obtain

$$\mathrm{d}p/\mathrm{d}X_{2k}^{i} = -(p/E)\left\{ \sum_{\substack{\ell=1 \\ \ell \neq k}}^{m^{i}} [1 - (\phi_{\ell}^{i}/p)(p - c_2^{i})]\lambda_{\ell}^{i} + \sum_{\ell=1}^{m^{j}} [1 - (\phi_{\ell}^{i}/p)(p - c_2^{j})]\lambda_{\ell}^{j} + [1 - (\phi_{\ell}^{i}/p)(p - c_2^{i})] \right\},$$

$$j \neq i;\ i, j = \alpha, \beta \quad (36)$$

where

$$E \equiv n^{\alpha}D_{2f}^{\alpha}\eta_f^{\alpha} + n^{\beta}D_{2f}^{\beta}\eta_f^{\beta} + \sum_{\ell=1}^{m^{\alpha}} D_{2m\ell}^{\alpha}\eta_{m\ell}^{\alpha} + \sum_{\ell=1}^{m^{\beta}} D_{2m\ell}^{\beta}\eta_{m\ell}^{\beta} - \sum_{\ell=1}^{m^{\alpha}} \phi_{\ell}^{\alpha}X_{2\ell}^{\alpha} - \sum_{\ell=1}^{m^{\beta}} \phi_{\ell}^{\beta}X_{2\ell}^{\beta} \quad (37a)$$

$$\lambda_{\ell}^{i} \equiv \mathrm{d}X_{2\ell}^{i}/\mathrm{d}X_{2k}^{i} \quad \text{for } \ell \neq k,\ \ell = 1, \ldots, m^{i} \quad (37b)$$

$$\lambda_{\ell}^{j} \equiv \mathrm{d}X_{2\ell}^{j}/\mathrm{d}X_{2k}^{i} \quad \text{for } j \neq i,\ \ell = 1, \ldots, m^{j}. \quad (37c)$$

Here we assume that

$$\lambda_{\ell}^{i} = \lambda_{\ell}^{j} = \lambda; \quad (38)$$

that is, the conjectural variations of the oligopolists in both countries are identical. It is assumed also that $E \neq 0$.

Since all oligopolists in both countries are faced with the same actual cost function and sell in the same world market, the world trading equilibrium must be symmetrical. All oligopolists produce the same output. It follows that in the world trading equilibrium there will be no trade and factor prices will be equalized across countries. Thus we arrive at our second proposition.

Proposition 2. *In any trading equilibrium, both countries are incompletely specialized and all oligopolists, whatever their nationalities, produce the same output. It follows that* *equilibrium factor prices as well as product prices are everywhere the same and that international trade is zero.*

It follows from proposition 2 that the first-order condition can be written as

$$p[\![1 - (X_2 - D_{2m})\{1 + [(1 + \mu)m^{\alpha} - 1]\lambda\}[(1 + \mu)\tilde{A}]^{-1}H]\!] = c_2(w, r) \quad (39)$$

where $\tilde{A}$ and H are defined in (21) and (22), respectively. Thus we can associate the opening of trade with a change in the scale parameter δ from 1 to $1 + \mu$ for oligopolists in country α and from μ to $1 + \mu$ for oligopolists in country β. That establishes proposition 3.

Proposition 3. *(i) If* $-[(1 + \mu)m^{\alpha} - 1]^{-1} \leq \lambda < 1$ *(including the Cournot model as a special case) and the trading equilibrium is unique, each oligopolist must produce more under free trade than in autarky and, at least in the case of identical homothetic preferences, the equilibrium world price must be lower than either equilibrium autarkic price. In each country, therefore, the allocational distortion created by oligopoly is less than in autarky and free trade is potentially gainful. Moreover, the more collusive are the conjectural variations of the oligopolists (i.e. the larger is* λ*), the less are the potential gains from trade. (ii) If* $\lambda = 1$, *the oligopolists are fully collusive and produce the same outputs in a trading equilibrium as in autarky. Hence there are no gains from trade.*

Unfortunately, proposition 3 does not survive the introduction of an additional imperfectly competitive industry. In particular, it is no longer true that free trade is always potentially gainful. The explanation lies in the theory of the second best. When there is a single distortion, a reduction in the distortion is potentially beneficial; but, when there are two or more distortions, a reduction in one or more distortions is not necessarily beneficial, even potentially.

5 FINAL REMARK

In a companion paper, Okawa (1994) has shown that propositions 1–3 remain valid if a constant number of oligopolists supply an intermediate good to one of two competitive final-goods industries and trade takes place in the final goods only or in all three goods; indeed he has shown that the world trading equilibrium is the same whether two or three goods are traded.

APPENDIX

In this appendix, it is shown that in our conjectural variations model, with each oligopolist a perfect competitor in the factor markets, the **perceived** marginal cost of each oligopolist is equal to the marginal rate of transformation evaluated at X_2^i.

The cost function of the kth oligopolist in the ith country may be defined as

$$C_2(w^i, r^i, X^i_{2k}) \equiv \min\{w^i L^i_2 + r^i K^i_2\}. \tag{A1}$$

Since the technologies display constant returns to scale,

$$\sum_{\ell=1}^{m^i} dC^i_{2\ell} = -dX^i_1. \tag{A2}$$

On the other hand,

$$\sum_{\ell=1}^{m^i} dC^i_{2\ell} = \sum_{\ell=1}^{m^i} (\partial C^i_{2\ell}/\partial X^i_{2\ell})(dX^i_{2\ell}/dX^i_{2k})dX^i_{2k}$$

$$= \left(MC^i_k + \sum_{\substack{\ell=1 \\ \ell \neq k}}^{m^i} \lambda^i_\ell MC^i_\ell \right) dX^i_{2k} \tag{A3}$$

where $\lambda^i_\ell \equiv (dX^i_{2\ell}/dX^i_{2k})$ $(\ell \neq k)$ is the conjectural variation which reflects the change in the ℓth $(\ell \neq k)$ oligopolist's output anticipated by the kth oligopolist in response to a unit change in his or her output.

Since all oligopolists are identical in all respects and perfect competitors in factor markets, the perceived marginal costs for all oligopolists must be identical:

$$MC^i_\ell = MC^i \quad \text{for all } \ell = 1, \ldots, k, \ldots, m^i. \tag{A4}$$

Moreover, the values of conjectural variations formed by the kth oligopolist with respect to other oligopolists are assumed to be identical:

$$\lambda^i_\ell = \lambda^i. \tag{A5}$$

Substituting from (A4) and (A5) into (A3),

$$\sum_{\ell=1}^{m^i} dC^i_{2\ell} = [1 + \lambda^i(m^i - 1)]MC^i dX^i_{2k}. \tag{A3}$$

Since

$$X^i_2 = \sum_{\ell=1}^{m^i} X^i_{2\ell},$$

$$dX^i_2 = \sum_{\ell=1}^{m^i} dX^i_{2\ell} = \sum_{\ell \neq k}^{m^i} (dX^i_{2\ell}/dX^i_{2k}) + dX^i_{2k} = [1 + \lambda^i(m^i - 1)]dX^i_{2k}. \tag{A6}$$

Thus, from (A2), (A3) and (A6),

$$MC^i = -(dX^i_1/dX^i_2). \tag{A7}$$

NOTES

1 In our formulation, the oligopolists are identical in all respects. Hence they would co-operate if binding agreements were feasible; see Kemp and Shimomura (1995).

For a nice summary of the virtues and limitations of the conjectural variations formulation, see Eaton and Grossman (1986: 386, n. 2).

2 It will be established in section 4 that when $\lambda = -[(1+\mu)m^{\alpha} - 1]^{-1}$ all oligopolists price according to marginal cost.

3 If the marginal benefit curve cuts the marginal cost curve from below, we reach the opposite conclusions. Thus we need to assume that $\partial B/\partial X_2 - \partial C/\partial X_2 < 0$.

REFERENCES

Bresnahan, T. F. (1981) 'Duopoly models with consistent conjectures', *American Economic Review* 71: 934–45.

Eaton, J. and Grossman, G. (1986) 'Optimal trade and industrial policy under oligopoly', *Quarterly Journal of Economics* 101: 383–406.

Helpman, E. and Krugman, P. R. (1985) *Market Structure and Foreign Trade*, Cambridge, MA: MIT Press.

Kemp, M. C. and Negishi, T. (1970, 1971) 'Variable returns to scale, commodity taxes, factor market distortions and their implications for trade gains', *Swedish Journal of Economics* 72: 1–11 and 73: 257–8.

Kemp, M. C. and Okawa, M. (1992) 'The gains from free trade under imperfect competition', University of New South Wales.

Kemp, M. C. and Shimomura, K. (1995) 'The apparently innocuous representative agent', *Japanese Economic Review*, 46: 247–56.

Okawa, M. (1994) 'The gains from free trade with an oligopolistic market for an intermediate good', Aichi University.

Perry, M. K. (1982) 'Oligopoly and consistent conjectural variations', *Bell Journal of Economics* 13: 197–205.

Seade, J. (1980) 'On the effects of entry', *Econometrica* 48: 479–89.

20

THE INTERNATIONAL DIFFUSION OF THE FRUITS OF TECHNICAL PROGRESS UNDER IMPERFECT COMPETITION*

1 INTRODUCTION

It has long been known that, in the familiar $2 \times 2 \times 2$ context of two primary factors, two no-joint-product constant-returns industries and two free-trading countries, uniform Hicksian technical progress in one country necessarily benefits the other country if preferences in the progressive country are homothetic and if initially there is some international trade; see, for example, Hicks (1953) and Ikema (1969). It is now known that the same is true if produced inputs are allowed, if capital is internationally mobile and even if one of the countries has an optimal tariff in place; see Kemp *et al.* (1993). And it may be added that the proposition remains true if joint production is allowed; indeed, the proof provided by Kemp *et al.* is already sufficiently general to accommodate joint production. Finally, it is worthy of emphasis that the proposition is global in scope, that is it is valid for technical improvements of all magnitudes; but the proof of this final proposition must wait for another occasion.

The proposition carries the interesting implication that neither country can hold an across-the-board absolute advantage over the other; see Kemp and Shimomura (1988).

In the earlier literature, to which reference has been made, the trading countries are bound together by a common competitive industrial structure. However, they are allowed to differ in relative factor endowments and in preferences.

In the present essay we examine the robustness of the Hicks–Ikema proposition to a change in industrial structure. In particular, we allow for the possibility that one of the two industries is oligopolistic. Of course, it was not to be expected that the proposition would survive in a second-best world without some qualification. However, it is known that the familiar gains-from-free-trade proposition survives the introduction of oligopoly, at least in a $2 \times 2 \times 2$ world, if the countries differ only in size; see Kemp and Okawa (1992). It might have been conjectured then that the same would be true of the Hicks–Ikema proposition. That expectation has not been realized. However, it has been shown that the Hicks–Ikema proposition survives if the economy is subjected to a simple additional restriction on the elasticity of substitution in consumption.

As an important by-product of our analysis it is shown how elements of oligopoly can be incorporated in a general-equilibrium model of trade with full allowance for feedbacks from the decisions of oligopolists through other markets. The neglect of such feedbacks mars some of the early treatments of the welfare economics of international trade under imperfect competition; see, for example, Markusen (1981).

It will ease our later task if we first record some of the properties of a **closed** economy. This step-by-step procedure will have the incidental advantage of allowing us to consider some unresolved issues in the general-equilibrium closed-economy analysis of oligopoly.

2 A CLOSED ECONOMY

In each of two countries (α and β) two homogeneous final goods (1 and 2) are produced by means of two primary factors of production (labour and capital) and a technology characterized by constant returns to scale and the absence of joint production. Both factor markets are competitive. Good 1 is produced for a competitive market and is chosen as the *numéraire*. Good 2 is sold on an oligopolistic market. The oligopolists are of the Cournot–Nash type.

There are n factor owners, each with the same endowment of capital and labour; and there are m oligopolists, each a sole proprietor but owning no capital and no labour. All factor owners and all oligopolists share the same homothetic preferences.

Each oligopolist chooses input and output levels to maximize his or her utility. If in equilibrium good 2 is produced then, from the identical homotheticity of preferences, it must be consumed by all individuals, including the m oligopolists; hence utility maximization does **not** imply profit maximization. The indirect utility function of the kth oligopolist is

$$V_k = V(p, \Pi_k) \tag{1}$$

where p is the relative price of good 2 and Π_k is the profit of the kth oligopolist. Differentiating (1) and invoking Roy's identity, we obtain

$$(\partial V/\partial \Pi_k)^{-1}\,\mathrm{d}V_k = -D_{2k}\mathrm{d}p + \mathrm{d}\Pi_k \tag{2}$$

where D_{2k} is the kth oligopolist's demand for good 2 and $\partial V/\partial \Pi_k > 0$.

The profit of the kth oligopolist is

$$\Pi_k = pX_{2k} - c(w, r)X_{2k} \tag{3}$$

where w and r are, respectively, the wage and capital-rental rates, and where X_{2k} and $c(w, r)$ are, respectively, the output of the kth oligopolist and his or her

perceived average and marginal cost of production. Differentiating (3), we find that

$$d\Pi_k = p\,dX_{2k} + X_{2k}\,dp - c(w, r)\,dX_{2k}. \qquad (3')$$

From (2) and (3′) we obtain the first-order condition for a maximum of the kth oligopolist's well-being:

$$p + (X_{2k} - D_{2k})(\partial p/\partial X_{2k}) = C'(X_2) \qquad (4)$$

where $X_2 \equiv \Sigma_{\ell=1}^{m} X_{2\ell}$ and $C'(X_2)$ is the marginal social opportunity cost of producing X_2. In equating $c(w, r)$ and $C'(X_2)$ we have relied on the Cournot–Nash assumption and on the perfect competitiveness of the factor markets.

The kth oligopolist is endowed with sufficient knowledge of the economy to allow him or her to compute accurately the feedback term $\partial p/\partial X_{2k}$ in (4). Thus the market-clearing condition for good 2 is

$$nD_2(p, y) + \sum_{\ell=1}^{m} D_2(p, \Pi_\ell) = \sum_{\ell=1}^{m} X_{2\ell} \equiv X_2 \qquad (5)$$

where $y \equiv wL + rK$ is the income of a typical factor owner, L and K are, respectively, the labour and capital endowments of a typical factor owner, and $D_2(\,,\,)$ is the Marshallian demand function for good 2. Differentiating (5) with respect to X_{2k}, holding constant $\Sigma_{\ell \neq k} X_{2\ell}$, w, r and, therefore, y,[1] we find that

$$\left(n \frac{\partial}{\partial p} D_2(p, y) + \sum_{\ell=1}^{m} \frac{\partial}{\partial p} D_2(p, \Pi_\ell)\right) dp$$
$$+ \sum_{\ell=1}^{m} \left(\frac{\partial}{\partial \Pi_\ell} D_2(p, \Pi_\ell)\right)(\partial \Pi_\ell/\partial X_{2k})dX_{2k} = dX_{2k}. \qquad (5')$$

However, from (3′)

$$\partial \Pi_\ell/\partial X_{2k} = X_{2\ell}(\partial p/\partial X_{2k}) \quad \text{if } \ell \neq k \qquad (6)$$

$$\partial \Pi_k/\partial X_{2k} = p + X_{2k}(\partial p/\partial X_{2k}) - C'(X_2). \qquad (7)$$

Hence, substituting from (6) and (7) into (5′), we can hope to solve for the required term $\partial p/\partial X_{2k}$.

Recalling that preferences are identical and homothetic, and that any equilibrium is bound to be symmetric (the same for all factor owners and the same for all oligopolists), the solution can be written as

$$\partial p/\partial X_{2k} = -(p/\varepsilon)[1 - (\phi/p)(p - C')] \qquad (8a)$$

where

$$\varepsilon(p, X_2) \equiv X_2(\eta - \phi) = X_2\bar{\eta}, \qquad (8b)$$

$$\eta(p) \equiv -[p/D_2(p, y)] \frac{\partial}{\partial p} D_2(p, y) = -[p/D_2(p, \pi)] \frac{\partial}{\partial p} D_2(p, \pi) > 0, \qquad (8c)$$

$$\phi(p) \equiv p \frac{\partial}{\partial y} D_2(p, y) = p \frac{\partial}{\partial \pi} D_2(p, \pi), \tag{8d}$$

$$\pi \equiv \left(\sum_{\ell=1}^{m} \Pi_\ell \right) / m \tag{8e}$$

is the common profit of each oligopolist and $\bar{\eta}$ is the compensated elasticity of demand. Substituting from (8) into the first-order condition (4), we obtain

$$p \left(1 - \frac{X_{2k} - D_{2k}}{\varepsilon + (X_{2k} - D_{2k})\phi} \right) = C'(X_2) = C'(mX_{2k}). \tag{9}$$

The equilibrium of a closed economy, if it exists,[2] is determined by the revised first-order condition (9) and the market-clearing condition (5).

Finally, to accommodate the possibility of uniform Hicksian improvements we introduce a shift parameter λ and rewrite (9) in the more elaborate form

$$p \left(1 - \frac{X_{2k} - D_2(p, \pi)}{\varepsilon + [X_{2k} - D_2(p, \pi)]\phi(p)} \right) = C'(mX_{2k}/\lambda). \tag{10}$$

Initially, $\lambda = 1$. Similarly, the market-clearing condition is rewritten as

$$nD_2(p, y_f) + mD_2(p, \pi) = mX_{2k} \tag{11a}$$

where

$$y_f = \lambda y(mX_{2k}/\lambda) \tag{11b}$$

is the income of the typical factor owner, and the profit earned by a typical oligopolist is rewritten as

$$\pi = pX_{2k} - C(mX_{2k}/\lambda)/m. \tag{12}$$

Equations (10)–(12) contain the three unknowns p, X_{2k} and π, as well as the two parameters λ and m. Together, they will serve as the basis of our comparative statical calculation. It will be convenient to have them in differential form. Thus, substituting in (10) for π, and differentiating totally, we obtain

$$\begin{aligned} &\{A + pB^{-2}[-(\varepsilon/p)(\eta D_{2k} - \phi X_{2k}) + X_2\bar{\eta}'(X_{2k} - D_{2k}) + (X_{2k} - D_{2k})^2\phi']\}\,\mathrm{d}p \\ &+ [\![pB^{-2}\{-\varepsilon[1 - \phi + (\phi/p)F'(X_2)] + m\bar{\eta}(X_{2k} - D_{2k})\} - mC'']\!]\,\mathrm{d}X_{2k} \\ &+ X_{2k}[B^{-2}\varepsilon\phi F'(X_2) + mC'']\mathrm{d}\lambda \\ &+ \{pB^{-2}\varepsilon[(\phi/p)(m^{-1}C - X_{2k}F') + (X_{2k} - D_{2k})] - X_2C''\}\,\hat{m} = 0 \end{aligned} \tag{13}$$

where $F(X_2) = wL_2 + rK_2$ is the total factor cost of producing X_2, L_2 and K_2 are the amounts of labour and capital employed in the second industry, $\hat{m} \equiv \mathrm{d}m/m$, $\phi' \equiv \mathrm{d}\phi/\mathrm{d}p$, $F' \equiv \mathrm{d}F/\mathrm{d}X_2$ and

$$A \equiv 1 - (X_{2k} - D_{2k})/B > 0 \tag{14}$$

$$B \equiv \varepsilon + (X_{2k} - D_{2k})\phi > 0. \tag{15}$$

It is shown in appendix 2 that $F' > 0$. Similarly, substituting in (11a) for π and y_f and differentiating totally, we find that

$$\begin{aligned} dp = &- (p/(\bar{\eta}X_{2k}))[1 - \phi - (\phi/p)(ny' - F')]dX_{2k} \\ &+ (p/(m\bar{\eta}X_{2k}))[n(\phi/p)y - mX_{2k}(\phi/p)(ny' - F')]d\lambda \\ &- (p/(\bar{\eta}X_2))(\phi/p)[(ny - C) - mX_{2k}(ny' - F')]\hat{m}. \end{aligned} \tag{16}$$

It is shown in appendix 2 that y' is positive.

Let us pause to examine the term $ny' - F'$ before returning to the main thread of our analysis. We have

$$\begin{aligned} dF/dX_2 &= d(wL_2 + rK_2)/dX_2 \\ &= [(w\, dL_2 + r\, dK_2) + (L_2\, dw + K_2\, dr)]/dX_2 \\ &= -(dX_1/dX_2) + (L_2\, dw + K_2\, dr)/dX_2 \end{aligned} \tag{17}$$

where X_1 is the total output of the first industry. On the other hand,

$$n(dy/dX_2) = [(nL)dw + (nK)dr]/dX_2. \tag{18}$$

Hence

$$\begin{aligned} (dF/dX_2) - n(dy/dX_2) &= -(dX_1/dX_2) + [(L_2\, dw + K_2\, dr)/dX_2] \\ &\quad - [(nL)dw + (nK)dr]/dX_2 \\ &= -(dX_1/dX_2) - L_1(dw + k_1\, dr)/dX_2 \end{aligned} \tag{19}$$

where $k_1 \equiv K_1/L_1$. From profit maximization in the first industry,

$$w = f_1(k_1) - k_1 f_1'(K_1) \quad \text{and} \quad r = f_1'(K_1) \tag{20}$$

where $f_1(k_1) \equiv F^1(K_1, L_1)/L_1$, $f_1'(k_1) \equiv df_1(k_1)/dk_1$ and $F^1(K_1, L_1)$ is the constant-returns production function for the first industry. From (20), $dw = -k_1 f_1''(k_1)dk_1$, $dr = f_1''(k_1)dk_1$ and, therefore,

$$dw + k_1\, dr = 0.$$

Thus, from (19) and (21),

$$(dF/dX_2) - n(dy/dX_2) = -(dX_1/dX_2) > 0 \tag{22}$$

and, in (16),

$$\partial p/\partial X_{2k} < 0, \quad \partial p/\partial \lambda > 0 \quad \text{and} \quad \partial p/\partial m < 0. \tag{23}$$

Returning now to the first-order condition (10), rewriting it in the general form

$$MB(p, X_{2k}, \lambda, m) = MC(X_{2k}, \lambda, m) \tag{24}$$

and differentiating, we obtain

$$(\partial MB/\partial p)\mathrm{d}p + (\partial MB/\partial X_{2k})\mathrm{d}X_{2k} + (\partial MB/\partial \lambda)\mathrm{d}\lambda + m(\partial MB/\partial m)\hat{m}$$

$$= (\partial MC/\partial X_{2k})\mathrm{d}X_{2k} + (\partial MC/\partial \lambda)\mathrm{d}\lambda + m(\partial MC/\partial m)\hat{m}. \tag{24'}$$

However in (16) we have the general form

$$\mathrm{d}p = \underset{(-)}{(\partial p/\partial X_{2k})}\mathrm{d}X_{2k} + \underset{(+)}{(\partial p/\partial \lambda)}\mathrm{d}\lambda + m\underset{(-)}{(\partial p/\partial m)}\hat{m}. \tag{25}$$

Hence, substituting from (25) into (24′),

$$[(\partial MB/\partial p)(\partial p/\partial X_{2k}) + \partial MB/\partial X_{2k} - \partial MC/\partial X_{2k}]\mathrm{d}X_{2k}$$

$$= -\ [\underset{(+)}{(\partial MB/\partial p)(\partial p/\partial \lambda)} + \underset{(+)}{\partial MB/\partial \lambda} - \underset{(-)}{\partial MC/\partial \lambda}]\mathrm{d}\lambda$$

$$-\ m[\underset{(-)}{(\partial MB/\partial p)(\partial p/\partial m)} + \partial MB/\partial m - \underset{(+)}{\partial MC/\partial m}]\hat{m} \tag{26}$$

where, from (13) and (16),

$$\partial MB/\partial p = A + pB^{-2}[-(\varepsilon/p)(D_{2k}\,\eta - \phi X_{2k})$$

$$+ (X_{2k} - D_{2k})X_2\bar{\eta}' + (X_{2k} - D_{2k})^2\phi'] \tag{27}$$

$$\partial MB/\partial X_{2k} = pB^{-2}\{-\varepsilon[1 - \phi + (\phi/p)F'(X_2) + m\bar{\eta}(X_{2k} - D_{2k})]\} \tag{28}$$

$$\partial MC/\partial X_{2k} = mC''(X_2) > 0 \tag{29}$$

$$\partial MB/\partial \lambda = pB^{-2}\varepsilon(\phi/p)X_{2k}F'(X_2) > 0 \tag{30}$$

$$\partial MC/\partial \lambda = -X_2C''(X_2) < 0 \tag{31}$$

$$m(\partial MB/\partial m) = pB^{-2}\varepsilon[(\phi/p)(m^{-1}C - X_{2k}F') + (X_{2k} - D_{2k})] \tag{32}$$

$$m(\partial MC/\partial m) = X_2C''(X_2) > 0 \tag{33}$$

$$\partial p/\partial X_{2k} = -(pm/(X_2\bar{\eta}))[1 - \phi + (\phi/p)(-\mathrm{d}X_1/\mathrm{d}X_2)] < 0 \tag{34}$$

$$\partial p/\partial \lambda = (p/(X_2\bar{\eta}))[n(\phi/p)y + X_2(\phi/p)(-\mathrm{d}X_1/\mathrm{d}X_2)] > 0 \tag{35}$$

$$m(\partial p/\partial m) = -(p/(X_2\bar{\eta}))(\phi/p)[ny - C - X_2(ny' - F')] < 0. \tag{36}$$

As our next step we determine the sign of the coefficient of $\mathrm{d}X_{2k}$ in (26). To this end, we consider the Marshallian adjustment process according to which, for each oligopolist, output is increasing (decreasing) if marginal benefit exceeds (falls short of) marginal cost:

$$\dot{X}_{2k} = \psi\cdot(MB - MC) = \delta(X_{2k})$$

for ψ a positive constant.

It is assumed that the process is stable:

$$\Delta \equiv (\partial MB/\partial p)(\partial p/\partial X_{2k}) + \partial MB/\partial X_{2k} - \partial MC/\partial X_{2k} < 0. \tag{37}$$

It then follows from (26) that, if $\partial MB/\partial p > 0$, $\mathrm{d}X_{2k}/\mathrm{d}\lambda > 0$; that is, technical progress stimulates the output of each oligopolist and therefore the total output of good 2,[3] implying that, given suitable lumpsum compensation, technical progress is welfare enhancing.

Is it plausible that $\partial MB/\partial p$ is positive? To help the reader form a judgement we proceed to derive a sufficient condition for positivity in terms of the elasticity of substitution in consumption. We begin with some additional technical apparatus. Thus, since preferences are homothetic, the ratio in which the two goods are consumed depends on the price ratio only:

$$D_{2k}/D_{1k} = f(p), \quad f'(p) < 0. \tag{38}$$

From (38) and the typical oligopolist's budget constraint

$$\pi = [p + f(p)^{-1}]D_{2k} \tag{39}$$

we find that

$$\eta = \frac{p + \sigma(p)f(p)^{-1}}{p + f(p)^{-1}} > 0 \tag{40a}$$

$$\phi = \frac{p}{p + f(p)^{-1}} > 0 \tag{40b}$$

and, therefore, that

$$\bar{\eta} = \eta - \phi = \frac{\sigma(p)f(p)^{-1}}{p + f(p)^{-1}} > 0 \tag{40c}$$

where

$$\sigma(p) \equiv -(p/f(p))(\mathrm{d}f(p)/\mathrm{d}p) > 0 \tag{40d}$$

is the elasticity of substitution in consumption.

Let us now return to (27) which, in view of (14) and (15), can be rewritten as

$$\begin{aligned}\partial MB/\partial p = B^{-2}\{&[\varepsilon + (X_{2k} - D_{2k})\phi]^2 - (X_{2k} - D_{2k})[\varepsilon + (X_{2k} - D_{2k})\phi] \\ &- \varepsilon(\eta D_{2k} - \phi X_{2k})\} \\ &+ pB^{-2}[(X_{2k} - D_{2k})X_2\bar{\eta}' + (X_{2k} - D_{2k})^2\phi'].\end{aligned} \tag{27'}$$

Consider the first term on the right-hand side of (27′). In view of (40) it can be expressed as

$$B^{-2}\{[\varepsilon + (X_{2k} - D_{2k})\phi]^2 - (X_{2k} - D_{2k})[\varepsilon + (X_{2k} - D_{2k})\phi] - \varepsilon(\eta D_{2k} - \phi X_{2k})\}$$

$$= B^{-2}\Big\{(X_{2k} - D_{2k})\phi\{\varepsilon + [(m-1)X_{2k} + D_{2k}]\bar{\eta}\} + (m-1)X_{2k}\varepsilon\bar{\eta}$$

$$+ B(X_{2k} - D_{2k})\frac{(\sigma - 1)f(p)^{-1}}{p + f(p)^{-1}}\Big\}$$

$$> 0 \text{ if } \sigma \geqslant 1 \qquad (41)$$

where $(\sigma-1)f(p)^{-1}/[p + f(p)^{-1}] = \eta - 1$ and $m \geqslant 1$. The inequality (41) is justified in appendix 2. Turning to the second term of (27′), we have

$$pB^{-2}\{(X_{2k} - D_{2k})X_2\bar{\eta}' + (X_{2k} - D_{2k})^2\phi'\}$$

$$= pB^{-2}[\![(X_{2k} - D_{2k})X_2\{f(p)[p + f(p)^{-1}]^{-1}\sigma'(p)$$

$$+ (X_{2k} - D_{2k})f(p)^{-1}[p + f(p)^{-1}]^{-2}(\sigma - 1)(\sigma X_2 - X_{2k} + D_{2k})]\!]$$

$$\geqslant 0 \text{ if } \sigma(p) \geqslant 1 \text{ and } \sigma'(p) \geqslant 0. \qquad (42)$$

It follows from the preceding argument that $\partial MB/\partial p > 0$ if

$$\sigma'(p) \geqslant 0 \qquad (43a)$$

and

$$\sigma(p) \geqslant 1. \qquad (43b)$$

From (40a), $\sigma \geqslant 1$ if and only if $\eta \geqslant 1$; hence (43b) can be alternatively stated as

$$\eta(p) \geqslant 1. \qquad (43b')$$

If preferences are of CES type, $\sigma' = 0$ and (43b) or (43b′) suffices. If the utility function is of Cobb–Douglas form then technical progress is necessarily welfare enhancing.

Proposition 1. *In a closed economy as specified in this section, a uniform Hicksian improvement is potentially beneficial (in the sense that, combined with suitable lumpsum transfers, it improves the well-being of all individuals) if* $\sigma(p) \geqslant 1$ *and* $\sigma'(p) \geqslant 0$ *in equilibrium.*

3 AN OPEN ECONOMY

We are now prepared to consider the robustness of the Hicks–Ikema theorem in a context of imperfect competition. Instead of one closed economy we now have two trading economies, α and β. Initially, the two economies are identical in all respects except size. In particular, all factor owners and all oligopolists, whatever their country of residence, share the same homothetic preferences; all factor owners, whatever their country of residence, have the same factor endowments; and all firms in an industry, whatever the country in which they produce, share a common, constant-returns technology. Thus if m_j and n_j are, respectively, the number of oligopolists and the number of factor owners in country j, $j = \alpha, \beta$, then $n^\alpha = \mu n^\beta$ and $m^\alpha = \mu m^\beta$, where μ is some positive number.

Our model of the world economy consists of the first-order conditions for oligopolists in each of the two countries as well as the world market-clearing condition for good 2. The first-order condition for oligopolists in country α is

$$p\left(1 - \frac{X^\alpha_{2k} - D_2(p, \pi^\alpha)}{\varepsilon^w + [X^\alpha_{2k} - D_2(p, \pi^\alpha)]\phi(p)}\right) = C^{\alpha\prime}(m^\alpha X^\alpha_{2k}/\lambda) \tag{44}$$

where

$$\varepsilon^w \equiv \sum_{j=\alpha,\beta} n^j D_2(p, y^j)\eta(p) + \sum_{j=\alpha,\beta} m^j D_2(p, \pi^j)\eta(p) - \sum_{j=\alpha,\beta} \phi(p) X^j_2. \tag{45}$$

Taking advantage of the symmetry of the equilibrium, (45) may be rewritten as

$$\begin{aligned}\varepsilon^w &= (X^\alpha_2 + X^\beta_2)\eta - (X^\alpha_2 + X^\beta_2)\phi \\ &= (X^\alpha_2 + X^\beta_2)\bar{\eta} \\ &= X^w_2\bar{\eta}.\end{aligned} \tag{45'}$$

Similarly, the first-order condition for oligopolists in country β is

$$p\left(1 - \frac{X^\beta_{2k} - D_2(p, \pi^\beta)}{\varepsilon^w + [X^\beta_{2k} - D_2(p, \pi^\beta)]\phi(p)}\right) = C^{\beta\prime}(m^\beta X^\beta_{2k}) \tag{46}$$

and the market-clearing condition for good 2 is

$$\begin{aligned}&n^\alpha D_2(p, y^\alpha_f) + n^\beta D_2(p, y^\beta_f) + m^\alpha D_2(p, \pi^\alpha) + m^\beta D_2(p, \pi^\beta) \\ &\quad = m^\alpha X^\alpha_{2k} + m^\beta X^\beta_{2k} \\ &\quad = (m^\alpha + m^\beta) X_{2k}\end{aligned} \tag{47}$$

where

$$y^\alpha_f = \lambda y^\alpha(m^\alpha X^\alpha_{2k}/\lambda) \tag{48}$$

$$y^\beta_f = y^\beta(m^\beta X^\beta_{2k}) \tag{49}$$

$$\pi^\alpha = pX^\alpha_{2k} - C^\alpha(m^\alpha X^\alpha_{2k}/\lambda)/m^\alpha \tag{50}$$

$$\pi^\beta = pX^\beta_{2k} - C^\beta(m^\beta X^\beta_{2k})/m^\beta. \tag{51}$$

Differentiating (44) with respect to λ, we find that

$$\begin{aligned}&\{A^w + p(B^w)^{-2}[-(\varepsilon^w/p)(D_{2k}\eta - X_{2k}\phi) + (X_{2k} - D_{2k})X^w_2\bar{\eta}' \\ &\quad + (X_{2k} - D_{2k})^2\phi']\}\mathrm{d}p\end{aligned}$$

$$+[\![p(B^w)^{-2}\{-\varepsilon^w[1-\phi+(\phi/p)(\mathrm{d}F/\mathrm{d}X_2^\alpha)]+(X_{2k}-D_{2k})m^\alpha\bar{\eta}\}-m^\alpha C'']\!]\mathrm{d}X_{2k}^\alpha$$

$$+p(B^w)^{-2}(X_{2k}-D_{2k})m^\beta\bar{\eta}\mathrm{d}X_{2k}^\beta$$

$$=-[pB^{-2}\varepsilon^w(\phi/p)(\mathrm{d}F/\mathrm{d}X_2^\alpha)X_{2k}+X_2^\alpha C'']\mathrm{d}\lambda \tag{52}$$

where

$$A^w\equiv(X_{2k}-D_{2k})(B)^{-1}>0 \tag{53}$$

$$B^w\equiv\varepsilon^w+(X_{2k}-D_{2k})\phi>0 \tag{54}$$

and where we again rely on the symmetry of the equilibrium to omit country superscripts from D_{2k} and X_{2k}. Similarly, we may differentiate (46), the first-order condition for β, to obtain

$$\{A^w+p(B^w)^{-2}[-(\varepsilon^w/p)(D_{2k}\eta-X_{2k}\phi)+(X_{2k}-D_{2k})X_2^w\bar{\eta}'$$

$$+(X_{2k}-D_{2k})^2\phi']\}\mathrm{d}p$$

$$+[\![p(B^w)^{-2}\{-\varepsilon^w[1-\phi+(\phi/p)(\mathrm{d}F/\mathrm{d}X_2^\beta)]+(X_{2k}-D_{2k})m^\beta\bar{\eta}\}-m^\beta C'']\!]\mathrm{d}X_{2k}^\beta$$

$$+p(B^w)^{-2}(X_{2k}-D_{2k})m^\alpha\bar{\eta}\,\mathrm{d}X_{2k}^\alpha$$

$$=0. \tag{55}$$

Finally, differentiating the market-clearing condition (47), bearing in mind the definitions (48)–(51), we find that

$$\mathrm{d}p=-(m^\alpha/\varepsilon^w)[p(1-\phi)-\phi(\mathrm{d}X_1^\alpha/\mathrm{d}X_2^\alpha)]\mathrm{d}X_{2k}^\alpha$$

$$-(m^\beta/\varepsilon^w)[p(1-\phi)-\phi(\mathrm{d}X_1^\beta/\mathrm{d}X_2^\beta)]\mathrm{d}X_{2k}^\beta$$

$$+(1/\varepsilon^w)[n^\alpha\phi y-X_2^\alpha\phi(\mathrm{d}X_1^\alpha/\mathrm{d}X_2^\alpha)]\mathrm{d}\lambda. \tag{56}$$

Since $-(\mathrm{d}X_1^j/\mathrm{d}X_2^j)>0$, we can infer from (56) that

$$\partial p/\partial X_{2k}^\alpha<0,\quad \partial p/\partial X_{2k}^\beta<0,\quad \partial p/\partial\lambda>0. \tag{57}$$

Returning now to the first-order condition (44), rewriting it in the general form

$$MB^\alpha(p,X_{2k}^\alpha,X_{2k}^\beta,\lambda)=MC^\alpha(X_{2k}^\alpha,\lambda) \tag{58}$$

and differentiating, we obtain

$$(\partial MB^\alpha/\partial p)\mathrm{d}p+(\partial MB^\alpha/\partial X_{2k}^\alpha)\mathrm{d}X_{2k}^\alpha+(\partial MB^\alpha/\partial X_{2k}^\beta)\mathrm{d}X_{2k}^\beta+(\partial MB^\alpha/\partial\lambda)\mathrm{d}\lambda$$

$$=(\partial MC^\alpha/\partial X_{2k}^\alpha)\mathrm{d}X_{2k}^\alpha+(\partial MC^\alpha/\partial\lambda)\mathrm{d}\lambda. \tag{59}$$

From (56), however,

$$\mathrm{d}p=(\partial p/\partial X_{2k}^\alpha)\mathrm{d}X_{2k}^\alpha+(\partial p/\partial X_{2k}^\beta)\mathrm{d}X_{2k}^\beta+(\partial p/\partial\lambda)\mathrm{d}\lambda. \tag{60}$$

Hence, substituting from (60) into (59),

$$[(\partial MB^{\alpha}/\partial p)(\partial p/\partial X^{\alpha}_{2k}) + (\partial MB^{\alpha}/\partial X^{\alpha}_{2k}) - (\partial MC^{\alpha}/\partial X^{\alpha}_{2k})]\mathrm{d}X^{\alpha}_{2k}$$
$$+ [(\partial MB^{\alpha}/\partial p)(\partial p/\partial X^{\beta}_{2k}) + (\partial MB^{\alpha}/\partial X^{\beta}_{2k})]\mathrm{d}X^{\beta}_{2k}$$
$$= - [(\partial MB^{\alpha}/\partial p)(\partial p/\partial \lambda) + (\partial MB^{\alpha}/\partial \lambda) - (\partial MC^{\alpha}/\partial \lambda)]\mathrm{d}\lambda. \tag{61}$$

Similarly, we can obtain a general form of the first-order condition for oligopolists in β:

$$[(\partial MB^{\beta}/\partial p)(\partial p/\partial X^{\alpha}_{2k}) + (\partial MB^{\beta}/\partial X^{\alpha}_{2k})]\mathrm{d}X^{\alpha}_{2k}$$
$$+ [(\partial MB^{\beta}/\partial p)(\partial p/\partial X^{\beta}_{2k}) + (\partial MB^{\beta}/\partial X^{\beta}_{2k}) - (\mathrm{d}MC^{\beta}/\mathrm{d}X^{\beta}_{2k})]\mathrm{d}X^{\beta}_{2k}$$
$$= - (\partial MB^{\beta}/\partial p)(\partial p/\partial \lambda)\mathrm{d}\lambda. \tag{62}$$

Combining (61) and (62),

$$\begin{bmatrix} H_{11} & H_{12} \\ H_{21} & H_{22} \end{bmatrix} \begin{bmatrix} \mathrm{d}X^{\alpha}_{2k} \\ \mathrm{d}X^{\beta}_{2k} \end{bmatrix} = \begin{bmatrix} T^{\alpha} \\ T^{\beta} \end{bmatrix} \mathrm{d}\lambda \tag{63}$$

where

$$H_{11} \equiv (\partial MB^{\alpha}/\partial p)(\partial p/\partial X^{\alpha}_{2k}) + (\partial MB^{\alpha}/\partial X^{\alpha}_{2k}) - (\partial MC^{\alpha}/\partial X^{\alpha}_{2k}) \tag{64}$$

$$H_{12} \equiv (\partial MB^{\alpha}/\partial p)(\partial p/\partial X^{\beta}_{2k}) + (\partial MB^{\alpha}/\partial X^{\beta}_{2k}) \tag{65}$$

$$H_{21} \equiv (\partial MB^{\beta}/\partial p)(\partial p/\partial X^{\alpha}_{2k}) + (\partial MB^{\beta}/\partial X^{\alpha}_{2k}) \tag{66}$$

$$H_{22} \equiv (\partial MB^{\beta}/\partial p)(\partial p/\partial X^{\beta}_{2k}) + (\partial MB^{\beta}/\partial X^{\beta}_{2k}) - (\mathrm{d}MC^{\beta}/\mathrm{d}X^{\beta}_{2k}) \tag{67}$$

$$T^{\alpha} \equiv - [(\partial MB^{\alpha}/\partial p)(\partial p/\partial \lambda) + (\partial MB^{\alpha}/\partial \lambda) - (\partial MC^{\alpha}/\partial \lambda)] \tag{68}$$

$$T^{\beta} \equiv - (\partial MB^{\beta}/\partial p)(\partial p/\partial \lambda). \tag{69}$$

Let Δ denote the determinant of the square matrix on the left-hand side of (63):

$$\Delta = H_{11}H_{22} - H_{12}H_{21}. \tag{70}$$

To pin down the sign of Δ, we assume the stability of the Marshallian adjustment process in which the output of an oligopolist is increasing (decreasing) if his or her marginal benefit exceeds (falls short of) his or her marginal cost:

$$\dot{X}^{j}_{2k} = \psi^{j} \cdot (MB^{j} - MC^{j}) = \delta^{j}(X^{\alpha}_{2k}, X^{\beta}_{2k}), \quad j = \alpha, \beta \tag{71}$$

for ψ^{j} a positive constant.

For stability it is sufficient and almost necessary that the trace of the square matrix in (63) be negative and that

$$\Delta > 0. \tag{72}$$

Solving (63), we find that

$$dX^{\alpha}_{2k}/d\lambda = \Delta^{-1}(H_{22}T^{\alpha} - H_{12}T^{\beta}) \tag{73}$$

$$dX^{\beta}_{2k}/d\lambda = \Delta^{-1}(-H_{21}T^{\alpha} + H_{11}T^{\beta}). \tag{74}$$

By straightforward calculations,

$$H_{22}T^{\alpha} - H_{12}T^{\beta} = -[\partial MB/\partial\lambda - \partial MC/\partial\lambda] \cdot H_{22}$$
$$+ \{\varepsilon(B^{w})^{-2}[p(1-\phi) + \phi(dF/dX^{\beta}_{2})] + m^{\beta}C''\}(\partial MB/\partial p)(\partial p/\partial\lambda) \tag{75}$$

where, by appeal to symmetry, country superscripts have been dropped from C and MB. The square-bracketed terms in (75) are known to be positive. Thus, if $H_{22} < 0$ and $\partial MB/\partial p > 0$ then $dX^{\alpha}_{2k}/d\lambda > 0$. We have already, in section 2, examined the sign of $\partial MB/\partial p$. Turning to H_{22}, we have

$$H_{22} \equiv (\partial MB/\partial p)(\partial p/\partial X^{\beta}_{2k}) + (\partial MB/\partial X^{\beta}_{2k}) - (\partial MC/\partial X^{\beta}_{2k})$$
$$= \partial MB/\partial X^{\beta}_{2k} - \partial MC/\partial X^{\beta}_{2k}. \tag{76}$$

That is, $H_{22} < 0$ if in the initial equilibrium the marginal benefit associated with an increase in output is less than the marginal cost. Moreover, $H_{22} < 0$ is the stability condition needed for gainful free trade; see Kemp and Okawa (1992). By further calculation,

$$-H_{21}T^{\alpha} + H_{11}T^{\beta} = \{(B^{w})^{-2}p(1-\phi)[\phi n^{\alpha}y + X^{\alpha}_{2}\phi(-dX_{1}/dX_{2})]$$
$$+ \phi C[(\varepsilon^{w})^{-1}m^{\alpha}C'' + (B^{w})^{-2}\phi(dF/dX^{\alpha}_{2})]\}(\partial MB/\partial p)$$
$$+ [(\partial MB/\partial\lambda) - (\partial MC/\partial\lambda)](\partial MB/\partial X^{\alpha}_{2k}) \tag{77}$$

where

$$[(\partial MB/\partial\lambda) - (\partial MC/\partial\lambda)](\partial MB/\partial X^{\alpha}_{2k})$$
$$= X^{\alpha}_{2}[\varepsilon^{w}(B^{w})^{-2}\phi(dF/dX^{\alpha}_{2}) + m^{\alpha}C'']p(B^{w})^{-2}(X_{2k} - D_{2k})\bar{\eta}m^{\alpha} > 0. \tag{78}$$

Thus, if $\partial MB/\partial p > 0$ then

$$dX^{\beta}_{2k}/d\lambda > 0 \tag{79}$$

and technical progress in α benefits β.

Proposition 2. *In a world trading economy as specified in this section, a uniform Hicksian improvement in one country is potentially beneficial to the other (in the sense that, combined with suitable lumpsum transfers confined to the unprogressive country, it improves the well-being of all individuals in that country) if* $\sigma(p) \geqslant 1$ *and* $\sigma'(p) \geqslant 0$ *in equilibrium.*

The common sense of proposition 2 is not hard to find, at least when the elasticity of substitution is constant. Thus suppose that the technical improvement gives rise to equiproportionate increases in both outputs in α and, therefore, to no change in the price ratio. The supposed allocation cannot form part of an equilibrium, for all oligopolists, wherever they produce, find that their marginal revenues exceed their marginal costs. Output of the second commodity therefore expands at the expense of the first commodity. Hence the relative price of the second good falls. Moreover, $X_2^\alpha/X_1^\alpha < X_2^\beta/X_1^\beta$ since, after the improvement, β is relatively well endowed with oligopolists. Hence β exports the second good. Evidently β benefits from an improved allocation and, if the elasticity of demand for the second good is sufficiently great, that gain will dominate any loss from the decline in its price.

Finally, we notice that, in the limiting case of perfect competition, the progressive country α necessarily benefits from uniform Hicksian improvements while country β is neither harmed nor benefited. This might seem to contradict the Hicks–Ikema proposition. Recall, however, that, in that proposition, it is assumed that, initially, the two countries trade non-zero amounts. If the two countries are identical except possibly for scale, as in our own analysis, that assumption is violated.

4 A FINAL REMARK

In the present essay, the number of oligopolists in each country has been treated as given: neither entry nor exit has been allowed. That assumption is, in turn, forced upon us by our decision to work with constant returns to scale; for constant returns and freedom of entry and exit together imply perfect competition. We hope to later re-examine our questions in a context of increasing returns to scale and free entry and exit.

APPENDIX 1: EXISTENCE OF EQUILIBRIUM

Consider a non-co-operative game in normal form. The set of players is $N = \{1, 2, \ldots, n\}$, n finite. The strategy space of player i is $S_i \subset R^p$ and the strategy space of the game is the Cartesian product of the strategy spaces of the individual players: $S = \times_{i \in N} S_i \subset R^m$, where $m = np$. The elements of S_i, called strategies, are denoted by $s_i \in S_i$. A strategy vector $s \in S$ is of the form $s = (s_1, s_2, \ldots, s_n)$, $s_i \in S_i$, and is sometimes written as $s = (s_i, \bar{s}_i)$ where $\bar{s}_i$ is the vector of strategies of all players except the ith. A payoff vector is written as $P(s) = (P_1(s), \ldots, P_n(s))$. The game has a non-co-operative solution if each of the following conditions is satisfied:

(A.1) the number of players n is finite,

(A.2) the strategy set of the ith player S_i is a compact and convex subset of R^m,

(A.3) the payoff of the ith player is a scalar-valued function $P_i(s)$ which is defined for all $s \in S$ and is continuous and bounded everywhere,

(A.4) $P_i(s)$ is quasi-concave with respect to s_i, $i = 1, 2, \ldots, n$.

For a proof, see Friedman (1977: 160–1).

In the above existence theorem, the strategy sets of the players are taken to be independent of each other. In the model of section 2, however, the strategy sets are made dependent on each other by the general resource constraint $\Sigma_{\ell=1}^{m} X_{2\ell} \leqslant \bar{X}_2$, where $\bar{X}_2$ is the greatest possible output of good 2. The theorem must be extended to accommodate the dependence of the individual strategy sets.

Let us assume that the payoff function of the ith player is defined on a subset T_i of S in such a way that, no matter what other players do, there are some strategies for which his or her payoff is defined. Formally, we have the further assumption

(A.5) $P_i(s)$ is continuous and bounded on $T_i \subset S$, where T_i is compact and convex, $i = 1, 2, \ldots, n$. For any $\bar{s}_i \in \bar{S}_i$, there is at least one $s_i \in S_i$ such that $(s_i, \bar{s}_i) \in T_i$.

It can then be shown that a game satisfying (A.1), (A.2), (A.4) and (A.5) has a non-co-operative equilibrium. If s^* is a strategy vector associated with such an equilibrium then $s^* \in \cap_{i=1}^{n} T_i$. For a detailed discussion, see Friedman (1977: 152–5).

Assumptions (A.1), (A.2) and (A.5) are not difficult to accept. However, (A.4) may be thought to be too restrictive in a general-equilibrium setting. Fortunately, Nishimura and Friedman (1981) have been able to replace (A.4) with a weak restriction on the 'best reply mapping'. The latter is defined as

$$r_i(\bar{s}_i) = \left\{ t_i \in S_i : P_i(t_i, \bar{s}_i) = \max_{s_i \in S_i} P_i(s_i, \bar{s}_i) \right\}.$$

Let $r(s) \equiv \times_{i \in N} r_i(\bar{s}_i)$, a mapping from S to subsets of S, so that the fixed points of r coincide with the equilibrium points of the game. And let $U(s) \subset S$ denote an open neighbourhood of S. Then the new, substitute assumption is as follows:

(A.6) For any $s \in S$ such that $s \notin r(s)$, there is at least one player i, co-ordinate k and open neighbourhood $U(s)$ such that, for any s^1, $s^2 \in U(s)$, $t_i^1 \in r(\bar{s}_i^1)$ and $t_i^2 \in r_i(\bar{s}_i^2)$, the condition $(t_{ik}^1 - s_{ik}^1)(t_{ik}^2 - s_{ik}^2) > 0$ holds. The implication of (A.6) for our model is that, given any $(X_{21}, \ldots, X_{2m})$ which is not an equilibrium, for at least our oligopolist k, either all optimal responses by k are strictly greater than X_{2k} or they are strictly less than X_{2k}.

For other extensions of the existence theorem, see Nishimura and Friedman (1981: 639).

APPENDIX 2: MISCELLANEOUS PROOFS

In this appendix it will be shown that (i) the total income of factor owners is a monotone increasing function of the total output of oligopolists, that (ii) the total social cost of producing good 2, $F(X_2)$, is a monotone increasing function of oligopolists' output, that (iii) the inequality (41) is valid, and that (iv) if a technical improvement in one country causes the output of every oligopolist (wherever located) to increase, and if in each country there is in place a suitable scheme of lumpsum compensation, then both countries benefit from the improvement.

Proof of (i). Each factor owner's income is

$$y = wL + rK = L(w + rk) \tag{A1}$$

where

$$w = f_1(k_i) - k_1 f_1'(k_1) \tag{A2}$$

$$r = f_1'(k_1) \tag{A3}$$

and

$$k \equiv K/L, \quad k_1 \equiv K_1/L_1. \tag{A4}$$

From (A2) and (A3), and the first-order conditions of the oligopolists,

$$\frac{f_1(k_1) - k_1 f_1'(k_1)}{f_1'(k_1)} = \frac{f_2(k_2) - k_2 f_2'(k_2)}{f_2'(k_2)}. \tag{A5}$$

To complete the specification of supply, we have the conditions of full employment

$$\ell_1 + \ell_2 = 1 \tag{A6}$$

$$\ell_1 k_1 + \ell_2 k_2 = k \tag{A7}$$

where $\ell_j = L_j/(nL)$ and the total output of good 2,

$$X_2 = nL\ell_2 f_2(k_2). \tag{A8}$$

From (A1),

$$dy = L(k - k_1) f_1''(k_1) dk_1 \tag{A9}$$

and, from (A6) and (A7),

$$d\ell_1 = (k_2 - k_1)^{-1}(\ell_1 dk_1 + \ell_2 dk_2) = -d\ell_2. \tag{A10}$$

Hence, from (A8) and (A10),

$$dX_2 = -nL(k_2 - k_1)^{-1} \{\ell_1 f_2 dk_1 + \ell_2 [f_2 - (k_2 - k_1) f_2'] dk_2\}. \tag{A11}$$

However, differentiating (A5),

$$f_1(f_1')^{-2} f_1'' dk_1 = f_2(f_2')^{-2} f_2'' dk_2 \tag{A12}$$

Hence, from (A9), (A11) and (A12),

$$dy/dX_2 = -n^{-1}(k_2 - k_1)^2 \ell_2 f_2'' \{\ell_1 f_2 + \ell_2[f_2 - (k_2 - k_1) f_2'] \chi\}^{-1} > 0 \tag{A13}$$

where

$$\chi \equiv (f_1(f_1')^{-2} f_1'')(f_2(f_2')^{-2} f_2'')^{-1} > 0. \tag{A14}$$

Proof of (ii). The total cost of producing X_2, the total output of the oligopolists, is

$$F = wL_2 + rK_2. \tag{A15}$$

Differentiating (A15) totally, we obtain

$$\begin{aligned} dF &= -(w\,dL_1 + r\,dK_1) + L_2(dw + k_2\,dr) \\ &= -dX_1 + L_2(dw + k_2\,dr). \end{aligned} \tag{A16}$$

On the other hand, from (A2) and (A3),

$$dw = -k_1 f_1''\, dk_1 \tag{A17}$$

$$dr = f_1''\, dk_1. \tag{A18}$$

Hence

$$dw + k\,dr = (k_2 - k_1) f_1''\, dk_1. \tag{A19}$$

Next, we notice that, from (A5) and (A11),

$$dk_1/dX_2 = -[\![[(nL)/(k_2 - k_1)]\{\ell_1 f_2 + \ell_2[f_2 - (k_2 - k_1) f_2']\chi\}]\!]^{-1}. \tag{A20}$$

Finally, from (A16), (A19) and (A20),

$$\begin{aligned} dF/dX_2 = &-(dX_1/dX_2) - n^{-1}\ell_2(k_2 - k_1)^2 f_1'' \{\ell_1 f_2 \\ &+ \ell_2[f_2 - (k_2 - k_1) f_2']\}^{-1} > 0. \end{aligned} \tag{A21}$$

Proof of (iii). The first term on the right-hand side of (27′) may be expressed as

$$\begin{aligned} &B^{-2}\{[\varepsilon + (X_{2k} - D_{2k})\phi]^2 - (X_{2k} - D_{2k})[\varepsilon + (X_{2k} - D_{2k})\phi] \\ &\quad - \varepsilon(\eta D_{2k} - \phi X_{2k})\} \\ &= B^{-2}\{B[\varepsilon + (X_{2k} - D_{2k})\phi - (X_{2k} - D_{2k})] - \varepsilon D_{2k}\eta + \varepsilon\phi X_{2k}\}. \end{aligned} \tag{A22}$$

Let us examine the square-bracketed term on the right-hand side of (A22). We have

$$\varepsilon + (X_{2k} - D_{2k})\phi - (X_{2k} - D_{2k})$$

$$= X_2\bar{\eta} - (X_{2k} - D_{2k})(1 - \phi) \quad [\text{since } \varepsilon \equiv X_2\bar{\eta}]$$

$$= [X_2 - (X_{2k} - D_{2k})]\bar{\eta} + (X_{2k} - D_{2k})\bar{\eta} - (X_{2k} - D_{2k})(1 - \phi)$$

$$= [X_2 - (X_{2k} - D_{2k})]\bar{\eta} + (X_{2k} - D_{2k})(\eta - 1) \quad [\text{from (8b)}]$$

$$= [X_2 - (X_{2k} - D_{2k})]\bar{\eta} + (X_{2k} - D_{2k})(\sigma - 1)f(p)^{-1}/[p + f(p)^{-1}]. \quad \text{(A23)}$$

Substituting now from (A23) into (A22),

$$B^{-2}\{B[\varepsilon + (X_{2k} - D_{2k})\phi - (X_{2k} - D_{2k})] - \varepsilon D_{2k}\eta + \varepsilon\phi X_{2k}\}$$

$$= B^{-2}[\![[\varepsilon + (X_{2k} - D_{2k})\phi]\{[X_2 - (X_{2k} - D_{2k})]\bar{\eta} + (X_{2k} - D_{2k})\}G]\!]$$

$$- \varepsilon D_{2k}\bar{\eta} - \varepsilon D_{2k}\phi + \varepsilon\phi X_{2k} \quad \text{(A24)}$$

where

$$G \equiv (\sigma - 1)f(p)^{-1}[p + f(p)^{-1}]^{-1} = \eta - 1. \quad \text{(A25)}$$

Evidently G has the sign of $\sigma - 1$. Omitting the terms involving G and summing all other terms between the open brackets of (A24), we obtain

$$[\varepsilon + (X_{2k} - D_{2k})\phi][(m - 1)X_{2k} + D_{2k}]\bar{\eta} - \varepsilon\bar{\eta}D_{2k} + (X_{2k} - D_{2k})\varepsilon\phi$$

$$= (X_{2k} - D_{2k})\phi[(m - 1)X_{2k} + D_{2k}]\bar{\eta} + \varepsilon(m - 1)\bar{\eta}X_{2k} + (X_{2k} - D_{2k})\varepsilon\phi$$

$$= (X_{2k} - D_{2k})\phi\{\varepsilon + [(m - 1)X_{2k} + D_{2k}]\bar{\eta}\} + (m - 1)X_{2k}\varepsilon\bar{\eta}. \quad \text{(A26)}$$

Finally, substituting from (A26) into (A24), we obtain inequality (41).

Proof of (iv).[4] Writing the kth oligopolist's first-order condition in general form, and dropping country superscripts,

$$MB(X_{2k}) = MC(X_{2k}) = MRT(X_2) \quad \text{(A27)}$$

where $MRT(X_2)$ is the marginal rate of transformation along a country's production possibility frontier. Thus the oligopolists are seen to be maximizing the value of national output with marginal benefit, as perceived by the typical oligopolist, as shadow price. Hence

$$X_1 + MB(X_{2k})X_2 \geqslant X_1^0 + MB(X_{2k})X_2^0 \quad \text{(A28)}$$

where X_j ($j = 1, 2$) now denotes the equilibrium output of good j after the technical improvement and X_j^0 ($j = 1, 2$) denotes the equilibrium output of good j before the improvement.

Now technical progress in one country, combined with suitable lumpsum compensation in each country, is gainful for each country if

$$\begin{aligned} ne(p, u_f) + me(p, u_m) &= X_1 + pX_2 \\ &\geqslant X_1^0 + pX_2^0 \\ &\geqslant ne(p, u_f^0) + me(p, u_m^0) \end{aligned} \tag{A29}$$

where u_f and u_m are the utility levels of factor owners and oligopolists after technical progress. On the other hand,

$$\begin{aligned} &(X_1 + pX_2) - (X_1^0 + pX_2^0) \\ &= (X_1 - X_1^0) - [MB(X_{2k}) - MB(X_{2k})](X_2 - X_2^0) + p(X_2 - X_2^0) \\ &= [p - MB(X_{2k})](X_2 - X_2^0) + [(X_1 - X_1^0) + MB(X_{2k})(X_2 - X_2^0)]. \end{aligned} \tag{A30}$$

In view of (A27), the second term on the right-hand side of (A30) is non-negative. Moreover, from the condition that profit be positive, $p > MB(X_{2k})$. Therefore, if $X_2 > X_2^0$, so that $X_{2k} > X_{2k}^0$ and the output of each oligopolist increases, then technical progress combined with suitable lumpsum compensation is beneficial to each country.

NOTES

* We acknowledge with gratitude the helpful comments of Makoto Tawada.

1 That is, it is assumed not only that each oligopolist has no **direct** power to influence factor prices but also that he or she is unaware of his or her power to influence them **indirectly**, through p and the demand for factors by the first industry. In effect, the oligopolist is unaware of the existence of the function $\lambda y(mX_{2k}/\lambda)$ that we later introduce in equation (11b).

2 Questions of existence are discussed in appendix 1.

3 A proof may be found in appendix 2.

4 See also Helpman and Krugman (1985: 96–7).

REFERENCES

Friedman, J. W. (1977) *Oligopoly and the Theory of Games*, Amsterdam: North-Holland.

Helpman, E. and Krugman, P. R. (1985) *Market Structure and Foreign Trade*, Cambridge, MA: MIT Press.

Hicks, J. R. (1953) 'An inaugural lecture', *Oxford Economic Papers* 5: 117–35.

Ikema, M. (1969) 'The effect of economic growth on the demand for imports: A simple diagram', *Oxford Economic Papers* 21: 66–9.

Kemp, M. C. and Okawa, M. (1992) 'The gains from free trade under imperfect competition', University of New South Wales.

Kemp, M. C. and Shimomura, K. (1988) 'The impossibility of global absolute advantage in the Heckscher–Ohlin model of international trade', *Oxford Economic Papers* 40: 575–6.

Kemp, M. C., Ng, K.-Y. and Shimomura, K. (1993) 'The international diffusion of the fruits of technical progress', *International Economic Review* 35: 381–6.

Markusen, J. R. (1981) 'Trade and gains from trade with imperfect competition', *Journal of International Economics* 11: 531–72.

Nishimura, K. and Friedman, J. W. (1981) 'Existence of Nash equilibrium in *n* person games without quasi-concavity', *International Economic Review* 22: 637–48.

21

DOES THE SET OF IMPERFECTLY COMPETITIVE GENERAL EQUILIBRIA DEPEND ON THE CHOICE OF PRICE NORMALIZATION?*

1 INTRODUCTION

It is well known that the choice of price normalization has no implications for the set of perfectly competitive general equlibria. In contrast, it has been argued by Volker Böhm (1994) that the set of **imperfectly** competitive general equlibria may depend on the choice of normalization. Böhm's article brings to centre stage an issue which has lurked in the wings ever since the appearance of Gabszewicz and Vial (1972).[1] The issue is an important one. How it is settled has implications not only for existence but for the whole of descriptive and welfare-theoretical comparative statics, including in the latter category propositions concerning the gainfulness of international trade and investment.

Böhm's supporting argument consists of a pair of pure-exchange examples which, were it not for the general-equilibrium setting and the normalization of prices, might be described as Cournot–Nash and Bertrand–Nash, respectively. The examples will be examined in turn.

It will be suggested that the 'Cournot–Nash' example does not bear on the questions raised by Böhm because the real objectives of imperfectly competitive firms are allowed to change with every change of normalization; and that the 'Bertrand–Nash' example is unsatisfactory because it incorporates the assumption that each oligopolist in choosing his or her best response to another oligopolist's nominal price takes the latter as given, even though he or she is aware that all nominal prices are subject to normalization.

2 THE 'COURNOT–NASH' EXAMPLE

In Böhm's 'Cournot–Nash' example each of two imperfectly competitive firms is the sole supplier of a commodity. A third commodity is widely held and competitively supplied by many individuals. Each firm seeks to maximize its **nominal** profit with respect to its own sales, on the assumptions (i) that the sales of the other firm are constant and (ii) that nominal prices adjust to clear the three markets and at the same time satisfy a given normalization.

In this example, every change of normalization entails a change in the **real** objectives of the two firms. (To understand this point, one need only consider normalizations which reduce to the choice of *numéraire*.) However, there is no reason, in logic or psychology, why firms should adjust their objectives in this way. We therefore conclude that Böhm's 'Cournot–Nash' example is irrelevant to the question he has posed.

3 THE 'BERTRAND–NASH' EXAMPLE

In Böhm's 'Bertrand–Nash' example there are, again, three commodities, each of the first two controlled by a single imperfectly competitive individual and the third widely held and competitively supplied by many identical individuals. Neither oligopolist wishes to consume the commodity sold by the other oligopolist; each therefore can optimize with respect to the **given** excess demand for his or her commodity by holders of the third commodity. Each of the two oligopolists seeks to maximize his or her utility with respect to the nominal price of the commodity in his or her possession, on the assumption that the **nominal** price charged by the other oligopolist is constant and, therefore, that the nominal price of the third commodity only adjusts to satisfy the normalization.

In the context of Böhm's example, the latter assumption is not plausible; for, in that example, neither oligopolist has a taste for the other's commodity. It would be more plausible to assume that each oligopolist seeks to maximize his or her utility on the assumption that the other oligopolist holds constant the price of his or her commodity in terms of the third commodity. In other words, oligopolists with the assumed preferences would not want to play Böhm's game, in which the strategic variables are nominal prices and the price normalization is part of the formal rules of the game. Instead, they would want to play a more conventional game, with relative prices as the strategic variables and with rules which say nothing about price normalization.

4 BEYOND BÖHM'S EXAMPLES

We have argued that Böhm has failed to demonstrate that under imperfectly competitive conditions the choice of price normalization determines the set of equilibria. His Cournot–Nash example incorporates 'irrational' oligopolists who fail to appreciate that the real content of nominal profit changes with every change of normalization, and his Bertrand–Nash game is uninteresting in the sense that agents with the specified preferences would prefer to play an alternative game with relative prices as strategic variables.

However, something has been learned. The objection that we have raised against Böhm's Cournot–Nash example can be opposed to any model of imperfectly competitive general equilibrium, whether of the Cournot–Nash or the Bertrand–Nash variety, if it incorporates nominal profit maximization. On the other hand, it has been shown by Gabszewicz and Michel (1993) that if each agent maximizes his or her utility then, for a very general Cournot–Nash model, the set of equlibria is independent of the normalization.[2]

That leaves for consideration models of Bertrand–Nash type with utility-maximizing agents and rules of the game which include a price normalization. Now we know from section 3 that, for some specifications of preferences and endowments, individuals will prefer to play an alternative game with relative prices as strategic variables and with a set of rules free of price normalization. We can now add that if each agent considers himself or herself to be in a strategic relationship to at least one other agent in each market then he or she cannot imagine varying his or her price, **all** other prices constant, without violating the normalization. Thus, in that extreme case, the notion of Bertrand–Nash equilibrium is internally inconsistent. Beyond special cases like Böhm's and that just described, the question remains open. However, whether or not there exist broad classes of cases in which the set of equilibria do depend on the normalization, there remains the awkward question: why should agents be interested in games in which the strategic variables are nominal prices and for which the rules include a price normalization?

NOTES

* I am grateful to Volker Böhm and Ngo Van Long for their patience and courtesy in responding to my questions as I struggled to formalize my intuitive misgivings about Böhm (1994).

1 Also relevant and noteworthy are Cornwall (1977), Roberts and Sonnenschein (1977) and Dierker and Grodal (1986).

2 If **all** industries are imperfectly competitive and if primary factors are inelastically supplied, no agent can contemplate a change in his or her offer with all other offers unchanged; that is, the Cournot–Nash formulation must be abandoned. Perhaps for that reason, Gabszewicz and Michel (1993) insist on at least one competitive market.

REFERENCES

Böhm, V. (1994) 'The foundations of the theory of monopolistic competition revisited', *Journal of Economic Theory* 63: 208–18.

Cornwall, R. R. (1977) 'The concept of general equilibrium in a market economy with imperfectly competitive producers', *Metroeconomica* 29: 55–72.

Dierker, H. and Grodal, B. (1986) 'Non-existence of Cournot–Walras equilibrium in a general equilibrium model with two oligopolists', in W. Hildenbrand and A. Mas-Collel (eds) *Contributions to Mathematical Economics. In Honour of Gérard Debreu*, pp. 167–85, Amsterdam, North-Holland.

Gabszewicz, J. J. and Michel, P. (1993) 'Oligopoly equilibrium in exchange economies', CORE discussion paper.

Gabszewicz, J. J. and Vial, J. P. (1972) 'Oligopoly "à la Cournot" in general equilibrium analysis', *Journal of Economic Theory* 49: 10–32.

Roberts, D. J. and Sonnenschein, H. (1977) 'On the foundation of the theory of monopolistic competition', *Econometrica* 45: 101–14.

22

LEARNING BY DOING

Formal tests for intervention in an open economy*

1 INTRODUCTION

Some ten years ago I offered a brief examination of the Mill–Bastable infant-industry dogma (Kemp, 1964).[1] Drawing a sharp distinction between the benefits of learning which are confined to the firm which is doing, and the benefits of learning which accrue to other firms, that is between dynamic internal and dynamic external economies of production, I argued that, under competitive conditions with complete knowledge by producers, dynamic internal economies could not serve to justify the protection of infant firms. I admitted that infants might lack the foresight and means to wait out the period of learning and, on social grounds, may deserve protection. However, I noted that the case for protection is then based not on dynamic internal economies but on the presence of uncertainty and the imperfection of capital markets.

During the intervening years this proposition has had its ups and downs. In particular, it has been denied by Negishi (1968, 1972) and Ohyama (1972), and upheld by Long (1975).

In this essay I propose to look again at the policy implications of dynamic internal economies without, however, burdening myself with the more special assumptions which pervade the infant-industry literature. In the context of a two-period model, I develop two general tests which may be applied to any proposal for intervention. The first test if failed disqualifies the proposal; the second test if passed justifies intervention. It is shown that the first test cannot be met if the policy-making country applies a system of optimal tariffs and if its producers have complete knowledge and are not myopic. The relevance of the analysis to economies with privately owned wasting resources is noted.

2 THE MODEL

Consider a country (the 'home' country) which potentially produces, consumes and trades (freely, with the rest of the world) n commodities. Time is divided into two periods, the present and the future. Symbols with the subscript 1 relate to the present, those with the subscript 2 to the future. Thus

c_1 = present consumption vector of the home country;
e_1 = present endowment vector of the home country;
y_1 = present net production vector of the home country, with the ith element positive, negative or zero as the ith commodity is on balance an output, an input or neither;
m_1 = present vector of net home imports with the ith element positive or zero as the ith commodity is on balance imported, exported or neither;
p_1 = vector of present consumers' prices in the home country, equal to producers' gross prices (i.e. gross of tax and subsidy), equal to world prices in the case of freely traded goods;
Y_1 = set of feasible present production vectors in the home country.

The symbols c_2, e_2, y_2, m_2, p^2, Y_2 are defined analogously. It is possible that some elements of m_i are inherently non-positive and that some elements of y_i are inherently zero ($i = 1, 2$). For example, given the home country's technology it may not be feasible to produce certain commodities in positive amounts, and some commodities may be non-tradable.

In each period non-increasing returns prevail, so that the net production possibility sets Y_i are convex; in addition they are assumed to be closed. Since there are no externalities of production it is unnecessary to distinguish individual firms.

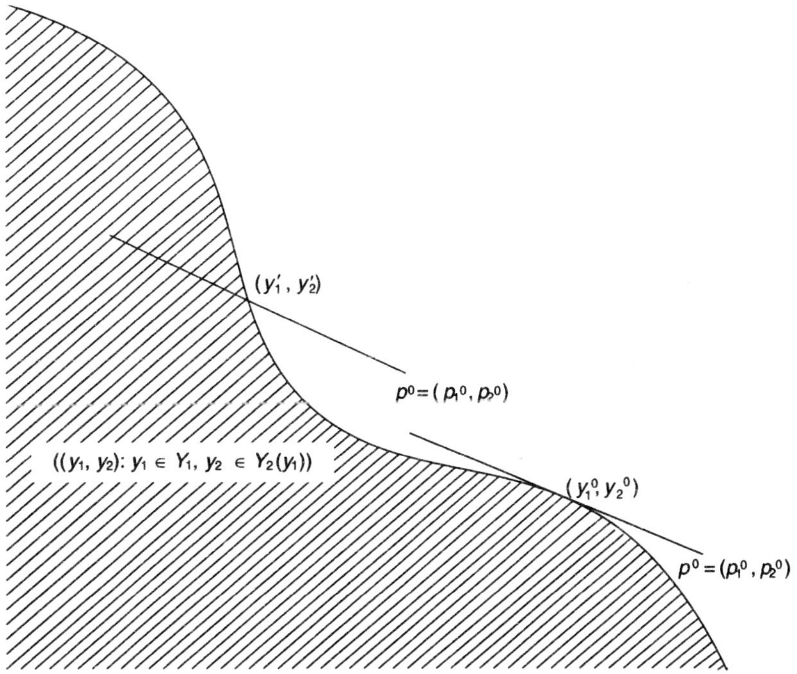

Figure 1

To give expression to the possibility of learning, the set of future production possibilities is supposed to be conditional upon the present net output vector and is therefore written $Y_2(y_1)$. It follows that the set of feasible production vectors $\{(y_1, y_2): y_1 \in Y_1, y_2 \in Y_2(y_1)\}$ need not be convex. Figure 1 illustrates.

Individual preferences are strictly convex.[2] Moreover, the distribution of income is so controlled that if interference with the allocation of resources leaves one individual better off (respectively, worse off) then it leaves no individual worse off (better off). It follows that the community behaves like a single individual with strictly convex preferences. The set $C(c_1, c_2)$ contains those two-period consumption vectors which are preferred to the given vector (c_1, c_2). The set $\bar{C}(c_1, c_2)$ contains those two-period consumption vectors which are preferred to or indifferent to (c_1, c_2).

Suppose that in an initial free-trade tax-free competitive equilibrium

$$c_i = c_i^0, \quad e_i = e_i^0, \quad y_i = y_i^0, \quad m_i = m_i^0, \quad p_i = p_i^0, \quad i = 1, 2. \tag{1}$$

Consider now any alternative feasible pattern of production which, we suppose, can be imposed on the economy by some mixture of taxes and subsidies on production. We wish to rank the associated competitive equilibrium against the initial equilibrium. Quantities associated with the new equilibrium will be indicated by primes. For example, the new pattern of production is denoted by (y_1', y_2') with $y_1' \in Y_1$ and $y_2' \in Y_2(y_1')$.

3 THE TESTS

3.1 A necessary condition

We begin by developing a condition which must be satisfied if the substitution of (y_1', y_2') for (y_1^0, y_2^0) is to be judged desirable. Now if the change is desirable, $(c_1', c_2') \in C(c_1^0, c_2^0)$ and $\Sigma p_i^0 c_i' > \Sigma p_i^0 c_i^0$. Noting that $c_i = y_i + e_i + m_i$ and that $e_i' = e_i^0$, this inequality may be written

$$\sum p_i^0(y_i' - y_i^0) + \sum p_i^0(m_i' - m_i^0) > 0. \tag{2a}$$

That is, interpreting m_i^0 and m_i' as input–output vectors of a special kind, if the change in allocation is desirable then it is profitable at the initial prices. Since $\Sigma p_i^0 y_i^0 \geqslant 0$ (non-negative profits in a competitive equilibrium) and since $\Sigma p_i^0 m_i^0 = 0$ (the balance of payments is zero), (2a) reduces to

$$\sum p_i^0 y_i' + \sum p_i^0 m_i' > \sum p_i^0 y_i^0 \geqslant 0. \tag{2b}$$

That is, if the change in allocation is desirable then the new allocation is profitable at the old prices. Of course, profitability at the old prices does not imply profitability at the new.

In the limiting small-country case the prices of tradable goods (but not necessarily of non-tradable goods) are independent of the allocation of resources in the home country. In another limiting case, $m_i' = 0$ ($i = 1, 2$); that is, the home economy is closed after intervention (but not necessarily before intervention). In each case $\Sigma p_i^0 m_i' = 0$ and (2b) reduces to

$$\sum p_i^0 y_i' > \sum p_i^0 y_i^0 \geqslant 0. \tag{2c}$$

That is, if the new consumption vector is preferred to the old then the new production vector is profitable at the old prices, as in Figure 1.

Suppose that producers have complete knowledge and are not myopic. Then at the old prices (y_1^0, y_2^0) is profit maximizing and

$$\sum p_i^0 y_i^0 \geqslant \sum p_i^0 y_i'. \tag{3}$$

It follows that, for a small country or for one which after intervention would be autarkic, inequality (2c) can never be satisfied and intervention never justified.[3] For a large open economy it is still possible that (2a) may be satisfied in spite of (3). However, this could be the case only if the home country had failed to take advantage (by tariffs on trade) of its monopoly–monopsony power in trade. The imposition of production taxes and subsidies might then be justified on second-best grounds.

The assumption that producers have complete knowledge and are not myopic is conventional in general economic theory, and also in the more rigorous treatments of the infant-industry dogma. However, in a context of learning by doing, where the hand teaches the brain and producers are of limited imagination, the assumption is not altogether plausible. Suppose then that producers are only local maximizers or are unaware that Y_2 depends on y_1. In the future producers must adjust to unforeseen changes in their production set Y_2. Present expectations of future spot prices will be falsified and any futures contracts concluded in the present will prove to be suboptimal. It follows that one can no longer infer from $(c_1', c_2') \in C(c_1^0, c_2^0)$ that $\Sigma p_i^0 c_i' > \Sigma p_i^0 c_i^0$, so that (2a) ceases to be a necessary condition of intervention and intervention cannot be ruled out even in a small or autarkic country.

3.2 A sufficient condition

Let us suppose that the necessary condition (2a) is either satisfied or irrelevant. That is, our attention is for the time being restricted to an economy which either is large, free trading and non-autarkic, or is guided by producers who are myopic or unaware of the learning process, or both.

For $(c_1^0, c_2^0) \notin \bar{C}(c_1', c_2')$ it suffices that $\Sigma p_i' c_i' > \Sigma p_i' c_i^0$ so that, following the reasoning behind (2a),

$$\sum p_i'(y_i' - y_i^0) + \sum p_i'(m_i' - m_i^0) > 0. \tag{4a}$$

That is, if the change in allocation is profitable at the new prices it is desirable. Alternatively, we may note that under free trade $\Sigma p_i'(m_i' - m_i^0)$ is positive or

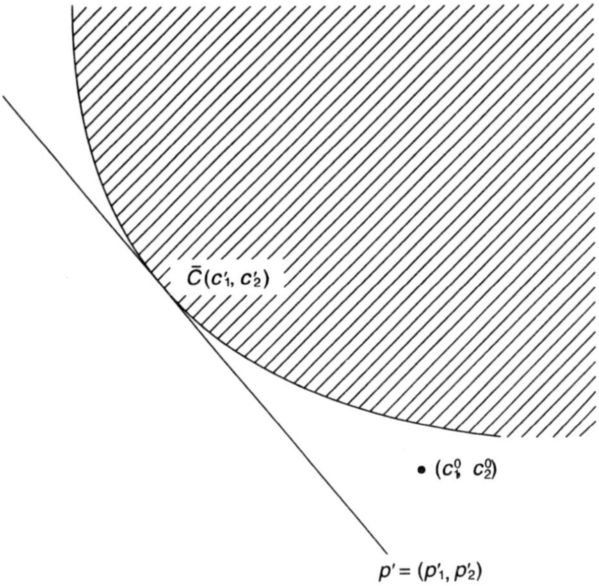

Figure 2

negative as the home country's terms of trade improve or deteriorate as a result of the change, and say that the change is desirable if the additional loss on pure production, calculated at the new prices, is more than offset by the gains from improved terms of trade. Since $\Sigma p'_i m'_i = 0$ (the balance of payments is zero), (4a) reduces to

$$\sum p'_i(y'_i - y^0_i) - \sum p'_i m^0_i > 0. \tag{4b}$$

Of course, (4a) and (4b) are sufficient but (in general) not necessary. Figure 2 suggests the possibility that the change is desirable but (4a) and (4b) are not satisfied.

In the limiting small-country case, $p'_i = p^0_i$ for tradable goods and (4b) reduces further to

$$\sum p'_i(y'_i - y^0_i) > 0. \tag{4c}$$

In that case intervention is desirable if the new production vector is less unprofitable than the old when evaluated at the new prices. The same inequality is obtained if in the **absence** of intervention the home country is self-sufficient, so that $m^0_i = 0$ $(i = 1, 2)$.

The conclusions reached so far are summarized in

Proposition 1. *For intervention to be justified it is necessary that the inequality*

$$\sum p_i^0 y_i' + \sum p_i^0 m_i' > \sum p_i^0 y_i^0 \geqslant 0 \tag{2b}$$

be satisfied. This inequality cannot be satisfied if the home country applies a system of optimal tariffs and if its producers have complete knowledge and are not myopic. Intervention is justified if the inequality

$$\sum p_i'(y_i' - y_i^0) - \sum p_i' m_i^0 > 0 \tag{4b}$$

is satisfied. If the home country is small or if after intervention it is self-sufficient, (2b) *reduces to*

$$\sum p_i^0 y_i' > \sum p_i^0 y_i^0 \geqslant 0 \tag{2c}$$

and (4b) *reduces to*

$$\sum p_i'(y_i' - y_i^0) > 0. \tag{4c}$$

Suppose that the home country is small but its producers myopic or ill-informed. They must be dislodged from (y_1^0, y_2^0) and driven to a preferred point (y_1', y_2'). Suppose that (y_1', y_2') is a global optimum for the community. Since the learning process is supposed to be internal to the firm, that point is also a global optimum for each firm. Suppose further that firms adjust without delay to price stimuli. Then the optimal tax–subsidy intervention is very short lived, a series of mere flash signals following closely one upon the other, each designed to move producers one step closer to (y_1', y_2'). Strictly, under the extreme conditions assumed, intervention spanning any finite interval of time results in suboptimal transitional production. In fact, of course, adjustment is not instantaneous; the optimal policy takes time to do its work and itself varies with time, in a manner determined by the speed with which firms react to price stimuli and by the properties of the production set.

In the more recent literature on infant industries it has been customary to 'decompose' the production set into two sets one of which (that of the infant industry) incorporates learning, the other not.[4] Producers employing activities included in the latter set are neither taxed nor subsidized; the pattern of their production is the same whether or not the infant industry is supported, provided only that prices do not change. Evidently this technology is a special case of that described in section 2. Let α and β relate production sets to the non-learning and learning (infant) sectors, respectively. Then we may write

$$Y_1 = Y^{\alpha} + Y_1^{\beta}, \quad Y_2 = Y^{\alpha} + Y_2^{\beta}(y_1^{\beta}).$$

The reader may develop the specialized forms of tests (2a) and (4a) without difficulty.

The argument of this section has been developed in terms of a model with just two periods, the present and the future. However, there is no difficulty in extending the argument to cover any number of periods. In general, the production set of the jth period is denoted by $Y_j(y_1, \ldots, y_{j-1})$ for $j > 1$; then the key formulae (2a) and (4a) carry over unchanged, with the summations running over the number of periods.

Finally, it may be noted that the description of the home country's technology offered in section 2 is sufficiently general to accommodate privately owned wasting resources not included in the endowment vectors e_i. The case for intervention in a context of wasting resources is identical (except for trivial matters of sign) with the case for intervention in a context of learning by doing.

4 PERSPECTIVE

Attention has been focused on dynamic **internal** economies of production. It is well known that, when the economies are **external** to the firm, intervention generally is justified. It remains to note, however, that if the externalities can be 'internalized' by bargaining then the conclusions of section 3 apply. In particular, in a small country with knowledgeable and non-myopic producers intervention is never justified.

NOTES

* This essay has its origin in talks given at the Delhi School of Economics in August 1967 and at the University of Essex in the spring of 1968. In its preparation I have been greatly influenced by the papers of Negishi (1968) and Long (1975). For most useful comments I am indebted to Jagdish Bhagwati (in Delhi) and to Henry Y. Wan, Jr, Geoffrey Fishburn, Ngo Van Long and Michihiro Ohyama.

1 The treatment in Kemp (1964) is a refined version of that in Kemp (1960).

2 For the necessary conditions derived in section 3 even convexity can be dispensed with.

3 Ohyama (1972: 63–4) has argued that even in small countries (with non-myopic business people) intervention may be justified. However, there appears to be a slip in his reasoning. The inequality at the bottom of p. 63 should be

$$p''(z'' - z') + p''(a'' - a') \geqslant -p''(w'' - w').$$

The first term on the left may be positive since p'' is the vector of domestic consumers' prices which by assumption differs from the vector of prices received by producers in the infant industry. I am grateful to Professor Ohyama for his assistance in tracking down the slip.

4 See, for example, Long (1975), Negishi (1968, 1972) and Ohyama (1972).

REFERENCES

Kemp, M. C. (1960) 'The Mill–Bastable infant-industry dogma', *Journal of Political Economy* 68: 65–7.

Kemp, M. C. (1964) *The Pure Theory of International Trade*, Ch. 12, Englewood Cliffs, NJ: Prentice Hall.

Long, N. Van (1975) 'Infant industry protection, dynamic internal economies and the non-appropriability of consumers' and producers' surpluses', *Economic Record* 51: 256–62.

Negishi, T. (1968) 'Protection of the infant industry and dynamic internal economies', *Economic Record* 44: 56–67.
Negishi, T. (1972) *General Equilibrium Theory and International Trade*, Ch. 6, Amsterdam: North-Holland.
Ohyama, M. (1972) 'Trade and welfare in general equilibrium', *Keio Economic Studies* 9: 37–73.

Part IV

COMPENSATION: LUMPSUM, NON-LUMPSUM OR NEITHER?

23

GAINS FROM TRADE WITH AND WITHOUT LUMPSUM COMPENSATION*

It is shown by example that there are situations in which free trade is Pareto-superior to autarky if and only if the compensation of losers is effected by lumpsum transfers and that there are situations in which free trade is Pareto-superior to autarky if and only if compensation is not lumpsum.

1 INTRODUCTION

According to the traditional gains-from-trade theorem, for any country entering trade there always exists a system of post-trade lumpsum compensating payments such that after compensation each member of the country is not worse off than under autarky. However, Dixit and Norman (1980) have considered the possibility of achieving trade gains with compensation effected by means of non-lumpsum taxes and subsidies. On the assumption that the authorities are restricted to the 'taxation of goods and factors', they argue that 'even this more limited set of instruments suffices to make free trade Pareto superior to autarky' and claim that '[t]his set of results [their finding combined with the traditional doctrine] constitutes a powerful argument in favour of trade . . .' (p. 76). In particular, they appear to suggest that if free trade is strictly gainful with lumpsum compensation then it is strictly gainful when compensation is effected by carefully chosen (non-lumpsum) taxes on goods and services. The suggestion is an interesting one for, if valid, it would imply that any internal misallocation generated by (carefully chosen) non-lumpsum taxes is always sufficiently offset by an improvement in the terms of trade. However, the Dixit–Norman analysis is quite informal; no proofs are provided. Indeed, it is not even clear just how broad is the class of economies they have in mind.

In the present essay we consider the following questions. Are there situations in which trade is strictly gainful with lumpsum compensation but not with any scheme of non-lumpsum compensation? Are there situations in which trade is strictly gainful with non-lumpsum compensation but not with any scheme of lumpsum compensation? To each question we give an affirmative answer. Thus, let us define a **situation** as an ordered pair $s = (\mathscr{E}, e^a)$, where $\mathscr{E}$ is a vector of characteristics of the world economy and e^a is an autarkic equilibrium state of that economy. In the space of all situations let A be the class for which trade is strictly gainful for a particular country under some scheme of internal lumpsum compensation, and let B be the class for which trade is strictly gainful for that country under some scheme of non-lumpsum compensation. Then it is our finding that neither class is contained in the other: there exists a situation s' which belongs to A but not to B, and there exists a situation s'' which belongs to B but not to A. The proof is by example; of three examples offered in section 2, the first pair establishes the existence of s' and the third establishes the existence of s''. None of the examples contains any out-of-the-ordinary (non-Arrow–Debreu) features.

Finally, in section 3 we offer a general comment on the work of Dixit and Norman. It is there argued that any useful proposition concerning the gains from trade, be it with lumpsum or with non-lumpsum compensation, must specify a scheme of compensation (as a function of s) and assert the existence of a compensated trading equilibrium under that scheme; and it is noted that Dixit and Norman have failed to provide such a proposition.

2 THREE EXAMPLES

The first two examples show that there are circumstances in which trade is strictly gainful if and only if compensation is lumpsum.

Example 1. There are three goods. In the country under observation (the 'home' country) each of the three goods may be consumed; and the first two may be combined to produce the third. In the home country there are six households with the common utility index

$$u^i = 2\sqrt{2}\,x_{i1}^{1/4}x_{i2}^{1/4}x_{i3}^{1/2},$$

where x_{ik} is the consumption of good k by household i. The commodity endowments of the six households are

$$\omega_1 = \omega_4 = (1, 0, 0), \quad \omega_2 = \omega_5 = (0, 1, 0), \quad \omega_3 = \omega_6 = (0, 0, 1).$$

Moreover, households 4, 5 and 6 share equally in the ownership of a single firm with the constant-returns production function

$$y_3 = 2(-y_1)^{1/2}(-y_2)^{1/2},$$

where y_k is the net output of good k and inputs are treated as negative outputs. The autarkic prices (normalized so that $p_1 + p_2 + p_3 = 1$) are $p^a = \left(\frac{1}{3}, \frac{1}{3}, \frac{1}{3}\right)$, the autarkic production vector is $y^a = \left(-\frac{1}{2}, -\frac{1}{2}, 1\right)$, and the autarkic consumption vector is $x_i^a = \left(\frac{1}{4}, \frac{1}{4}, \frac{1}{2}\right)$, all i.

Since households 1–3 own no shares in the firm, their indirect utility functions are

$$v_1 = p_1^{3/4}/[p_2^{1/4}(1 - p_1 - p_2)^{1/2}],$$

$$v_2 = p_2^{3/4}/[p_1^{1/4}(1 - p_1 - p_2)^{1/2}],$$

$$v_3 = (1 - p_1 - p_2)^{1/2}/(p_1^{1/4}p_2^{1/4}),$$

where p_3 is written as $1 - p_1 - p_2$. It is easy to verify that the autarkic utility $v_i^a = 1$, $i = 1, 2, 3$. Figure 1 displays the set $\mathscr{P}_i(v_i^a)$ of prices (p_1, p_2) such that household i, $i = 1, 2, 3$, is not better off than under autarky. Neither the three price sets nor their complements have an element in common other than p^a. Thus, whatever the world price vector (and, therefore, whether or not trade with lumpsum compensation is strictly gainful), it is impossible to find a set of domestic prices such that all individuals are better off than under autarky. □

Example 1 demonstrates that there can be no general gains-from-trade proposition without lumpsum compensation. However, the example may strike some trade theorists as unconventional in that there is no good for which the firm appears alone on one side of the market. Our second example therefore is taken from the familiar class of two-by-two economies.

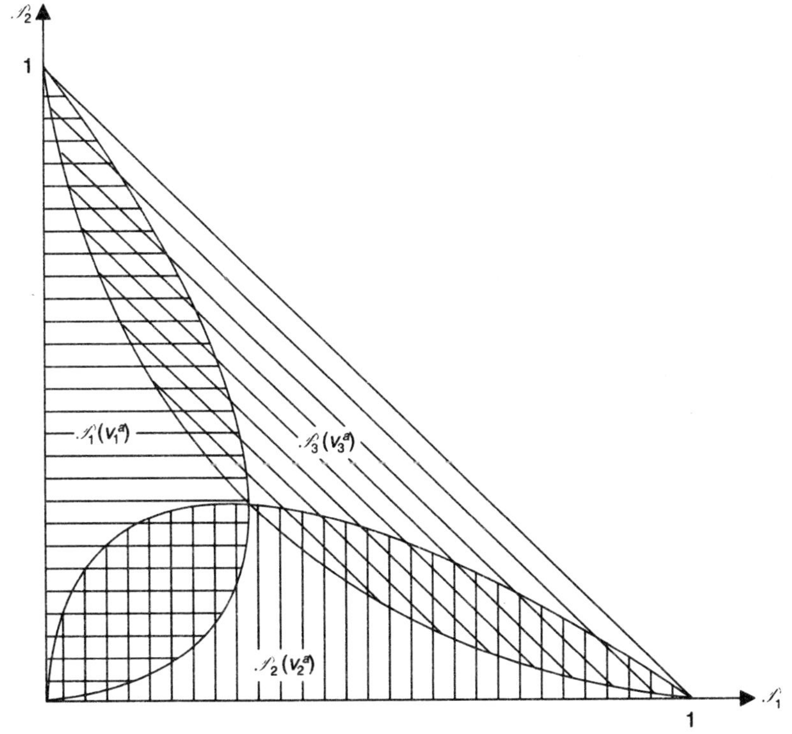

Figure 1

Example 2. Two tradable consumption goods 1 and 2 are produced by two inelastically supplied primary or non-produced factors (goods 3 and 4) in a Heckscher–Leontief technology:

$$\begin{bmatrix} \frac{4}{5} & \frac{1}{5} \\ \frac{1}{5} & \frac{4}{5} \end{bmatrix} \begin{bmatrix} y_1 \\ y_2 \end{bmatrix} \leqslant \begin{bmatrix} -y_3 \\ -y_4 \end{bmatrix}.$$

There are two households, with utility indices

$$u_1 = (3/4^{1/3}) x_{11}^{2/3} x_{12}^{1/3}, \quad u_2 = (3/4^{1/3}) x_{21}^{1/3} x_{22}^{2/3}.$$

Thus the consumption of household i is 'intensive' in commodity i, $i = 1, 2$. The community has an endowment of primary factors but no endowment of producible commodities; moreover, the endowment is shared equally by the two households:

$$\omega_1 = \left(0, 0, \frac{1}{2}, \frac{1}{2}\right) = \omega_2.$$

It follows that households supply primary factors and demand produced consumption goods. Firms, on the other hand, demand primary factors and supply produced consumption goods. Thus, firms and households are on opposite sides of each market. In addition, the two households share ownership of the firms equally. However, under constant returns to scale and freedom of entry, profits are zero in equilibrium, so this assumption plays no role.

Let us normalize domestic prices so that $p_1 + p_2 = 1$, write $p_1 = p$ and $p_2 = 1 - p$, and denote by w_i the income of household i. Then, in autarkic equilibrium,

$$p^a = \frac{1}{2} = 1 - p^a, \quad w_1^a = \frac{1}{2} = w_2^a,$$

$$x_{11}^a = \frac{2}{3}, \quad x_{12}^a = \frac{1}{3}, \quad x_{21}^a = \frac{1}{3}, \quad x_{22}^a = \frac{2}{3},$$

$$y_1^a = 1 = y_2^a,$$

$$u_1^a = 1 = u_2^a.$$

Now let the economy be opened to trade, and suppose that it is small in relation to the rest of the world, so that world prices for the two tradables are given numbers. Indicating world prices by primes, we have $p_1' = kp'$ and $p_2' = k(1 - p')$ for some $k > 0$. Let $\frac{1}{3} < p' < \frac{1}{2}$. Then $\frac{1}{2} \leqslant p'/(1 - p') < 1$ so that, if firms face world prices, production remains at the autarkic point; but, since $p'/(1 - p') \neq 1$, international trade is possible.

Consider Figure 2. In the absence of compensation, the post-trade budget line for each household is SS′, which passes through the common per capita output point P and has a slope of $p'/(1 - p') < 1$. It is easy to see that household 1

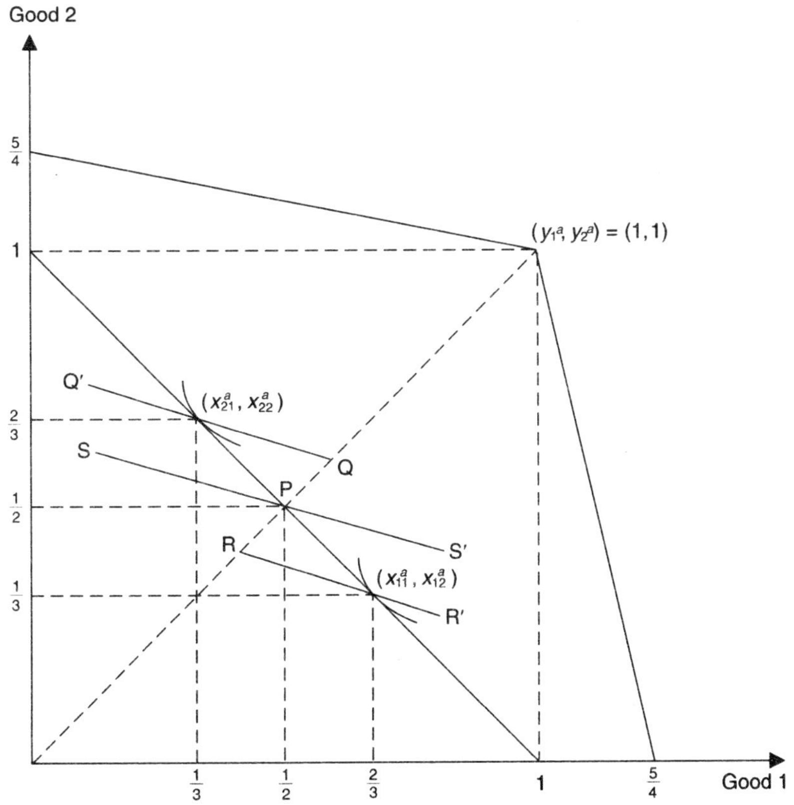

Figure 2

gains from trade and that household 2 loses. It is easy to see also that if lumpsum compensation were feasible then trade would be strictly gainful; for a post-trade transfer of PQ = RP of the output bundle from household 1 to household 2 would leave both households better off than under autarky.

Suppose, alternatively, that only non-discriminatory non-lumpsum taxes are allowed. We notice at once that, since the two households are equally endowed and since primary factors of production enter neither of the utility functions, taxes on the sale or initial holdings of factors can do nothing to redistribute income; such taxes are equivalent to poll taxes and can be useful only in achieving balance in the government's tax–subsidy budget. Ruling out import and export taxes on the ground that they distort production, we are left with taxes on consumption as the effective devices for redistributing real income.

Now in any tax-ridden trading equilibrium, since the two household endowments are equal, $w_1 = w_2$. Moreover, from the log-linearity of the utility functions, in equilibrium

$$px_{11} = \frac{2}{3}w_1, \quad (1-p)x_{12} = \frac{1}{3}w_1,$$

$$px_{21} = \frac{1}{3}w_2, \quad (1-p)x_{22} = \frac{2}{3}w_2.$$

Hence,

$$p(x_{11} + x_{21}) = (1-p)(x_{12} + x_{22}).$$

On the other hand, since international payments balance,

$$p'(x_{11} + x_{21}) + (1-p')(x_{12} + x_{22}) = p' \cdot 1 + (1-p') \cdot 1 = 1.$$

Hence, solving the last four equations,

$$x_{11} = 2x_{21} = 2(1-p)/(3D)$$

$$2x_{12} = x_{22} = 2p/(3D),$$

where $D \equiv p + p' - 2pp'$, and

$$u_1 = p^{1/3}(1-p)^{2/3}/D,$$

$$u_2 = p^{2/3}(1-p)^{1/3}/D.$$

It is easy to verify that (i) u_1 and u_2 are zero at $p = 0$ and $p = 1$, (ii) u_1 is increasing up to $p = p'/(2-p') < p'$ and thereafter decreasing, (iii) u_2 is increasing up to $p = 2p'/(1+p') > p'$ and thereafter decreasing, and (iv) $u_1 = u_2 = 1$ at $p = \frac{1}{2}$. Moreover, by assumption, $\frac{1}{3} < p' < \frac{2}{3}$; hence (v) $2p'/(1+p') > \frac{1}{2} > 0$ and $p'/(2-p') < \frac{1}{2} < 1$. It follows from (ii), (iv) and (v) that if $\frac{1}{2} \leqslant p \leqslant 1$, then $u_1 \leqslant 1$, the autarkic level of utility; and it follows from (iii), (iv) and (v) that if $0 \leqslant p \leqslant \frac{1}{2}$, then $u_2 \leqslant 1$. Hence, not both households can be better off than under autarky. □

In example 2 it was assumed that coefficients of production are rigidly fixed. However, that extreme assumption was made only for convenience. All that is needed is that autarkic output have multiple supporting price lines. As Kemp *et al.* (1985) have shown, the production frontier can contain sharp points even when the underlying production functions are smooth.

Remark 1 about examples 1 and 2. In the construction of examples 1 and 2 it was assumed that the government runs a balanced tax–subsidy budget. However, it will be obvious that our conclusion, that non-lumpsum compensation cannot always be substituted for lumpsum compensation, holds *a fortiori* if there is a surplus which is spent on goods which are then removed from the system.

Remark 2 about examples 1 and 2. It is well known from the recent literature on tax reform that if and only if there is a single or composite good such that all consumers are on the same side of the market, then there is a direction of change of consumer prices such that, if the change is sufficiently small, all individuals are left better off. (See, in particular, Weymark (1979: theorem 1), which refines Diamond and Mirrlees (1971).) It is easy to verify that the condition is violated by example 1. However, example 1 provides more than a simple illustration of Weymark's theorem, for the example is global in scope, whereas the theorem applies only to infinitesimal price changes. In example 2, on the other hand, the condition of Weymark's theorem is satisfied but there are no **feasible** Pareto-improving price changes.

Our third example shows that there are circumstances in which trade is strictly gainful if and only if compensation is non-lumpsum.

Example 3. In each of two countries there is a single non-tradable factor of production, labour, which produces two tradable consumption goods in a constant-returns no-joint-products technology. The technology differs from country to country; in particular, each country has a comparative advantage in producing some commodity. Moreover, at home all individuals are alike both in their labour endowments and in their preferences. For concreteness it is assumed that preferences can be summarized by a Mill–Cobb–Douglas utility function. Finally, the home country is larger than the foreign country, in the limited sense that the tax-free world trading equilibrium lies on the linear segment of the home offer curve.

For the home country, trade without taxes means only a change in production; the consumption and well-being of each individual is unchanged. Suppose, however, that the home country imposes a tax on the consumption of the imported commodity and a subsidy on the consumption of the exported commodity, with the rates of tax and subsidy nicely calculated to equate home consumer prices to foreign autarkic prices and to balance the government's tax–subsidy budget. Then trade takes place at **foreign** autarkic prices, home production shifts marginally, if at all, and each home individual is better off than before trade. Diagrammatically, the home offer curve is so distorted by the tax that it passes through the straight segment of the foreign offer curve. □

3 COMMENT ON DIXIT AND NORMAN

Examples 1 and 2 show conclusively that it is not generally the case that trade with suitable non-lumpsum compensation is strictly gainful whenever trade with lumpsum compensation is strictly gainful. This does not mean that valid and policy-relevant propositions about the gains from trade with non-lumpsum compensation are beyond our reach. However, such propositions must state sufficient conditions (restrictions on $s = (\mathscr{E}, e^a)$ for the existence of equilibrium with strictly gainful trade with specified schemes of compensation (vectors of taxes which depend on s); thus any useful gains-from-trade theorem under non-lumpsum compensation is an existence theorem.[1] Dixit and Norman have failed to specify carefully either the class of economies or the redistributive scheme and therefore cannot even approach the all-important question of existence.

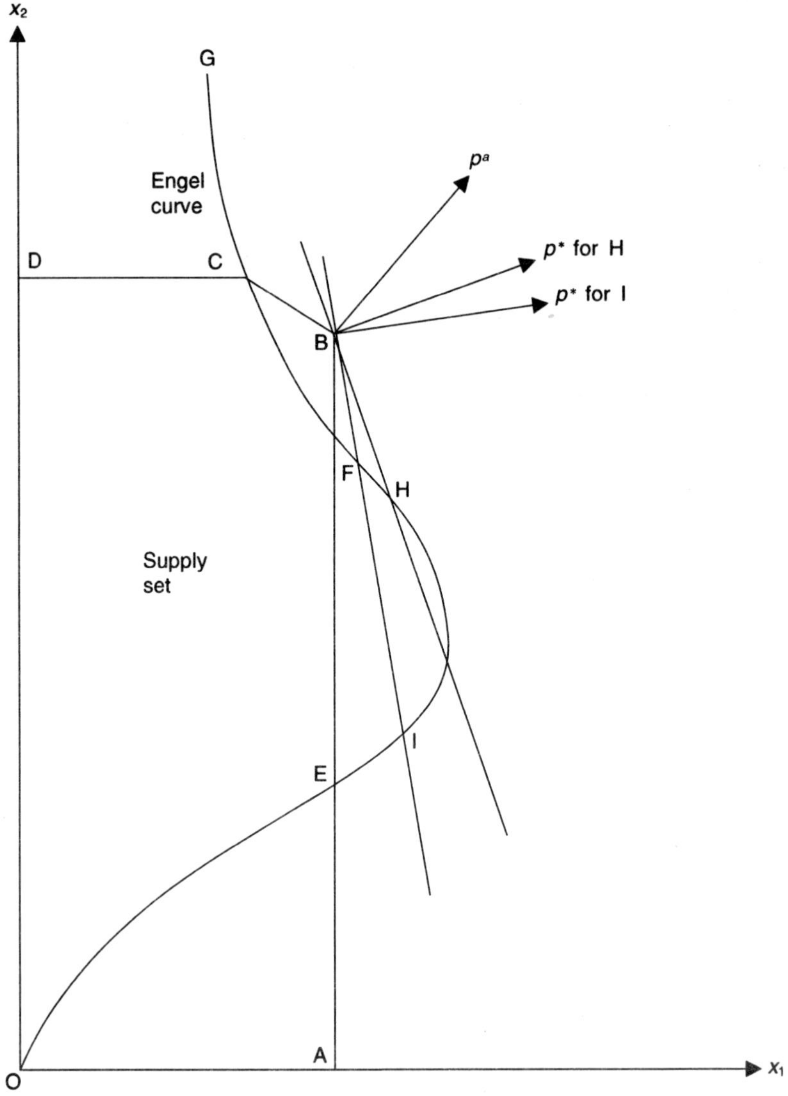

Figure 3(a)

That question presents technical difficulties.[2] More important, for present purposes, is the problem of finding a suitable scheme of compensation. Consider, by way of illustration, the two-step procedure which Dixit and Norman seem to have in mind. At the first step one searches for an 'interim equilibrium' in which each household faces the same prices and consumes the same quantities as under autarky, each firm achieves maximum profit at equilibrium world prices and the government applies its tax surplus to stockpile all l goods, spending the same amount on each good. At the next step, one reduces the tax surplus by $1/l$ in some non-discriminatory manner (e.g. by a negative poll tax). The households then buy back the stockpiled goods at autarkic prices. The remaining stockpiles may be disposed of physically. If no good is inferior, this procedure works; that is, it yields a trading equilibrium which is Pareto-superior to autarky. (Of course, the procedure is very wasteful.) Otherwise, households buying less inferior goods may increase spending on one good by more than the entire tax surplus. With households' preferences unrevealed, no stockpile is adequate in all events. Try now a one-step procedure without disposal. Again, it may break down as the following example demonstrates.

Example 4. In a world of three goods, tradable consumption goods are produced under constant returns by the non-tradable primary good 3. Thus $y_1 + y_2 \leqslant -y_3$, where y_k is the net output of the kth good. There is a single type of household or, equivalently, a single price-taking household; the household owns both the production sector and the endowment vector $\omega = (8, 19, 1)$. The Engel curve defined by the autarkic prices $\left|\frac{1}{3}, \frac{1}{3}, \frac{1}{3}\right|$ is described by the equation

$$x_1 = 5 + 50(x_2 - 5)/[25 + (x_2 - 5)^2].$$

In Figure 3(a), the supply set OABCD contains those pairs of goods 1 and 2 which can be represented as the sum of the endowment vector (8, 19, 1) and the feasible output vector (y_1, y_2), where $y_1 + y_2 \leqslant 1$. The Engel curve is labelled OEFCG. In the companion Figure 3(b), the offer curve of the 'home' country consists of two branches: both (i) the curve B′C′G′ and (ii) the curve E′F′ indicate possible trades when output is at point B in Figure 3(a). We now superimpose the offer curve of the world, αB′γ; that curve exhibits no peculiarity at all. Since the home country would not trade at any price ratio $p_1/p_2 < 1$, point B′ is an equilibrium (without trade); so are points H′ and I′, which correspond to points H and I for Figure 3(a). Clearly, trade does not improve welfare in any of these three cases; at H and I it is welfare reducing. □

The purpose of this exercise is not simply to reinforce example 2, by showing again that non-lumpsum compensation cannot always be substituted for lumpsum compensation. Rather, its purpose is to reveal the possibility that an apparently innocuous scheme of compensation may yield an 'inappropriate' equilibrium in which everyone loses from trade, and this in spite of the presence of a production gain (at equilibrium world prices, post-trade output at B dominates pre-trade output at C), in spite of the fact that producers and consumers are on opposite sides of each market, and in the absence of any need for redistribution (all individuals are identical in preferences and endowments). Of course there may well be some other non-lumpsum scheme which, **for this example**, guarantees that everyone gains from trade. But that is beside the

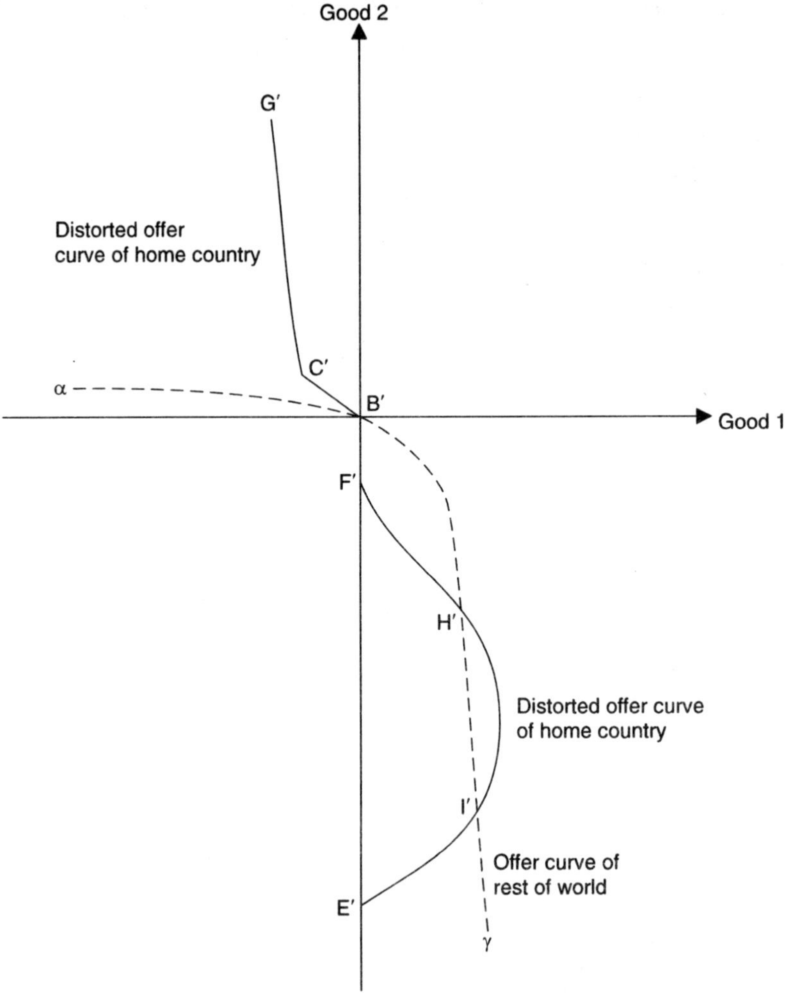

Figure 3(b)

point. What we wish to emphasize is the need to specify an operational rule which assigns to any situation $s = (\mathscr{E}, e^a)$ a policy vector $t = f(s)$ of tax rates etc. so that each equilibrium e^* in the class of policy-assisted equilibria $E^*(s, t) = E^*(s, f(s))$ is Pareto-not-worse than autarky.

There remains for comment the suggestion of Dixit and Norman that their proposition, if valid, would constitute a 'powerful argument in favour of trade'. Why this should be so is not made clear. The only hint we have is their remark that non-lumpsum redistributive instruments are 'weaker' than lumpsum transfers (p. 80). If by this it is meant that the proper deployment of non-lumpsum instruments presupposes less information, or less costly information, than does the proper deployment of lumpsum instruments, then we must ask for a demonstration. In this connection it is worth recalling that the Grandmont–McFadden (1972) and Grinols (1981) schemes of **lumpsum** compensation require knowledge of autarkic equilibrium quantities only.

That completes our discussion of the Dixit–Norman proposition concerning the gains from trade. In concluding we merely note that their related proposition concerning the formation of customs unions (pp. 192–4) is vulnerable to similar comment; see also Kemp and Wan (1986).

NOTES

* We acknowledge with gratitude the helpful comments of J. Bhagwati, A. Dixit, D. Easley, W. Ethier, E. Grinols, E. Helpman, R. Jones, A. Khan, R. Manning, T. Mitra, A. Woodland and M. Yano.

1 It will be recalled that the propositions of Grandmont and McFadden (1972) and of Kemp and Wan (1972) were of precisely this kind.

2 Dixit and Norman (1980) appear to believe that the question of existence with non-lumpsum compensation contains no novelties. 'Having seen the manner in which the existence of equilibrium can be checked when treating lump-sum transfers, we will not repeat the *same* argument' (p. 79, italics added). As the contributions of Sontheimer (1971), Shoven (1974), Mantel (1975) and Shafer and Sonnenschein (1976) suggest, questions of existence cannot be simply brushed aside in this manner.

REFERENCES

Diamond, P. A. and Mirrlees, J. A. (1971) 'Optimal taxation and public production I: Tax rules', *American Economic Review* 70: 8–27.

Dixit, A. K. and Norman, V. (1980) *Theory of International Trade*, Welwyn, Herts.: James Nisbet.

Grandmont, J. M. and McFadden, D. (1972) 'A technical note on classical gains from trade', *Journal of International Economics* 2: 109–25.

Grinols, E. L. (1981) 'An extension of the Kemp–Wan theorem on the formation of customs unions', *Journal of International Economics* 11: 259–66.

Kemp, M. C. and Wan, H. Y., Jr (1972) 'The gains from free trade', *International Economic Review* 13: 509–22.

Kemp, M. C. and Wan, H. Y., Jr (1986) 'The comparison of second-best equilibria: The case of customs unions', in D. Bös and C. Seidl (eds) *Welfare Economics of the Second Best*, Suppl. 5 of *Zeitschrift für Nationalökonomie* 161–7, Vienna: Springer-Verlag.

Kemp, M. C., Long, N. V. and Tawada, M. (1985) 'Sharp points in production surfaces', *Oxford Economic Papers*, 37: 375–81.

Mantel, R. R. (1975) 'General equilibrium and optimal taxes', *Journal of Mathematical Economics* 11: 187–200.

Shafer, W. and Sonnenschein, H. (1976) 'Equilibrium with externalities, commodity taxation and lumpsum transfers', *International Economic Review* 17: 601–11.

Shoven, J. B. (1974) 'General equilibrium with taxes', *Journal of Economic Theory* 8: 1–25.

Sontheimer, K. C. (1971) 'The existence of international trade equilibrium with trade tax-subsidy distortions', *Econometrica* 39: 1015–35.

Weymark, J. A. (1979) 'A reconciliation of recent results in optimal taxation theory', *Journal of Public Economics* 12: 171–89.

24

ON LUMPSUM COMPENSATION*

1 INTRODUCTION

Almost any disturbance to an economy benefits some individuals and harms others. Following Pareto we may then ask concerning any particular disturbance whether there is a scheme of compensation such that, after compensation, all individuals are better off than they would have been in the absence of the disturbance. Going beyond Pareto, we may want to know in addition the types of information needed to implement the scheme.

From Pareto until quite recently the focus has been on questions of the first kind and on schemes of **lumpsum** compensation. Implicitly, it has been assumed that the authorities have all the information needed for implementation of such schemes.

However, there is now a widespread belief among economists that the implementation of lumpsum compensation requires detailed and reliable information about the preferences of individuals and the technical capabilities of firms, information which, practically speaking, is unattainable and is likely to remain so. It is believed also that there are preferred alternatives to lumpsum compensation. In this connection, the demonstration by Diamond and Mirrlees (1971), that schemes of **non**-lumpsum compensation can be both feasible and compatible with efficiency in production, has been influential. Since the appearance of their paper, the focus of theoretical work has shifted away from lumpsum towards non-lumpsum compensation; see, for example, the well-known texts by Atkinson and Stiglitz (1980) and Dixit and Norman (1980). Implicit in the trend is the perception that the implementation of non-lumpsum compensation requires less information, or more accessible information, than does the implementation of lumpsum compensation.

It has been shown elsewhere that, in a context of international trade, this perception is mistaken; see Kemp and Wan (1993). In particular, it has been shown that if the disturbance to the economy fails to yield a production gain, that is an increase in the value of output at post-disturbance prices, then schemes of non-lumpsum compensation like those proposed by Dixit and Norman (DN) are inapplicable; that if the Weymark (1979) condition for a welfare-enhancing direction of price change is not satisfied then DN non-lumpsum compensation is infeasible; and, most important, that DN compensation for a finite disturbance can be implemented only if the authorities have global information about individual preferences, information that is not and never will be available to them. Taken together, or one at a time, these observations imply that DN non-lumpsum compensation is not generally implementable. It has been shown also that there is a scheme of lumpsum compensation which is successful over a wider domain, and the implementation of which relies on more accessible information than any of its competitors, lumpsum or non-lumpsum. This is the Grandmont–McFadden–Grinols (GMG) scheme of compensation, so named after Grandmont and McFadden (1972) and Grinols (1981, 1984), which accords to each individual the value at cum-disturbance prices of trades that would have been chosen in the absence of the disturbance and to each firm the value at cum-disturbance prices of the net inputs that would have been chosen in the absence of the disturbance. In particular, it has been shown that, in contrast to earlier schemes of lumpsum compensation, like the *princeps* scheme of Vanek (1965: appendix to Ch. 4) and Kemp and Wan (1972), the GMG scheme of compensation incorporates detailed instructions for implementation; that the scheme can handle discrete disturbances characteristic of institutional rearrangements such as the opening of trade or the formation of a customs union; and that, whatever the extent of the disturbance, the scheme is relatively modest in its informational needs – specifically, it requires information about individuals' pre-disturbance trades and shareholdings and about firms' pre-disturbance production vectors, but it does not require further knowledge of preferences or technologies. Moreover, the GMG scheme of compensation may be feasible even when there is no production gain and even when the Weymark condition is not satisfied. Thus it is free of some of the weaknesses that we have attributed to schemes of non-lumpsum compensation.[1]

Kemp and Wan (1993) focused on disturbances to the conditions of international trade. However, the above appraisal of GMG and alternative schemes of compensation is valid over a broader domain; indeed, it is quite general. Thus, in comparison with alternative schemes, GMG compensation is both **more powerful** (has a wider domain) and **informationally less oppressive**.

In the present essay we provide a proposition which marks out a broad field within which GMG compensation is feasible. Specifically, it is shown that if the technical capabilities of some firms unexpectedly expand, and those of no firms contract, then GMG compensation is feasible.[2] The proposition is then fitted into a two-stage, two-period allocation mechanism which accommodates both the social decision to accept or reject the additional technical capabilities as well as the allocation of resources contingent on that decision. It is noted that the implementation of compensation requires historical information and that therefore compensation can be sensibly discussed only in a dynamic context. Ironically, it is shown also that the relevant historical information is available for a finite economy only if the economy is 'essentially repetitive' and that it is available for an economy with overlapping generations only if, before the disturbance, the economy is in a steady state. Thus the allowed dynamics is severely limited.

In summary, lumpsum compensation of GMG type is a preferred alternative to any scheme of non-lumpsum compensation. However, deeper difficulties do exist for both lumpsum and non-lumpsum schemes, and in fact for any welfare analysis based on comparative statics. These difficulties flow from the possibility of changing preferences and technologies, which make observable data from the past irrelevant to decisions concerning the future.

For the most part (i.e. throughout section 2), we work with a finite economy of Arrow–Debreu–McKenzie type. However, the analysis is briefly reworked (in section 3) to accommodate overlapping generations and an infinite horizon. Moreover, recent work by Kemp and Wong (1992) on the gains from international trade suggests that our conclusions are valid for economies with an incomplete set of markets.

2 ANALYSIS

To effect GMG compensation the authorities must know the trade vectors of firms as they would have been in the absence of a disturbance. Since they relate to a hypothetical situation, the vectors cannot be directly observed. However, for a restricted class of economies it suffices to observe choices in an earlier period. This is the class of **essentially repetitive economies** (EREs), that is economies which decompose into one-period economies which are identical except for the disturbance or perturbation under scrutiny. We proceed to describe a two-period ERE for the case in which there is an optional expansion of the aggregate production set. At least two periods must be accommodated; for, otherwise, the economy will lack the minimum dynamics specified in the introduction. On the other hand, longer-lasting EREs can be built up straightforwardly from one-period and two-period economies.

2.1 Essentially repetitive economies

Let there be m individuals, n firms and H goods in each of two adjacent and equal intervals of time (periods), and let $I \equiv \{1, \ldots, m\}$ and $J \equiv \{1, \ldots, n\}$. The two periods are indicated by the superscripts 0 and 1. The disturbance occurs at the end of period 0.

A two-period ERE is then an array

$$\mathscr{E} = ((X_i, \succsim_i, e_i)_{i \in I}, (Y_j)_{j \in J}, (\theta_{ij})_{i \in I, j \in J}) \tag{1}$$

where

$X_i \subset R_+^{2H}$ is the consumption set of individual i

$\succsim_i \subset R_+^{2H} \times R_+^{2H}$ is the preference pre-ordering of i
$e_i \in R_+^{2H}$ is the endowment vector of i
$Y_j \subset R^{2H}$ is the production set of firm j
$\theta_{ij} \geqslant 0$ is the share of i in the ownership of $j\,(\Sigma_j \theta_{ij} = 1)$

and where the essentially repetitive structure of $\mathscr{E}$ is captured in the following specifications:

$$X_i = X_i^0 \times X_i^1, \quad X_i^0 = X_i^1 \subset R_+^H \tag{2}$$

where X_i^k is the component consumption set for period k, $k = 0, 1$;

$$\succsim_i^0 = \succsim_i^1 \subset R^{2H} \tag{3}$$

is the component preference ordering for periods 0 and 1;

$$\succsim_i^0 \times \succsim_i^1 \subset \succsim_i \tag{4a}$$

$$((X_i^0)^2 \backslash \succsim_i^0) \times \overline{((X_i^1)^2 \backslash \succsim_i^1)} \subset (X_i)^2 \backslash \succsim_i \tag{4b}$$

$$\overline{((X_i^0)^2 \backslash \succsim_i^0)} \times ((X_i^1)^2 \backslash \succsim_i^1) \subset (X_i)^2 \backslash \succsim_i \tag{4c}$$

where $(X_i^k)^2$ is the set of all comparable pairs of sub-bundles;

$$e_i = (e_i^0, e_i^1), \quad e_i^0 = e_i^1 \in R_+^H \tag{5}$$

where e_i^k is the component endowment of i in period k, $k = 0, 1$;

$$Y_j = Y_j^0 \times Y_j^1, \quad Y_j^0, Y_j^1 \subset R^H \tag{6}$$

where Y_j^k is the component production set of firm j for period k, $k = 0, 1$;

$$Y_j^1 = Y_j^0 \cup (d)\, Y_j^\Delta, \quad Y_j^0 \cap Y_j^\Delta = \emptyset, \quad d \in \{0, 1\} \tag{7}$$

where Y_j^Δ is the set of additional production vectors which may be available to firm j and d is the community's decision parameter ($d = 0$ if the addition to the production set is rejected, $d = 1$ if the addition is accepted);

$$Y_j^\Delta \neq \{0\} \text{ for } j \in J' \subset J, \quad Y_j^\Delta = \{0\} \text{ for } j \in J \backslash J'. \tag{8}$$

A few explanatory remarks are offered concerning specifications (2)–(8). Thus (2) states that what is consumable in one period is consumable in the other; (3) and (4) provide a partially specified standard for the evaluation of two-period prospects. According to (3), the consumption bundles of each period are ranked by the same criterion. Thus if the ordered pair (a, b) is in $\succsim^k$ for period k then a is 'not worse than' b in a sense to be completed only by (4): (4) specifies intertemporal independence of preferences in terms of the orthogonality of the one-period 'orderings'. Thus a is said to be 'not worse than' b if, for any c from the other period, a paired with c is not worse than b paired with c. Moreover,

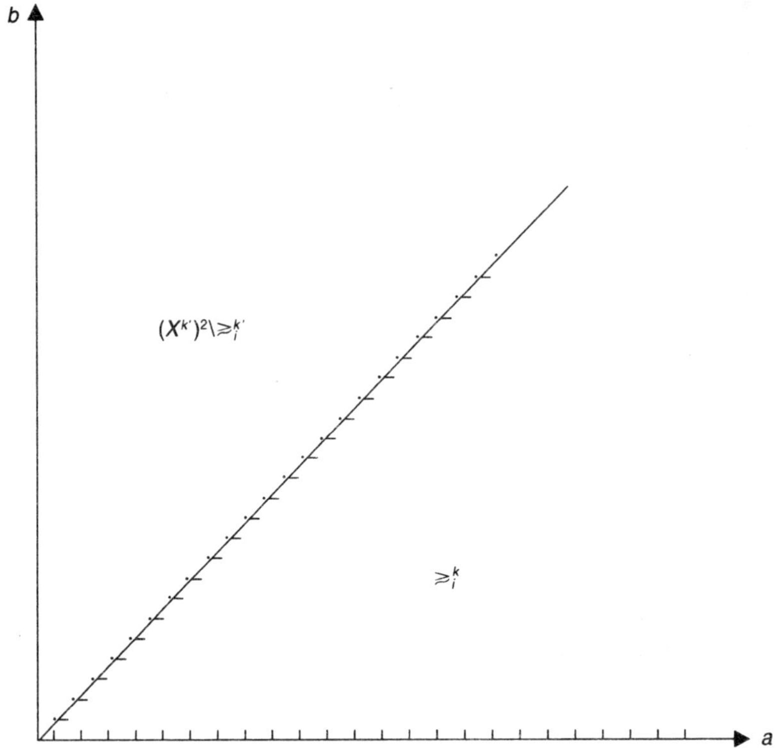

Figure 1(a) Period k

(4a) specifies that if *a* is 'not worse than' *b* and, in the other period, *c* is 'not worse than' *d* then *a* paired with *c* is 'not worse than' *b* paired with *d*; and (4b–c) require that if *a* is 'worse than' *b* and *c* is 'not better than' *d* then *a* paired with *c* is 'worse than' *b* paired with *d*. (Figure 1 illustrates (4) when $H = 1$ and preferences are insatiable.) Specification (4) is only a partial specification; it leaves open the ordering of *a* paired with *c* and *b* paired with *d* when in one-period comparisons *a* is 'better than' *b* and *c* 'worse than' *d*. However, it suffices for our purposes. Specification (5) needs no explanation. The orthogonal form of Y_j in (6) implies that no activity today can affect the supply possibilities of tomorrow. For example, the construction and operation of artesian wells today has no bearing on the level of tomorrow's water table or on tomorrow's water pressure. Specification (7) concerns the expansion of the individual firm's production set while (8) states that not all firms need participate in the economy's expansion.

Having specified the physical conditions which must be satisfied by an ERE, we must make precise the institutional framework within which the economy operates:

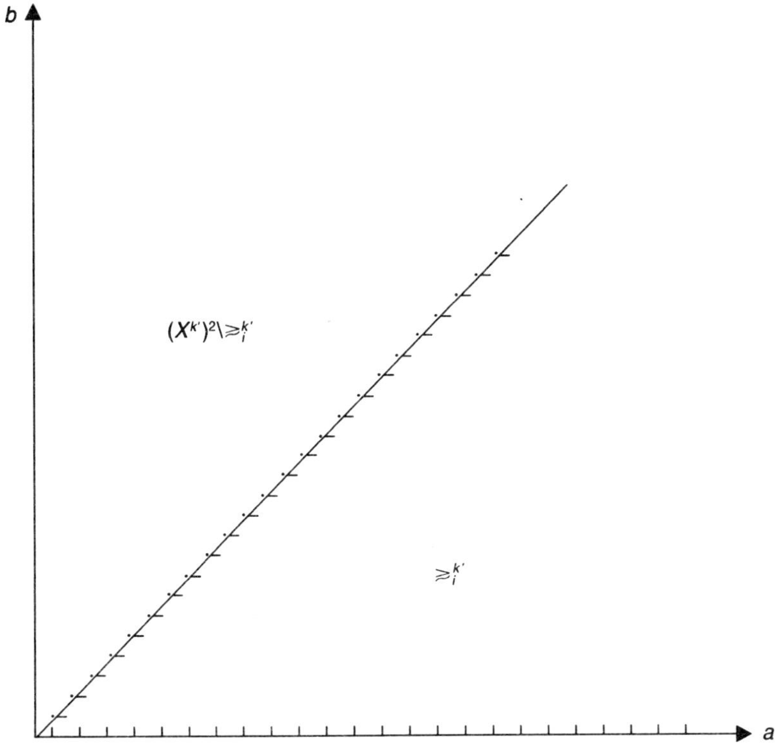

Figure 1(b) Period k'

the only markets are spot markets for commodities. (9)

Thus at the end of period 0 there can be no outstanding commitments or indebtedness:

all profits earned during period 0 are distributed and spent during that period. (10)

We now have two period-specific component economies, say $\mathscr{E}^0$ and $\mathscr{E}^1$. Let $Y_j' = Y_j^0 \cup Y_j^\Delta$. Then we may specify that

$$\mathscr{E}^1 = \mathscr{E}^0 \text{ if } d = 0 \text{ and } \mathscr{E}^1 = \mathscr{E}^\Delta \equiv ((X_i^1, \precsim_i^1, e_i^1)_{i \in I}, (Y_j')_{j \in J}, (\theta_{ij})_{i \in I, j \in J})$$

if $d = 1$.

Thus $\mathscr{E}^\Delta$ differs from $\mathscr{E}^0$ only in the expansion of the production sets of some firms. $\mathscr{E}^0$ and $\mathscr{E}^1$ are completely isolated from each other, except that in period 1 the **equilibrium attainable state** of period 0 will be known. In particular, it is **not** known in period 0 that the production sets will expand in period 1. Let t_{ik}^0 denote the amount of commodity k purchased by individual i

in period 0. Then an equilibrium attainable set of period 0 is an array of $(m+n)H$ numbers

$$\begin{bmatrix} t_{11}^0 & \dots & t_{m1}^0; & y_{11}^0 & \dots & y_{n1}^0 \\ \vdots & & \vdots & \vdots & & \vdots \\ t_{1H}^0 & \dots & t_{mH}^0; & y_{1H}^0 & \dots & y_{nH}^0 \end{bmatrix} \equiv [t_1^0, \dots, t_m^0; y_1^0, \dots, y_n^0] \equiv a^0$$

which satisfies the conditions

$$e_i^0 + t_i^0 \in X_i^0 \ (i \in I), \quad y_j^0 \in Y_j^0 \ (j \in J) \quad \text{[microphysical attainability]} \quad (11)$$

$$\sum_{i \in I} t_i^0 = \sum_{j \in J} y_j^0 \quad \text{[macrophysical attainability].} \quad (12)$$

Let $\mathscr{P}$ be the $(H-1)$-dimensional natural simplex, and let

$$p^0 = (p_1^0, \dots, p_H^0) \in \mathscr{P} \quad (13)$$

be an H-dimensional vector such that

$$\text{for all } i, \ p^0 \cdot t_i^0 \leqslant \sum_{j \in J} \theta_{ij} p^0 \cdot y_j^0 \quad \text{[microfiscal attainability]} \quad (14)$$

$$\text{for all } i, \ e_i^0 + t_i^0 \succsim_i^0 e_i^0 + t^0 \text{ for all } t^0 \in \{t^0 : t^0 + e_i^0 \in X_i^0,$$

$$p^0 \cdot t^0 \leqslant \sum_{j \in J} \theta_{ij} p^0 \cdot y_j^0\} \quad \text{[micro-optimality for consumers]} \quad (15)$$

$$\text{for all } j, \ p^0 \cdot y_j^0 \geqslant p^0 \cdot y^0 \text{ for all } y^0 \in Y_j^0 \quad \text{[micro-optimality for firms].} \quad (16)$$

Any array a^0 that satisfies conditions (11)–(16) is a **market equilibrium** of $\mathscr{E}^0$. A market equilibrium of $\mathscr{E}^\Delta$ is similarly defined. Shortly, we shall introduce sufficient conditions for the existence of market equilibrium.

2.2 Grandmont–McFadden–Grinols compensation

First, however, we must formally introduce, and establish some of the properties of, GMG compensation.

Definition. *The GMG scheme of lumpsum compensation* $\sigma^\#$ *assigns*

(i) to each individual i, $\sigma_I^\#(p^1, i) = p^1 \cdot t_i^0$
(ii) to each firm j, $\sigma_J^\#(p^1, j) = -p^1 \cdot y_j^0$.

Thus the GMG scheme gives each individual a cost-of-living adjustment and takes from each firm its 'base period' profits indexed by 'current period' prices.

Proposition 1. *The GMG scheme of lumpsum compensation* $\sigma^\#$ *has the following properties:*

(i) *It is* ***Pareto-non-deteriorating****, that is it ensures that in the new situation* ($d = 1$) *each individual can afford a consumption bundle 'not inferior to' that chosen in the old situation* ($d = 0$).

(ii) *It is* ***self-financing****, that is* $\Sigma_{i \in I} \sigma_b^{\#}(p^1, i) + \Sigma_{j \in J} \sigma_f^{\#}(p^1, j) = 0$.

(iii) *Both* $\sigma_f^{\#}(p^1, j)$ *and* $\sigma_b^{\#}(p^1, i)$ *are* ***continuous*** *in* p^1.

(iv) *It is* ***privacy preserving****, in the sense that* $\sigma_b^{\#}(., i)$ *and* $\sigma_f^{\#}(., j)$ *are determined by past choices as reflected in the array* a^0*, not by* $\mathscr{E}^{\Delta}$.

Proof. *(i) The income of i under* p^1 *is*

$$w_i(p^1, \sigma^{\#}) = p^1 \cdot \left(e_i^1 + \sum_{j \in J} \theta_{ij} y_j^1\right) + p^1 \cdot \left(x_i^0 - e_i^0 - \sum_{j \in J} \theta_{ij} y_j^0\right) \quad \text{[from the definitions of } \sigma^{\#} \text{ and } t_i^0\text{]}$$

$$= p^1 \cdot x_i^0 + \sum_{j \in J} \theta_{ij} \left(\max_{y \in Y_j^1} p^1 \cdot y - p^1 y_j^0\right) \quad \text{[since } y_j^1 \text{ is profit maximizing and } e_i^0 = e_i^1\text{]}$$

$$\geqslant p^1 \cdot x_i^0 \quad \text{[since, for all } j,\ y_j^0 \in Y_j^0 \subseteq Y_j^1\text{]}. \qquad (17)$$

Hence $x_i^1 \succsim_i^0 x_i^0$ *for any* x_i^1 *chosen at prices* p^1 *and income* $w_i(p^1, \sigma^{\#})$.
Parts (ii)–(iv) are obvious. □

2.3 Existence of market equilibrium

To ensure that $\mathscr{E}^0$ has a market equilibrium we simply adopt the assumptions made by Debreu (1959) for his Theorem 5.7(1), with the exception of his (c), which will be modified to accommodate the possibility of compensation in kind. Debreu's assumptions are as follows. For every individual i,

(a) X_i^1 is closed, convex and has a lower bound for $\leqslant$,
(b.1) there is no saturation consumption in X_i^1,
(b.2) for every x_i' in X_i^1, the sets $\{x_i \in X_i^1 : x_i \succsim_i^1 x_i'\}$ and $\{x_i \in X_i^1 : x_i \precsim_i^1 x_i'\}$ are closed in X_i^1,
(b.3) if x_i^1 and x_i^2 are two points in X_i^1 and if λ is a real number in (0, 1) then $x_i^2 \succ_i^1 x_i^1$ implies $\lambda x_i^2 + (1 - \lambda) x_i^1 \succ_i^1 x_i^1$,
(c) there is an $\hat{x}_i$ in X_i^1 such that $\hat{x}_i \ll e_i^1$;

and, for every firm j,

(d.1) $0 \in Y_j^1$,
(d.2) $Y^1 = \Sigma_{j \in J} Y_j^1$ is closed and convex,
(d.3) $Y^1 \cap (-Y^1) \subseteq \{0\}$,
(d.4) $Y^1 \supseteq (-R_+^H)$.

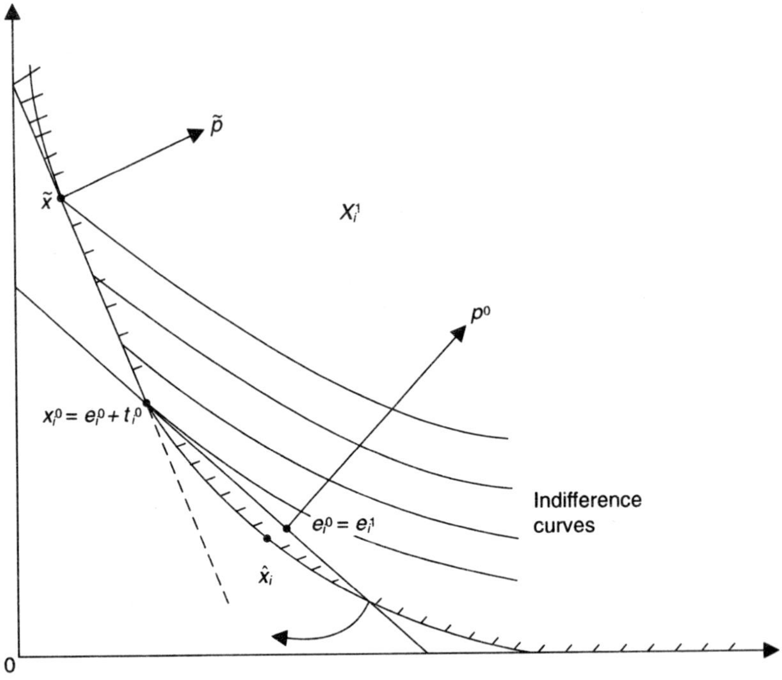

Figure 2

To ensure that $\mathscr{E}^{\Delta}$ has a market equilibrium, assumption (c) must be slightly modified to allow for compensation in kind. Specifically, it is required not that there is an $\hat{x}_i$ in X_i^1 such that $\hat{x}_i \ll e_i^1$ but that

(c′) there is an $\hat{x}_i$ in X_i^1 such that $\hat{x}_i \ll e_i^1 + t_i^0$.

To make clear the need to vary Debreu's assumption (c), we modify a diagram devised by Koopmans (1957: 30). In Figure 2, $\hat{x}_i \ll e_i^1$, so Debreu's (c) is satisfied. However, our (c′) is not satisfied. After compensation in kind of t_i^0, the 'virtual endowment' becomes x_i^0. As the price line sweeps from p^0 to $\tilde{p}$, the intersection of the budget set and the consumption set is steadily compressed until the price line coincides with the linear edge of X_i^1. Implosion then occurs and the point chosen jumps from $x_i^0 = e_i^0 + t_i^0$ to $\tilde{x}$; both upper and lower hemi-continuity are lost.

Proposition 2. *$\mathscr{E}^0$ has an equilibrium, and $\mathscr{E}^{\Delta}$ supplemented by the GMG scheme of lumpsum compensation $\sigma^{\#}$ has an equilibrium.*

Proof. *In view of proposition 1(iii), we can apply Theorem 5.7(1) of Debreu (1959).* □

It is not assumed that the equilibrium is unique, either in $\mathscr{E}^0$ or in $\mathscr{E}^1$. However, it is assumed that if $\mathscr{E}^1 = \mathscr{E}^0$ then any realized equilibrium from period 0 will be replicated in period 1.

Assumption. *All individuals share the common belief that if $\mathscr{E}^1 = \mathscr{E}^0$ then the attainable substate a^0 will recur under market co-ordination.*

Proposition 3. *If*

$$y^0 \text{ is in the interior of } Y^1 = \sum_{j \in J} Y_j^1 \tag{18}$$

then the new equilibrium is Pareto-superior to the old.

Proof. *By construction, $p^1 \cdot y_j^1 > p^1 \cdot y_j^0$ for some j, say $j = 1$. Moreover, $\theta_{ij} > 0$ for some i, say $i = 1$. From (17), therefore, $w_1(p^1, \sigma^{\#}) > p^1 \cdot x_1^0$. From Debreu's assumption (b.1), which rules out saturation consumption in X_1^1, $x_1^1 >_1^1 x_1^0$. Hence, from (4a), individual 1 is strictly better off in the new equilibrium.* □

Remark 1. *It has been assumed that the community must choose between two production sets, one of which is included in the other ($Y^0 \subset Y^0 \cup Y^\Delta$); and in proving proposition 3 use has been made of that relationship. However, the assumption of inclusion is not necessary to the proof: outside a neighbourhood of the equilibrium production of period 0, any amount of technical regress or amnesia can be allowed; in short, only (18) is needed.*

Figure 3, which is based on the assumptions that there are just two produced goods, both consumable, and that primary factors are not consumable and therefore are inelastically supplied, establishes the plausibility of that assertion. The upper boundary of the aggregate production set of period 0 is represented by the curve ABC; the upper boundary of the alternative production set for period 1 is represented by A′B′C′; and the period 0 (alternative period 1) equilibrium is represented by point B (point B′), where the Scitovsky indifference curve SS (S′S′) forms a tangent with ABC (A′B′C′). Since SS and S′S′ cannot intersect, B′ must lie between D and E.

Remark 2. *In the GMG-compensated equilibrium of period 1, some individuals are better off, and none is worse off, than in the equilibrium of period 0. However, without more restrictive assumptions about preferences, or redistribution beyond that implicit in GMG compensation, there is no assurance that every individual, or even a majority of individuals, is better off in the GMG-compensated equilibrium. Thus GMG compensation alone does not ensure that a majority would be in favour of accepting the additional technical possibilities.*

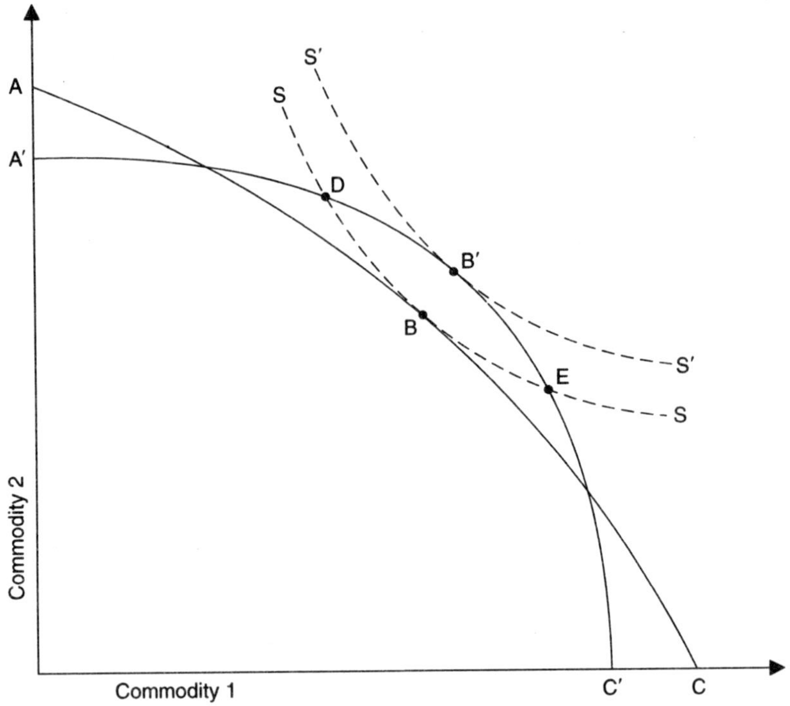

Figure 3

To ensure that **all** individuals are better off in the compensated equilibrium, it suffices that the government engage in lumpsum redistribution of the type dubbed 'sagacious' by Grandmont and McFadden (1972). The latter may be financed from the profit, $\max p^1 Y^\Delta$. To verify that the profit is positive, notice that there exists $\delta > 0$ such that $y^0 + \delta(1, 1, \ldots, 1) \equiv (y^0 + y^\delta) \in Y^\Delta$ and that, for any $p^1 \in \mathscr{P}$,

$$\begin{aligned} \max p^1 Y^\Delta &\geqslant p^1 \cdot y^\delta \\ &= \delta(p_1^1 + p_2^1 + \ldots + p_H^1) \\ &= \delta. \end{aligned}$$

Alternatively, by restricting preferences and production sets, we can ensure that no individual is able to predict that $p^1 = p^0$ or that $p^1 \neq p^0$ and, therefore, that all individuals will be in favour of accepting the additional technical possibilities. For example, attention might be restricted to smooth economies in which (i) the preferences of each individual i are representable by a smooth utility function u_i with strictly positive first derivatives and a strictly quasi-concave bordered Hessian

$$\begin{bmatrix} \partial^2 u_i/\partial x_{ij}\partial x_{ik} & \partial u_i/\partial x_{ij} \\ \partial u_i/\partial x_{ik} & 0 \end{bmatrix}$$

and in which (ii) for each firm j, the relative interior of the set of efficient production points, say

$$(Y_j \cup Y_j^{\Delta})_{\text{eff}},$$

is an open smooth surface embedded in R^H with Gaussian curvature everywhere non-zero; see Balasko (1988: 45–8, 202). This specification rules out the possibility that Y^{Δ} contains a linear (Ricardian) facet which might be decisive in determining p^1. Moreover, no individual knows the preferences of other individuals; hence no individual can predict that $p^1 = p^0$ or that $p^1 \neq p^0$. However, no individual is worse off if $p^1 = p^0$ and, in view of (i) above, all

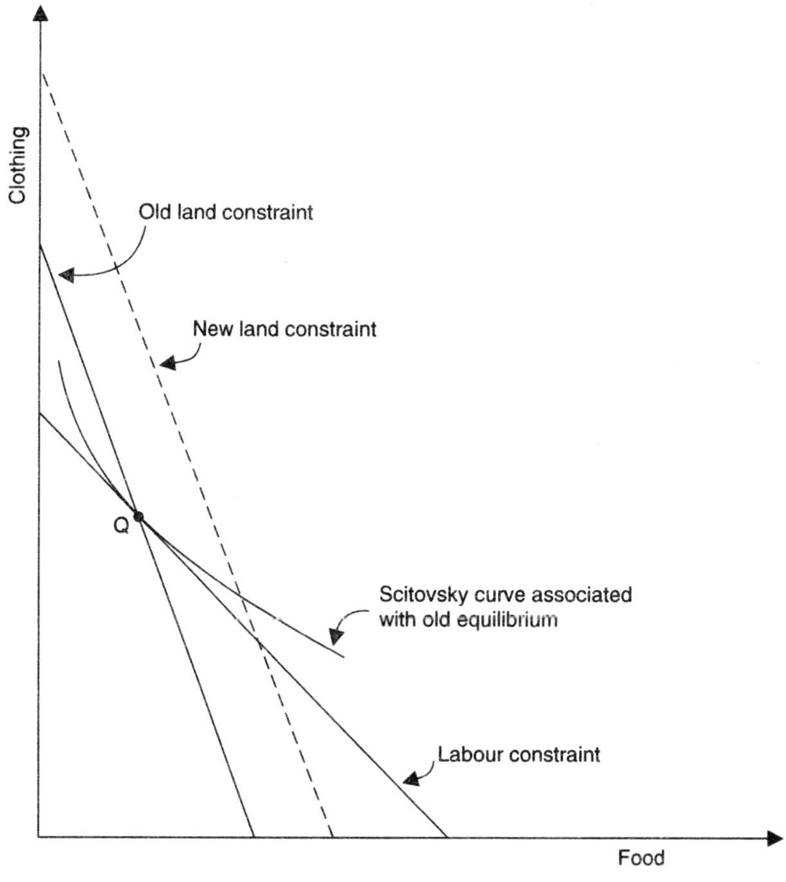

Figure 4

individuals are better off if $p^1 \neq p^0$. It follows that all individuals will be in favour of accepting the additional technical possibilities. It is worth emphasizing that the foregoing argument does not require that individuals assess the likelihood that $p^1 = p^0$. Finally, the assumption of smoothness ((i) and (ii)) is sufficient but not necessary; an alternative sufficient condition consists of (i) and the strict convexity of $Y^0 \cup Y^\Delta$.

Remark 3. *Suppose that y^0 is in $Y^0 \cup Y^\Delta$ but not in the interior of $Y^0 \cup Y^\Delta$. Then it is not generally true that the GMG-compensated equilibrium of period 1 is Pareto-preferred to the equilibrium of period 0. Thus in the example of Figure 4, which incorporates preferences which are smooth and of full dimensionality, there is no compensated equilibrium that is Pareto-preferred to the period 0 equilibrium at Q. In that equilibrium, land is a free good. This suggests that by imposing suitable restrictions on p^0 one might ensure that the compensated equilibrium is Pareto-preferred to the equilibrium of period 0 even when y^0 is in the boundary of $Y^0 \cup Y^\Delta$. Let H^0 denote the preferred open half-space defined by the hyperplane through y^0 with normal p^0, and let R^c denote the commodity subspace for consumables. Then the condition*

$$R^c \cap (H^0 \cap Y^\Delta) \neq \emptyset, \tag{19}$$

added to the requirement that preferences be smooth and of full dimensionality, ensures that the GMG-compensated equilibrium of period 1 is Pareto-preferred to the equilibrium of period 0. It should be noted that (18) implies (19) and that (19) is equivalent to $\max p^0 Y^\Delta > 0$.

At this point we draw the reader's attention to the appendix which contains a simple worked example. The example is designed to clarify the role and properties of GMG compensation.

2.4 An allocation mechanism

Finally, we can consider a mechanism which encompasses the social decision to accept or reject the additional production possibilities $Y_j^\Delta, j \in J$, as well as the allocation of resources subsequent to that decision. Following Hurwicz (1979) and Green and Laffont (1979), the mechanism combines a game and a quasi-game, played in sequence.

In the first stage, which is completed in period 0, each individual has a yea-or-nay choice: $d_i = 0$ or 1 for each i, with the understanding that 0 is for the status quo, that is the repetition in period 1 of the allocation of period 0, and 1 is for supply augmentation with a GMG-compensated Walrasian allocation. In the absence of a veto, the additional production possibilities are accepted. Thus the **social choice function** is

$$d = f(d_i, d_{)i(}) = \prod_{i \in I} d_i$$

where $d_{)i(} = (d_1, \ldots, d_{i-1}, d_{i+1}, \ldots, d_n)$ and where $d = 1$ means that the compensated supply augmentation is to be implemented and $d = 0$ means that the status quo is to be preserved. It is worth emphasizing that in the foregoing account it is **not** assumed that $\mathscr{E}^0$ has a unique equilibrium. However, it **is** assumed that if $d = 0$ then any realized equilibrium from period 0 will be replicated in period 1; see the assumption of subsection 2.3.

Let us pass to the second stage, which occupies period 1. If $d = 0$, the period 0 allocation is re-established, with individual i enjoying the status quo consumption x_i^0; and, if $d = 1$, individual i participates in the quasi-game defined by Hurwicz (1979: Sec. 4), in which $Y^1 = Y^0 \cup Y^\Delta$ and the GMG scheme of compensation $\sigma^{\#}$ is in force. In the latter case, the economy will reach one of the set of compensated Walrasian allocations $W(a^0, \mathscr{E}^\Delta)$, which one depending on the co-ordination provided by the market. However, for all possible i and for all possible equilibria in $W(a^0, \mathscr{E}^\Delta)$, $x_i^1 \succsim_i^1 x_i^0$ but not necessarily $x_i^0 \succsim_i^0 x_i^1$. The **outcome function** can be rendered in the form shown in Table 1.

Table 1

Choices of individual i	Choices of other individuals: $d_{)i(} = (1, 1, \ldots, 1)$	Choices of other individuals: $d_{)i(} \neq (1, 1, \ldots, 1)$
$d_i = 1$	$d = 1$ $\mathscr{E}^1 = \mathscr{E}^\Delta$ Compensation	$d = 0$ $\mathscr{E}^1 = \mathscr{E}^0$
$d_i = 0$	$d = 0$ $\mathscr{E}^1 = \mathscr{E}^0$	$d = 0$ $\mathscr{E}^1 = \mathscr{E}^0$

Suppose that $\mathscr{E}^1 = \mathscr{E}^\Delta$ and let $A(\mathscr{E}^\Delta)$ be the set of substates attainable in a GMG-compensated equilibrium, with the generic element $a^k = (t_1^k, \ldots, t_m^k; y_1^k, \ldots, y_n^k)$, $k = 1, \ldots, K \geqslant 1$.

Proposition 4. *$d = 1$ is a dominant-strategy equilibrium.*

Proof. *Let the preferences of individual i be represented by the utility function u^i. Suppose that $a^k \in A(\mathscr{E}^\Delta)$ prevails. From proposition 3,*

$$(u_i(e_i^0 + t_i^0, e_i^0 + t_i^k))_{i \in I} \geqslant (u_i(e_i^0 + t_i^0, e_i^0 + t_i^0))_{i \in I} \quad \text{for all } k.$$

From Table 1, then, $(d_i)_{i \in I} = (1, 1, \ldots, 1)$ is the dominant-strategy equilibrium, notwithstanding the fact that the value of the utility allocation cannot be known to any individual, even in a probabilistic sense. □

2.5 A generalization

In subsection 2.4 we studied an economy the population of which has the option of accepting or rejecting an increase in its productive capacity. We now modify the context by supposing that the enlarged capacity is conditional on the provision of a public or semi-public good the availability of which benefits some producers. It will be shown that our earlier analysis continues to apply.

Suppose that, to produce the public good, the authorities must choose a vector $y^- \in Y^- \subset R^H$, where the set Y^- is closed and bounded for $\leqslant$. If the public good is provided, $Y_j^1 = Y_j' = Y_j^0 \cup Y_j^\Delta$ for all $j \in J' \subset J$ while $Y_j^1 = Y_j^0$ for $j \in J \backslash J'$. Thus, if the public good is provided, $Y' \equiv \Sigma_{j \in J} Y_j'$ describes the gross productive capacity of the private sector and $Y' - Y^-$ describes the net productive capacity. If, on the other hand, the public good is not provided, $Y_j^1 = Y_j^0$ for all $j \in J$. Suppose further that the authorities know with certainty that

$$y^0 \equiv \sum_{j \in J} y_j^0 \in Y' - Y^-. \tag{20}$$

Formally, then, the community is in the same situation as in earlier subsections. (There, it was presented by nature with the option of accepting or rejecting an enlargement of its overall productive capacity; here, it is presented by nature with the option of embarking on an activity which will enlarge its net productive capacity.) Given (19), individual i will choose the strategy $d_i = 1$, and the community will produce the public good at minimum cost *ex post*

$$y^{-*} \in \arg\min p^1 Y^- \tag{21}$$

and then supplement the economy $\mathscr{E}^\Delta$ with a GMG scheme of lumpsum compensation.

3 REFORMULATION IN TERMS OF OVERLAPPING GENERATIONS

Throughout section 2 it was assumed that there are just two periods of time and that the lifetime of each individual coincides with the lifetime of the economy. However, by viewing the population as a set of partially overlapping generations it is possible to reformulate the model without these limiting features. Moreover, the introduction of overlapping generations allows us to relax the assumption that each individual has the same endowment and preferences in each period of this life; and it allows us to accommodate foreseen technical expansion without creating an incentive for compensation-seeking individuals to manipulate their pre-disturbance choices.

In each period k, $k = 0, 1, 2, \ldots, m$ individuals are born and n firms are established by them. Each individual and each firm survives for two periods. Associated with each period there are H goods. The index sets for individuals and firms are, respectively,

$$I = \{(i', k)\}_{i' = 1,\ldots, m;\ k = 0, 1, 2,\ldots} \quad \text{and} \quad J = \{(j', k)\}_{j' = 1,\ldots, n;\ k = 0, 1, 2,\ldots}.$$

A technical disturbance occurs at the end of period 1. Our overlapping-generations economy is then an array like (1). However, the following changes are needed to accommodate individuals and firms of generation 0, that is individuals $i = (i', 0)$, $i' = 1,\ldots, m$, and firms $j = (j', 0)$, $j' = 1,\ldots, n$:

$$X_{(i', 0)} \subset R_+^H, \quad \succsim_{(i', 0)} \subset R_+^H \times R_+^H, \quad e_{(i', 0)} \in R_+^H, \quad Y_{(j', 0)} \subset R^H.$$

Specifications (2)–(5) of section 2 then apply only to (i', k), $k > 0$. However, we no longer need insist that $X_i^0 = X_i^1$ in (2), that $\succsim_i^0 = \succsim_i^1$ in (3), or that $e_i^0 = e_i^1$ in (5), where superscripts 0 and 1 now denote the young (individual (i', k) during period k) and the old (individual (i', k) during period $k + 1$). Moreover, (6) must be replaced by

$$\begin{aligned} &\text{for all } j' = 1,\ldots, n,\\ &Y_{(j', 0)} = Y_{j'}^0, \quad Y_{(j', 1)} = Y_{j'}^0 \times Y_{j'}^1\\ &Y_{(j', k)} = Y_{j'}^1 \times Y_{j'}^1 \quad \text{for } k > 1\\ &Y_{j'}^0, Y_{j'}^1 \subset R^H \end{aligned} \tag{6'}$$

and, in (7) and (8), the subscript j should be replaced by j' and the set J by the set $\{1,\ldots, n\}$. Finally, we rule out indebtedness between contemporaries, as in (9) and (10); borrowing and lending across generations is, of course, incompatible with the overlapping structure of the population.

Our story starts at the beginning of period 1, when individual $i = (i', 0)$ is already old. At the end of that period a technical improvement becomes available. Depending on the public choice between $d = 0$ and $d = 1$, $Y_{j'}^1 = Y_{j'}^0$ for all j' **or** $Y_{j'}^1 = Y_{j'}^0 \cup Y_{j'}^\Delta$ for all j'. Thus we are confronted with two alternative sequence economies, each with an overlapping-generations structure and differing from each other during and after period 2. Each such economy operates like a countable sequence of one-period economies. Thus in period k, $k \geqslant 1$, all individuals $(i', k - 1)$ and (i', k) behave as if they live during that period only; they achieve a momentary equilibrium which, for period 1, resembles the equilibrium of the period 0 component economy of ERE, described by (11)–(16).[3]

The critical flow matrix is

$$a^0 \equiv [t_{(1,0)}^0,\ldots, t_{(m,0)}^0, t_{(1,1)}^0,\ldots, t_{(m,1)}^0; y_{(1,0)}^0,\ldots, y_{(n,0)}^0, y_{(1,1)}^0,\ldots, y_{(n,1)}^0]$$

where, for any j', $y_{(j', 0)} = y_{(j', 1)} \equiv y_{j'}^0$, say. Thus, in period k, $k = 2, 3,\ldots,$ GMG compensation assigns

to each individual $i = (i', k - 1)$, $\sigma_b^{\#}(p^1, i) = p^1 \cdot t^0_{(i', 0)}$
to each individual $i = (i', k)$, $\sigma_b^{\#}(p^1, i) = p^1 \cdot t^0_{(i', 1)}$
to each firm $j = (j', k - 1)$, $\sigma_j^{\#}(p^1, j) = -p^1 \cdot y^0_{j'}$
to each firm $j = (j', k)$, $\sigma_j^{\#}(p^1, j) = -p^1 \cdot y^0_{j'}$.

The self-financing property of GMG compensation (proposition 1(ii)) now takes on the special meaning of **contemporaneous** self-financing. Thus, for all $k \geqslant 2$,

$$\sum_{i'=1}^{m} \sigma_b^{\#}(p^1, (i', k-1)) + \sum_{i'=1}^{m} \sigma_b^{\#}(p^1, (i', k)) + \sum_{j'=1}^{n} \sigma_j^{\#}(p^1, (j', k-1)) + \sum_{j'=1}^{n} \sigma_j^{\#}(p^1, (j', k)) = 0.$$

Existence can be established if (c′) is replaced by the Gale–McKenzie assumption of irreducibility, in the form given it by Balasko and Shell (1980) in a context of overlapping generations. It can then be shown that, for the overlapping-generations economy, $d = 1$ is a dominant-strategy equilibrium. Moreover, this is so whether or not the expansion of production opportunities is expected, for no individual agent can profitably manipulate his or her choices in period 1, the base period for GMG compensation: no member of generation 0 has the motivation to manipulate his or her choices because the GMG scheme of compensation does not apply to that generation; nor will any member of generation 1 manipulate his or her choices because the manipulation affects only generations not yet born.

The equilibrium is not coalition proof, since generation 1 can bribe generation 0. However, one can imagine the economy growing in scale, with an unchanging list of types in each generation and with compensation based on group data, that is on generation-specific, type-specific averages. Then, as each individual recedes into insignificance, any coalition for the manipulation of choices must grow in size or lose effectiveness. One may suppose that the larger the economy the less likely is the coalition issue to arise.

4 SUMMARY AND PROSPECT

We have sought to demonstrate that lumpsum compensation of the GMG type is both more powerful and less demanding of unattainable information than any of its lumpsum or non-lumpsum competitors and, basing ourselves on that finding, we have suggested that the recent tendency to focus on non-lumpsum compensation in theoretical welfare economics should be reversed. Of greater importance, we have argued that the applicability and policy relevance of post-Paretian comparative-statical welfare economics, including the compensation principle, is confined to the highly restricted class of essentially repetitive economies and to the only slightly less restricted class of stationary economies with overlapping generations.

Throughout section 2 it was assumed that the disturbance is unexpected. The assumption was convenient for it deprived households of the incentive to manipulate their pre-disturbance choices. However, the assumption is unnecessarily strong. There is an incentive to manipulate choices only if the disturbance is foreseen with some degree of confidence and if it is known that compensation will be computed on the basis of choices made after the point of time at which the disturbance is first anticipated. For a more thorough discussion of the possibility of choice manipulation, the reader is referred to Kemp and Wan (1993: Ch. 3).[4]

Our discussion has been thoroughly traditional in its assumption that all costs of adjusting to technical change and compensation are negligible. The assumption is unrealistic. Typically, the processes of hiring and firing divert resources from their productive uses both in the expanding sector and in the contracting; see Kemp and Wan (1973). Thus it is conceivable that during the process of adjustment there will be a decline in the outputs of all final goods. In that event, GMG compensation cannot be always self-financing.

Evidently there is need of a more capacious theory. One might try to make do with present-value compensation. However, the relevant rates of time preference may be known only to the agents in question; if so, the issue of manipulation must be faced again. Moreover, in a context of overlapping generations, it is necessary to compensate individuals during their lifetimes.

An alternative approach is more promising. It begins with the recognition that costs of adjustment depend on the rate at which the disturbance takes place and that the rate of disturbance is often under the control of the authorities. It is then noted that the choice facing the community is between alternative time paths of technical change, each of them compatible with sustained GMG compensation. Of course, public choice must now be exercised not over two alternatives but over many. Can one devise sagacious redistributions or restrictions on preferences and technologies which ensure that a unanimous choice is made? This issue, and others like it, deserve further study.

APPENDIX: A NUMERICAL EXAMPLE

Consider a farm economy in which a single crop is produced in amount y_1 by means of labour and land inputs $-y_2$ and $-y_3$, respectively. For convenience only, it is assumed that there is a single price-taking worker, a single price-taking landlord, and a single farm. The farm is owned by the landlord. The commodity endowment of the worker is

$$e_w = (e_{w1}, e_{w2}, e_{w3}) = (0, 8/27, 0)$$

and that of the landlord is

$$e_\ell = (e_{\ell 1}, e_{\ell 2}, e_{\ell 3}) = (0, 0, 8/27).$$

The production function is $y_1 = (-y_2)^{2/3}(-y_3)^{1/3}$ before the disturbance and $y_1 = (-y_2)^{1/3}(-y_3)^{1/3}$ after the disturbance, where the disturbance is the adoption of a technical improvement which reduces the dependence of output on labour. Finally, the common utility index is $u = y$.

In the absence of compensation, the competitive equilibrium quantities, before and after the disturbance, are as shown in Table A1. Thus

Table A1: Compensation not paid

	Before disturbance	*After disturbance*	*Gain*
Output	8/27	4/9	
Share of labour	2/3	1/3	
Share of land	1/3	1/3	
Share of profit	0	1/3	
Worker's share	2/3	1/3	
Landlord's share	1/3	2/3	
Worker's income	16/81	4/27	−4/81
Landlord's income	8/81	8/27	+16/81

$$t_w^0 = (16/81, -8/27, 0)$$

$$t_l^0 = (8/81, 0, -8/27)$$

$$y^0 = (8/27, -8/27, -8/27).$$

Computed at the post-disturbance, cum-compensation equilibrium prices

$$p^1 = (1, 1/2, 1/2),$$

the GMG transfer to the worker is

$$(16/81, -8/27, 0) \cdot (1, 1/2, 1/2) = 4/81$$

and the GMG transfer to the landlord is

$$(8/81, 0, -8/27) \cdot (1, 1/2, 1/2) = -4/81.$$

The net post-disturbance income of the worker, after compensation, is therefore

$$(4/27) + (4/81) = 16/81,$$

which is equal to the pre-disturbance income; and the net post-disturbance income of the landlord, after compensation, is

$$(8/27) - (4/81) = 20/81,$$

which exceeds the pre-disturbance income of 8/81.

NOTES

* We recall with pleasure the stimulation provided by a series of articles, on post-Paretian welfare economies and the compensation principle in particular, written in the 1970s by John Chipman, usually in collaboration with James Moore. We have in mind Chipman and Moore (1971, 1972, 1973, 1978) and Chipman (1976).

For helpful comments we are grateful to Jürgen Eichberger and Kar-yiu Wong, and to participants in the conference in honour of John Chipman, held at the University of Minnesota, 25 and 26 September 1992.

1 After the presentation of our paper in Minneapolis, we came across Hammond and Sempere (1992). In their carefully argued paper, Hammond and Sempere modify the DN scheme of compensation by introducing poll subsidies which mop up excess supplies of goods and render the Weymark condition unnecessary. (In ancient correspondence with the authors, Bill Ethier proposed a similar modification of the DN scheme.) However, the modified scheme involves the freezing of consumer prices by means of commodity taxes of some specific structure, and this requires unattainable global information about preferences. If, lacking such information, the authorities were to impose taxes which fail to freeze prices, they would find themselves locked into a sequential process of tinkering with real prices (not just the price quotations of an auctioneer). In contrast, GMG compensation never requires the authorities to trade out of equilibrium.

2 Alternatively, it might have been shown that if the endowments of some households unexpectedly expand, and that of no household contracts, then GMG compensation is feasible.

3 A formal definition of a competitive equilibrium can be obtained by extending the definition of Balasko and Shell (1980: 285) to cover production.

4 Households might misrepresent their actual choices, whether or not those choices have been manipulated. However, the possibility of false reporting is not peculiar to lumpsum compensation; it dogs all branches of economic policy. Moreover, GMG compensation is partially protected against false reporting by the 'double-entry' property of transactions: each transaction involves at least two parties with opposing interests in overstating or understating the extent of the transaction.

REFERENCES

Atkinson, A. B. and Stiglitz, J. E. (1980) *Lectures on Public Economics*, New York: McGraw-Hill.

Balasko, Y. (1988) *Foundations of the Theory of General Equilibrium*, Boston: Academic Press.

Balasko, Y. and Shell, K. (1980) 'The overlapping-generations model, I: The case of pure exchange without money', *Journal of Economic Theory* 23: 281–306.

Chipman, J. S. (1976) 'The Paretian heritage', *Revue européennes de sciences sociales et Cahiers Vilfredo Pareto* 14: 65–71.

Chipman, J. S. and Moore, J. C. (1971) 'The compensation principle in welfare economics', in A. M. Zarley (ed.) *Papers in Quantitative Economics*, Vol. 1, pp. 1–77, Lawrence, Manhattan and Wichita, Kansas: The University Press of Kansas.

Chipman, J. S. and Moore, J. C. (1972) 'Social utility and the gains from trade', *Journal of International Economics* 2: 157–72.

Chipman, J. S. and Moore, J. G. (1973) 'Aggregate demand, real national income, and the compensation principle', *International Economic Review* 14: 153–81.

Chipman, J. S. and Moore, J. C. (1978) 'The new welfare economics, 1939–1974', *International Economic Review*, 19: 547–84.

Debreu, G. (1959) *Theory of Value*, New York: Wiley.

Diamond, P. A. and Mirrlees, J. A. (1971) 'Optimal taxation and public production, I and II', *American Economic Review* 61: 8–27 and 261–78.

Dixit, A. K. and Norman, V. D. (1980) *Theory of International Trade*, Cambridge: Cambridge University Press.

Grandmont, J. M. and McFadden, D. (1972) 'A technical note on classical gains from trade', *Journal of International Economics* 2: 109–25.

Green, J. R. and Laffont, J.-J. (1979) *Incentives in Public Decision-Making*, Amsterdam: North-Holland.

Grinols, E. L. (1981) 'An extension of the Kemp-Wan theorem on the formation of customs unions', *Journal of International Economics* 11: 259–66.

Grinols, E. L. (1984) 'A thorn in the lion's paw: Has Britain paid too much for common market membership?', *Journal of International Economics* 16: 217–93.

Hammond, P. J. and Sempere, J. (1992) 'Limits to the potential gains from market integration and other supply-side policies', European University Institute, Florence, Working Paper ECO 92/79.

Hurwicz, L. (1979) 'On allocations attainable through Nash equilibria', *Journal of Economic Theory* 21: 140–65.

Kemp, M. C. and Wan, H. Y., Jr (1972) 'The gains from free trade', *International Economic Review* 13: 509–22.

Kemp, M. C. and Wan, H.Y., Jr (1973) 'Hysteresis of long-run equilibrium from realistic adjustment costs', in G. Horwich and P. A. Samuelson (eds) *Trade, Stability and Macroeconomics. Essays in Honor of Lloyd A. Metzler*, pp. 221–42, New York: Academic Press.

Kemp, M. C. and Wan, H. Y., Jr (1993) *The Welfare Economics of International Trade*, London: Harwood Academic.

Kemp, M. C. and Wong, K.-Y. (1992) 'The gains from trade when markets are possibly incomplete', University of Washington, this volume.

Koopmans, T. C. (1957) *Three Essays on the State of Economic Science*, New York: McGraw-Hill.

Vanek, J. (1965) *General Equilibrium of International Discrimination*, Cambridge, MA: Harvard University Press.

Weymark, J. A. (1979) 'A reconciliation of recent results in optimal taxation theory', *Journal of Public Economics* 12: 171–89.

25

LUMPSUM COMPENSATION IN A CONTEXT OF INCOMPLETE MARKETS

1 INTRODUCTION

In an earlier essay (Kemp and Wan, 1992) it was shown that if the production sets of some firms unexpectedly expand and if those of all other firms remain unchanged then it is possible by means of Grandmont–McFadden–Grinols (GMG) lumpsum compensation[1] to achieve a strict Pareto improvement. The twin of this theorem states that if the endowment vectors of some households unexpectedly expand and if those of all other households remain unchanged then it is possible by means of GMG compensation to achieve a strict improvement; and it can be established by means of a similar argument. Together, the two theorems form the centrepiece of Paretian comparative-statical welfare economics.

The demonstration by Kemp and Wan relied on the assumption that there is a complete set of markets. However, it is known that, when markets are incomplete, competitive equilibria may not exist, even under assumptions which, in all other respects, coincide with those of Arrow and Debreu; and it is also known that, even when equilibria do exist, they are generally constrained suboptimal (Hart, 1975; Geanakoplos and Polemarchakis, 1986). The latter observation suggests that the two propositions might not survive the absence of markets.

In the present essay it is argued that the propositions remain valid even when there is an incomplete set of securities markets. We again focus on the first of the two propositions.

In the absence of a complete set of securities markets the proper objectives of a firm are, in general, unclear. If the production set of the firm satisfies a spanning condition, there can be found a set of weights, one for each state of nature, such that the firm's shareholders can unanimously agree to maximize expected profit defined in terms of those weights; see Magill and Shafer (1991: Section 4) and Geanakoplos *et al.* (1990). However, the spanning condition is restrictive. In the present analysis, therefore, it is assumed that production is carried on by households; that is, attention is confined to cottage industry. Given that assumption, production decisions are by-products of expected utility maximization. One might then wish to say that each household owns its own firm or firms. However, it must be understood that, generally, such firms do not maximize the present values of their cash flows. Moreover, there is no reason why two or more identical households should not combine their productive activities, thus leaving the number of firms indeterminate.

2 GENERAL EQUILIBRIUM WITH MISSING MARKETS

The economy is assumed to extend through $T+1$ periods of time, $T \geqslant 1$, beginning with period 0. The values of variables in period 0 are known with certainty, but which of several mutually exclusive states of nature occurs in period t, $0 < t \leqslant T$, is not known until period t. For simplicity, it is assumed that there is the same number of states, S, in each period. Let us define $\mathbf{S} = (1, \ldots, S)$, $\mathbf{T}^a = (0, 1, \ldots, T)$, $\mathbf{T}^b = (0, 1, \ldots, T-1)$, $\mathbf{T}^c = (1, \ldots, T)$ and $\mathbf{T}^d = (1, \ldots, T-1)$.

In each period and in each state of nature, N goods, $N \geqslant 2$, are bought and sold. The price of the nth good in period 0 (in period t when state s occurs) is denoted by $p_{0,n}$ (by $p_{ts,n}$); and the vector of goods prices in period 0 (in period t when state s occurs) is denoted by $\mathbf{p}_0 \in R_+^N$ (by $\mathbf{p}_{ts} \in R_+^N$); and $\mathbf{p}_t = \{\mathbf{p}_{ts}\}$, $\mathbf{p} = (\mathbf{p}_0, \mathbf{p}_1, \ldots, \mathbf{p}_T)$.

There are M one-period securities which are bought and sold in each period t, $t \in \mathbf{T}^b$. In period t and state s, security m delivers an amount $a_s^m \geqslant 0$ of good 1, the *numéraire*; in at least one state a_s^m is positive. The monetary payment by security m in period t and state s is therefore $p_{ts,1} a_s^m \geqslant 0$.[2] Let us define $\mathbf{a}_s = \{a_s^m\}$ and the $S \times M$ matrix $\mathbf{A} = \{\mathbf{a}_s\}$. It is assumed without loss that $\mathbf{A}$ has full column rank, implying that $S \geqslant M$. (When $S = M$ markets are complete.)

The price of the mth security in period 0 (in period t and state s) is denoted by $r_{0,m}$ ($r_{ts,m}$); the vector of security prices is denoted by $\mathbf{r}_0 \in R_+^M$ ($\mathbf{r}_{ts} \in R_+^M$); and we define $\mathbf{r}_t = \{\mathbf{r}_{ts}\}$ and $\mathbf{r} = (\mathbf{r}_0, \mathbf{r}_1, \ldots, \mathbf{r}_{T-1})$.

On the assumptions that each security delivers a positive amount in at least one state and that $\mathbf{A}$ has full column rank, Geanakoplos and Polemarchakis (1986) were able to show that there exists a closed, convex cone $\Theta = \{\mathbf{r}_t \in R_{++}^M: \mathbf{r}_t = \mathbf{A}'\mathbf{v}, \mathbf{v} \in R_{+}^S\}$. The interior of Θ, denoted by Θ^o, is the set of non-arbitrage security prices. It is clear that, in equilibrium, $\mathbf{r}_t \in \Theta^o$.

There are I households. Let us define the set of households $\mathbf{I} = (1, \ldots, I)$. The ith household is endowed with commodity vectors $\mathbf{w}_0^i$, $\mathbf{w}_{ts}^i \in R_+^N$ in period 0 and in period t if state s occurs, respectively. Moreover, the ith household receives from the government lumpsum transfers $b_0^i \in R$ in period 0, $b_{1s}^i \in R$ in period 1 if state s occurs, and $b_{tss'}^i \in R$ in period t, $t \in \mathbf{T}^c$, if states s and s' occur in periods t and $t-1$, respectively. Let us define $\mathbf{b}^i = (b_0^i, b_{11}^i, \ldots, b_{1S}^i, b_{211}^i, \ldots, b_{TSS}^i)$.

Each household engages in production, making use both of its own and of purchased resources. Let $\mathbf{y}_0^i$, $\mathbf{y}_{ts}^i \in R^N$ be the net output vectors of the ith household in period 0 and in period t if state s occurs, respectively; and let $\mathbf{y}_t^i = \{\mathbf{y}_{ts}^i\}$, $\mathbf{y}^i = (\mathbf{y}_0^i, \mathbf{y}_1^i, \ldots, \mathbf{y}_T^i)$. The choice of net outputs is subject to the production constraint

$$\mathbf{y}^i \in \mathbf{Y}^i, \tag{1}$$

where $\mathbf{Y}^i$ is a closed and convex subset of $R^{N(1+ST)}$. Irreversibility and free disposal are assumed.

Turning to household expenditure, let $\mathbf{x}_0^i$, $\mathbf{x}_{ts}^i \in R_+^N$ denote the consumption vectors of the ith household in period 0 and in period t if state s occurs, respectively; and let $\mathbf{z}_0^i$, $\mathbf{z}_{ts}^i \in R^M$ denote the vectors of securities purchased in period 0 and in period t if state s occurs, respectively. Let $\mathbf{x}_t^i = \{\mathbf{x}_{ts}^i\}$, $\mathbf{x}^i = (\mathbf{x}_0^i, \mathbf{x}_1^i, \ldots, \mathbf{x}_T^i)$, $\mathbf{z}_t^i = \{\mathbf{z}_{ts}^i\}$, $\mathbf{z}^i = (\mathbf{z}_0^i, \mathbf{z}_1^i, \ldots, \mathbf{z}_{T-1}^i)$. Then the ith household is subject to the budget constraints

$$\mathbf{p}_0 \cdot (\mathbf{x}_0^i - \mathbf{y}_0^i) + \mathbf{r}_0 \cdot \mathbf{z}_0^i \leqslant \mathbf{p}_0 \cdot \mathbf{w}_0^i + b_0^i \tag{2a}$$

$$\mathbf{p}_{1s} \cdot (\mathbf{x}_{1s}^i - \mathbf{y}_{1s}^i) + \mathbf{r}_{1s} \cdot \mathbf{z}_{1s}^i \leqslant \mathbf{p}_{1s} \cdot \mathbf{w}_{1s}^i + p_{1s,1}\mathbf{a}_s \cdot \mathbf{z}_0^i + b_{1s}^i \tag{2b}$$

$$\mathbf{p}_{ts} \cdot (\mathbf{x}_{ts}^i - \mathbf{y}_{ts}^i) + \mathbf{r}_{ts} \cdot \mathbf{z}_{ts}^i \leqslant \mathbf{p}_{ts} \cdot \mathbf{w}_{ts}^i + p_{ts,1}\mathbf{a}_s \cdot \mathbf{z}_{t-1,s'}^i + b_{tss'}^i \tag{2c}$$

$$t \in \mathbf{T}^d, \quad s, s' \in \mathbf{S}.$$

It is assumed that the preferences of the ith household can be represented by a utility function $U^i(\mathbf{x}^i)$ which is increasing, continuous and concave in all goods and strictly increasing in the *numéraire*. Endowed with perfect conditional foresight, the household chooses $(\mathbf{x}^i, \mathbf{y}^i, \mathbf{z}^i)$ to maximize its utility subject to (1) and (2).

Let us further define $\mathbf{x}_0 = \Sigma_i \mathbf{x}_0^i$, $\mathbf{x}_{ts} = \Sigma_i \mathbf{x}_{ts}^i$, $\mathbf{w}_0 = \Sigma_i \mathbf{w}_0^i$, $\mathbf{w}_{ts} = \Sigma_i \mathbf{w}_{ts}^i$, $\mathbf{y}_0 = \Sigma_i \mathbf{y}_0^i$, $\mathbf{y}_{ts} = \Sigma_i \mathbf{y}_{ts}^i$, $\mathbf{x} = \Sigma_i \mathbf{x}^i$, $\mathbf{y} = \Sigma_i \mathbf{y}^i$, $\mathbf{w} = \Sigma_i \mathbf{w}^i$ and $\mathbf{z} = \Sigma_i \mathbf{z}^i$.

That completes our description of the economy.

A competitive equilibrium is said to exist if

(1) all households are maximizing their expected utility subject to their production and budget constraints (1) and (2);
(2) $\mathbf{x}_t \leqslant \mathbf{y}_t + \mathbf{w}_t$ for all $t \in \mathbf{T}^a$; and
(3) $\Sigma_i \mathbf{z}_t^i \leqslant 0$ for all $t \in \mathbf{T}^b$.

Proposition 1. *The present model has a competitive equilibrium if* $\Sigma_i b_0^i = \Sigma_i b_{ts}^i = 0$ *for all* $t \in \mathbf{T}^c$ *and* $s \in \mathbf{S}$.

Proposition 1, which is proved by Kemp and Wong (1992), does not rule out the possibility that some equilibrium security prices are zero. However, the assumption that each security delivers a positive amount of the *numéraire* in some state combines with the assumption of non-satiation of preferences to ensure that the equilibrium prices of all securities are positive.

3 TECHNICAL IMPROVEMENTS AND COMPENSATING TRANSFERS

We now consider the effect on well-being of improvements in the technology of some firms. We contrast two situations. In the first situation, the production set of the ith household is $\hat{\mathbf{Y}}^i$, $i \in \mathbf{I}$; and in the second situation the production set of the ith household is

$$\mathbf{Y}^i = \hat{\mathbf{Y}}^i \cup \mathbf{Y}^{\Delta i}, \quad i \in \mathbf{I}, \tag{3}$$

where $\mathbf{Y}^{\Delta i}$ is the set of newly feasible production vectors, so that

$$\hat{\mathbf{Y}}^i \cap \mathbf{Y}^{\Delta i} = \emptyset, \quad i \in \mathbf{I}. \tag{4a}$$

To avoid triviality it is assumed that

$$\mathbf{Y}^{\Delta i} \neq \emptyset \quad \text{for some } i \in \mathbf{I}. \tag{4b}$$

For each i, $\mathbf{Y}^i$ satisfies the same restrictions as $\hat{\mathbf{Y}}^i$. Hence proposition 1 applies to both situations.

Henceforth, the values of all variables in the first situation will be distinguished by circumflexes.

For simplicity only, it is assumed that in the first or initial situation there are no transfers, so that $\hat{b}_0^i = \hat{b}_{ts}^i = 0$ for all $i \in \mathbf{I}$, $t \in \mathbf{T}^c$ and $s \in \mathbf{S}$. In the second or final situation, the ith household receives from the government

$$b_0^i = \mathbf{p}_0 \cdot (\hat{\mathbf{x}}_0^i - \hat{\mathbf{y}}_0^i - \mathbf{w}_0^i) + \mathbf{r}_0 \cdot \hat{\mathbf{z}}_0^i \tag{5a}$$

$$b_{1s}^i = \mathbf{p}_{1s} \cdot (\hat{\mathbf{x}}_{1s}^i - \hat{\mathbf{y}}_{1s}^i - \mathbf{w}_{1s}^i) + \mathbf{r}_{1s} \cdot \hat{\mathbf{z}}_{1s}^i - p_{1s,1} \mathbf{a}_s \cdot \hat{\mathbf{z}}_0^i \tag{5b}$$

$$b_{tss'}^i = \mathbf{p}_{ts} \cdot (\hat{\mathbf{x}}_{ts}^i - \hat{\mathbf{y}}_{ts}^i - \mathbf{w}_{ts}^i) + \mathbf{r}_{ts} \cdot \mathbf{z}_{ts}^i - p_{ts,1} \mathbf{a}_s \cdot \mathbf{z}_{(t-1)s'}^i \tag{5c}$$

$$b_{Tss'}^i = \mathbf{p}_{Ts} \cdot (\hat{\mathbf{x}}_{Ts}^i - \hat{\mathbf{y}}_{Ts}^i - \mathbf{w}_{Ts}^i) - p_{Ts,1} \mathbf{a}_s \cdot \mathbf{z}_{(T-1)s'}^i\,. \tag{5d}$$

This scheme of compensation is a special case of scheme (6) in Kemp and Wong (1992). We therefore may avail ourselves of their lemma 1.

Lemma 1 (Kemp and Wong). *The scheme of lumpsum transfers (5) implies a zero government deficit and therefore is feasible.*

By virtue of proposition 1 and lemma 1 there exists a competitive equilibrium in each situation.

4 MAIN PROPOSITION

Let us say that the final situation weakly Pareto-dominates the initial situation if, under the scheme of lumpsum transfers (5), no household is worse off in the final situation; and that the final situation Pareto-dominates the initial situation if, under the same scheme of transfers, some households are better off, and none worse off, in the final situation.

Proposition 2. *Given the scheme of lumpsum transfers (5), the final situation Pareto-dominates the initial situation.*

Proof. *It is easy to verify, by substitution from (5) into (2), that the final situation weakly Pareto-dominates the initial situation. It then follows from revealed preference that, if consumption and/or production substitution takes place in at least one household, the final situation Pareto-dominates the initial situation. The proof is completed by the observation that, as an implication of (3) and (4), production substitution, and therefore consumption substitution, must take place in at least one household.* □

That completes our formal presentation. It is therefore a suitable place for a warning sign: our central welfare statement, embodied in proposition 2, is in terms of **prospective** improvements, not in terms of **realized** improvements. The household utility functions $U^i(\mathbf{x}^i)$ have meaning only in period 0, before the states of the world in periods $1,\ldots, T$ are known. After the states are known, utility depends only on consumption planned for the realized states, and that may be less in the final situation (with compensation) than it would have been in the initial situation. The scheme of compensation (5) allows each household to choose its cum-improvement final-situation consumption at least as great as its pre-improvement initial-situation consumption; but it does not require it to do so. Of course, this remark applies whether or not securities markets are complete.

5 FINAL REMARKS

When markets are incomplete, the spreading of risks is suboptimal. What we have shown, in effect, is that the scheme of lumpsum transfers described in section 4 is such that there remains enough risk spreading to ensure the gainfulness of a technical improvement. Can one claim more? Does that scheme of transfers in fact eliminate **all** distortions associated with the incompleteness of markets and generate the same allocation of risks as a complete complement of markets? If that conjecture were valid proposition 2 would be uninteresting, for it would simply restate its complete-markets counterpart. In fact, the conjecture is incorrect. Transfers are tied to the equilibrium quantities of the initial situation and therefore cannot be freely chosen to achieve Pareto optimality.

This does not mean that there is no scheme of lumpsum compensation which eliminates all distortions associated with the incompleteness of markets. However, any such scheme must be based on the trades of individuals in a **complete-markets** initial equilibrium. Such trades are not observable, even ideally. The remarkable thing about proposition 2 is that a scheme of compensation based solely on the trades of the pre-disturbance equilibrium, and not relying in the least on knowledge of preferences or technologies, has been shown to be efficacious.

NOTES

1 GMG lumpsum compensation ensures that pre-disturbance consumption baskets remain available at post-disturbance prices.

2 As noted by Geanakoplos and Polemarchakis (1986: 71, 73–9), the assumption that each security delivers a non-negative amount of a **single** commodity (the *numéraire*) in all states excludes Hart's (1975) example of non-existence. The assumption that each security delivers a non-negative amount of the *numéraire* in all states and a positive amount of the *numéraire* in at least one state greatly simplifies the analysis. With preferences which are non-satiated in the *numéraire*, and with arbitrage, the prices of the securities are positive. However, the assumption is stronger than is needed. An alternative assumption is that the expected payment by each security is positive. A more general analysis, which relies on neither of these assumptions, has been provided by Geanakoplos and Polemarchakis (1986).

REFERENCES

Geanakoplos, J. and Polemarchakis, H. (1986) 'Existence, regularity, and constrained suboptimality of competitive allocations when markets are incomplete', in W. Heller, R. Starr and D. Starrett (eds) *Essays in Honor of Kenneth Arrow*, Vol. 3, pp. 65–95, Cambridge: Cambridge University Press.

Geanakoplos, J., Magill, M. Quinzii, M. and Drèze, J. (1990) 'Generic inefficiency of stock market equilibrium when markets are incomplete', *Journal of Mathematical Economics* 19: 113–51.

Hart, O.D. (1975) 'On the optimality of equilibrium when the market structure is incomplete', *Journal of Economic Theory* 11: 418–43.

Kemp, M. C. and Wan, H. Y., Jr (1992) 'On lumpsum compensation', University of New South Wales, this volume.

Kemp, M. C. and Wong, K.-Y. (1992) 'The gains from trade when markets are possibly incomplete', University of Washington, this volume.

Magill, M. and Shafer, W. (1991) 'Incomplete markets', in W. Hildenbrand and H. Sonnenschein (eds) *Handbook of Mathematical Economics*, Vol. IV, pp. 1524–614, Amsterdam: North-Holland.

26

LUMPSUM COMPENSATION IN A CONTEXT OF OVERLAPPING GENERATIONS

1 INTRODUCTION

In earlier papers (Kemp and Wan, 1992, 1993a) it was shown that if the production sets of some firms unexpectedly expand and if those of all other firms remain unchanged then it is possible by means of Grandmont–McFadden–Grinols (GMG) lumpsum compensation[1] to achieve a strict Pareto improvement. The twin of this theorem states that if the endowment vectors of some households unexpectedly expand and if those of all other households remain unchanged then it is possible by means of GMG compensation to achieve a strict improvement; and it can be established by means of a similar argument. Together, the two theorems form the core of Paretian comparative-statical welfare economics.

Those demonstrations relied on assumptions of the Arrow–Debreu–McKenzie type, although the possibility of incomplete markets was admitted. The economies under study were finite. Whether the propositions survive the recognition that economies go on for ever, with populations composed of overlapping generations of mortal individuals, was not considered. However, popular models of economies with overlapping generations are characterized by Pareto-suboptimal competitive equilibria; and it is well known that, for economies with distortions, an expansion of endowments or production sets might leave all households worse off. These possibilities raise questions about the robustness of each of the two core welfare propositions listed above.

The purpose of this essay is to show that, for a broad class of economies with overlapping generations, the two propositions remain valid. As in the Kemp–Wan papers, the focus will be on the first of the two propositions.

2 GENERAL EQUILIBRIUM WITH OVERLAPPING GENERATIONS

Time is discrete. In every period of time $t \in \mathbf{N}$, where $\mathbf{N}$ is the set of all positive integers, there is a constant finite number $N \geqslant 2$ of completely perishable goods. These are bought and sold in spot markets in each period.

The price of good n in period t is denoted by p_n^t; and the vector of goods prices in period t is denoted by $p^t \in \mathbf{R}_+^N$. The set of all possible price sequences is then $\mathbf{P} = \{p: p = (p^1, p^2, \ldots) \in \times_{t=1}^{\infty} \mathbf{R}_+^N\}$.

At the beginning of any period t, $t \in \mathbf{N}$, a generation of finitely many households $\mathbf{H}_t$ appears; let us define $\mathbf{H}_t = \{1, \ldots, H_t\}$. Each member of each generation lives for two periods. In addition, therefore, there is a single generation $\mathbf{H}_0$ that survives into period 1. Thus the set of all households is $\mathbf{H} = \cup_{t \in \mathbf{N}_0} \mathbf{H}_t$, where $\mathbf{N}_0$ is the set of non-negative integers. Sometimes reference will be made to the subset $\mathbf{H}_{\leq T} = \cup_{t=0}^{t=T} \mathbf{H}_t$, where $T \in \mathbf{N}$.

Household h chooses its lifetime consumption vector x_h from its consumption set $\mathbf{X}_h$, which is simply the non-negative orthant of the relevant finite-dimensional Euclidean space. Specifically,

$$x_h = (x_h^t, x_h^{t+1}) \in \mathbf{X}_h = \mathbf{R}_+^{2N} \quad \text{for } h \in \mathbf{H} \backslash \mathbf{H}_0$$

$$x_h = x_h^1 \in \mathbf{X}_h = \mathbf{R}_+^N \quad \text{for } h \in \mathbf{H}_0$$

where the superscripts refer to the time period in which consumption takes place. Whenever it is convenient, we also denote by x_h the sequence $(0, \ldots, x_h, 0, \ldots)$. Throughout the essay, and without further mention, this convention will be applied to other symbols too. The preferences of household h are represented by a complete, transitive and reflexive binary relation $\succcurlyeq_h$ on $\mathbf{X}_h$.

Each generation $\mathbf{H}_t$, $t \in \mathbf{N}$, establishes a finite set of firms $\mathbf{F}_t$. The set $\mathbf{F}_t$ is taken as given, as is the ownership of firms. Each firm survives for two periods. In addition, during period 1 there is a set $\mathbf{F}_0$ of old firms owned by members of $\mathbf{H}_0$. The set of all firms is $\mathbf{F} = \cup_{t \in \mathbf{N}_0} \mathbf{F}_t$. Sometimes reference will be made to the subset $\mathbf{F}_{\leq T} = \cup_{t=0}^{t=T} \mathbf{F}_t$. Firm $f \in \mathbf{F}$ chooses a profit-maximizing point y_f in its production set $\mathbf{Y}_f$. In particular,

$$y_f = (y_f^t, y_f^{t+1}) \in \mathbf{Y}_f \subset \mathbf{R}^{2N} \quad \text{for } f \in \mathbf{F} \backslash \mathbf{F}_0$$

$$y_f = y_f^1 \in \mathbf{Y}_f \subset \mathbf{R}^N \quad \text{for } f \in \mathbf{F}_0.$$

The social production possibility set is $\mathbf{Y} = \Sigma_{f \in \mathbf{F}} \mathbf{Y}_f$.

Household $h \in \mathbf{H}_t$ is endowed with a vector of resources $e_h = (e_h^t, e_h^{t+1}) \in \mathbf{X}_h$. Included in e_h may be labour of several types. Any profits made by firms $f \in \mathbf{F}_t$ are completely distributed among the households $h \in \mathbf{H}_t$ according to the given shares $\theta_{hf} \geq 0$ $(\Sigma_{h \in \mathbf{H}_t} \theta_{hf} = 1)$.

Later we shall want to introduce a particular scheme of lumpsum compensatory transfers. Let b_h be the vector of transfers to household h, with positive elements for quantities received, negative elements for quantities taken. Then

$$b_h = (b_h^t, b_h^{t+1}) \in \mathbf{R}^{2N} \quad \text{for } h \in \mathbf{H}_t, \ t \in \mathbf{N}$$

$$b_h = b_h^1 \in \mathbf{R}^N \quad \text{for } h \in \mathbf{H}_0.$$

A scheme of compensatory lumpsum transfers is **balanced** if

$$\sum_{h \in \mathbf{H}_{t-1} \cup \mathbf{H}_t} b_h^t = 0.$$

Given prices p and the profit-maximizing production plans $(y_f)_{f \in \mathbf{F}}$, the wealth of household h is then

$$w_h(p) = p \cdot e_h + \sum_{f \in \mathbf{F}} \theta_{hf} p \cdot y_f + p \cdot b_h. \tag{1}$$

This provides an upper bound for the household's expenditure on consumption. Thus the household's budget set is

$$B_h(p) = \{x \in \mathbf{X}_h : p \cdot x_h \leqslant w_h(p)\}.$$

The aggregate resource vector of period t is $e^t = \Sigma_{h \in \mathbf{H}_{t-1} \cup \mathbf{H}_t} e_h^t$; similarly, $x^t = \Sigma_{h \in \mathbf{H}_{t-1} \cup \mathbf{H}_t} x_h^t$ and $y^t = \Sigma_{f \in \mathbf{F}_{t-1} \cup \mathbf{F}_t} y_f^t$ denote the aggregate consumption and production vectors of period t. Resources aggregated to period T are denoted by $e_{\leqslant T} = \Sigma_{h \in \mathbf{H}_{\leqslant T}} e_h$. This notation is extended to other quantities in an obvious way.

Assumption H. *The preferences of each household are continuous and convex. There is no satiation.*

Assumption F. *The production possibility sets of firms are closed and convex and include the origin. Free production is impossible* ($\mathbf{Y}_f \cap \mathbf{R}_+^\infty \subseteq \{0\}$).

Assumption S. *For each household* $h \in \mathbf{H}$, $e_h + b_h > 0$.

Assumption I. *For each* $T \in \mathbf{N}$ *there is* $\bar{y} \in \mathbf{Y}_{\leqslant T}$: $e_{\leqslant T} + \bar{y} \gg 0$.

Assumption I requires that the resources and technologies of the subeconomies with time horizon T permit the supply of a positive amount of each good.

Definition (feasible allocation). *A feasible allocation is a pair of sequences* $(x, y) = ((x_h)_{h \in \mathbf{H}}, (y_f)_{f \in \mathbf{F}})$ *such that* $x_h \in \mathbf{X}_h$ *for all* h, $y_f \in \mathbf{Y}_f$ *for all* f *and* $x^t = y^t + e^t$ *for all* t.

Definition (competitive equilibrium). *A competitive equilibrium is a feasible allocation* $(x^*, y^*) = ((x_h^*)_{h \in \mathbf{H}}, (y_f^*)_{f \in \mathbf{F}})$ *and a non-zero price sequence* $p^* \in \mathbf{P}$ *such that, for all* h *and* f,

(a) $p^* \cdot y_f^* \geqslant p^* \cdot y_f$ *for all* $y_f \in \mathbf{Y}_f$
(b) x_h^* *is a greatest element of* $B_h(p^*)$ *for* $\succcurlyeq_h$.

It should be noted that competitive equilibrium as defined is compatible with intra-generational borrowing and lending. Intergenerational borrowing and lending are ruled out by the assumption of a two-period life expectancy.

Definition (irreducibility). *The economy is irreducible if and only if for any feasible allocation* (x, y) *and for any non-trivial partition of households* $\mathbf{H}^1$, $\mathbf{H}^2$ *there is a* $\bar{t} \in \mathbf{N}$ *and an* $\bar{h} \in \mathbf{H}_{\bar{t}} \cap \mathbf{H}^1$ *such that*

$$x'_{\bar{h}} >_{\bar{h}} x_{\bar{h}}$$

where

$$x'_{\bar{h}} = x_{\bar{h}} + \sum_{\mathbf{H}^2 \cap \mathbf{H}_{\bar{t}-1}} e_h^{\bar{t}} + \sum_{\mathbf{H}^2 \cap \mathbf{H}_{\bar{t}}} e_h + \sum_{\mathbf{H}^2 \cap \mathbf{H}_{\bar{t}+1}} e_h^{\bar{t}+1}.$$

McKenzie (1959) developed the concept of irreducibility to ensure that every household has positive wealth in equilibrium: 'In loose terms, an economy is irreducible if it cannot be divided into two groups of consumers where one group is unable to supply any goods which the other group wants'. The present definition is an adaptation of McKenzie's to accommodate overlapping generations. It is similar to the definition introduced by Geanakoplos and Polemarchakis (1991) in their study of abstract exchange economies.

We can now state our basic existence theorem.

Theorem 1. *If the economy is irreducible, if assumptions H, F, S and I are satisfied and if any scheme of lumpsum transfers is balanced then there exists a competitive equilibrium.*

A proof may be found in Kemp and Wolik (1994).

3 TECHNICAL IMPROVEMENTS AND COMPENSATING TRANSFERS

We now consider the effect on well-being of improvements in the technologies of some firms. We contrast two situations. In the first situation, the production set of firm f, $f \in \mathbf{F}$, is $\hat{\mathbf{Y}}_f$; and in the second situation the production set of firm f is

$$\mathbf{Y}_f = \hat{\mathbf{Y}}_f \cup \mathbf{Y}_f^{\Delta}, \quad f \in \mathbf{F} \tag{2}$$

where $\mathbf{Y}_f^{\Delta}$ is the set of newly feasible production vectors, so that

$$\hat{\mathbf{Y}}_f \cap \mathbf{Y}_f^{\Delta} = \emptyset, \quad f \in \mathbf{F}. \tag{3a}$$

To avoid triviality, it is assumed that

for some $f \in \mathbf{F}$, $\mathbf{Y}_f^{\Delta} \neq \emptyset$ *and* $\hat{y}_f$ *is in the interior of* $\mathbf{Y}_f$; *for each* f, $\mathbf{Y}_f$ *satisfies the same assumptions as* $\hat{\mathbf{Y}}_f$, *hence theorem 1 applies to both situations.* (3b)

Henceforth, the values of all variables in the first situation will be distinguished by circumflexes.

For simplicity only, it will be assumed that in the first or initial situation there are no transfers, so that $\hat{b}_h = 0$, $h \in \mathbf{H}$. In the second or final situation household h receives from the government

$$b_h^t = \hat{x}_h^t - \sum_{f \in \mathbf{F}_t} \theta_{hf} \hat{y}_f^t - e_h^t, \quad \text{if } h \in \mathbf{H}_t,\ t \in \mathbf{N} \tag{4a}$$

$$b_h^{t+1} = \hat{x}_h^{t+1} - \sum_{f \in \mathbf{F}_t} \theta_{hf} \hat{y}_f^{t+1} - e_h^{t+1}, \quad \text{if } h \in \mathbf{H}_t,\ t \in \mathbf{N} \tag{4b}$$

and

$$b_h^1 = \hat{x}_h^1 - \sum_{f \in \mathbf{F}_0} \theta_{hf} \hat{y}_f^1 - e_h^1, \quad \text{if } h \in \mathbf{H}_0. \tag{4c}$$

Lemma 1. *The scheme of GMG lumpsum transfers (1) is balanced.*

A proof may be found in Kemp and Wolik (1994).

By virtue of theorem 1 and lemma 1 there exists a competitive equilibrium in each situation.

4 MAIN PROPOSITION

Let us say that the final situation weakly Pareto-dominates the initial situation if, under the scheme of compensatory transfers (1), no household is worse off in the final situation; and that the final situation Pareto-dominates the initial situation if, under the same scheme of transfers, some households are better off, and none worse off, in the final situation.

Theorem 2. *Given the scheme of GMG lumpsum transfers (1), the final situation Pareto-dominates the initial situation.*

Proof. *It is easy to verify, by substitution from (4) into (1), that the final situation weakly Pareto-dominates the initial situation. It then follows from revealed preference that, if consumption substitution takes place in at least one household and/or production substitution in at least one firm, the final situation Pareto-dominates the initial situation. The proof is completed by the observation that, as an implication of (2) and (3), production substitution must take place in at least one firm and therefore consumption substitution in at least one household.* □

5 DURABLE CAPITAL GOODS

The proof of theorem 2 rests on the fiction that all goods perish within one period of time. However, the fiction was introduced merely as a simplification; none of the conclusions requires it.

For suppose that, in addition to the N perishable goods already distinguished, there are M produced capital goods, each with a fixed and finite lifetime of θ periods. Then, admitting age as an economically relevant characteristic of such goods, we may distinguish θM additional goods, M of them newly produced and the remainder used or second-hand. In the first period of their existence, firms buy vectors of such goods; then, in their maturity, they either scrap the goods (if the latter have reached age θ) or sell them to a new generation of firms. It is straightforward but cumbersome to show that theorems 1 and 2 remain valid when the list of marketable goods is extended in this way.

Similarly, stocks of exhaustible resources can be accommodated without disturbing our conclusions. For example, in any period, a deposit of iron ore can be left underground (transformed by storage into the same stock with a later time subscript), or it can be extracted and stored above ground (transformed, with the aid of other inputs, into an intermediate good), or it can be extracted and used as an input to a conventional productive process.

6 FINAL REMARKS

Throughout earlier sections it was assumed that the technical improvement is unexpected. Whatever its realism, that is not an assumption forced on us by logical considerations. The analysis could be reworked on the assumption that at $t = 1$ it is known with certainty that an improvement will take place at $t = t' > 1$. Specifically, it could be shown that there is a scheme of GMG lumpsum compensation which ensures that all households on stage during or after $t = 1$ are better off in the final situation. That is, it could be shown that what matters in determining which households enjoy the fruits of a technical improvement is not the period during which the improvement occurs but the period during which it is foretold. Of course, this proposition relies on the assumption of irreducibility.

In Kemp and Wan (1992, 1993a, 1993b) the relative merits of lumpsum and non-lumpsum compensation have been discussed, with special attention to the informational requirements of the two alternatives. The balance of advantages seemed to favour lumpsum compensation. However, that discussion was restricted to economies in which all individuals are alive at the time at which the disturbance is announced; it does not apply to economies of the kind discussed in this essay. In a context of overlapping generations there may be households which will be in need of compensation but which will be born after the announcement of the disturbance; and for such households it will not be possible, even ideally, to collect the information needed for GMG compensation. Whether it be lumpsum or non-lumpsum, compensation will impose impossible informational requirements.

NOTE

1 GMG lumpsum compensation ensures that pre-disturbance consumption baskets remain available at post-disturbance prices.

REFERENCES

Geanakoplos, J. D. and Polemarchakis, H. M. (1991) 'Overlapping generations', in W. Hildenbrand and H. Sonnenschein (eds) *Handbook of Mathematical Economics*, Vol. IV, pp. 1899–960, Amsterdam: North-Holland.

Kemp, M. C. and Wan, H. Y. (1992) 'On lumpsum compensation', University of New South Wales, this volume.

Kemp, M. C. and Wan, H. Y. (1993a) 'Lumpsum compensation in a context of incomplete markets', University of New South Wales, this volume.

Kemp, M. C. and Wan, H. Y. (1993b) *The Welfare Economics of International Trade*, London: Harwood Academic.

Kemp, M. C. and Wolik, N. (1994) 'The gains from international trade in a context of overlapping generations', University of New South Wales, this volume.

McKenzie, L. W. (1959) 'On the existence of general equilibrium for a competitive market', *Econometrica* 27: 54–71.

Part V

INTERNATIONAL AID

27

THE STATIC WELFARE ECONOMICS OF FOREIGN AID

A consolidation*

1 INTRODUCTION

In the 1950s, when the profession of development economics was in its infancy, it was widely believed that chronically poor countries could be set on the path of self-sustaining growth only by means of an initial 'big push', with substantial technical and financial support from abroad. Today's practitioners have greater confidence in the efficacy of small stimuli; for them, 'haste makes waste'. However, most of them would accord to foreign aid an important facilitating role in the growth process. They also emphasize its role in achieving more equitable intra-national and international distributions of income. This being so, it is remarkable that nowhere in the vast literature on the economics of development can one find a systematic theoretical examination of questions relating to the incidence of aid or to the optimal level and timing of aid.

In the present essay I seek to remedy this deficiency, at least in part. The exposition is systematic; that is, a large number of related questions are examined from a fixed point of view and by means of a unified theoretical analysis. However, the treatment is far from comprehensive; important questions remain out of reach of the apparatus employed and, doubtless, others have simply not occurred to me. Thus the entire discourse is static, with no provision for the passage of time: nothing is said about the optimal **timing** of aid, including its division into stock and flow components;[1] nothing is said about the important concept of 'absorptive capacity';[2] and nothing is said about the role of aid in promoting research into the process of economic development and in gradually raising the quality of civil services in the recipient countries.[3] Moreover, the analysis rests on the traditional but unsatisfactory assumption of complete and competitive markets. Finally, aid is treated throughout as a parameter to be varied at the policy-maker's will, not as a variable to be explained by the analysis. Nevertheless it may be useful to have a consolidation of information; at a minimum, it can serve as a starting point for further, more policy-relevant analysis.

In a world economy in which everything depends on everything else, there are as many means of international aid as there are instruments of economic policy. However, to keep the discussion within reasonable bounds attention is restricted to (i) transfers of goods or of command over goods, and (ii) transfers of information ('technical assistance').[4] Transfers of goods have been much discussed by trade theorists as the raw material of the 'transfer problem' and the 'reparations problem'. They are the archetypical instruments of aid, although in practice they are rarely used in isolation. Of course, access to valuable information is also a good. However it is a public good, not a private good, and therefore merits our special attention.

If the essay has a theme it is that some of the folklore of international aid – that is, the body of propositions treated as self-evident – must be given up. Consider the proposition that one country can always help another by a transfer of private goods. It will emerge that, in a wide variety of contexts, this proposition is invalid; indeed, it will be shown that a particular country may be unable to help **any** other country by that means. Moreover, even if one particular country can help another by a direct transfer of goods, it yet may be optimal (i.e. it may entail least utility cost to the donor) to give only part of the aid by direct transfer, the rest indirectly, by direct transfer to third countries. (However, it is never optimal to give all aid indirectly.) Finally, even if each direct transfer does good when viewed as an isolated act, one cannot be sure that the sum of all gifts by all donors does good.

Similarly, a country with a global absolute advantage over all other countries may be unable to help any other country by technical assistance. Moreover, even if one particular country can help another by direct technical assistance, it yet may be optimal (i.e. it may entail least utility cost or greatest utility gain to the donor) to give only part of the aid by direct transfer, the rest indirectly. Finally, even if each direct transfer hurts the donor when viewed as an isolated act, one cannot be sure that the aggregate of all gifts by all donors hurts any donor.

2 AID BY TRANSFER OF GOODS – THE SIMPLEST CASE

It is easy to see that, in general, an international transfer of goods will bring about a change in world prices. Only in the singular situation in which marginal propensities are the same, commodity by commodity, in donor and recipient, will this not be so. The change in prices might favour the recipient, thus reinforcing the initial welfare impact of the transfer; or it might be to the advantage of the donor, thus offsetting, more or less, the initial impact. For a long time it was unclear whether the change in prices might so favour the donor that, on balance, it would be better off after the transfer and the recipient worse off. Evidently there could be no firmly based welfare economics of international aid until this question had been answered.

Professional discussion of the question reached a local peak with the appearance in 1947 of Paul Samuelson's *Foundations*. Earlier, Leontief (1936) had produced a two-by-two example in which a transfer worked to the net advantage of the donor and, therefore, to the net disadvantage of the recipient.

Samuelson's contribution was to note that if the assumption of Walrasian stability is added to Leontief's specification then his conclusions are reversed. Much later, Balasko (1978) showed that, in quite general two-by-two contexts, the donor benefits if and only if the system is unstable.

It will be useful to have a proof of Samuelson's proposition to which we can later refer. There are two free-trading countries, α and β, and there are two commodities, 1 and 2. The population of each country is completely homogeneous, both in preferences and in asset holdings. Each commodity is a private consumption good. In an initial world trading equilibrium, α exports commodity 1 and β exports commodity 2; this assumption is for concreteness only. The initial equilibrium is disturbed when α extends aid to β. The following notation will be employed:

$T^{\alpha\beta}$ the amount of aid, in terms of commodity 2, from α (the donor) to β (the recipient); initially, $T^{\alpha\beta} = 0$

p the price of commodity 1 in terms of commodity 2

u^j the utility derived from consumption in country j ($j = \alpha, \beta$)

e^j the expenditure function of country j, expenditure in terms of commodity 2 ($j = \alpha, \beta$)

r^j the revenue function of country j, revenue in terms of commodity 2 ($j = \alpha, \beta$)

z^{ji} the excess demand by country j for commodity i ($i = 1, 2; j = \alpha, \beta$).

The aid is financed in α and distributed in β by means of lumpsum taxes and subsidies. Hence the private budget constraint of α is

$$e^{\alpha}(p, u^{\alpha}) = r^{\alpha}(p) - T^{\alpha\beta} \tag{1}$$

and that of β is

$$e^{\beta}(p, u^{\beta}) = r^{\beta}(p) + T^{\alpha\beta}. \tag{2}$$

The description of world equilibrium is then completed by the market-clearing condition[5]

$$z^{\alpha 1}(p, u^{\alpha}) + z^{\beta 1}(p, u^{\beta}) = 0. \tag{3}$$

Equations (1)–(3) contain the three variables p, u^{α} and u^{β}, as well as the parameter $T^{\alpha\beta}$. The system is assumed to possess a unique solution (p^*, $u^{\alpha*}$, $u^{\beta*}$) with p^* positive and finite.

We wish to know how each of the three variables responds to a small change in $T^{\alpha\beta}$. Differentiating (1)–(3) with respect to $T^{\alpha\beta}$, we find that

$$\begin{bmatrix} e_p^{\alpha} - r_p^{\alpha} & e_u^{\alpha} & 0 \\ e_p^{\beta} - r_p^{\beta} & 0 & e_u^{\beta} \\ z_p^{\alpha 1} + z_p^{\beta 1} & z_u^{\alpha 1} & z_u^{\beta 1} \end{bmatrix} \begin{bmatrix} dp \\ du^{\alpha} \\ du^{\beta} \end{bmatrix} = \begin{bmatrix} -1 \\ 1 \\ 0 \end{bmatrix} dT^{\alpha\beta} \tag{4}$$

where subscripts indicate differentiation (e.g. $e_p^{\alpha} \equiv \partial e^{\alpha}/\partial p$ and $r_p^{\alpha} \equiv dr^{\alpha}/dp$). Recalling the envelope result that $e_p^j - r_p^j = z^{j1}$ ($j = \alpha, \beta$), choosing units of utility so that $e_u^j = 1$, defining $z_p^1 \equiv z_p^{\alpha 1} + z_p^{\beta 1}$, and noting that $T^{\alpha\beta} = 0$, we can rewrite (4) in the more streamlined form

$$\begin{bmatrix} z^{\alpha 1} & 1 & 0 \\ z^{\beta 1} & 0 & 1 \\ z_p^1 & z_u^{\alpha 1} & z_u^{\beta 1} \end{bmatrix} \begin{bmatrix} \mathrm{d}p \\ \mathrm{d}u^{\alpha} \\ \mathrm{d}u^{\beta} \end{bmatrix} = \begin{bmatrix} -1 \\ 1 \\ 0 \end{bmatrix} \mathrm{d}T^{\alpha\beta}. \tag{5}$$

Solving,

$$\begin{aligned} \Delta(\mathrm{d}p/\mathrm{d}T^{\alpha\beta}) &= (pz_u^{\alpha 1} - pz_u^{\beta 1})/p \\ \Delta(\mathrm{d}u^{\alpha}/\mathrm{d}T^{\alpha\beta}) &= -z_p^1 = -\Delta(\mathrm{d}u^{\beta}/\mathrm{d}T^{\alpha\beta}) \end{aligned} \tag{6}$$

where

$$\Delta \equiv z_p^1 + z^{\beta 1}(pz_u^{\alpha 1} - pz_u^{\beta 1})/p \tag{7}$$

is the determinant of the matrix of coefficients in (5). We note that $pz_u^{j1}/e_u^j = pz_u^{j1}$ is the marginal propensity to consume commodity 1 in country j and may be of either sign, and that z_p^1 is the sum of two pure (or 'compensated') price slopes, one for each country, and is necessarily negative. Moreover, it can be shown that $\Delta < 0$ is a sufficient and almost necessary[6] condition for the local Walrasian stability of the system; let us assume that $\Delta < 0$. Applying this information to (6), we see that aid necessarily hurts the donor α and benefits the recipient β. Thus, it seems, common sense has been vindicated and a firm foundation provided for the welfare economics of international aid.

However, Samuelson's proposition is based on very strict assumptions. There are only two commodities. Moreover, only two countries, the donor and the recipient, are recognized; there are no bystanders. Finally, markets are not only competitive but free of all distortions. In particular, the aid is financed and disbursed by means of non-distorting lumpsum taxes and subsidies; and it is spent in a manner determined by the preferences of the recipient, unconstrained by tying conditions of any kind. Until recently it was simply taken for granted that the proposition survives under more realistic assumptions.

The proposition can be generalized to a limited extent. Thus it can be shown that the number of commodities is immaterial[7] and that in a world of many countries the proposition remains valid if the donor and recipient are small. However, we now know, principally from the work of Michihiro Ohyama (1972, 1974) and David Gale (1974), that, in general, the proposition does not survive outside the context in which Samuelson proved it.

3 AID BY TRANSFER OF GOODS – TIED AID

Externalities, commodity taxes, factor-market distortions, aid tying and elements of monopoly power (including the monopoly power of labour unions) can all generate outcomes which, in the light of Samuelson's result, appear to be paradoxical. Space does not allow me to consider in detail all types of distortions. Here I perturb the basic model in just one respect, by allowing for the possibility that aid is tied.[8]

The provision of aid may be conditional on the recipient meeting conditions imposed by the donor. The recipient may be required to spend the aid in a particular way – on defence or on commodities exported by the donor, for example; or it may be required to modify its commercial policy – aid may then be viewed as compensation for forgone tariff revenue. In general, aid may be tied to any variable under the control of the recipient government. Here the focus is on just one of several possibilities.[9] It is assumed that the recipient β is required to spend a proportion m^{β} of the aid on the commodity exported by the donor α; as in section 2, it is assumed that commodity 1 is exported by α.

As in the simple case studied by Samuelson, the aid is financed in α by means of lumpsum taxes. The private budget constraint of α is, therefore,

$$e^{\alpha}(p, u^{\alpha}) = r^{\alpha}(p) - T^{\alpha\beta}. \tag{1}$$

The aid is spent by the government of β; it influences the welfare w^{β} of β but does not enter the private budget constraint

$$e^{\beta}(p, u^{\beta}) = r^{\beta}(p) \tag{8}$$

where u^{β} must now be interpreted as that part of β-well-being derived from private expenditure. The description of world equilibrium is completed by the condition of market clearance,

$$z^{\alpha 1}(p, u^{\alpha}) + z^{\beta 1}(p, u^{\beta}) + m^{\beta} T^{\alpha\beta}/p = 0. \tag{9}$$

Differentiating our new system ((1), (8), (9)) with respect to $T^{\alpha\beta}$, we find that

$$\begin{bmatrix} z^{\alpha 1} & 1 & 0 \\ z^{\beta 1} & 0 & 1 \\ z_p^{\alpha 1} + z_p^{\beta 1} & z_u^{\alpha 1} & z_u^{\beta 1} \end{bmatrix} \begin{bmatrix} dp \\ du^{\alpha} \\ du^{\beta} \end{bmatrix} = \begin{bmatrix} -1 \\ 0 \\ -m^{\beta}/p \end{bmatrix} dT^{\alpha\beta}. \tag{4'}$$

Solving,

$$\begin{aligned} \Delta(dp/dT^{\alpha\beta}) &= -(m^{\beta} - p z_u^{\alpha 1})/p \\ \Delta(du^{\alpha}/dT) &= -z_p^{1} - z^{\beta 1}(m^{\beta} - p z_u^{\beta 1})/p \\ \Delta(du^{\beta}/dT) &= z^{\beta 1}(m^{\beta} - p z_u^{\alpha 1})/p. \end{aligned} \tag{10}$$

From (7) and (10) we see that for both $\Delta < 0$ and $du^{\alpha}/dT > 0$ it is necessary and sufficient that

$$-z^{\beta 1}(m^{\beta} - p z_u^{\beta 1})/p < z_p^{\alpha 1} + z_p^{\beta 1} < -z^{\beta 1}(z_u^{\alpha 1} - z_u^{\beta 1}). \tag{11}$$

Evidently this condition can be satisfied without inferiority. However, it does imply that the recipient's offer curve is inelastic at the initial equilibrium. Consider the first inequality of (11). Making use of a well-known relationship between substitution terms

$$pz_p^{\beta 1} + z_p^{\beta 2} = 0 \tag{12}$$

and of the identity between marginal propensities to consume

$$pz_u^{\beta 1} + z_u^{\beta 2} = 1$$

that inequality can be rewritten as

$$z_p^{\beta 2} - z^{\beta 1} z_u^{\beta 2} < p z_p^{\alpha 1} - (1 - m^{\beta}) z^{\beta 1} < 0. \tag{13}$$

But the left-hand expression in (13) is the total derivative $dz^{\beta 2}/dp$; hence $-dz^{\beta 2}/d(1/p) < 0$. Thus the recipient's offer of its export commodity decreases when its terms of trade improve, implying that the recipient's offer curve is inelastic.

The fate of the recipient is easily determined. Since the initial equilibrium is Pareto-efficient, a small change in the real income of one country must be accompanied by an opposite change in the real income of the other country. Indeed, given the normalization $e_u^{\alpha} = e_u^{\beta} = 1$, we have

$$dw^{\beta}/dT^{\alpha\beta} = 1 + du^{\beta}/dT^{\alpha\beta} = -du^{\alpha}/dT^{\alpha\beta} \tag{14}$$

where, it will be recalled, w^{β} is the total well-being of β.

Thus we have established that, if and only if condition (11) is satisfied, the economy is locally stable but the donor benefits from aid and the recipient suffers. Let us try to construct the common sense of the proposition. Because the aid is marginal it has the same direct welfare effect however it is spent by the government of β. But its indirect effects, through prices, do depend on how it is spent. If $m^{\beta} \neq pz_u^{\beta 1}$, that is if the government's tied marginal propensity to spend on the first commodity differs from the corresponding marginal propensity to consume of individuals in β, then, in effect, the Engel curve of β contains a kink at the initial equilibrium point. The kink serves to moderate or magnify the price effects of the transfer. In particular, if $m^{\beta} > pz_u^{\beta 1}$, that is if the marginal propensity of the β-government is greater than that of β-individuals, then any aid-induced increase in p (improvement in α terms of trade) must be exaggerated and it is this exaggeration of the price change that lies behind any perverse welfare outcomes.

It must be emphasized that, in the above formulation, aid is tied to **marginal** consumption. To verify that the tying requirement has been satisfied the donor must know a great deal about the recipient's economy – often, more than can be known. Verification would be much easier if aid were tied to the recipient's **total** consumption, as in Schweinberger (1990); for then only post-aid consumption need be known. However, tying in that sense has little to do with real-world tying, which is typically of the marginal kind. Relevant information may be found in the OECD document *Development Cooperation, 1986 Review*, December 1986. In particular, it is there shown that two-thirds of the 'bilateral official development assistance' given by members of the Development Assistance Committee is directed to specific projects while only 5 per cent is programme assistance.

It must be emphasized also that, in a two-country formulation, the tying of aid necessarily assumes a larger-than-life importance. In practice, there are many recipients and many potential donors. Each recipient does much preliminary shopping about, seeking to match its particular needs to donors with the appropriate comparative advantages. Thus the formal tying of aid might disrupt world allocation hardly at all.

More will be said about the tying of aid in section 4.

4 AID BY TRANSFER OF GOODS – BYSTANDERS

In Samuelson's world there is a donor and there is a recipient, but there are no other countries. It was David Gale's great contribution to show that when aid is given in the presence of bystanders it is no longer inevitable that the donor suffers and the recipient benefits – even if the world economy is stable and free of distortions, including tying; see Gale (1974).[10] Of course, the Samuelsonian outcome is still possible; indeed, that outcome is inevitable if donor and recipient are small or if they have the same marginal propensities to consume. But paradoxes can no longer be ruled out by appeal to stability alone.

4.1 Aid in the absence of distortions

Adding a bystander γ to system (1)–(3), we obtain

$$e^{\alpha}(p, u^{\alpha}) = r^{\alpha}(p) - T^{\alpha\beta} \tag{1}$$

$$e^{\beta}(p, u^{\beta}) = r^{\beta}(p) + T^{\alpha\beta} \tag{2}$$

$$e^{\gamma}(p, u^{\gamma}) = r^{\gamma}(p) \tag{15}$$

$$\sum_{j=\alpha,\beta,\gamma} z^{j1}(p, u^{j}) = 0. \tag{16}$$

Differentiating this system totally with respect to $T^{\alpha\beta}$, and redefining z_p^1 as $\Sigma_{j=\alpha,\beta,\gamma} z_p^{j1}$, we obtain

$$\begin{bmatrix} z^{\alpha 1} & 1 & 0 & 0 \\ z^{\beta 1} & 0 & 1 & 0 \\ z^{\gamma 1} & 0 & 0 & 1 \\ z_p^1 & z_u^{\alpha 1} & z_u^{\beta 1} & z_u^{\gamma 1} \end{bmatrix} \begin{bmatrix} dp \\ du^{\alpha} \\ du^{\beta} \\ du^{\gamma} \end{bmatrix} = \begin{bmatrix} -1 \\ 1 \\ 0 \\ 0 \end{bmatrix} dT^{\alpha\beta}. \tag{17}$$

Solving,

$$\Delta''(dp/dT^{\alpha\beta}) = z_u^{\alpha 1} - z_u^{\beta 1} \tag{18}$$

$$\Delta''(du^{\alpha}/dT^{\alpha\beta}) = -z_p^1 - z^{\gamma 1}(z_u^{\beta 1} - z_u^{\gamma 1}) \tag{19}$$

$$\Delta''(du^{\beta}/dT^{\alpha\beta}) = z_p^1 + z^{\gamma 1}(z_u^{\alpha 1} - z_u^{\gamma 1}) \tag{20}$$

$$\Delta''(du^{\gamma}/dT^{\alpha\beta}) = -z^{\gamma 1}(z_u^{\alpha 1} - z_u^{\beta 1}) \tag{21}$$

where

$$\Delta'' \equiv \sum_{j=\alpha,\beta,\gamma} (z_p^{j1} - z^{j1} z_u^{j1}) \equiv z_p^1 - \sum_{j=\alpha,\beta,\gamma} z^{j1} z_u^{j1} \tag{22}$$

is negative as a sufficient condition of local stability.

We see at a glance that the donor might benefit and/or the recipient suffer. For the donor to benefit it is necessary that the bystander be a net trader in the initial equilibrium, with marginal propensities to consume which differ from those of the recipient; if either condition fails to be satisfied, we are effectively back to Samuelson's two-countries model. Similarly, for the recipient to suffer, it is necessary that the bystander be a net trader, with marginal propensities which differ from those of the donor; if either condition fails to hold, we again are back to the two-countries model. Finally, we notice that the donor might benefit even when initially it does not trade, so that $z^{\alpha 1} = 0$; and that the recipient might suffer even when initially it does not trade, so that $z^{\beta 1} = 0$. Of course, it is not possible for both outcomes to occur simultaneously.

Alternative necessary conditions can be obtained by making use of the Slutzky decomposition of the uncompensated net demand function $\tilde{z}^{j1}(p)$:

$$\tilde{z}_p^{j1} = z_p^{j1} - z^{j1} z_u^{j1}, \quad j = \alpha, \beta, \gamma. \tag{23}$$

Thus, substituting for $z_p^{\gamma 1}$, equations (19) and (20) can be rewritten as

$$\Delta''(\mathrm{d}u^{\alpha}/\mathrm{d}T^{\alpha\beta}) = -(z_p^{\alpha 1} + z_p^{\beta 1}) - \tilde{z}_p^{\gamma 1} - z^{\gamma 1} z_u^{\beta 1} \tag{24}$$

and

$$\Delta''(\mathrm{d}u^{\beta}/\mathrm{d}T^{\alpha\beta}) = (z_p^{\alpha 1} + z_p^{\beta 1}) + \tilde{z}_p^{\gamma 1} + z^{\gamma 1} z_u^{\alpha 1}. \tag{25}$$

However, differentiating the jth country's budget constraint $p\tilde{z}^{j1} + \tilde{z}^{j2} = 0$, we obtain

$$\tilde{z}^{j1} + p\tilde{z}_p^{j1} + \tilde{z}_p^{j2} = 0, \quad j = \alpha, \beta, \gamma. \tag{26}$$

Applying (26) to (24) and (25), and recalling that the marginal propensities to consume pz_u^{j1} and z_u^{j2} add to one, we obtain, respectively,

$$\Delta''(\mathrm{d}u^{\alpha}/\mathrm{d}T^{\alpha\beta}) = -(z_p^{\alpha 1} + z_p^{\beta 1}) + (\tilde{z}_p^{\gamma 2}/p) - z^{\gamma 1} z_u^{\beta 2}/p \tag{27}$$

and

$$\Delta''(\mathrm{d}u^{\beta}/\mathrm{d}T^{\alpha\beta}) = (z_p^{\alpha 1} + z_p^{\beta 1}) - (\tilde{z}_p^{\gamma 2}/p) - z^{\gamma 1} z_u^{\alpha 2}/p. \tag{28}$$

Suppose that $z^{\gamma 1}$ is negative (positive): that is, that the bystander exports the first (second) commodity. Then, from (24) (from (27)), we can infer that if a transfer enriches the donor then either the commodity exported by the bystander is inferior to the recipient, or the bystander's export supply is backward bending, or both; and from (25) (from (28)) we can infer that if a transfer impoverishes the recipient then either the commodity exported by the bystander is inferior to the donor or the bystander's export supply is backward bending, or both.

Gale's contribution was to show that, in the presence of bystanders, it is not always possible for one country to enrich another by means of a direct international transfer. This answer to one question suggests a further question: given that α cannot help β by means of a direct transfer, can α help β in a roundabout way, by directing the transfer to bystander γ? More generally, whether or not α can help β directly, is it possible that a given amount of aid (in terms of β-utility) can be given at less utility cost to α if it is given indirectly? It will be shown that each of the following outcomes is possible; necessary and sufficient conditions for each outcome will be provided.

1 Any transfer from α, whether to β or to γ or to both, impoverishes β. In this case, clearly, it is impossible for α to play Good Samaritan to β. (Negative transfers by α are ruled out.)
2 A transfer from α to β impoverishes β but a transfer from α to γ enriches β. In this case α can aid β only indirectly, by making a grant to γ.
3 A transfer from to α to β enriches β but a transfer from α to γ impoverishes β. In this case α can aid β only directly, by making a grant to β.
4 Any transfer from α, whether to β or to γ, enriches β. In some circumstances a transfer of given size will do most good to β if it is made directly; in other circumstances the transfer will be most efficacious if made indirectly.

Of these possibilities, 1 and 4 are of special interest. It is not always feasible for a potential donor to enrich another country by a direct transfer; and, even if a direct transfer is efficacious, it yet may be less efficacious than an indirect transfer.

Equation (20) gives us the effect on β's welfare of a direct transfer from α; and equation (21), with the superscripts β and γ permuted, describes the effect on β's welfare of an indirect transfer. Thus

$$\begin{aligned} \Delta''(\mathrm{d}u^{\beta}/\mathrm{d}T^{\alpha\beta}) &= z_p^1 + z^{\gamma 1}(z_u^{\alpha 1} - z_u^{\gamma 1}) \\ \Delta''(\mathrm{d}u^{\beta}/\mathrm{d}T^{\alpha\gamma}) &= -\, z^{\beta 1}(z_u^{\alpha 1} - z_u^{\gamma 1}) \end{aligned} \qquad (29)$$

where $T^{\alpha\gamma}$ is, of course, the amount transferred by α to γ. Inspection of (29) reveals that, even with Δ'' constrained to be negative, $\mathrm{d}u^{\beta}/\mathrm{d}T^{\alpha\beta}$ and $\mathrm{d}u^{\beta}/\mathrm{d}T^{\alpha\gamma}$ can be both negative, both positive or (either) one positive, the other negative; that is, none of the outcomes 1–4 distinguished above can be ruled out.

We can look beyond the binary possibilities 1–4 and show that if α cannot help β (outcome 1) then γ **can** do so, at least indirectly. In other words, β always has at least one potential friend. (Of course, the potential friend may be even poorer than β.) The plausibility of this proposition can be established by observing that indirect aid from γ to β reverses the direction of indirect aid from

α to β; in effect, the former removes the natural sign restriction from $T^{\alpha\beta}$. Whether γ can also help β directly is another matter. It can be verified that if α and γ export the same commodity then at least one of them can help β directly.[11] On the other hand, α may be able to help neither β nor γ, either by directing all aid to β or by directing all aid to γ or, therefore, by dividing aid between β and γ.[12] While each country has a potential friend, it is not always the case that each country can serve as a friend. This finding is of some theological and ethical interest; not every country can play the part of Good Samaritan. Finally, we note that, if $z^{\alpha 1} = 0$ and under other sufficient conditions, the donor's utility may increase, both when aid is given wholly to β or γ and therefore when it is divided in any manner between them. This possibility serves as a warning that the textbook practice of lumping together all countries but one as 'the rest of the world' does not necessarily bring back the orthodox Samuelsonian conclusions.

To this point we have confined our attention to aid directed wholly to one country. It remains to consider the **optimal** mode of assistance, optimality being defined in terms of the utility cost to α to a given small increase in the welfare of β.[13] Suppose that u^{β} has been raised to the required level by setting $T^{\alpha\beta} = \bar{T}^{\alpha\beta} > 0$ and $T^{\alpha\gamma} = \bar{T}^{\alpha\gamma} > 0$. Let $T^{\alpha} = T^{\alpha\beta} + T^{\alpha\gamma}$ and $\varepsilon \equiv T^{\alpha\beta}/T^{\alpha}$, so that (2) and (15) take the more general form

$$e^{\beta}(p, u^{\beta}) = r^{\beta}(p) + \varepsilon T^{\alpha} \tag{30}$$

and

$$e^{\gamma}(p, u^{\gamma}) = r^{\gamma}(p) + (1 - \varepsilon) T^{\alpha}. \tag{31}$$

We are interested in the response of u^{α} to a small change in ε, with u^{β} held constant and T^{α} allowed to vary. Differentiating the system ((1), (30), (31), (16)) with respect to ε, we obtain

$$\begin{bmatrix} z^{\alpha 1} & 1 & 0 & 1 \\ z^{\beta 1} & 0 & 0 & -\varepsilon \\ z^{\gamma 1} & 0 & 1 & -(1-\varepsilon) \\ z_p^1 & z_u^{\alpha 1} & z_u^{\gamma 1} & 0 \end{bmatrix} \begin{bmatrix} \mathrm{d}p \\ \mathrm{d}u^{\alpha} \\ \mathrm{d}u^{\gamma} \\ \mathrm{d}T \end{bmatrix} = \begin{bmatrix} 0 \\ T \\ -T \\ 0 \end{bmatrix} \mathrm{d}\varepsilon. \tag{32}$$

Solving,

$$\Delta'''(\mathrm{d}p/\mathrm{d}\varepsilon) = -T^{\alpha}(z_u^{\alpha 1} - z_u^{\gamma 1}) \tag{33a}$$

$$\Delta'''(\mathrm{d}u^{\alpha}/\mathrm{d}\varepsilon) = T^{\alpha} z_p^1 = -\Delta'''(\mathrm{d}u^{\gamma}/\mathrm{d}\varepsilon) \tag{33b}$$

$$\Delta'''(\mathrm{d}T^{\alpha}/\mathrm{d}\varepsilon) = -T^{\alpha}[z_p^1 - z^{\alpha 1}(z_u^{\alpha 1} - z_u^{\gamma 1})] \tag{33c}$$

where

$$\Delta''' \ \varepsilon z_p^1 - z_u^{\alpha 1}(\varepsilon z^{\alpha 1} + z^{\beta 1}) - z_u^{\gamma 1}[\varepsilon z^{\gamma 1} - (1-\varepsilon) z^{\beta 1}] \tag{34}$$

is negative as a sufficient condition of local stability.

Equation (33b) tells us that **for all permissible** ε $\mathrm{d}u^{\alpha}/\mathrm{d}\varepsilon$ is positive. This implies that it is never optimal to give all aid indirectly, through γ. It is possible that the optimal value of ε is one. However, it is also possible that at some value of ε less than one, say $\varepsilon(u^{\beta})$, T^{α} reaches its maximum feasible value; in that case, the optimal value of ε is $\varepsilon(u^{\beta})$. Thus we know that there are circumstances in which α can help β by giving all aid indirectly but cannot help β by giving all aid directly. In those circumstances, we can make use of (29) to write

$$z_p^1 + z^{\gamma 1}(z_u^{\alpha 1} - z_u^{\gamma 1}) > 0$$

$$- z^{\beta 1}(z_u^{\alpha 1} - z_u^{\gamma 1}) < 0$$

so that, subtracting the second inequality from the first, and appealing to (33c),

$$z_p^1 - z^{\alpha 1}(z_u^{\alpha 1} - z_u^{\gamma 1}) > 0$$

and $\mathrm{d}T^{\alpha}/\mathrm{d}\varepsilon > 0$; eventually, at $\varepsilon = \varepsilon(u^{\beta}) < 1$, the T^{α} required to maintain the given level of u^{β} is infeasible. In general, the optimal ε must lie in the half-open interval (0,1].

4.2 Tied aid again

We have seen that it may be impossible for α to aid β, either directly or indirectly (or by a mixture of the two modes). However, that conclusion was derived from the assumption that aid is 'clean' or untied. Now it is usually taken for granted that aid is most beneficial to the recipient when it is completely untied. In fact this is not the case. In particular, even when it is impossible for α to help β by means of an untied transfer it yet may be possible to help with a tied transfer. Thus, while tying can create paradoxes in a two-country setting, it can remove them when there are three or more countries.

To see this, let us suppose that $\varepsilon = 1$ and that α requires the government of β to spend a proportion m^{β} of the aid on the first commodity ($0 \leqslant m^{\beta} \leqslant 1$). Then the conditions of international equilibrium become

$$e^{\alpha}(p, u^{\alpha}) - r^{\alpha}(p) = -T^{\alpha\beta} \tag{1}$$

$$e^{\beta}(p, u^{\beta}) - r^{\beta}(p) = 0 \tag{8}$$

$$e^{\gamma}(p, u^{\gamma}) - r^{\gamma}(p) = 0 \tag{15}$$

$$z^{\alpha 1}(p, u^{\alpha}) + z^{\beta 1}(\mathrm{p}, u^{\beta}) + z^{\gamma 1}(p, u^{\gamma}) + m^{\beta}T^{\alpha\beta}/p = 0. \tag{35}$$

It should be recalled that (8) is the private budget constraint of β and u^{β} that part of β's welfare generated by that budget. The total welfare of β, w^{β}, is greater than u^{β} by the contribution of α's aid. Initially, $T^{\alpha\beta} = 0$.

Differentiating ((1), (8), (15), (35)) with respect to $T^{\alpha\beta}$ and solving for $\mathrm{d}u^{\alpha}/\mathrm{d}T^{\alpha\beta}$ and $\mathrm{d}u^{\gamma}/\mathrm{d}T^{\alpha\beta}$, we find that

$$(\mathrm{d}u^{\alpha}/\mathrm{d}T^{\alpha\beta}) = (1/\Delta'')(-z_p^1 + z^{\gamma 1}z_u^{\gamma 1} + z^{\beta 1}z_u^{\beta 1} + z^{\alpha 1}m^{\beta}/p) \tag{36a}$$

$$(du^{\gamma}/dT^{\alpha\beta}) = (1/\Delta'')[(z^{\gamma 1}/p)(m^{\beta} - pz_u^{\alpha 1})]. \tag{36b}$$

Since $T^{\alpha\beta} = 0$ the initial equilibrium is Pareto-efficient; hence an infinitesimal transfer has the same effect on the recipient's welfare **however it is spent** and

$$\Delta''(dw^{\beta}/dT^{\alpha\beta}) = -(du^{\alpha}/dT^{\alpha\beta} + du^{\gamma}/dT^{\alpha\beta})$$
$$= z_p^1 + z^{\gamma 1}(z_u^{\alpha 1} - z_u^{\gamma 1}) + (z^{\beta 1}/p)(m^{\beta} - pz_u^{\beta 1}). \tag{37}$$

It is easy to verify that (36a) may be negative even when $du^{\alpha}/dT^{\alpha\beta}|_{\varepsilon=1}$ and $du^{\alpha}/dT^{\alpha\beta}|_{\varepsilon=0}$ are positive, and that (37) may be positive even when $du^{\beta}/dT^{\alpha\beta}|_{\varepsilon=1}$ and $du^{\beta}/dT^{\alpha\beta}|_{\varepsilon=0}$ are negative. For those comforting outcomes it is necessary that $z^{\beta 1}(m^{\beta} - pz_u^{\beta 1})$ be negative; that is, that the government of β be required marginally to spend more on β's exported commodity than would β-individuals. This is a thoroughly plausible condition. If the aid had been tied both in the donor country and in the recipient country, the condition would have been even weaker.

Thus by tying its aid a donor can circumvent the impossibility results of this section. Notice, however, that if α and β export different commodities then circumvention can be achieved only by unconventionally tying aid to the good **imported** by the donor.

4.3 Joint donors and joint recipients

So far, I have concentrated on a few basic questions raised by the desire of a single country to aid another. However, the poorer countries typically receive aid from several quarters, and most wealthy countries spread their aid widely. These well-known facts suggest additional questions. If both α and γ help β and wish to extend their aid, co-operatively sharing the utility burden, equally or in any other fashion, how should the additional aid be shared among the donors? If α helps both β and γ and wishes to extend the aid, dividing the additional utility benefits equally or in some other fashion, how should the additional aid be shared by the recipients? Each question is grist for the mill constructed in this section.

Thus suppose that in an initial equilibrium β receives $T^{\alpha\beta}$ from α and $T^{\gamma\beta}$ from γ, both $T^{\alpha\beta}$ and $T^{\gamma\beta}$ positive. The equilibrium is described by the equations

$$e^{\alpha}(p, u^{\alpha}) - r^{\alpha}(p) = -T^{\alpha\beta} \tag{38}$$

$$e^{\beta}(p, u^{\beta}) - r^{\beta}(p) = T^{\alpha\beta} + T^{\gamma\beta} \tag{39}$$

$$e^{\gamma}(p, u^{\gamma}) - r^{\gamma}(p) = -T^{\gamma\beta} \tag{40}$$

$$z^{\alpha 1}(p, u^{\alpha}) + z^{\beta 1}(p, u^{\beta}) + z^{\gamma 1}(p, u^{\gamma}) = 0. \tag{21}$$

Treating u^{β} as a parameter and $T^{\alpha\beta}$, $T^{\gamma\beta}$ as variables, we can differentiate the system with respect to u^{β}, add the equality-of-sharing condition $du^{\alpha} = du^{\gamma}$, and solve for the additional contributions of the donors α and γ. Omitting the detailed calculations, we have

$$\Delta''''(\mathrm{d}T^{\alpha\beta}/\mathrm{d}u^{\beta}) = -z^{\alpha 1}(z_u^{\alpha 1} - 2z_u^{\beta 1} + z_u^{\gamma 1}) + z_p^1 \tag{41a}$$

$$= \Delta'' - (z^{\alpha 1} - z^{\gamma 1})(z_u^{\gamma 1} - z_u^{\beta 1}) \tag{41b}$$

$$\Delta''''(\mathrm{d}T^{\gamma\beta}/\mathrm{d}u^{\beta}) = -z^{\gamma 1}(z_u^{\alpha 1} - 2z_u^{\beta 1} + z_u^{\gamma 1}) + z_p^1 \tag{42a}$$

$$= \Delta'' - (z^{\gamma 1} - z^{\alpha 1})(z_u^{\alpha 1} - z_u^{\beta 1}) \tag{42b}$$

where $\Delta'''' \equiv 2z_p^1 < 0$. If $z^{\alpha 1} = z^{\gamma 1}$ or if $z_u^{\beta 1}$ lies midway between $z_u^{\alpha 1}$ and $z_u^{\gamma 1}$ then $\mathrm{d}T^{\alpha\beta}/\mathrm{d}u^{\beta} = \mathrm{d}T^{\gamma\beta}/\mathrm{d}u^{\beta} > 0$. Otherwise, the vector $(\mathrm{d}T^{\alpha\beta}, \mathrm{d}T^{\gamma\beta})$ of incremental aid can have any pattern of signs. In particular, it is possible that the recipient β can be made better off with less aid from each donor. However, for that outcome it is necessary that the recipient's offer curve be inelastic and/or that the commodity exported by the recipient be inferior in at least one of the donor countries;[14] and, as (41b) and (42b) reveal, it is necessary also that the recipient's marginal propensity to buy any good fall between the donors' marginal propensities to buy the same good. Of course, whatever the manner in which aid changes, both donors find themselves worse off: $\mathrm{d}u^{\alpha} = \mathrm{d}u^{\gamma} = -\mathrm{d}u^{\beta}/2$.[15]

Suppose alternatively that in an initial equilibrium the single donor α gives $T^{\alpha\beta}$ to β and $T^{\alpha\gamma}$ to γ, both $T^{\alpha\beta}$ and $T^{\alpha\gamma}$ positive. The equilibrium is described by the equations

$$e^{\alpha}(p, u^{\alpha}) - r^{\alpha}(p) = -T^{\alpha\beta} - T^{\alpha\gamma} \tag{43}$$

$$e^{\beta}(p, u^{\beta}) - r^{\beta}(p) = T^{\alpha\beta} \tag{44}$$

$$e^{\gamma}(p, u^{\gamma}) - r^{\gamma}(p) = T^{\alpha\gamma} \tag{45}$$

$$z^{\alpha 1}(p, u^{\alpha}) + z^{\beta 1}(p, u^{\beta}) + z^{\gamma 1}(p, u^{\gamma}) = 0. \tag{16}$$

Treating u^{α} as a parameter and $T^{\alpha\beta}$, $T^{\alpha\gamma}$ as variables, both positive, we can differentiate ((43)–(45), (16)) with respect to u^{α}, add the equality-of-benefit condition $\mathrm{d}u^{\beta} = \mathrm{d}u^{\gamma}$, and solve for the aid received by the recipients β and γ. Thus

$$-\Delta''''(\mathrm{d}T^{\alpha\beta}/\mathrm{d}u^{\alpha}) = z^{\beta 1}(-2z_u^{\alpha 1} + z_u^{\beta 1} + z_u^{\gamma 1}) - z_p^1 \tag{46a}$$

$$= -\Delta'' + (z^{\beta 1} - z^{\gamma 1})(z_u^{\gamma 1} - z_u^{\alpha 1}) \tag{46b}$$

$$-\Delta''''(\mathrm{d}T^{\alpha\gamma}/\mathrm{d}u^{\alpha}) = z^{\gamma 1}(-2z_u^{\alpha 1} + z_u^{\beta 1} + z_u^{\gamma 1}) - z_p^1 \tag{47a}$$

$$= -\Delta'' + (z^{\beta 1} - z^{\gamma 1})(z_u^{\alpha 1} - z_u^{\beta 1}). \tag{47b}$$

If $z^{\beta 1} = z^{\gamma 1}$ or if $z_u^{\alpha 1} = z_u^{\beta 1} = z_u^{\gamma 1}$ then $\mathrm{d}T^{\alpha\beta}/\mathrm{d}u^{\alpha} = \mathrm{d}T^{\alpha\gamma}/\mathrm{d}u^{\alpha} < 0$. Otherwise, the vector $(\mathrm{d}T^{\alpha\beta}, \mathrm{d}T^{\alpha\gamma})$ of incremental aid can have any pattern of signs. In particular, it is possible that both recipients can be made better off with a smaller total outlay by the donor. However, for that outcome it is necessary that the donor's offer curve be inelastic and/or that the commodity exported by the donor be inferior in at least one of the recipient countries;[16] and, as (46b) and (47b) reveal, it is necessary also that the donor's marginal propensity to buy any good fall between the recipients' marginal propensities to buy the same good. Of course, whatever the manner in which aid changes, the donor is left worse off: $du^{\alpha} = -du^{\beta}/2 = -du^{\gamma}/2$.

4.4 Summary

In the traditional stable two-country setting additional aid implies an additional transfer. What we have established in this section is that, when there are more than two countries, there is no comparable result, even when donors and recipients share the burden or benefit equally. In particular, incremental binary aid may bring about paradoxical changes in the well-being of donor and/or recipient. However, this finding should not be taken quite literally. In the world about us, there are dozens of countries; in that world, incremental binary aid almost always will bring about welfare changes of the Samuelson kind. Rather, the α, β and γ of our models should be interpreted as aggregates of aid-giving countries, aid-receiving countries and bystander countries. **Even if each gift of each donor does good when considered as an isolated act, one cannot be sure that the sum of all gifts by all donors does good.**

5 AID BY TRANSFER OF INFORMATION – THE SIMPLEST CASE

Let us turn now to the welfare implications of international technical assistance. Aid of this kind differs in at least one important respect from aid by the transfer of goods. By spreading useful information it makes the world economy more efficient. This suggests that there are circumstances in which technical assistance improves the well-being of all countries simultaneously. On the other hand, the transfer of information improves the recipient's productive capacity and, as we know from the work of J. S. Mill and Edgeworth, this may give rise to such an adverse change in the recipient's terms of trade that, on balance and paradoxically, the recipient is impoverished.

In the present section, these and related questions are considered in the familiar setting of two countries and two commodities. Now, however, it is specified that one country (α) is technically advanced, the other (β) technically backward, in the sense that, in each industry, α is more efficient than β. Thus if v^{ij} denotes the vector of primary inputs used in the ith industry and jth country and $F^{ij}(v^{ij})$ the production function of that industry and country then

$$\text{for all } v^{i\alpha} = v^{i\beta} = v^{i} > 0, \quad F^{i\alpha}(v^{i}) = \mu(v^{i})F^{i\beta}(v^{i}) \quad \text{and} \quad \mu(v^{i}) > 1.$$

Suppose now that α makes a free gift of part of its technology to β such that in each industry the new production function is a constant $\lambda > 1$ times the old production function and β's production set expands in uniform proportion. We wish to know how the gift affects the terms of trade and the well-being of each country.

Introducing the β-productivity parameter λ, we rewrite the model of section 2 as

$$e^{\alpha}(p, u^{\alpha}) - r^{\alpha}(p) = 0 \tag{48}$$

$$e^{\beta}(p, u^{\beta}) - \lambda r^{\beta}(p) = 0 \tag{49}$$

$$z^{\alpha 1}(p, u^{\alpha}) + e^{\beta}_{p}(p, u^{\beta}) - \lambda r^{\beta}_{p}(p) = 0 \tag{50}$$

where λ is initially equal to one and increases when technical assistance takes place. Equation (50) is a less compact version of the market-clearing condition (3). Differentiating this system totally with respect to λ, and recalling that $\lambda = 1$ and that $e^j_p - r^j_p = z^{j1}$, we obtain

$$\begin{bmatrix} z^{\alpha 1} & 1 & 0 \\ z^{\beta 1} & 0 & 1 \\ z^{1}_{p} & z^{\alpha 1}_{u} & z^{\beta 1}_{u} \end{bmatrix} \begin{bmatrix} \mathrm{d}p \\ \mathrm{d}u^{\alpha} \\ \mathrm{d}u^{\beta} \end{bmatrix} = \begin{bmatrix} 0 \\ r^{\beta} \\ r^{\beta}_{p} \end{bmatrix} \mathrm{d}\lambda. \tag{51}$$

Solving,

$$\begin{aligned} \Delta(\mathrm{d}p/\mathrm{d}\lambda) &= r^{\beta}_{p} - r^{\beta} z^{\beta 1}_{u} \\ &= [(px^{\beta 1}/r^{\beta}) - p z^{\beta 1}_{u}]\, r^{\beta}/p \\ &= (\theta^{\beta 1} - m^{\beta 1})(r^{\beta}/p) \end{aligned} \tag{52a}$$

$$\Delta(\mathrm{d}u^{\alpha}/\mathrm{d}\lambda) = (m^{\beta 1} - \theta^{\beta 1})(z^{\alpha 1} r^{\beta}/p) \tag{52b}$$

$$\Delta(\mathrm{d}u^{\beta}/\mathrm{d}\lambda) = (m^{\beta 1} - \theta^{\beta 1})(z^{\beta 1} r^{\beta}/p) + r^{\beta} z^{1}_{p} \tag{52c}$$

where $x^{\beta 1} \equiv r^{\beta}_{p}$ is β's output of the first commodity, $\theta^{\beta 1} \equiv px^{\beta 1}/r^{\beta}$ is the share of the first industry in β's national product and $m^{\beta 1} \equiv p z^{\beta 1}_{u}$ is β's marginal propensity to consume the first commodity.

We see at once that at least one of the countries benefits from the transfer of knowledge. Otherwise, the vector of welfare changes $(\mathrm{d}u^{\alpha}, \mathrm{d}u^{\beta})$ can have any pattern of signs. Either country can suffer; in particular, the recipient can suffer, confirming the Mill–Edgeworth discovery. However, it is possible also that both countries benefit; for that outcome it is necessary and sufficient that

$$p z^{1}_{p} < -z^{\beta 1}(m^{\beta 1} - \theta^{\beta 1}) < 0.$$

Suppose that preferences in β are homothetic. Then $m^{\beta 1} = a^{\beta 1}$, where $a^{\beta 1}$ is β's average propensity to consume the first commodity, and $z^{\beta 1}(m^{\beta 1} - \theta^{\beta 1}) \geqslant 0$. Bearing in mind that Δ is negative, we see from (52b) that the donor is never impoverished and, if there is some initial trade, is necessarily enriched by its act of generosity. Moreover, the incentive to transfer information persists, both at the level of government and at the level of the individual firm, for as long as α is more efficient in each industry, that is for as long as α has a global absolute advantage. This finding has destructive implications for textbook trade theory.[17] Whether economists interested in economic development should pay attention to it will depend on its robustness under less restrictive assumptions.

It is easy to see that the proposition is impervious to the addition of commodities. If preferences in β are homothetic, the transfer of information by α causes β to increase its demand for imports and increase its supply of exports. The upshot is an improvement in α's terms of trade and well-being.

In the following section we shall check the robustness of the finding to the addition of countries.

6 AID BY TRANSFER OF INFORMATION – BYSTANDERS

Adding a third country γ, we arrive at the system

$$e^{\alpha}(p, u^{\alpha}) - r^{\alpha}(p) = 0 \tag{1}$$

$$e^{\beta}(p, u^{\beta}) - \lambda r^{\beta}(p) = 0 \tag{49}$$

$$e^{\gamma}(p, u^{\gamma}) - r^{\gamma}(p) = 0 \tag{15}$$

$$z^{\alpha 1}(p, u^{\alpha}) + e^{\beta}_{p}(p, u^{\beta}) - \lambda r^{\beta}_{p}(p) + z^{\gamma 1}(p, u^{\gamma}) = 0. \tag{53}$$

Differentiating with respect to λ, we obtain

$$\begin{bmatrix} z^{\alpha 1} & 1 & 0 & 0 \\ z^{\beta 1} & 0 & 1 & 0 \\ z^{\gamma 1} & 0 & 0 & 1 \\ z^{1}_{p} & z^{\alpha 1}_{u} & z^{\beta 1}_{u} & z^{\gamma 1}_{u} \end{bmatrix} \begin{bmatrix} dp \\ du^{\alpha} \\ du^{\beta} \\ du^{\gamma} \end{bmatrix} = \begin{bmatrix} 0 \\ r^{\beta} \\ 0 \\ r^{\beta}_{p} \end{bmatrix} d\lambda. \tag{54}$$

Solving,

$$\Delta''(dp/d\lambda) = -(m^{\beta 1} - \theta^{\beta 1})r^{\beta}/p \tag{55a}$$

$$\Delta''(du^{\alpha}/d\lambda) = (m^{\beta 1} - \theta^{\beta 1})r^{\beta} z^{\alpha 1}/p \tag{55b}$$

$$\Delta''(du^{\beta}/d\lambda) = -[\Delta'' - (m^{\beta 1} - \theta^{\beta 1})z^{\beta 1}/p]r^{\beta} \tag{55c}$$

$$\Delta''(du^{\gamma}/d\lambda) = (m^{\beta 1} - \theta^{\beta 1})z^{\gamma 1} r^{\beta}/p. \tag{55d}$$

We notice the strong symmetry between $du^{\alpha}/d\lambda$ and $du^{\gamma}/d\lambda$; the identity of the donor is of no significance. We see also that, given homotheticity of the recipient's preferences, the donor benefits if and only if the donor and recipient export different commodities. When there are just two countries, that condition is necessarily satisfied; but when there are three or more countries the condition need not be satisfied.

As a corollary of these propositions, both donor and bystander benefit if and only if they export the same commodity. To the extent that wealthy countries tend to export the same commodities and to the extent that aid flows from wealthy to poor countries, **the corollary gives some basis for believing that wealthy countries are individually enriched by their collective generosity.**

We now know that when there are just two countries and the recipient's preferences are homothetic, the donor is necessarily enriched; and that, when there are three countries, technical assistance to one country may impoverish the donor even though the recipient's preferences are homothetic. Can we infer from these findings that if preferences are homothetic in both β and γ then the transfer of information by α to both β and γ must enrich α? If the answer to that question were in the affirmative then we would know that, the more widespread its generosity, the more likely is the donor to benefit from its generosity. Unfortunately the inference is not generally valid; the inclusion of γ in α's programme of technical assistance might or might not work to α's advantage. Thus we find again that the practice of lumping together all other countries as 'the rest of the world' does not bring back the orthodox two-country conclusions. However, if both recipients export the same commodity then the inference can be made. To verify that this is so, we write the revised system

$$e^{\alpha}(p, u^{\alpha}) - r^{\alpha}(p) = 0 \tag{56}$$

$$e^{\beta}(p, u^{\beta}) - \lambda r^{\beta}(p) = 0 \tag{57}$$

$$e^{\gamma}(p, u^{\gamma}) - \lambda r^{\gamma}(p) = 0 \tag{58}$$

$$z^{\alpha 1}(p, u^{\alpha}) + e_p^{\beta}(p, u^{\beta}) - \lambda r_p^{\beta}(p) + e_p^{\gamma}(p, u^{\gamma}) - \lambda r_p^{\gamma}(p) = 0. \tag{59}$$

Differentiating with respect to λ, we obtain

$$\begin{bmatrix} z^{\alpha 1} & 1 & 0 & 0 \\ z^{\beta 1} & 0 & 1 & 0 \\ z^{\gamma 1} & 0 & 0 & 1 \\ z_p^1 & z_u^{\alpha 1} & z_u^{\beta 1} & z_u^{\gamma 1} \end{bmatrix} \begin{bmatrix} \mathrm{d}p \\ \mathrm{d}u^{\alpha} \\ \mathrm{d}u^{\beta} \\ \mathrm{d}u^{\gamma} \end{bmatrix} = \begin{bmatrix} 0 \\ r^{\beta} \\ r^{\gamma} \\ r_p^{\beta} + r_p^{\gamma} \end{bmatrix} \mathrm{d}\lambda. \tag{60}$$

Solving,

$$\Delta''(\mathrm{d}p/\mathrm{d}\lambda) = -(r_p^{\beta} + r_p^{\gamma}) + (r^{\beta} z_u^{\beta 1} + r^{\gamma} z_u^{\gamma 1}) \tag{61a}$$

$$\Delta''(\mathrm{d}u^{\alpha}/\mathrm{d}\lambda) = (z^{\alpha 1}/p)[r^{\beta}(m^{\beta 1} - \theta^{\beta 1}) + r^{\gamma}(m^{\gamma 1} - \theta^{\gamma 1})] \tag{61b}$$

$$\Delta''(\mathrm{d}u^{\beta}/\mathrm{d}\lambda) = r^{\beta}\Delta'' + [r^{\beta}(m^{\beta 1} - \theta^{\beta 1}) + r^{\gamma}(m^{\gamma 1} - \theta^{\gamma 1})](z^{\beta 1}/p) \tag{61c}$$

$$\Delta''(\mathrm{d}u^{\gamma}/\mathrm{d}\lambda) = r^{\gamma}\Delta'' + [r^{\beta}(m^{\beta 1} - \theta^{\beta 1}) + r^{\gamma}(m^{\gamma 1} - \theta^{\gamma 1})](z^{\gamma 1}/p). \tag{61d}$$

Evidently $\mathrm{d}u^{\alpha}/\mathrm{d}\lambda$ may be negative, even if preferences are homothetic in both β and γ. However, for that outcome it is necessary that β and γ export different commodities. In other words, for donor enrichment it suffices that both recipients export the same commodity. On the other hand, even that condition does not ensure that both recipients gain; indeed, it does not ensure that one of them gains.

Many additional questions, most of them with counterparts in section 5, might be addressed to the model of this section. To work through the details would be tedious. Here we simply note[18] that, even if α has a global absolute advantage over both β and γ, it may be unable to help β directly (by technical assistance to β) or indirectly (by technical assistance to γ); indeed α may be unable to help β or γ, either by extending technical assistance to one of them or by assisting both according to some sharing formula. Thus a country may be incapable of playing the Good Samaritan, either by gifts of private goods or by technical assistance.

7 THE RESOURCE-USING ADMINISTRATION OF FOREIGN AID

It is inevitable that some part of every programme of foreign aid will be absorbed by administrative procedures or in downright waste. Indeed there may have been historical instances in which the net aid received was negative.[19] In the present section, I briefly rework the two-country analysis of section 2 to accommodate resource leakages of this sort. Several unexpected possibilities come to light. In particular it emerges that if only a proportion ω, $\omega < 1$, of the aid reaches the recipient then it is possible that (i) the donor is enriched by its act of charity, the extent of the enrichment increasing with the extent of the leakage, and that (ii) the recipient is impoverished by aid, the extent of the impoverishment increasing with the extent of the leakage. Indeed it is possible that outcomes (i) and (ii) are realized simultaneously. Of course, it is also possible that both donor and recipient are impoverished by a particular programme of aid; but it is not possible that they are both enriched.

Suppose, for the sake of simplicity only, that the costs of administering aid are borne by the recipient and that the administration of aid is subject to the same laws of production as the *numéraire*. Then the equilibrium of the world economy is described by equations (1)–(3), with one small change – the aid received by β is now $\omega T^{\alpha\beta}$, not $T^{\alpha\beta}$:

$$e^{\alpha}(p, u^{\alpha}) = r^{\alpha}(p) - T^{\alpha\beta} \tag{1}$$

$$e^{\beta}(p, u^{\beta}) = r^{\beta}(p) + \omega T^{\alpha\beta} \tag{62}$$

$$z^{\alpha 1}(p, u^{\alpha}) + z^{\beta 1}(p, u^{\beta}) = 0. \tag{3}$$

Differentiating the system with respect to $T^{\alpha\beta}$, we obtain

$$\begin{bmatrix} z^{\alpha 1} & 1 & 0 \\ z^{\beta 1} & 0 & 1 \\ z_p^1 & z_u^{\alpha 1} & z_u^{\beta 1} \end{bmatrix} \begin{bmatrix} dp \\ du^{\alpha} \\ du^{\beta} \end{bmatrix} = \begin{bmatrix} -1 \\ \omega \\ 0 \end{bmatrix} dT^{\alpha\beta}. \tag{63}$$

Solving,

$$\Delta(dp/dT^{\alpha\beta}) = z_u^{\alpha 1} - \omega z_u^{\beta 1} \tag{64a}$$

$$\Delta(\mathrm{d}u^{\alpha}/\mathrm{d}T^{\alpha\beta}) = (1 - \omega)z^{\beta 1}z_u^{\beta 1} - z_p^1 \tag{64b}$$

$$\Delta(\mathrm{d}u^{\beta}/\mathrm{d}T^{\alpha\beta}) = (1 - \omega)z^{\alpha 1}z_u^{\alpha 1} + \omega z_p^1. \tag{64c}$$

Inspection of (64b) reveals that if $z^{\beta 1}z_u^{\beta 1} < 0$, that is if β imports (exports) the first or non-*numéraire* good and that good is inferior (normal) in β-consumption, then $\mathrm{d}u^{\alpha}/\mathrm{d}T^{\alpha\beta}$ is a declining function of ω, with $\mathrm{d}u^{\alpha}/\mathrm{d}T^{\alpha\beta}$ positive if $\omega < 1 - z_p^1/(z^{\beta 1}z_u^{\beta 1}) < 1$ and $\mathrm{d}u^{\alpha}/\mathrm{d}T^{\alpha\beta}$ negative if $\omega > 1 - z_p^1/(z^{\beta 1}z_u^{\beta 1})$. Equation (64c), on the other hand, reveals that if $z^{\alpha 1}z_u^{\alpha 1} > 0$, that is if α imports (exports) the first good and if that good is normal (inferior) in α-consumption, then $\mathrm{d}u^{\beta}/\mathrm{d}T^{\alpha\beta}$ is an increasing function of ω, with $\mathrm{d}u^{\beta}/\mathrm{d}T^{\alpha\beta}$ negative if $\omega < z^{\alpha 1}z_u^{\alpha 1}/(z^{\alpha 1}z_u^{\alpha 1} - z_p^1) < 1$ and positive if $z^{\alpha 1}z_u^{\alpha 1}/(z^{\alpha 1}z_u^{\alpha 1} - z_p^1) < \omega \leqslant 1$. Since both countries cannot benefit from a programme of aid, we can be sure that

$$[1 - z_p^1/(z^{\beta 1}z_u^{\beta 1})] < z^{\alpha 1}z_u^{\alpha 1}/(z^{\alpha 1}z_u^{\alpha 1} - z_p^1) = [1 - z_p^1/(z^{\alpha 1}z_u^{\alpha 1})]^{-1}$$

and, therefore, that if $\omega < 1 - z_p^1/(z^{\beta 1}z_p^{\beta 1})$ then the conventional or Samuelsonian welfare responses are reversed. In the special case $z_p^1 = 0$, if $z^{\beta 1}z_u^{\beta 1} < 0$ then, for Walrasian stability, it is necessary that $z^{\alpha 1}z_u^{\alpha 1} > 0$; from (64b) and (64c), therefore, for $\mathrm{d}u^{\alpha}/\mathrm{d}T^{\alpha\beta} > 0$ and $\mathrm{d}u^{\beta}/\mathrm{d}T^{\alpha\beta} < 0$ it suffices that $\omega < 1$ and $z^{\beta 1}z_u^{\beta 1} < 0$.

Thus it has been verified that (i) and (ii) are possible outcomes. Just as the Samuelsonian conclusions failed to survive the introduction of bystanders and of market distortions like aid tying, so they fail in a context of administrative costs and wastage.

The paradoxical flavour of (i) and (ii) can be removed by reflecting that resource-absorbing administration represents a loss of β-income. Thus superimposed on the Samuelsonian costs and benefits of aid are the costs and benefits associated with a Mill–Edgeworth country-specific loss of income. The latter can dominate the former, leaving the donor α better off and the recipient β worse off than in the absence of aid.[20]

8 NEXT STEPS

The welfare economics of international aid, as expounded in sections 2–7, is deficient on several counts. As noted in the introduction, the theory is static, with no time dimension; it is based on the assumption of well-functioning competitive markets failing to accommodate the market aberrations characteristic of all countries; and it treats the level and world-wide allocation of aid as parameters, not as variables the equilibrium values of which are determined on a network of imperfectly competitive markets in which the usual prices (rates of interest) are replaced by vectors of broadly defined tying conditions. It must now be added that the theory is based on the assumption that aid is financed and distributed by lumpsum taxes and subsidies. The assumption is unrealistic;

moreover, such devices create problems of incentives not recognized in the theory. Finally, the entire analysis makes sense only if all trading countries are solvent. It does not apply if, before or after aid, one or more of the countries finds itself in the disequilibrium condition of insolvency.

There is plenty of useful work to be done.

NOTES

* To Ben Higgins I offer thanks for forty years of friendship, instruction and fun; and for two hours of expert technical assistance in getting this essay into shape.

Helpful conversations and correspondence with Horst Herberg and Albert Schweinberger are also gratefully acknowledged.

1 For a preliminary treatment of these matters, the reader may consult Kemp *et al.* (1990).

2 For an authoritative discussion of the concept, the reader is referred to Higgins (1960) and (1962: Ch. 2).

3 For a persuasive statement concerning the importance of this role, see Higgins (1989).

4 For a related welfare analysis of concessionary commercial policy, the reader may consult Kemp and Shimomura (1990).

5 Alternatively, we may make use of the market-clearing condition

$$z^{\alpha 2}(p, u^{\alpha}) + z^{\beta 2}(p, u^{\beta}) = 0. \qquad (*)$$

However, (1) and (2) can be rewritten as

$$pz^{\alpha 1} + z^{\alpha 2} = -T^{\alpha\beta}$$

and

$$pz^{\beta 1} + z^{\beta 2} = T^{\alpha\beta}$$

respectively, so that, adding,

$$p(z^{\alpha 1} + z^{\beta 1}) + (z^{\alpha 2} + z^{\beta 2}) = 0.$$

Hence (1)–(3) imply (*).

6 In the singular case in which $\Delta = 0$, the system may be locally stable or unstable; it all depends then on the non-linear terms in the expansion of the functions in (1)–(3) about the equilibrium point.

7 This proposition seems to be missing from the literature. For an unpublished statement and proof of the proposition, see Safra (1983).

8 The analysis of the *Foundations* has been extended by Wang (1985) to accommodate factor-market distortions and by Samuelson (1954), Ohyama (1974) and Bhagwati *et al.* (1985) to allow for import duties. Recently, Turunen-Red and Woodland (1988) have shown that in a protectionist world it may be possible to find a Pareto-improving multilateral transfer.

9 For a more detailed treatment, see Kemp and Kojima (1985b, 1987); the reader may also consult Kemp and Kojima (1985a) and, for a pioneering treatment of other forms of tying, Ohyama (1974).

10 Gale's example involves pure exchange, two commodities and individual preferences of the fixed-proportions type. However, perverse outcomes are possible without those special features. Thus, Léonard and Manning (1983) have shown how to

construct whole families of two-commodity examples characterized by smooth preferences, market stability and perverse welfare outcomes of Gale's type. The phenomenon of perversity in three-country economies is further discussed by Yano (1983) and by Bhagwati *et al.* (1983). The exposition of the next subsection follows that of Bhagwati *et al.*

11 Suppose that α cannot help β directly. Then, from (20),

$$z^{\gamma 1}(z_u^{\alpha 1} - z_u^{\gamma 1}) > 0. \qquad (*)$$

Permuting the subscripts α and γ in (19), we see that a transfer from γ to β helps β if

$$z^{\alpha 1}(z_u^{\alpha 1} - z_u^{\gamma 1}) > 0. \qquad (**)$$

But if α and γ export the same commodity, (*) implies (**).

12 For α to be a friend to neither β nor γ it is **necessary** that β and γ export different commodities and that, for each commodity, α's marginal propensity to consume be intermediate to those of β and γ. By way of proof, assume that (20) and (21) are positive with and without the superscripts β and γ interchanged and then note that the four inequalities imply the conditions for the proposition.

To establish beyond doubt that both β and γ might be made worse off, however the aid is divided between them, we offer the following example: $z_p^1 = 0 = z^{\alpha 1}$, $z^{\beta 1} > 0$, $z_u^{\gamma 1} < z_u^{\alpha 1} < z_u^{\beta 1}$.

13 This paragraph contains a corrected version of the analysis of Kemp and Kojima (1987: 102–4).

14 If both $dT^{\alpha\beta}/du^{\beta}$ and $dT^{\gamma\beta}/du^{\beta}$ are negative then, adding (41) and (42) and making use of (16),

$$-z^{\beta 1}(z_u^{\alpha 1} - 2z_u^{\beta 1} + z_u^{\gamma 1}) - 2z_p^1 < 0.$$

Substituting from the Slutzky equation $z_p^{\beta 1} = \tilde{z}_p^{\beta 1} + z^{\beta 1} z_u^{\beta 1}$,

$$-z^{\beta 1}(z_u^{\alpha 1} + z_u^{\gamma 1}) - 2\tilde{z}_p^{\beta 1} - 2(z_p^{\alpha 1} + z_p^{\gamma 1}) < 0. \qquad (\dagger)$$

If $z^{\beta 1} < 0$, the proposition follows immediately. Suppose then that $z^{\beta 1} > 0$. By Walras' law,

$$p\tilde{z}^{\beta 1}(p) + \tilde{z}^{\beta 2}(p) - T^{\alpha\beta} - T^{\gamma\beta} = 0$$

so that, differentiating with respect to p,

$$z^{\beta 1} + p\tilde{z}_p^{\beta 1} + \tilde{z}_p^{\beta 2} = 0. \qquad (\dagger\dagger)$$

Substituting from (††) and recalling that, for each country, the two marginal propensities to consume add to one, (†) becomes

$$(z^{\beta 1}/p)(z_u^{\alpha 2} + z_u^{\gamma 2}) + (2/p)\tilde{z}_p^{\beta 2} - 2(z_p^{\alpha 1} + z_p^{\gamma 1}) < 0.$$

The proposition then follows from the twin facts that

$$z^{\beta 1} > 0 \quad \text{and} \quad z_p^{\alpha 1} + z_p^{\gamma 1} < 0.$$

15 In this paragraph we have answered the question: how does equal utility sharing translate into aid sharing (where aid is measured in terms of the *numéraire*)? The question can be turned about: how does equal aid sharing translate into utility

sharing? To answer the second question, one treats u^{β} as a parameter and u^{α}, u^{γ}, $T^{\alpha\beta}$ and $T^{\gamma\beta}$ as variables, with the revised equality-of-sharing condition $dT^{\alpha\beta} = dT^{\gamma\beta}$. Again omitting the detailed calculations, we have

$$\Delta'''''(du^{\alpha}/du^{\beta}) = (z^{\alpha 1} - z^{\gamma 1})(z_u^{\beta 1} - z_u^{\gamma 1}) - z_p^1$$

$$\Delta'''''(du^{\gamma}/du^{\beta}) = (z^{\gamma 1} - z^{\alpha 1})(z_u^{\beta 1} - z_u^{\alpha 1}) - z_p^1$$

$$\Delta'''''(dT^{\alpha\beta}/du^{\beta}) = \Delta''''(dT^{\gamma\beta}/du^{\beta}) = \Delta''$$

where

$$\Delta''''' \equiv -(z_u^{\alpha 1} - z_u^{\gamma 1})(z^{\alpha 1} - z^{\gamma 1}) + 2z_p^1 < 0.$$

If $z^{\alpha 1} = z^{\gamma 1}$ or if $z_u^{\beta 1}$ lies midway between $z_u^{\alpha 1}$ and $z_u^{\gamma 1}$ then $du^{\alpha}/du^{\beta} = du^{\gamma}/du^{\beta} < 0$; otherwise, the vector $(du^{\alpha}/du^{\beta}, du^{\gamma}/du^{\beta})$ may contain one positive term. In general, it is possible that the recipient β can be made better off with less aid from each donor.

16 The proof follows the general lines of note 14.

17 See Kemp and Shimomura (1988).

18 The following assertions can be verified on the basis of (55) only.

19 See Bauer (1971: 99–100).

20 For a more detailed reconciliation of (i) and (ii) with Samuelson's findings, the reader may consult Kemp and Wong (1993).

REFERENCES

Balasko, Y. (1978), 'The transfer problem and the theory of regular economies', *International Economic Review* 19: 687–94.

Bauer, P. T. (1971) *Dissent on Development*, London: Weidenfeld and Nicolson.

Bhagwati, J. N., Brecher, R. A. and Hatta, T. (1983) 'The generalized theory of transfers and welfare: Bilateral transfers in a multilateral world', *American Economic Review* 83: 606–18.

Bhagwati, J. N., Brecher, R. A. and Hatta, T. (1985) 'The generalized theory of transfers and welfare: Exogenous (policy-imposed) and endogenous (transfer-induced) distortions', *Quarterly Journal of Economics* 100: 697–714.

Gale, D. (1974) 'Exchange equilibrium and coalitions: An example', *Journal of Mathematical Economics* 1: 63–6.

Higgins, B. H. (1960) 'Assistance étrangère et capacité d'absorption', *Développement et Civilisations* Octobre–Décembre: 28–43.

Higgins, B. H. (1962) *United Nations and U.S. Foreign Economic Policy*, Homewood, IL: Irwin.

Higgins, B. H. (1989) *The Road Less Travelled*, Vol. 2 of the series *History of Development Studies*, Canberra: National Centre for Development Studies, Australian National University.

Kemp, M. C. and Kojima, S. (1985a) 'The welfare economics of foreign aid', in G. R. Feiwel (ed.) *Issues in Contemporary Microeconomics and Welfare*, pp. 470–83, London: Macmillan.

Kemp, M. C. and Kojima, S. (1985b) 'Tied aid and the paradoxes of donor-enrichment and recipient-impoverishment', *International Economic Review* 26: 721–9.

Kemp, M. C. and Kojima, S. (1987) 'More on the welfare economics of foreign aid', *Journal of the Japanese and International Economies* 1: 97–109.

Kemp, M. C. and Shimomura, K. (1988) 'The impossibility of global absolute advantage in the Heckscher–Ohlin model of trade', *Oxford Economic Papers* 40, 575–6.

Kemp, M. C. and Shimomura, K. (1990) ' "Trade" or "aid"?', in H. Ohta *et al.* (eds) *Trade, Policy, and International Adjustments*, pp. 19–35, New York: Academic Press.

Kemp, M. C. and Wong, K.-Y. (1993) 'Paradoxes associated with the administration of foreign aid', *Journal of Development Economics* 42: 197–204.

Kemp, M. C., Long, N. V. and Shimomura, K. (1990) 'On the optimal timing of foreign aid', *Kobe Economic and Business Review* 35: 31–49.

Léonard, D. and Manning, R. (1983) 'Advantageous reallocations: A constructive example', *Journal of International Economics* 15: 291–5.

Leontief, W. (1936) 'Note on the pure theory of capital transfer', in *Explorations in Economics: Notes and Essays Contributed in Honor of F. W. Taussig*, pp. 84–92, New York: McGraw-Hill.

Ohyama, M. (1972) 'Trade and welfare in general equilibrium', *Keio Economic Studies* 9: 37–73.

Ohyama, M. (1974) 'Tariffs and the transfer problem', *Keio Economic Studies* 11: 29–45.

Safra, Z. (1983) 'The transfer paradox: Stability, uniqueness and smooth preferences', Harvard University.

Samuelson, P. A. (1954) 'The transfer problem and transfer costs', *Economic Journal* 64: 264–9.

Schweinberger, A. G. (1990) 'On the welfare effects of tied aid', *International Economic Review* 31: 457–62.

Turunen-Red, A. H. and Woodland, A. D. (1988) 'On the multilateral, transfer problem: Existence of Pareto improving international transfers', *Journal of International Economics* 25: 249–69.

Wang, L. F. S. (1985) 'Factor market distortions, the transfer problem, and welfare', *Keio Economic Studies* 22: 57–64.

Yano, M. (1983) 'Welfare aspects of the transfer problem', *Journal of International Economics* 15: 277–89.

28

CONDITIONS FOR THE LOCAL IMPOTENCE OF LUMPSUM TRANSFERS TO EFFECT A REDISTRIBUTION OF WELFARE BETWEEN NATIONS*

Suppose that N countries collectively produce and trade m private consumption goods and t pure public consumption goods. Here it is understood that $N \geqslant 2$, $m \geqslant 0$, $t \geqslant 1$ and $m + t \geqslant 2$; thus it is not required that either countries or commodities exceed the traditional two in number. Suppose further that the governments of the trading countries have only two functions: they impose corrective taxes to ensure that, from the national point of view, private consumption of public goods is optimal; and they may engage in international lumpsum transfers. On the basis of these assumptions we can establish the following proposition.

Proposition. *If in international equilibrium each country purchases at least one public good then any pattern of sufficiently small international transfers leaves unchanged (a) world prices of both private and public goods, (b) the consumption by each country of both private and public goods, and therefore (c) the welfare of each country.*

That is, within limits the world equilibrium is independent of the international distribution of income; a small international transfer is completely absorbed in offsetting changes in the private consumption of public goods in those countries which are parties to the transfer.

On reflection the proposition makes a strong appeal to common sense. Thus suppose that an initial equilibrium is disturbed by the transfer of one dollar from country 1 to country 2. If the donor cuts its expenditure on public goods by exactly the amount transferred and if the recipient increases its expenditure on public goods by the same amount then, in each country, the total consumption of each good, public and private, is unchanged and no country has an incentive to make further adjustments to its expenditure.

Warr (1983) proved a version of the proposition suited to a closed economy with $t = 1$; but he claimed that the proposition is invalid for $t > 1$, thus implying that it is negligible. Kemp and Kojima (1985), on the other hand, examined the welfare economics of international transfers under the polar specification that public goods are provided only by governments and are public within the borders of a single country.

Proof of the proposition. *Let c^i be the vector of the consumption of private goods in country i; and let g^i be the vector of purchases of public goods in country i, so that Σg^i is the vector of consumption of public goods in each country. Let p be the vector of world prices of private goods, q the vector of world prices of public goods, and y^i the income of country i. The task of the typical individual in country i is then to find*

$$\max_{c^i, g^i} u^i\left(c^i, \sum g^j\right) \tag{P}$$

subject to

$$pc^i + qg^i \leqslant y^i \tag{1}$$

$$c^i \geqslant 0, \quad g^i \geqslant 0, \tag{2}$$

where u^i is taken to be an increasing and strictly quasi-concave function. By assumption, any solution to (P) is interior in g^i; for simplicity only, suppose that it is interior in c^i also. The first-order conditions consist of (1) and

$$u^i_k = \lambda^i p_k, \quad k = 1, \ldots, m$$

$$u^i_l = \lambda^i p_l, \quad l = 1, \ldots, t$$

whence

$$J^i_k\left(c^i, \sum g^j\right) \equiv u^i_k / u^i_t = p_k / q_t, \quad k = 1, \ldots, m \tag{3a}$$

$$J^i_l\left(c^i, \sum g^i\right) \equiv u^i_l / u^i_t = p_l / q_t \quad l = 1, \ldots, t-1. \tag{3b}$$

Recalling that $i = 1, \ldots, N$, we see that in (1) and (3) there are $n + n(m + t - 1) = n(m + t)$ equations in the same number of unknowns (nm c^i_k's and nt g^i_l's). If $t = 1$ we can reasonably require (1) and (3) to be uniquely solvable. When $t > 1$ we cannot expect to solve for the g^i_l's, for to individual countries the source of supply of a particular public good is a matter of indifference; however, even when $t > 1$, we can reasonably require both the aggregate world supply of individual public goods and the value of all public goods supplied by each particular country to be uniquely determined, and that is all we need. Let the unique solution be indicated by asterisks. From (3a),

$$c^{i*} = H^i\left(p, q, \sum g^{j*}\right) \equiv H^i(p, q, g^*). \tag{4}$$

From (1),

$$y \equiv \sum y^j = p \sum H^j(p, q, g^*) + qg^*. \tag{5}$$

From (5) and (3b), the latter with solution values inserted,

$$g^* = D(p, q, y). \tag{6}$$

Thus g^* depends on aggregate income only. From (4) and (6),

$$c^{i*} = H^i(p, q, D(p, q, y)) \equiv E^i(p, q, y). \tag{7}$$

Hence

$$c^* = \sum c^{j*} = \sum E^j(p, q, y) \equiv E(p, q, y). \tag{8}$$

Thus c^{i*} and therefore c^* depend on aggregate income only. The conclusions of the proposition follow immediately. □

As already noted, the proposition does not rely on the assumption that country *i* purchases the whole range of private consumption goods; in fact it is not required that country *i* purchases **any** private consumption goods. Of much greater importance, it is not required that the intra-national publicness of public consumption goods be offset by corrective taxes. That assumption merely simplifies the proof by allowing one to treat each country as a single coherent maximizer.

We note also that the proposition is valid for any international equilibrium, whether stable or unstable, whether or not some goods are inferior in consumption, and whether or not there are more than two countries. Thus it contrasts sharply with the literature on the welfare paradoxes of international transfers. (The key contributions are those of Ohyama (1972, 1974) and Gale (1974). For further references, see Kemp and Kojima (1985).)

What **is** indispensable is the assumed uniqueness of the world equilibrium. Without that assumption there are many ways of choosing the post-transfer equilibrium, and associated with each choice is a different vector of equilibrium national welfares.

NOTE

* The first part of this essay appeared, in preliminary form, in Kemp (1984). However, in that earlier version the generality of the central proposition was rather played down. In particular, it was not noted that the proposition is valid whether or not the intra-national publicness of public consumption goods is neutralized by suitable commodity taxation.

REFERENCES

Gale, D. (1974) 'Exchange equilibrium and coalitions: An example', *Journal of Mathematical Economics* 1: 63–6.

Kemp, M. C. (1984) 'A note on the theory of international transfers', *Economic Letters* 14: 259–62.

Kemp, M. C. and Kojima, S. (1985) 'The welfare economics of foreign aid', in G. R. Feiwel (ed.) *Issues in Contemporary Microeconomics and Welfare*, pp. 470–83, London: Macmillan.

Ohyama, M. (1972) 'Trade and welfare in general equilibrium', *Keio Economic Studies* 9: 37–73.

Ohyama, M. (1974) 'Tariffs and the transfer problem', *Keio Economic Studies* 11: 29–45.

Warr, P. G. (1983) 'The private provision of a public good is independent of the distribution of income', *Economics Letters* 13: 207–11.

29

THE TRANSFER PROBLEM IN A CONTEXT OF PUBLIC GOODS*

1 INTRODUCTION

It is widely accepted that in a stable and distortion-free competitive world, with just two trading countries and constant returns to scale, any feasible lumpsum transfer between countries must reduce the well-being of the donor and enhance that of the recipient. However, proofs of the proposition have relied on the twin assumptions

1. that each of the two countries is **egalitarian** and therefore behaves like a single price-taking individual, and
2. that all goods are **private** or non-public.

Assumption (1) is essential. That much has been known, or should have been known, since the appearance of Johnson (1960). We now introduce a pure (non-excludable, non-rivalrous) public good and show that the proposition remains valid; that is, we show that assumption (2) is inessential. Only one public good is formally recognized. However, our conclusion is valid whatever the number of such goods.

Of course, the assumption of egalitarianism is maintained. This enables us to take advantage of an insight of Kemp and Long (1992), that in egalitarian societies the private provision of public goods coincides with the socially optimal provision of public goods.

Two cases are studied. We deal in detail with the case of a pure intermediate good which, in the country of its production, is freely available without congestion to all producers of private goods in that country but which is unavailable to producers in the other country. Then, more briefly, we consider the case of a pure public consumption good confined to consumers in the country of production. Our analysis ends with the passing notice of pure **international** public goods, that is public goods which are freely available without congestion to the consumers or producers of both countries, whatever the place of production.

2 A PURE PUBLIC INTERMEDIATE GOOD

Let there be two countries, α and β, two private goods and one pure public intermediate good the benefits of which are confined to the country in which it is produced. The two private goods are traded internationally. The second private good is chosen as *numéraire*. The price of the first private good in terms of the second is denoted by p; the amount transferred from α to β, in terms of the second good, is denoted by T.

Each country is inhabited by households which are identical in all respects and by firms which have access to a common technology. However, the preferences and endowments of α-households may differ in any way from those of β-households, and the technology available in α may differ in any way from that available in β. The expenditure function of the jth country may therefore be written simply as $e^j(p, u^j)$ where e^j is the minimum aggregate expenditure by households on the two private goods, in terms of the second commodity, given the world price ratio p and given the well-being of the typical family u^j. The restricted revenue function of the jth country is denoted by $R^j(p, g^j, v^j)$, where R_j is the maximum value of private output, in terms of the second commodity, given the amount of the public good produced g^j and the vector of factor endowments v^j. The excess demand function for the first private commodity in the jth country is then $z^{j1}(p, g^j, u^j) = \partial e^j(p, u^j)/\partial p - \partial R^j(p, g^j, v^j)/\partial p$. Notice that the revenue functions R^α and R^β are defined for **given** g^α and g^β and, in that sense, are **restricted** revenue functions. Henceforth we shall delete the constant endowment vectors as explicit arguments of the revenue functions and write the latter more simply as $r^\alpha(p, g^\alpha)$ and $r^\beta(p, g^\beta)$.

A transfer T from α to β is financed in each country by lumpsum taxes on individual households. The equilibrium of the world economy is then described by the system of equations

$$e^\alpha(p, u^\alpha) - r^\alpha(p, g^\alpha) + T = 0 \tag{1}$$

$$r_g^\alpha(p, g^\alpha) = 0 \tag{2}$$

$$e^\beta(p, u^\beta) - r^\beta(p, g^\beta) - T = 0 \tag{3}$$

$$r_g^\beta(p, g^\beta) = 0 \tag{4}$$

$$z^{\alpha 1}(p, g^\alpha, u^\alpha) + z^{\beta 1}(p, g^\beta, u^\beta) = 0 \tag{5}$$

where $r_g^j \equiv \partial r^j/\partial g^j, j = \alpha, \beta$. Here equations (1) and (3) are the aggregate budget constraints of households. They say that household expenditure on private goods is constrained by the sum of household earnings in the private sector and the amount received by transfer (negative for α, positive for β). Equations (2) and (4), on the other hand, state that the public good is subject to Lindahl pricing in each country. (This explains why, in (1) and (3), only earnings in the private sector are included.) Finally, equation (5) expresses the requirement that the world market for the first private good must clear; it then follows from a suitably generalized Walras' law that the world market for the second private good must also clear.

Equations (2) and (4) can be solved for g^j in terms of p. Thus

$$g^j = g^j(p), \quad j = \alpha, \beta \tag{6a}$$

where

$$g_p^j \equiv \mathrm{d}g^j/\mathrm{d}p = -r_{gp}^j/r_{gg}^j, \quad j = \alpha, \beta. \tag{6b}$$

Substitution for g^j in (1), (3) and (5) yields the condensed system

$$e^\alpha(p, u^\alpha) - r^\alpha(p, g^\alpha(p)) + T = 0 \tag{7}$$

$$e^\beta(p, u^\beta) - r^\beta(p, g^\beta(p)) - T = 0 \tag{8}$$

$$z^{\alpha 1}(p, g^\alpha(p), u^\alpha) + z^{\beta 1}(p, g^\beta(p), u^\beta) = 0. \tag{9}$$

Totally differentiating (7)–(9), and recalling (2) and (4), we obtain

$$\begin{bmatrix} e_p^\alpha - r_p^\alpha & e_u^\alpha & 0 \\ e_p^\beta - r_p^\beta & 0 & e_u^\beta \\ z_p^{\alpha 1} + z_p^{\beta 1} - r_{pg}^\alpha g_p^\alpha - r_{pg}^\beta g_p^\beta & z_u^{\alpha 1} & z_u^{\beta 1} \end{bmatrix} \begin{bmatrix} \mathrm{d}p \\ \mathrm{d}u^\alpha \\ \mathrm{d}u^\beta \end{bmatrix} = \begin{bmatrix} -1 \\ 1 \\ 0 \end{bmatrix} \mathrm{d}T \tag{10}$$

where, except in the case of $g_p^j \equiv \mathrm{d}g^j/\mathrm{d}p$, subscripts indicate partial derivatives. Choosing units of utility so that $e_u^j = 1$, and defining $z_p^1 \equiv z_p^{\alpha 1} + z_p^{\beta 1}$, (10) can be written more compactly as

$$\begin{bmatrix} z^{\alpha 1} & 1 & 0 \\ z^{\beta 1} & 0 & 1 \\ z_p^1 - r_{pg}^\alpha g_p^\alpha - r_{pg}^\beta g_p^\beta & z_u^{\alpha 1} & z_u^{\beta 1} \end{bmatrix} \begin{bmatrix} \mathrm{d}p \\ \mathrm{d}u^\alpha \\ \mathrm{d}u^\beta \end{bmatrix} = \begin{bmatrix} -1 \\ 1 \\ 0 \end{bmatrix} \mathrm{d}T. \tag{10'}$$

Solving (10′) for $\mathrm{d}p/\mathrm{d}T$ and $\mathrm{d}u^j/\mathrm{d}T$, and recalling (6b),

$$\Delta(\mathrm{d}p/\mathrm{d}T) = z_u^{\alpha 1} - z_u^{\beta 1} \tag{11a}$$

$$\Delta(\mathrm{d}u^\alpha/\mathrm{d}T) = -[z_p^1 + (r_{pg}^\alpha)^2/r_{gg}^\alpha + (r_{pg}^\beta)^2/r_{gg}^\beta] \tag{11a}$$

$$= -\Delta(\mathrm{d}u^\beta/\mathrm{d}T) \tag{11b}$$

where $r_{gg}^j < 0$ is the second-order condition for the optimal supply of the public good in the jth country and

$$\Delta = z_p^1 + (r_{pg}^\alpha)^2/r_{gg}^\alpha + (r_{pg}^\beta)^2/r_{gg}^\beta - z^{\alpha 1} z_u^{\alpha 1} - z^{\beta 1} z_u^{\beta 1} < 0 \tag{11c}$$

is a sufficient and almost necessary condition of Walrasian stability. Since $z_p^1 < 0$ and $r_{gg}^j < 0$, (11b) yields the desired result:

$$\mathrm{d}u^\alpha/\mathrm{d}T < 0, \quad \mathrm{d}u^\beta/\mathrm{d}T > 0. \tag{12}$$

3 A PURE PUBLIC CONSUMPTION GOOD

If the public good is directly consumed, g^j enters the restricted expenditure function of the jth country and Lindahl pricing implies that $e_g^j - r_g^j = 0$. Hence our system of equations (2)–(5) takes the more elaborate form

$$e^{\alpha}(p, g^{\alpha}, u^{\alpha}) - r^{\alpha}(p, g^{\alpha}) + T = 0 \tag{13}$$

$$e_g^{\alpha}(p, g^{\alpha}, u^{\alpha}) - r_g^{\alpha}(p, g^{\alpha}) = 0 \tag{14}$$

$$e^{\beta}(p, g^{\beta}, u^{\beta}) - r^{\beta}(p, g^{\beta}) - T = 0 \tag{15}$$

$$e_g^{\beta}(p, g^{\beta}, u^{\beta}) - r_g^{\beta}(p, g^{\beta}) = 0 \tag{16}$$

$$z^{\alpha 1}(p, g^{\alpha}, u^{\alpha}) + z^{\beta 1}(p, g^{\beta}, u^{\beta}) = 0. \tag{17}$$

Nevertheless, by following essentially the same logical steps as in section 2, we arrive again at the traditional result contained in inequalities (12).

4 A PURE INTERNATIONAL PUBLIC GOOD

If the public good is international in scope and if the world is egalitarian in the sense that 1′: each household, wherever it is found, has the same composition, endowment and preferences, and has access to the same technology, then, from the Kemp–Long proposition already alluded to, the public good, whether an intermediate good or a consumption good, will be optimally supplied, each household contributing equally and benefiting equally and, therefore, each country contributing and benefiting in proportion to its size. No international transfer is needed, at least on compassionate grounds. If nevertheless a small transfer were made the qualitative welfare effects would be as in sections 2 and 3. In the case of an international public intermediate good, for example, the relevant model of the world economy is

$$N^{\alpha} e(p, u^{\alpha}) - N^{\alpha} r(p, g) + T = 0 \tag{18}$$

$$N^{\beta} e(p, u^{\beta}) - N^{\beta} r(p, g) - T = 0 \tag{19}$$

$$r_g(p, g) = 0 \tag{20}$$

$$N^{\alpha} z^1(p, g, u^{\alpha}) + N^{\beta} z^1(p, g, u^{\beta}) = 0 \tag{21}$$

where e, r and z^1 are the common **per household** expenditure, revenue and excess demand functions, now written without country superscripts, and where N^j is the number of households in the jth country ($j = \alpha, \beta$) and g is the world production of the public good.

Calculations along the lines of section 2 reveal that $du^{\alpha}/dT < 0$ and $du^{\beta}/dT > 0$.

NOTE

The present essay is a revised version of Kemp and Abe (1994). It differs from that paper chiefly in the revision and extension of section 4.

REFERENCES

Johnson, H. G. (1960) 'Income distribution, the offer curve and the effects of tariffs', *Manchester School of Economics* 28: 223–42.

Kemp, M. C. and Abe, K. (1994) 'The transfer problem in a context of public goods', *Economics Letters* 45: 223–6.

Kemp, M. C. and Long, N. V. (1992) 'Some properties of egalitarian economies', *Journal of Public Economics* 49: 383–7.

30

ON THE OPTIMAL TIMING OF FOREIGN AID

This essay develops a model of foreign aid in a dynamic framework. It is shown that there will be an initial stock transfer followed by a continuous flow transfer. If the donor is wealthier than the recipient, both before and after aid, and if there is no restriction on the sign of the latter, then along the optimal path the flow transfer is opposite in sign to the stock transfer.

1 INTRODUCTION

The available formal analysis of foreign aid is static, with no provision for the passage of time. Its chief weakness is its inability to address questions of phasing or timing. In particular, it has nothing to say about the **optimal timing** of aid, including its division into stock and flow components.

A similar criticism can be directed to the analysis of reparations, indeed of all forms of unrequited transfer between governments. However, we shall employ throughout the concrete terminology of aid.

Here we offer a dynamic formulation in which questions of timing are central. The formulation has the virtue and defect of being simple. Thus, for the most part, we recognize just two countries, each producing a single commodity (the same in each country) by means of homogeneous capital and labour, and differing only in their initial factor endowments. Of course, in such a world there is no scope for conventional trade; in the absence of private international investment and of transfers between governments, each economy would be isolated. However, at the end, we do broaden our analysis by introducing a second traded commodity.

The country offering aid will be referred to as the donor, the other country as the recipient. The donor seeks that combination of initial stock transfer Ω and continuous flow transfer $\langle \omega(t) \rangle$ which achieves a given improvement in the recipient's welfare at least welfare cost to the donor. In its search for the optimal pair $(\Omega, \langle \omega(t) \rangle)$ the donor may or may not enjoy the co-operation of the recipient. If the recipient co-operates, Ω and $\omega(t)$ are unrestricted in sign; in the absence of co-operation, Ω and $\omega(t)$ are constrained to be non-negative. The optimal pair will prove to be sensitive to changes in assumptions about co-operation and to changes in the assumed degree of capital mobility.

It is shown that in most cases it is optimal to combine stock and flow aid, that is to give the aid partly in a lump, at the outset, and partly as a flow, over time. However, if the two countries co-operate, stock and flow aid may be of opposite sign. It is shown also that when marginal utility is of constant elasticity, the rate of flow of aid increases (decreases) if and only if the initial world stock of capital is less than (greater than) its steady-state value.

2 PRIVATE CAPITAL IMMOBILE BETWEEN COUNTRIES

In many real world situations the case for foreign aid rests in part on the reluctance of private capital to migrate. Indeed, 'for most of the least developed countries, foreign aid has become more important than borrowing as a source of funds from abroad' (Levy 1988: 152). We therefore begin our analysis under the assumption that private capital is internationally immobile.

Without loss, it is assumed that the labour force in each country is initially equal to one. The following standard notation will be employed:

- ρ the rate of time preference in each country
- n the rate of growth of the labour force in each country
- k_i the capital : labour ratio and capital stock in the ith country, $i = 1, 2$
- $f(k_i)$ the common production function, assumed to be increasing, strictly concave and to satisfy the Inada conditions
- c_i the level of consumption per capita in the ith country
- $u(c_i)$ the common individual utility function, assumed to be increasing, strictly concave, with marginal utility tending to infinity as consumption tends to zero.

In a state of isolation, the ith country finds the time path of consumption that maximizes

$$\int_0^{\infty} u(c_i)\exp(-\delta t)\mathrm{d}t \quad (\delta \equiv \rho - n > 0) \tag{P.1}$$

subject to

$$\dot{k}_i = f(k_i) - nk_i - c_i$$

$$k_i(0) = k_{i0}, \text{ given.}$$

Let the maximum value of the integral be denoted by $v(k_{i0})$.

The first country (the donor) wants to (or is required to) increase $v(k_{20})$ to $v(k_{20}) + \Delta$, $\Delta > 0$. The problem facing the donor is then to find the least utility-cost way of doing this. Formally, the donor's problem is to find Ω and the time paths of c_1, c_2, and ω that maximize

$$\int_0^{\infty} u(c_1)\exp(-\delta t)\mathrm{d}t \tag{P.2}$$

subject to

$$\dot{k}_1 = f(k_1) - nk_1 - c_1 - \omega \tag{1}$$

$$\dot{k}_2 = f(k_2) - nk_2 - c_2 + \omega \tag{2}$$

$$k_i(0) = \Omega = k_{i0}, \text{ given } (i = 1, 2),$$

$$\int_0^\infty u(c_2)\exp(-\delta t)\mathrm{d}t \geqslant v(k_{20}) + \Delta.$$

The reasoning behind this formulation is as follows: for any Ω and $\langle\omega(t)\rangle$ there is an optimal consumption path $\{\langle c_2(t)\rangle: \Omega, \langle\omega(t)\rangle\}$ which the recipient would choose; however, the donor would select the **same** path if, as we have assumed, the donor controls $\langle c_2(t)\rangle$, for it is in the donor's interest that any aid be used efficiently.

Alternatively, the donor's task is to find, for some $\lambda > 0$, the time path of c_1, c_2, ω, and the values $k_1(0)$ and $k_2(0)$ that maximize

$$\int_0^\infty u(c_1)\exp(-\delta t)\mathrm{d}t + \lambda \int_0^\infty u(c_2)\exp(-\delta t)\mathrm{d}t \tag{P.2'}$$

subject to (1), (2) and

$$k_1(0) + k_2(0) \leqslant k_{10} + k_{20}, \text{ given.} \tag{3}$$

Evidently $\lambda \gtrless 1$ if and only if, in the optimum,

$$\int_0^\infty u(c_1)\exp(-\delta t)\mathrm{d}t \lesseqgtr \int_0^\infty u(c_2)\exp(-\delta t)\mathrm{d}t.$$

In (P.2) and (P.2′) the controls ω and Ω are unrestricted in sign. This implies a high degree of co-operativeness between donor and recipient. In some situations it may be more realistic to require both ω and Ω to be non-negative, so that to the constraints of (P.2′) are added

$$\omega \geqslant 0 \tag{4}$$

$$k_2(0) \geqslant k_{20}. \tag{5}$$

In the analysis to follow we shall consider both the case in which (4) and (5) are imposed (the non-co-operative case) and the case in which they are not imposed (the co-operative case).

The current-value Hamiltonian associated with (P.2′) is

$$H = u(c_1) + \lambda u(c_2) + \psi_1[f(k_1) - nk_1 - c_1 - \omega] + \psi_2[f(k_2) - nk_2 - c_2 + \omega] \tag{6}$$

and, if the full complement of constraints (1) to (5) is recognized, we have as necessary conditions

$$\frac{\partial H}{\partial c_1} = u'(c_1) - \psi_1 = 0 \tag{7}$$

$$\frac{\partial H}{\partial c_2} = \lambda u'(c_2) - \psi_2 = 0 \tag{8}$$

$$\frac{\partial H}{\partial \omega} = -\psi_1 + \psi_2 \leqslant 0, \quad \omega \geqslant 0, \quad \omega(-\psi_1 + \psi_2) = 0 \tag{9}$$

$$\dot{\psi}_1 = \delta\psi_1 - \psi_1[f'(k_1) - n] \tag{10}$$

$$\dot{\psi}_2 = \delta\psi_2 - \psi_2[f'(k_2) - n]. \tag{11}$$

It follows from (9) that

$$\psi_1(0) \geqslant \psi_2(0). \tag{12}$$

Suppose, realistically in the case of foreign aid, that, before and after aid, the donor is the wealthier of the two countries so that $\lambda < 1$. In the absence of aid, $k_1(t) > k_2(t)$ for all $t \geqslant 0$ and the marginal product of capital is always greater in the second country. The same is true if all aid is given in a lump, at $t = 0$. It is intuitively clear, then, that all aid should be given in a lump and that the optimal $\omega(t)$ is identically zero. More formally, suppose that there is a non-degenerate interval $[t_1, t_2]$ on which $\omega(t) > 0$. Then, from (9),

$$\psi_1(t) = \psi_2(t) \quad \text{for } t \in [t_1, t_2] \tag{13}$$

so that, bearing in mind (7) and (8),

$$u'(c_1) = \lambda u'(c_2). \tag{14}$$

Since $\lambda < 1$, $u'(c_1(t)) < u'(c_2(t))$ and

$$c_1(t) > c_2(t) \quad \text{for } t \in [t_1, t_2]. \tag{15}$$

From (9) to (11), on the other hand, if $\omega(t) > 0$ then $k_1(t) = k_2(t)$ and $\dot{k}_1(t) = \dot{k}_2(t)$ so that, from (1) and (2), $c_1 + \omega = c_2 - \omega$ or

$$c_1(t) = c_2(t) - 2\omega(t) < c_2(t) \quad \text{for } t \in [t_1, t_2]. \tag{16}$$

Evidently (15) and (16) cannot both be true. Hence $\omega(t)$ cannot be positive on a non-degenerate interval.

Thus our intuitive conclusion, that the whole of the aid should be given in a lump, is justified. However, in arriving at that conclusion it was assumed that constraints (4) and (5) are satisfied. If those constraints are not imposed then, instead of (9), we have $\psi_1(t) = \psi_2(t)$ for all t. It then follows from (10) and (11) that $k_1(t) = k_2(t)$ for all t. Hence

$$\Omega = \frac{1}{2}(k_{10} - k_{20}) \tag{17}$$

and, since the donor remains the wealthier country, $\omega(t)$ must be negative on some interval. In fact, the optimal $\omega(t)$ is always negative. For, suppose that $\omega(t) = 0$ at $t = t_1$, so that $c_1(t_1) = c_2(t_1)$. From (7) and (10),

$$\frac{\alpha(c_1(t_1))\,(\dot{c}_1(t_1))}{c_1(t_1)} = f'(k_1(t_1)) - \rho \tag{18}$$

where

$$\alpha(c) \equiv \frac{-u''(c)c}{u'(c)} > 0$$

is the elasticity of marginal utility. Similarly, from (8) and (13),

$$\frac{\alpha(c_2(t_1))\,(\dot{c}_2(t_1))}{c_2(t_1)} = f'(k_2(t_1)) - \rho. \tag{19}$$

Hence

$$\frac{\dot{c}_1(t_1)}{c_1(t_1)} = \frac{\dot{c}_2(t_1)}{c_2(t_1)}. \tag{20}$$

It follows that $c_1(t) = c_2(t)$ for all t. This in turn implies that the two countries enjoy the same level of well-being, a contradiction.

If marginal utility is of constant elasticity then these results can be considerably sharpened. For, then, (18) and (19) imply that c_1 and c_2 change at the same proportional rate, increasing (decreasing) if and only if the initial world capital stock is smaller than (greater than) its steady-state value, that is if and only if $k_{10} + k_{20}$ is less than (greater than) $2k^*$, where k^* is defined by $f'(k^*) = \rho$; it then follows that $-\omega(t)$ steadily rises (falls) under the same necessary and sufficient conditions.

Let us summarize our conclusions to this point. Suppose that, before and after aid, the donor is the wealthier of the two countries. In the non-co-operative solution, all aid is offered at the outset. In the co-operative solution, there is an 'excessive' initial pulse of aid, followed by a flow of aid which is always negative; if marginal utility is of constant elasticity, then consumption in each country, as well as $-\omega(t)$, rises (falls) if and only if the initial world capital stock is less than (greater than) its steady-state value.

Other cases can now be treated relatively briefly. Thus suppose that before aid the donor is the wealthier country, but after aid, the recipient is wealthier, so that $\lambda > 1$. Then, whether or not the recipient is co-operative, it is optimal to set $\Omega = (k_{10} - k_{20})/2 > 0$ and to supplement this lump of aid with a flow which is always positive. If marginal utility is of constant elasticity, then optimal consumption changes at the same proportional rate in each country; if and only if $k_{10} + k_{20}$ is less than (greater than) $2k^*$, then $c_1(t)$, $c_2(t)$ and $\omega(t)$ are increasing (decreasing).

Suppose, finally, that, before and after aid, the recipient is the wealthier country, as it might be in the event of post-war reparations. In the non-co-operative (co-operative) case, $\Omega = 0$ ($\Omega = (k_{10} - k_{20})/2 < 0$) and $\omega(t)$ is positive for all t. If the elasticity of marginal utility is constant, then optimal consumption changes at the same proportional rate in each country, with $c_1(t)$, $c_2(t)$ and $\omega(t)$ increasing (decreasing) if and only if $k_{10} + k_{20}$ is less than (greater than) $2k^*$.

3 PRIVATE CAPITAL MOBILE BETWEEN COUNTRIES

If capital is completely mobile between countries, so that the marginal product of capital is always the same everywhere, then it is a matter of indifference to the donor whether aid is given in a lump or as a flow or as a mixture of both; moreover, if some or all of the aid is given as a flow, it is of no importance to the donor whether it is increasing or decreasing, positive or negative, for the difference between one aid profile and another will be continuously offset by an equal and opposite difference between the associated profiles of capital flow. Nevertheless, the many optimal patterns of aid have one thing in common – they are all associated with the same pair of optimal consumption paths.

If marginal utility is of constant elasticity, then $c_1(t)$ and $c_2(t)$ change at the same proportional rate, increasing or decreasing according as $k_{10} + k_{20}$ is smaller or greater than $2k^*$.

These conclusions hold whether or not the donor and the recipient co-operate; however, the extent of the indeterminacy is less in the absence of co-operation, for then Ω and $\omega(t)$ are constrained to be non-negative.

4 FINAL REMARKS

Our analysis can be extended in several directions. Thus the donor and recipient might be allowed to differ not only in initial endowments but also in technology and the rate of time preference; and they might be allowed to produce more than one good, so that trade and aid could be seen to interact. Finally, one might recognize that the absorption of aid is costly, with the cost increasing with the rate of absorption; then the sharp distinction between stock and flow would disappear.

Here we briefly indicate how the analysis must be modified to accommodate the possibility that the donor is more productive than the recipient and the possibility that there are two commodities, one a pure consumption good, the other a pure investment good. In addition, we record a fact which will come as no surprise to the attentive reader of sections 2 and 3. Problem (P.2) contains the *a priori* restriction that a stock transfer can occur only at $t = 0$. If the problem is formulated more flexibly, it still can be shown that $t = 0$ is the only date at which a stock transfer would occur in an optimal plan.

4.1 The donor more productive than the recipient

We confine our attention to the case in which $k_{10} > k_{20}$ and private capital is immobile. Let the donor's production function be denoted by $f(k_1)$ and the recipient's by $\beta f(k_2)$, with $0 < \beta < 1$. In isolation, k_1 approaches k^*, which is defined by $f'(k^*) = \rho$, and k_2 approaches k^{**}, defined by $\beta f'(k^{**}) = \rho$. Clearly, $k^* > k^{**}$. The donor seeks the solution to (P.2′), with $\beta f(k_2)$ replacing $f(k_2)$. The new necessary conditions consist of (7) to (11), with (11) modified to

$$\dot{\psi}_2 = \delta\psi_2 - \psi_2[\beta f'(k_2) - n]. \tag{11'}$$

In the co-operative case, the solution is characterized by $u'(c_1(t)) < u'(c_2(t))$; hence $c_1(t) > c_2(t)$ for all t, $f'(k_1(t)) = \beta f'(k_2(t))$ for all t, and k_1 and k_2 approach k^* and k^{**} respectively. It follows that if $f'(k_{10}) > \beta f'(k_{20})$ then it is optimal to set $\Omega < 0$ and $\omega(t) > 0$ for all t; that is, it is optimal to shift capital to the more productive donor country and if $f'(k_{10}) < \beta f'(k_{20})$ then it is optimal to set Ω equal to the positive solution of the equation

$$f'(k_{10} - \Omega) - \beta f'(k_{20} + \Omega) = 0$$

and to set $\omega(t) > 0$ for all t or $\omega(t) < 0$ for all t, depending on the values of β and λ.

In the non-co-operative case, capital cannot be shifted to the donor country; it follows that if $f'(k_{10}) > \beta f'(k_{20})$ then it is optimal to set $\Omega = 0$ and $\omega(t)$ always positive but smaller than in the co-operative case.

4.2 A second commodity

When a second commodity is recognized, we have the additional complication of variable terms of trade. However, if the two countries co-operate, so that $k_1(t) = k_2(t)$ for all t, then the relevant analysis remains straightforward and yields conclusions similar to those of section 2. The appendix contains a complete examination of the case in which private capital is internationally immobile. Here we merely list the main conclusions.

First, except when the initial world capital : labour ratio greatly exceeds its steady-state value, production is always incompletely specialized in both countries.

Second, when production is incompletely specialized, then $c_1(t) > c_2(t)$ and $\omega(t) < 0$ if and only if $\lambda > 1$. If the consumption good is capital intensive, both c_1 and c_2 increase (decrease) if the world capital : labour ratio is less than (greater than) its steady-state value. If, in addition, the elasticity of marginal utility is constant, then $|\omega(t)|$ monotonely increases.

APPENDIX

In this appendix, we extend the analysis of section 2 to accommodate a second commodity. One of the two commodities is a pure consumption good, the other a pure investment good. Both can be traded internationally. With each commodity there is an associated production function with the same properties as f; however, the two commodities differ in their relative factor intensities.

Let p denote the relative price of the consumption good in terms of the investment good and $g(p, k_i)$ denote the GNP function of the ith country. The flow of aid is recorded in terms of the consumption good. It is assumed that private capital is internationally immobile, but intersectorally mobile. Moreover, we assume that the donor and the recipient co-operate so that there are no restrictions on the sign of flow and stock aid.

Define

$$\bar{c}_1 = c_1 + \omega \quad \text{and} \quad \bar{c}_2 = c_2 - \omega.$$

Then, for some $\lambda > 0$, the two countries seek to maximize

$$\int_0^\infty [u(\bar{c}_1 - \omega) + \lambda u(\bar{c}_2 + \omega)] \exp(-\delta t)\, dt \tag{P.3}$$

subject to

$$\dot{k}_1 = g(p, k_1) - nk_1 - p\bar{c}_1 \tag{21}$$

$$\dot{k}_2 = g(p, k_2) - nk_2 - p\bar{c}_2 \tag{22}$$

$$g_p(p, k_1) + g_p(p, k_2) - \bar{c}_1 - \bar{c}_2 \geqslant 0 \tag{23}$$

$$k_1(0) + k_2(0) \leqslant k_{10} + k_{20}, \quad \text{given.} \tag{24}$$

Let ψ_i be the shadow price of k_i, and let γ be the multiplier associated with (23). We have the necessary conditions

$$\frac{\partial L}{\partial \bar{c}_1} = u'(\bar{c}_1 - \omega) - p\psi_1 - \gamma = 0 \tag{25}$$

$$\frac{\partial L}{\partial \bar{c}_2} = \lambda u'(\bar{c}_2 + \omega) - p\psi_2 - \gamma = 0 \tag{26}$$

$$\frac{\partial L}{\partial \omega} = -\, u'(\bar{c}_1 - \omega) + \lambda u'(\bar{c}_2 + \omega) = 0 \tag{27}$$

$$\frac{\partial L}{\partial p} = \sum_{i=1}^{2} \psi_i [g_p(p, k_i) - \bar{c}_i] + \gamma \sum_{i=1}^{2} g_{pp}(p, k_i) = 0 \tag{28}$$

$$\dot{\psi}_1 = \psi_1 [\rho - g_k(p, k_1)] - \gamma g_{pk}(p, k_1) \tag{29}$$

$$\dot{\psi}_2 = \psi_2 [\rho - g_k(p, k_2)] - \gamma g_{pk}(p, k_2). \tag{30}$$

We begin our study of these equations by stating a useful lemma.

Lemma. *On the optimal path, $p > 0$.*

Proof. *Suppose that $p(t) = 0$ for some t, say t'. From the assumed properties of the production functions, $g_p(0, k_i) = 0$. Hence, from (23), $\bar{c}_1 + \bar{c}_2 = 0$. From this result, and the non-negativity of c_i, $c_1 = c_2 = 0$, contradicting the assumed properties of the utility function.* □

From (25) to (27), with $p > 0$,

$$\psi_1 = \psi_2 \equiv \psi. \tag{31}$$

Hence,

$$\psi g_k(p, k_1) + \gamma g_{pk}(p, k_1) = \psi g_k(p, k_2) + \gamma g_{pk}(p, k_2). \tag{32}$$

It is convenient to consider separately the two cases $\gamma > 0$ and $\gamma = 0$.

Case A: $\gamma > 0$

In this case, (23) holds with equality

$$g_p(p, k_1) + g_p(p, k_2) - \bar{c}_1 - \bar{c}_2 = 0. \tag{33}$$

Together with (28) and (31), this implies that

$$g_{pp}(p, k_1) + g_{pp}(p, k_2) = 0. \tag{34}$$

But g_{pp} is non-negative, and hence

$$g_{pp}(p, k_i) = 0 \quad (i = 1, 2). \tag{35}$$

Thus production must be completely specialized in each country when $\gamma > 0$.

Given the restrictions imposed on the utility function, it is impossible that both countries produce only the investment good. And since capital can be co-operatively shifted internationally and the same production functions prevail everywhere, it is inefficient for the countries to specialize in producing different goods. Thus we are left with just one possibility: both countries produce the consumption good only. Then

$$\dot{k}_i = -nk_i \tag{36}$$

and

$$f_c(k_i) = \bar{c}_i \quad (i = 1, 2) \tag{37}$$

where f_c is the per capita production function for thc consumption good. Therefore (32) reduces to

$$(p\psi + \gamma)f_c'(k_1) = (p\psi + \gamma)f_c'(k_2) \tag{38}$$

which implies that $k_1 = k_2$. From (37), therefore, $\bar{c}_1 = \bar{c}_2$. In the absence of a switch of regime, both consumption and capital converge monotonely to zero.

Case B: $\gamma = 0$

From (25) and (26), $\psi > 0$. Hence, from (28),

$$g_p(p, k_1) + g_p(p, k_2) - \bar{c}_1 - \bar{c}_2 = 0. \tag{39}$$

Equation (32) becomes

$$g_k(p, k_1) = g_k(p, k_2). \tag{40}$$

As we have noted, it would be inefficient for the two countries to specialize in producing different commodities. We therefore focus on the remaining possibilities:

(B_i) that each country produces only the consumption good
(B_{ii}) that each country produces both commodities

Consider the case (B_i) first. Then (40) reduces to

$$pf_c'(k_1) = pf_c'(k_2). \tag{41}$$

Since p is positive, (41) implies that

$$k_1 = k_2 \tag{42}$$

and hence

$$\bar{c}_1 = \bar{c}_2. \tag{43}$$

Evidently, the trajectory is the same as in case A.

Consider now the case (B_{ii}). Since neither country specializes, we can write

$$g(p, k_i) = r(p)k_i + w(p) \tag{44}$$

where $r(p)$ and $w(p)$ are the rental rate and wage rate, respectively. From (21) and (22), defining $k \equiv k_1 + k_2$, we have

$$\dot{k} = r(p)k + 2w(p) - nk - p(\bar{c}_1 + \bar{c}_2). \tag{45}$$

Furthermore, from (39) and (44),

$$r'(p)k + 2w'(p) = \bar{c}_1 + \bar{c}_2. \tag{46}$$

On the other hand, from (25) and (26),

$$\bar{c}_1 + \bar{c}_2 = \phi(p\psi) + \phi(p\psi/\lambda) \tag{47}$$

where ϕ is the inverse of the u' function. Hence, from (46) and (47)

$$r'(p)k + 2w'(p) = \phi(p\psi) + \phi(p\psi/\lambda). \tag{48}$$

Equation (48) determines p as a function of k and ψ. Thus (45) can be rewritten as

$$\begin{aligned}\dot{k} = {} & [r(p(k, \psi)) - p(k, \psi)r'(p(k, \psi))]k + 2[w(p(k, \psi)) \\ & - p(k, \psi)w'(p(k, \psi))] - nk\end{aligned} \tag{49}$$

and, from (29) and (30),

$$\dot{\psi} = \psi[\rho - r(p(k, \psi))]. \tag{50}$$

We now have all the pieces needed for the construction of the phase diagram. Let us begin with case (B_{ii}). From (48),

$$\frac{dp}{d\psi} = \frac{p[\phi'(p\psi) + (1/\lambda)\phi'(p\psi/\lambda)]}{r''(p)k + 2w''(p) - [\phi'(p\psi) + (1/\lambda)\phi'(p\psi/\lambda)]\psi} < 0. \tag{51}$$

Now, from (44), $r(p)k + 2w(p) = g(p, k)$. Hence

$$r''(p)k + 2w''(p) = g_{pp}(p, k) \tag{52}$$

which is strictly positive.

For any given k, if ψ takes on a sufficiently small value, then only the consumption good is produced. At that point, $p = p^*$ (the absolute value of the slope of the world production possibility curve at the point where the output of the investment good is zero). Thus we have the pair of equations

$$r(p^*)k + 2w(p^*) = p^*[r'(p^*)k + 2w'(p^*)] \tag{53}$$

$$p^*[r'(p^*)k + 2w'(p^*)] = \phi(p^*\psi) + \phi(p^*\psi/\lambda). \tag{54}$$

These two equations determine the locus of (k, ψ) at which production switches from diversification to complete specialization in the consumption good. Differentiating them with respect to p^*, ψ and k, and eliminating dp^*, we obtain the slope of that locus:

$$\frac{d\psi}{dk} = \frac{r(p^*)[r''(p^*)k + 2w''(p^*)] - [\phi'(p^*\psi) + (1/\lambda)\phi'(p^*\psi/\lambda)][r(p^*) - p^*r'(p^*)]\psi}{(p^*)^2[\phi'(p^*\psi) + (1/\lambda)\phi'(p^*\psi/\lambda)][r''(p^*)k + 2w''(p^*)]}. \tag{55}$$

If the consumption good is capital intensive, so that $r' > 0$, then the right-hand side of (55) is negative; otherwise its sign is ambiguous. Denote this locus by HJ in the (k, ψ)-plane; see Figures 1 and 2. Below HJ only the consumption good is produced, above HJ both goods are produced.

Returning to (49) and (50), we seek the loci for $\dot{k} = 0$ and $\dot{\psi} = 0$. Differentiating (48), we obtain

$$dp = -(1/\Delta)r'(p)dk + (p/\Delta)[\phi'(p\psi) + (1/\lambda)\phi'(p\psi/\lambda)]d\psi \tag{56}$$

where Δ is the denominator of (51). Differentiating (49), we obtain

$$d\dot{k} = -p[r''(p)k + 2w''(p)]dp + [r(p) - pr'(p) - n]dk. \tag{57}$$

And, finally, differentiating (50) with respect to p and ψ, with p satisfying $\rho = r(p)$, we obtain

$$d\dot{\psi} = -\psi r'(p)dp. \tag{58}$$

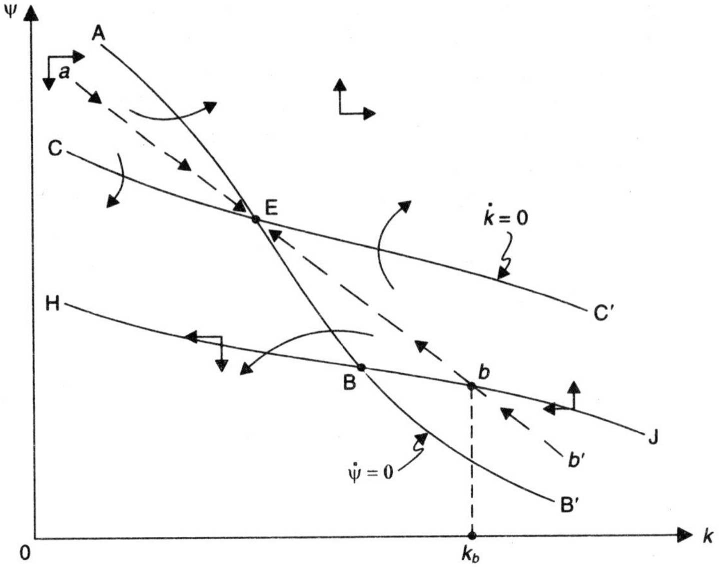

Figure 1 $r'(p) > 0$

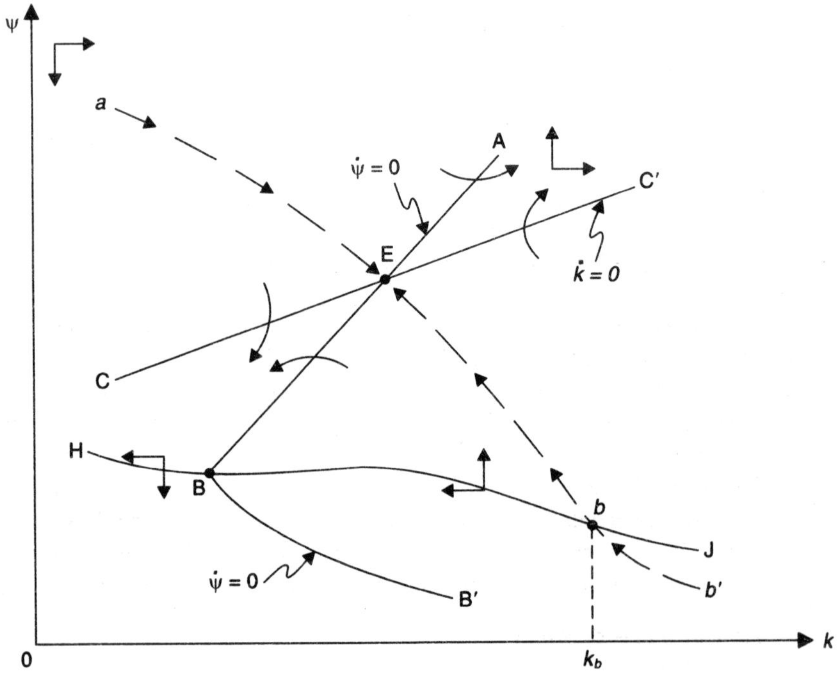

Figure 2 $r'(p) < 0$

Substituting from (56) into (57) and (58), and noting that at the steady state $r(p) - n = \rho - n = \delta > 0$, it can be verified that the saddle-point property holds.

Figures 1 and 2 are the phase diagrams associated with (P.3) when n is sufficiently small but positive. In each figure the optimal trajectory is a negatively sloped curve, denoted by $a\mathrm{E}bb'$, where E is the steady-state equilibrium, and b is the intersection of the stable arm of the saddle with the locus HJ. On bb' only the consumption good is produced; on $a\mathrm{E}b$, both goods are produced in each country. Moreover, $k_1 = k_2$ on bb', implying that, if $k_{10} + k_{20}$ exceeds the capital stock at the point b, which we denote by k_b, there is an initial stock transfer such that

$$k_1(0) = k_2(0) = \frac{1}{2}(k_{10} + k_{20}).$$

We now study the manner in which aid and consumption behave through time. We know, from our earlier discussion of case A, that, when both countries produce only the consumption good, the rate of flow of aid and the two rates of consumption go monotonely to zero. If $\lambda < 1$, then $c_1 > c_2$ for all t, and $\omega < 0$ for all t. It remains to study the behaviour of aid and consumption above HJ, where each country produces both goods.

From (27), we know that, if and only if $\lambda < 1$, $c_1 > c_2$ for all t. What more can be said? Differentiating (48) with respect to time, we find that

$$[(1/\psi)(r''k + 2w'') - \phi'(p\psi) - (1/\lambda)\phi'(p\psi/\lambda)]p\dot{\psi}$$
$$= (p/\psi)(r''k + 2w'')\dot{\psi} - r'\dot{k}. \qquad (59)$$

Now recall that $\dot{\psi} < 0$ on $a\mathrm{E}$ and $\dot{\psi} > 0$ on Eb and $\dot{k}$ is of opposite sign to $\dot{\psi}$ along the stable arm of the saddle. These facts together with (59) imply that, if the consumption good is capital intensive, so that $r'(p) > 0$, then $\mathrm{d}(p\psi)/\mathrm{d}t$ is negative on $a\mathrm{E}$ and positive on Eb. Since $u'(c_1) = p\psi$ and $u'(c_2) = p\psi/\lambda$, we can infer that, if $r'(p) > 0$, c_i monotonely increases on $a\mathrm{E}$ and monotonely decreases on Eb.

Let us now consider the behaviour of aid above HJ. Suppose that $k(0) > k_b$ and $\lambda < 1$, so that $c_1(t) > c_2(t)$ for all t. When k reaches k_b at $t = t^*$, $k_1 = k_2$ and $\omega < 0$. At t^*, each country produces the same amount of the consumption good, and c_1 exceeds c_2 by ω, the amount of the transfer. After t^*, each country produces both goods. However, the transfer will continue to be effected by a net shipment of the consumption good only; if the recipient were to ship both goods, the donor would simply sell back all the investment goods received. Since $c_1 > c_2$ for all t, the flow of aid is negative for all t. Moreover, from the equations of accumulation and the equality of k_1 and k_2, we deduce that

$$2\omega = \phi(p\psi) - \phi(p\psi/\lambda).$$

Differentiating this equation with respect to time, and assuming that the elasticity of marginal utility is a constant, we have

$$\dot{\omega} = \frac{[\phi(p\psi/\lambda) - \phi(p\psi)][d(p\psi)/dt]}{2\alpha p\psi}.$$

Thus, if $r' > 0$ then on aE, ω monotonely increases (decreases) and on Eb, ω monotonely decreases (increases) if $\lambda < 1$ ($\lambda > 1$). In short, if the consumption good is capital intensive, we reach conclusions very similar to those obtained in the one good case.

It remains to consider the possibility that the population is declining or stationary. If the population is declining, there is only the steady state with $k = 0$. If the population is stationary we have a more interesting case. For the locus $\dot{k} = 0$ is determined by (49) and (50); and the locus HJ is determined by (53) and (54). Comparing the two pairs of equations, one sees that, if $n = 0$, the locus $\dot{k} = 0$ coincides with HJ. Moreover, differentiating (49) and (50) with respect to p, ψ and n, we find that

$$\frac{d\psi}{dn} = -\frac{r''k + 2w'' - [\phi'(p\psi) + \phi'(p\psi/\lambda)/\lambda](r''k + 2w'')^{-1}k}{[\phi'(p\psi) + \phi'(p\psi/\lambda)/\lambda]\,p} > 0$$

thus confirming that the locus $\dot{k} = 0$ lies above HJ if $n > 0$.

REFERENCE

Levy, V. (1988) 'Does concessionary aid lead to higher investment rates in low-income countries?', *Review of Economics and Statistics* 69: 152–6.

31

'TRADE' OR 'AID'?

1 INTRODUCTION

The title of this essay can be construed as posing a moral question. Indeed, a preference for 'trade' is often defended on the ground that it encourages self-reliance. But it is also possible to consider the title from a purely economic point of view, as posing a question about the relative efficiencies of two alternative methods of aiding a country.

We consider the latter question in its simplest setting: a world economy comprising two countries, α and β, each capable of producing two tradable consumption goods and each imposing a border tax (possibly zero or negative) on its imported commodity. Country α wants to secure for β an increment of utility Δu^{β}. In an ideal co-operative world this would be achieved at least utility cost to α by first eliminating both border taxes and then moving along the world contract locus by means of an international transfer. But that degree of co-operation is too much to expect; indeed, it may be more realistic to assume that β is completely passive, simply maintaining its border duty in the face of the initiative of α. Then Δu^{β} can be attained by means of a non-negative lumpsum transfer by α to β ('aid') and/or by means of an adjustment of the rate at which the α border tax is levied ('trade'). Which instrument imposes the smaller utility cost on α?

In some extreme cases the answer is clear. Thus if both countries are initially free trading, then any feasible improvement in the well-being of β can be achieved at least cost to α by means of a lumpsum transfer. In terms of Figure 1, the movement from P_0 to P_1 is less costly to α than the movement from P_0 to P_1'. On the other hand, if α has set its border tax at its Edgeworth–Bickerdike optimal level (given the level of the β tax) then any sufficiently small Δu^{β} can be achieved at least utility cost to α by means of an adjustment of the α tax. In the limit, as Δu^{β} goes to zero, the cost (in terms of α utility) per unit of additional β utility also goes to zero.

In general, however, both countries impose effective but suboptimal taxes on trade and one cannot determine the least-cost method of helping β without calculation. In the present essay we offer two complementary constructions. In section 3, the set of possible border-tax pairs is partitioned into three subsets,

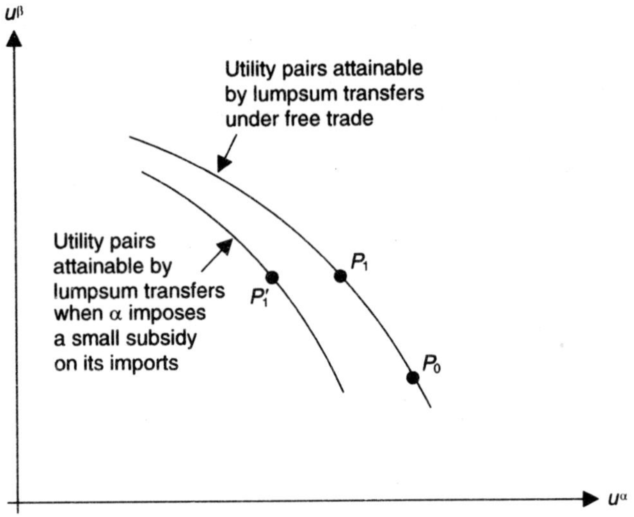

Figure 1

one containing pairs such that a sufficiently small increase in u^β can be achieved at least cost to α by means of a lumpsum transfer, one containing pairs such that an adjustment of the border tax of α is the less costly method, and one containing pairs such that the two instruments are equally costly. The analysis of that section is local or marginal in scope. In section 4, on the other hand, a global analysis is provided. Viewing the welfare of each country as a function of the two instruments, the α border tax, and the amount of its lumpsum transfer to β, we cover the instrument plane with two sets of indifference curves, one for each country, and deduce the least-cost mixture of instruments for any feasible and positive Δu^β. It is shown that in general it is suboptimal for α to adjust only one instrument, never optimal for α to subsidize its imports, and optimal for α to tax its imports only if it is optimal for it to choose a zero net transfer.

In his well-known study of economic policies towards less developed countries, Harry Johnson compared the effects of equal amounts of aid and trade on the welfare of the recipient. He noted that 'trade can never provide as large a flow of resources as foreign financial aid of the same real value' (see Johnson, 1967: 57; also Thirlwall, 1976; Yassin, 1982). However this finding, by itself, is of little interest. Policy implications emerge only when aid and trade are costed in terms of the donor's forgone utility.

2 THE MODEL

Two countries, α and β, produce two tradable consumption goods, 1 and 2. Under conditions of free trade with no international transfers, α imports the first commodity; β, the second. The second commodity serves as *numéraire*. Thus p is the world price of the first commodity in terms of the second and q^j is the relative price of the first commodity in the jth country. Relating the several price ratios are the conditions of arbitrage equilibrium

$$q^{\alpha} = p(1 + t^{\alpha}) \tag{1}$$

$$q^{\beta} = \frac{p}{1 + t^{\beta}} \tag{2}$$

where t^j is the rate of import duty imposed by the jth country.

The following additional notation will be employed:

u^j the utility of the jth country ($j = \alpha, \beta$)
$e^j(q^j, u^j)$ the expenditure of the jth country, in terms of the second commodity ($j = \alpha, \beta$)
$r^j(q^j)$ that part of the revenue of the jth country derived from production ($j = \alpha, \beta$)
$x^{ji}(q^j)$ the supply of the ith commodity by the jth country ($i = 1, 2; j = \alpha, \beta$)
$c^{ji}(q^j, u^j)$ the compensated demand for the ith commodity by the jth country ($i = 1, 2; j = \alpha, \beta$)
$z^{ji}(q^j, u^j) \equiv c^{ji}(q^j, u^j) - x^{ji}(q^j)$ the excess demand for the ith commodity by the jth country ($i = 1, 2; j = \alpha, \beta; z^{\alpha 1} > 0$)
T the net transfer from α to β, in terms of the second commodity (initially, $T = 0$).

The transfer is financed in α and distributed in β by means of lumpsum taxes and subsidies. On the other hand, the import duty yields revenue, in terms of the second commodity, which amounts to $t^{\alpha}pz^{\alpha 1}$ in α and to $[t^{\beta}/(1 + t^{\beta})]z^{\beta 2}$ in β; this, too, is distributed in lumpsum fashion. The budget constraints of the typical individuals in α and β are, therefore,

$$\begin{aligned} e^{\alpha}(q^{\alpha}, u^{\alpha}) &= r^{\alpha}(q^{\alpha}) + t^{\alpha}pz^{\alpha 1}(q^{\alpha}, u^{\alpha}) - T \\ e^{\beta}(q^{\beta}, u^{\beta}) &= r^{\beta}(q^{\beta}) + \frac{t^{\beta}}{1 + t^{\beta}} z^{\beta 2}(q^{\beta}, u^{\beta}) + \frac{T}{1 + t^{\beta}} \end{aligned} \tag{3}$$

respectively. However, in world balance-of-payments equilibrium, $pz^{\beta 1} + z^{\beta 2} = T$. Hence the private budget constraint for β can be written as

$$\begin{aligned} e^{\beta}(q^{\beta}, u^{\beta}) &= r^{\beta}(q^{\beta}) + \frac{t^{\beta}}{1 + t^{\beta}} [T - pz^{\beta 1}(q^{\beta}, u^{\beta})] + \frac{T}{1 + t^{\beta}} \\ &= r^{\beta}(q^{\beta}) - \frac{t^{\beta}}{1 + t^{\beta}} pz^{\beta 1}(q^{\beta}, u^{\beta}) + T. \end{aligned} \tag{4}$$

The description of world equilibrium is completed by the condition of market clearance:

$$z^{\alpha 1}(q^{\alpha}, u^{\alpha}) + z^{\beta 1}(q^{\beta}, u^{\beta}) = 0. \tag{5}$$

Equations (1)–(5) contain the five variables u^{α}, u^{β}, q^{α}, q^{β} and p, as well as the parameters T, t^{α} and t^{β}. It is assumed that the system possesses a unique solution with a positive price ratio.

3 LOCAL ANALYSIS

The required partition of the (t^{α}, t^{β})-plane will be obtained in stages.

We begin by constructing the boundary of the set of pairs (t^{α}, t^{β}), which eliminate all trade. Let (q_*^j, u_*^j) be the autarkic value of (q^j, u^j); it is obtained as the solution of the pair of equations

$$e^j(q^j, u^j) = r^j(q^j)$$

$$z^{j1}(q^j, u^j) = 0.$$

Then

$$\frac{q_*^{\alpha}}{q_*^{\beta}} = (1 + t^{\alpha})(1 + t^{\beta})$$

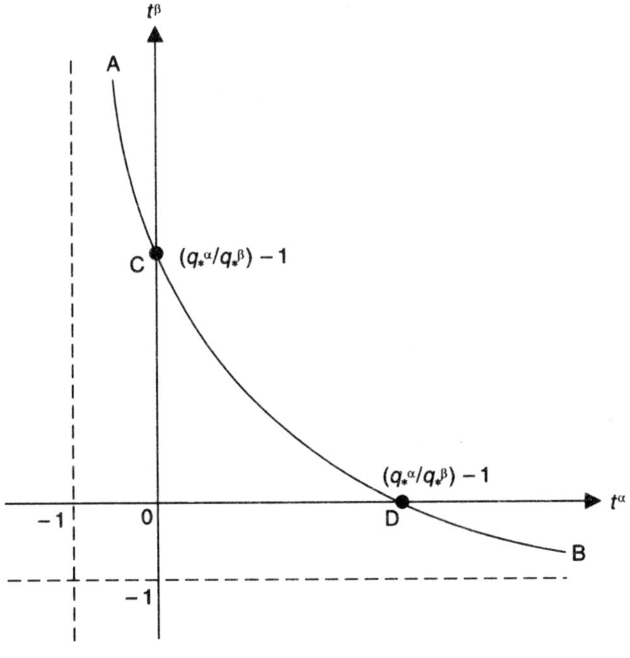

Figure 2

is the equation to the required boundary. It is represented in Figure 2 by the rectangular hyperbola *ACDB*. For all (t^α, t^β) on or above that curve, trade is annihilated.

Next we trace on Figure 2 the locus of points that satisfy $\partial u^\alpha/\partial t^\alpha = 0$ and the locus of points that satisfy $\partial u^\beta/\partial t^\alpha$. Substituting from (1) and (2) into (3)–(5) and differentiating with respect to t^α and T, we obtain

$$= \begin{bmatrix} p^2 t^\alpha z_q^{\alpha 1} \\ 0 \\ -p z_q^{\alpha 1} \end{bmatrix} \mathrm{d}t^\alpha + \begin{bmatrix} -1 \\ 1 \\ 0 \end{bmatrix} \mathrm{d}T \tag{6}$$

where the subscripts indicate differentiation ($e_q^\alpha \equiv \partial e^\alpha/\partial q^\alpha$, $r_q^\alpha \equiv dr^\alpha/dq^\alpha$, etc.). Recalling the envelope result that $e_q^j - r_q^j = z^{j1}$ ($j = \alpha, \beta$) and choosing units of utility so that $e_u^j = 1$, (6) reduces to

$$\begin{bmatrix} 1 - t^\alpha p z_u^{\alpha 1} & 0 & z^{\alpha 1} - (1 + t^\alpha) t^\alpha p z_q^{\alpha 1} \\ 0 & 1 + p \dfrac{t^\beta}{1 + t^\beta} z_u^{\beta 1} & z^{\beta 1} + p \dfrac{t^\beta}{(1 + t^\beta)^2} z_q^{\beta 1} \\ z_u^{\alpha 1} & z_u^{\beta 1} & (1 + t^\alpha) z_q^{\alpha 1} + \dfrac{z_q^{\beta 1}}{1 + t^\beta} \end{bmatrix} \begin{bmatrix} \mathrm{d}u^\alpha \\ \mathrm{d}u^\beta \\ \mathrm{d}p \end{bmatrix}$$

$$= \begin{bmatrix} p^2 t^\alpha z_q^{\alpha 1} \\ 0 \\ -p z_q^{\alpha 1} \end{bmatrix} \mathrm{d}t^\alpha + \begin{bmatrix} -1 \\ 1 \\ 0 \end{bmatrix} \mathrm{d}T. \tag{7}$$

Solving for the responses of u^α, u^β and p to changes in t^α and T, we obtain

$$\Delta \frac{\partial u^\alpha}{\partial t^\alpha} = p z_q^{\alpha 1} \left[p \frac{t^\alpha}{1 + t^\beta} z_q^{\beta 1} - z^{\beta 1} \left(1 + p \frac{t^\beta}{1 + t^\beta} z_u^{\beta 1} + p t^\alpha z_u^{\beta 1} \right) \right] \tag{8}$$

$$\Delta \frac{\partial u^\beta}{\partial t^\alpha} = p z_q^{\alpha 1} \left(z^{\beta 1} + p \frac{t^\beta}{(1 + t^\beta)^2} z_q^{\beta 1} \right) \tag{9}$$

$$\Delta \frac{\partial p}{\partial t^\alpha} = - p z_q^{\alpha 1} \left(1 + p \frac{t^\beta}{1 + t^\beta} z_u^{\beta 1} \right) \tag{10}$$

$$\Delta \frac{\partial u^\alpha}{\partial T} = - \frac{z_q^{\beta 1}}{1 + t^\beta} - \frac{z_q^{\alpha 1}}{1 + t^\beta} [p z_u^{\beta 1} (t^\alpha + t^\beta + t^\alpha t^\beta) + (1 + t^\alpha)] \tag{11}$$

$$\Delta \frac{\partial u^\beta}{\partial T} = (1 + t^\alpha) z_q^{\alpha 1} + \frac{z_q^{\beta 1}}{1 + t^\beta} \left(- p z_u^{\alpha 1} \frac{t^\alpha + t^\beta + t^\alpha t^\beta}{1 + t^\beta} + 1 \right) \tag{12}$$

$$\Delta \frac{\partial p}{\partial T} = z_u^{\alpha 1} \left(1 + p \frac{t^\beta}{1 + t^\beta} z_u^{\beta 1} \right) - z_u^{\beta 1} (1 - t^\alpha p z_u^{\alpha 1}) \tag{13}$$

where Δ is the determinant of the coefficient matrix in (7) and is negative as a sufficient condition of local Walrasian stability, and where $q^j z_u^{j1}/e_u^j = q^j z_u^{j1}$ is the marginal propensity to buy the first good in the jth country.

Let us return to Figure 2. Consider first the locus $\partial u^{\alpha}/\partial t^{\alpha} = 0$. On AB, $z^{\beta 1} = 0$; from (8), therefore

$$\Delta \left.\frac{\partial u^{\alpha}}{\partial t^{\alpha}}\right|_{AB} \quad \frac{t^{\alpha}}{1 + t^{\beta}} p^2 z_q^{\alpha 1} z_q^{\beta 1}. \tag{14}$$

However, both Δ and the pure substitution term z_q^{j1} are negative; hence

$$\left|\frac{\partial u^{\alpha}}{\partial t^{\alpha}}\right|_{AB} \lesseqqgtr 0 \quad \text{if and only if} \quad t^{\alpha} \gtreqqless 0. \tag{15}$$

On the vertical axis (ordinate), on the other hand, $t^{\alpha} = 0$ and

$$\Delta \left|\frac{\partial u^{\alpha}}{\partial t^{\alpha}}\right|_{t^{\alpha} = 0} = -p z^{\beta 1} z_q^{\alpha 1}\left(1 + p \frac{t^{\beta}}{1 + t^{\beta}} z_u^{\beta 1}\right). \tag{16}$$

The bracketed term of (16) can be written as $1 + [p/(1 + t^{\beta})] z_u^{\beta 1} t^{\beta}$, where $[p/(1 + t^{\beta})] z_u^{\beta 1}$ is the marginal propensity of β to consume the first commodity; moreover, Δ, $z^{\beta 1}$ and $z_q^{\alpha 1}$ are all negative. In the absence of inferiority and for $1 + t^{\beta} > 0$, therefore,

$$\left.\frac{\partial u^{\alpha}}{\partial t^{\alpha}}\right|_{t^{\alpha} = 0,\, z^{\beta 1} \neq 0} > 0. \tag{17}$$

From (15) and (17) we can infer that the locus $\partial u^{\alpha}/\partial t^{\alpha} = 0$ leaves point C in a south-easterly direction with slope steeper than that of AB at C.

Consider next the locus $\partial u^{\beta}/\partial t^{\alpha} = 0$. On AB, $z^{\beta 1} = 0$; from (9), therefore,

$$\Delta \left.\frac{\partial u^{\beta}}{\partial t^{\alpha}}\right|_{AB} = \frac{t^{\beta}}{(1 + t^{\beta})^2} p^2 z_q^{\alpha 1} z_q^{\beta 1} \tag{18}$$

implying that

$$\operatorname{sign}\left(\left.\frac{\partial u^{\beta}}{\partial t^{\alpha}}\right|_{AB}\right) = \operatorname{sign}(-t^{\beta}). \tag{19}$$

On the horizontal axis, on the other hand, $t^{\beta} = 0$ and

$$\Delta \left.\frac{\partial u^{\beta}}{\partial t^{\alpha}}\right|_{t^{\beta} = 0} = p z^{\beta 1} z_q^{\alpha 1} > 0. \tag{20}$$

Hence

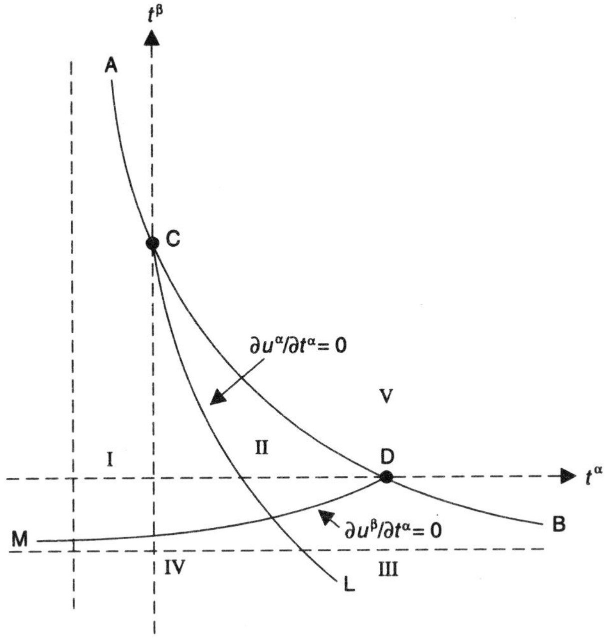

Figure 3

$$\left.\frac{\partial u^{\beta}}{\partial t^{\alpha}}\right|_{t^{\beta}=0} < 0. \tag{21}$$

From (19) and (20), the locus $\partial u^{\beta}/\partial t^{\alpha} = 0$ leaves D either with a positive slope or with a negative slope greater than that of AB at D. Moreover, from (9), the locus remains everywhere above the line $t^{\beta} = -1$.

Suppose for the time being that the two loci intersect only once. Then we can distinguish the five regions depicted in Figure 3. In region I, $\partial u^{\alpha}/\partial t^{\alpha}$ and $\partial u^{\beta}/\partial t^{\alpha}$ are of opposite sign; hence α can help β at some utility cost to itself. The positivity of $\partial u^{\alpha}/\partial t^{\alpha}$ indicates that the tariff imposed by α is less than the optimal tariff for given t^{β}. (The optimal t^{α} for each t^{β} is indicated by the locus CL, along which $\partial u^{\alpha}/\partial t^{\alpha} = 0$.) In region III, likewise, $\partial u^{\alpha}/\partial t^{\alpha}$ and $\partial u^{\beta}/\partial t^{\alpha}$ are of opposite sign and α can help β only at some cost to itself. However, in region III, $\partial u^{\alpha}/\partial t^{\alpha}$ is negative, indicating that, for each t^{β}, t^{α} exceeds its optimal value. In regions II and IV, on the other hand, the two derivatives are of the same sign, implying that, by adjusting t^{α}, it is possible to improve the well-being of both countries. In region II, the tariff of α exceeds its optimal value; hence a Pareto improvement can be achieved by reducing t^{α}. In region IV, on the other hand, t^{α} lies below its optimal level and a Pareto improvement can be achieved by raising t^{α}. Finally, in region V, there is no trade and it is impossible to change the countries' utilities by marginally adjusting t^{α}.

It is plain that in region V only transfers are efficacious. What can be said about regions II and IV? It is tempting to assert that in those regions α can help β at least cost by adjusting the level of its import duty. However, such an assertion can be justified only by showing that a transfer to β would both benefit β and entail some cost to α (or a benefit to α, per unit increase in u^{β}, smaller than that associated with an adjustment to t^{α}). Let us return to equations (11) and (12). It is easy to verify that, if inferiority is ruled out, both the square- and large-bracketed terms are positive. Hence $\partial u^{\alpha}/\partial T < 0$ and $\partial u^{\beta}/\partial T > 0$, whatever the values of t^{α} and t^{β}.[1] Thus α can help β by means of a transfer only at some utility cost to itself. We therefore can be sure that, in regions II and IV, the least-cost method of helping β is by adjustment of t^{α}.

This leaves regions I and III. There, whatever the manner of helping β, α suffers some loss of welfare. What is needed is a partitioning of those regions into subregions in which a transfer is the less costly method of achieving a given increment of u^{β} and subregions in which an adjustment of the import duty of α is the less costly method. We can guess that for points in region I and near region II, and for points in region III and near region IV, an adjustment of t^{α} will be the more efficient method. More precisely, we can verify with the aid of (8), (9), (11) and (12) that, when $t^{\alpha} = -t^{\beta}/(1 + t^{\beta})$

$$\frac{\partial u^{\alpha}}{\partial t^{\alpha}} + \frac{\partial u^{\beta}}{\partial t^{\alpha}} = 0 = \frac{\partial u^{\alpha}}{\partial T} + \frac{\partial u^{\beta}}{\partial T}.$$

This implies that, along the locus $t^{\alpha} = -t^{\beta}/(1 + t^{\beta})$, the two methods are equally efficient for small amounts of aid (strictly, for infinitesimal aid).

Thus we arrive at Figure 4. In the shaded regions of the figure, α can help β at least cost to itself by adjusting its import duty; in the unshaded regions, α can help β at least cost by means of a transfer. As t^{α} increases, with t^{β} given and non-negative, there is a single switch of regime, from aid to trade; as t^{α} increases, with t^{β} given and negative, there are two switches, from aid to trade and then back to aid.

That almost completes our analysis. However, it has been assumed that the loci $\partial u^{\alpha}/\partial t^{\alpha} = 0$ and $\partial u^{\beta}/\partial t^{\alpha} = 0$ intersect only once. It remains to comment briefly on other possibilities. If the loci intersect several times, we encounter a multiplicity of subregions; but nothing new in principle emerges. If the loci never meet, our map resembles Figure 5.

4 GLOBAL ANALYSIS

Given t^{β}, and bearing in mind the assumption of uniqueness, the welfare of the jth country can be represented as a function of the instruments t^{α} and T or, equivalently, as a function of p and T. In principle, therefore, we can cover that

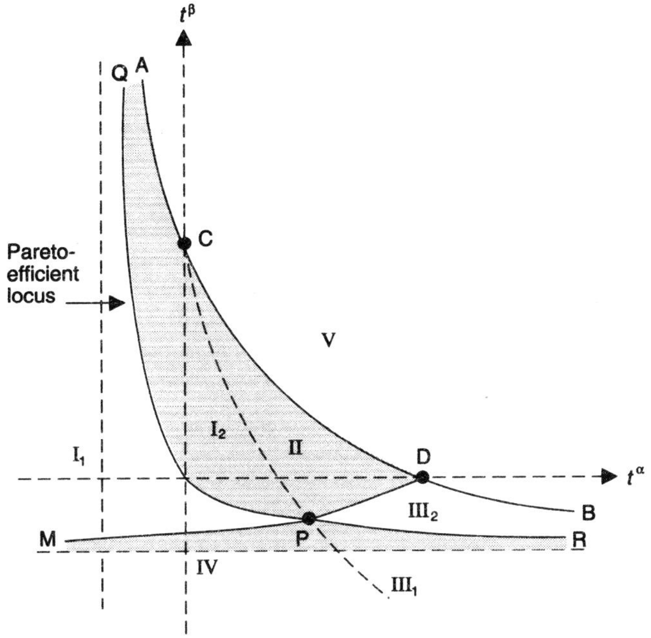

Figure 4

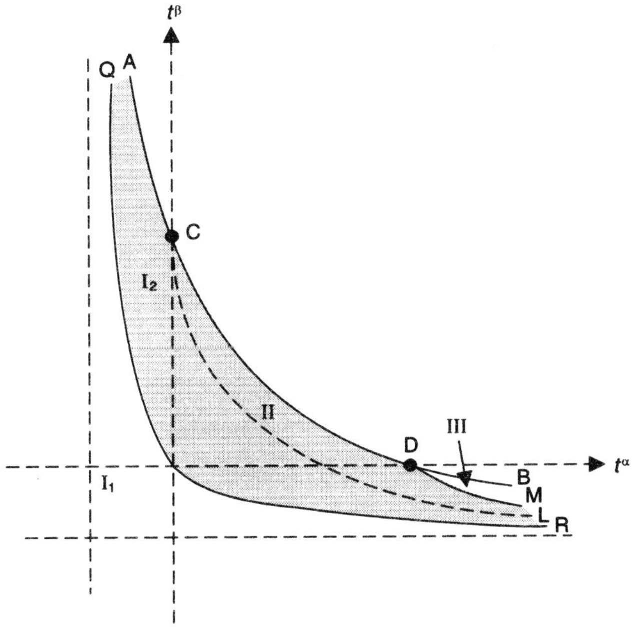

Figure 5

part of the (p, T)-plane defined by $p > 0$ with two families of indifference curves, one for each country. If we could discover the properties of the indifference curves we might then determine the optimal (least-cost) mixture of instruments for each feasible Δu^{β}, large or small.

For simplicity, let us set $t^{\beta} = 0$, so that our model of the world economy reduces to

$$z^{\alpha}(q^{\alpha}, u^{\alpha}) \equiv e^{\alpha}(q^{\alpha}, u^{\alpha}) - r^{\alpha}(q^{\alpha}) - t^{\alpha} p z^{\alpha 1}(q^{\alpha}, u^{\alpha}) = -T \tag{22}$$

$$z^{\beta}(p, u^{\beta}) \equiv e^{\beta}(p, u^{\beta}) - r^{\beta}(p) = T \tag{23}$$

$$z^{\alpha 1}(q^{\alpha}, u^{\alpha}) + z^{\beta 1}(p, u^{\beta}) = 0 \tag{24}$$

$$q^{\alpha} = p(1 + t^{\alpha}). \tag{25}$$

Moreover, it will be assumed that the expenditure function e^i satisfies the following regularity conditions:

$$\lim_{q^i \to \infty} e^i(q^i, u^i) = \infty \quad \text{for all } u^i \tag{26a}$$

$$\lim_{q^i \to 0} e^i(q^i, u^i) = 0 \quad \text{for all } u^i \tag{26b}$$

$$\lim_{u^i \to \infty} e^i(q^i, u^i) = \infty \quad \text{for all } q^i > 0 \tag{26c}$$

$$\lim_{u^i \to -\infty} e^i(q^i, u^i) = 0 \quad \text{for all } q^i > 0. \tag{26d}$$

It will be assumed also that neither good is inferior, that is that

$$\left.\begin{aligned} z_u^{i1} &= \frac{\partial^2 e^i}{\partial u^i \partial q^i} > 0 \\ z_u^i - p z_u^{i1} &= \frac{\partial e^i}{\partial u^i} - p \frac{\partial^2 e^i}{\partial u^i \partial q^i} > 0 \end{aligned}\right\} \quad \text{for all } (q^i, u^i),\ q^i > 0. \tag{27}$$

Finally, it will be assumed that marginal propensities to consume are everywhere the same, so that

$$z_u^{\alpha i}(p, u^{\alpha}) \equiv z_u^{\beta 1}(p, u^{\beta}) \quad \text{in } p, u^{\alpha}, u^{\beta}. \tag{28}$$

The indifference map for country β is obtained straightforwardly from (23). Given the standard properties of expenditure and revenue functions, and the additional restrictions (26), we easily obtain Figure 6. Since the expenditure function shifts up with increases in u^{β}, we can construct the family of indifference curves displayed in Figure 7, the level of utility associated with Al_i being less than the level of utility associated with Al_j if and only if $i < j$. Since

$$\lim_{u^{\beta} \to -\infty} z^{\beta}(p, u^{\beta}) = -r^{\beta}(p)$$

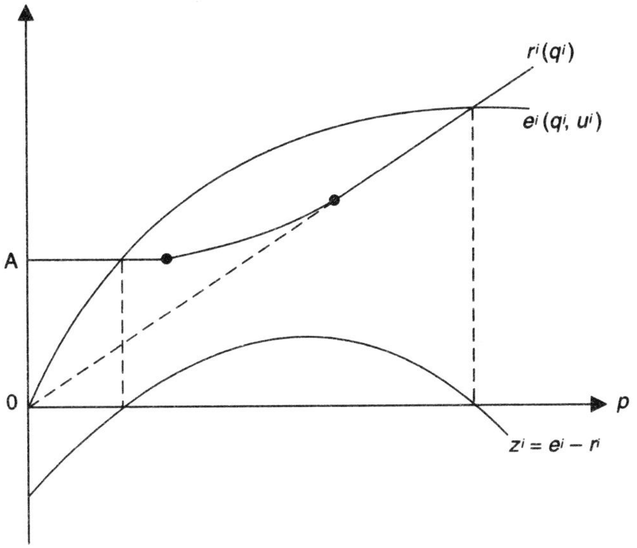

Figure 6

the family of curves is bounded below by the curve AC. The autarkic equilibrium price ratio in β is p^β, for at $(q^\beta, T) = (p^\beta, 0)$ we have $z^\beta(p^\beta, u^\beta) = T = 0$ and $\partial z^\beta(p^\beta, u^\beta)/\partial q^\beta = z^{\beta 1}(p^\beta, u^\beta) = 0$.

The construction of the indifference map of α is not so easy. Let p^e be the free-trade world equilibrium price. By assumption, in that equilibrium β exports the first commodity; hence $p^e > p^\beta$. In any world equilibrium to the left of the line $p = p^e$ in Figure 7, $t^\alpha > 0$; and in any equilibrium to the right of the line, $t^\alpha < 0$. Eliminating q^α from (22)–(25) and differentiating totally, we obtain

$$\begin{bmatrix} 0 & -t^\alpha p^2 z_q^{\alpha 1} & 1 \\ 1 & 0 & -1 \\ z_u^{\beta 1} & p z_q^{\alpha 1} & 0 \end{bmatrix} \begin{bmatrix} \mathrm{d}u^\beta \\ \mathrm{d}t^\alpha \\ \mathrm{d}T \end{bmatrix} = \begin{bmatrix} z^{\alpha 1} - p t^\alpha (1 + t^\alpha) z_q^{\alpha 1} \\ z^{\beta 1} \\ (1 + t^\alpha) z_q^{\alpha 1} + z_q^{\beta 1} \end{bmatrix} \mathrm{d}p - \begin{bmatrix} 1 - t^\alpha p z_u^{\alpha 1} \\ 0 \\ z_u^{\alpha 1} \end{bmatrix} \mathrm{d}u^\alpha. \quad (29)$$

Hence, solving,

$$\left.\frac{\partial T}{\partial p}\right|_{(29)} = -\left(z^{\alpha 1} + \frac{t^\alpha p z_q^{\beta 1}}{1 + t^\alpha p z_u^{\beta 1}} \right) \quad (30)$$

$$\left.\frac{\partial T}{\partial u^\alpha}\right|_{(29)} = -\frac{1}{1 + t^\alpha p z_u^{\beta 1}}. \quad (31)$$

Lemma. $1 + t^\alpha p z_u^{\beta 1} > 0$ *if* $t^\alpha > -1$.

Proof. *By assumption,* $z_u^{\beta 1} > 0$. *Hence*

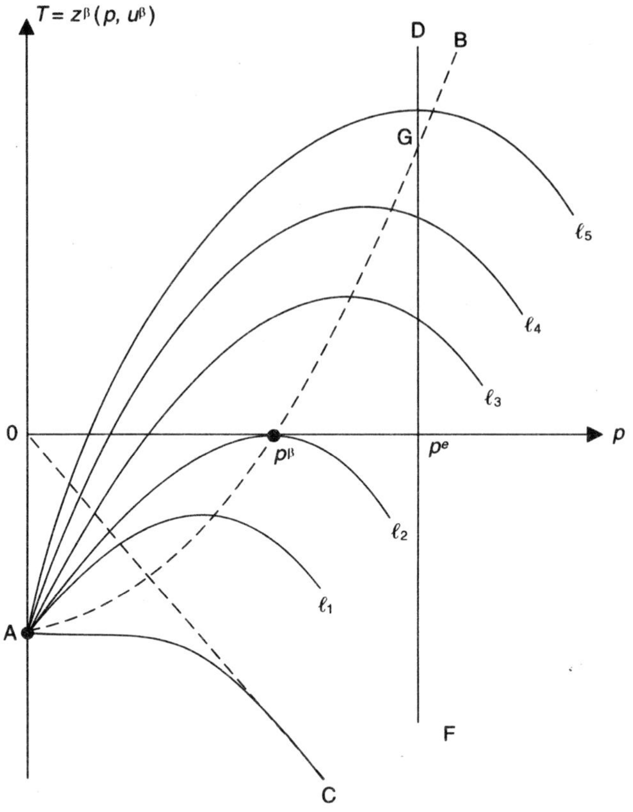

Figure 7

$$1 + t^{\alpha} p z_u^{\beta 1} > 0 \quad \textit{if} \quad t^{\alpha} \geqslant 0$$

and

$$1 + t^{\alpha} p z_u^{\beta 1} > 1 - p z_u^{\beta 1} > 0 \quad \textit{if} \quad -1 < t^{\alpha} < 0. \qquad \square$$

Equation (30) gives the slope of the indifference curves of α. Along $Ap^{\beta}GB$ in Figure 7, $z^{\alpha 1} = 0$; from (30) and the lemma, therefore

$$\left.\frac{\partial T}{\partial p}\right|_{(29),\, z^{\alpha 1} = 0} = -\frac{t^{\alpha} p z_q^{\beta 1}}{1 + t^{\alpha} p z_q^{\beta 1}} \begin{cases} > 0 & \text{on } Ap^{\beta}G \\ = 0 & \text{at } G \\ < 0 & \text{on } GB. \end{cases} \tag{32}$$

Similarly, along $DGp^{e}F$, $t^{\alpha} = 0$ and, from (30), we obtain

$$\left.\frac{\partial T}{\partial p}\right|_{(29),\, t^{\alpha} = 0} = -\, z^{\alpha 1} \begin{cases} > 0 & \text{on } DG \\ = 0 & \text{at } G \\ < 0 & \text{on } Gp^{e}F. \end{cases} \tag{33}$$

Finally, from (23)

$$\left.\frac{\partial T}{\partial p}\right|_{(23)} = z^{\beta 1} = - z^{\alpha 1}$$

so that

$$\left.\frac{\partial T}{\partial p}\right|_{(29)} - \left.\frac{\partial T}{\partial p}\right|_{(23)} = - \frac{t^{\alpha} p z_q^{\beta 1}}{1 + t^{\alpha} p z_u^{\beta 1}} \begin{cases} > 0 & \text{to the left of } DGp^eF \\ = 0 & \text{on } DGp^eF \\ < 0 & \text{to the right of } DGp^eF. \end{cases} \qquad (34)$$

From (32)–(34) we construct Figure 8, in which the solid curve $m_i m_i'$ is a typical indifference curve of country α and the dashed curve $l_i l_i'$ is a typical

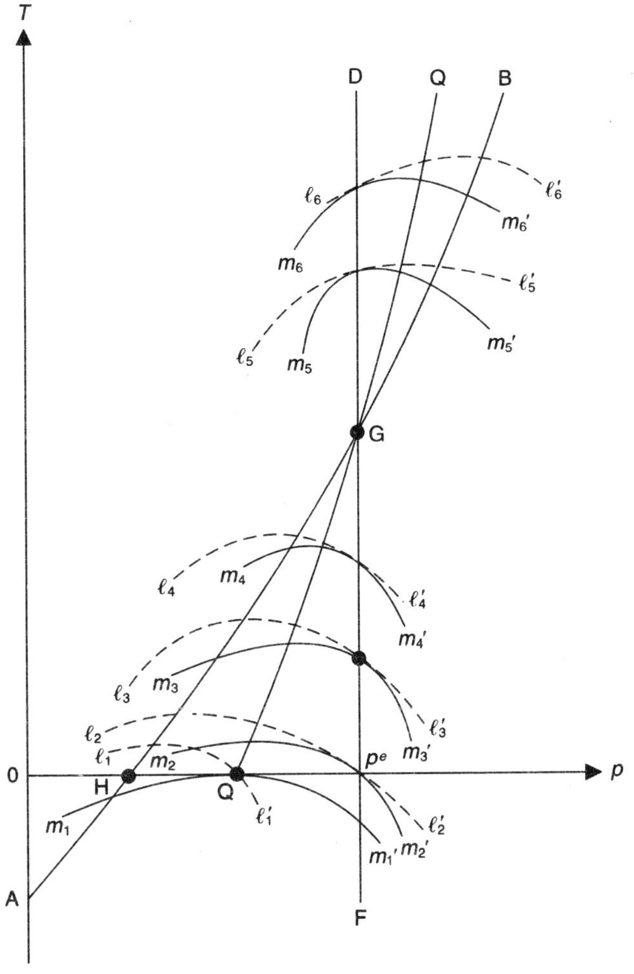

Figure 8

indifference curve of β. As we have already noted, higher β curves represent greater β utility; and, from (31), higher α curves represent lower α utility. Points on the contract locus DGp^eF are Pareto-optimal.

From Figure 8 we see immediately that if in the initial equilibrium $t^\alpha < 0$, then any feasible and positive Δu^β is achieved at least cost to α by setting $t^\alpha = 0$ and then moving along the contract locus by increasing the level of T. It is also clear that if in the initial equilibrium $t^\alpha > 0$, then any feasible and sufficiently large Δu^β is achieved by setting $t^\alpha = 0$ and T at some positive level. However, if in the initial equilibrium $t^\alpha > 0$ and Δu^β is feasible but small, then Δu^β could be attained with $t^\alpha = 0$ only if T were negative; ruling out negative T, Δu^β is attained at least cost to α by setting $T = 0$ and t^α equal to some positive but smaller value. Suppose, for example, that an initial world equilibrium is represented by point H in Figure 8, with $t^\alpha > 0$ and $T = 0$; and that α seeks to raise u^β to the level represented by the indifference curve l_1l_1'. This can be achieved at least cost to α by setting t^α at a lower but still positive level while maintaining $T = 0$, thus guiding the economy to the new equilibrium represented by point Q.

Summarizing, it is never optimal to set $t^\alpha < 0$; it is optimal to choose $t^\alpha > 0$ only if it is optimal to set $T = 0$. These conclusions are, of course, fully compatible with our earlier local results, summarized by Figures 4 and 5.

5 A FINAL REMARK

Many stones have been left unturned. In particular, we draw attention to the desirability of moving beyond the traditional two-goods, two-countries framework and of accommodating strategic behaviour on the part of the donor and the recipient.

ACKNOWLEDGEMENTS

The present essay is one of a series of papers devoted to the economics of foreign aid. Already published are Kemp (1984) and Kemp and Kojima (1985a, b, 1987). We acknowledge with gratitude the helpful comments of Ngo Van Long and Albert Schweinberger.

NOTE

1 The assumption of non-inferiority is essential to this conclusion. That tariffs combined with consumption inferiority might give rise to two-country transfer paradoxes was first noted by Ohyama (1972, 1974).

REFERENCES

Johnson, H. G. (1967) 'Economic policies toward less developed countries', The Brookings Institute, Washington, DC.

Kemp, M. C. (1984) 'A note on the theory of international transfers', *Economic Letters* 14: 259–62.

Kemp, M. C. and Kojima, S. (1985a) 'The welfare economics of foreign aid', in G. R. Feiwel (ed.) *Issues in Contemporary Microeconomics and Welfare*, pp. 470–83, London: Macmillan.

Kemp, M. C. and Kojima, S. (1985b) 'Tied aid and the paradoxes of donor-enrichment and recipient-impoverishment', *International Economic Review* 26: 721–9.

Kemp, M. C. and Kojima, S. (1987) 'More on the welfare economics of foreign aid', *Journal of the Japanese and International Economies* 1: 97–109.

Ohyama, M. (1972) 'Trade and welfare in general equilibrium', *Keio Economic Studies* 9: 37–73.

Ohyama, M. (1974) 'Tariffs and the transfer problem', *Keio Economic Studies* 11: 29–45.

Thirlwall, A. P. (1976) 'When is trade more valuable than aid?', *Journal of Development Studies* 12(5): 35–41.

Yassin, I. H. (1982) '"When is trade more valuable than aid?": Revisited', *World Development* 10: 161–6.

AUTHOR INDEX

Abe, K. 364
Aliprantis, C. D. 138
Arrow, K. J. x, 22, 45, 138, 139, 140, 317
Atkinson, A. B. 296

Balasko, Y. D. 138, 145, 307, 312, 315, 335
Bastable, C. F. 274
Batra, R. N. 48
Bauer, P. T. 354
Bhagwati, J. N. 27, 38, 40, 45, 163, 203, 204, 216, 280, 295, 352, 353
Bickerdike, C. F. 19
Binh, T. N. xi, xii, 105, 106, 110, 129, 130
Böhm, V. xiii, 271, 272
Bresnahan, T. F. 246
Brock, W. A. 76
Burke, J. 138

Caves, R. E. 19, 38
Chiarella, C. 158
Chipman, J. S. xv, 40, 45, 315
Clarke, H. R. 150
Cooper, C. A. 38
Cornwall, R. R. 273
Cournot, A. 183
Croushore, D. 76

Debreu, G. x, 34, 38, 42, 43, 45, 138, 139, 303, 304, 305, 317
Diamond, P. A. xiv, 291, 296
Dierker, H. 273
Diewert, W. E. 240
Dixit, A. K. xvi, 45, 106, 285, 286, 291, 292, 294, 295, 296
Drazen, A. 76

Easley, D. 295
Eaton, J. 252
Edgeworth, F. Y. 19, 346, 347, 351
Eichberger, J. 99, 315
Ethier, W. J. 230, 231, 234, 295, 315

Feenstra, R. 76
Fishburn, G. 280
Foster, E. 216
Friedman, J. W. 266

Gale, D. 101, 312, 336, 339, 341, 352, 353, 358
Galor, O. 138
Gabszewicz, J. J. 271, 273
Geanakoplos, J. 47, 48, 53, 70, 99, 126, 132, 138, 145, 317, 318, 322, 326
Graaff, J. de V. 19
Graham, F. D. 228
Grandmont, J. M. xiv, 34, 70, 99, 105, 126, 295, 296, 306, 324
Green, J. R. 308
Grinols, E. L. xiv, 44, 45, 48, 295, 296, 324
Grodal, B. 273
Grossman, G. M. 47, 78, 105, 129, 252

Haberler, G. 19
Hahn, F. H. 138, 139, 140
Hamada, K. 188
Hammond, P. J. 315
Hansen, B. 188
Hart, O. D. xi, 47, 48, 70, 72, 317, 322
Helpman, E. 48, 230, 231, 234, 242, 270, 295
Herberg, H. vi, 228, 352
Hicks, J. R. 160, 253, 254
Higgins, B. H. 352

Hotelling, H. 152
Hurwicz, L. 308

Ikema, M. 160, 253, 254

Johnson, H. G. 27, 38, 150, 151, 216, 360, 380
Jones, R. W. 188, 295

Khan, A. 295
Kimura, Y. xv
Kindleberger, C. P. ix
Kojima, S. 352, 353, 356, 358, 392
Koopmans, T. 304
Krueger, A. O. 28, 30, 47, 78, 105, 211, 212, 218, 228
Krugman, P. 230, 234, 242, 270

Laffont, J.-J. 308
Léonard, D. 188, 352
Leontief, W. 334, 335
Lerner, A. P. 150, 175
Levy, V. 366
Lindahl, E. 363
Lloyd, P. J. 233
Long, N. V. xi, xii, 77, 105, 106, 110, 129, 145, 152, 158, 273, 274, 280, 360, 363, 392

McCallum, B. T. 76
McFadden, D. xiv, 34, 70, 99, 105, 129, 295, 297, 306, 324
McKenzie, L. W. x, 132, 138, 312, 323, 326
Magill, M. 48, 79, 85, 317
Malinvaud, E. xii
Manning, R. 295, 352
Mantel, R. R. 295
Markusen, J. R. 230, 234, 240, 254
Marshall, A. 27
Massell, B. F. 38
Matthews, R. C. O. 19
Meade, J. E. 163
Melvin, J. R. 234
Michel, P. 273
Mill, J. S. 19, 34, 274, 346, 347, 351
Mirrlees, J. A. xiv, 291, 296
Muller, W. J. 138

Neary, J. P. xv, 233, 236, 237
Negishi, T. xiii, 228, 230, 231, 234, 238, 242, 274, 280
Newbery, D. M. G. xi, 48, 51, 55, 78, 79
Ng, Y.-K. 150, 188
Nishimura, K. 266
Norman, V. xvi, 45, 105, 285, 286, 291, 292, 294, 295, 296

Ohyama, M. x, 45, 47, 78, 105, 129, 150, 230, 274, 280, 336, 352, 392
Okawa, M. 242, 243, 250, 253, 358
Olsen, E. 18

Pareto, V. xvi, 296
Perry, M. K. 246
Polak, J.-J. 17
Pomery, J. 48
Prebisch, R. 167, 181

Quibria, M. G. 150
Quinzii, M. 79, 85

Razin, A. 48
Roberts, D. J. 273
Roy, R. 254
Russell, W. R. 48
Rybczynski, T. 124
Ryder, H. 138

Safra, Z. 312
Samuelson, P. A. ix, xii, xv, xvi, 3, 4, 5, 7, 18, 24, 29, 34, 47, 78, 105, 126, 129, 130, 216, 218, 228, 334, 335, 336, 351, 352
Schweinberger, A. G. 233, 236, 237, 240, 338, 352, 392
Scitovsky, T. 27, 33, 216
Seade, J. 246
Sempere, J. 315
Serra, P. 105, 106, 110, 111, 126, 129
Shafer, W. 48, 295, 317
Shell, K. 138, 312, 315
Shimomura, K. 77, 150, 158, 160, 163, 252, 253, 352, 354
Shoven, J. B. 295
Shy, O. 48, 51, 55, 78, 79
Sidgwick, H. 19
Singer, H. W. 167, 181
Sinn, H.-W. 59
Snape, R. 188
Solow, R. M. 156, 157
Sonnenschein, H. 28, 30, 47, 78, 105, 211, 212, 216, 218, 228, 273, 295
Sontheimer, K. 26, 295
Spraos, J. 199
Stackelberg, H. 183

Stephan, G. 138
Stiglitz, J. E. xi, 48, 51, 55, 78, 296

Tawada, M. 158, 270
Thirlwall, A. P. 380
Tinbergen, J. 228
Tu, P. N. V. 150
Turnovsky, S. 48
Turunen-Red, A. H. 352

Vanek, J. x, 34, 40, 45, 47, 78, 105, 129, 203, 216, 296
Vial, J.-P. 273
Viner, J. 27

Wagenhals, G. 138
Walras, L. 26
Wan, H. Y. ix, x, xiv, xv, 27, 34, 39, 40, 41, 45, 46, 47, 60, 62, 70, 72, 78, 92, 103, 105, 126, 129, 137, 148, 150, 280, 295, 296, 297, 313, 317, 323, 328
Wang, L. F. S. 352
Warr, P. 356
Wegge, L. L. ix
Weymark, J. A. 291, 296, 297
Wigle, R. M. 230
Wilson, C. 138
Wolik, N. 145, 326, 327
Wong, K.-Y. xi, xii, 47, 72, 77, 78, 105, 126, 130, 137, 148, 150, 315, 319, 320, 354
Woodford, M. 138, 352
Woodland, A. 295

Yamamoto, H. 77
Yano, M. 45, 295, 353
Yassin, I. H. 380

SUBJECT INDEX

allocation mechanism 308

Bertrand process 272

compensation: incomplete markets 317–29; lumpsum xii–xv, 6–7, 24, 57, 61, 68, 89, 110–15, 133–4, 149, 285–329; non-lumpsum 117–19, 285–95, 297; overlapping generations 310–12, 323–9
Cournot process 183–6, 271–2
customs unions: gainfulness 37–46, 59–61, 136, 144–5; quality standards 39–40; second best 41–6

diffusion of technical progress: free trade 161–2; imperfect competition 253–70; optimal tariffs 162–3; perfect competition 160–4

economic imperialism 167, 170–5
economies: barter ix–x, 47–72; essentially repetitive 298–302; imperfectly competitive xiii, 242–73; incomplete markets xi, 47–72, 78–100; monetary xi–xii, 73–100, 120; overlapping generations xii, 101–47

factor trade expenditure function 233
foreign aid: joint donors and recipients 344–6; optimal timing 365–78; trade *versus* aid 379–93; transfer of goods 334–6, 339–46; transfer of information 346–50

gains from trade: commodity taxes 223–5; demand variations 27–33; factor market distortions 226–8; free trade 4–7, 12–13, 24–34; imperfect competition 242–52; incomplete markets 47–72; learning by doing 274–81; licensing of technology 33–4; migration 147–51; monetary economies 73–100; overlapping generations 101–47; sharing between nations 167–99, 253–69; variable returns to scale 219–23, 230–41
good Samaritan: impossibility result 342, 350

imperialism 167, 170–5
implicit factoral terms of trade 235
incomplete markets xi, 47–72, 78–100
irreducibility 132, 326, 328

learning by doing 274–81

monetary economies xi–xii, 73–100

nationalism 167, 175–7

optimal tariffs 14–17
overlapping generations xii, 101–46, 310–12

Pareto dominance 135
price normalization: bearing on existence 271–3
public goods: bearing on transfer problem 356–64

quality standards in customs unions 39–40

reparations 326
resource nationalism 167, 175–7

second best 41–6
Stackelberg process 187–8
survival in open economies 152–9
technical assistance 326–7, 346–50
tied aid 336–9, 343–4
transfer problem 334–64